Financial Accounting Version 2.0

By
Joe Hoyle and C.J. Skender

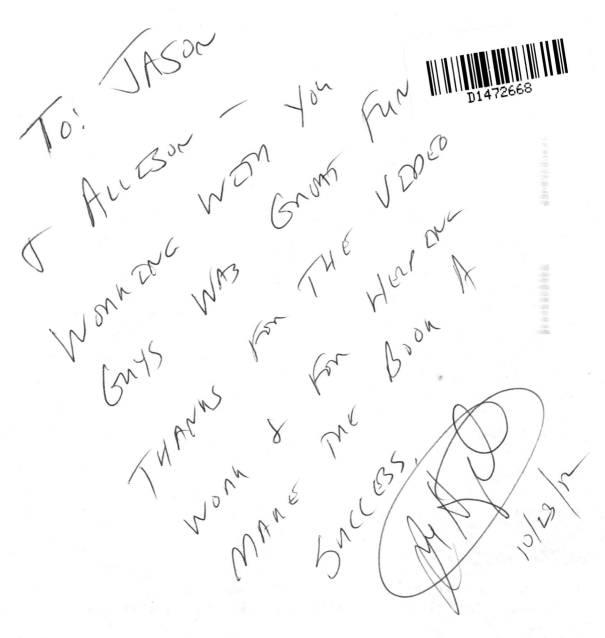

P-690860-BW-3

9 781453 326817

flatworld
KNOWLEDGE

Financial Accounting Version 2.0

Joe Hoyle and C.J. Skender

Published by:

Flat World Knowledge, Inc.
One Bridge Street
Irvington, NY 10533

Printed in North America

Brief Contents

Contents

About the Authors

JOE BEN HOYLE, UNIVERSITY OF RICHMOND

Joe Hoyle is an associate professor of accounting at the Robins School of Business at the University of Richmond. In 2006, he was named by *BusinessWeek* as one of twenty-six favorite undergraduate business professors in the United States. In 2007, he was selected as the Virginia Professor of the Year by the Carnegie Foundation for the Advancement of Teaching and the Council for the Advancement and Support of Education. In 2009, he was judged to be one of the one hundred most influential members of the accounting profession by *Accounting Today*.

Joe has two market-leading textbooks published with McGraw-Hill—*Advanced Accounting* (11th edition, 2012) and *Essentials of Advanced Accounting* (5th edition, 2012), both coauthored with Tom Schaefer of the University of Notre Dame and Tim Doupnik of the University of South Carolina.

At the Robins School of Business, Joe teaches Fundamentals of Financial Accounting, Intermediate Financial Accounting I, Intermediate Financial Accounting II, and Advanced Financial Accounting. He earned his BA degree in accounting from Duke University and his MA degree in business and economics, with a minor in education, from Appalachian State University. He has written numerous articles and continues to make many presentations around the country on teaching excellence. He maintains a blog on teaching at http://www.joehoyle-teaching.blogspot.com/.

Joe also has three decades of experience operating his own CPA (Certified Public Accountant) Exam review programs. In 2008, he created CPA Review for Free (http://www.CPAreviewforFREE.com), which provides thousands of free questions to help accountants around the world prepare for the CPA Exam.

Joe and his wife, Sarah, have four children and four grandchildren.

C. J. SKENDER, UNIVERSITY OF NORTH CAROLINA AT CHAPEL HILL

C. J. Skender has received two dozen teaching awards at the University of North Carolina's Kenan-Flagler Business School (fourteen awards), at Duke University's Fuqua School of Business (five awards), and at North Carolina State University (five awards). He has been included among the outstanding Fuqua faculty in four editions of the *Businessweek Guide to the Best Business Schools*. His classes were highlighted in *Businessweek* (http://www.businessweek.com) and *Sports Illustrated* (http://sportsillustrated.cnn.com) in 2006. C. J. was featured in "The Last Word" in the April 2008 *Journal of Accountancy*. He was voted best professor in *The Daily Tar Heel: Carolina's Finest* annual awards issue in 2011.

C. J. has served as a training consultant on three continents for organizations, such as **GlaxoSmithKline**, **IBM**, **Siemens**, **Starwood**, and **Wells Fargo**. He was inducted into the **Wells Fargo** Hall of Fame in 2003 for lifetime achievement. C. J. has developed and delivered various executive education seminars as well as CPA, CMA (Certified Management Accountant), and CIA (Certified Internal Auditor) review courses. For six years, he lectured simultaneously in the state, Carolina, and Duke CPA preparatory classes. For seven years, C. J. taught financial accounting and managerial accounting on cable television in the Research Triangle area. His scholarly work has been published in *TAXES* and the *Journal of Accounting Education*.

C. J. Skender was born in Harrisburg, Pennsylvania, in 1954. He captained three sports at Susquehanna Township High School. C. J. holds academic degrees from Lehigh University and Duke University. He attended Lehigh on a basketball scholarship and graduated magna cum laude. C. J. worked as an auditor for Deloitte Haskins & Sells in Philadelphia. He has attained eleven professional designations in accounting, financial planning, insurance, and management. C. J. has taught more than five hundred sections of college courses and more than twenty-five thousand students in his academic career. He was tapped into the Golden Chain Honor Society at North Carolina State University in 1985 and was named Alumni Distinguished Professor there in 1992. C. J. was presented the Outstanding Educator Award by the North Carolina Association of Certified Public Accountants in 1995. At the University of North Carolina, he has received three Weatherspoons (2000, 2004, and 2007) as well as the James M. Johnston Teaching Excellence Award in 2005.

C. J. and his wife, Mary Anne, are the parents of two sons and one daughter: Charles (1979), Timothy (1983), and Corey (1987). They have one granddaughter: Riley (2010). C. J. and his wife reside in Raleigh, North Carolina.

Acknowledgments

A textbook of this size owes a genuine debt of gratitude to a long list of wonderful people. We want to acknowledge the time, energy, ideas, and patience invested by each of the following individuals.

SECOND EDITION BOOK DEVELOPMENT AND SUPPORT

A warm thank you to Jeff Shelstad, Michael Boezi, Pam Hersperger, Becky Knauer, Chrissy Chimi, Ellen Bohnstengel, and Jason Kypros.

TEXTBOOK REVIEWERS

- James John Aitken, Central Michigan University
- Pervaiz Alam, Kent State University
- Somer Anderson, Fontbonne University
- Jane Austin, Oklahoma City University
- Richard Baldwin, Johnson & Wales University, Friedman Center, Graduate School
- Sheila Bedford, American University
- Bruce Branson, North Carolina State University
- Rada Brooks, University of California, Berkeley, Haas School of Business
- Helen Brubeck, San Jose State University
- Charles Bunn, Wake Technical Community College
- Stan Clark, University of Southern Mississippi
- Sue Cunningham, Rowan Cabarrus Community College
- Betty David, Francis Marion University
- Carolyn Dreher, Southern Methodist University, Cox School of Business
- Wilbert Harri, Pima Community College
- Lori Holder-Webb, Simmons College School of Management
- Ethan Kinory, Baruch College, City University of New York
- Pamela Legner, College of DuPage
- Randall Lewis, Spring Arbor University
- Chao-Shin Liu, University of Notre Dame
- Jane Mooney, Simmons College
- Jason Nielsen, Harrisburg Area Community College
- Larry Sayler, Greenville College
- Rachel Siegel, Lyndon State College
- David Sulzen, Ferrum College
- Diane Tanner, University of North Florida
- Steven Thoede, Texas State University
- Robin Thomas, North Carolina State University
- Joyce van der Laan Smith, Richmond University
- Wendy Wilson, Southern Methodist University
- Gregory Yost, University of West Florida

The authors also appreciate the efforts of Claude Laflamme and Mike Donohue from Lyryx Learning. Their team helped develop the FLYX product that accompanies this textbook.

Preface

HOW TO USE THIS BOOK: FROM THE AUTHORS TO THE STUDENTS

If we have done our job properly during the creation of this textbook, it will be like no other educational material that you have ever experienced. We literally set out to rethink the nature, structure, and purpose of college textbooks. Every feature that you find here was designed to enhance student learning. We want this material to be presented in a manner that is both innovative and effective.

The two of us have taught in college for over sixty years. Year in and year out, financial accounting has always seemed to us to be both interesting and relevant to everyday life. We believe it is knowledge well worth acquiring. From the day we started this project, we hoped to share our enthusiasm with you, to develop a book that you will find to be both readable and worth reading.

Historically, textbooks have been presented as dry monologues, a one-way conversation that often seems to talk to the teacher more than to the student. "Boring" and "confusing" should never be synonymous with any aspect of education. Instead, we seek to promote an active dialogue. Authors, teachers, and students should work together to create an environment where education flourishes. We want you, the student, to understand the nature of our endeavor. After all, the only reason that this book exists is to aid you in learning financial accounting. If you do not read the chapters because you find them boring or if you do not understand the material that is included, no one benefits. We will have wasted our time.

We view this textbook as a guide. In constructing these seventeen chapters, we have worked to lead you on a voyage through the world of business and financial reporting. We want to help you attain a usable knowledge of the principles of financial accounting as well as an appreciation for its importance and logic. By learning its theory, presentation, and procedures, individuals become capable of using financial accounting to make prudent business decisions. That is an important goal regardless of the direction of your career. We have relied on our experience as teachers to highlight the aspects of this material that make it interesting, logical, and relevant.

Talk, though, is cheap. Saying that this book is different and interesting does not make it so. Be a wise consumer. When someone tries to sell you something, force them to back up their claims.

SO HOW DOES THIS BOOK WORK? WHAT MAKES IT SPECIAL?

1. Every chapter is introduced with a short video in which one of the authors provides an overview of the material and a discussion of its importance. Thus, students are never forced to begin reading blindly, struggling to put new subjects into an understandable context. Even before the first written word, each chapter is explained through the opening video. Simply put, this introduction makes the subject matter more understandable and your reading more interesting and efficient. We attempt to remove the mystery from every aspect of financial accounting because we want you to be an effective learner.

2. This textbook is written entirely in a question-and-answer format. The Socratic method has been used successfully for thousands of years to help students develop critical thinking skills. We do that here on every page of every chapter. A question is posed and the answer is explained. Then, the next logical question is put forth to lead you through the material in a carefully constructed sequential pattern. Topics are presented and analyzed as through a conversation. This format breaks each chapter down into easy-to-understand components. A chapter is not thirty pages of seemingly unending material. Instead, it is twenty to forty questions and answers that put the information into manageable segments with each new question logically following the previous one.

3. All college textbooks present challenging material. However, that is no excuse for allowing readers to become lost. Educational materials should be designed to enhance learning and not befuddle students. At key points throughout each chapter, we have placed multiple-choice ("Test Yourself") questions along with our own carefully constructed answers. These questions allow you to pause at regular intervals to verify that you understand the material that has been covered. Immediate feedback is always a key ingredient in successful learning. These questions and answers are strategically placed throughout every chapter to permit ongoing review and reinforcement of knowledge.

4. For a course such as financial accounting, each subject should relate in some manner to the real world of business. Therefore, every chapter includes a discussion with a successful investment analyst about the material that has been presented. This expert provides an honest and open assessment of financial accounting straight from the daily world of high finance and serious business decisions. Every question, every answer, and every topic need to connect directly to the world we all face. Students should always be curious about the relevance of every aspect of a textbook's coverage. We believe that it is helpful to consider this material from the perspective of a person already working in the business environment of the twenty-first century.

5. In many chapters, we talk about the current evolution occurring in financial accounting as the United States considers the possibility of moving from following U.S. rules (U.S. GAAP) to international standards (IFRS). The world is getting smaller as companies and their operations become more global. At the same time, technology makes the amount of available

information from around the world almost beyond comprehension. Accountants work to help make this mass of information easier to understand and manage. Consequently, throughout this textbook, we interview one of the partners of a large international accounting firm about the impact of possibly changing financial accounting in this country so that all reporting abides by international accounting rules rather than solely U.S. standards.

6. Each chapter ends with a final video. However, instead of merely rehashing the material one last time in a repetitive fashion, we challenge you to select the five most important elements of each chapter. Some coverage is simply more important than others. That is a reasonable expectation. Part of a successful education is gaining the insight to make such evaluations. Then, we provide you with our own top five. The lists do not need to match; in fact, it is unlikely that they will be the same. That is not the purpose. This exercise should encourage you to weigh the significance of the material. What really makes a difference based on your understanding of financial accounting? In what areas should you focus your attention?

IS THIS BOOK UNIQUE?

We truly believe so. We believe that it has an educationally creative structure that will promote your learning and make the educational process more effective and more interesting:

- Opening videos for the chapters
- Socratic method used consistently throughout the book
- Embedded multiple-choice questions
- Discussions with both an investment analyst and an international accounting expert
- Closing videos establishing top-five lists for each chapter
- Two end-of-chapter "video problems" in each chapter where questions are posed and a video is available so students can watch one of the authors explain his version of the answer
- A "research assignment" at the end of each chapter designed to help students uncover and analyze the wealth of information available on the Internet

In addition, all the end-of-chapter material in the second edition (questions, true or false, multiple-choice, and problems) has been rewritten and expanded. The sheer number of available end-of-chapter material has been doubled and, in some chapters, tripled.

Every page of this book, every word in fact, has been created to encourage and enhance your understanding. We want you to benefit from our coverage, but just as importantly, we want you to enjoy the process. When presented correctly, learning can be fun and, we believe, should be fun.

Please feel free to contact us if you have any suggestions for improvement. We would love to hear from you.

Finally, this book is dedicated to our wives and our families. It is also dedicated to the thousands of wonderful teachers across the world who walk into countless college classrooms each day and make learning happen for their students. You make the world a better place to be.

Joe Hoyle, University of Richmond (Jhoyle@richmond.edu)

C. J. Skender, University of North Carolina at Chapel Hill

CHAPTER 1
What Is Financial Accounting, and Why Is It Important?

 Video Clip

In this video, Professor Joe Hoyle introduces the essential points covered in Chapter 1.

View the video online at: http://bit.ly/hoyle1-1

1. MAKING GOOD FINANCIAL DECISIONS ABOUT AN ORGANIZATION

LEARNING OBJECTIVES

At the end of this section, students should be able to meet the following objectives:

1. Define "financial accounting."
2. Understand the connection between financial accounting and the communication of information about an organization.
3. Explain the importance of gaining an understanding of financial accounting.
4. List decisions that an individual might make about an organization.
5. Differentiate between financial accounting and managerial accounting.
6. Provide reasons for individuals to study the financial accounting information supplied by their employers.

1.1 Financial Accounting and Information

Question: In the June 30, 2011, edition of The Wall Street Journal, *numerous headlines described the recent activities of various business organizations. Here are just a few:*

"TMX and LSE Give Up on Planned Merger"
"Ally Financial Faces Charge for Mortgage Losses"
"HomeAway Jumps 49% in Debut"

"Ad-Seller Acquiring Myspace for a Song"

Millions of individuals around the world read such stories each day with rapt interest. From teenagers to elderly billionaires, this type of information is analyzed obsessively. How are these people able to understand all the data and details being provided? For most, the secret is straightforward: a strong knowledge of financial accounting.

This textbook provides an introduction to financial accounting. A logical place to begin such an exploration is to ask the obvious question: **What is financial accounting?**

> **financial accounting**
>
> The communication of financial information about a business or other type of organization to external audiences to help them assess its financial health and future prospects.

Answer: In simplest terms, financial accounting is the communication of information about a business or other type of organization (such as a charity or government) so that individuals can assess its financial health and future prospects. No single word is more relevant to financial accounting than "information." Whether it is gathering monetary information about a specific organization, putting that information into a format designed to enhance communication, or analyzing the information that is conveyed, financial accounting is intertwined with information.

In today's world, information is king. Financial accounting provides the rules and structure for the conveyance of financial information about businesses (and other organizations) to maximize clarity and understanding. Although a wide array of organizations present financial information to interested parties, this book primarily focuses on the reporting of businesses because that is where the widest use of financial accounting occurs.

organization → reports information based on the principles of financial accounting → interested individuals assess financial health and future prospects

At any point in time, some businesses are poised to prosper while others teeter on the verge of failure. Many people want to be able to evaluate the degree of success achieved to date by a particular organization as well as its prospects for the future. They seek information and the knowledge that comes from understanding that information. How well did **The Coca Cola Company** do last year, and how well should this business do in the coming year? Those are simple questions to ask, but the answers can make the difference between earning millions and losing millions.

Financial accounting provides data that these individuals need and want.

1.2   Financial Accounting and Wise Decision Making

Question: Every semester, most college students are enrolled in several courses as well as participate in numerous outside activities. All of these compete for the hours that make up each person's day. Why should a student invest valuable time to learn the principles of financial accounting? Why should anyone be concerned with the information communicated about an organization? **What makes financial accounting important?**

Answer: Many possible benefits can be gained from acquiring a strong knowledge of financial accounting because it provides the accepted methods for communicating relevant information about an organization. In this book, justification for the serious study that is required to master this subject matter is simple and straightforward. Obtaining a working knowledge of financial accounting and its underlying principles enables a person to understand the information conveyed about an organization so that better decisions can be made.

Around the world each day, millions of individuals make critical judgments about the businesses and other organizations they encounter. Developing the ability to analyze financial information and then making use of that knowledge to arrive at sound decisions can be critically important. Whether an organization is as gigantic as **Walmart** or as tiny as a local convenience store, individuals have many, varied reasons for studying the information that is available.

As just a single example, a recent college graduate looking at full-time employment opportunities might want to determine the probability that Company A will have a brighter economic future than Company B. Although such decisions can never be correct 100 percent of the time, knowledge of financial accounting and the information being communicated greatly increases the likelihood of success. As Kofi Annan, former secretary-general of the United Nations, has said, "Knowledge is power. Information is liberating."[1]

Thus, the ultimate purpose of this book is to provide students with a rich understanding of the rules and nuances of financial accounting so they can evaluate available information about organizations and then make good decisions. In the world of business, most successful individuals have developed this ability and are able to use it to achieve their investing and career objectives.

1.3   Common Decisions about Organizations

Question: Knowledge of financial accounting assists individuals in making informed decisions about businesses and other organizations. What kinds of evaluations are typically made? For example, assume that a former student—one who recently graduated from college—has been assigned the task of analyzing financial data provided by the Acme Company. **What real-life decisions could a person be facing where an understanding of financial accounting would be beneficial?**

Answer: The number of possible judgments that an individual might need to make about a business or other organization is close to unlimited. However, many of these decisions deal with the current financial health and prospects for future success. In order to analyze available data to make such assessments, a working knowledge of financial accounting is invaluable. The more in-depth the understanding is of those principles, the more likely the person will be able to use the information to arrive at the best possible choices. Common examples include the following:

- Should a bank loan money to the Acme Company? The college graduate might be employed by a bank to work in its corporate lending department. Assume, for example, that the Acme Company is a local business that has applied to the bank for a large loan so that it can expand. The graduate has been instructed by bank management to prepare an assessment of Acme to determine if it is likely to be financially healthy in the future so that it will be able to repay the borrowed money when due. A correct decision to provide the loan eventually earns a profit for the bank because Acme will be required to pay an extra amount (known as **interest**) on the money borrowed. Conversely, an incorrect analysis of the information could lead to a substantial loss if the loan is granted and Acme is unable to fulfill its obligation. Bank officials must weigh the potential for profit against the risk of loss. That is a daily challenge in virtually all businesses. The former student's career with the bank might depend on the ability to analyze financial accounting data and then make appropriate choices about the actions to be taken. Should a loan be made to this company?

- Should another business make sales on credit to the Acme Company? The college graduate might hold a job as a credit analyst for a manufacturing company that sells its products to retail stores. Assume that Acme is a relatively new retailer that wants to buy goods (inventory) on credit from this manufacturer to sell in its stores. The former student must judge whether to permit Acme to buy merchandise now but wait until later to remit the money. If payments are received on a timely basis, the manufacturer will have found a new outlet for its merchandise. Profits will likely increase. Unfortunately, Acme could also make expensive purchases but then be unable to make payment, creating significant losses for the manufacturer. Again, the possibility of profit must be measured against the chance for loss.

- Should an individual invest money to become one of the owners of the Acme Company? The college graduate might be employed by a firm that provides financial advice to its clients. Assume that the firm is presently considering whether to recommend acquisition of ownership shares of Acme as a good investment strategy. The former student has been assigned to gather and evaluate relevant financial information as a basis for this decision. If Acme is poised to become larger and more profitable, its ownership shares will likely rise in value over time, earning money for the firm's clients. Conversely, if the prospects for Acme appear to be dim, the value of these shares might start to drop (possibly precipitously) so that the investment firm should avoid suggesting the purchase of an ownership interest in this business.

Success in life—especially in business—frequently results from being able to make appropriate decisions. Many economic choices, such as those described earlier, depend on a person's ability to understand and make use of financial information about organizations. That financial information is produced and presented in accordance with the rules and principles underlying financial accounting.

interest

The charge for using money over time, often associated with long-term loans; even if not specifically mentioned in the debt agreement, financial accounting rules require it to be computed and reported based on a reasonable rate.

T E S T   Y O U R S E L F

Question:

James Esposito is a college student who has just completed a class in financial accounting. He earned a good grade and wants to make use of his knowledge. He wants to invest $10,000 that he recently inherited from a distant uncle. In which of the following decisions is Esposito most likely to have used his understanding of financial accounting?

    a. He decides to deposit the money in a bank to earn interest.

    b. He decides to buy ownership shares in **Microsoft Corporation** in hopes that they will appreciate in value.

    c. He decides to trade in his old car and buy a new one that uses less gasoline.

    d. He decides to buy a new computer so that he can make money by typing papers for his classmates.

Answer:

The correct answer is choice b: He decides to buy ownership shares in **Microsoft Corporation** in hopes that they will appreciate in value.

Explanation:

All of these are potentially good economic decisions. However, financial accounting focuses on conveying data to help reflect the financial health and prospects of organizations. His decision to buy ownership shares of **Microsoft** rather than any other company indicates that he believes that **Microsoft** is poised to grow and prosper. This decision is exactly the type that investors around the world make each day with the use of their knowledge of financial accounting.

1.4   Financial Accounting versus Managerial Accounting

Question: A great number of possible decisions could be addressed in connection with any business. **Is an understanding of financial accounting relevant to all decisions made about an organization?** *What about the following?*

- *Should a business buy a building to serve as its new headquarters or rent a facility instead?*
- *What price should a data processing company charge customers for its services?*
- *Should advertisements to alert the public about a new product be carried on the Internet or on television?*

Answer: Decisions such as these three are extremely important for the success of any organization. However, these examples are not made about the reporting organization. Rather, they are made within the organization in connection with some element of its operations.

> **managerial accounting**
>
> The communication of financial information within an organization so internal decisions can be made in an appropriate manner.

The general term "accounting" refers to the communication of financial information for decision-making purposes. Accounting is then further subdivided into (a) financial accounting and (b) **managerial accounting**.[2] Financial accounting is the subject explored in this textbook. It focuses on conveying relevant data (primarily to external parties) about an organization (such as **Motorola Mobility** or **Starbucks**) as a whole so that wise decisions can be made. Thus, questions such as the following all fall within the discussion of financial accounting:

- Do we loan money to the Acme Company?
- Do we sell on credit to the Acme Company?
- Do we recommend that our clients buy the ownership shares of the Acme Company?

These decisions pertain to an overall evaluation of the financial health and future prospects of the Acme Company.

Managerial accounting is the subject of other books and other courses. This second branch of accounting refers to the communication of information within an organization so that internal decisions (such as whether to buy or rent a building) can be made in an appropriate manner. Individuals studying an organization as a whole have different goals than do internal parties making operational decisions. Thus, many unique characteristics have developed in connection with each of these two branches of accounting. Financial accounting and managerial accounting have evolved independently over the decades to address the specific needs of the users being served and the decisions being made. This textbook is designed to explain those attributes that are fundamental to attaining a useable understanding of financial accounting.

It is not that one of these areas of accounting is more useful or more important than the other. Financial accounting and managerial accounting have simply been created to achieve different objectives. They both do their jobs well, but they do not have the same jobs.

TEST YOURSELF

Question:

Janet Wineston is vice president of the State Bank of Main Street. Here are four decisions that she made at her job today. Which of these decisions was likely to have required her to make use of her knowledge of financial accounting?

a. She gave one of the tellers who works at the bank a pay raise.

b. She hired an advertising consultant to produce a television commercial for the bank.

c. She granted a $300,000 loan to one company but not another.

d. She decided on the rate of interest that would be paid to customers on a new type of savings account.

Answer:

The correct answer is choice c: She granted a $300,000 loan to one company but not another.

Explanation:

Financial accounting focuses on decisions about organizations. When money was loaned to one company but not the other, Wineston was making decisions about both. She must have viewed one as more financially healthy than the other. Her other three decisions all relate to internal operations. Accounting information can certainly help in arriving at proper choices for these three, but it is managerial accounting that is designed to produce the needed data for such decisions.

1.5   Financial Accounting Information and Company Employees

Question: Financial accounting refers to the conveyance of information about an organization as a whole and is most frequently distributed to assist outside decision makers. **Does a person who is employed by an organization care about the financial accounting data that is reported?** *Why should an employee in the marketing or personnel department of the Acme Company be interested in the financial information that this business generates and distributes?*

Answer: Financial accounting is designed to portray the overall financial condition and prospects of an organization. Virtually every employee should be interested in studying that information to judge future employment prospects. A business that is doing well will possibly award larger pay raises or perhaps significant end-of-year cash bonuses. A financially healthy organization can afford to hire new employees, buy additional equipment, or pursue major new initiatives. Conversely, when a business is struggling and prospects are dim, employees might anticipate layoffs, pay cuts, or reductions in resources.

Thus, although financial accounting information is directed to outside decision makers, employees should be keenly interested in the financial health of their own organization. No one wants to be clueless as to whether their employer is headed for prosperity or bankruptcy. In reality, employees are often the most avid readers of the financial accounting information distributed by employers because the results can have such an immediate and direct impact on their jobs and, hence, their lives.

KEY TAKEAWAY

Financial accounting encompasses the rules and procedures covering the conveyance of monetary information to describe a business or other organization. Individuals who attain a sufficient level of knowledge of financial accounting can then utilize this information to make decisions based on the organization's perceived financial health and future prospects. Such decisions might include assessing employment potential, lending money, granting credit, and buying or selling ownership shares. However, financial accounting does not address issues that are purely of an internal nature, such as whether an organization should buy or lease equipment or the level of pay raises. Information to guide such internal decisions is generated according to managerial accounting rules and procedures that are introduced in other books and courses. Although financial accounting is not directed toward the inner workings of an organization, most employees are interested in the resulting information because it helps them assess the future of their employer.

2. INCORPORATION AND THE TRADING OF CAPITAL SHARES

2.1 The Ownership Shares of an Incorporated Business

Question: In discussing possible decisions that could be made about a business organization, ownership shares were mentioned. Virtually every day, on television, in newspapers, or on the Internet, mention is made that the shares of one company or another have gone up or down in price because of trading on one of the stock markets. **Why does a person acquire ownership shares of a business such as Capital One or Intel?**

Answer: In the United States, as well as in many other countries, owners of a business can apply to the state government to become identified as an entity legally set apart from its owners. This process is referred to as **incorporation**. Therefore, a **corporation** is an organization that has been formally recognized by the state government as a separate legal entity that can act independently of its owners. A business that has not been incorporated is either a **sole proprietorship** (one owner) or a **partnership** (more than one owner). These businesses are not separate from their ownership.

incorporation

Legal process by which owners of an organization apply to a state government to have it identified as an entity legally separate from its owners (a corporation); corporations are the legal form of most businesses of any size in the United States.

corporation

An organization that has been formally recognized by the state government as a separate legal entity so that it can sell ownership shares to raise money for capital expenditures and operations.

sole proprietorship

An unincorporated business created, owned, and operated by a single individual; the business is not legally separate from its owner.

partnership

An unincorporated business created, owned, and operated by more than one individual; the business is not legally separate from its owners.

As will be discussed in detail in a later chapter, several advantages are gained from incorporation. One is especially important in connection with the study of financial accounting. A corporation has the ability to obtain monetary resources by selling (also known as issuing) capital shares that allow investors to become owners. They are then known as **stockholders** or **shareholders**.

Millions of corporations operate in the United States. **The Walt Disney Company** and **General Electric** are just two well-known examples of corporations. They exist as legal entities completely distinct from the multitude of individuals and organizations that possess their ownership shares (also known as equity or **capital stock**).

Any investor who acquires one or more shares of the capital stock of a corporation becomes an owner and has all of the rights that are specified by the state government or on the stock certificate. The number of shares and owners can be staggering. At the end of 2010, stockholders held over 2.3 billion shares of **The Coca-Cola Company**. Thus, possession of one share of the capital stock of **The Coca-Cola Company** provided a person with approximately a 1/2,300,000,000th part of the ownership.

One of the great advantages of incorporation is the ease by which most capital stock can be exchanged. For most companies, investors are able to buy or sell ownership shares on stock exchanges in a matter of moments. In contrast, sole proprietorships and partnerships rarely sell capital shares. Without the separation provided by incorporation, a clear distinction between owner and business does not exist. For example, debts incurred by a business that is a sole proprietorship or partnership may ultimately have to be satisfied by the owner personally. Thus, individuals tend to avoid making investments in unincorporated businesses unless they can be involved directly in the management. However, partnerships and sole proprietorships still remain popular because they are easy to create and offer possible income tax benefits as will be described in a later chapter.

If traded on a stock exchange, shares of the capital stock of a corporation continually go up and down in value based on myriad factors, including the perceived financial health and future prospects of the organization. As an example, during trading on July 1, 2011, the price of an ownership share of **Intel** rose by $0.37 to $22.53, while a share of **Capital One** went up by $0.98 to $52.65.

For countless individuals and groups around the world, the most popular method of investment is through the purchase and sell of these capital shares of corporate ownership. Although many other types of investment opportunities are available (such as the acquisition of gold or land), few come close to evoking the level of interest of capital stock.[3] On the **New York Stock Exchange** alone, billions of shares are bought and sold every business day at a wide range of prices. As of June 30, 2011, an ownership share of **Sprint Nextel** was trading for $5.39, while a single share of **Berkshire Hathaway** sold for $116,105.00.

stockholders

Individuals or organizations that hold the ownership shares of capital stock of a corporation; same as shareholders.

shareholders

Individuals or organizations that hold the ownership shares of capital stock of a corporation; same as stockholders.

capital stock

Ownership (equity) shares of stock in a corporation that are issued to raise monetary financing for capital expenditures and operations.

New York Stock Exchange

Organized stock market that efficiently matches buyers and sellers of capital stock at a mutually agreed-upon price allowing ownership in companies to change hands easily. The New York Stock Exchange is the largest stock exchange in the world followed by NASDAQ, the London Stock Exchange, the Tokyo Stock Exchange, and the Shanghai Stock Exchange.

TEST YOURSELF

Question:

Ray Nesbitt owns a store in his hometown of Charlotte, North Carolina, that sells food and a variety of other goods. He has always operated this store as a sole proprietorship because he was the only owner. Recently, he went to his lawyer and began the legal process of turning his business into a corporation. Which of the following is the most likely reason for this action?

a. He can sell a wider variety of goods as a corporation.

b. He has plans to build a second, and maybe a third, store in the area.

c. The store has reached a size where incorporation has become mandatory.

d. He hopes his son will one day decide to become a member of the management.

Answer:

The correct answer is choice b: He has plans to build a second, and maybe a third, store in the area.

Explanation:

One of the most important reasons to incorporate a business is that additional sources of capital can be tapped by issuing stock. Nesbitt may be planning to get the money needed to build the new stores by encouraging others to acquire stock and become owners. There is no size limit for incorporation, and the decision has little or nothing to do with operations. Neither the selection of goods nor the members of the management team is affected by the legal form of the business.

2.2   The Operational Structure of a Corporation

Question: The owners of most small corporations can operate their businesses effectively as both stockholders and managers. For example, two friends might each own half of the capital stock of a bakery or a retail clothing store. Those individuals probably work together to manage this business on a day-to-day basis.

Because of the number of people who can be involved, large corporations offer a significantly different challenge. **How do millions of investors possessing billions of capital shares of a corporation ever serve in any reasonable capacity as the owners and managers of that business?**

Answer: Obviously, a great many corporations like **The Coca-Cola Company** have an enormous quantity of capital shares held by tens of thousands of investors. Virtually none of these owners can expect to have any impact on the daily operations of the business. A different operational structure is needed. In a vast number of such organizations, stockholders vote to elect a representative group to oversee operations. This body—called the **board of directors**[4] —is made up of approximately ten to twenty-five knowledgeable individuals.

As shown in Figure 1.1, the board of directors hires the members of management who run the business on a daily basis. The board then meets periodically (often quarterly) to review operating, investing, and financing results as well as to approve strategic policy initiatives.

FIGURE 1.1 Company Operational Structure

Ownership	Each capital share is the equivalent of one unit of ownership.
Board of Directors	Elected by shareholders to hire and oversee the management of the company and make policy decisions.
Management	Officials such as the president, the chief financial officer, and the director of marketing who are in charge of daily operations.
Employees	All individuals who work for a company who are not deemed to be members of the management.

Occasionally, the original founders of a business (or their descendants) continue to hold enough shares to influence or actually control operating and other significant decisions of a business. Or wealthy outside investors might acquire enough shares to gain this same level of power. Such owners have genuine authority within the corporation. Even that degree of control, though, is normally carried out through membership on the board of directors. For example, at the end of 2010, the **Ford Motor Company** had fifteen members on its board of directors, three of whom were named Ford. Except in rare circumstances, the hierarchy of owners, board of directors, management, and employees remains intact. Thus, most stockholders are not involved with the operating decisions of any large corporation.

2.3 Predicting the Appreciation of Capital Stock Values

Question: The acquisition of capital shares of a corporation is an extremely popular investment strategy for a wide range of the population. A buyer becomes one of the owners of the business. Why spend money in this way especially since very few stockholders can ever hope to hold enough shares to participate in managing or influencing operations? Ownership shares sometimes cost small amounts but can also require hundreds if not thousands of dollars. **What is the potential benefit of buying capital stock issued by a business organization such as PepsiCo or Chevron?**

Answer: Capital shares of thousands of corporations trade each day on markets around the world such as the New York Stock Exchange or NASDAQ (National Association of Securities Dealers Automated Quotations). One party is looking to sell shares whereas another is seeking shares to buy. Stock markets match up these buyers and sellers so that a mutually agreed-upon price can be negotiated. This bargaining process allows the ownership interests of these companies to change hands with relative ease.

When investors believe a business is financially healthy and its future is bright, they expect prosperity and growth to continue. If that happens, the negotiated price for the capital shares of the corporation should rise over time. Investors around the world attempt to anticipate such movements in order to buy the stock at a low price and sell later at a higher one. Conversely, if predictions are not optimistic, then a business's share price is likely to drop so that owners will experience losses in the value of their investments.

Financial accounting information plays an invaluable role in this market process as millions of investors attempt to assess the financial condition and prospects of various business organizations on an ongoing basis. Being able to understand and make use of reported financial data helps improve the investor's knowledge of a corporation and, thus, the chance of making wise decisions about the buying and selling of capital shares. Ignorance often leads to poor decisions and much less lucrative outcomes.

In the United States, such investment gains—if successfully generated—are especially appealing to individuals when ownership shares are held for over twelve months before being sold. For income tax purposes, the difference between the buy and sale prices for such investments is referred to as a long-term capital gain or loss. Under certain circumstances, significant tax reductions are attributed to long-term capital gains.[5] The U.S. Congress created this tax incentive to encourage additional investment so that businesses could more easily obtain money for growth purposes. When businesses prosper and expand, the entire economy tends to do better.

> **NASDAQ (National Association of Securities Dealers Automated Quotations)**
>
> An electronic market that allows for the trading of capital shares in approximately three thousand companies, providing instantaneous price quotations to efficiently match buyers and sellers allowing ownership in companies to change hands.

TEST YOURSELF

Question:

Mr. and Mrs. Randolph Ostar buy one thousand shares of a well-known company at $25 per share on July 1, Year One. They hold no other investments. The stock is traded on the New York Stock Exchange, and the price goes up over time to $36 per share. On June 27, Year Two, the couple is considering the sale of these shares so that they can buy a new car. At the last moment, they postpone these transactions for one week. What is the most likely reason for this delay?

  a. Automobile prices tend to go down after July 1 each year.
  b. It normally takes several weeks to sell the shares of a large corporation.
  c. Laws delay the immediate use of money from the sale of investments for several weeks.
  d. They are hoping to reduce the amount of income taxes to be paid.

Answer:

The correct answer is choice d: They are hoping to reduce the amount of income taxes to be paid.

Explanation:

For individuals who own stock, gains on the sale of capital assets (such as these shares) are taxed at low rates, but only if long-term (held for over one year). The Ostars anticipate making an $11,000 profit ($36 − $25 × 1,000 shares). Currently, the shares have been held for slightly less than one year. If sold in June, the gain is short-term and taxed at a higher rate. By holding them for just one more week, the gain becomes long-term, and a significant amount of tax money is saved.

2.4 The Receipt of Dividends

Question: Investors acquire ownership shares of selected corporations hoping that the stock price will rise over time. This investment strategy is especially tempting because long-term capital gains are often taxed at a relatively low rate. **Is the possibility for appreciation in value the only reason that investors choose to acquire capital shares?**

dividends

Distributions made by a
corporation to its
shareholders as a reward
when income has been
earned; decision to pay is
made by the board of
directors; shareholders often
receive favorable tax
treatment when cash
dividends are collected.

Answer: Many corporations—although certainly not all—pay cash **dividends** to their stockholders periodically. A dividend is a reward for being an owner of a business that is prospering. It is not a required payment; it is a sharing of profits with the stockholders. As an example, for 2010, **Duke Energy** reported earning profits (net income) of $1.32 billion. During that same period, the corporation distributed total cash dividends of approximately $1.28 billion to the owners of its capital stock.[6]

The board of directors determines whether to pay dividends. Some boards prefer to leave money within the business to stimulate future growth and additional profits. For example, **Google Inc.** reported profits (net income) for 2010 of $8.51 billion but distributed no dividends to its owners. Newer companies often choose to pay less dividends than older companies as they try to grow quickly to a desired size.

Not surprisingly, a variety of investing strategies abound. Many investors acquire ownership shares almost exclusively in hopes of benefiting from an anticipated appreciation of stock prices. Another large segment of the investing public is more likely to be drawn to the possibility of dividend payments. Unless an owner has the chance to influence or control the operations of a business, only these two potential benefits can accrue from the ownership of capital shares: appreciation in the value of the stock price and cash dividends.

2.5   Annual Rate of Return on an Investment in Capital Stock

Question: An investor can put money into a savings account at a bank and earn a small but relatively risk-free profit. For example, $100 could be invested on January 1 and then be worth $102 at the end of the year because interest is added to the balance. The extra $2 means that the investor earned an annual return of 2 percent ($2 increase/$100 investment). This computation helps in comparing one possible investment opportunity against another. **How is the annual rate of return computed when the capital stock of a corporation is acquired as an investment and then held for a period of time?**

Answer: Capital stock investments are certainly not risk free. Profits can be high, but losses always loom as a possibility. The annual rate of return measures those profits and losses in the past and is often anticipated for the future as a way of making investment decisions.

To illustrate, assume that on January 1, Year One, an investor spends $100 for one ownership share of the Ace Company and another $100 for a share of the Base Company. During the year, Ace distributes a dividend of $1.00 per share to each of its owners while Base pays a dividend of $5.00 per share. On December 31, the capital stock of the Ace Company is selling on a stock market for $108 per share whereas the stock of the Base Company has a price of only $91 per share.

This investor now holds a total value of $109 as a result of the purchase of the share of the Ace Company: the cash dividend of $1 and a share of capital stock worth $108. In one year, the total value has risen by $9 ($109 less $100) so that the annual rate return was 9 percent ($9 increase/$100 investment).

The shares of the Base Company did not perform as well. At the end of the year, the total value of this investment is only $96: the cash dividend of $5 plus one share of stock worth $91. That is a drop of $4 during the year ($96 less $100). The annual rate of return on this investment is a negative 4 percent ($4 decrease/$100 investment).

As a result of this first year, buying a share of Ace obviously proved to be a better investment than buying a share of Base because of the higher annual rate of return. However, a careful analysis of the financial accounting data available at the start of the year might have helped this investor realize in advance that the rate of return on the investment in Ace would be higher. An assessment of the financial health and future prospects of both businesses could have shown that a higher return was expected in connection with the investment in Ace.

Therefore, estimating the annual rate of return is important for investors because it helps them select from among multiple investment opportunities. This computation provides a method for quantifying the financial benefit earned in the past and expected in the future. Logically, investors should simply choose the investment that provides the highest anticipated rate of return. However, as with all predictions, the risk that actual actions will not follow the expected course must be taken into consideration. Investing often breaks down to anticipating profits while measuring the likelihood and amount of potential losses.

> **KEY TAKEAWAY**
>
> Incorporation allows an organization to be viewed legally as a separate entity apart from its ownership. In most large corporations, few owners are able to be involved in the operational decision making. Instead, stockholders elect a board of directors to oversee the business and direct the work of management. Corporations can issue shares of capital stock that give the holder an ownership right and enables the business to raise monetary funds. If the organization is financially healthy and prospering, these shares can increase in value over time—possibly by a significant amount. In addition, a profitable organization may well share its good fortune with its ownership through the distribution of cash dividends. Investors often attempt to estimate the annual rate of return that can be expected from an investment as a way of comparing it to other investment alternatives. This computation takes the profit for the year (stock appreciation and dividends) and divides it by the amount of the investment at the start of the period.

3. USING FINANCIAL ACCOUNTING FOR WISE DECISION MAKING

> **LEARNING OBJECTIVES**
>
> At the end of this section, students should be able to meet the following objectives:
>
> 1. List the predictions that investors and potential investors want to make about a business organization.
> 2. List the predictions that creditors and potential creditors want to make about a business organization.
> 3. Explain the reporting of monetary amounts as a central focus of financial accounting.
> 4. Explain how financial accounting information is enhanced and clarified by verbal explanations.
> 5. Understand the function played by the annual report published by many businesses and other organizations.

3.1   Financial Accounting Information and Investments in Capital Stock

Question: Investors are interested (sometimes almost obsessively interested) in the financial information that is produced by a business organization according to the rules and principles of financial accounting. They want to use this information to make wise investing decisions. **What do investors actually hope to learn about a business by analyzing published financial information?**

Answer: The information reported by financial accounting is similar to a giant, complex portrait painted of the organization. There are probably hundreds, if not thousands, of aspects of the picture that can be examined, analyzed, and evaluated to help assess the financial health and future prospects of the model. Theories abound as to which pieces of information are best to use when studying a business. One investor might prefer to focus on a particular portion of the data almost exclusively (such as profitability) whereas another may believe that entirely different information is most significant (such as the sources and uses of cash).

Ultimately, in connection with the buying and selling of capital stock, all investors are trying to arrive at the same two insights. They are attempting to use the provided financial accounting data to estimate the following:

1. The price of the corporation's capital stock in the future
2. The amount of cash dividends that will be paid over time by the business

Despite the complexity of the information, these two goals are rather simplistic. If an investor owns capital shares of a business and feels that the current accounting information signals either a rise in stock prices or strong dividend distributions, holding the investment or even buying more shares is probably warranted. Conversely, if careful analysis indicates a possible drop in stock price or a reduction in dividend payments, sale of the stock is likely to be the appropriate action.

Interestingly, by the very nature of the market, any exchange of ownership shares means that the buyer has studied available information and believes the future to be relatively optimistic for the business in question. In contrast, the seller has looked at similar data and arrived at a different, more pessimistic outlook.

TEST YOURSELF

Question:

An investor is currently studying the financial information produced by Company A and also by Company B. The investor holds ownership shares of Company A but not Company B. After studying all the available data, the investor sells her shares of Company A and uses the proceeds to buy shares of Company B. What is the most likely explanation for these actions?

a. Company B has been more profitable than Company A in the past.

b. Company B has paid a larger dividend than Company A in the past.

c. Last year, the price of Company B's stock rose faster than that of Company A.

d. Company B is poised to be more profitable than Company A in the future.

Answer:

The correct answer is choice d: Company B is poised to be more profitable than Company A in the future.

Explanation:

Investors use data to anticipate changes in stock prices and dividend payments. Such events are affected by an organization's financial health and future prospects. Historical data, such as profitability, dividends, and stock prices, are helpful but only if they provide guidance as to what will happen in the future. If Company B is expected to be more profitable in the coming year, that outcome may well translate into a strong appreciation in the price of the stock or high dividend payments.

3.2 Financial Accounting Information and Other Interested Parties

*Question: **Are there reasons to analyze the financial accounting information produced by a particular business other than to help investors predict stock prices and cash dividend payments?***

Answer: The desire to analyze an organization's financial situation is not limited to investors in the stock market. For example, as discussed previously, a loan might be requested from a bank, or one business could be considering the sale of its merchandise to another on credit. Such obligations require eventual payment. Therefore, another portion of the individuals and groups that study the financial information reported by an organization wants to assess the likelihood that money will be available in the future to pay debts. Stock prices and cash dividend distributions are much less significant to a creditor.

The same financial data utilized by investors who are buying or selling capital stock will also be of benefit to current and potential creditors. However, this group is likely to focus attention on particular elements of the information such as the sheer amount of the debt owed, when that debt is scheduled to come due, and the perceived ability to generate sufficient cash to meet those demands in a timely fashion. Ultimately, creditors attempt to anticipate the organization's future cash flows to measure the risk that debt principal and interest payments might not be forthcoming when due.[7]

Therefore, millions of individuals and groups use reported financial information to assess business organizations in order to make three predictions:

- Future stock market prices for the capital shares issued by the business
- Future cash dividend distributions
- Future ability to generate sufficient cash to meet debts as they mature

The first two relate to investors in the capital stock issued by the corporation; the third is of more significance to the creditors of that organization.

3.3 The Nature of Financial Information

*Question: The term "financial information" comes up frequently in these discussions. **What is meant by financial information?***

Answer: Financial information reported by and about an organization consists of data that can be measured in monetary terms. For example, if a building costs $4 million to acquire, that is financial information, as is the statement that a debt of $700,000 is owed to a bank. In both cases, relevant information is communicated to decision makers as a monetary balance. However, if a business has eight thousand employees, that fact might be interesting, but it is not financial information. The figure is not a dollar amount; it is not stated in the form that is most useful for decision-making purposes by either investors or creditors. Assuming that those workers were paid a total of $500 million during the most recent year, then that number is financial information because it reflects the amount of money spent.

Likewise, a men's clothing store does not include in its financial accounting information that it holds ten thousand shirts to be sold. Instead, the business reports that it currently owns shirts for sale (frequently referred to as **inventory**) with a cost of, perhaps, $300,000. Or, after having sold these items to customers, it could explain that total sales of $500,000 were made during the period.

> **inventory**
>
> A current asset bought or manufactured for the purpose of selling in order to generate revenue.

3.4 Financial Accounting and Verbal Explanations

Question: The value of reported data seems somewhat restricted if only amounts measured in dollars is included. **Is financial accounting information limited solely to figures that can be stated in monetary terms?**

Answer: Although financial accounting starts by reporting balances as monetary amounts, the communication process does not stop there. Extensive verbal explanations as well as additional numerical data are also provided to clarify or expand the monetary information where necessary. To illustrate, assume that an organization is the subject of a lawsuit and estimates an eventual loss of $750,000. This is financial information that must be reported based on the rules of financial accounting. However, the organization should also communicate other nonfinancial information such as the cause of the lawsuit and the likelihood that the loss will actually occur. The dollar amount alone does not provide sufficient information for either investors or creditors.

Thus, accounting actually communicates to decision makers in two distinct steps:

1. Financial information is provided in monetary terms
2. Further explanation is given to clarify and expand on those monetary balances

3.5 The Annual Report

Question: Businesses and other organizations must have some structural method for conveying financial information and additional verbal explanations to outside decision makers. **If a potential investor or creditor wants to assess a business organization such as Johnson & Johnson or Colgate-Palmolive, in what form is that information delivered?**

Answer: Most companies regardless of size prepare and distribute an annual report shortly after the end of each year. For example, the 2010 annual report of the **McDonald's Corporation** can be downloaded from the Internet at http://www.aboutmcdonalds.com/mcd/investors/ annual_reports.html.[8]

This publication is over fifty pages in length and contains virtually any financial accounting information that a potential investor or creditor could need to make an estimation of the future stock price for the capital stock issued by **McDonald's** as well as future dividend distributions and cash inflows and outflows. For example, here are some of the most relevant pieces of information included in the company's 2010 annual report.

- Pages 1 through 3 is a letter to shareholders from the chief executive office, the person who is the head of **McDonald's** management.
- Page 4 is a letter to shareholders from the chair of the board of directors.
- Pages 9 through 25 present management's discussion and analysis of the company's financial condition and results of operations.
- Pages 26 through 29 contain the financial accounting information formally reported by **McDonald's**.
- Pages 30 through 42 provide verbal explanations and other additional information to help clarify the monetary balances reported on pages 26 through 29.
- Page 46 identifies the executive members of management and the officers who work for **McDonald's**.
- Page 47 lists the members of the board of directors.

This textbook will focus on helping students gain an understanding of the financial accounting information that is produced by a business organization as exemplified by **McDonald's** on pages 26 through 29 and then explained further in pages 30 through 42. Those seventeen pages form the heart of the financial reporting process for this organization. Here in Chapter 1, most students will understand very little of the available data about **McDonald's**. However, with careful reading, thought, and work, by the conclusion of Chapter 17, students should have a working knowledge of financial accounting and its rules and procedures. They will then be able to analyze a good percentage of the information reported by any business as a basis for making wise decisions about the buying and selling of its capital stock and the extension of credit and loans.

KEY TAKEAWAY

Throughout the world each day, investors buy and sell the capital stock shares of thousands of businesses. Other individuals choose to loan money or grant credit to these same organizations. Such decisions are based on assessing potential risks and rewards. Financial accounting provides information to these decision makers to help them evaluate the possibility of capital stock price appreciation, cash dividend distributions, and the business's ability to generate cash to meet obligations as they come due. This information is financial in nature, meaning that it is stated in monetary terms. However, numerical data alone is of limited value. Thus, financial accounting provides monetary balances as well as clarifying verbal explanations to assist users in assessing the financial health and future prospects of a particular business. This information is made available to interested parties as one portion of the annual report that most business corporations produce each year.

Talking with a Real Investing Pro

Kevin G. Burns is a partner in his own registered investment advisory firm, the **LLBH Private Wealth Management Group**, an organization that specializes in asset management, concentrated stock strategies, and wealth transfer. **LLBH** consults on investing strategies for assets of nearly $1 billion. Before starting his own firm in October 2008, he was first vice president of **Merrill Lynch Private Banking and Investment Group**. Burns began his career on Wall Street in 1981 at **Paine Webber**. He has also worked at **Oppenheimer & Co.** and **Smith Barney**. Burns has appeared several times on the CBS Evening News. He has been kind enough to agree to be interviewed about his opinions and experiences in using financial accounting information. His thoughts will appear at the end of each chapter. His firm's Web site is http://www.LLBHprivatewealthmanagement.com.

Question: You majored in accounting in college but you never worked in the accounting field. Instead, you became an investment advisor. If you never planned to become an accountant, why did you major in that subject?

Kevin Burns: In my view, accounting is the backbone of any business major in college. Being able to translate the information that a company provides, prepare a budget, understand the concept of revenues and expenses, and the like has been enormously helpful in my investment management business. Anyone majoring in any aspect of business needs that knowledge. I also liked being able to know I had the right answers on the tests that my accounting professors gave me when all the numbers added up properly.

Question: Why do you prefer to invest in the capital stock of a business rather than put your client's money in other forms of investment such as gold or real estate?

KB: I think it is very important to diversify investments. In my world, that includes stocks as well as other types of investments. Of course, there is a place for investments in real estate, commodities, and the like. My personal preference is to invest only in very liquid assets; those—such as capital shares—that can be turned into cash quickly through trades on a stock exchange. I like to know, even if I am investing for the long term, that I can sell my investments five minutes after I buy them should I change my mind. I simply prefer liquid investments. Real estate is not very liquid as the housing market has recently shown. Gold, of course, is liquid. However, while it has appreciated lately, it was selling for around $800 an ounce when I was in high school and is now about $1,800 an ounce. Over a thirty-year period of time, that is not a very big profit. If my clients earned that small of a return on their money over thirty years, they would fire me.

What Was Truly Important?

To students of Financial Accounting:

You have now read Chapter 1. What were the five points that you discovered in this chapter that seemed most important to you? A lot of information is provided here. What stood out as truly significant? After you make your choices, go to the following link and watch a short video clip where Professor Joe Hoyle will choose his top five points from Chapter 1. You can learn his rationale for these picks and see whether you agree or disagree with those selections.

Video Clip

Professor Joe Hoyle talks about the five most important points in Chapter 1.

INVESTORS: SHOULD OWNERSHIP SHARES BE BOUGHT OR SOLD?

View the video online at: http://bit.ly/hoyle1-2

4. END-OF-CHAPTER EXERCISES

QUESTIONS

1. James Watkins is signing up for classes at his college for the upcoming semester and is thinking of taking a course in financial accounting. What is financial accounting?

2. What decisions are often associated with financial accounting?

3. How does financial accounting differ from managerial accounting?

4. Who are some of the most likely users of the information provided by financial accounting?

5. Betsy Ligando and Cynthia Zvyvco are planning to start a business where they will sell greeting cards in a leased space at the local shopping center. A friend told them that they should create their business as a corporation. What is a corporation?

6. From question 5, assume that the owners choose not to incorporate their business. What type of business will they create and what risks are involved?

7. From question 5, assume that the owners decide that their business will be created as a corporation. How does a business become a corporation?

8. What are the advantages of operating a business as a corporation?

9. What purpose does a board of directors serve in a corporation?

10. Tyrone Waters works part time during the school year and has saved up cash amounting to $2,000. He wants to invest that money in the capital stock of a business such as **Walmart**. Why would Waters use his money to buy ownership shares of this business?

11. An investor in the capital stock of a business will often look at available financial accounting information in a different way than a creditor or lender. How do the needs of these two groups differ?

12. What is financial information?

13. What is a dividend? Who makes the decision for a business corporation to distribute a dividend? Why is a dividend distributed?

14. Daisy Miller owns one hundred shares of the capital stock of Aground International, a business organization with its headquarters in her hometown. The company mails her a copy of its latest annual report. What is the purpose of the annual report?

15. Jimi Tattaro puts $500 into a savings account and closes it out one year later by removing all $515 that is now in the account. He also spent $600 to invest in the capital shares of the YxWho Corporation. He sold those shares one year later for $638. Before the sale, he received a $4 cash dividend from YxWho. What is the annual return on each of these investments?

TRUE OR FALSE

1. _____ Financial accounting information is generated primarily to help with decisions made inside a business or by some other organization.

2. _____ Typically, a business operated as a sole proprietorship will be able to raise money from issuing capital shares easier than will a business operated as a corporation.

3. _____ Employees have no reason to be interested in any financial accounting information provided by their employer.

4. _____ Most investors in the capital stock of a business want to be involved in the daily operations.

5. _____ The board of directors of a corporation is elected by its shareholders.

6. _____ Investors who hold investments in capital stock for longer than a year may enjoy a tax benefit.

7. _____ In analyzing a business, creditors are most interested in the possibility that the corporation's stock price might decline.

8. _____ Corporations that report earning additional profits are required by law to pay dividends to their shareholders.

9. _____ Purchasing the capital stock of a business is typically a riskier investment than opening a savings account.

10. _____ Financial information is communicated in monetary terms but may be explained verbally.

11. _____ Most businesses report their financial accounting information as part of an annual report released to owners and other interested parties.

12. _____ Accountants are the primary users of the information provided by financial accounting.

13. _____ An entity that loans money to a business is referred to as a "shareholder."

MULTIPLE CHOICE

1. Ramon Sanchez is a loan officer at Washington Bank. He is in the process of deciding whether or not to loan money to Medlock Corporation. Which of the following would have the most influence on Sanchez when making this decision?

    a. Medlock generated positive cash flows last year.

    b. Medlock paid dividends last year.

    c. Medlock's stock price increased last year.

    d. The number of stockholders in Medlock increased last year.

2. Which of the following is not a reason for an investor to purchase capital stock in a relatively large corporation?

    a. To receive dividend payments

    b. To sell the stock for a gain if the share price increases

    c. To earn a return on their investment

    d. To participate in the day-to-day operations of the business

3. Which of the following is not a decision that is normally made using financial accounting information?

    a. An investor decided to acquire shares of the capital stock of Rayburn Corporation.

    b. A credit analyst at Mayfield Corporation rejected a request for credit from Rayburn Corporation.

    c. A Rayburn Corporation manager decided to increase the quantity of widgets produced each month for sales purposes.

    d. A loan officer at Fairburn Bank chose to grant a loan request made by Rayburn Corporation so the company could expand.

4. Which of the following individuals is most likely to have a say in the policy decisions made by a large corporation?

    a. A stockholder

    b. A member of the board of directors

    c. An employee

    d. A creditor

5. Leon Williams is an investor in Springfield Corporation. On January 1, Year One, he purchased 150 shares of the corporation's capital stock at a price of $45 per share. On October 15, Year One, Springfield distributed a cash dividend of $1.50 per share to its stockholders. On December 31, Year One, Springfield's stock is selling for $47 per share. What is the annual rate of return on William's investment during Year One, rounded to one decimal point?

    a. 3.3 percent

    b. 4.4 percent

    c. 5.5 percent

    d. 7.8 percent

6. At the beginning of the current year, the capital stock of the Ajax Corporation was selling for $24 per share, but, by the end of the year it was selling for $35 per share. Which of the following individuals is the least likely to pay significant attention to this jump in stock price?

    a. The vice president in charge of advertising working on the budget for this coming year

    b. The loan officer at the bank who granted Ajax a loan late last year

    c. Chair of the board of directors

    d. Head of a local investment advisory company

7. Which of the following is least likely to be found in the financial information provided in the annual report of a large corporation?

    a. The amount of cash dividends paid in each of the last three years.

    b. The total amount of debt owed by the corporation.

    c. The rationale for deciding to rent a new airplane rather than buying it.

    d. The amount of cash held by the business at the end of the year.

8. William Alexander invests money to become one of the owners of a local restaurant. He sells his interest three months later because he wants to invest in a bookstore. Which is the most likely legal structure for the restaurant?

    a. Sole proprietorship

    b. Partnership

c. Standard operating business

d. Corporation

VIDEO PROBLEMS

Professor Joe Hoyle discusses the answers to these two problems at the links that are indicated. After formulating your answers, watch each video to see how Professor Hoyle answers these questions.

1. Your roommate is an English major. The roommate has just learned that you are taking a course in financial accounting. The roommate has never once considered taking a class in business and is mystified that you have chosen to spend your time learning this material. One evening, over pizza, you two are discussing your classes for the semester. The roommate wants to know why anyone could possibly benefit from a class in financial accounting. How would you respond?

View the video online at: http://bit.ly/hoyle1-3

2. Your uncle has worked for a large office supply business for twenty years. They have approximately one hundred retail stores located across the country. He is responsible for a small team of employees who do the interior design work in each of these stores. One day he sends you the following e-mail: "As a reward for twenty years of service, my company has offered to sell me one thousand shares of their capital stock for $23 per share. That's $23,000, and that is a lot of money. I've never been interested in this aspect of business. I understand you are taking a financial accounting course in college. What are capital shares? More importantly, how can I determine whether to spend $23,000 for these shares?"

View the video online at: http://bit.ly/hoyle1-4

PROBLEMS

1. Explain how each of the following individuals might use the information provided by financial accounting about the Nguyen Company, which is located in Falls Church, Virginia.

   a. Bank loan officer considering loaning money to Nguyen Company

   b. Current employee of Nguyen Company

   c. Potential employee of Nguyen Company

   d. Current investor in Nguyen Company

   e. Potential investor in Nguyen Company

   f. A credit analyst of company wanting to sell inventory to Nguyen Company

2. Mark each of the following with an (F) to indicate if it is financial information or an (N) to indicate if it is nonfinancial information.

   Metro Corporation has the following:

   a. ____ Cash of $4,000,000

   b. ____ A building that cost $50,000,000

   c. ____ 2,000 employees

   d. ____ Inventory with a cost of $16,000,000

   e. ____ 500 shares of capital stock

   f. ____ 1,000 trucks

   g. ____ Sales of merchandise for $45,000,000

   h. ____ 2,000 cans of beans for resale purposes

   i. ____ 2,000 cans of beans to be used in the employee cafeteria

3. Assume that a person you know tells the following story: "I inherited $3,000 from a distant uncle. I took that money and invested it all in the capital shares of **Ford Motor Co.** I had looked at several other corporations including **Intel**, **PepsiCo**, **Microsoft**, and **Google**. Eventually, though, I put my money into **Ford**."

   Answer the following questions:

   a. What is meant by "the capital shares of **Ford Motor Co.**?"

   b. Why would a person spend $3,000 to buy the capital shares of any business?

   c. Provide some possible reasons for this person to have invested in **Ford** rather than in those other corporations.

   d. In what way might the annual report of **Ford Motor Co.** have helped the person to make this decision?

RESEARCH ASSIGNMENTS

1. The chapter introduced several forms of business, including a corporation, sole proprietorship, and partnership. Other forms of business exist as well. Do an Internet search to learn as much as you can about each of the following business forms:

   - Sole proprietorship
   - Partnership
   - Limited partnership
   - C corporation
   - S corporation
   - Limited liability corporation (LLC)

   For each of these legal forms, discuss the following issues: ease of organization and maintenance of form, number of people involved, government involvement, liability to owners, ease of exit, taxation, day-to-day management, and funding sources.

2. A great amount of financial information is available on the Internet about most business corporations of any significant size. For example, visit http://www.google.com/finance/. In the "Get Quotes" box, type in "**Starbucks Corporation**."

   Answer each of the following questions based on the information provided at this site:

   a. For what price is the capital stock issued by **Starbucks** currently selling?

   b. On what stock market or exchange are the shares of **Starbucks** bought and sold?

   c. For convenience, the names of corporations that are listed on stock markets have a ticker symbol. This symbol is a shorthand method of identifying the business. What is the ticker symbol for **Starbucks**?

   d. Investors are often interested in the movement of the price of a share of stock during recent months. What is the fifty-two week range in the price of **Starbucks'** stock? Is the current price closer to the high or to the low in that range?

   e. Investors are also interested in comparing a business operation to other businesses in the same or related industry. Investors want to know how the company does in comparison to its chief competitors. List three corporations that may be competitors of **Starbucks**.

   f. Read the description of this business and list three things that you found most interesting.

   g. Provide the names of three officers and three members of the board of directors.

3. The U.S. Department of Labor has a page on its Web site at http://www.bls.gov/oco/ocos001.htm that is titled "Accountants and Auditors." Go to this site and read this page. Use that information to answer the following questions:

   a. In general, what functions do accountants perform?

   b. Briefly list the different types of accountants and what they do.

   c. What education is required to become an accountant or an auditor?

   d. What is a CPA?

   e. What are the typical requirements to become a CPA?

   f. What other certifications are available for accountants?

   g. What is the current job outlook for the accounting profession?

4. Go to http://www.target.com/. At the **Target Corporation** Web site, scroll to the bottom of that page, find "Company Information," and click on "Investors." Then, click on "Annual Reports." Click on the 2010 annual report and answer the following question:

   Starting on page 2, a two-page letter is included "to our shareholders" from the chairman, president, and CEO. Read that letter. Assume you are thinking about buying shares of the capital stock of **Target**. List two or three pieces of information that you found in this letter that you felt were especially relevant to your decision.

ENDNOTES

1. See http://www.deepsky.com/~madmagic/kofi.html.

2. Tax accounting is another distinct branch of accounting. It is less focused on decision making and more on providing information needed by a business to comply with all government rules and regulations. Even in tax accounting, though, decision making is important as businesses seek to take all possible legal actions to minimize tax payments.

3. The most prevalent form of capital stock is common stock so that these two terms have come to be used somewhat interchangeably. As will be discussed in a later chapter, the capital stock of some corporations is made up of both common stock and preferred stock.

4. A story produced by National Public Radio on the roles played by a board of directors can be found at http://www.npr.org/templates/story/story.php?storyId=105576374.

5. This same tax benefit is not available to corporate taxpayers, only individuals.

6. The receipt of cash dividends is additionally appealing to stockholders because, in most cases, they are taxed at the same reduced rates as are applied to net long-term capital gains.

7. Cash flows also influence stock prices and dividend payments and would, thus, be information useful for potential investors in the capital stock of a company as well as its creditors.

8. The annual report for the **McDonald's Corporation** can also be found by following these steps:

   1. Go to http://www.mcdonalds.com.
   2. Scroll to the bottom of the page and click on "Corporate."
   3. At the top of the next screen, click on "Investors" at the top of the page.
   4. A picture of **McDonald's** latest annual report should be on the next screen. Click on that picture for it to download.

What Should Decision Makers Know in Order to Make Good Decisions about an Organization?

 Video Clip

In this video, Professor Joe Hoyle introduces the essential points covered in Chapter 2.

View the video online at: http://bit.ly/hoyle2-1

1. CREATING A PORTRAIT OF AN ORGANIZATION THAT CAN BE USED BY DECISION MAKERS

LEARNING OBJECTIVES

At the end of this section, students should be able to meet the following objectives:

1. Explain the comparison of financial accounting to the painting of a portrait.
2. Understand the reasons why financial accounting information does not need to be exact.
3. Define the term "material" and describe its fundamental role in financial accounting.
4. Define the term "misstatement" and differentiate between the two types of misstatements: errors and fraud.

1.1 Financial Statements: The Portrait of an Organization

Question: In Chapter 1, mention was made that financial accounting is somewhat analogous to the painting of a giant, complex portrait. **How could financial accounting possibly be compared to an artistic endeavor such as the creation of a painted portrait?**

representational faithfulness

A reasonable agreement between reported information and the event or balance it purports to represent; this term refers to the communication of an appropriate picture of an organization, which can serve as the basis for appropriate decisions.

presents fairly

Financial information that contains no material misstatements in accordance with an accepted standard for financial reporting.

financial statements

Quantitative reports and related verbal disclosures that convey monetary information describing the operations, financial position, and cash flows of an organization as a basis for representing its financial health and future prospects.

Answer: The purpose of a portrait—as might have been created by Rembrandt, van Gogh, or even Picasso—is to capture a likeness of the artist's model. In a somewhat parallel fashion, financial accounting attempts to present a portrait of an organization that can be used by interested parties to assess its financial health and future prospects. If well painted, this picture should enable individuals to estimate future stock prices, dividend payments, and cash flows. Accounting even has specific terms (such as **representational faithfulness** and **presents fairly**) that are used to indicate that financial information successfully provides a reasonable likeness of the reporting organization.

In accounting, this portrait is most often presented in the form of **financial statements**. The accountant takes all appropriate monetary information and constructs a set of financial statements to be distributed to decision makers. Financial statements are a representation of an organization's operations, financial position, and cash flows. These statements provide the form and structure for the conveyance of financial information that will create a likeness of the reporting organization. This textbook is about the preparation of those financial statements and the meaning of their contents.

1.2 A Likeness Does Not Have to Be Exact

Question: *Financial accounting deals with numbers that are exact. A 3 is a 3 and nothing else.* **In describing the production of financial statements, why are the results not compared to a photograph rather than a painted portrait?** *After all, a photograph is a much more precise likeness than a painting.*

Answer: A human portrait, even by a master such as Rembrandt, will not be completely accurate. The shape of the person's chin or the turn of the neck may be off slightly. The color of the eyes and hair cannot possibly be a perfect replica of life. It is a painted portrait, not a photograph (which is much more mechanically accurate). Fortunately, absolute exactness is not necessary for capturing the essence of a model. A likeness is achieved when a viewer exclaims, "I know that person!" Exact precision is not required to meet that objective.

Despite public perception to the contrary, financial accounting information is rarely an exactly accurate portrait. The accountant's goal is to create financial statements that present a likeness of an organization that can be used to make decisions. For example, the reported cost of constructing a building may be off slightly because of the sheer volume of money being spent on the many different aspects of the project. No one expects the reported cost of a $50 million manufacturing plant to be accurate to the penny. As with the painted portrait, that does not necessarily reduce the usefulness of the data. If financial information provides a fair representation, an interested party should be able to make use of it to arrive at the desired projections such as future stock prices. A potential investor or creditor does not need numbers that are absolutely accurate in order to assert, "Based on the information available in the financial statements, I understand enough about this business to make informed decisions. Even if I could obtain figures that were more accurate, I believe that I would still take the same actions."

An artist applies oil paints, pastels, or watercolors to a canvas to present a likeness of a subject. An accountant does something quite similar in constructing financial statements with numbers and words. The goal is much the same: to produce a likeness that truly reflects the essence of the model, which, in this case, is an entire organization.

TEST YOURSELF

Question:

For the year ending January 31, 2011, **Walmart** reported having made sales to its customers (net of returns and allowances) of $418,952,000,000. James Forrest is studying the available information in order to decide whether to buy ownership shares of **Walmart** on the New York Stock Exchange at the current price. Which of the following statements is true about the figure reported as the company's net sales?

a. **Walmart** made net sales during these twelve months of exactly $418,952,000,000.

b. The $418,952,000,000 is accurate, although the number has been rounded to the nearest million.

c. Net sales were probably not $418,952,000,000 for the year, but that figure is close enough to be a fair presentation, one that Forrest can rely on in making his decision.

d. If this net sales figure had not been correct, **Walmart's** accountants would not have allowed the company to report the amount.

Answer:

The correct answer is choice c: Net sales were probably not $418,952,000,000 for the year, but that figure is close enough to be a fair presentation, one that Forrest can rely on in making his decision.

Explanation:

Accounting data are rarely accurate. That degree of exactness is often impossible to achieve and is not required when assessing a company's financial health. Financial statements are created to provide a fair presentation. Forrest ultimately wants to estimate stock prices and dividend payments. Net sales were almost certainly not as reported, but any difference between this number and the actual amount is not expected to be large enough to have an impact on the decisions that will be made.

1.3 Material Misstatements

Question: This is a surprising, possibly shocking, revelation. Financial accounting information has universally been branded as exhibiting rigid exactness. In fact, accountants are often referred to as "bean counters" because of their perceived need to count every bean in the bowl to arrive at obsessively accurate numbers. Here, though, the assertion is made that accounting information is not a precise picture but merely a fair representation of an organization's financial health and future prospects. **How correct or exact is the financial information that is reported by a business or other organization?**

Answer: In financial accounting, the data presented to decision makers by an organization should never contain any **misstatements** that are deemed to be **material**. This basic standard has long served as the required level for accuracy in financial reporting. Decision makers want financial statements—such as those prepared by **Starbucks** or **Intel**—that they can trust and use. That requires the statements to be free of any material misstatements. In that condition, reported financial information will be viewed as a likeness of the organization that is presented fairly. Thus, financial statements do not need exact accuracy. However, they must be free of material misstatements in order to be of use to decision makers.

misstatements

Errors or frauds that cause reported financial information to differ from the approach required by an official standard for reporting such as the U.S. Generally Accepted Accounting Principles (U.S. GAAP) or International Financial Reporting Standards (IFRS).

material

The magnitude of an omission or misstatement of accounting information that makes it probable that the judgment of a reasonable person relying on the information would have been changed or influenced by that omission or misstatement.

error

An unintentional misstatement of financial information.

fraud

An intentional misstatement of financial information; it can result from misappropriation of assets (theft) or fraudulent financial reporting.

A misstatement is an **error** (made accidentally) or **fraud** (done intentionally) where reported figures or words actually differ from the underlying reality. In simple terms, the information is wrong.

For example, a corporate official could erroneously record a $100,000 expenditure that was made in connection with the construction of a new building as if it pertained to the purchase of land. Consequently, the building's cost might be reported as only $2.3 million when it was actually $2.4 million. This reported number is misstated; it is wrong. The balance presented for the building contains a $100,000 error, as does the figure shown for land. This misstatement, though, might not be viewed as material.

A misstatement is deemed to be material if it is so significant that its presence would impact a decision made by an interested party. Using the previous illustration, assume the accidental $100,000 reduction in the reported cost of this building leads an outside decision maker to alter a choice being made (such as whether to buy or sell the business's capital stock or whether to grant a loan). Because of the change in the decision, the misstatement is judged to be material by definition. If no decision is affected, a misstatement is not material, and its existence does not prevent the reported information from still being fairly presented. The reported information is usable for decision making.

Financial information can (and almost always does) contain misstatements. However, the reporting entity must take adequate precautions to ensure that reported information holds no material misstatements for the simple reason that it is no longer fairly presented. If any material misstatements exist within the information, the portrait of the organization is not a proper likeness of the model. The decision maker is being misled.

The concept of materiality can seem rather nebulous. For the financial statements of a small convenience store, a $10 misstatement is not material whereas a $10 million one certainly is. For a business with real estate holdings of $30 billion, even a $10 million misstatement is probably not material. The problem for the accountant is determining where to draw the line for a particular organization. That is one of the most difficult decisions for any financial accountant. An exact dollar amount for materiality is virtually impossible to identify because it is a measure of the effect of a misstatement on an external party's judgment.

Other than sheer magnitude, the cause of the problem must also be taken into consideration. An accidental mistake of $100,000 is less likely to be judged material than one of $100,000 that resulted from a fraudulent act. Fraud occurs when someone wants to misrepresent reported numbers to make the organization look differently than it is or to cover theft. Fraud includes the intent to deceive and is more troublesome to decision makers than a mere error. Thus, both size and cause should be weighed in considering whether the presence of a misstatement has the ability to impact the actions of any decision makers.

Consequently, a financial accountant never claims that reported information is correct, accurate, or exact. Such precision is rarely possible and not needed when decision makers are analyzing the financial health and future prospects of an organization. However, the accountant must take all precautions necessary to ensure that reported data contain no material misstatements. Financial figures are never released without reasonable assurance being obtained that no errors or other mistakes are included that could be material, or in other words, that could impact the decisions that are made. All parties need to believe that reported information can be used with confidence because it presents a fair likeness of the organization as a whole.

When a company reports that a building was constructed at a cost of $2.3 million, the real message is that the actual cost was not materially different from $2.3 million. This figure is a fair representation of the amount spent, one that can be used in making decisions about the organization such as whether to invest in its capital stock or provide it with a loan.

TEST YOURSELF

Question:

For the year ending January 31, 2011, **Walmart** reported earning net income of $16,389,000,000. Which of the following statements is not true?

a. Net income is probably not $16,389,000,000, but it is not materially different than the reported figure.

b. To aid investors, actual net income could be lower than $16,389,000,000 but should not be any higher.

c. Decision makers should feel comfortable making decisions about the company based on this figure.

d. With companies of such size, determining an exact net income is impossible.

Answer:

The correct answer is choice b: To aid investors, actual net income could be lower than $16,389,000,000 but should not be any higher.

Explanation:

Net income reflects a likeness of a company's earnings that a decision maker can use. With so many complex transactions, precisely accurate figures are impossible. Company officials do need to have sufficient evidence to indicate that net income contains no material misstatements. Accountants tend to be conservative, which is likely to reduce reported income figures. Therefore, actual net income is more likely to be slightly higher than the reported figure rather than lower.

KEY TAKEAWAY

Financial accounting does not attempt to provide exact numbers because such accuracy is often impossible to achieve and not really required by decision makers. Instead, reported accounting information is intended to provide a likeness of an organization and its operations—a type of portrait. To achieve this goal, financial accountants must ensure that reported balances and other data cannot contain any material misstatements. A misstatement is inaccurate information included by accident (an error) or intentionally (fraud). Materiality refers to the point at which the size or the nature of such misstatements would cause a change in the decisions made by an individual using that information. If all material misstatements can be eliminated, the information is considered to be presented fairly. That likeness can then be used by interested parties to make considered decisions.

2. DEALING WITH UNCERTAINTY

LEARNING OBJECTIVES

At the end of this section, students should be able to meet the following objectives:

1. **Discuss the challenge created for financial accountants by the presence of uncertainty.**
2. **List examples of uncertainty that an accountant might face in reporting financial information about an organization.**
3. **Explain how financial accounting resembles a language, such as Spanish or Japanese.**

2.1 Uncertainty, the True Challenge for Reporting

*Question: Financial accounting figures can certainly be exact. If a cash register is bought for $836.54, the reported cost is $836.54. However, decision makers do not need financial figures with such absolute accuracy. If reported information is presented fairly, in other words if it contains no material misstatements, it can be used to estimate a corporation's future stock prices, cash dividend payments, and cash flows. **Even if not necessary for decision makers, what prevents reported financial information from being correct in an absolute sense?** Why are all reported figures not as precise as the reporting of the cash register?*

Answer: In truth, a reasonable percentage of numbers reported in a set of financial statements are exact. Materiality is not an issue in such cases. The cash register mentioned here has a reported cost of $836.54—a precise measure of the amount paid. Likewise, a cash balance shown as $2,785.16 is exact to the penny. However, many of the other figures reported by an organization do not lend themselves to such accuracy.

The primary reason that exactness is not a goal—often not even a possibility in financial accounting—can be summed up in a single word: uncertainty. Many of the events encountered every day by an organization contain some degree of uncertainty. Unfortunately, no technique exists to report uncertain events in precise terms.

When first introduced to financial accounting, many students assume that it is little more than the listing of cash receipts and disbursements in much the same way that elementary school children report how they spent their weekly allowances. That is a misconception. Financial accounting is a structured attempt to paint a fairly presented portrait of an organization's overall operations, financial condition, and cash flows. This requires the reporting of many events where a final resolution might not occur for months or even years. Here are just a few examples of the kinds of uncertainty that virtually every business (and financial accountant) faces in creating financial statements.

- A business is the subject of a lawsuit. Perhaps a customer has filed this legal action claiming damage as a result of one of the company's products. Such legal proceedings are exceedingly common and can drag on in the courts for an extended period of time before a settlement is reached. The actual amount won or lost (if either ever occurs) might not be known for years. What should the business report *now*?

- A sale of merchandise is made today for $300 with the money to be collected from the customer in several months. Until the cash is received, no one can be sure of the exact amount that will be collected. What should the business report *now*?

- An employee is promised a cash bonus next year that will be calculated based on any rise in the market price of the corporation's capital stock. Until the time passes and the actual increase (if any) is determined, the amount of this bonus remains a mystery. What should the business report *now*?

- A retail store sells a microwave oven today with a warranty. If the appliance breaks at any time during the next three years, the store has to pay for the repairs. No one knows whether the microwave will need to be fixed during this period. What should the business report *now*?

Any comprehensive list of the uncertainties faced regularly by most organizations would require pages to enumerate. Many of the most important accounting rules have been created to establish requirements for the reporting of uncertain situations. Because of the quantity and variety of such unknowns, exactness simply cannot be an objective of financial reporting.

For many accountants, dealing with so much uncertainty is the most interesting aspect of their job. Whenever an organization encounters a situation of this type, the accountant must first come to understand what has happened and then determine a logical method to communicate a fair representation of that information within the framework provided by financial accounting rules. Thus, reporting events in the face of uncertainty is surely one of the major challenges of being a financial accountant.

2.2   Accounting as the Language of Business

Question: Accounting is sometimes referred to as the "language of business." However, in this book, financial accounting has already been compared to the painting of a fairly presented portrait of an organization. **Given the references throughout this chapter to painting, is accounting really a type of language?** *Is it possible for accounting to paint portraits and also be a language?*

Answer: The simple answer to this question is that accounting is a language, one that enables an organization to communicate a portrait of its financial health and future prospects to interested parties by using words and numbers rather than oils or watercolors. The formal structure of that language becomes especially helpful when an organization faces the task of reporting complex uncertainties.

Any language, whether it is English, Spanish, Japanese, or the like, has been developed through much use to allow for the effective transfer of information between two or more parties. If a sentence such as "I drive a red car" is spoken, communication is successful but only if both the speaker and the listener have an adequate understanding of the English language. Based solely on the arrangement of these five words, information can be passed from one person to the another.

This process succeeds because English (as well as other languages) relies on relatively standardized terminology. Words such as "red," "car," and "drive" have defined meanings that the speaker and the listener both know with a degree of certainty. In addition, grammar rules such as syntax and punctuation are utilized to provide a framework for the communication. Thus, effective communication is possible in a language when

1. Set terminology exists
2. Structural rules and principles are applied

As will be gradually introduced throughout this textbook, financial accounting has its own terminology. Many words and terms (such as "LIFO" and "accumulated depreciation") have very specific meanings. In addition, a comprehensive set of rules and principles has been established over the decades to provide structure and standardization. They guide the reporting process so that the resulting information will be fairly presented and can be readily understood by all interested parties, both inside and outside of the organization.

Some students who read this textbook will eventually become accountants. Those individuals must learn specific terminology, rules, and principles in order to communicate financial information about an organization that is presented fairly. Others (probably most readers) will become external decision makers. They will make financial decisions. They will evaluate loan applications, buy capital stock, grant credit, make employment decisions, provide investment advice, and the like. They will not present financial information with all of its uncertainties but rather they will need to make use of it. The more such individuals know about financial accounting terminology, rules, and principles, the more likely it is that they will arrive at appropriate decisions.

To communicate a portrait properly in any language, both the speaker and the listener must understand the terminology as well as the structural rules and principles. That holds true even if the language is financial accounting.

KEY TAKEAWAY

At any point in time, organizations face numerous uncertain outcomes, such as the settlement of litigation or the collection of a receivable. The conveyance of useful information about these uncertain situations goes beyond the simple reporting of exact numbers. To communicate a fair representation of such uncertainty, financial accounting must serve as a language. Thus, it will have established terminology and structural rules much like that of any language. For successful communication of financial information, both the terminology and the structural rules must be understood by all parties involved.

3. THE NEED FOR ACCOUNTING STANDARDS

LEARNING OBJECTIVES

At the end of this section, students should be able to meet the following objectives:

1. Describe the purpose of accounting standards such as U.S. Generally Accepted Accounting Principles (U.S. GAAP) and International Financial Reporting Standards (IFRS) and the benefits that these rules provide.
2. Explain the importance of accounting standards to the development of a capitalistic economy.
3. Understand the role played by the Financial Accounting Standards Board (FASB) in the ongoing evolution of accounting standards in the United States.
4. Discuss the advantages and the possibility that financial reporting will switch from U.S. GAAP to IFRS.

3.1 The Existence of Formal Accounting Standards

Question: Rules and principles exist within financial accounting that must be followed. They provide the structural guidance that is essential for achieving effective communication. For example, assume that a reporting organization encounters an uncertainty (such as a lawsuit) and is now preparing financial information to portray the reality of that event. **When faced with such complexity, how does the financial accountant know which method of reporting is appropriate?** *How does a decision maker who analyzes that reported information know what guidelines were used in its preparation?*

Answer: The existence of financial accounting standards is essential to ensure that all communicated information is understood properly. Both the accountants within the reporting organization and the decision makers analyzing the resulting financial statements must understand those rules. The question that has haunted the accounting profession in recent times is, who should have the authority to create those standards?

For decades, a wide variety of formal accounting principles were developed in the United States as well as throughout the rest of the world. Japanese accounting rules evolved differently from those in Australia while Australian standards were not consistent with those in the United States. In earlier times, such country-by-country rules caused few problems because most businesses operated solely within their country's boundaries. During the past ten years or so, as a truly global economy became a reality, two primary systems of accounting rules emerged. **U.S. Generally Accepted Accounting Principles (U.S. GAAP)** are applied to most financial information presented within the United States. International Financial Reporting Standards (IFRS) are now used almost exclusively in the rest of the world. In accounting at the present time, two languages exist rather than one.

Having two bodies of rules causes problems for decision makers. For example, on its Web site, **BP** presents a 2010 set of financial statements prepared according to IFRS. One of its biggest competitors, **Exxon Mobil**, posted its own 2010 financial statements, but those amounts and explanations were created by following U.S. GAAP. Clarity and understanding are not enhanced when different communication standards are applied by such similar businesses.

Not surprisingly, many corporate officials and decision makers would prefer to see one universal set of accounting standards. If that were to happen, a corporation in Michigan and a corporation in Germany would produce comparable financial information that could be utilized for all reporting purposes around the world.

Over the past few years, extensive progress has been made in bringing these two sets of standards into alignment. However, a number of significant differences continue to exist. Many interested parties want to see IFRS adopted exclusively in the United States. According to this group, it is unlikely that the rest of the world will choose to follow U.S. GAAP so harmony can only be achieved by a general acceptance of IFRS. Others believe that U.S. GAAP is a superior system and should not be abandoned.

The debate has been intense and promises to continue to be so until some type of official resolution occurs.

Typical Opinions on Moving to the Use of IFRS

- "**Ford (Motor Co.)** supports the move to International Financial Reporting Standards, saying the company would save money by simplifying and standardizing its accounting across all 138 countries where **Ford** operates."

- "Companies like **Hallador Energy Co.**, a small Denver coal-mining company that doesn't do business outside the United States (opposes) moving to the international standards. 'We didn't join the metric system when everybody else did,' says W. Anderson Bishop, **Hallador's** chief financial officer. U. S. accounting rules are 'the gold standard, and why would we want to lower our standards just to make the rest of the world happy?'"

- "Larger companies, big accounting firms, and top rule makers favor the switch. They contend that global unity would save companies money by consolidating bookkeeping and make it easier to raise capital around the world."

- "James Barlow, chief financial officer of drug company **Allergan Inc.** and an opponent of IFRS, estimates the change could cost companies as much as 1 percent of revenues."[1]

At the time of this writing, U.S. GAAP continues to be the required system for most of the financial reporting found in the United States although a mandated switch to IFRS (in some form) during the next few years is quite possible. Because of the current situation and the uncertainty as to how legal requirements will eventually change, this textbook is primarily a presentation of U.S. GAAP. For the most part, U.S. GAAP and IFRS are based on the same accounting principles. However, varying interpretations of those principles have resulted in differences between U.S. GAAP and IFRS standards. In areas where IFRS disagrees with U.S. GAAP in significant ways, both methods of reporting will be described in this textbook.

3.2   The Development of Accounting Standards

Question: Whether in the form of U.S. GAAP or IFRS, financial accounting standards must be created in some logical fashion. **Who is in charge of the production of formal accounting standards?** *How often do these official standards come into existence?*

Answer: The Financial Accounting Standards Board (FASB) has held the authority to develop U.S. GAAP since 1973. An abundance of information can be found about this board and its activities by going to http://www.fasb.org/ and clicking on "About FASB."

IFRS are produced by the London-based International Accounting Standards Board (IASB). This group took over responsibility for international standards from a predecessor group in 2001.

Information about the resulting official pronouncements and the standard setting process is available at http://www.iasb.org/ by clicking on "About us."

Although some basic elements of accounting standards have been in use almost throughout history, many reporting rules are relatively new—often developed within the last few decades. Whether U.S. GAAP or IFRS, accounting standards evolve quite quickly as the nature of business changes and new reporting issues, problems, and resolutions arise. The growth of advanced technology speeds this process even more quickly. Fairly important changes in the formal structure of accounting rules occur virtually every year.

In the United States, the existence of U.S. GAAP means that a business in Seattle, Washington, and a business in Atlanta, Georgia, must account for financial information in much the same manner. As will be discussed later in this textbook, a few allowed alternatives do exist in connection with specific reporting challenges.

Because standardization exists in most areas of the reporting process, any decision maker with an adequate knowledge of financial accounting—whether located in Phoenix, Arizona, or in Portland, Maine—should be able to understand the fairly presented financial information conveyed by a wide variety of organizations. They all speak the same language. Put simply, the existence of accounting standards enables organizations and other interested parties to communicate successfully.

TEST YOURSELF

Question:

An investor is studying a set of financial statements prepared for a company. He is considering buying some of its ownership shares. While studying the financial statements, he notices that they have been prepared in accordance with U.S. GAAP. Which of the following statements is true?

a. The rules and principles that make up U.S. GAAP have been the same now for over forty years.

b. The rules and principles that make up U.S. GAAP are consistent throughout the United States.

c. The rules and principles that make up U.S. GAAP are used consistently throughout the world.

d. The rules and principles that make up U.S. GAAP are the same as those used for income tax purposes.

Answer:

The correct answer is choice b: The rules and principles that make up U.S. GAAP are consistent throughout the United States.

Explanation:

U.S. GAAP provides a standardization of rules so that information can be better understood. These rules evolve rapidly; thus, much of U.S. GAAP is less than ten to fifteen years old. A different set of rules known as IFRS is used in much of the rest of the world and might eventually be applied in the United States. Income tax laws help governments raise revenues, a completely different purpose than U.S. GAAP. U.S. GAAP is designed to help organizations produce fairly presented financial statements.

3.3   The Importance of Accounting Standards

Question: Several years ago, a front page article in the Wall Street Journal *contained a controversial assessment of U.S. GAAP: "When the intellectual achievements of the 20th century are tallied, GAAP should be on everyone's Top 10 list. The idea of GAAP—so simple yet so radical—is that there should be a standard way of accounting for profit and loss in public businesses, allowing investors to see how a public company manages its money. This transparency is what allows investors to compare businesses as different as* McDonald's, IBM *and* Tupperware, *and it makes U.S. markets the envy of the world."*[2]

Could formal accounting standards be so very important? *Can the development of U.S. GAAP possibly be one of the ten most important intellectual achievements of the entire twentieth century? A list of other accomplishments during this period includes air travel, creation of computers, birth of the Internet, landing on the moon, and the development of penicillin. With that level of competition, U.S. GAAP does not seem an obvious choice to be in the top ten. How can it be so important?*

Answer: The United States has a capitalistic economy, which means that businesses are (for the most part) owned by private citizens and groups rather than by the government. To operate and grow, these companies must convince investors and creditors to contribute huge amounts of their own money voluntarily. Not surprisingly, such financing is only forthcoming if the possible risks and rewards can be assessed and then evaluated with sufficient reliability. Before handing over thousands or even millions of dollars, decision makers must believe that they are using reliable data to make reasonable estimations of future stock prices, cash dividends, and cash flows. Otherwise, buying stocks and granting credit is no more than gambling. As this quote asserts, U.S. GAAP enables these outside parties to obtain the financial information they need to reduce their perceived risk to acceptable levels. Thus, money can be raised, and businesses can grow and prosper.

Without U.S. GAAP, investors and creditors would encounter significant difficulties in evaluating the financial health and future prospects of an organization.[3] Because of that uncertainty, they would be more likely to hold on to their money or invest only in other, safer options. Consequently, if accounting standards did not exist, the development and expansion of thousands of the businesses that have become a central part of today's society might be limited or impossible simply because of the lack of available resources. An expanding economy requires capital investment. That funding is more likely to be available when financial information can be understood because it is stated in a common language: U.S. GAAP.

By any method of measurement, the explosive development of the U.S. economy during the twentieth century (especially following World War II) has been spectacular, close to unbelievable. This growth has been fueled by massive amounts of money flowing from inside and outside the United States into the country's businesses. Much of the vitality of the U.S. economy results from the willingness of people to risk their money by buying capital stock or making loans or extending credit to such companies as **McDonald's**, **IBM**, and **Tupperware**. Without those resources, most businesses would be small or nonexistent, and the United States would surely be a radically different country.

3.4 The Evolution of Accounting Standards

Question: Accounting standards are important to businesses and decision makers alike. FASB is in charge of the creation of U.S. GAAP. As stated, all accounting standards tend to evolve over time. Official rules are modified, deleted, or added every year. ***How do new accounting standards come into existence?***

Answer: As indicated earlier, since 1973, FASB has served as the primary authoritative body in charge of producing U.S. GAAP for nongovernmental entities such as businesses and private not-for-profit organizations. FASB is an independent group supported by the U.S. government, various accounting organizations, and many private businesses.

Typically, accounting problems arise over time within the various areas of financial reporting. New types of financial events can be created, for example, that are not covered by U.S. GAAP or, perhaps, weaknesses in earlier rules start to become evident. If such concerns grow to be serious, FASB steps in to study the issues and alternatives. After a period of study, the board might pass new rules or make amendments to previous ones. FASB is methodical in its deliberations, and the entire process can take years. Changes to U.S. GAAP are never made without proper consideration.

Several other official bodies also play important roles in the creation of U.S. GAAP. They are normally discussed in detail in upper-level accounting textbooks. However, the major authority for the ongoing evolution of U.S. GAAP lies with FASB and its seven-member board. It has released scores of official statements during its first four decades of existence. The impact that those rulings have had on U.S. GAAP and the financial reporting process in this country is almost impossible to overemphasize.

As just one example, FASB recently made a number of changes in the required reporting of receivables because of the chance that some (perhaps many) of these balances would not be collected. Possibly as a result of the current economic difficulties around the world, the members of FASB felt that more information was needed from organizations to inform decision makers about the risk involved with the collection of these receivables. This type of evolution takes place frequently in the language known as financial accounting. Whether U.S. GAAP or IFRS, financial accounting rules must be updated as needed to meet current informational needs.

In 2009, FASB combined all authoritative accounting literature into a single source for U.S. GAAP, which is known as the *Accounting Standards Codification*. By bringing together hundreds of authoritative documents, FASB has made U.S. GAAP both more understandable and easier to access. A multitude of pronouncements has been woven together in a logical fashion so that all rules on each topic are now gathered in one location.

KEY TAKEAWAY

No language can enable communication without some standardization of terminology and rules. At present, U.S. GAAP plays this role in the United States. The availability of these authoritative guidelines has served a central role in the growth of the U.S. economy since the end of the Great Depression and World War II. These uniform accounting rules allow investors and creditors to assess the possible risks and rewards they face. U.S. GAAP is constantly evolving as accountants seek better methods of providing financial information in an ever-changing business world. The main authority for the development of U.S. GAAP lies with the Financial Accounting Standards Board (FASB). FASB looks constantly for reporting issues that need to be studied so that needed changes can be made in official accounting rules. IFRS plays this same role in much of the rest of the world. The future of IFRS rules in the United States is yet to be determined, but acceptance of a single set of accounting standards in some form has many supporters.

Talking with an Independent Auditor about International Financial Reporting Standards

Robert A. Vallejo is a partner in the assurance (audit) practice of the public accounting firm **Pricewaterhouse-Coopers (PwC)**. Rob began his career with **PwC** in 1992 and has spent five years working in Europe (two in Paris and three in Amsterdam). Because of his time in Europe, he has extensive practical experience dealing with International Financial Reporting Standards (IFRS) and actively helps his U.S. clients understand the significant differences between U.S. accounting standards and IFRS. He currently works in the firm's Richmond, Virginia, office. Rob is the founder of the Philadelphia Chapter of ALPFA (the Association of Latino Professionals in Finance and Accounting) and is a member of the American Institute of Certified Public Accountants (AICPA) and the Virginia Society of CPAs.

Question: Over the past fifty years or so, the accounting profession in the United States has developed a very comprehensive set of official guidelines referred to collectively as U.S. GAAP. Recently, a strong push has developed to move away from those principles and adopt the pronouncements of the International Accounting Standards Board. If U.S. GAAP has worked successfully for so many years, why should we now think about abandoning it in favor of IFRS, a system that is not necessarily well understood in the United States?

Rob Vallejo: Economic events continue to illustrate how interrelated the world's economies really are. Therefore, it makes common sense that all companies around the world should report their financial information in accordance with the same set of accounting standards. For investors and creditors, it is hard to compare two companies that use different reporting standards unless the individual has a truly in-depth understanding of the differences. Unfortunately, both sets of standards are complex, which makes it very difficult to have a solid grasp of both. The United States is one of the few remaining jurisdictions that has not adopted IFRS, limiting the understanding and usefulness of our standards beyond our borders. Another argument in favor of the adoption of IFRS is the complexity of U.S. GAAP. It is a very rules-based set of standards that has evolved over many decades to address the ever-changing world of business, creating a maze of standards that is difficult to navigate. IFRS is more principles-based, allowing the preparers of financial information more judgment in applying general rules to a wide variety of situations. Lastly, U.S. standard setters have become more involved in the evolution of IFRS. FASB has been working with the IASB in many instances to converge U.S. GAAP and IFRS even if formal adoption of IFRS never occurs in the United States.

Question: Rob, at key spots throughout this textbook, you have agreed to explain the impact that a possible change to IFRS will have on financial reporting in the United States. Obviously, the future is always difficult to anticipate with precision. However, what is your best guess as to when IFRS will start to be used in the financial statements issued by U.S. companies? At a basic level, as is appropriate in an introductory financial accounting course, how much real difference will be created by a change from U.S. GAAP to IFRS?

RV: The move to IFRS is being driven by the Securities and Exchange Commission (SEC), which has legal responsibility for much of the financial reporting in the United States. In 2008, the SEC published a road map that called for the largest U.S. publicly traded companies to publish their annual results for the year ending December 31, 2014, in accordance with IFRS. In February 2010, the SEC decided that IFRS would not be required of U.S. public companies prior to 2015 and, even then, only after additional study. A final decision is now expected from the SEC relatively soon, but the momentum leading to an inevitable switch to IFRS has subsided. Many believe that a much slower convergence approach, ensuring that all newly issued standards are the same under U.S. GAAP and IFRS, seems to be gaining traction. In general, any move to IFRS will not have a substantial impact on the financial information being reported by most U.S. companies. However, because of the many subtle differences between IFRS and U.S. GAAP, preparers of financial information have a lot of work to do to transition the reporting properly. As is the case many times, the devil is in the details.

Note: The role played in the U.S. economy by public accounting firms will be described in a later chapter. Some of these organizations have grown to an enormous size. According to its Web site as of July 14, 2011 (http://www.pwc.com/), **PricewaterhouseCoopers** employs approximately 161,000 individuals working in over 150 countries. During 2010, the firm earned in excess of $26 billion in revenues from customers as a result of the services that it rendered for them.

4. FOUR ESSENTIAL TERMS ENCOUNTERED IN FINANCIAL ACCOUNTING

LEARNING OBJECTIVES

At the end of this section, students should be able to meet the following objectives:

1. Define "asset" and provide examples found in financial reporting.
2. Define "liability" and provide examples found in financial reporting.
3. Define "revenue" and provide examples found in financial reporting.
4. Define "expense" and provide examples found in financial reporting.

4.1 Assets, Liabilities, Revenues, and Expenses

Question: Attaining a thorough understanding of financial accounting and its underlying standards is a worthwhile endeavor especially if a person hopes to become successful at making decisions about businesses or other organizations. **Where should the journey to gain knowledge of financial accounting and its principles begin?**

Answer: The study of a language usually starts with basic terminology. That is also an appropriate point of entry for an exploration into financial accounting. Consequently, four fundamental terms are introduced here in this section. Knowledge of these words is essential in gaining an understanding of accounting because they serve as the foundation for a significant portion of the financial information provided by any organization.

To illustrate, when examining the financial statements presented by **Sears** (formally known as **Sears Holdings Corporation**) for January 29, 2011, and the year then ended, four monetary balances immediately stand out because of their enormous size. On this date, the corporation reported $24.3 billion in **assets** along with $15.6 billion in **liabilities**. During that year, **Sears** generated **revenues** of $43.3 billion and incurred **expenses** of $43.2 billion.

- Assets
- Liabilities
- Revenues
- Expenses

There are thousands of words and concepts found in accounting. No terms are more crucial to a comprehensive understanding of the reporting process than these four. Almost all discussions concerning financial information, whether practical or theoretical, come back to one or more of these words.

4.2 Definition of the Term "Asset"

Question: The first essential term presented here is "asset." Is an asset a complicated accounting concept? What general information is conveyed to a decision maker by the term "asset"?

assets

Probable future economic benefits owned or controlled by an organization.

liabilities

Probable future sacrifices of economic benefits arising from present obligations; the debts of an organization.

revenues

Measures of the increases in or inflows of net assets (assets minus liabilities) resulting from the sale of goods and services.

expenses

Measures of decreases in or outflows of net assets (assets minus liabilities) incurred in connection with the generation of revenues.

Answer: Simply put, an asset is a probable future economic benefit that an organization either owns or controls.[4] On January 29, 2011, **Sears** reported holding over $24.3 billion of these economic benefits. If a customer walks into one of the company's retail stores, many of these assets are easy to spot. The building itself may well be owned by **Sears** and certainly provides a probable future economic benefit by allowing the company to display merchandise and make sales. Other visible assets are likely to include cash registers, the cash held in those machines, available merchandise from jewelry to car tires to children's clothing (usually referred to as **inventory** in financial accounting), shopping carts, delivery trucks, and the shelves and display cases. Each of those assets is acquired with the hope that it will help **Sears** prosper in the future.

inventory

A current asset bought or manufactured for the purpose of selling in order to generate revenue.

4.3 Examples of Typical Assets

Question: All decision makers who evaluate the financial health and future prospects of an organization should be interested in learning about its assets because those balances reflect the economic resources held at the present time. This is valuable information. **What are some of the largest asset balances that a business like Sears is likely to report?**

Answer: Every business has its own particular mix of assets. Virtually all have cash and accounts receivable (money due from customers). Many also have inventory (merchandise held for resale). The size and type of other assets will vary significantly based on the company and the industry in which it operates.

However, as a result of financial reporting and the existence of the Internet, such information is readily available to anyone wanting to learn about virtually any business. The assets are reported in the financial statements. As of January 29, 2011, the following four assets were reported by **Sears** as having the highest dollar amounts. Each of these asset categories will be discussed in detail later in this textbook.

Merchandise inventories	$9.1 billion
Buildings and improvements	$6.3 billion
Trade names and other intangible assets	$3.1 billion
Furniture, fixtures, and equipment	$2.9 billion

TEST YOURSELF

Question:

Alice Roanoke has decided to start an Internet business to provide expert financial advice to customers who sign up and pay a monthly fee. She hires Matt Showalter, a renowned expert in setting up investment strategies. She rents a building, paying for the next two years in advance. She also buys several large computers and a small library of books on investing and providing financial advice. Which of the following is not an asset to her new company?

a. Having Showalter as an employee
b. Owning the investment books
c. Paying the rent on the building for the subsequent two-year period
d. Acquiring the computers

Answer:

The correct answer is choice a: Having Showalter as an employee.

Explanation:

An asset is a future economic benefit that an organization owns or controls. A person cannot be owned or controlled and therefore is not deemed an asset for reporting purposes regardless of how smart or helpful the person is. Showalter could quit tomorrow. Company officials cannot force him to work for them; slavery was outlawed approximately 150 years ago. The books, the building, and the computers all have future economic benefit, and the company does have ownership or control.

4.4 Definition of the Term "Liability"

Question: As of January 29, 2011, **Sears** *also reports owing more than $15.6 billion in liabilities. Does this figure reflect the total amount that the reporting company will eventually have to pay to outside parties?* **What does the balance reported as liabilities represent?**

Answer: A more formal definition of a liability is that it is a probable future sacrifice of economic benefits arising from present obligations, but, for coverage here at the introductory level, liabilities can be viewed as the debts of the organization.

The $15.6 billion liability total disclosed by **Sears** most likely includes (1) amounts owed to the vendors who supply merchandise to the company's stores, (2) notes due to banks as a result of loans, (3) income tax obligations, and (4) balances to be paid to employees, utility companies, advertising agencies, and the like. The amount of such liabilities owed by many businesses can be staggering. **Walmart**, for example, disclosed approximately $109 billion in liabilities as of January 31, 2011. Even that amount pales in comparison to the $627 billion liability total reported by **General Electric** at the end of 2010. To ensure that a fairly presented portrait is shown to decision makers, businesses such as **Sears**, **Walmart**, and **General Electric** must make certain that the reported data contain no material misstatements. Thus, all the information that is provided about liabilities should be based on the rules and principles to be found in U.S. GAAP.

Another term that is often encountered in financial reporting is "net assets." The net asset total for an organization is simply its assets (future benefits) less its liabilities (debts). This balance is also known as "equity" in reference to the owners' rights to all assets in excess of the amount owed on liabilities. A business's net assets will increase if assets go up or if liabilities decrease. Changes in net assets show growth (or shrinkage) in the size of the organization over time. For example, **IBM** reported net assets of $22.7 billion at the end of 2009 (assets of $109.0 billion and liabilities of $86.3 billion). That number had risen to $23.2 billion by the end of 2010 (assets of $113.5 billion and liabilities of $90.3 billion). The ability of this business to increase its net assets by $500 million ($33.2 billion less $32.7 billion) during 2010 is certainly of interest to every decision maker analyzing the financial health and future prospects of **IBM**.

TEST YOURSELF

Question:

The Jackson Corporation is a women's clothing store located in Upper Lakeview. On Friday, the company's accountant is looking at four recent events so that the amount of liabilities can be reported as of the end of this week. Which of the following is not a liability for reporting purposes?

a. A new sales person was hired this morning, will begin work on the following Monday, and will be paid $600 per week.

b. Twenty dresses were received three days ago at a cost of $80 each, but they will not be sold until next week and payment will be made then.

c. The cost of renting the company's sales room is $1,300 per week, but the amount for this week will not be paid until next week.

d. The company borrowed $900,000 to build a new store, but construction will not start until next week.

Answer:

The correct answer is choice a: A new sales person was hired this morning, will begin work on the following Monday, and will be paid $600 per week.

Explanation:

With the dresses, the rent, and the loan, an event has already occurred that created an obligation. The dresses have been received, the room has been used, and money from the loan has been collected. In each case, the company has a debt. The new employee has not yet begun the job, so no debt has accrued. A commitment has been made to pay this person, but only if work is done. At that time, as the sales person works, the company does begin to have a debt (or liability) that must be reported.

4.5 Definition of the Term "Revenue"

Question: In financial accounting, a business or other organization reports its assets, which are probable future economic benefits, such as buildings, equipment, and cash. Liabilities (debts) are also included in the financial information being disclosed. Both of these terms seem relatively straightforward. The third *essential term to be discussed at this time—revenue—is one that initially appears to be a bit less clear. Sears reported that its stores generated revenues of $43.3 billion in 2010 alone. What does that tell a decision maker about Sears?* **What information is conveyed by the reporting of a revenue balance?**

Answer: "Revenue" is a measure of the financial impact on an organization that results from a particular process. This process is a sale. A customer enters a **Sears** store at the local mall and pays $100 to purchase several items, such as hammers, shirts, socks, and scarves. **Sears** receives an asset—possibly $100 in cash. This asset inflow into the business results from a sale and is called revenue. Revenue is *not* an asset; it is a measure of the increase in net assets created by the sale of inventory and services. Thus, for **The Coca-Cola Company**, revenues are derived (net assets are increased) from the sale of soft drinks. For **The Hershey Company**, revenues come from sales of chocolate whereas **The Walt Disney Company** generates revenue by selling admission to its amusement parks and movies.

For timing purposes, as will be discussed in a later chapter, revenue is recognized when the earning process takes place. That is normally when the goods or services are delivered. Therefore, throughout each day of the year, **Sears** makes sales to customers and accepts cash, checks, or credit card payments. The reported revenue figure is merely a total of all sales made during the period, clearly relevant information to any decision maker attempting to determine the financial prospects of this company. During 2010, the multitude of **Sears** stores located both inside and outside the United States sold inventory and services and received $43.3 billion in assets in exchange. That is the information communicated by the reported revenue balance. To reiterate, this figure is not exact, precise, accurate, or correct. However, according to **Sears**, $43.3 billion is a fairly presented total determined according to the rules of U.S. GAAP so that it contains no material misstatement. Any outside party analyzing **Sears** should be able to rely on this number with confidence in making possible finanical decisions about this business as a whole.

TEST YOURSELF

Question:

The Rowe Company is a restaurant in a remote area of Tennessee. The owner buys a steak from a local farmer for $7. The chef is paid $2 to cook this meat. A waitress is paid $1 to deliver the steak to a customer. The customer is charged $18, which is paid in cash. The customer leaves a tip for the waitress of $3. According to U.S. GAAP, what amount of revenue should the Rowe Company report in connection with this series of events?

a. $8

b. $10

c. $13

d. $18

Answer:

The correct answer is choice d: $18.

Explanation:

The term "revenue" refers to the increase in net assets brought into an organization as a result of a sale. There is a lot of interesting and relevant information here. However, only the payment made by the customer to the business is reported as revenue because that is the increase in net assets brought into the company by the sale.

Question:

The McCutcheon Company is a restaurant in a remote area of Montana. The owner buys a steak from a local farmer for $7. On Tuesday, the chef is paid $2 to cook this meat. A waitress is paid $1 to deliver the steak to a customer. The customer is charged $18. The customer does not have any money with him and tells the owner that he will pay the amount in the following week. The owner knows the customer and allows the payment to be delayed. According to U.S. GAAP, what amount of revenue should the McCutcheon Company report on Tuesday when the sale is made?

a. Zero

b. $8

c. $10

d. $18

Answer:

The correct answer is choice d: $18.

Explanation:

The term "revenue" refers to the increase in net assets as a result of the sale of a good or service. Here, the business received a promise to pay that is viewed as an asset because it has future economic benefit. Although no cash was collected, the business did gain an $18 asset (a receivable) as a result of the sale. Revenue was $18. Some very small organizations use cash systems that only recognize revenues when cash is received, but they are not reporting according to the rules of U.S. GAAP.

4.6 Definition of the Term "Expense"

Question: That leaves "expense" as the last of the four essential accounting terms introduced at this point. Sears reported $43.2 billion in total expenses during 2010. This figure apparently is important information that helps paint a proper portrait of the company, a portrait that can be used by decision makers. What is an expense?

Answer: An expense is an outflow or reduction in net assets[5] that was incurred by an organization in hopes of generating revenue. To illustrate, assume that—at the end of a week—a local business pays its employees $12,000 for the work performed during the previous few days. A $12,000 salary expense must be reported. Cash (an asset) was reduced by that amount, and this cost was incurred because the company employed those individuals to help generate revenues. That is an expense. The same general logic can be applied in recording insurance expense, rent expense, advertising expense, utility expense (such as for electricity and water), and many other similar costs. For each, net assets are reduced (assets go down or liabilities go up) to help create sales.

In some ways, expenses are the opposite of revenues that measure the inflows or increases in net assets that are created by sales. Expense figures reflect outflows or decreases in net assets incurred in hopes of generating revenues.

TEST YOURSELF

Question:

The Hathaway Corporation started business on January 1, Year One, as a restaurant in Toledo, Ohio. During Year One, the company paid $10,000 each month to rent a building to serve as its kitchen and dining room. Because operations were so successful, on the final day of Year One, the company paid $150,000 to buy a new building for the restaurant. The company hopes to move over the New Year's Day holiday from the old rental facility to the newly acquired one. In connection with these events, how much should Hathaway report as its total expenses for Year One?

a. Zero
b. $120,000
c. $150,000
d. $270,000

Answer:

The correct answer is choice b: $120,000.

Explanation:

The company's net assets decreased by $10,000 per month as a result of renting the first space. The benefit from that rental has passed because the restaurant was used at that time to generate revenue. That is an expense. In contrast, the new building is an asset. In acquiring the building, one asset (cash) was exchanged for another (building). Net assets did not change; one asset went up and one went down. Thus, no expense resulted. The expense for Year One is $120,000 in rent.

4.7 Four Essential Terms Encountered in Financial Accounting

Question: To reiterate, four terms are basic to an understanding of financial accounting. Almost any coverage of accounting starts with these four. **What is the meaning of asset, liability, revenue, and expense?**

Answer:

- **Asset.** A probable future economic benefit owned or controlled by the reporting company, such as inventory, land, or equipment.
- **Liability.** A probable future economic sacrifice or, in simple terms, a debt.
- **Revenue.** A measure of the inflow or increase in net assets generated by the sales made by a business. It is a reflection of the amounts brought in by the sales process during a specified period of time.
- **Expense.** A measure of the outflow or reduction in net assets caused by a business's attempt to generate revenue and includes many common costs, such as rent expense, salary expense, and insurance expense.

KEY TAKEAWAY

A strong knowledge of basic accounting terminology is essential for successful communication to take place in the reporting of financial information. Four terms provide a foundational core around which much of the accounting process is constructed. Assets are probable future economic benefits owned or controlled by an organization. Assets typically include cash, inventory, land, buildings, and equipment. Liabilities are the debts of the reporting entity, such as salary payable, rent payable, and notes payable. Revenue figures indicate the increase in a company's net assets (its assets minus its liabilities) created by the sale of goods or services. Revenues are the lifeblood of any organization. Without the inflow of cash or receivables that comes from generating sales, a business cannot exist for long. Expenses are decreases in net assets that are incurred in hopes of generating revenues. Expenses incurred by most companies run a full gamut from rent and salary to insurance and electricity.

Talking with a Real Investing Pro (Continued)

Following is a continuation of our interview with Kevin G. Burns.

Question: Financial accountants tend to place a heavy emphasis on the importance of generally accepted accounting principles (U.S. GAAP) to the world of business. After nearly three decades as an investment advisor, what is your opinion of the relevance of U.S. GAAP?

Kevin Burns: Before the accounting scandals of the late 1990s—such as **Enron** and **WorldCom**—financial information that adhered to U.S. GAAP was trusted worldwide. Investors around the globe took comfort in a standard that had such a great reputation for integrity. In the 1990s, though, I felt that U.S. GAAP become somewhat muddied because investors wanted to depend too heavily on one or two figures rather than judging the company as a whole. In the last several years, FASB has moved back to stressing clearer transparency for reported information. That objective enables investors to better see and understand the organization standing behind those statements. That is very important in order to maintain investor confidence.

As for the current state of the U.S. GAAP, it is certainly superior to the majority of the world's standards. Unfortunately, it is getting more complicated every year, which is not always a good goal.

Question: Your answer is quite interesting because of the push in recent years toward International Financial Reporting Standards as a single global set of standards for all businesses. Some people love the idea of the same accounting rules for everyone. Others hate the idea that IFRS could replace U.S. GAAP. What is your feeling?

KB: For an investor, that is a very interesting question. Given that we truly are a global economy I would love a worldwide standard but only if it was equal to or more transparent than the current U.S. standards. As an investment advisor, I would love to be able to compare business valuations here and in China (for example) side by side and have confidence that I am truly comparing apples to apples.

Question: When you begin to study the financial data reported by a company that you are analyzing as an investment possibility, which do you look at first: revenues, expenses, assets, or liabilities?

KB: For me, assets have always been the most important determination in the investments that I have chosen. However, that is because I have always been strictly a value investor. There are many different styles of investing. Value investors look at the value of a company's assets and then look for bargains based on current stock market prices. In comparison, growth investors look at earnings momentum and don't care too much about asset values. They like to see a consistent rise in profitability each year. Over the years, being a value investor has worked well for my clients and me.

 Video Clip

Professor Joe Hoyle talks about the five most important points in Chapter 2.

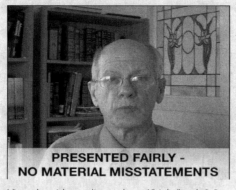

View the video online at: http://bit.ly/hoyle2-2

5. END-OF-CHAPTER EXERCISES

QUESTIONS

1. Why is the information reported by financial accounting not necessarily correct or accurate?
2. What is a misstatement?
3. In reference to a misstatement, what is meant by materiality?
4. How is materiality determined?
5. When is a misstatement considered fraud?
6. Provide several examples of uncertainties faced by businesses that can impact the financial reporting process.
7. Why is financial accounting compared to the painting of a portrait?
8. Why is financial accounting compared to a language?
9. What is U.S. GAAP and how has U.S. GAAP developed over the years?
10. Why is U.S. GAAP so important to the capital market system in the United States?
11. Why is there a push to accept International Financial Reporting Standards (IFRS) as the universal standards for financial accounting?
12. Define "asset" and give several examples.
13. Define "liability" and give several examples.
14. What is meant by the term "net assets?"
15. Define "revenue."
16. Define "expense."

TRUE OR FALSE

1. ____ Most countries require companies that operate within their borders to follow U.S. GAAP in preparing their financial statements.
2. ____ Companies face many uncertainties when preparing their financial statements.
3. ____ If a company reports equipment costing $122,756,255, that is the amount that it actually did cost.
4. ____ A liability is defined as a probable future economic benefit that an organization owns or controls.
5. ____ Creation of U.S. GAAP is primarily done by the U.S. government.
6. ____ IFRS has been in wide use in many countries since 1976.
7. ____ In order for investors to properly evaluate the financial information of a business or other organization, it is vital that the financial information be exact.
8. ____ A corporation reports sales of $33,453,750 when the actual figure was $33,453,843. This information contained a misstatement.
9. ____ Materiality depends on the size of the organization.
10. ____ A material misstatement that is made in a set of financial statements is acceptable as long as there is only one.
11. ____ A misstatement has to be caused by fraud.
12. ____ The reporting of a pending lawsuit is relatively simple.
13. ____ One business has a misstatement of $10,000 that is caused by fraud. It also has another misstatement of $10,000 that is caused by error. If one of these misstatements is material, then they both are.
14. ____ Only accountants need to understand the terminology that is found in accounting.
15. ____ For a business or other organization, an employee is an example of an asset.
16. ____ A sales transaction is normally considered revenue even if cash is not collected until the following year.
17. ____ The purchase of a building for $2.4 million is recorded as an expense.

MULTIPLE CHOICE

1. Which of the following is not an example of an uncertainty that companies often face in their financial reporting?

    a. Sales that have not yet been collected in cash

    b. Warranties

    c. A loan due to a bank

    d. A lawsuit that has been filed against the company

2. Which of the following is true about U.S. GAAP?

    a. U.S. GAAP has been developed over the past ten years.

    b. U.S. GAAP allows financial statement users to compare the financial information of companies around the world.

    c. U.S. GAAP helps accountants achieve an exact presentation of a company's financial results.

    d. U.S. GAAP helps investors and creditors evaluate the financial health of a business.

Questions 3, 4, and 5 are based on the following:

Mike Gomez owns a music store called Mike's Music and More. The store has inventory for sale that includes pianos, guitars, and other musical instruments. Mike rents the building in which his store is located, but owns the equipment and fixtures inside it. Last week, Mike's Music made sales of $3,000. Some of the sales were made in cash. Some were made to customers who have an account with Mike's Music and are billed at the end of the month. Last month, Mike's Music borrowed $10,000 from a local bank to expand the amount of inventory being sold.

3. Which of the following is not an asset owned by Mike's Music?

    a. The inventory of musical instruments

    b. The building in which the store is located

    c. The amount owed to Mike's Music by its customers

    d. The equipment and fixtures in the store

4. Which of the following is a liability to Mike's Music?

    a. The loan amount that must be repaid to the bank

    b. The amount owed to Mike's Music by its customers

    c. The sales Mike's Music made last week

    d. The cash collected from customers on the sales made last week

5. Which of the following statements is true?

    a. Mike's Music is too small for any outside party to care about its financial information.

    b. The sales Mike's Music made last week are considered revenue.

    c. The intent of Mike's Music to expand is an asset.

    d. The sales Mike's Music made on credit last week is viewed as a liability.

6. The Acme Company reports financial information to potential investors. The information is said to be "presented fairly according to U.S. GAAP." What does that mean?

    a. The information contains no material misstatements according to the rules and standards of U.S. GAAP.

    b. The information is correct and follows the rules of U.S. GAAP.

    c. The information contains neither errors nor fraudulent numbers as specified by U.S. GAAP.

    d. The information is comparable to that reported by other companies around the world.

7. Which of the following statements is true?

    a. Accounting rules referred to as IFRS are more complex than those existing within U.S. GAAP.

    b. Accounting rules referred to as IFRS have been developed for as long a period of time as the rules that make up U.S. GAAP.

    c. Accounting rules referred to as IFRS have become dominant in the world of accounting outside of the United States.

    d. Accounting rules referred to as IFRS will become mandatory in the United States in 2014.

8. The Remingshire Corporation paid $2,000 at the end of the week to employees who worked for the business during that week. The corporation also paid another $3,000 at the end of the week for rent on the retail space that was occupied that week. Which of the following statements is true?

    a. The $2,000 is an expense for this period, but the $3,000 is not.

    b. The $3,000 is an expense for this period, but the $2,000 is not.

    c. Neither the $2,000 nor the $3,000 is an expense for this period.

    d. Both the $2,000 and the $3,000 are expenses for this period.

9. Officials for the Boston Company have just borrowed $25,000 on a three-year loan from a bank. Which of the following is true?

    a. The company has an expense as a result of this transaction.

    b. The company's net assets have gone down as a result of this transaction.

    c. The company's net asserts have gone up as a result of this transaction.

    d. No change took place in this company's net assets as a result of this transaction.

VIDEO PROBLEMS

Professor Joe Hoyle discusses the answers to these two problems at the links that are indicated. After formulating your answers, watch each video to see how Professor Hoyle answers these questions.

1. Your roommate is an English major. The roommate knows that you are taking a course in financial accounting. The roommate has never once considered taking a class in business and is interested in what you are learning. One evening, while listening to some music on the Internet, you mention that financial accounting is a type of language. The roommate is completely baffled by this assertion and wants to know how anything in accounting could possibly resemble a language such as English. How would you respond?

View the video online at: http://bit.ly/hoyle2-3

2. Your uncle has worked for a large office supply business for the past twenty years. He is responsible for a small team of employees who do the interior design work for each of the company's stores located around the country. One day he sends you the following e-mail:. "As a reward for twenty years of service, my company has offered to sell me one thousand shares of their capital stock for $23 per share. That's $23,000, and that is a lot of money. I've never been interested in this aspect of business, but I don't want to make a dumb decision. The company furnished me with a set of financial statements that are just full of numbers and odd terms. At one point, I found a statement that this information was presented fairly in conformity with U.S. Generally Accepted Accounting Principles. I understand you are taking a financial accounting course in college. What is meant by 'presented fairly'? What is meant by 'U.S. Generally Accepted Accounting Principles'? Most important, why is this important to me as I look through financial statements in hopes of making a good decision?"

View the video online at: http://bit.ly/hoyle2-4

PROBLEMS

1. Mark each of the following with an (A) to indicate it is an asset, an (L) to indicate it is a liability, an (R) to indicate it is revenue, or an (E) to indicate it is an expense.

    a. _____ Cash

    b. _____ Building

    c. _____ Loan due to the bank

    d. _____ Inventory

    e. _____ Salary expense

    f. _____ Rent expense

    g. _____ Amounts owed to employees for work done

    h. _____ Equipment

    i. _____ Amounts owed to suppliers

    j. _____ Sales

2. For each of the following, indicate at least one area of uncertainty that would impact the financial reporting of the balance.

    a. Inventory

    b. Receivable from a customer

    c. Equipment

    d. Income taxes payable

    e. Liability from lawsuit

3. The Winslow Corporation operates a jewelry store in Topeka, Kansas. The business has recently issued a set of financial statements. One asset, inventory, was reported at $1.5 million. Later, it was determined that this balance was misstated. Describe several reasons why this misstatement might have happened.

4. For each of the following events, indicate whether the net assets of the reporting company increase, decrease, or remain the same.

    a. The company owes $1,000 for some purchases made last month and pays that amount now.

    b. The company borrows $220,000 from a bank on a loan.

    c. The company sells a service to a customer for $30,000 with payment made immediately.

    d. The company sells a service to a customer for $40,000, but payment will not be made for several months.

    e. The company pays $8,000 in cash for several pieces of equipment.

    f. The company rented a large truck for one day for $500, which it paid at the end of the work day.

RESEARCH ASSIGNMENTS

1. Go to http://www.aboutmcdonalds.com/. At the **McDonald's** Web site, click on "Investors" at the left of the page. Click on "Annual Reports" on the right of the next screen. Finally, click on "2010 Annual Report" to download. Answer the following questions:

   a. On page 26 of the 2010 annual report for **McDonald's**, you will see a list of revenues and expenses. What is the largest revenue and what is the amount? What is the largest expense and what is the amount?

   b. On page 27 of the 2010 annual report for **McDonald's**, you will see a list of assets and liabilities. What is the largest asset and what is the amount? What is the largest liability and what is the amount?

2. **IBM Corporation** provides information about accounting to help decision makers understand the financial statements that the business provides. Go to the following URL and read the sections presented on "Assets" and on "Liabilities."

   http://www.ibm.com/investor/help/guide/statement-basics.wss#assets

   For the coverage of assets, and then also for liabilities, list two pieces of information that you already knew based on the coverage here in Chapter 2. Next, list one piece of information about both assets and liabilities that you learned from the **IBM** essay.

3. Go to http://www.google.com/finance/. In the box labeled "Get quotes," enter "**Johnson & Johnson**." On the page that appears, scroll down and find "Investor Relations" on the right side. Click on that link and then click on "Annual Reports" on the left side of the next page. Click on "2010 Annual Report" in the middle of the next page that appears. After the annual report downloads, scroll to page 41. You should find a listing of the company's assets and liabilities.

   a. What is the total amount reported for the company's assets?

   b. What is the total amount reported for the company's liabilities?

   c. Determine the net assets for **Johnson & Johnson**.

ENDNOTES

1. Michael Rapoport, "Accounting Move Pits Big vs. Small," *The Wall Street Journal*, July 6, 2011, C1.

2. Clay Shirky, "How Priceline Became a Real Business," *Wall Street Journal*, August 13, 2001, A-12.

3. The wide-scale financial meltdown in the world economy that began to be evident in 2008 put a serious strain on the traditional capitalist model. The United States and other governments had to spend billions of dollars to bail out (and, in some cases, take over) major enterprises. Whether U.S. GAAP could have done a better job to help avoid this calamity will probably not be fully known for years.

4. This is one of the opening chapters in an introductory financial accounting textbook. Definitions are somewhat simplified here so that they will be more understandable to students who are just beginning their exploration of accounting. Many terms and definitions will be expanded in later chapters of this textbook or in upper-level financial accounting courses.

5. An expense often causes an immediate reduction in assets, especially if cash is paid. Frequently, though, an expense creates an increase in liabilities instead of a reduction in assets. That happens if the cost is incurred but payment is delayed until a later date. In either case—the reduction of an asset or the creation of a liability—the amount of net assets held by the organization decreases as a result of the expense.

CHAPTER 3

How Is Financial Information Delivered to Decision Makers Such as Investors and Creditors?

 Video Clip

In this video, Professor Joe Hoyle introduces the essential points covered in Chapter 3.

View the video online at: http://bit.ly/hoyle3-1

1. CONSTRUCTION OF FINANCIAL STATEMENTS BEGINNING WITH THE INCOME STATEMENT

LEARNING OBJECTIVES

At the end of this section, students should be able to meet the following objectives:

1. Understand that financial statements provide the physical structure for the financial information reported to decision makers by businesses and other organizations.
2. Identify each of the four financial statements typically produced by a reporting entity.
3. List the normal contents of an income statement.
4. Define "gains" and "losses" and explain how they differ from "revenues" and "expenses."
5. Explain the term "cost of goods sold."
6. Compute gross profit and the gross profit percentage.

1.1 Financial Statements Provide Physical Structure for Financial Reporting

Question: The revenues, expenses, assets, and liabilities reported by an organization provide essential data for decision making. These figures and related information enable a thorough analysis and evaluation of the organization's financial health and future prospects. How do outsiders learn of these amounts? How do decision makers obtain this data? **How is financial information actually conveyed to interested parties?**

For example, a company such as **Marriott International Inc.** *(the hotel chain) has millions of current and potential shareholders, creditors, and employees. How does such a business communicate vital financial information to all of the groups and individuals that might want to make some type of evaluation?*

Answer: Businesses and other organizations periodically produce financial statements that provide a formal structure for conveying financial information to decision makers. Smaller organizations distribute such statements each year, frequently as part of an annual report prepared by management. Larger companies, like **Marriott International**, issue yearly statements but also prepare interim statements, usually on a quarterly basis.[1]

Regardless of the frequency, financial statements serve as the vehicle to report all monetary balances and explanatory information required according to the rules and principles of U.S. GAAP (or IFRS, if applicable). When based on these standards, such statements create a fairly presented portrait of the organization—one that contains no material misstatements. In simple terms, an organization's revenues, expenses, assets, liabilities, and other balances are reported to outsiders by means of financial statements.

Typically, a complete set of financial statements produced by a business includes four separate statements along with pages of comprehensive notes. When financial statements and the related notes are studied with knowledge and understanding, a vast array of information is available to decision makers who want to predict future stock prices, cash dividend payments, and cash flows.

1.2 Financial Statements and Accompanying Notes

Because final figures shown on the income statement and the statement of retained earnings are necessary to produce subsequent statements, the preparation of financial statements is carried out in the sequential order shown here.

- Income statement (also called a statement of operations or a statement or earnings)[2]
- Statement of retained earnings (or the more inclusive statement of stockholders' equity)
- Balance sheet (also called a statement of financial position)
- Statement of cash flows
- Notes to clarify and explain specified information further

The financial statements prepared by **Marriott International** as of December 31, 2010, and the year then ended were presented in just five pages of its annual report (pages 45 through 49) whereas the notes accompanying those statements made up the next twenty-eight pages. Although decision makers often focus, almost obsessively, on a few individual figures easily located in a set of financial statements, the vast wealth of information provided by the notes should never be ignored.

TEST YOURSELF

Question:

The Winston Corporation has prepared an annual report for the past year that includes a complete set of financial statements. Which of the following is not likely to be included?

a. Statement of changes in liabilities
b. Balance sheet
c. Income statement
d. Statement of cash flows

Answer:

The correct answer is choice a: Statement of changes in liabilities.

Explanation:

The balance sheet reports assets and liabilities at the end of the year. The income statement shows the revenues and expenses incurred during the year. The statement of retained earnings explains the change in the reported retained earnings figure for the year. The statement of cash flows indicates how the organization gained cash during this period and how it was used. There is no statement of changes in liabilities, although information about liabilities is available on the balance sheet.

1.3   Reporting Revenues and Expenses on an Income Statement

Question: Assume that an individual is analyzing the most recent income statement prepared by a business in hopes of deciding whether to buy its capital stock or, possibly, grant a loan application. Or, perhaps, this person is a current employee who must decide whether to stay with the company or take a job offer from another organization. Regardless of the reason, the decision maker wants to assess the company's financial health and future prospects. Certainly, all of the available financial statements need to be studied but, initially, this individual is looking at the income statement. **What types of financial data will be available on a typical income statement such as might be produced by a business like** IBM, **Apple, Papa John's,** *or* **Pizza Hut?**

Answer: The main contents of an income statement are rather straightforward: a listing of all revenues earned and expenses incurred by the reporting organization during the period specified. As indicated previously in Chapter 2, revenue figures disclose increases in net assets (assets minus liabilities) that were created by the sale of goods or services. For **IBM**, revenues are derived from the sale and servicing of computers (a total of $99.9 billion in 2010) while, for **Papa John's International**, the reported revenue figure for 2010 (a bit over $1.1 billion) measures the increase in net assets created by the sale of pizzas and related items.

Conversely, expenses are decreases in net assets incurred by reporting organization in hopes of generating revenues. For example, salaries paid to sales people for the work they have done constitute an expense. The cost of facilities that have been rented is also an expense as is money paid for utilities, such as electricity, heat, and water.

For example, **IBM** reported selling, general, and administrative expenses during 2010 of $21.8 billion. That was just one category of expenses disclosed within the company's income statement for this period.[3] During the same year, **Papa John's** reported salaries and benefits as an expense for its domestic company-owned restaurants of $137.8 million. Financial accounting focuses on providing

---

income statement

A listing of all revenues earned and expenses incurred during a specific period of time as well as all gains and losses; also called statement of operations or statement of earnings.

statement of retained earnings

A financial statement that reports the change in a corporation's retained earnings account from the beginning of a period to the end; the account is increased by net income and decreased by a reported net loss and/or any dividends declared.

balance sheet

A listing of all asset, liability, and stockholders' equity accounts at a specific point in time; also called statement of financial position.

statement of cash flows

A listing of all cash inflows (sources) and cash outflows (uses) during a specific period of time categorized as operating activities, investing activities, and financing activities.

useful information about an organization, and both of these figures will help decision makers begin to glimpse a portrait of the underlying business.

Accounting is often said to provide transparency—the ability to see straight through the words and numbers to gain a vision of the actual company and its operations.

1.4 Reporting Gains and Losses

*Question: **Is nothing else presented on an income statement other than revenues and expenses?***

Answer: An income statement also reports gains and losses for the same period of time. A gain is an increase in the net assets of an organization created by an occurrence that is outside its primary or central operations. A loss is a decrease in net assets from a similar type of incidental event.

When **Apple** sells or repairs a computer, it reports revenue because that is the sale of a good or service provided by this company. However, if **Apple** disposes of a piece of land adjacent to a warehouse, a gain is reported (if sold above cost) or a loss (if sold below cost). Selling computers falls within **Apple's** primary operations whereas selling land does not.

If **Pizza Hut** sells a pepperoni pizza, the transaction increases net assets. Revenue has been earned and should be reported. If the company disposes of one of its old ovens, the result is reflected as either a gain or loss. **Pizza Hut** is not in the business of selling appliances. This classification split between revenues/expenses and gains/losses helps provide decision makers with a clearer portrait of what actually happened during the reporting period.

An example of an income statement for a small convenience store (Davidson Groceries) is shown in Figure 3.1. Note that the name of the company, the identity of the statement, and the period of time reflected are apparent. Although this is an illustration, it is quite similar structurally to the income statements created by virtually all business organizations in the United States and most other countries.

FIGURE 3.1 Income Statement

Davidson Groceries Income Statement for Year Ended December 31, 2009		
Revenues:		
Sales of groceries		$1,400,000
Expenses:		
Cost of goods sold	$900,000	
Salary	120,000	
Rent	20,000	
Advertising	30,000	
Insurance	15,000	
Others	25,000	
Total Expenses		(1,110,000)
Operating income		290,000
Other gains and losses:		
Gain on sale of delivery truck	5,000	
Loss on sale of land behind building	(15,000)	(10,000)
Income before income taxes		280,000
Income tax expense		(50,000)
Net income		$230,000

TEST YOURSELF

Question:

The Bartolini Company has recently issued a set of financial statements. The company owns several restaurants that serve coffee and donuts. Each of the following balances appears in the company's financial statements. Which was not included in the company's reported income statement?

  a. Loss from fire in warehouse—$4,000

  b. Rent expense—$13,000

  c. Cash—$9,000

  d. Gain on sale of refrigerator—$1,000

Answer:

The correct answer is choice c: Cash—$9,000.

Explanation:

Revenues, expenses, gains, and losses all appear in a company's income statement. Cash is an asset, and assets are shown on the balance sheet.

1.5   Cost of Goods Sold and Gross Profit

Question: A review of the sample income statement in Figure 3.1 raises a number of questions. The meaning of balances such as salary expense, rent expense, advertising expense, and the like are relatively clear. These figures measure specific outflows or decreases in net assets that were incurred in attempting to generate revenue. However, the largest expense reported on this income statement is referred to as cost of goods sold. **What does the cost of goods sold figure represent?** *What information is communicated by this $900,000 balance?*

Answer: This convenience store generated sales of $1.4 million in Year 2XX4. Customers came in during that period and purchased merchandise for that amount. That is the first step in the sale and is reflected within the revenue balance. The customers then take their goods and leave the store. This merchandise no longer belongs to Davidson Groceries. In this second step, a decrease occurred in the company's net assets; the goods were removed. Thus, an expense has occurred. As the title implies, "cost of goods sold" (sometimes referred to as "cost of sales") is an expense reflecting the cost of the merchandise that customers purchased during the period. It is the amount that Davidson paid for inventory items—such as apples, bread, soap, tuna fish, and cheese—that were then sold. In the language of accounting, that is the meaning of "cost of goods sold."

Note that the timing of expense recognition is not tied to the payment of cash but rather to the loss of the asset. As a simple illustration, assume Davidson Groceries pays $2 in cash for a box of cookies on Monday and then sells it to a customer for $3 on Friday. The income statement will recognize revenue of $3 (the increase in the net assets created by the sale) and cost of goods sold of $2 (the decrease in net assets resulting from the sale). Both the revenue and the related expense are recorded on Friday when the sale took place and the inventory was removed. That is when the change in net assets occurred. **Apple**, **Pizza Hut**, and thousands of other American businesses report the sale of merchandise in this manner because they all follow the same set of rules: U.S. GAAP.

The difference in revenue and cost of goods sold is often referred to as the company's **gross profit**, **gross margin**, or **markup**. It is one of the reported figures studied carefully by decision makers. If a business buys inventory for $50 or $5,000, how much revenue can be generated by its sale? That difference is the gross profit.

As an example, assume that an investor or creditor is comparing two large home improvement companies: **Lowe's** and **Home Depot**. For the year ended January 28, 2011, **Lowe's** reported net sales revenues of $48.8 billion along with cost of goods sold of $31.7 billion. Thus, **Lowe's** earned gross profit during that period of $17.1 billion. Sales of merchandise and services ($48.8 billion) exceeded the cost of those goods ($31.7 billion) by that amount. **Lowe's** reported a gross profit that was 35.0 percent of sales ($17.1 million/$48.8 million). Thus, on the average, when a customer bought goods at **Lowe's** for $100 during this period the markup above cost earned by the company was $35.00 (35.0 percent of $100 sales price). Any decision maker will find such numbers highly informative especially when compared with the company's prior years or with competing enterprises.

For the year ended January 30, 2011, **Home Depot** reported net sales of $68.0 billion, cost of sales of $44.7 billion, and gross profit of $23.3 billion. Its gross profit percentage was 34.3 percent ($23.3 million/$68.0 million). On the average, when a customer bought goods at **Home Depot** for $100 during this period the markup above cost earned by the company was $34.30 (34.3 percent of $100 sales price).

gross profit

Difference between sales and cost of goods sold; also called gross margin or markup.

gross margin

Difference between sales price and cost of goods sold; also called gross profit or markup.

markup

Difference between sales price and cost of goods sold on an item of inventory; also called gross profit or gross margin.

Home Depot is clearly a bigger business than **Lowe's**, but during this year it earned a slightly smaller profit on each sales dollar than did its competitor.

Such reported information is studied carefully and allows decision makers to compare these two companies and their operations.

TEST YOURSELF

Question:

The Hayes Corporation is a car dealer. A new car is received from the manufacturer during September at a cost of $33,000. This vehicle is sold in October to a customer for $42,000. In connection with this transaction, which of the following statements is correct?

  a. The company will report cost of goods sold of $42,000.
  b. The company will report gross profit of $42,000.
  c. The company will report cost of goods sold of $33,000.
  d. The company will report gross profit of $33,000.

Answer:

The correct answer is choice c: The company will report cost of goods sold of $33,000.

Explanation:

On the company's income statement, revenue of $42,000 (the sales price) and cost of goods sold of $33,000 (the cost paid to acquire the inventory) will be reported. Gross profit is the difference in these two figures, or $9,000.

1.6 Placement of Income Taxes on an Income Statement

*Question: In Figure 3.1, revenues and expenses are listed first to arrive at an operating income figure. That is followed by gains and losses. This sequencing is appropriate since revenues and expenses relate to the primary or central operations of the business and gains and losses are created by more incidental events. **Why then is income tax expense listed last, by itself, on the bottom of the income statement and not with the other expenses?***

Answer: State, federal, and international income taxes cost businesses considerable sums of money each year. **Exxon Mobil Corp.** reported income taxes of $21.6 billion at the bottom of its 2010 income statement. The income tax figure is segregated in this manner because it is not an expense in a traditional sense. As previously described, an expense—like cost of goods sold, advertising, or rent—is incurred in order to generate revenues. Income taxes do not create revenues. Instead, they are caused by a company's revenues and related profitability.

Because the financial impact is the same as an expense (an outflow or decrease in net assets), "income tax expense" is often used for labeling purposes. A more appropriate title would be something like "income taxes assessed by government." Because the nature of this "expense" is different, the income tax figure is frequently isolated at the bottom of the income statement, separate from true expenses.

KEY TAKEAWAY

Financial information is gathered about an organization, but the resulting figures must then be structured in some usable fashion that can be conveyed to interested decision makers. Financial statements serve this purpose. A typical set of financial statements is made up of an income statement, statement of retained earnings, balance sheet, statement of cash flows, and explanatory notes. The income statement reports revenues from the sale of goods and services as well as expenses such as rent and advertising. Gains and losses that arise from incidental activities are also included on the income statement but separately so that the income generated from primary operations is apparent. Cost of goods sold is an expense that reflects the cost of all inventory items acquired by customers. Income tax expense is reported at the bottom of the income statement because it is actually a government assessment rather than a true expense.

2. REPORTED PROFITABILITY AND THE IMPACT OF CONSERVATISM

LEARNING OBJECTIVES

At the end of this section, students should be able to meet the following objectives:

1. Describe the method used to differentiate assets from expenses.
2. Discuss the rationale for the practice of conservatism and its effect on financial reporting.
3. Explain the reason dividend distributions are not reported as expenses within net income.
4. Discuss the need for decision makers to study an entire set of financial statements rather than focus exclusively on one or two numbers such as net income or gross profit.

2.1 Differentiating between an Asset and an Expense

Question: Previously, the term "asset" was defined as a probable future economic benefit owned or controlled by a reporting entity. On an income statement, items such as rent and advertising are listed as expenses. Why are such costs not grouped with the assets on the balance sheet? For example, rent paid for a building could provide a probable future economic benefit but it is included in Figure 3.1 as an expense. The same is true for advertising. **How does an organization determine whether a cost represents an asset or an expense?**

Answer: Deciding whether a particular cost should be classified as an asset or an expense is not always easy for an accountant. If a business makes a $10,000 rent payment, an expense might have been incurred because an outflow of an asset (cash) has taken place. However, the cost of this rent could also be reported as an asset if it provides probable future economic benefit.

A cost is identified as an asset if the benefit clearly has value in generating *future* revenues whereas an expense is a cost that has already helped earn revenues in the *past*. With an asset, the utility associated with a cost is yet to be consumed completely. With an expense, the utility has already been consumed. To illustrate, assume that on December 31, Year One, a business pays $10,000 for rent on a building that was used during the previous month as a retail outlet. The benefit gained from occupying that space has already occurred. Use of the building helped the business make sales during December. The reduction in net assets to pay for the rent is reflected on the income statement as a rent expense. The benefit is in the past.

If on that same day, another $10,000 is paid to rent this building again during the upcoming month of January Year Two, the acquired benefit relates directly to the future. The building will be occupied in January in hopes of creating additional revenue. Until consumed, this second cost is shown as a $10,000 asset (referred to as "prepaid rent").

- **Expense.** A cost that helped a business generate revenue in the past.
- **Asset.** A cost expected to help generate additional revenue in the future.

When a cost is incurred, the accountant must investigate its purpose to determine when the related benefit is expected. This timing—as guided by U.S. GAAP or IFRS—indicates whether an asset should be recognized or an expense.

TEST YOURSELF

Question:

In a set of financial statements, a company reports an account balance of $19,000 labeled as "prepaid insurance." Which of the following is not true in connection with this account?

   a. The account appears on the company's income statement.
   b. The money was paid in the past but will provide benefit in the future.
   c. The account is an asset.
   d. The cost is expected to help generate future revenue.

Answer:

The correct answer is choice a: The account appears on the company's income statement.

Explanation:

The account title implies a benefit to the company in the future. A payment has been made for insurance coverage on assets such as buildings and equipment over the next few months or years. Because the benefits are yet to be derived, this cost cannot be reported on the income statement; rather, it must be reported as an asset on the balance sheet.

2.2 Conservatism in Financial Accounting

Question: A business or other organization can face many complicated situations. Determining fair presentation is often not easy. For example, at times, the decision whether a cost will generate revenue in the future (and be reported as an asset) or has already helped create revenue in the past (and is, thus, an expense) is difficult. When an accountant encounters a case that is "too close to call," what reporting is appropriate? To illustrate, assume that a business agrees to pay $24,000 but corporate officials cannot ascertain the amount of the related benefit that has already occurred versus the amount that will take place in the future. **When clear delineation of a cost between asset and expense appears to be impossible, what reporting is made?**

practice of conservatism

Preference of accountants to avoid making an organization look overly good; when faced with multiple reporting options that are equally likely, the worse possible outcome is reported to help protect the decision maker from information that is too optimistic.

Answer: Working as an accountant is a relatively easy job when financial events are distinct and easily understood. Unfortunately, in real life, situations often arise where two or more outcomes seem equally likely. The distinction raised in this question between an asset and an expense is simply one of numerous possibilities where multiple portraits could be envisioned. At such times, financial accounting has a long history of following the **practice of conservatism**.

The conservative nature of accounting influences many elements of U.S. GAAP and must be understood in order to appreciate the meaning of financial information conveyed about an organization. Simply put, conservatism holds that whenever an accountant faces two or more *equally likely* possibilities, the one that makes the reporting company look worse should be selected. In other words, financial accounting attempts to ensure that an organization never looks significantly better than it actually is.

Differentiating between an asset and an expense provides a perfect illustration of conservatism. If a cost is incurred that might have either a future value (an asset) or a past value (an expense), the accountant always reports the most likely possibility. That is the only appropriate way to paint a portrait of an organization that is the fairest representation. However, if neither scenario appears more likely to occur, the cost is classified as an expense rather than an asset because of conservatism. Reporting a past benefit rather than a future benefit has a detrimental impact on the company's appearance to a decision maker. This handling reduces reported income as well as the amount shown as the total of the assets.

Conservatism can be seen throughout financial accounting. When the chance of two possibilities is the same, accounting prefers that the more optimistic approach be avoided.

2.3 The Reason for Conservatism

Question: **Why does conservatism exist in financial accounting?** *Every organization must want to look as successful as possible. Why does a bias exist for reporting outcomes in a negative way?*

Answer: Accountants are well aware that the financial statements they produce are relied on by decision makers around the world to determine future actions that will place significant amounts of money at risk. For example, if a company appears to be prosperous, an investor might decide to allocate scarce cash resources to obtain shares of its capital stock. Similarly, a creditor is more willing to make a loan to a business that seems to be doing well economically.

Such decision makers face potential losses that can be substantial. Accountants take their role in this process quite seriously. As a result, financial accounting has traditionally held that the users of financial statements are best protected if the reporting process is never overly optimistic in picturing an organization's financial health and future prospects. Money is less likely to be lost if the accountant paints a portrait that is no more rosy than necessary. The practice of conservatism is simply an attempt by financial accounting to help safeguard the public.

The problem that can occur when a business appears excessively profitable can be seen in the downfall of **WorldCom** where investors and creditors lost billions of dollars. A major cause of this accounting scandal, one of the biggest in history, was the fraudulent decision by members of the company's management to record a cost of nearly $4 billion as an asset rather than as an expense. Although any future benefit resulting from those expenditures was highly doubtful, the cost was reported to outsiders as an asset. Conservatism was clearly not followed.

Consequently, in its financial statements, **WorldCom** appeared to have $4 billion more in assets and be that much more profitable than was actually true. At the same time that its two chief rivals were reporting declines, **WorldCom** seemed to be prospering. Investors and creditors risked incredible amounts of their money based on the incorrect information they had received. Later, in 2002, when the misstatement was uncovered, the stock price plummeted, and **WorldCom** went bankrupt. Conservatism is designed to help prevent such unnecessary losses. If no outcome is viewed as most likely, the accountant should always work to prevent an overly optimistic picture of the reporting entity and its financial health.

TEST YOURSELF

Question:

Which of the following is not an example of the effect of the practice of conservatism?

a. A company has revenue, but the revenue is not reported because of some uncertainty.

b. A company has a liability, but the liability is not reported because of some uncertainty.

c. A company has an asset, but the asset is not reported because of some uncertainty.

d. A company has a cost that is reported as expense because of an uncertainty about the future benefit.

Answer:

The correct answer is choice b: A company has a liability, but the liability is not reported because of some uncertainty.

Explanation:

The practice of conservatism holds that when outcomes are equally likely, the option that makes the reporting entity look worse should be reported. Delaying the revenue in A and the asset in C are both examples of conservative reporting. Recognizing an expense in D rather than an asset also reduces reported income and total assets. However, delaying the reporting of the liability in B improves the way the company's financial position appears. Reporting fewer debts makes the company look better.

2.4 Reporting Dividend Distributions

Question: Previously, the term "dividends" was introduced and discussed. Dividend distributions made to owners reduce the net assets held by an organization. In Figure 3.1, a number of expenses are listed, but no dividends are mentioned. **Why are dividend payments not included as expenses of a corporation on its income statement?**

Answer: Dividends are not expenses and, therefore, are omitted in preparing an income statement. Such distributions obviously reduce the amount of net assets owned or controlled by a company. However, they are not related in any way to generating revenues. A dividend is a reward paid by a corporation (through the decision of its board of directors) to the owners of its capital stock. A dividend is a sharing of profits and not a cost incurred to create revenue.

In Figure 3.1, Davidson Groceries reports net income for the year of $230,000. The board of directors might look at that figure and opt to make a cash dividend distribution to company owners. That is one of the most important decisions for any board. Such payments usually please the owners but reduce the size of the company and—possibly—its future profitability.

An income statement reports revenues, expenses, gains, and losses. Dividend distributions do not qualify and must be reported elsewhere in the company's financial statements.

TEST YOURSELF

Question:

A company has the following reported balances at the end of the current year: revenues—$100,000, rent expense—$40,000, dividends paid—$12,000, loss on sale of truck—$2,000, salary expense—$19,000, gain on sale of land—$9,000, and prepaid insurance—$8,000. What should be reported by this company as its net income for the year?

  a. $28,000
  b. $36,000
  c. $40,000
  d. $48,000

Answer:

The correct answer is choice d: $48,000.

Explanation:

Net income is made up of revenues ($100,000) less expenses ($40,000 plus $19,000, or $59,000) plus gains ($9,000) less losses ($2,000), or $48,000. Dividends paid is not an expense, and prepaid insurance is an asset.

2.5 The Significance of Reported Net Income

*Question: The final figure presented on the income statement is net income. This balance reflects the growth in an organization's net assets during the period resulting from all revenues, expenses, gains, and losses. More specifically, it is the revenues and gains less the expenses and losses. For example, in 2010, the income statement reported by the **Kellogg Company** indicated that the size of that company's net assets grew in that one year by $1.24 billion as a result of net income (revenues and gains less expenses and losses). In evaluating the operations of any business, this figure seems to be incredibly significant. It reflects the profitability for the period. **Is net income the most important number to be found in a set of financial statements?***

Answer: The net income figure reported for any business is an eagerly anticipated and carefully analyzed piece of financial information. It is the most discussed number disclosed by virtually any company. It is reported in newspapers and television, on the Internet and the radio.

However, financial statements present a vast array of data and the importance of any one balance should never be overemphasized. A portrait painted by an artist is not judged solely by the small section displaying the model's ear or mouth but rather by the representation made of the entire person. Likewise, only the analysis of all information conveyed by a set of financial statements enables an interested party to arrive at the most appropriate decisions about an organization.

Some creditors and investors seek shortcuts when making business decisions rather than doing the detailed analysis that is appropriate. Those individuals often spend an exorbitant amount of time focusing on reported net income. Such a narrow view shows a fundamental misunderstanding of financial reporting and the depth and breadth of the information being conveyed. In judging a company's financial health and future prospects, an evaluation should be carried out on the entity as a whole. Predicting stock prices, dividends, and cash flows requires a complete investigation. That is only possible by developing the capacity to work with all the data presented in a set of financial statements. If a single figure such as net income could be used reliably to evaluate a business organization, creditors and investors would never incur losses.

> **KEY TAKEAWAY**
>
> Conservatism is an often misunderstood term in financial reporting. Despite a reputation to the contrary, financial accounting is not radically conservative. However, when two reporting options are equally likely, the one that makes the company look best is avoided. The portrait that results is less likely to be overly optimistic. In this way, decision makers are protected. Their chance of incurring losses is reduced. For example, expenses refer to costs that helped generate revenue in the past while assets reflect costs that provide future economic benefits. If the timing of these benefits cannot be ascertained, the cost should be recognized as an expense. This assignment reduces both reported income and total assets. The resulting net income figure (revenues and gains less expenses and losses) is useful in evaluating the financial health and prospects of a company but no single figure should be the sole source of information for a decision maker. Dividend distributions are not included in this computation of net income because they reflect a sharing of profits with owners and not a cost incurred to generate revenue.

3.   INCREASING THE NET ASSETS OF A COMPANY

> **LEARNING OBJECTIVES**
>
> At the end of this section, students should be able to meet the following objectives:
>
> 1. Define "retained earnings" and explain its composition.
> 2. Define "capital stock" and explain the meaning of its reported account balance.
> 3. Explain the lack of financial impact that the exchange of ownership shares between investors has on a corporation.

3.1   The Meaning of Retained Earnings

*Question: The second financial statement is known as the statement of **retained earnings**.*[4] *The term retained earnings has not yet been introduced.* **What information does a retained earnings balance communicate to an outside decision maker?** *For example, on May 1, 2010,* **Barnes & Noble** *reported retained earnings of aproximately $681.1 million, one of the largest amounts found in the company's financial statements. What does that figure tell decision makers about this bookstore chain?*

Answer: The retained earnings account (sometimes referred to as "reinvested earnings") is one of the most misunderstood figures in all of financial reporting. As shown in Figure 3.2, this balance is the total amount of all net income earned by a business since it first began operations, less all dividends paid to stockholders during that same period of time. Retained earnings is a measure of the profits left in a business throughout its existence to create growth. For an organization like **The Coca-Cola Company** with a long history of profitability, much of its enormous expansion over the years has come from its own operations. That growth is reflected by the retained earnings balance, which is $49.2 billion for **Coca-Cola** as of December 31, 2010.

FIGURE 3.2

Total net income since organization began operations
Less: total of all dividends paid to owners

Retained earnings balance

When a business earns income, it becomes larger because net assets have increased. Even if a portion of the profits is distributed to shareholders as a dividend, the company has grown in size as a result of its own operations. The retained earnings figure informs decision makers of the amount of that internally generated expansion. This reported balance answers the question: How much of the company's net assets have been derived from operations during its life?

If a company reports an annual net income of $10,000 and then pays a $2,000 dividend to its owners each year, it is growing in size at the rate of $8,000 per year. After four years, for example, $32,000 ($8,000 × four years) of its net assets will have been generated by its own operating activities. That information is communicated through the retained earnings balance.

As of May 1, 2010, **Barnes & Noble** reported total assets of $3.7 billion and liabilities of $2.8 billion. Thus, the company had net assets of $900 million. Assets exceeded liabilities by that amount. Those additional assets did not appear by magic. They had to come from some source. One of the primary ways to increase the net assets of a business is through profitable operations. The balance for retained earnings shown by **Barnes & Noble** lets decision makers know that approximately $681 million of its net assets were generated by the total net income earned since the company's inception, after all dividend distributions to shareholders were subtracted.

TEST YOURSELF

Question:

On January 1, Year One, the Green River Company was started when owners contributed $100,000 cash to start operations. During the first year, the company earned a reported net income of $23,000 and paid a $2,000 dividend. During the second year, the company earned another $31,000 and paid a $5,000 dividend. What is reported on the company's balance sheet as the total retained earnings at the end of Year Two?

  a. $47,000

  b. $54,000

  c. $147,000

  d. $154,000

Answer:

The correct answer is choice a: $47,000.

Explanation:

Retained earnings are a measure of a company's growth in net assets because of its operations. Since its beginning, Green River made a total profit of $54,000 ($23,000 plus $31,000) and paid a total dividend of $7,000 ($2,000 plus $5,000). As a result, net assets rose by $47,000 ($54,000 less $7,000). This balance is reported as retained earnings. The increase from the money the owners put into the business is known as contributed capital (or capital stock), which is a separately reported figure.

3.2 The Reporting of Retained Earnings

Question: In Figure 3.2, Davidson Groceries calculated its net income for 2XX4 as $230,000. Assume that this company began operations on January 1, 2XX1, and reported the balances shown in Figure 3.3 over the years:

FIGURE 3.3

Year	Reported Net Income	Dividends Distributed	Growth in Company (income minus dividends)
Past Years			
2XX1	$140,000	$50,000	$90,000
2XX2	180,000	70,000	110,000
2XX3	210,000	90,000	120,000
Totals	$530,000	$210,000	$320,000
Current Year			
2XX4	$230,000	$100,000	$130,000

How is the growth of this company's net assets reported? What is the structure of the statement of retained earnings as it appears within a set of financial statements?

Answer: In the three prior years of its existence, Davidson Groceries' net assets increased by $320,000 as a result of operating activities. As can be seen in Figure 3.3, the company generated total profit during this earlier period of $530,000 while distributing dividends to shareholders of $210,000, a net increase of $320,000. During the current year (2XX4), net assets continued to rise as Davidson Groceries made an additional profit (see also Figure 3.1) of $230,000 but distributed another $100,000 in dividends. Thus, the net assets of Davidson Groceries increased in 2XX4 by $130,000 ($230,000 less $100,000) as a result of business operations. For all four years combined, net assets went up by $450,000 ($320,000 + $130,000), all net income for these years minus all dividends.

Figure 3.4 shows the format by which this retained earnings information is conveyed to the decision makers who are evaluating Davidson Groceries. As can be seen here, this structure first presents the previous growth in net assets ($320,000) followed by the net income ($230,000) and dividends ($100,000) for just the current year.

FIGURE 3.4 Statement of Retained Earnings

Davidson Groceries Statement of Retained Earnings for Year Ended December 31, 2009		
Retained earnings balance, January 1, 2009		$320,000
Net income reported for 2009	$230,000	
Dividends distributed during 2009	100,000	
Net income less dividends for 2009		130,000
Retained earnings balance, December 31, 2009		$450,000

TEST YOURSELF

Question:

The London Corporation has just produced a set of financial statements at the end of its fifth year of operations. On its balance sheet, it shows assets of $700,000 and liabilities of $200,000. The retained earnings balance within stockholders' equity is $100,000. Net income for the current year was reported as $90,000 with dividends of $50,000 distributed to the company's owners. Which of the following statements is true?

a. The company's net income for the previous four years can be determined from this information.

b. The company's dividend payments for the previous four years can be determined from this information.

c. The company's retained earnings balance at the beginning of its fifth year was $10,000.

d. Total income less dividends paid during the previous four years was $60,000.

Answer:

The correct answer is choice d: Total income less dividends paid during the previous four years was $60,000.

Explanation:

Retained earnings at the end of the fifth year was reported as $100,000. Of that, $40,000 is the growth in net assets during the current year from net income ($90,000) less dividends ($50,000). Retained earnings at the beginning of the year must have been $60,000 ($100,000 total less $40,000 increase). That represents the growth in net assets in all prior years from net income less dividends. The exact amount of income during this earlier period or the total dividends cannot be derived, only the net figure.

3.3   Assets Contributed to Gain Ownership Shares

*Question: In the information provided, **Barnes & Noble** reported holding net assets of $900 million, but only $681 million of that amount was generated through operations as shown by the retained earnings* *balance. That raises an obvious question: How did **Barnes & Noble** get the rest of its net assets? Clearly, additional sources must have enabled the company to attain the $900 million reported total. Increases in net assets are not the result of magic or miracles. **Other than through operations, how does a company derive net assets?***

Answer: Beyond operations (as reflected by the retained earnings balance), a business accumulates net assets by receiving contributions from investors who become owners through the acquisition of capital stock.[5] This is the other major method that an organization like **Barnes & Noble** uses to gather millions in net assets. In financial statements, the measure of this inflow is usually labeled something like **capital stock**, **common stock**, or **contributed capital**. Regardless of the exact title, the reported amount indicates the portion of the net assets that came into the business directly from stockholders who made the contribution to obtain an ownership interest.

The amount of a company's net assets is the excess of its assets over its liabilities. For most businesses, two accounting balances indicate the primary sources of those net assets.

- **Capital stock (or contributed capital).** This is the amount invested in the business by individuals and groups in order to become owners. For example, as of September 25, 2010, **Apple Inc.** reported assets of $75 billion and liabilities of $27 billion. Thus, the company was holding $48 billion in net assets ($75 billion less $27 billion). How did **Apple** get that amount of net assets? That is a question that should interest virtually any investor or creditor analyzing this business. A reported capital stock balance of nearly $11 billion shows that this portion of the $48 billion came from owners contributing assets in order to purchase shares of the company's stock directly from **Apple**.

- **Retained earnings.** This figure is the total net income earned by the organization over its life less amounts distributed as dividends to owners. On September 25, 2010, **Apple Inc.** reported a retained earnings balance of approximately $37 billion (see Figure 3.5). A growth in net assets of that amount resulted from the operating activities since the day **Apple** first got started.

FIGURE 3.5 Apple Inc.

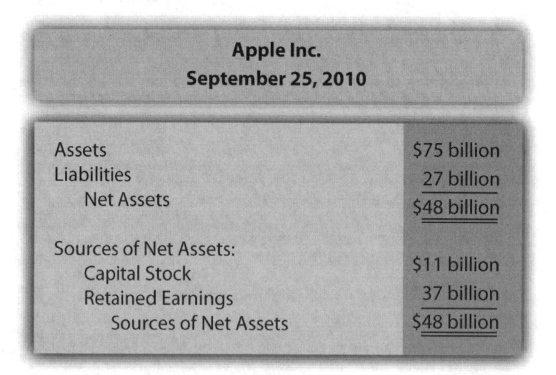

These numbers reconcile because the total amount of net assets ($48 billion) must have a source of the same amount ($48 billion).

3.4 The Trading of Shares of Capital Stock

*Question: A corporation issues (sells) ownership shares to investors to raise money. The source of the resulting inflow of assets into the business is reflected in financial accounting by the reporting of a capital stock (or contributed capital) balance. Thus, over its life, **Apple** has received assets of $11 billion in* *exchange for shares of capital stock.* **Does a company receive money when its shares are sold each day on the New York Stock Exchange, NASDAQ (National Association of Securities Dealers Automated Quotations), or other stock exchanges?**

Answer: No, purchases and sales on stock markets normally occur between two investors and not directly with the company. Only the initial issuance of the ownership shares to a stockholder creates the inflow of assets reported by a capital stock or contributed capital account.

To illustrate, assume that Investor A buys one thousand shares of capital stock shares directly from Business B for $179,000 in cash. This transaction increases the net assets of Business B by that amount. The source of the increase is communicated to decision makers by adding $179,000 to the capital stock balance reported by the company. Business B is bigger by $179,000, and the capital stock account provides information about that growth.

Subsequently, these shares may be exchanged between investors numerous times without any additional financial impact on Business B. For example, assume Investor A later sells the 1,000 shares to Investor Z for $200,000 using a stock market such as the New York Stock Exchange. Investor A earns a $21,000 gain ($200,000 received less $179,000 cost), and Investor Z has replaced Investor A as an owner of Business B. However, the financial condition of the company has not been affected by this new exchange. Business B did not receive anything. From its perspective, nothing happened except for a change in the identity of an owner. Thus, a corporation's capital stock balance only measures the initial investment contributed directly to the business.

KEY TAKEAWAY

The source of a company's net assets (assets minus liabilities) is of interest to outside decision makers. The reported retained earnings figure indicates the amount of these net assets that came from the operations of the company. This growth in size was internally generated. The reported retained earnings balance is all the net income earned since operations began less all dividend distributions. Net assets can also be derived from contributions made by parties seeking to become owners. The capital stock (or contributed capital) balance measures this source of net assets. There is no reported impact unless these assets go directly from the owners to the company. Hence, exchanges between investors using a stock exchange do not affect a business's net assets or its financial reporting.

---

4.   REPORTING A BALANCE SHEET AND A STATEMENT OF CASH FLOWS

LEARNING OBJECTIVES

At the end of this section, students should be able to meet the following objectives:

1. List the types of accounts presented on a balance sheet.
2. Explain the difference between current assets and liabilities and noncurrent assets and liabilities.
3. Calculate working capital and the current ratio.
4. Provide the reason for a balance sheet to always balance.
5. Identify the three sections of a statement of cash flows and explain the types of events included in each.

4.1   Information Reported on a Balance Sheet

Question: The third financial statement is the balance sheet. **If a decision maker studies a company's balance sheet (on its Web site, for example), what information can be discovered?**

Answer: The primary purpose of a balance sheet is to report a company's assets and liabilities at a particular point in time. The format is quite simple. All assets are listed first—usually in order of liquidity[6]—followed by all liabilities. A portrait is provided of each future economic benefit owned or controlled by the company (its assets) as well as its debts (liabilities).

FIGURE 3.6 Balance Sheet[7]

Davidson Groceries Balance Sheet, December 31, 2009		
Assets		
Current Assets		
Cash	$22,000	
Accounts Receivable	24,000	
Inventory	103,000	
Prepaid Rent	12,000	
Total Current Assets		$161,000
Noncurrent Assets		
Land	210,000	
Equipment (net)	155,000	
Buildings (net)	680,000	
Total Noncurrent Assets		1,045,000
Total Assets		$1,206,000
Liabilities and Stockholders' Equity		
Liabilities		
Current Liabilities		
Accounts Payable	$33,000	
Salaries Payable	9,000	
Insurance Payable	15,000	
Total Current Liabilities		$57,000
Noncurrent Liabilities		
Note Payable—Third National Bank	300,000	
Note Payable—State Bank	220,000	
Total Noncurrent Liabilities		520,000
Total Liabilities		$577,000
Stockholders' Equity		
Capital Stock	$179,000	
Retained Earnings	450,000	
Total Stockholders' Equity		$629,000
Total Liabilities and Stockholders' Equity		$1,206,000

working capital

Formula measuring an organization's liquidity (the ability to pay debts as they come due); calculated by subtracting current liabilities from current assets.

A typical balance sheet is reported in Figure 3.6 for Davidson Groceries. Note that the assets are divided between current (those expected to be used or consumed within the following year) and noncurrent (those expected to remain with Davidson for longer than a year). Likewise, liabilities are split between current (to be paid during the upcoming year) and noncurrent (not to be paid until after the next year). This labeling is common and aids financial analysis. Davidson Groceries' current liabilities ($57,000) can be subtracted from its current assets ($161,000) to arrive at a figure often studied by interested parties known as **working capital** ($104,000 in this example). It reflects short-term financial strength, the ability of a business or other organization to generate sufficient cash to pay debts as they come due.

Current assets can also be divided by current liabilities ($161,000/$57,000) to determine the company's **current ratio** (2.82 to 1.00), another figure calculated by many decision makers as a useful measure of short-term operating strength.

The balance sheet shows the company's financial condition on one specific date. All of the other financial statements report events occurring over a period of time (often a year or a quarter). However, the balance sheet discloses all assets and liabilities as of the one specified point in time.

current ratio

Formula measuring an organization's liquidity (the ability to pay debts as they come due); calculated by dividing current assets by current liabilities.

TEST YOURSELF

Question:

Which of the following statements is true?

a. Rent payable appears on a company's income statement.

b. Capital stock appears on a company's balance sheet.

c. Gain on the sale of equipment appears on a company's balance sheet.

d. Accounts receivable appears on a company's income statement.

Answer:

The correct answer is choice b: Capital stock appears on a company's balance sheet.

Explanation:

Assets and liabilities such as accounts receivable and rent payable are shown on a company's balance sheet at a particular point in time. Revenues, expenses, gains, and losses are shown on an income statement for a specified period of time. Capital stock, a measure of the amount of net assets put into the business by its owners, is reported within stockholders' equity on the balance sheet.

4.2 The Accounting Equation

Question: Considerable information is included on the balance sheet presented in Figure 3.6. Assets such as cash, inventory, and land provide future economic benefits for the reporting entity. Liabilities for salaries, insurance, and the like reflect debts that are owed at the end of the fiscal period. The $179,000 capital stock figure indicates the amount of assets that the original owners contributed to the business. The retained earnings balance of $450,000 was computed earlier in Figure 3.4 and identifies the portion of the net assets generated by the company's own operations over the years. For convenience, a general term such as "stockholders' equity" or "shareholders' equity" usually encompasses the capital stock and the retained earnings balances.

Why does the balance sheet balance? *This agreement cannot be an accident. The asset total of $1,206,000 is exactly the same as the liabilities ($577,000) plus the two stockholders' equity accounts ($629,000—the total of capital stock and retained earnings). Thus, assets equal liabilities plus stockholders' equity. What creates this monetary equilibrium?*

Answer: The balance sheet will always balance unless a mistake is made. This is known as the **accounting equation.**

Accounting Equation (Version 1):

$$\text{assets} = \text{liabilities} + \text{stockholders' equity}.$$

Or, if the stockholders' equity account is broken down into its component parts:

Accounting Equation (Version 2):

$$\text{assets} = \text{liabilities} + \text{capital stock} + \text{retained earnings}.$$

accounting equation

Assets = liabilities + stockholders' equity. The equation balances because all assets must have a source: a liability, a contribution from an owner (contributed capital), or from operations (retained earnings).

As discussed previously, this equation stays in balance for one simple reason: assets must have a source. If a business or other organization has an increase in its total assets, that change can only be caused by (a) an increase in liabilities such as money being borrowed, (b) an increase in capital stock such as additional money being contributed by stockholders, or (c) an increase created by operations such as a sale that generates a rise in net income. No other increases occur.

One way to understand the accounting equation is that the left side (the assets) presents a picture of the future economic benefits that the reporting company holds. The right side provides information to show how those assets were derived (from liabilities, from investors, or from operations). Because no assets are held by a company without a source, the equation (and, hence, the balance sheet) must balance.

Accounting Equation (Version 3):

$$\text{assets} = \text{the total source of those assets.}$$

4.3   The Statement of Cash Flows

Question: The fourth and final financial statement is the statement of cash flows. Cash is so important to an organization and its financial health that a complete statement is devoted to presenting the changes that took place in this one asset. As can be inferred from the title, this statement provides a portrait of the various ways the reporting company generated cash during the year and the uses that were made of it. **How is the statement of cash flows structured?**

Answer: Decision makers place considerable emphasis on a company's ability to generate significant cash inflows and then make wise use of that money. Figure 3.7 presents an example of that information in a statement of cash flows for Davidson Groceries for the year ended December 31, 2XX4. Note that all the cash changes are divided into three specific sections:

- Operating activities
- Investing activities
- Financing activities

operating activities

A statement of cash flow category relating to cash receipts and disbursements arising from the primary activities of the organization.

investing activities

A statement of cash flow category relating to cash receipts and disbursements arising from an asset transaction other than one related to the primary activities of the organization.

financing activities

A statement of cash flow category relating to cash receipts and disbursements arising from a liability or stockholders' equity transaction other than one related to the primary activities of the organization.

FIGURE 3.7   Statement of Cash Flows[8]

Davidson Groceries Statement of Cash Flows for Year Ended December 31, 2XX4		
Cash Flows from Operating Activities		
Cash Collected from Customers	$1,396,000	
Cash Paid for Inventory	(935,000)	
Cash Paid for Salaries	(138,000)	
Cash Paid for Rent	(27,000)	
Cash Paid for Advertising	(30,000)	
Cash Paid for Insurance and Other Expenses	(48,000)	
Cash Paid for Income Taxes	(50,000)	$168,000
Cash Flows from Investing Activities		
Cash Received from Sale of Delivery Truck	40,000	
Cash Received from Sale of Land	35,000	
Cash Paid in Purchase of Building	(280,000)	(205,000)
Cash Flows from Financing Activities		
Cash Paid to Owners as Dividends	(100,000)	
Cash Received from Bank on a Loan	120,000	20,000
Cash Reduction During Year		(17,000)
Cash Balance—January 1, 2XX4		39,000
Cash Balance—December 31, 2XX4		$22,000

4.4   Classification of Cash Flows

Question: In studying the statement of cash flows, a company's individual cash flows relating to selling inventory, advertising, selling land, buying a building, paying dividends and the like can be readily understood. For example, when the statement indicates that $120,000 was the "cash received from bank on a loan," a decision maker should have a clear picture of what happened. There is no mystery.

All cash flows are divided into one of the three categories:

1. *Operating activities*
2. *Investing activities*
3. *Financing activities*

How are these distinctions drawn? **On a statement of cash flows, what is the difference in an operating activity, an investing activity, and a financing activity?**

Answer: Cash flows listed as the result of operating activities relate to receipts and disbursements that arose in connection with the central activity of the organization. For Davidson Groceries, these cash changes were created by daily operations and include selling goods to customers, buying merchandise, paying salaries to employees, and the like. This section of the statement shows how much cash the primary business function generated during this period of time, a figure that is watched closely by virtually all financial analysts. Ultimately, a business is only worth the cash that it can create from its normal operations.

Investing activities report cash flows created by events that (1) are separate from the central or daily operations of the business and (2) involve an asset. Thus, the amount of cash collected when either equipment or land is sold is reported within this section. A convenience store does not participate in such transactions as a regular part of operations and both deal with an asset. Cash paid to buy a building or machinery will also be disclosed in this same category. Such purchases do not happen on a daily operating basis and an asset is involved.

Like investing activities, the third section of this statement—cash flows from financing activities—is unrelated to daily business operations but, here, the transactions relate to either a liability or a stockholders' equity balance. Borrowing money from a bank meets these criteria as does distributing a dividend to shareholders. Issuing stock to new owners for cash is another financing activity as is payment of a noncurrent liability.

Any decision maker can study the cash flows of a business within these three separate sections to receive a picture of how company officials managed to generate cash during the period and what use was made of it.

TEST YOURSELF

Question:

In reviewing a statement of cash flows, which one of the following statements is not true?

a. Cash paid for rent is reported as an operating activity.
b. Cash contributed to the business by an owner is an investing activity.
c. Cash paid on a long-term note payable is a financing activity.
d. Cash received from the sale of inventory is an operating activity.

Answer:

The correct answer is choice b: Cash contributed to the business by an owner is an investing activity.

Explanation:

Cash transactions such as the payment of rent or the sale of inventory that are incurred as part of daily operations are included within operating activities. Events that do not take place as part of daily operations are either investing or financing activities. Investing activities are carried out in connection with an asset such as a building or land. Financing activities impact either a liability (such as a note payable) or a stockholders' equity account (such as contributed capital).

KEY TAKEAWAY

The balance sheet is the only one of the four financial statements that is created for a specific point in time. It reports the company's assets as well as the source of those assets: liabilities, capital stock, and retained earnings. Assets and liabilities are divided between current and noncurrent. This classification system permits the reporting company's working capital and current ratio to be computed for analysis purposes. The statement of cash flows explains how the cash balance changed during the year. All cash transactions are classified as falling within operating activities (daily activities), investing activities (nonoperating activities that affect an asset), or financing activities (nonoperating activities that affect either a liability or a stockholders' equity account).

Talking with a Real Investing Pro (Continued)

Following is a continuation of our interview with Kevin G. Burns.

Question: Warren Buffett is one of the most celebrated investors in history and ranks high on any list of the richest people in the world. When asked how he became so successful at investing, Buffett answered quite simply: "We read hundreds and hundreds of annual reports every year."[9]

Annual reports, as you well know, are the documents that companies produce each year containing their latest financial statements. You are an investor yourself, one who provides expert investment analysis for your clients. What is your opinion of Mr. Buffett's advice?

Kevin Burns: Warren Buffet—who is much richer and smarter than I am—is correct about the importance of annual reports. Once you get past the artwork and the slick photographs and into the "meat" of these reports, the financial statements are a treasure trove of information. Are sales going up or down? Are expenses (such as cost of goods sold) increasing or decreasing as a percentage of sales? Is the company making money? How much cash is the business generating? How are the officers compensated? Do they own stock in the company?

I actually worry when there are too many pages of notes. I prefer companies that don't need so many pages to explain what is happening. I like companies that are able to keep their operations simple. Certainly, a great amount of important information can be gleaned from a careful study of the financial statements in any company's annual report.

One of the great things about our current state of technology is that an investor can find a company's annual report on the Internet in a matter of seconds. You can download information provided by two or three companies and make instant comparisons. That is so helpful for analysis purposes.

 Video Clip

Professor Joe Hoyle talks about the five most important points in Chapter 3.

ASSETS CAN COME FROM OPERATIONS (RETAINED EARNINGS)

View the video online at: http://bit.ly/hoyle3-2

5. END-OF-CHAPTER EXERCISES

QUESTIONS

1. Why do businesses produce financial statements?
2. What are the four financial statements that are typically prepared and distributed by a business or other organization?
3. What is the purpose of the notes that are attached to financial statements?
4. On which financial statement are revenues and expenses reported?
5. How does a gain differ from a revenue?
6. What is a loss?
7. The Bestron Corporation has a loss of $32,000 and an expense of $74,000. How does a loss differ from an expense?
8. In producing an income statement, why are revenues and expenses reported separately from gains and losses?
9. What three pieces of information are typically listed at the top of a financial statement?
10. Define "cost of goods sold."
11. The Amherst Company reported a "gross profit" of $743,800. What is the meaning of this term?
12. The Algernon Corporation incurs a cost of $327,000. The company's accountant is now trying to decide whether to report this balance as an asset or an expense. How do companies determine if a cost is an expense or an asset?
13. From an accounting perspective, define "conservatism."
14. A company has experienced a situation where it is going to incur a loss. Officials believe the chances are 60 percent that the loss will be $13,000. However, there is also a 40 percent chance that the loss might be $98,000. What reporting should be made?
15. Explain why dividends are not reported on the income statement.
16. What are retained earnings?
17. A business has been in operation for nine years and is now reporting a retained earnings balance of $127,000. What makes up that figure?
18. The Olson Company reports a $116,000 figure that is labeled "capital stock" on its balance sheet. What information is being communicated?
19. On which financial statement would assets and liabilities be reported?
20. What differentiates a current asset from a noncurrent asset?
21. What is the accounting equation, and explain why it is true.
22. What are the three categories of cash flows that are reported on the statement of cash flow?
23. On its statement of cash flows, the Jackson Company reported a total cash inflow of $226,000 from operating activities. It also reported a cash outflow of $142,000 from investing activities and a cash inflow of $34,000 from financing activities. How do operating, investing, and financing cash flows differ from one another?

TRUE OR FALSE

1. _____ The income statement reports a company's revenues and expenses for one particular day of the year.

2. _____ An increase in the net assets of a business that results from the sale of inventory is reported as a gain.

3. _____ A business reports a retained earnings balance of $156,000. This figure represents the monetary amounts contributed to the business by its owners.

4. _____ Assets and liabilities can be broken down into the categories of current and noncurrent.

5. _____ Income tax expense is typically reported separately from other expenses.

6. _____ Conservatism helps reporting companies look better to potential investors.

7. _____ The dividends paid balance is reported on the balance sheet.

8. _____ Companies receive money each time their stock is sold on a stock exchange such as the New York Stock Exchange.

9. _____ A balance sheet must always balance.

10. _____ The statement of cash flows is broken up into operating, investing, and financing activities.

11. _____ If a business reports current assets of $300,000 and current liabilities of $200,000, it has working capital of $500,000.

12. _____ Sales revenue less cost of goods sold is referred to as net income.

13. _____ A gain is the amount of net income earned by a company over its life less any dividends it has paid.

14. _____ The purpose of the balance sheet is to report the assets and liabilities of a company on a specific date.

15. _____ The accounting equation identifies how retained earnings are calculated.

16. _____ If a company has a possible loss, conservatism requires that this loss must always be reported.

17. _____ A company buys merchandise for $175,000 and sells it to various customers for $240,000. The gross profit is $65,000.

18. _____ The Bagranoff Company has a current ratio of 3:1. The company collects a $20,000 accounts receivable. The current ratio will rise as a result of this collection.

19. _____ The Clikeman Company has been in business for several years. The company starts the current year with net assets of $300,000 and ends the year with net assets of $430,000. For the current year, the company's net income less its dividends must have been $130,000.

20. _____ The Richmond Company has been in business for five years and now reports contributed capital as $310,000. This figure means that the owners put $310,000 worth of assets (probably cash) into the business five years ago when it was created.

21. _____ A company needs money to build a new warehouse. Near the end of the current year (Year One), the company borrows $900,000 in cash from a bank on a ten-year loan. The company does not start the construction project until the next year (Year Two). On a statement of cash flows for Year One, a cash inflow of $900,000 should be reported as a financing activity.

22. _____ Near the end of the current year, a company spent $27,000 in cash on a project that the accountant believed had future economic benefit. The accountant reported it in that manner. In truth, the project only had past economic benefit. The company went on to report net income of $200,000 for the current year along with total assets of $800,000. The company should have reported net income of $227,000 for the year and total assets of $773,000.

23. _____ Assume the Albemarle Company buys inventory for $9,000. It pays 60 percent immediately and will pay the rest next year. The company then spends $900 in cash on advertising in order to sell 70 percent of the inventory for $14,000. Of that amount, it collects 80 percent immediately and will collect the remainder next year. The company pays a cash dividend this year of $2,000. As a result of just the operating activities, the company will report that its cash increased by $4,900 during the period.

24. _____ A company is being sued because a product it made has apparently injured a few people. The company believes that it will win the lawsuit, but there is uncertainty. There is some chance (a 33 percent chance) that the company might lose $20,000. To arrive at fairly presented financial statements in connection with this uncertainty, this lawsuit should be reported on the income statement of this year as a $6,600 loss.

25. _____ A company has the following account balances: revenues—$120,000, salary payable—$7,000, cost of goods sold—$50,000, dividends paid—$3,000, rent expense—$12,000, gain on sale of land—$4,000, accounts receivable—$13,000, cash—$15,000, and advertising expense—$8,000. Reported net income for the period is $54,000.

26. _____ A company gets $10,000 cash from its owners when it is started at the beginning of Year One. It gets another $15,000 from a bank loan. Revenues for that year were $70,000, expenses were $39,000, and dividends paid to the owners were $3,000. The retained earnings balance at the start of Year Two was $38,000.

27. _____ The Watson Corporation reported net income of $334,000. During the year, a $10,000 expenditure was erroneously recorded by this business as an asset when it should have been reported as an expense. For an error, $10,000 is not viewed as material by this company. Therefore, net income is fairly presented as reported at $334,000.

MULTIPLE CHOICE

1. You are the chief executive officer of Fisher Corporation. You are very concerned with presenting the best financial picture possible to the owners so you can get a big bonus at the end of this year. Unfortunately, Fisher has a lawsuit pending that could result in the company having to pay a large sum of money. Lawyers believe the company will win and pay nothing. However, they believe there is a 20 percent chance of a $100,000 loss and a 10 percent chance of a $300,000 loss. What amount should be reported?

    a. Zero
    b. $50,000
    c. $100,000
    d. $300,000

2. Henderson Inc. reports the following: assets of $500,000, liabilities of $350,000 and capital stock of $100,000. What is the balance reported as retained earnings?

    a. $50,000
    b. $250,000
    c. $450,000
    d. $750,000

3. Giles Corporation borrowed $675,000 from Midwest Bank during the year. Where is this event be reported on Giles's statement of cash flows?

    a. Operating activities
    b. Investing activities
    c. Financing activities
    d. It would not be reported on the statement of cash flows

4. You are considering investing in the stock of Mogul Corporation. On which of the following statements would you find information about what the company holds in inventory at the end of the most recent year?

    a. Income statement
    b. Statement of retained earnings
    c. Balance sheet
    d. Statement of cash flows

5. You are considering investing in the stock of the Maintland Corporation. On which of the following statements would you find information about the cost of the merchandise that the company sold to its customers this past year?

    a. Income statement
    b. Statement of retained earnings
    c. Balance sheet
    d. Statement of cash flows

6. The Drexel Company began operations on January 1, Year One. In Year One, the company reported net income of $23,000 and, in Year Two, reported net income of another $31,000. In the current year of Year Three, the company reported net income of $37,000. Drexel paid no dividends in Year One but paid $10,000 in Year Two and $12,000 in Year Three. On the December 31, Year Three, balance sheet, what is reported as retained earnings?

    a. $22,000
    b. $25,000
    c. $69,000
    d. $91,000

7. The Shelby Corporation has been in business now for six years. At the end of its latest fiscal year, the company reported $560,000 in assets, $320,000 in liabilities, $100,000 in contributed capital, and $140,000 in retained earnings. What is the total of stockholders' equity?

    a. $140,000
    b. $240,000
    c. $420,000
    d. $560,000

8. The Valdese Corporation operates a restaurant and has sales revenue of $300,000, cost of goods sold of $170,000, other expenses of $50,000, and a gain on the sale of a truck of $14,000. Which of the following statements is true?

    a. Gross profit is $80,000, and net income is $80,000.

    b. Gross profit is $80,000, and net income is $94,000.

    c. Gross profit is $130,000, and net income is $94,000.

    d. Gross profit is $144,000, and net income is $80,000.

9. Which of the following is true about the usual reporting of income taxes?

    a. They are reported within cost of goods sold.

    b. They are reported the same as any other expense.

    c. They are netted against sales revenue.

    d. They are reported separately at the bottom of the income statement.

10. A company had a number of cash transactions this year. It paid $22,000 in dividends to its owners, borrowed $100,000 from a bank on a long-term loan, bought a building for $288,000, sold equipment for $23,000, sold inventory for $16,000, and issued capital stock to an investor for $35,000. On a statement of cash flows, what is the net amount to be reported as financing activities?

    a. Cash inflow of $78,000

    b. Cash inflow of $113,000

    c. Cash inflow of $157,000

    d. Cash inflow of $265,000

11. A company had a number of cash transactions this year. It paid $43,000 in dividends to its owners, borrowed $200,000 from a bank on a long-term loan, bought a building for $312,000, sold equipment for $51,000, sold inventory for $25,000, and issued capital stock to an investor for $85,000. On a statement of cash flows, what is the net amount to be reported as investing activities?

    a. Cash outflow of $112,000

    b. Cash outflow of $176,000

    c. Cash outflow of $242,000

    d. Cash outflow of $261,000

12. A company reports total assets of $500,000 ($300,000 current and $200,000 noncurrent). The same company reports total liabilities of $350,000 ($75,000 current and $275,000 noncurrent). What is the amount of working capital?

    a. $150,000

    b. $225,000

    c. $300,000

    d. $500,000

13. A company is producing financial statements. Which statements should be prepared initially?

    a. Income statement and balance sheet

    b. Income statement and statement of retained earnings

    c. Statement of cash flows and statement of retained earnings

    d. Statement of cash flows and balance sheet

VIDEO PROBLEMS

Professor Joe Hoyle discusses the answers to these two problems at the links that are indicated. After formulating your answers, watch each video to see how Professor Hoyle answers these questions.

1. Your roommate is an English major. The roommate's parents own an ice cream shop in a resort community in Florida. They often try to talk with your roommate about their business and use terms such as financial statements, inventory, assets, liabilities, revenue, expenses, contributed capital, and gross profit. The roommate is usually lost in these conversations and feels dumb. One evening on the way to see a movie, your roommate mentions that you are taking a financial accounting course and asks you to explain these terms in some relatively simple fashion. How would you respond?

View the video online at: http://bit.ly/hoyle3-3

2. Your uncle and two friends started a small office supply store three years ago (January 1, Year One). They each invested $20,000 in cash. They then rented a building for $2,000 per month and hired an employee for $3,000 per month. The business buys $9,000 in merchandise per month and sells it for cash of $16,000 in that same month. For convenience, assume that all transactions are for cash. Each owner takes out $4,000 in cash each year as a dividend.

   At the end of Year Three, the owners decide to apply for a loan so they can purchase a building that will allow them to expand operations. The bank has asked for several pieces of information, and your uncle recently sent you an e-mail asking that you help him determine the appropriate amounts to report. What figures should be provided for each of the following?

   a. Gross profit for Year Three

   b. Gross profit percentage for Year Three

   c. Net income for Year Three

   d. Contributed capital as of the end of Year Three

   e. Retained earnings as of the end of Year Three

View the video online at: http://bit.ly/hoyle3-4

PROBLEMS

1. On which financial statement will a decision maker find each of the following account balances?

   a. _____ Sales revenue
   b. _____ Cash
   c. _____ Gain on sale of building
   d. _____ Retained earnings
   e. _____ Salary expense
   f. _____ Salary payable
   g. _____ Capital stock
   h. _____ Dividends paid
   i. _____ Loss on the sale of land
   j. _____ Income tax expense
   k. _____ Net income

2. The following relate to the Farr Corporation for the month of April:

Sales Revenue	$170,000
Gain on the Sale of Land	$20,000
Equipment	$125,000
Tax Expense	$14,000
Inventory	$10,000
Dividends Paid	$7,000
Loss on Lawsuit	$24,000
Cost of Goods Sold	$82,000
Advertising Expense	$15,000

   a. Determine Farr's gross profit for the month of April.
   b. Determine Farr's net income for the month of April.
   c. If retained earnings at the beginning of April is reported as $800,000, what should retained earnings be reported as at the end of April?

3. The Maverick Company has the following account balances at the end of December. Show that Maverick's balance sheet does balance using the accounting equation.

Cash	$8,000
Capital Stock	$120,000
Inventory	$16,000
Note Payable	$45,000
Retained Earnings	$29,000
Building	$158,000
Equipment	$30,000
Accounts Payable	$11,000
Salary Payable	$7,000

4. The Ramond Company has hired you to prepare financial statements for the year ending December 31 of the current year. On your first day of work, your assistant uncovers several items that could be classified as expenses or could be classified as assets. The assistant has asked for your help. Determine whether the following items should be recorded as an expense or an asset within the financial statements currently being prepared.

   a. On December 31, Ramond paid $14,000 to rent office space for the next twelve months.
   b. On October 1, Ramond paid $40,000 for fire insurance that covered the company's property for the last quarter of the year.
   c. On July 1, Ramond purchased $27,000 in supplies, all of which were used by the end of the year.
   d. On December 31, Ramond purchased $5,000 worth of supplies for the coming month.

5. For each of the following, determine the missing balance.

a.

Net Income	$82,900
Cost of Goods Sold	$459,030
Advertising Expense	$56,000
Gain on Sale of Equipment	$5,000
Income Tax Expense	$50,000
Sales Revenue	?

b.

Net Income	$6,500
Retained Earnings, 12/31	$16,200
Dividends	$2,900
Retained Earnings, 1/1	?

c.

Cash	$460,000
Accounts Receivable	$540,200
Current Assets	$1,670,000
Inventory	?

d.

Total Assets	$54,000
Total Liabilities	$32,000
Capital Stock	$15,000
Retained Earnings	?

6. Rescue Records needs rescuing. The downloading of songs over the Internet is killing its business. The owners of Rescue want to know if they made a net income or a net loss during the current year that ended on December 31, Year One. Given the following account balances, prepare an income statement for Rescue similar to the example shown in Figure 3.1.

Advertising Expense	$4,600
Salary Expense	$25,470
Cost of Goods Sold	$109,000
Sales Revenue	$197,000
Income Tax Expense	$3,800
Loss on Sale of Land	$12,090
Rent Expense	$35,000

7. Your lawn care business, A Cut Above, has grown beyond your wildest dreams—to the point where you would like to buy some new equipment and hire some people to help you. Unfortunately, you don't have that kind of money sitting around, so you are applying for a loan. The bank has requested financial statements, including, of course, a balance sheet. The following are the balances you have on December 31, Year One. Prepare a classified balance sheet to submit to the bank.

Cash	$2,400
Prepaid Insurance	$1,600
Note Payable Due Two Years from Now (Loan from Mom)	$5,000
Capital Stock (Money You Invested to Start Business)	$2,000
Accounts Receivable	$500
Supplies Inventory	$300
Equipment	$3,000
Accounts Payable	$200
Retained Earnings, 12/31	$600

8. Maria Sanchez, an accountant by trade, earns extra cash by working in the evenings as a personal trainer at the local gymnasium. Maria is curious about her cash inflows and outflows from this extra work. The following is the information that she gathered for the month of February. Prepare a statement of cash flows for Maria.

Cash Paid for Supplies Inventory	$500
Cash Paid for Advertising	$400
Cash Paid for Equipment	$900
Cash Received from Bank Loan	$1,000
Cash Paid for Insurance	$700
Cash Received from Customers	$2,200
Cash Paid for Taxes	$400
Cash Balance, Beginning of February	$500

9. The Eli Company started business on January 1, Year One. In Year One, the company made a net income of $100,000 and paid cash dividends of $30,000. At the end of Year Two, the company has the following accounts and their appropriate balances:

Repair Expense	$10,000
Cost of Goods Sold	$170,000
Advertising Expense	$10,000
Inventory	$120,000
Dividends Paid in Year Two	$80,000
Accounts Payable	$40,000
Salary Payable	$10,000
Land and Equipment	$300,000
Contributed Capital (Capital Stock)	$120,000
Notes Payable (Due in Year Six)	$210,000
Salary Expense	$40,000
Loss on Sale of Equipment	$10,000
Sales Revenue	$470,000
Income Tax Expense	$30,000
Cash	$50,000
Accounts Receivable	$100,000

Retained earnings at the beginning of Year Two can be computed from the information provided at the beginning of the problem.

     a. Prepare an income statement for the Eli Company for Year Two in the form presented in Figure 3.1.

     b. Prepare a statement of retained earnings for the Eli Company for Year Two in the form presented in Figure 3.4.

     c. Prepare a balance sheet for the Eli Company for the end of Year Two (December 31) in the form presented in Figure 3.6.

RESEARCH ASSIGNMENT

1. Go to http://www.hersheys.com/. At **The Hershey Company** Web site, click on "Corporate Information" at the bottom of the page. Click on "Investors" on the top of the next screen. Then, click on "Financial Reports" on the left side of the screen. You should see a drop-down menu. Click on "Annual & Quarterly Reports." Finally, click on "2010 Annual Report to Stockholders/Form 10-K" to download the form. The Form 10-K is the document that many businesses must file with the U.S. government each year. Because it requires that financial statements be included, some companies like **Hershey** also use it as the annual report for their stockholders.

    Using **The Hershey Company's** Form 10-K, answer the following questions:

    a. On page 54 of the 2010 financial statements for **The Hershey Company**, an income statement is presented. For 2008 and also for 2010, determine the following balances. Has this company's income picture improved from 2008 to 2010?

    - Gross profit
    - Gross profit percentage
    - Provision for income taxes (income tax expense)
    - Net Income

    b. On page 55 of the 2010 financial statements, a balance sheet is presented. Determine the following balances as of December 31, 2009, and also December 31, 2010.

    - Working capital
    - Current ratio
    - Retained earnings

    c. On page 56 of the 2010 financial statements, a statement of cash flows is presented. Determine the amount of cash that **Hershey** generated from its operating activities during 2010.

    d. On page 57 of the 2010 financial statements, a statement of stockholders' equity is presented. The middle column is for retained earnings and serves the same purpose as a statement of retained earnings. How much did **Hershey** pay its stockholders as dividends in 2008, 2009, and 2010?

ENDNOTES

1. Financial statements for many of the businesses that have their capital stock traded publicly on stock exchanges are readily available on corporate Web sites. For example, the statements released by **Marriott International** can be located through the following path. The financial statements issued by most large companies will be found by using similar steps.·

   1. Go to http://www.marriott.com.
   2. Click on "About Marriott" (probably at the bottom of the homepage).
   3. Click on "Investor."
   4. Click on "Financial Information."
   5. Click on "Financial Reports & Proxy."
   6. Click on "Annual Report" (for the year desired).

2. As will be discussed in a later chapter of this textbook, a statement of comprehensive income is also sometimes attached to or presented with an income statement.

3. Financial information reported by large publicly traded companies tends to be highly aggregated. Thus, the expense figure shown by **IBM** is a summation of several somewhat related expenses. Those individual balances would be available within the company for internal decision making.

4. As indicated earlier, many businesses actually report a broader statement of changes in stockholders' equity. At this initial point in the coverage, focusing solely on retained earnings makes the learning process easier.

5. Other events can also impact the reported total of a company's net assets. They will be discussed in other chapters. The two sources described here—capital stock and retained earnings—are shown by all corporations and are normally significantly large amounts.

6. Liquidity refers to the ease with which assets can be converted into cash. Thus, cash is normally reported first followed by investments in stock that are expected to be sold soon, accounts receivable, inventory, and so on.

7. As will be discussed in detail later in this textbook, noncurrent assets such as buildings and equipment are initially recorded at cost. This figure is then systematically reduced as the amount is moved gradually each period into an expense account over the life of the asset. Thus, balance sheet figures for these accounts are reported as "net" to show that only a portion of the original cost still remains recorded as an asset. This shift of the cost from asset to expense is known as depreciation and mirrors the using up of the utility of the property.

8. The cash flows resulting from operating activities are being shown here using the direct method, an approach recommended by the FASB. This format shows the actual amount of cash flows created by individual operating activities such as sales to customers and purchases of inventory. In the business world, an alternative known as the indirect method is more commonly encountered. This indirect method will be demonstrated in detail in Chapter 17.

9. See http://www.minterest.com/warren-buffet-quotes-quotations-on-investing/.

CHAPTER 4

How Does an Organization Accumulate and Organize the Information Necessary to Create Financial Statements?

Video Clip

In this video, Professor Joe Hoyle introduces the essential points covered in Chapter 4.

View the video online at: http://bit.ly/hoyle4-1

1. THE ESSENTIAL ROLE OF TRANSACTION ANALYSIS

LEARNING OBJECTIVES

At the end of this section, students should be able to meet the following objectives:

1. Define "transaction" and provide several common examples.
2. Define "transaction analysis" and explain its importance to the accounting process.
3. Identify the account changes created by the purchase of inventory, the payment of a salary, and the borrowing of money.
4. Understand that corporate accounting systems can be programmed to record expenses such as salary automatically as they accrue.

1.1 The Nature of a Transaction

Question: Information provided by a set of financial statements is essential to any individual analyzing a business or other organization. The availability of a fair representation of a company's financial position, operations, and cash flows is invaluable for a wide array of decision makers. However, the sheer volume of data that a business such as **General Mills, McDonald's,** *or* **PepsiCo** *must gather in order to prepare these statements has to be astronomical. Even a small enterprise—a local convenience store, for* *example—generates a significant quantity of information virtually every day. **How does an accountant begin the process of accumulating all the necessary data so that financial statements can be produced and distributed to decision makers?***

transactions

Events that have a financial impact on an organization; information on the resulting changes must be gathered, sorted, classified, and turned into financial statements by means of an accounting system.

Answer: The accounting process starts by analyzing the effect of transactions—any event that has an immediate financial impact on a company. Large organizations participate in literally millions of transactions each year. The resulting information must be gathered, sorted, classified, and turned into a set of financial statements that cover a mere four or five pages. Over the decades, accountants have had to become very efficient to fulfill this seemingly impossible assignment. Despite the volume of transactions, the goal remains the same: to prepare financial statements that are presented fairly because they contain no material misstatements according to U.S. GAAP or IFRS.

For example, all the occurrences listed in Figure 4.1 are typical transactions that any business might encounter. Each causes some measurable effect on the company's assets, liabilities, revenues, expenses, gains, losses, capital stock, or dividends paid. The accounting process begins with an analysis of each transaction to determine the specific financial changes that took place. Was revenue earned? Did a liability increase? Has an asset been acquired? What changed as a result of this event?

FIGURE 4.1 Transactions Frequently Encountered by a Business

1—Buy inventory on credit for $2,000
2—Pay regular salary of $300 to an employee for work done during the past week; no amount had previously been recorded
3—Borrow $9,000 in cash from bank by signing a loan agreement
4—Make a sale of the inventory bought in (1) to a customer for $5,000 on credit
5—Pay $700 for insurance coverage for the past few months; this amount has previously been recognized in the company's accounting system as it was incurred
6—Buy a new automobile for the company for a price of $40,000 by paying $10,000 in cash and signing a note for the remainder
7—Issue ownership shares to a new stockholder for cash of $19,000
8—Collect cash from customer on earlier sale in (4)
9—Pay cash for the inventory acquired in (1)
10—Pay $4,000 to rent a building for the next four months

In any language, successful communication is only possible if the information to be conveyed is properly understood. Likewise, in accounting, transactions must be analyzed so that their impact is understood. A vast majority of transactions are relatively straightforward so that, with experience, the accountant can ascertain the financial impact almost automatically. Within this process, each individual asset, liability, revenue, expense, and the like is referred to as an account. For example, rent expense and salary expense are both expense accounts. The monetary amount attributed to an account is known as an account balance.

For transactions with greater complexity, the necessary analysis becomes more challenging. However, the importance of this initial step in the production of financial statements cannot be overstressed. The well-known computer aphorism captures the essence quite succinctly: "garbage in, garbage out." There is little hope that financial statements can be fairly presented unless the entering information is based on an appropriate identification of the changes in account balances created by each transaction.

TEST YOURSELF

Question:

Each of the following events took place this week in connection with the operations of the Hammond Corporation. Which does not qualify as a transaction?

a. An employee is hired who will be paid $1,000 per month.

b. Inventory is bought on account for $2,000 with payment to be made next month.

c. An owner invests $3,000 cash in the business to receive capital stock.

d. A truck is bought for $39,000 by signing a note payable.

Answer:

The correct answer is choice a: An employee is hired who will be paid $1,000 per month.

Explanation:

A transaction is any event that has a financial impact on an organization. The purchase of inventory increases that asset and the company liabilities. The investment increases the company's cash. The acquisition of the truck raises the assets as well as the note payable. However, hiring an employee is not, by itself, a transaction because there is no financial impact at that time. There will be an impact only after the person has done work and earned a salary.

1.2   Analyzing the Impact of a Transaction

Question: Transaction 1—A company buys inventory on credit for $2,000. How does transaction analysis work here? **What accounts are affected by the purchase of merchandise?**

Answer: Inventory, which is an asset, increases by $2,000 because of the purchase. The organization has more inventory than it did previously. Because no money was paid for these goods when bought, a liability for the same amount has been created. The term **accounts payable** is often used in financial accounting to represent debts resulting from the acquisition of inventory and supplies.

accounts payable

Short-term liabilities to pay for goods and services that have been acquired on credit.

Transaction 1: Inventory Purchased on Credit

Inventory (asset) increases by $2,000

Accounts Payable (liability) increases by $2,000

Note that the accounting equation described in the previous chapter remains in balance here. Assets have gone up by $2,000 while the liability side of the equation has also increased by the same amount to reflect the source of this increase.

TEST YOURSELF

Question:

A company incurred a transaction where its assets as well as its liabilities increased. Which of the following transactions does not result in this impact?

a. Money is borrowed from a bank.

b. A sale is made to a customer for cash.

c. Supplies are bought and will be paid for next week.

d. A truck is bought by signing a note payable.

Answer:

The correct answer is choice b: A sale is made to a customer for cash.

Explanation:

In all four of these cases, assets increase. Cash goes up in the first two, while supplies and a truck increase assets in the last two, respectively. The company owes the bank in A and the supplier in C. In D, the company has a liability to the party that provided the money for the truck. In B, there is no debt or other obligation to any party.

1.3   The Financial Impact of Paying an Employee

Question: Transaction 2—A company pays a salary of $300 to one of its employees for work performed during the past week. No amount had previously been recorded by the accounting system for this amount. **What accounts are affected by payment of a salary?**

Answer: Cash (an asset) is decreased here by $300. Whenever cash is involved in a transaction, identifying that change is a good place to start the analysis. Increases and decreases in cash are often obvious.

The cash balance declined because salary was paid to an employee. Assets were reduced as a result of the payment. That is a cost to the company. Recognizing an expense as a result is appropriate rather than an asset because the employee's work reflects a past benefit. The person's effort has already been carried out, generating revenues for the company in the previous week rather than in the future. Thus, a salary expense of $300 is reported.

Transaction 2: Salary Paid to Employee

Salary Expense (expense) increases by $300

Cash (asset) decreased by $300

The continued equilibrium of the accounting equation does exist here although it is less apparent. Assets are decreased. At the same time, an expense is recognized. This expense reduces reported net income. On the statement of retained earnings, current net income becomes a component of retained earnings. The reduction in income serves to decrease retained earnings. An expense ultimately reduces reported retained earnings. Because both assets and retained earnings go down by the same amount as a result of this transaction, the accounting equation continues to balance.

1.4   Recording Accrued Expenses

Question: In Transaction 2, the company paid a salary of $300 that it owed to a worker. **Why does a payment to an employee not always reduce a salary payable balance?**

Answer: Costs such as salary, rent, or interest increase gradually over time and are often referred to as **accrued expenses** because the term "accrue" means "to grow." How should the very slow growth of an expense be recognized? An accounting system can be mechanically structured to record such costs in either of two ways. On the financial statements, reported results are the same but the steps in the process differ.

- Some companies simply ignore accrued expenses until paid. At that time, the expense is recognized and cash is reduced. No liability is entered into the accounting system or removed. Because the information provided specifies that nothing has been recorded to date, this approach was apparently used here. When financial statements are produced, any amount that is still owed must be recognized for a fair presentation.

- Other companies choose to program their computer systems so that both the expense and the related liability are recognized automatically as the amount grows. For salary, as an example, this increase could literally be recorded each day or week based on the amount earned by employees. At the time payment is finally conveyed, the expense has already been recorded. Thus, the liability is removed because that debt is being settled. Later, in Transaction 5, this second possible approach to recording accrued expenses is illustrated.

A company can recognize an accrued expense (such as a salary) as it is incurred or wait until payment is made. This decision depends on the preference of company officials. The end result (an expense is reported and cash decreased) is the same, but the recording procedures differ. As mentioned, if no entry has been made prior to the production of financial statements (the first alternative), both the expense and the payable have to be recognized at that time so that all balances are properly included for reporting purposes.

TEST YOURSELF

Question:

The Abraham Company rents a building for $4,000 per month with payment being made on the tenth day following that month. The accounting system is organized so that the expense and liability are recorded throughout the month. In that way, the accounting records are kept up to date. However, when the appropriate payment was made for November on December 10 of the current year, the accountant increased the rent expense and decreased cash. Which of the following statements is true in connection with this recording?

   a. Reported expenses are understated by $4,000.
   b. Net income is understated by $4,000.
   c. Liabilities are understated by $4,000.
   d. All account balances are stated properly.

Answer:

The correct answer is choice b: Net income is understated by $4,000.

Explanation:

Because the expense and the liability have already been recorded as incurred in November, the accountant should have decreased the liability rather than increased the expense when payment was made. The liability balance was not properly reduced; it is overstated. The expense was erroneously increased, so it is overstated. Simply stated, the expense was recorded twice and is overstated by $4,000. That causes reported net income to be understated by that amount.

1.5 Borrowing Money from the Bank

Question: Transaction 3—A company borrows $9,000 from a bank on a long-term note. **What is the financial impact of signing a loan agreement with a bank or other lending institution?**

   Answer: In this transaction, cash is increased by the amount of money received from the lender. The company is obligated to repay this balance and, thus, has incurred a new liability. As with many common transactions, the financial impact is reasonably easy to ascertain.

Transaction 3: Money Borrowed on Loan

Cash (asset) increases by $9,000

Note Payable (liability) increases by $9,000

KEY TAKEAWAY

Most organizations must gather an enormous quantity of information as a prerequisite for the periodic preparation of financial statements. This process begins with an analysis of the impact of each transaction (financial event). After the effect on all account balances is ascertained, the recording of a transaction is relatively straightforward. The changes caused by most transactions—the purchase of inventory or the signing of a note, for example—can often be determined quickly. For accrued expenses, such as salary or rent that grow over time, the accounting system can record the amounts gradually as incurred or only at the point of payment. However, the figures to be reported on the financial statements are not impacted by the specific mechanical steps that are taken.

2. UNDERSTANDING THE EFFECTS CAUSED BY COMMON TRANSACTIONS

2.1 Recording the Sale of Inventory

Question: Transaction 4—Assume that the inventory items bought in Transaction 1 for $2,000 are now sold to a customer for $5,000 on credit. **What account balances are impacted by the sale of merchandise in this manner?**

Answer: Two connected events actually take place in the sale of inventory. First, revenue of $5,000 is generated by the sale. This account is frequently labeled as "Sales" or "Sales revenue."

In this example, because the money will not be collected until a later date, accounts receivable (an asset) is initially increased. The reporting of a receivable balance indicates that this amount of money is due from a customer and should be collected at some subsequent point in time.

Transaction 4, Part 1: Sale Occurs on Credit

Accounts Receivable (asset) increases by $5,000

Sales (revenue) increases by $5,000

perpetual inventory system
Accounting system that maintains an ongoing record of all inventory items both in total and individually; records increases and decreases in inventory accounts as they occur as well as the cost of goods sold to date.

Second, the inventory is removed. Companies have an option in the method by which inventory balances are monitored. Here, a **perpetual inventory system** is utilized. That approach is extremely common due to the prevalence of computer systems in the business world. It maintains an ongoing record of the inventory held and the amount that has been sold to date. All changes in inventory are recorded immediately. However, in a later chapter, an alternative approach—still used by some smaller businesses—known as a **periodic inventory system** will also be demonstrated.

periodic inventory system
Accounting system that does not maintain an ongoing record of all inventory items; instead, ending inventory is determined by a physical count so that a formula (beginning inventory plus purchases less ending inventory) can be used to calculate cost of goods sold.

Because a perpetual system is used here, the reduction in inventory is recorded simultaneously with the sale. Inventory costing $2,000 is taken away by the customer. The company's net assets are reduced by this amount. Therefore, a $2,000 expense is recognized. That inventory no longer provides a future benefit for the company but rather is a past benefit. Cost of goods sold is reported to reflect this decrease in the amount of merchandise on hand.

Transaction 4, Part 2: Inventory Acquired by Customer

Cost of Goods Sold (expense) increases by $2,000

Inventory (asset) decreases by $2,000

As discussed in the previous chapter, the $3,000 difference between the sales revenue of $5,000 and the related cost of goods sold of $2,000 is known as the gross profit (or gross margin or mark up) on the sale.

TEST YOURSELF

Question:

The Hashan Company buys inventory for $7,000 that it eventually sells to a customer for $8,000 in cash. The company's accountant increases cash by $8,000, reduces inventory by $7,000, and records a "gain on sale of inventory" for $1,000. Which of the following statements is true?

a. The company's reported net income is stated properly.

b. The company's reported revenues are too high.

c. The company's reported expenses are too high.

d. All reported figures are properly stated.

Answer:

The correct answer is choice a: The company's reported net income is stated properly.

Explanation:

The company should have recognized revenues of $8,000 and a cost of goods sold of $7,000 so that a gross profit of $1,000 would be reported on the company's income statement. Both the revenue and the expense were omitted and are too low. Instead, a gain of $1,000 was recorded. That gain has the same impact as the $1,000 gross profit, so net income was not affected by the mistake.

2.2   The Dual Effect of Transactions

Question: In each of the events studied so far, two accounts have been affected. **Are two accounts impacted by every possible transaction?**

Answer: In every transaction, a cause-and-effect relationship is always present. For example, the accounts receivable balance increases because of a sale. Cash decreases as a result of paying salary expense. Cost of goods sold increases because inventory is removed. No account balance can possibly change without some identifiable cause. Thus, every transaction must touch a minimum of two accounts. Many transactions actually affect more than two accounts but at least two are impacted by each of these financial events.

2.3   Paying a Previously Recorded Expense

Question: Transaction 5—In this transaction, the reporting company pays $700 for insurance coverage relating to the past few months. The information provided indicates that the cost was previously recorded in the company's accounting system as incurred. Apparently, the computers were programmed to accrue this expense periodically. **What is the financial impact of paying an expense if the balance has already been recognized over time as the liability grew larger?**

Answer: Several pieces of information should be noted in analyzing this example.

■ Cash declined by $700 as a result of the payment.

■ This cost relates to a past benefit. Thus, an expense must be recorded. No future economic benefit is created by the insurance payment. Cash was paid for coverage over the previous months.

■ The company's accounting system has already recorded this amount. Thus, $700 in insurance expense and the related liability were recognized as incurred. This is clearly a different mechanical procedure than that demonstrated in Transaction 2 for the salary payment.

The expense cannot be recorded again or it will be double counted. Instead, cash is reduced along with the liability that was established through the accrual process. The expense was recorded already so no additional change in that balance is needed. Instead, the liability is removed and cash decreased.

Transaction 5: Payment of Amount Owed for Insurance

Insurance Payable (liability) decreases by $700

Cash (asset) decreases by $700

Note that accounting recognition is dependent on the recording that has already taken place. The final results to be reported should be the same (here an expense is recognized and cash decreased), but the steps in the process can vary.

TEST YOURSELF

Question:

Sara Frances is the accountant for National Lumber Company of Cleveland. She receives an invoice for three months' rent for one of the warehouses that the company uses. This bill is for $3,000 per month, or $9,000 in total. The check is written, and Ms. Frances is getting ready to record the payment but is not sure whether the expense has been previously accrued. Which one of the following statements is not true?

a. If the expense has been accrued, a rent payable balance of $9,000 should be present in the accounting records.
b. If the expense has not been accrued, no rent payable balance should currently be present in the accounting records.
c. If the expense has been accrued, the net income figure should already be properly stated before the payment is recorded.
d. If the expense has not been accrued, a liability will need to be established when the payment is recorded.

Answer:

The correct answer is choice d: If the expense has not been accrued, a liability will need to be established when the payment is recorded.

Explanation:

If the accounting system recognized the rent as it accrued, the expense balance and the related liability have already been recorded. The expense recognition means that net income can be determined appropriately based on the reported balances. If no accrual has been recorded to date, there is neither an expense nor a liability. At the time of payment, cash is decreased and the expense is recorded. Because the liability was never entered into the records, no change is made in that balance.

2.4 Acquisition of an Asset

*Question: Transaction 6—According to the original information, a truck is acquired for $40,000, but only $10,000 in cash is paid by the company. The other $30,000 is covered by signing a note payable. This transaction seems a bit more complicated because more than two accounts are involved. **What is the financial impact of buying an asset when only a portion of the cost is paid on that date?***

Answer: In this transaction, for the first time, three accounts are impacted. A truck is bought for $40,000 so the balance recorded for this asset is increased by that cost. Cash decreases $10,000 while the notes payable balance rises by $30,000. These events each happened. To achieve a fair presentation, the accounting process seeks to reflect the actual occurrences that took place. As long as the analysis is performed properly, recording a transaction is no more complicated when more than two accounts are affected.

Transaction 6: Acquisition of Truck for Cash and a Note

Truck (asset) increases by $40,000

Cash (asset) decreases by $10,000

Notes Payable (liability) increases by $30,000

2.5 Recording a Capital Contribution by an Owner

*Question: Transaction 7—Assume that several individuals approach the company and offer to contribute $19,000 in cash to the business in exchange for capital stock so that they can join the ownership. The offer is accepted. **What accounts are impacted by the issuance of capital stock to the owners of a business?***

Answer: When cash is contributed to a company for a portion of the ownership, cash obviously goes up by the amount received. This money was not generated by revenues or by liabilities but rather represents assets given freely so that new ownership shares could be obtained. This inflow is reflected in financial accounting as increases in both the cash and capital stock accounts. Outside decision makers can see that this amount of the company's net assets came from investments made by owners.

Transaction 7: Cash Contributed in Exchange for Capital Stock

Cash (asset) increases by $19,000

Capital Stock (stockholders' equity) increases by $19,000

TEST YOURSELF

Question:

The Hamilton Company issues capital stock to new owners in exchange for a cash contribution of $34,000. The company's accountant thought the money came from a sale and recorded an increase in cash and an increase in revenue. Which of the following statements is not true as a result of this recording?

a. The company's assets are overstated on the balance sheet.
b. The company's net income is overstated on the income statement.
c. The company's capital stock account is understated on the balance sheet.
d. The company's expenses are correctly stated on the income statement.

Answer:

The correct answer is choice a: The company's assets are overstated on the balance sheet.

Explanation:

The company should have increased cash, and it did, so that balance (as well as the other assets) is properly stated. The revenue balance was overstated, so that reported net income is also overstated. The capital stock account should have been increased but was not, so it is understated. Expenses were not affected by either the transaction or the recording, so that total is correct.

2.6 The Collection of an Account Receivable

Question: Transaction 8—A sale of merchandise was made previously in Transaction 4 for $5,000. No cash was received at that time, but the entire amount is collected now. **What accounts are affected by the receipt of money from an earlier sale?**

Answer: The revenue from this transaction was properly recorded in Transaction 4 when the sale originally took place and the account receivable balance was established. Revenue should not be recorded again or it will be double counted, causing reported net income to be overstated. In simple terms, revenue is recorded when earned, and that has already taken place. Instead, for recording purposes, the accountant indicates that this increase in cash is caused by the decrease in the accounts receivable balance established in Transaction 4.

Transaction 8: Collection of Account Receivable

Cash (asset) increases by $5,000

Accounts Receivable (asset) decreases by $5,000

2.7 Payment Made on an Earlier Purchase

Question: Transaction 9—Inventory was bought in Transaction 1 for $2,000 and later sold in Transaction 4. Now, however, the company is ready to make payment of the amount owed for this merchandise. **When cash is delivered to settle a previous purchase of inventory, what is the financial effect of the transaction?**

Answer: As a result of the payment, cash is decreased by $2,000. The inventory was recorded previously when acquired. Therefore, this subsequent transaction does not replicate that effect. Instead, the liability established in number 1 is now removed from the books. The company is not buying the inventory again but simply paying off the debt established for these goods when they were purchased.

Transaction 9: Payment of a Liability for a Purchase

Accounts Payable (liability) decreases by $2,000

Cash (asset) decreases by $2,000

2.8 Payment of Rent in Advance

Question: Transaction 10—The company wants to rent a building to use for the next four months and pays the property's owner $4,000 to cover this cost. **When payment is made for rent (or a similar cost) with a future economic benefit, what recording is appropriate in financial accounting?**

Answer: In acquiring the use of this property, the company's cash decreases by $4,000. The money was paid to utilize the building for four months in the future. The anticipated economic benefit is an asset, and that information should be reported to decision makers by establishing a prepaid rent balance. Money has been paid to use the property at a designated time in the future to help generate revenues.

Transaction 10: Payment of Rent in Advance

Prepaid Rent (asset) increases $4,000

Cash (asset) decreases by $4,000

3.   DOUBLE-ENTRY BOOKKEEPING

3.1   Double-Entry Bookkeeping

Question: Transaction analysis determines the changes that occur in accounts whenever various events take place. Financial statements eventually provide a formal structure to communicate the resulting balances to an array of interested parties.

- *Revenues, expenses, gains, and losses are presented on an income statement where they are combined to arrive at reported net income for the period.*
- *Total income earned and dividends distributed by the company over its entire life are netted to compute the retained earnings balance to be reported.*
- *Assets, liabilities, capital stock, and retained earnings are all displayed on a balance sheet.*
- *Changes in cash are separated into operating activities, investing activities, and financing activities and disclosed on a statement of cash flows.*
- *Notes offer pages of additional explanatory information.*

The amount of financial data that is readily available to any decision maker is impressive.

*Accountants for a business of any significant size face a daunting challenge in creating financial statements. They must gather, measure, and report the impact of the many varied events that occur virtually every day. As an example, for 2010, **Xerox Corporation** disclosed revenues of over $21.6 billion and operating expenses and other costs of $20.8 billion. At the end of 2010, the **Kellogg Company** reported holding $1.1 billion in inventory—which is a lot of cereal—and indicated that its operating activities that year generated a net cash inflow of approximately $1 billion. **How can any organization possibly amass and maintain such an enormous volume of data so that financial statements can be produced with no material misstatements?***

Answer: Over five hundred years ago, Venetian merchants in Italy developed a system that continues to serve in the twenty-first century as the basis for accumulating financial data throughout much of the world. Today, when every aspect of modern society seems to be in a constant state of flux, a process that has remained in use for over five centuries is almost impossible to comprehend. However, the **double-entry bookkeeping** procedures that were first documented in 1494 by Fra Luca Bartolomeo de Pacioli (a friend of Leonardo da Vinci) remain virtually unchanged by time. Organizations, both small and large, use the fundamentals of double-entry bookkeeping to gather the monetary information needed to produce financial statements that are fairly presented according to the rules of U.S. GAAP or IFRS.

double-entry bookkeeping

A mechanical process created over five hundred years ago and documented by Fra Luca Bartolomeo de Pacioli that facilitates the gathering and reporting of financial information.

3.2   Analyze, Record, Adjust, and Report

*Question: This assertion sounds like science fiction. It hardly seems believable that **Xerox** keeps up with over $21.6 billion in revenue (approximately $59 million per day) using the same methods that Venetian merchants applied to their transactions during the Renaissance. **How can a five-hundred-year-old bookkeeping system possibly be usable in today's modern world?***

Answer: State-of-the-art computers and other electronic devices are designed to refine and accelerate the financial accounting process, but the same basic organizing procedures have been utilized now for hundreds of years. In simplest terms, accounting systems are all created to follow four sequential steps:

- Analyze
- Record
- Adjust
- Report

The first two of these steps are studied in this chapter. As explained previously, financial accounting starts by analyzing each transaction—every event that has a monetary impact on the organization—to ascertain the changes created in accounts such as rent expense, cash, inventory, and dividends paid. Fortunately, a vast majority of any company's transactions are repetitive so that many of the effects can be easily anticipated. A sale on credit always increases both accounts receivable and revenue. Regardless of the time or place, a cash purchase of a piece of equipment increases the balance reported for equipment while decreasing cash. Computer systems can be programmed to record the impact of these events automatically allowing the accountant to focus on analyzing more complex transactions.

3.3 Debits, Credits, and T-Accounts

Question: The second step in the financial accounting process is "record." At the beginning of this chapter, a number of transactions were presented and their impact on individual accounts determined. Following this analysis, some method must be devised to capture the information in an orderly fashion. Officials could just list the effect of each transaction on a sheet of paper:
"Increase inventory $2,000 and increase accounts payable $2,000."
"Increase salary expense $300 and decrease cash $300."
"Increase cash $9,000 and increase note payable $9,000."
However, this process is slow and poorly organized. A more efficient process is required for companies like Xerox and Kellogg. **After all monetary changes are identified, how are these effects accumulated?**

Answer: An essential step in understanding double-entry bookkeeping is to realize that financial information is accumulated by **accounts**. As mentioned previously, every balance to be reported in a set of financial statements is maintained in a separate account. Thus, for assets, an individual account is established to monitor cash, accounts receivable, inventory, and so on. To keep track of expenses, a number of additional accounts are needed, such as cost of goods sold, rent expense, salary expense, and repair expense. The same is true for revenues, liabilities, and other categories. A small organization might utilize only a few dozen accounts in its entire record-keeping system. A large business probably has thousands.

Based on the original Venetian model, the balance for each account is monitored in a form known as a **T-account** as displayed in Figure 4.2. This structure provides room for recording on both the left side (known as the **debit** side) and the right side (the **credit** side).

FIGURE 4.2 Examples of Common T-Accounts

One side of every T-account records increases; the other side records decreases. For over five hundred years, the following rules have applied.

In some accounts, debits indicate an increase and credits indicate a decrease. They are grouped together because they all refer to costs.

Increase Shown with a Debit:

- Expenses and losses
- Assets
- Dividends paid[1]

---

accounts

Detailed records of the transactions and current balances of individual assets, liabilities, stockholders' equity, revenues and expenses.

T-account

Maintains the monetary balance for each of the accounts reported by an organization with a left (debit) side and a right (credit) side used to show increases and decreases.

debit

Left side of a T-account; it indicates increases in assets, expenses, and dividends paid as well as decreases in liabilities, capital stock, and revenue and gains.

credit

Right side of a T-account; it indicates increases in liabilities, capital stock, retained earnings, and revenue and gains as well as decreases in assets, expenses, and dividends paid.

In other accounts, credits indicate an increase and debits indicate a decrease. They are grouped together because they all reflect sources of funding.

Increase Shown with a Credit:

- Liabilities
- Capital stock
- Revenues and gains
- Retained earnings[2]

The debit and credit rules for these seven general types of accounts provide a short-hand method for recording the financial impact that a transaction has on any account. They were constructed in this manner so that the following would be true:

Basic Rule for Double-Entry Bookkeeping

Debits must always equal credits for every transaction.

At first view, the debit and credit rules might seem completely arbitrary. However, they are structured to mirror the cause-and-effect relationship found in every transaction. This is the basis of what the Venetian merchants came to understand so long ago: every effect must have a cause.

- Assume an asset (such as cash) increases. As shown here, that change is recorded on the debit side of the T-account for that asset. What could cause an asset to become larger? A reason must exist. A liability—possibly a bank loan—could have been incurred (recorded as a credit); capital stock could have been issued to an owner (a credit); revenue could have been earned from a sale (a credit). The list of possible reasons is relatively short. In each case, the debit (increase) to the asset is caused by an equal and offsetting credit.

- Assume an asset (such as cash) decreases. This change is recorded on the credit side of the asset's T-account. What might cause this reduction? An expense could have been paid (recorded as a debit); a dividend could have been distributed to shareholders (a debit); a liability could have been extinguished (a debit); another asset could have been acquired (a debit). Once again, the cause-and-effect relationship is reflected; the debits equal the credits. Each effect is set equal and opposite to its cause.

There are only seven types of accounts. Therefore, a mastery of debit and credit rules can be achieved with a moderate amount of practice. Because of the fundamental role that debits and credits play within every accounting system, this knowledge is well worth the effort required to obtain it.

TEST YOURSELF

Question:

A company incurs a transaction that is reflected in its accounting system through a debit to salary expense and a credit to salary payable for salary for one month. Which one of the following is the best description of the transaction that took place?

a. Employee salaries for the past month were paid.

b. Employee salaries for the upcoming month were paid.

c. Employee salaries for the past month are recognized but not paid.

d. Employee salaries for the past month have been accrued and are now paid.

Answer:

The correct answer is choice c: Employee salaries for the past month are recognized but not paid.

Explanation:

A debit to an expense is an increase, while a credit to a liability is also an increase. The expense increased, indicating that salary for the past month has been incurred. The payable also increased, which means that the amount owed to the employees has risen. Recognition is made here that an expense has been incurred but not yet paid.

KEY TAKEAWAY

Most companies participate in numerous transactions each day that must be examined and organized so that financial statements can eventually be prepared. This process requires four steps: analyze, record, adjust, and report. Over five hundred years ago, double-entry bookkeeping was created as a mechanical process to facilitate this gathering and reporting of financial information. A T-account is maintained for each account (such as cash, accounts payable, and rent expense) to be reported by a company. The left side of the T-account is the debit side, and the right side is the credit. Expenses and losses, assets, and dividends paid increase with debits. Liabilities, revenues and gains, capital stock, and retained earnings increase with credits. Debits always equal credits because every transaction must have both an effect and a cause for that effect.

4. RECORDING TRANSACTIONS USING JOURNAL ENTRIES

LEARNING OBJECTIVES

At the end of this section, students should be able to meet the following objectives:

1. Describe the purpose and structure of a journal entry.
2. Identify the purpose of a journal.
3. Define trial balance and indicate the source of its monetary balances.
4. Prepare journal entries to record the effect of acquiring inventory, paying salary, borrowing money, and selling merchandise.
5. Define accrual accounting and list its two components.
6. Explain the purpose of the revenue realization principle.
7. Explain the purpose of the matching principle.

4.1 The Purpose of a Journal Entry

Question: In an accounting system, the impact of each transaction is analyzed and must then be recorded. Debits and credits are used for this purpose. **How does the actual recording of a transaction take place?**

journal entry

The physical form used in double-entry bookkeeping to record the financial changes caused by a transaction; each must have at least one debit and one credit and the total debit(s) must always equal the total credit(s).

journal

The physical location of all journal entries; it is the financial diary of an organization capturing the impact of transactions as they took place; it is also referred to as the general journal.

general journal

The physical location of all journal entries; it is the financial diary of an organization capturing the impact of transactions as they took place; it is also referred to as the journal.

Answer: The effects produced on various accounts by a transaction should be entered into an accounting system as quickly as possible so that information is not lost and mistakes have less time to occur. After each event is analyzed, the financial changes caused by a transaction are initially recorded as a **journal entry**.[3] A list of a company's journal entries is maintained in a **journal** (also referred to as a **general journal**), which is one of the most important components within any accounting system. The journal is a financial diary for a company. It provides a history of the impact of all financial events, recorded as they took place.

A journal entry is no more than an indication of the accounts and balances that were changed by a single transaction.

4.2 Practicing with Debits and Credits

Question: Debit and credit rules are best learned through practice. **In order to master the use of debits and credits for recording purposes, where should the needed work begin?**

Answer: When faced with debits and credits, everyone has to practice at first. That is normal and to be expected. These rules can be learned quickly but only by investing a bit of effort. Earlier in this chapter, a number of common transactions were presented (Figure 4.1) and then analyzed to demonstrate their impact on account balances. Assume now that these same transactions are to be recorded as journal entries.

To provide more information for this illustration, the reporting company will be a small farm supply store known as the Lawndale Company that is located in a rural area. For convenience, assume that the business incurs each of these transactions during the final two days of Year Four, just prior to preparing financial statements.

Assume further that this company already has the various T-account balances as of December 29, Year Four, presented in Figure 4.3 before recording the impact of this last group of transactions. A company keeps its T-accounts together in a ledger (or general ledger). This listing of the account balances found in the ledger is known as a **trial balance**. Note that the total of all the debit and credit balances do agree ($360,700) and that every account shows a positive balance. In other words, the current figure being reported is either a debit or credit based on what reflects an increase in that particular type of account. Few T-accounts contain negative balances.

> **trial balance**
>
> List of account balances at a specific point in time for each of the T-accounts maintained in a company's ledger; eventually, financial statements are created using these balances.

FIGURE 4.3 Balances From T-accounts in Ledger

Lawndale Company Trial Balance (prior to recording new transactions) December 29, Year Four		
Account	Debit	Credit
Cash	$20,000	
Accounts Receivable	50,000	
Iventory	65,000	
Accounts Payable		$18,000
Insurance Payable		700
Notes Payable (long-term)		40,000
Capital Stock		30,000
Retained Earnings (beginning of year)		32,000
Sales of Merchandise		250,000
Cost of Goods Sold	150,000	
Rent Expense	12,000	
Salary Expense	60,000	
Utilities Expense	10,000	
Insurance Expense	3,700	
Totals	$370,700	$370,700

4.3 Journal Entry for Acquisition of Inventory on Credit

*Question: After the balances in Figure 4.3 were determined, several additional transactions took place during the last two days of Year Four. The first transaction analyzed at the start of this chapter (Figure 4.1) was the purchase of inventory on credit for $2,000. This acquisition increases the recorded amount of inventory while also raising one of the company's liabilities (accounts payable). **How is the acquisition of inventory on credit recorded in the form of a journal entry?***

Answer: Following the transactional analysis, a journal entry is prepared to record the impact that the event has on the Lawndale Company. Inventory is an asset. An asset always uses a debit to note an increase. Accounts payable is a liability so that a credit indicates that an increase has occurred. Thus, the journal entry shown in Figure 4.4 is appropriate.[4]

FIGURE 4.4 Journal Entry 1: Inventory Acquired on Credit

Inventory	2,000		(increase an asset—debit)
Accounts Payable		2,000	(increase a liability—credit)

Notice that the word "inventory" is physically on the left of the journal entry and the words "accounts payable" are indented to the right. This positioning clearly shows which account is debited and which is credited. In the same way, the $2,000 numerical amount added to the inventory total appears on the left (debit) side whereas the $2,000 change in accounts payable is clearly on the right (credit) side.

Preparing journal entries is a mechanical process but one that is fundamental to the gathering of information for financial reporting purposes. Any person familiar with accounting could easily "read" the previous entry: Based on the debit and credit, both inventory and accounts payable have gone up so a purchase of merchandise for $2,000 on credit is indicated. Interestingly, with translation of the words, a Venetian merchant from the later part of the fifteenth century would be capable of understanding the information captured by this journal entry even if prepared by a modern company as large as **Xerox** or **Kellogg**.

4.4 Recording Payment of an Expense

Question: In Transaction 2, the Lawndale Company pays its employees salary of $300 for work performed during the past week. **If no entry has been recorded previously for this amount, what journal entry is appropriate when a salary payment is made?**

Answer: Because the information provided indicates that no entry has yet been made, neither the $300 salary expense nor the related salary payable already exists in the accounting records. Apparently, the $60,000 salary expense appearing in the trial balance reflects earlier payments made during the period to company employees.

Payment is made here for past work so this cost represents an expense rather than an asset. Thus, the balance recorded as salary expense goes up while cash decreases. As shown in Figure 4.5, increasing an expense is always shown by means of a debit. Decreasing an asset is reflected through a credit.

FIGURE 4.5 Journal Entry 2: Salary Paid to Employees

| Salary Expense | 300 | | (increase an expense—debit) |
| Cash | | 300 | (decrease an asset—credit) |

In practice, the date of each transaction could also be included here. For illustration purposes, this extra information is not necessary.

4.5 Journal Entry When Money Is Borrowed

Question: According to Transaction 3, $9,000 is borrowed from a bank when officials sign a note payable that will have to be repaid in several years. **What journal entry is prepared by a company to reflect the inflow of cash received from a loan?**

Answer: As always, recording begins with an analysis of the transaction. Cash—an asset—increases $9,000, which is shown as a debit. The notes payable balance also goes up by the same amount. As a liability, this increase is recorded through a credit. By using debits and credits in this way, a record of the financial effects of this transaction are entered into the accounting records.

FIGURE 4.6 Journal Entry 3: Money Borrowed from Bank

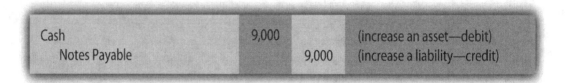

| Cash | 9,000 | | (increase an asset—debit) |
| Notes Payable | | 9,000 | (increase a liability—credit) |

TEST YOURSELF

Question:

An accountant looks at a journal entry found in a company's journal that shows a debit to notes payable and a credit to cash. Which of the following events is being recorded?

  a. Money has been borrowed from a bank.
  b. Money has been contributed by an owner.
  c. Money has been received from a sale.
  d. Money has been paid on a liability.

Answer:

The correct answer is choice d: Money has been paid on a liability.

Explanation:

Cash is an asset that decreases by means of a credit. Notes payable is a liability that decreases with a debit. Both cash and notes payable decreased, indicating that a payment was made.

4.6 Recording Sale of Inventory on Credit

Question: In Transaction 1, inventory was bought for $2,000. That journal entry is recorded earlier. Now, in Transaction 4, these goods are sold for $5,000 to a customer with payment to be made at a later date. How is the sale of merchandise on credit recorded in journal entry form?

Answer: As discussed previously, two events happen when inventory is sold. First, the sale is made and, second, the customer takes possession of the merchandise from the company. Assuming again that a perpetual inventory system is in use, both the sale and the related expense are recorded immediately.

In the initial part of the transaction, the accounts receivable balance goes up $5,000 because the money from the customer will not be collected until a future point in time. The increase in this asset is shown by means of a debit. The new receivable resulted from a sale. Thus, revenue is also recorded (through a credit) to indicate the cause of that effect.

FIGURE 4.7   Journal Entry 4A: Sale of Inventory Made on Account

| Accounts Receivable | 5,000 | | (increase an asset—debit) |
| Sales of Merchandise | | 5,000 | (increase revenue—credit) |

At the same time, inventory costing $2,000 is surrendered by the company. The reduction of any asset is recorded by means of a credit. The expense account that represents the outflow of inventory has been identified previously as "cost of goods sold." Like any expense, it is entered into the accounting system through a debit.

FIGURE 4.8   Journal Entry 4B: Merchandise Acquired by Customers

| Cost of Goods Sold | 2,000 | | (increase an expense—debit) |
| Inventory | | 2,000 | (decrease an asset—credit) |

4.7 The Role of Accrual Accounting

Question: In the previous transaction, the Lawndale Company made a sale but no cash was to be collected until some later date. Why is revenue reported at the time of sale rather than when cash is

eventually collected? Accounting is conservative. Delaying recognition of sales revenue (and the resulting increase in net income) until the $5,000 is physically received seems logical. Why is the revenue recognized here before the cash is collected?

Answer: This question reflects a common misconception about the information conveyed through financial statements. As shown in Journal Entry 4A, the reporting of revenue is not tied directly to the receipt of cash. One of the most important components of U.S. GAAP is **accrual accounting**. It serves as the basis for timing the recognition of revenues and expenses. Because of the direct impact on net income, such issues are among the most complicated and controversial in accounting. The accountant must constantly monitor events as they occur to determine the appropriate point in time for reporting each revenue and expense. Accrual accounting provides standard guidance for that process.

Accrual accounting is really made up of two distinct elements. The **revenue realization principle** provides authoritative direction as to the proper timing for the recognition of revenue. The **matching principle** establishes similar guidelines for expenses. These two principles have been utilized for decades in the application of U.S. GAAP. Their importance within financial accounting can hardly be overstated.

Revenue realization principle. Revenue is properly recognized at the point that (1) the earning process needed to generate the revenue is substantially complete and (2) the amount eventually to be received can be reasonably estimated. As the study of financial accounting progresses into more complex situations, both of these criteria will require careful analysis and understanding.

Matching principle. Expenses are recognized in the same time period as the revenue they help to create. Thus, if specific revenue is to be recognized in the year 2019, all associated costs should be reported as expenses in that same year. Expenses are matched with revenues. However, when a cost cannot be tied directly to identifiable revenue, matching is not possible. In those cases, the expense is recognized in the most logical time period, in some systematic fashion, or as incurred—depending on the situation.

Revenue is reported in Journal Entry 4A. Assuming that the Lawndale Company has substantially completed the work required of this sale and $5,000 is a reasonable estimate of the amount that will be collected, recognition at the time of sale is appropriate. Because the revenue is reported at that moment, the related expense (cost of goods sold) should also be recorded as can be seen in Journal Entry 4B.

Accrual accounting provides an excellent example of how U.S. GAAP guides the reporting process in order to produce fairly presented financial statements that can be understood by all possible decision makers.

TEST YOURSELF

Question:

Which of the following statements is not true?

a. Accrual accounting is a component of U.S. GAAP.

b. According to the matching principle, revenues should be recognized in the same period as the expenses that help to generate those revenues.

c. The revenue realization principle and the matching principle are components of accrual accounting.

d. Revenues should not be recognized until the amount to be realized can be reasonably estimated.

Answer:

The correct answer is choice b: According to the matching principle, revenues should be recognized in the same period as the expenses that help to generate those revenues.

Explanation:

Accrual accounting is the U.S. GAAP that structures timing for reporting revenues and expenses. It is made up of the revenue realization principle and the matching principle. Revenues are reported when the earning process is substantially complete and the amount to be received can be reasonably estimated. Expenses are recognized in the same period as revenues they help generate. The answer is b; it is stated backward. Expenses are matched with revenues; revenues are not matched with expenses.

5. CONNECTING THE JOURNAL TO THE LEDGER

LEARNING OBJECTIVES

At the end of this section, students should be able to meet the following objectives:

1. Prepare journal entries for basic transactions such as the payment of insurance, the acquisition of a long-lived asset, the contribution of capital by owners, the distribution of a dividend, and the like.
2. Explain the recording of a gain or loss.
3. Describe the recording of an unearned revenue.
4. Understand the purpose within an accounting system of both the journal and the ledger.
5. Discuss the posting of journal entries to T-accounts in the ledger and describe the purpose of that process.

5.1   Payment of a Previously Recognized Expense

*Question: In Transaction 5, the Lawndale Company pays $700 for insurance coverage received over the past few months. Here, though, the amount has already been recognized. Both the insurance expense and an insurance payable were recorded as incurred. That information was provided in Figure 4.1, and both amounts can be seen on the trial balance in Figure 4.3. Apparently, Lawndale's accounting system was programmed to recognize this particular expense as it grew over time. **When an expense has already been recorded, what journal entry is appropriate at the time payment is made?***

Answer: Because of the previous recognition, the expense should not now be recorded a second time. Instead, this payment eliminates the liability that was established by the accounting system. Cash—an asset—is decreased, which is shown in accounting by means of a credit. At the same time, the previously recorded payable is removed. Any reduction of a liability is communicated by a debit. To reiterate, no expense is included in this entry because that amount has already been recognized as incurred.

FIGURE 4.9 Journal Entry 5: Payment of Liability for Insurance Coverage

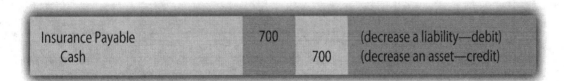

| Insurance Payable | 700 | | (decrease a liability—debit) |
| Cash | | 700 | (decrease an asset—credit) |

Note that Journal Entries 2 and 5 differ although the events are similar. As discussed previously, specific recording techniques are influenced by the manner in which the accounting system has handled earlier events. In Journal Entry 2, neither the expense nor the payable had yet been recorded. Thus, the expense was recognized at the time of payment. Conversely, in Journal Entry 5, both the expense and payable had already been entered into the records as the amount gradually grew over time. Hence, when paid, the liability is settled, but no further expense is recognized. The proper amount is already present in the insurance expense T-account.

5.2   Acquisition of an Asset

Question: In Transaction 6, a new truck is acquired by the Lawndale Company for $40,000. Cash of $10,000 is paid at the time of purchase but a note payable—due in several years—is signed for the remaining $30,000. This transaction impacts three accounts rather than just two. **How is a journal entry constructed when more than two accounts are affected?**

Answer: As has been discussed, every transaction changes at least two accounts because of the cause-and-effect relationship underlying all financial events. However, beyond that limit, any number of accounts can be impacted. Complex transactions often touch numerous balances. Here, the truck account (an asset) is increased and must be debited. Part of the acquisition was funded by paying cash (an asset) with that decrease recorded as a credit. The remainder of the cost was covered by signing a note payable (a liability). Any increase in a liability is recorded by means of a credit. Note that the debits do equal the credits even when more than two accounts are affected by a transaction.

FIGURE 4.10   Journal Entry 6: Truck Acquired for Cash and by Signing a Note

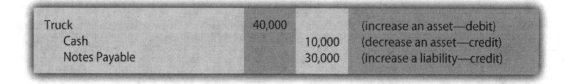

Truck	40,000		(increase an asset—debit)
Cash		10,000	(decrease an asset—credit)
Notes Payable		30,000	(increase a liability—credit)

5.3   Issuance of Capital Stock

Question: In Transaction 7, the Lawndale Company needs additional financing so officials go to current or potential shareholders and convince them to contribute cash of $19,000 in exchange for new shares of the company's capital stock. These individuals invest their money in order to join the ownership or increase the number of shares they already hold. **What journal entry does a business record when capital stock is issued?**

Answer: The asset cash is increased in this transaction, a change that is always shown as a debit. Capital stock also goes up because new shares are issued to company owners. As indicated in the debit and credit rules, the capital stock account increases by means of a credit.

FIGURE 4.11   Journal Entry 7: Capital Stock Issued for Cash

| Cash | 19,000 | | (increase an asset—debit) |
| Capital Stock | | 19,000 | (increase a capital stock—credit) |

TEST YOURSELF

Question:

A corporation issues a balance sheet on December 31, Year Ten. Within stockholders' equity, a balance of $89,000 is reported in the capital stock account. What does this figure represent?

a. The current market value of the company's own stock.

b. The current market value of stocks the company holds in other companies.

c. The amount of assets contributed to the business by its owners since the company was created.

d. The amount of assets contributed to the business by its owners in the current year.

Answer:

The correct answer is choice c: The amount of assets contributed to the business by its owners since the company was created.

Explanation:

The stockholders' equity balances indicate the source of the company's net assets (the amount by which assets exceed liabilities). Normally, the net assets come either from the owners or from the operations of the business (total net income minus all dividends). The capital stock account (sometimes shown as contributed capital) is the amount of net assets put into the company by the owners since the company was started.

5.4   Collection Made on Account Receivable

Question: In Journal Entry 4A, a sale was made on credit. An account receivable was established at that time for $5,000. Assume that the customer now pays this amount to the Lawndale Company. **How does the collection of an amount from an earlier sales transaction affect the account balances?**

Answer: When a customer makes payment on a previous sale, the cash balance increases while accounts receivable decrease. Both are assets; one balance goes up (by a debit) while the other is reduced (by a credit).

FIGURE 4.12   Journal Entry 8: Money Collected on Account

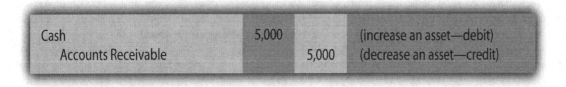

| Cash | 5,000 | | (increase an asset—debit) |
| Accounts Receivable | | 5,000 | (decrease an asset—credit) |

Note that cash is collected here, but no additional revenue is recorded. Based on the requirements of accrual accounting, revenue of $5,000 was recognized previously in Journal Entry 4A. Apparently, the revenue realization principle was met at that time, the earning process was substantially complete, and a reasonable estimation could be made of the amount to be received. Recognizing the revenue again at the current date would incorrectly inflate reported net income. Instead, the previously created receivable balance is removed.

5.5   Paying for a Previous Purchase

Question: In Journal Entry 1, inventory was purchased on credit for $2,000. Assume, now, in Transaction 9, that Lawndale makes payment of the entire amount that is due. **How is a cash outflow to pay for inventory previously acquired shown in a company's journal?**

Answer: Inventory was bought at an earlier time, and payment is now being made. The inventory was properly recorded when acquired and should not be entered again. The merchandise was only obtained that one time. Here, cash is reduced (a credit). The liability set up in Journal Entry 1 (accounts payable) is removed by means of a debit.

FIGURE 4.13 Journal Entry 9: Money Paid for Previous Purchase

| Accounts Payable | 2,000 | | (decrease a liability—debit) |
| Cash | | 2,000 | (decrease an asset—credit) |

5.6 Prepayment of an Expense

Question: Company officials like the building that is being used for operations and decide to rent it for four additional months at a rate of $1,000 per month. An immediate payment of $4,000 is made. This cost provides a future economic benefit rather than a past value. Recognition of an expense is not yet appropriate. **What recording is appropriate when rent or other costs such as insurance or advertising are paid in advance?**

Answer: Cash is decreased by the payment made here to rent this building. As an asset, a reduction in cash is reported by means of a credit. However, this rent provides a future value for Lawndale Company. The cost is not for past usage of the building but rather for the upcoming months. Therefore, the amount paid creates an asset. The probable economic benefit is the ability to make use of this facility over the next four months to generate new revenue. When the $4,000 is paid, an asset—normally called prepaid rent—is recorded through a debit.

FIGURE 4.14 Journal Entry 10: Money Paid for Future Rent

| Prepaid Rent | 4,000 | | (increase an asset—debit) |
| Cash | | 4,000 | (decrease an asset—credit) |

Note that Lawndale does not record the building itself because the company does not gain ownership or control (beyond these four months). The payment only provides the right to make use of the building for the specified period in the future so that a prepaid rent balance is appropriate.

5.7 Acquisition of Land

Question: Before this illustration of typical journal entries is completed, four additional transactions will be examined. In total, these fourteen provide an excellent cross-section of basic events encountered by most businesses and the journal entries created to capture that information. An understanding of the recording of these transactions is of paramount importance in mastering the mechanical rules for debits and credits.

Officials of the Lawndale Company decide to purchase a small tract of land by paying $8,000 in cash. Perhaps they think the space might be used sometime in the future as a parking lot. **What recording is made to reflect the cash purchase of a plot of land?**

Answer: The transaction here is straightforward. As an asset, land increases with a debit. The company's cash balance goes down because of the acquisition. That drop is recorded using a credit. As stated earlier in this section, Venetian merchants would probably have made the same recording five hundred years ago (although not in U.S. dollars).

FIGURE 4.15 Journal Entry 11: Land Acquired for Cash

| Land | 8,000 | | (increase an asset—debit) |
| Cash | | 8,000 | (decrease an asset—credit) |

5.8 Sale of an Asset Other Than Inventory

Question: Now, assume that—for demonstration purposes—this same piece of land is sold almost imme-diately to an outside party for cash of $11,000. A sale occurs but the land is not inventory. It was not bought specifically to be resold within the normal course of business. As a farm supply store, selling land is not the primary operation of the Lawndale Company. **Should revenue be recorded along with cost of goods sold when land rather than inventory is sold?** *These two accounts are used in journalizing the sale of inventory. Does the same reporting apply to the sale of other assets such as land or equipment?*

Answer: Because the sale of land is not viewed as a central portion of this company's operations, neither revenue nor cost of goods sold is reported as in the sale of inventory. An $11,000 increase in cash is recorded along with the removal of the $8,000 cost of the land that was conveyed to the new owner. However, to alert decision makers that a tangential or incidental event has taken place, a gain (if the sales price is more than the cost of the land) or a loss (if sales price is less than cost) is recognized for the difference. The effect on net income is the same (a net increase of $3,000), but the method of re-porting has changed.

The resulting gain or loss is then separated from revenues and expenses on the income statement to more clearly communicate information as to the nature of the transaction. The decision maker can see the operating income earned by the reporting company from the normal sale of goods and services distinct from any other gains and losses. For example, if an investor or creditor is looking at the finan-cial statements produced by an Italian restaurant, the amount of income from selling pizzas, spaghetti, and the like is important information apart from any gains and losses that were not part of typical op-erations. Consequently, neither revenue nor cost of goods sold is found in the following entry as was demonstrated in Journal Entries 4A and 4B.

FIGURE 4.16 Journal Entry 12: Land Sold for Cash in Excess of Cost

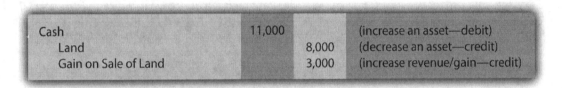

Cash	11,000		(increase an asset—debit)
Land		8,000	(decrease an asset—credit)
Gain on Sale of Land		3,000	(increase revenue/gain—credit)

TEST YOURSELF

Question:

A company buys and sells pots and pans for the kitchen. This same company bought land for a possible ware-house for $43,000. Several years later, the land was sold for $54,000 cash when the decision was made not to construct the new warehouse. In its accounting system, the company increased revenues by $54,000 (along with cash). Cost of goods sold was also recorded as $43,000 (along with a decrease in the land account). Which of the following statements is true?

a. Net income is correctly reported.

b. Gross profit is correctly reported.

c. The reported total for assets is overstated.

d. The journal entry was properly made.

Answer:

The correct answer is choice a: Net income is correctly reported.

Explanation:

The company's entry increased revenues and the cost of goods sold so that the gross profit was raised by $11,000 ($54,000 minus $43,000). However, a gain of $11,000 should have been reported instead. Thus, the components of net income are wrong, but the total impact of $11,000 is properly shown. The balance sheet accounts (cash and land) were recorded in an appropriate fashion.

5.9 Receiving Cash before the Earning Process Is Complete

Question: Accrual accounting, as specified in the revenue realization principle, mandates that revenues should not be recognized until the earning process is substantially complete. Assume a customer gives the

Lawndale Company $3,000 in cash for some type of service to be performed at a future date. The work has not yet begun. Thus, Lawndale cannot report revenue of $3,000. **How is a cash inflow recorded if received for work before the earning process is substantially complete?**

Answer: Although cash is received, accrual accounting dictates that revenue cannot be recognized until the earning process is substantially complete. Here, the earning process will not take place for some time in the future. As an asset, the cash account is increased (debit) but no revenue can yet be recorded. Instead, an unearned revenue account is established for the $3,000 credit. This balance is reported by the Lawndale Company as a liability. Because the money has been accepted, the company is obliged to provide the service or return the $3,000 to the customer. Recording this liability mirrors that responsibility.

FIGURE 4.17 Journal Entry 13: Money Received for Work to Be Done Later

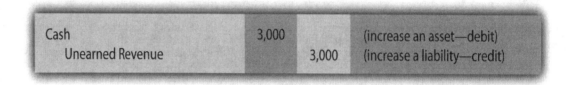

| Cash | 3,000 | | (increase an asset—debit) |
| Unearned Revenue | | 3,000 | (increase a liability—credit) |

5.10 Distribution of a Dividend

Question: Here is one final transaction to provide a full range of basic examples at this preliminary stage of coverage. Many additional transactions and their journal entries will be introduced throughout this textbook, but these fourteen form a strong core of the typical events encountered by most businesses.

Assume that the Lawndale Company has been profitable. As a result, at the end of the year, the board of directors votes to distribute a cash dividend to all owners, a reward that totals $600. Payment is made immediately. **What recording is appropriate when a dividend is distributed to the owners of a corporation?**

Answer: Cash is reduced by this payment to the company's owners. As an asset, a credit is appropriate. The cause of the decrease in cash was a dividend. Hence, a "dividends paid" account is established to measure this particular outflow of net assets. According to the debit and credit rules, an increase in this account is shown through a debit. Thus, the recording of this last illustration is as follows.

FIGURE 4.18 Journal Entry 14: Dividend Distributed to Owners

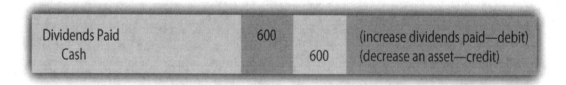

| Dividends Paid | 600 | | (increase dividends paid—debit) |
| Cash | | 600 | (decrease an asset—credit) |

To help visualize the components of an accounting system, all of the journal entries presented here have been gathered into an actual journal in Figure 4.19 as the accountant for the Lawndale Company might have kept. Normally, a date for each entry is included for reference purposes, but that has been omitted here.

FIGURE 4.19 Lawndale Company Journal—Final Days of Year Four

Journal Entry	Accounts	Debit	Credit
1	Inventory	$2,000	
	Accounts Payable		$2,000
2	Salary Expense	300	
	Cash		300
3	Cash	9,000	
	Notes Payable		9,000
4A	Accounts Receivable	5,000	
	Sales of Merchandise		5,000
4B	Cost of Goods Sold	2,000	
	Inventory		2,000
5	Insurance Payable	700	
	Cash		700
6	Truck	40,000	
	Cash		10,000
	Notes Payable		30,000
7	Cash	19,000	
	Capital Stock		19,000
8	Cash	5,000	
	Accounts Receivable		5,000
9	Accounts Payable	2,000	
	Cash		2,000
10	Prepaid Rent	4,000	
	Cash		4,000
11	Land	8,000	
	Cash		8,000
12	Cash	11,000	
	Land		8,000
	Gain on Sale of Land		3,000
13	Cash	3,000	
	Unearned Revenue		3,000
14	Dividends Paid	600	
	Cash		600

5.11 Current T-Account Balances

Question: With adequate practice, obtaining an understanding of the rules for debits and credits is a reasonable goal. However, these journal entries do not provide the current balance of any account. They record the effect of each transaction but not the updated account totals, figures that could change many times every day. **How does an accountant keep track of the current balance of cash, inventory, rent expense, or the myriad other accounts that appear on a set of financial statements?**

Answer: In an accounting system, the recording process is composed of two distinct steps.

1. After analyzing the financial impact of a transaction, a journal entry is created to reflect the monetary impact on relevant accounts.

2. Then, each individual debit and credit is added to the specific T-account being altered, a process known as "posting." A debit to cash in a journal entry is listed as a debit in the cash T-account. A credit made to notes payable is recorded as a credit within the corresponding T-account. After all entries are posted, the current balance for any account can be determined by adding the debit and the credit sides of the T-account and netting the two.

Historically, posting the individual changes shown in each journal entry to the specific T-accounts was a tedious and slow process performed manually. Today, automated systems are designed so that the impact of each entry is simultaneously recorded in the proper T-accounts found in the ledger.

For illustration purposes, all of the journal entries recorded earlier have been posted into the ledger T-accounts shown in Figure 4.19. Each account includes the previous balance (PB) found in the trial balance in Figure 4.3. The new debits and credits are then posted for each of the fourteen sample transactions. For cross-referencing purposes, the number of the corresponding journal entry is included. The debit and credit sides of each account are summed and netted to determine the current balance (CB). For example, the cash T-account has $67,000 as the total of all debits and $25,600 for all credits, which net to a current balance of $41,400.

After all of the additional journal entries have been posted into the ledger, an updated trial balance can be drawn from the individual T-account balances. No change is created by this process, but, as can be seen in Figure 4.21, the accounts and their current balances are much easier to see. Simply the clarity of the information can help accountants spot accounts that may contain errors because of unusual or unexpected totals.

FIGURE 4.20   Lawndale Company Ledger—December 31, Year Four

CASH		
PB 20,000		
(3) 9,000	(2)	300
(7) 19,000	(5)	700
(8) 5,000	(6)	10,000
(12) 11,000	(9)	2,000
(13) 3,000	(10)	4,000
	(11)	8,000
	(14)	600
67,000		25,600
CB 41,400		

ACCOUNTS RECEIVABLE	
PB 50,000	
(4A) 5,000	(8) 5,000
14,000	5,000
CB 50,000	

INVENTORY	
PB 65,000	
(1) 2,000	(4B) 2,000
10,000	2,000
CB 65,000	

PREPAID RENT	
(10) 4,000	
CB 4,000	

TRUCK	
(6) 40,000	
CB 40,000	

LAND	
(11) 8,000	(12) 8,000
8,000	8,000
CB 0	

INSURANCE PAYABLE	
	PB 700
(5) 700	
700	700
	CB 0

ACCOUNTS PAYABLE	
	PB 18,000
(9) 2,000	(1) 2,000
2,000	4,600
	CB 18,000

NOTES PAYABLE	
	PB 40,000
	(3) 9,000
	(6) 30,000
	CB 79,000

UNEARNED REVENUE	
	(13) 3,000
	CB 3,000

CAPITAL STOCK	
	PB 30,000
	(7) 19,000
	CB 49,000

RETAINED EARNINGS	
	PB 32,000
	CB 32,000

DIVIDENDS PAID	
14 600	
CB 600	

SALES OF MERCHANDISE	
	PB 250,000
	(4A) 5,000
	CB 255,000

COST OF GOODS SOLD	
PB 150,000	
(4B) 2,000	
CB 152,000	

RENT EXPENSE	
PB 12,000	
CB 12,000	

SALARY EXPENSE	
PB 60,000	
(2) 300	
CB 60,300	

INSURANCE EXPENSE	
PB 3,700	
CB 3,700	

GAIN ON SALE OF LAND	
	(12) 3,000
	CB 3,000

UTILITIES EXPENSE	
PB 10,000	

FIGURE 4.21 Lawndale Company Trial Balance (after all journal entries have been posted)—December 31, Year Four

Lawndale Company Updated Trial Balance December 31, Year Four		
Account	Debit	Credit
Cash	$41,400	
Accounts Receivable	50,000	
Inventory	65,000	
Prepaid Rent	4,000	
Truck	40,000	
Accounts Payable		$18,000
Unearned Revenue		3,000
Notes Payable (long-term)		79,000
Capital Stock		49,000
Retained Earnings (beginning of year)		32,000
Dividends Paid	600	
Sales of Merchandise		255,000
Cost of Goods Sold	152,000	
Rent Expense	12,000	
Salary Expense	60,300	
Utilities Expense	10,000	
Insurance Expense	3,700	
Gain on Sale of Land		3,000
Totals	$439,000	$439,000

KEY TAKEAWAY

Initial coverage of the recording of basic transactions is concluded here through analysis of the payment of insurance, the contribution of capital, the purchase and sale of land, the receipt of cash prior to work being performed, the payment of dividends to owners, and the like. After the impact of each event is ascertained, debits and credits are used to record these changes within the journal. These journal entries are then posted to the appropriate T-accounts to monitor the ever-changing account balances. All T-accounts are physically located in a ledger, which is also known as a general ledger. Journal entries document the effect of transactions. T-accounts maintain the current balance of every account.

Talking with a Real Investing Pro (Continued)

Following is a continuation of our interview with Kevin G. Burns.

Question: When you were a college student majoring in accounting, you learned all the debit and credit rules as well as about the role of journal entries and the general ledger. In your years as an investment advisor, has this knowledge ever proven to be helpful to you and your career?

Kevin Burns: Although I never planned to be an accountant when I was in college, I found the internal logic of the debit and credit rules quite fascinating. Thinking through transactions and figuring out the proper recording process was a great introduction to business operations. In all honesty, as an investment advisor, I pay more attention to asset values and other balance sheet information than the accounting process that is used to gather this information. However, I also happen to own a restaurant and I always find it interesting when I dig through the specific expense accounts looking for ways to be more efficient.

For instance, recently when I saw that we had spent a lot of money last year on building maintenance, I could not imagine how that was possible. I dug through the T-account myself and found a recording error that needed to be fixed that changed our net income. My background allowed me to understand the entire process. Frequently, as I study the various debits within our expenses, I am able to spot areas where the restaurant can save money. I am always amazed that some business owners seem almost scared to look into their own financial information. I think they are afraid of feeling stupid. But, the more information you have, the more likely it is that you will make money.

 Video Clip

Professor Joe Hoyle talks about the five most important points in Chapter 4.

View the video online at: http://bit.ly/hoyle4-2

6.   END-OF-CHAPTER EXERCISES

QUESTIONS

1. What is a transaction?
2. When and where was the basic accounting system developed that is still used by organizations today?
3. What is meant by the term "double-entry bookkeeping"?
4. What are the four basic steps followed in an accounting system?
5. How is information about the impact of a transaction initially captured in an accounting system?
6. How is information about specific account balances accumulated?
7. Which accounts are increased with a debit?
8. Which accounts are increased with a credit?
9. Susan Osgood works as an accountant and maintains the journal for the Nelson Corporation. What is the purpose of a journal?
10. In a journal entry, why do the debit figures always agree with the credit figures?
11. What is a trial balance?
12. What function does accrual accounting serve?
13. Accrual accounting is composed of which two principles? Define each.
14. An accountant indicates that a certain expense was recognized in the current year because of the matching principle. What does that mean?
15. The Abraham Company receives $27,000 to do a job. However, the work is not yet completed. How is the receipt of this money recognized for financial reporting purposes?

TRUE OR FALSE

1. _____ Debits and credits must equal for every transaction.

2. _____ A list of all recorded journal entries is recorded in the ledger, which is maintained by a company.

3. _____ Revenue may not be recorded until cash is collected.

4. _____ A transaction is any event that has a financial impact on a company.

5. _____ The balance of an expense account is increased with a credit.

6. _____ Examples of accrued expenses include salary, rent, and interest.

7. _____ The term "revenue" and the term "gain" are interchangeable.

8. _____ Posting refers to the process of analyzing transactions and producing journal entries.

9. _____ A company must recognize each accrued expense as it is incurred.

10. _____ The matching principle states that expenses should be recognized in the same period as the revenue they help generate.

11. _____ Unearned revenue is reported on the balance sheet as a liability account.

12. _____ The Hampstone Company buys 20,000 pieces of inventory (all identical) for $70,000. The company sells 8,000 units of this inventory for $5 each in cash. The company should debit cash for $40,000, credit inventory for $28,000, and credit gain for $12,000.

13. _____ Assume a company buys inventory for $8,000 for cash. It then spends $700 in cash on advertising in order to sell 60 percent of the inventory for $11,000. Of that amount, it collects $5,000 immediately and will collect the remaining $6,000 next year. The company pays a cash dividend of $1,000. The amount of net income to be recognized this year will be $5,500.

14. _____ A company buys inventory for $6,000 on credit on December 31, Year One. By accident, the journal entry is made backward (debits are shown as credits and credits are shown as debits). The company reports working capital of $140,000. The correct amount of working capital is $134,000.

15. _____ A matching principle is the portion of U.S. GAAP that sets the rule for the timing of recognition of revenues.

16. _____ Assume a company buys inventory for $3,000 on credit. It then spends $400 on advertising in order to sell 30 percent of the inventory for $9,000. Of that amount, it collects $5,000 immediately and will collect the remaining $4,000 next year. The amount of gross profit to be recognized this year will be $7,700.

MULTIPLE CHOICE

1. Which of the following is **not** true about double-entry bookkeeping?

   a. It originated in Italy.
   b. Debits and credits must equal.
   c. It is still used today by most businesses.
   d. Each entry can have only one credit and one debit.

2. Which of the following entries could Yeats Company not make when they perform a service for a client?

   a. **FIGURE 4.22**

   b. **FIGURE 4.23**

   c. **FIGURE 4.24**

   d. **FIGURE 4.25**

3. Which of the following is a transaction for Tyler Corporation?

   a. Tyler pays its employees $400 for work done.
   b. Tyler considers renting office space that will cost $1,500 per month.
   c. Tyler agrees to perform services for a client, which will cost $7,000.
   d. Tyler places an order for supplies that will be delivered in two weeks. The supplies cost $200.

4. Elenor Company sells 400 units of inventory for $40 each. The inventory originally cost Elenor $26 each. What is Elenor's gross profit on this transaction?

   a. $ 5,600
   b. $ 9,600
   c. $10,400
   d. $16,000

5. Which of the following increases with a debit?

    a. Retained earnings

    b. Sales revenue

    c. Inventory

    d. Note payable

6. In January, Rollins Company is paid $500 by a client for work that Rollins will not begin until February. Which of the following is the correct journal entry for Rollins to make when the $500 is received?

    a. **FIGURE 4.26**

    b. **FIGURE 4.27**

    c. **FIGURE 4.28**

    d. **FIGURE 4.29**

7. The accountant for the Babson Corporation determines that the current Cash balance held by the company is $32,564. Which of the following could not have been the source of that information?

    a. Trial balance

    b. Journal

    c. T-account

    d. Ledger

8. In the accounting system for the Caldwell Company, which of the following comes first?

    a. Journal

    b. Financial statements

    c. T-account

    d. Ledger

9. Which of the following T-accounts is least likely to have a credit balance?

    a. Revenue

    b. Equipment

    c. Accounts payable

    d. Capital stock

10. The Brooklyn Corporation rents a building for $100 per day. The company's accounting system accrues this expense each day. After twelve days, payment is made. What account is debited when that payment is made?

    a. Rent expense

    b. Rent payable

    c. Cash

    d. Cannot be determined based on the information provided

11. The Bronx Corporation rents a building for $100 per day. The company's accounting system makes no recognition of this expense as it accrues. After twelve days, payment is made. What account is debited when that payment is made?

    a. Rent expense

    b. Rent payable

    c. Cash

    d. Cannot be determined based on the information provided

VIDEO PROBLEMS

Professor Joe Hoyle discusses the answers to these two problems at the links that are indicated. After formulating your answers, watch each video to see how Professor Hoyle answers these questions.

1. Your roommate is an English major. One of the roommate's parents works as an accountant for the family's business, a corporation that owns a number of ice cream stores in Florida. The parent is constantly talking about working with debits and credits, which seems like some foreign language to your roommate. One day, on the way to the fitness center, your roommate blurts out this question: "What in the world are debits and credits? How can they possibly be so important?" How would you respond?

View the video online at: http://bit.ly/hoyle4-3

2. Your uncle and two friends started a small office supply store at the beginning of the current year. Almost immediately, it becomes obvious to them that they need some system for keeping their financial records. They will eventually have to report their income taxes, and they may well need monetary information for a bank loan. Your uncle knows that you are taking a financial accounting course in college. He sends you an e-mail and asks if you can provide some suggestions on getting started with this record-keeping process. He realizes that you have just started your course, but he hopes that you can give him some basic ideas on how to gather the needed information. How would you respond?

View the video online at: http://bit.ly/hoyle4-4

PROBLEMS

1. For each of the following transactions of the Hamner Corporation, indicate what accounts are affected and whether they increase or decrease.

   a. Owners put $30,000 in cash into the business.

   b. The company borrows $15,000 in cash from the bank on a note payable.

   c. The company buys equipment for $19,000 using cash.

   d. The company buys machinery at a cost of $11,000 that will be paid within thirty days.

   e. The company sells services for $14,000. It collects $2,000 immediately (when the work is done) with the rest due at the end of the month.

   f. The company pays $5,000 in rent on a building that was used during the past month. The expense has not been accrued over that time.

   g. The company pays a $3,000 dividend to its owners.

   h. The company buys inventory for $10,000 on credit.

   i. The company sells the above inventory for $18,000. It collects $7,000 immediately with the rest to be received within the next few weeks.

   j. The company pays for inventory bought in transaction h.

   k. The company collects money due from the sale in transaction i.

2. For each of the following is a debit or credit needed to reflect the impact?

   a. Equipment increases

   b. Salary payable increases

   c. Cash decreases

   d. Rent expense increases

   e. Sales revenue increases

   f. Accounts receivable decreases

   g. Capital stock increases

   h. Inventory decreases

   i. Accounts payable decreases

   j. Salary expense decreases

3. Record the following journal entries for Taylor Company for the month of March:

   a. Borrowed $4,500 from Local Bank and Trust

   b. Investors contributed $10,000 in cash for shares of the company's stock.

   c. Bought inventory costing $2,000 on credit

   d. Sold inventory that originally cost $400 for $600 on credit

   e. Purchased a new piece of equipment for $500 cash

   f. Collected $600 in cash from sale of inventory in (d)

   g. Paid for inventory purchased in (c)

   h. Paid $1,200 in cash for an insurance policy that covers the next year

   i. Employees earned $3,000 during the month but have not yet been paid; this amount has been recorded by the company as it was earned.

   j. Paid employees $2,900 of the wages earned and recorded during February

4. For each of the following transactions, determine if Raymond Corporation has earned revenue during the month of May and, if so, how much has been earned.

   a. Customer A paid Raymond $1,500 for work Raymond will perform in June.

   b. Customer B purchased $6,000 in inventory with the total payment expected to be received in four weeks. Those items had cost Raymond $3,600 in February.

   c. Raymond performed a service for Customer C and was paid $3,400 in cash.

   d. Customer D paid Raymond $2,300 for inventory that was purchased previously in April.

5. Record the journal entries for the transactions in number 4 above.

6. The following are the account balances for the Ester Company for December 31, Year Four, and the year that ended. All accounts have normal debit or credit balances. For some reason, company accountants do not know the amount of sales revenue earned this year. What is the balance of that account?

FIGURE 4.30 Trial Balance—Ester Company

Ester Company T-Account Balances
December 31, Year Four

Account	Balance
Cash	$22,000
Accounts Receivable	85,000
Inventory	113,000
Land	175,000
Accounts Payable	14,000
Salary Payable	7,000
Notes Payable	125,000
Capital Stock	90,000
Retained Earnings, 1/1/04	114,000
Sales Revenue	not given
Cost of Goods Sold	185,000
Salary Expense	89,000
Utilities Expense	15,000
Dividends Paid	6,000

7. State whether a debit or credit balance is normal for each of the following T-accounts:

    a. Cash

    b. Dividends paid

    c. Notes payable

    d. Unearned revenue

    e. Cost of goods sold

    f. Prepaid rent

    g. Accounts receivable

    h. Capital stock

8. Near the end of her freshman year at college, Heather Miller is faced with the decision of whether to get a summer job, go to summer school, or start a summer dress-making business. Heather has some experience designing and sewing and believes that third option might be the most lucrative of her summer alternatives. Consequently, she starts "Sew Cool."

    During June, the first month of business, the following occur:

    a. Heather deposits $1,000 of her own money into Sew Cool's checking account.

    b. Sew Cool purchases equipment for $1,000. The company signs a note payable for this purchase.

    c. Sew Cool purchases $1,000 in sewing supplies and material paying cash.

    d. Sew Cool gives Heather's parents a check for $80 for rent ($70) and utilities ($10) for the past four weeks.

    e. Heather sews and sells twenty dresses during the month. Each dress has a price of $60. Cash is received for twelve of the dresses, with customers owing for the remaining eight.

    f. The dresses sold cost $35 each to make.

    g. Sew Cool purchases advertising for $50 cash.

    h. Sew Cool pays Heather a cash dividend of $10 cash.

    i. Sew Cool's taxes, paid in cash, amount to $87.
        Required:

        A. Prepare journal entries for the previous transactions.

        B. Prepare t-accounts for each account used.

        C. Prepare a trial balance for June.

9. Bowling Corporation had the following transactions occur during January:

    a. Bowling purchased $450,000 in inventory on credit.

b. Bowling received $13,000 in cash from customers for subscriptions that will not begin until the following month.

c. Bowling signed a note from Midwest Bank for $67,000.

d. Bowling sold all the inventory purchased in (a) for $700,000 on account.

e. Bowling paid employees $120,000 for services performed (and recorded) during the previous year.

f. Bowling purchased land for $56,000 in cash.

g. Bowling received $650,000 in cash from customers paying off previous accounts receivable.

h. Bowling paid dividends to stockholders in the amount of $4,000.

i. Bowling owes its employees $123,000 for work performed during the current month but not yet paid.

j. Bowling paid $300,000 on its accounts payable.

k. Bowling paid taxes in cash of $45,000.

> *Required:*
>
> A. Prepare journal entries for the previous transactions.
>
> B. Complete the following T-accounts. Numbers already under the accounts represent the prior balance in that account.

FIGURE 4.31 Opening T-Account Balances

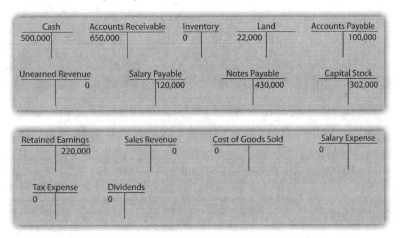

C. Prepare a trial balance for the end of January.

10. The following events occurred during the month of January for McLain Company.

    a. McLain purchases inventory costing $1,800 on account.

    b. McLain sells 240 units for $20 each. McLain collects cash for 200 of these units. These specific units cost McLain $8 each to purchase.

    c. McLain collects $500 in cash on its accounts receivable.

    d. McLain takes out a loan for $400.

    e. McLain pays out $350 cash in dividends.

    f. McLain receives a contribution of $600 in cash from its owners in exchange for capital stock shares.

    g. McLain purchased a new piece of equipment. The new equipment cost $1,000 and was paid for in cash.

    h. McLain pays $500 of its accounts payable.

    i. McLain incurs $500 in salaries expense, but will not pay workers until next month.

    j. McLain incurs $300 in rent expense and pays it in cash.

    k. McLain prepays $200 in cash for insurance.

    l. Taxes, paid in cash, are $110.

Required:

A. Prepare journal entries for the earlier transactions.

B. Complete the following T-accounts. Numbers already under the accounts represent the prior balance in that account.

FIGURE 4.32 Opening T-Account Balances

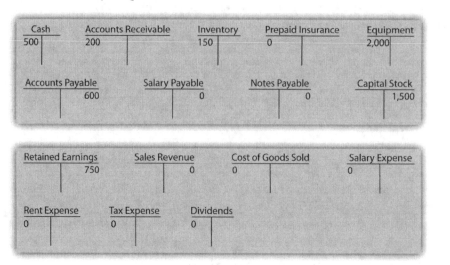

C. Prepare a trial balance for January.

RESEARCH ASSIGNMENT

A newspaper company collects money for subscriptions before its newspapers are physically delivered. How large is that liability, and when does it become revenue?

Go to http://www.nytimes.com/. At **The New York Times** Web site, scroll to the bottom of the screen and click on "The New York Times Company." Click on "Investors" at the top of the next screen. Click on "Financials" on the left side of the next screen. In the center of the next page, click on "2010 Annual Report & Form 10-K" to download.

After the document has downloaded, scroll to page 63 to look at the company's balance sheet. Does **The New York Times Company** report any unearned revenue within its liabilities?

Next, scroll to page 72. Within the notes to financial statements, a description is provided of the revenue recognition procedures used by **The New York Times Company**. What information is presented to decision makers by the last sentence in the fourth bullet point?

ENDNOTES

1. One method to keep track of these accounts initially is to remember them as the "DEAD" accounts: **d**ebits increase, **e**xpenses and losses, **a**ssets, and **d**ividends paid. Quickly, though, through practice, such mnemonic devices will not be needed.

2. Changes in the balance reported for retained earnings normally do not come as a direct result of a transaction. As discussed previously, this account reflects all the net income earned to date reduced by all dividend payments. Income is made up of revenues, expenses, gains, and losses. Accounting recognition of revenues and gains (which increase with credits) lead to a larger retained earnings balance. Expenses, losses, and dividends paid (which all increase with debits) reduce retained earnings. Consequently, credits cause an increase in retained earnings whereas debits produce a decrease.

3. In larger organizations, similar transactions are often grouped, summed, and recorded together for efficiency. For example, all cash sales at one store might be totaled automatically and recorded at one time at the end of each day. To help focus on the mechanics of the accounting process, the journal entries in this textbook will be prepared for transactions individually.

4. The parenthetical information is included here only for clarification purposes and does not appear in a true journal entry.

CHAPTER 5
Why Is Financial Information Adjusted Prior to the Production of Financial Statements?

 Video Clip

In this video, Professor Joe Hoyle introduces the essential points covered in Chapter 5.

PREPAID EXPENSE - ASSET GRADUALLY USED UP OVER TIME

View the video online at: http://bit.ly/hoyle5-1

1. THE NEED FOR ADJUSTING ENTRIES

LEARNING OBJECTIVES

At the end of this section, students should be able to meet the following objectives:

1. Explain the purpose and necessity of adjusting entries.
2. List examples of several typical accounts that require adjusting entries.
3. Provide examples of adjusting entries for various accrued expenses.

1.1 Accounting for the Passage of Time

Question: The first two steps of the accounting process were identified in Chapter 4 as "analyze" and "record." A transaction occurs and the resulting financial effects are ascertained through careful analysis. Once determined, the monetary impact on specific accounts is recorded in the form of a journal entry. Each of the debits and credits is then posted to the corresponding T-accounts located in the ledger. As needed, current balances can be determined for any of these accounts by netting the debits and credits. It is a system as old as the painting of the Mona Lisa.

The third step in this process was listed as "adjust." **Why do ledger account balances require adjustment?** *Why are the T-account totals found in the trial balance at the end of Chapter 4 (Figure 4.21) not* *simply used by the accountant to produce Year Four financial statements for that business (Lawndale Company)?*

Answer: Financial events take place throughout the year. As indicated, journal entries record the individual debit and credit effects that are then entered into the proper T-accounts. However, not all changes in these balances occur as the result of physical events. Some accounts increase or decrease because of the passage of time. The impact can be so gradual that producing individual journal entries is not reasonable.

For example, salary is earned by employees every day (actually every minute), but payment is not made until the end of the week or month. Many other expenses, such as utilities, rent, and interest, are incurred over time in much the same way. Accounting for supplies such as pens and envelopes is only slightly different. This asset is slowly depleted because of usage rather than time, but the impact on accounts is basically the same. As indicated in Chapter 4, unless an accounting system is programmed to record tiny incremental changes, none of these financial effects is captured as they occur.

Following each day of work, few companies take the trouble to record the equivalent amount of salary, rent, or other expense along with the related liability. When a pad of paper is consumed within an organization, debiting supplies expense for a dollar and crediting supplies for the same amount hardly seems worth the effort.

Therefore, prior to producing financial statements, the accountant must search for any such changes that have not yet been recognized. These incremental increases or decreases must also be recorded in a debit and credit format (called **adjusting entries** rather than journal entries) with the impact then posted to the appropriate ledger accounts. The updating process continues until all balances are presented fairly. These adjustments are a prerequisite step in the preparation of financial statements. They are physically identical to the journal entries recorded for transactions, but they occur at a different time and for a different reason.

adjusting entries

Changes in account balances recorded prior to preparing financial statements to update T-accounts because some amounts have increased or decreased over time but have not been recorded through a journal entry.

TEST YOURSELF

Question:

On Monday morning, a company hires a person and promises to pay $300 per day for working Monday through Friday. The first payment of $1,500 is made at the end of the workday on Friday. The person quits on Saturday. Which of the following statements is true?

a. An adjusting entry is needed when the person is hired if financial statements are prepared at that time.

b. An adjusting entry is needed at the end of work on Monday if financial statements are prepared at that time.

c. An adjusting entry is needed at the end of work on Friday when payment is made if financial statements are prepared at that time.

d. An adjusting entry is needed on Saturday when the person quits if financial statements are prepared at that time.

Answer:

The correct answer is choice b: An adjusting entry is needed at the end of work on Monday if financial statements are prepared at that time.

Explanation:

When financial statements are prepared, adjusting entries recognize changes created by the passage of time. Hiring an employee creates no change; money has not been earned. Payment is an actual transaction recorded by a journal entry. The person quitting requires no entry because further work was not done after Friday's payment. When an employee works on Monday, salary is owed for that day. The amount is probably not recorded by the accounting system, so an adjusting entry is needed.

1.2 Examples of Adjusting Entries

*Question: Adjusting entries update ledger accounts for any financial changes that occur gradually over time so that they are not recorded through a journal entry. Large companies will make hundreds, if not thousands, of adjustments at the end of each fiscal period. **What kinds of adjustments are normally needed before a set of financial statements is prepared?***

Answer: A variety of adjusting entries will be examined throughout the remainder of this textbook. One of the accountant's primary responsibilities is the careful study of all financial information to ensure that it is presented fairly before being released. Such investigation can lead to the preparation of numerous adjusting entries. Here, in Chapter 5, only the following four general types of adjustments are introduced to demonstrate the process and also reflect the importance of the revenue recognition principle and the matching principle. In later chapters, additional examples will be described and analyzed.

- Accrued expenses (also referred to as accrued liabilities)
- Prepaid expenses (including supplies)
- Accrued revenue
- Unearned revenue (also referred to as deferred revenue)

Usually, at the start of the adjustment process, the accountant prepares an updated trial balance to provide a visual, organized representation of all ledger account balances. This listing aids the accountant in spotting figures that might need adjusting in order to be fairly presented. Therefore, Figure 4.21 is replicated here in Figure 5.1 because this trial balance holds the December 31, Year Four, account balances for the Lawndale Company determined at the end of Chapter 4. All transactions have been recorded and posted, but no adjustments have yet been made.

FIGURE 5.1 Updated Trial Balance for the Lawndale Company

Lawndale Company Updated Trial Balance December 31, Year Four

Account	Debit	Credit
Cash	$41,400	
Accounts Receivable	50,000	
Inventory	65,000	
Prepaid Rent	4,000	
Truck	40,000	
Accounts Payable		$18,000
Unearned Revenue		3,000
Notes Payable (long-term)		79,000
Capital Stock		49,000
Retained Earnings (beginning of year)		32,000
Dividends Paid	600	
Sales of Merchandise		255,000
Cost of Goods Sold	152,000	
Rent Expense	12,000	
Salary Expense	60,300	
Utilities Expense	10,000	
Insurance Expense	3,700	
Gain on Sale of Land		3,000
Totals	$439,000	$439,000

1.3 Adjusting Entry to Recognize an Accrued Expense

accrued expense

Expenses (and related liabilities) that grow gradually over time; if not recognized automatically by the accounting system, the monetary impact is recorded prior to preparing the company's financial statements by means of an adjusting entry.

Question: The first type of adjustment listed is an **accrued expense.** *Previously, the word "accrue" was defined as "to grow." Thus, an accrued expense is one that increases gradually over time. As has been indicated, some companies program their accounting systems to record such expenses as incurred. This accrual process eliminates the need for subsequent adjusting entries. Other companies make few, if any, accruals and update all balances through numerous adjustments when financial statements are to be prepared.*

The mechanical recording process for such expenses should be designed to meet the informational needs of company officials. Some prefer to have updated balances readily available in the ledger at all times while others are inclined to wait for periodic financial reports to be issued. **What are some typical accrued expenses, and what is the appropriate adjusting entry if they are not recorded as incurred by the accounting system?**

Answer: If a reporting company's accounting system recognizes an expense as it grows, no adjustment is necessary. The balances are recorded properly. They are ready to be included in financial statements. Thus, when statements are prepared, the accountant only needs to search for accrued expenses that have not yet been recognized.

Numerous expenses get slightly larger each day until paid, including salary, rent, insurance, utilities, interest, advertising, income taxes, and the like. For example, on its December 31, 2010, balance sheet, **The Hershey Company** reported accrued liabilities of approximately $593 million. In the notes to the financial statements, this amount was explained as debts owed by the company on that day for payroll, compensation and benefits ($219 million), advertising and promotion ($211 million), and other accrued expenses ($163 million).

Assume, for illustration purposes, that the accountant reviews the trial balance presented in Figure 5.1 and realizes that utility expenses (such as electricity and water) have not been recorded since the most recent payment early in December of Year Four. Assume that Lawndale Company currently owes $900 for those utilities. The following adjustment is needed before financial statements can be created. It is an adjusting entry because no physical event took place. This liability simply grew over time and has not yet been paid.

FIGURE 5.2 Adjusting Entry 1: Amount Owed for Utilities

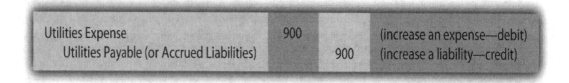

| Utilities Expense | 900 | | (increase an expense—debit) |
| Utilities Payable (or Accrued Liabilities) | | 900 | (increase a liability—credit) |

TEST YOURSELF

Question:

A company owes its employees $7,300 at the end of Year One, which it pays on January 8, Year Two. This balance was not accrued by the company's accounting system in Year One, nor was it recorded as an adjusting entry on December 31, Year One. Which of the following is not true for the Year One financial statements?

a. Reported expenses are too low by $7,300.

b. Reported net income is too high by $7,300.

c. Reported total assets are too high by $7,300.

d. Reported total liabilities are too low by $7,300.

Answer:

The correct answer is choice c: Reported total assets are too high by $7,300.

Explanation:

Neither the expense nor the payable was recorded in Year One, and those reported balances are too low. Because the expense was too low, reported net income will be overstated by $7,300. This accrual does not impact an asset until paid in Year Two. Therefore, the Year One asset balance is properly stated.

KEY TAKEAWAY

Adjusting entries are often necessary to update account balances before financial statements can be prepared. These adjustments are not the result of physical events or transactions but are caused by the passage of time or small changes in account balances. The accountant examines all current account balances as listed in the trial balance to identify amounts that need to be changed prior to the preparation of financial statements. Although numerous adjustments are studied in this textbook, four general types are especially common: accrued expenses, prepaid expenses, accrued revenues, and unearned revenues. Any expense (such as salary, interest, or rent) that grows gradually over time but has not yet been paid is known as an accrued expense (or accrued liability). If not automatically recorded by the accounting system as incurred, the amount due must be entered into the records by adjustment prior to producing financial statements.

2.   PREPARING VARIOUS ADJUSTING ENTRIES

LEARNING OBJECTIVES

At the end of this section, students should be able to meet the following objectives:

1. Explain the need for an adjusting entry in the reporting of prepaid expenses and be able to prepare that adjustment.
2. Explain the need for an adjusting entry in the reporting of accrued revenue and be able to prepare that adjustment.
3. Describe the challenge of determining when the earning process for revenue is substantially complete and discuss possible resolutions.
4. Explain the need for an adjusting entry in the reporting of unearned revenue and be able to prepare that adjustment.

2.1   Recording and Adjusting Prepaid Expenses

*Question: The second adjustment to be considered here involves the handling of **prepaid expenses**. For example, as of May 29, 2011, **General Mills Inc.** reported "prepaid expenses and other current assets" of $483.5 million. A decision maker studying this business needs to understand what information is conveyed by such balances.*

In the transactions that were recorded in the previous chapter, Journal Entry 10 reported a $4,000 payment made by the Lawndale Company for four months of rent to use a building. An asset—prepaid rent—was recorded at that time through the normal accounting process. The resulting account is listed on the trial balance in Figure 5.1. Such costs are common and often include payments for insurance and supplies.

*Assume, at the end of Year Four, the company's accountant examines the invoice that was paid and determines that this $4,000 in rent covered the period from December 1, Year Four, until March 31, Year Five. As a result, an adjusting entry is now necessary so that all balances are presented fairly. **Why is a year-end adjusting entry often needed in connection with a prepaid expense?***

prepaid expenses

A future economic benefit created when an expense is paid in advance; reported as an asset initially and then gradually reassigned to expense over time through adjusting entries.

Answer: During these four months, the Lawndale Company will use the rented facility to help generate revenue. Over that time, the future economic benefit established by the payment gradually becomes a past benefit. The asset literally changes into an expense day by day. In this example, one month of the rent from this payment has now been consumed. The benefit provided by using this building during December to gain revenue no longer exists. That portion of the rent ($1,000 or $4,000/four months) reflects a past benefit and should be reported as an expense in Year Four in accordance with the matching principle. Expenses are recognized in the same period as the revenue they help to generate.

As a preliminary step in preparing financial statements, an adjusting entry is needed to reclassify $1,000 from the asset (prepaid rent) into an expense (rent expense). This adjustment leaves $3,000 in the asset (for the remaining three months of rent on the building) while $1,000 is now reported as an expense (for the previous one month of rent).

FIGURE 5.3 Adjusting Entry 2 (Version 1): Use Is Made of a Rented Facility (Original Entry to Prepaid Rent)

| Rent Expense | 1,000 | | (increase an expense—debit) |
| Prepaid Rent | | 1,000 | (decrease an asset—credit) |

Adjusting entries are created to take whatever amounts reside in the ledger and align them with the requirements of U.S. GAAP (or IFRS, if those standards are being applied). For this illustration, the original $4,000 payment was classified as a prepaid rent and the adjustment was created in response to that initial entry. After $1,000 is moved from asset to expense, the balances are presented fairly: an asset of $3,000 for the future benefit and an expense of $1,000 for the past.

In recording transactions, some accounting systems mechanically handle events in a different manner than others. Thus, construction of each adjusting entry depends on the recording that previously took place. To illustrate, assume that when this $4,000 payment was made, the company entered the debit to rent expense rather than prepaid rent. Perhaps an error was made or, more likely, a computerized accounting system was programmed to record all money spent for rent as an expense. For convenience, many companies prefer to automate the recording process wherever possible knowing that adjusting entries can then be made to arrive at proper balances. The initial accounting has no impact on the figures to be reported but does alter the adjustment process.

If a $4,000 expense was recorded here initially rather than a prepayment, an adjusting entry is still needed. The expense appearing on the income statement should be $1,000 (for the past one month) while the appropriate asset on the balance sheet should be $3,000 (for the subsequent three months). If the entire cost of $4,000 is located in rent expense, the following alternative is necessary to arrive at proper balances. This adjustment shifts $3,000 out of the expense and into the asset.

FIGURE 5.4 Adjusting Entry 2A (Version 2): Use Is Made of a Rented Facility (Original Entry to Rent Expense)

| Prepaid Rent | 3,000 | | (increase an asset—debit) |
| Rent Expense | | 3,000 | (decrease an expense—credit) |

This adjusting entry leaves the appropriate $1,000 in expense and puts $3,000 into the asset account. Those are the proper balances as of the end of the year. Regardless of the account, the accountant first determines the balance that is present in the ledger and then creates the specific adjustment needed to arrive at fairly presented figures.

TEST YOURSELF

Question:

A company pays $4,000 to rent a building on October 1, Year One, for four months. The amount was recorded as prepaid rent, and no further change was made in the balance. When preparing to produce Year One financial statements, the accountant erroneously believed that the entire $4,000 was originally recorded as a rent expense and made an adjustment based on that assumption. Which of the following is a result of the accountant's action?

  a. The prepaid rent is overstated on the balance sheet by $4,000.

  b. The rent expense is overstated on the income statement by $4,000.

  c. The prepaid rent is overstated on the balance sheet by $1,000.

  d. The rent expense is overstated on the income statement by $1,000.

Answer:

The correct answer is choice a: The prepaid rent is overstated on the balance sheet by $4,000.

Explanation:

Rent was $1,000 per month. Three months have passed. The rent expense should be reported as $3,000 with the prepaid rent as $1,000. All $4,000 was recorded as prepaid rent. The accountant thought the rent expense was recorded as $4,000, so $1,000 was moved from expense to prepaid rent. That entry raised the prepaid rent to $5,000 ($4,000 plus $1,000) and dropped the expense to a negative $1,000. The prepaid rent is overstated by $4,000 ($5,000 rather than $1,000); the rent expense is understated by $4,000.

2.2 Recognizing Accrued Revenue

Question: The third general type of adjustment to be covered here is accrued revenue. As the title implies, this revenue is one that grows gradually over time. If not recorded by a company's accounting system as earned, an adjusting entry to update the balances is necessary before financial statements are prepared. This process mirrors that of accrued expenses. **What adjustment is used by a reporting organization to recognize any accrued revenue that has not previously been recorded?**

Answer: Various types of revenue are earned as time passes rather than through a physical event such as the sale of inventory. To illustrate, assume that a customer visited the Lawndale Company five days before the end of Year Four to ask for assistance. The customer must be away from his ranch for thirty days and wanted company employees to feed, water, and care for his horses during the period of absence. Everything needed for the job is available in the customer's barn. The Lawndale Company just provides the service. The parties agreed that the company will receive $100 per day for this work with payment to be made upon the person's return.

No asset changes hands at the start of this task. Thus, the company's accounting system is not likely to make any entry until payment is eventually received. However, after the first five days of this work, the Lawndale Company is ready to prepare Year Four financial statements. For that reason, the company needs to recognize all revenue earned to date. Service to this customer has been carried out for five days at a rate of $100 per day. The company has performed the work to earn $500 although the money will not be received until later. Consequently, a receivable and revenue for this amount should be recognized through an adjusting entry. The earning process for the $500 occurred in Year Four and should be recorded in this year.

FIGURE 5.5 Adjusting Entry 3: Revenue Earned for Work Done

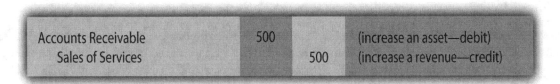

| Accounts Receivable | 500 | | (increase an asset—debit) |
| Sales of Services | | 500 | (increase a revenue—credit) |

The $500 receivable will be removed in the subsequent period when the customer eventually pays Lawndale for the services rendered. No recognition is needed in this adjusting entry for cost of goods sold because a service, rather than inventory, is being sold.

2.3   The Earning Process

Question: As discussed in a previous chapter, the revenue realization principle (within accrual accounting) provides formal guidance for the timing of revenue reporting. It states in part that the earning process must be substantially complete before revenue is recognized. That seems reasonable. In the previous example, the work has been performed for only five days out of a total of thirty. That does not appear to qualify as substantially complete. Is accrued revenue recognized if the earning process is not substantially complete?

Answer: This example draws attention to one of the most challenging questions that accountants face in creating a fair portrait of a business. When should revenue be recognized? The revenue realization principle is established by U.S. GAAP, but practical issues remain. For example, when does an earning process become substantially complete? Here, the simplest way to resolve this accounting issue is to consider the nature of the task to be performed by the Lawndale Company.

Is the job of caring for the horses a single task to be carried out by the company over thirty days or is it thirty distinct tasks to be performed each day over this period of time?

If the work is viewed as one large task like painting a house, then the earning process here is only one-sixth of the way finished and not substantially complete. No revenue should be recognized until the remainder of the work has been performed. In that case, the adjusting entry is not warranted.

Conversely, if this assignment is actually thirty separate tasks, then five of them are substantially complete at the end of the year, and revenue of $500 is properly recorded by the previous adjustment. Unfortunately, the distinction is not always clear. Because accounting is conservative, revenue should never be recognized unless evidence predominates that the individual tasks are clearly separate events.

TEST YOURSELF

Question:

The Acme Company paints houses in and around San Antonio, Texas. In December of Year One, the company was hired to paint the outside of a five-story apartment building for $100,000. All money was to be paid when the work was finished. By December 31, Year One, the company had painted the first three floors of the building and recognized accrued revenue of $60,000 ($100,000 × 3/5). Which of the following is not true?

a. The reported net income is overstated in Year One.

b. The reported assets are overstated at the end of Year One.

c. The reported liabilities are overstated at the end of Year One.

d. The reported revenue is overstated in Year One.

Answer:

The correct answer is choice c: The reported liabilities are overstated at the end of Year One.

Explanation:

Through the entry that was made, Acme recognized a receivable and revenue. The revenue increases net income. However, painting this building is a single job that is only 3/5 complete. That is not the same as "substantially complete." Individual floors do not represent separate jobs. Based on accrual accounting, no justification exists for recognizing revenue. The receivable, revenue, and net income are all too high. This job does not impact liabilities, which continue to be reported properly.

2.4   The Revenue Recognition Principle

Question: In practice, how does an accountant determine whether a specific job is substantially complete? Because of the direct impact on net income, this judgment must be critical in financial reporting.

Answer: Accountants spend a lot of time searching for credible evidence as to the true nature of the events they encounter and report. Their goal is to ensure that all information included in financial statements is presented fairly according to U.S. GAAP (or IFRS). The timing of revenue recognition can be a special challenge that requires analysis and expertise.

Is a job substantially complete so that revenue should be recognized or not?

That question can often be difficult to answer. Here is one technique that might be applied in analyzing this particular example. Assume that after five days, Lawndale had to quit feeding the customer's horses for some legitimate reason. Should the company be able to demand and collect $500 for the work done to that point? If so, then those five days are distinct tasks that have been completed.

However, if no money would be due based on working just five days, substantial completion has not been achieved by the services performed to date. Thus, revenue recognition would be inappropriate.

In Adjusting Entry 3 (Figure 5.5), the assumption is made that the daily tasks are separate and that the company could collect for the work accomplished to date. However, this type of judgment can be extremely difficult in the real world. It is often the product of much thought and discussion. The impact on the financial statements can be material, which increases pressure on the accountant. Even with standard rules, painting a fairly presented portrait is not always easy.

Students frequently enroll in a financial accounting course believing that little is required other than learning set rules and then following them mechanically. As will be demonstrated many times in this textbook, nothing ever replaces the need for experienced judgment on the part of the accountant.

2.5   Unearned Revenue

Question: The last adjusting entry to be covered at this time is unearned (or deferred) revenue. Some companies operate in industries where money is received first and then earned gradually over time. Newspaper and magazine businesses, for example, are paid in advance by their subscribers and advertisers. The earning process becomes substantially complete by the subsequent issuance of their products.

*For example, the January 2, 2011, balance sheet of **The Washington Post Company** reported deferred revenues as a liability of over $379 million. The notes to the company's financial statement provided clear information about the accounting process: "Amounts received from customers in advance are deferred as liabilities" or "Revenues from newspaper subscriptions and retail sales are recognized upon the later delivery or publication date."*

*In Journal Entry 13 in Chapter 4, the Lawndale Company reported receiving $3,000 in cash for services to be rendered at a later date. An unearned revenue account was recorded as a liability for that amount and appears in the trial balance in Figure 5.1. **When is an adjusting entry needed in connection with the recognition of previously unearned revenue?***

Answer: As indicated by **The Washington Post Company**, unearned revenue represents a liability recognized when money is received before work is done. After the required service is carried out so that the earning process is substantially complete, an appropriate amount is reclassified from unearned revenue on the balance sheet to revenue on the income statement. For example, in connection with the $3,000 payment collected by Lawndale, assume that all the work necessary to recognize the first $600 was performed by the end of Year Four. Prior to preparing financial statements, an adjusting entry reduces the liability and recognizes the earned revenue.

FIGURE 5.6 Adjusting Entry 4: Money Previously Received Has Now Been Earned

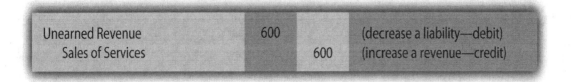

| Unearned Revenue | 600 | | (decrease a liability—debit) |
| Sales of Services | | 600 | (increase a revenue—credit) |

TEST YOURSELF

Question:

The Midlothian Trash Company of Richmond, Virginia, charges customers $100 per month to pick up trash for one month. Money is due on the first day of each month. By the beginning of the current month, the company has received $49,000. If financial statements are made immediately, what reporting is appropriate for the company?

a. Assets increase and liabilities increase

b. Assets increase and revenues increase

c. Expenses increase and revenues increase

d. Expenses increase and liabilities increase

Answer:

The correct answer is choice a: Assets increase and liabilities increase.

Explanation:

The company receives cash, so reported assets are higher. However, the earning process at the first day of the month is not substantially complete, so no revenue can be recognized yet. Instead, an unearned revenue is recorded that increases the company's liabilities. The company owes the service to its customers, or it owes them their money back.

KEY TAKEAWAY

To align reported balances with the rules of accrual accounting, adjusting entries are created as a step just prior to the preparation of financial statements. Prepaid expenses are normally recorded first as assets when paid and then reclassified to expense as time passes to satisfy the matching principle. The mechanics of this process can vary somewhat based on the initial recording of the payment, but the reported figures should be the same regardless of the company's accounting system. Accrued revenue and the corresponding receivable are recognized when the earning process is deemed to be substantially complete even though cash is not yet received. The time at which this benchmark is achieved can depend on whether a single job or a collection of independent tasks is under way. As with many areas of financial reporting, this decision by the accountant often relies heavily on professional judgment rather than absolute rules. Companies occasionally receive money for services or goods before they are provided. In such cases, unearned revenue is recorded as a liability to indicate the obligation to the customer. Over time, as the earning process becomes substantially complete, the unearned revenue is reclassified as revenue.

3. PREPARATION OF FINANCIAL STATEMENTS

LEARNING OBJECTIVES

At the end of this section, students should be able to meet the following objectives:

1. **Prepare an income statement, statement of retained earnings, and balance sheet based on the balances in an adjusted trial balance.**
2. **Explain the purpose and construction of closing entries.**

3.1 Preparing Financial Statements

Question: The accounting process is clearly a series of defined steps that take a multitude of monetary transactions and eventually turn them into fairly presented financial statements. **After all adjusting entries have been recorded in the journal and posted to the appropriate T-accounts in the ledger, what happens next in the accounting process?**

Answer: After the adjusting entries are posted, the accountant should believe that all material misstatements have been removed from the accounts. Thus, they are presented fairly according to U.S. GAAP (or IFRS) and can be used by decision makers. As one final check, an adjusted trial balance is produced for a last, careful review. Assuming that no additional concerns are uncovered, the accountant prepares an income statement, a statement of retained earnings, and a balance sheet.

The basic financial statements are then completed by the production of a statement of cash flows. In contrast to the previous three, this statement does not report ending ledger account balances but rather discloses and organizes all of the changes that took place during the period in the composition of the cash account. As indicated in Chapter 3, cash flows are classified as resulting from operating activities, investing activities, or financing activities.

The reporting process is then finalized by the preparation of explanatory notes that accompany a set of financial statements.

The final trial balance for the Lawndale Company (including the four adjusting entries produced earlier) is presented in Figure 5.7. The original trial balance in Figure 5.1 has been updated by the four adjusting entries that were discussed in this chapter.

Adjusting Entry 1

- Utilities expense increases by $900
- Utilities payable increases by $900

Adjusting Entry 2 (Version 1)

- Rent expense increases by $1,000
- Prepaid rent decreases by $1,000

Adjusting Entry 3

- Accounts receivable increases by $500
- Sales of services increases by $500

Adjusting Entry 4

- Unearned revenue decreases by $600
- Sales of services increases by $600

These changes are entered into Figure 5.1 to bring about the totals presented in Figure 5.7.

FIGURE 5.7 Updated Trial Balance for Lawndale Company—December 31, Year Four (after posting four adjusting entries to Figure 5.1)

Lawndale Company Updated Trial Balance December 31, Year Four		
Account	Debit	Credit
Cash	$41,400	
Accounts Receivable	50,500	
Inventory	65,000	
Prepaid Rent	3,000	
Truck	40,000	
Accounts Payable		$18,000
Utilities Payable		900
Unearned Revenue		2,400
Notes Payable (long-term)		79,000
Capital Stock		49,000
Retained Earnings (beginning of year)		32,000
Dividends Paid	600	
Sales of Merchandise		255,000
Sales of Services		1,100
Cost of Goods Sold	152,000	
Rent Expense	13,000	
Salary Expense	60,300	
Utilities Expense	10,900	
Iinsurance Expense	3,700	
Gain on Sale of Land		3,000
Totals	$440,400	$440,400

After that, each of the final figures is appropriately placed within the first three financial statements. Revenues and expenses appear in the income statement, assets and liabilities in the balance sheet, and so on. The resulting statements for the Lawndale Company are exhibited in Figure 5.8.

FIGURE 5.8 Year Four Financial Statements for Lawndale Company

Lawndale Company
Income Statement
Year Ended December 31, Year Four

Revenues		
Sales of Merchandise	$255,000	
Sales of Services	1,100	$256,100
Expenses		
Cost of Goods Sold	152,000	
Rent Expense	13,000	
Salary Expense	60,300	
Utilities Expense	10,900	
Insurance Expense	3,700	(239,900)
Operarting Income		16,200
Other Gains and Losses		
Gain on Sale of Land		3,000
Net Income		$19,200

Lawndale Company
Statement of Retained Earnings
Year Ended December 31, Year Four

Retained Earnings Balance, January 1, Year Four		$32,000
Net Income, Year Four	$19,200	
Dividends Paid	(600)	18,600
Retained Earnings Balance, December 31, Year Four		$50,600

Lawndale Company
Balance Sheet
December 31, Year Four

Assets		
Current Assets		
Cash	$41,400	
Accounts Receivable	50,500	
Inventory	65,000	
Prepaid Rent	3,000	
Total Current Assets		$159,900
Noncurrent Assets		
Truck		40,000
Total Assets		$199,900
Liabilities and Stockholders' Equity		
Liabilities		
Current Liabilities		
Accounts Payable	$18,000	
Utilities Payable	900	
Unearned Revenue	2,400	
Total Current Liabilities		$21,300
Noncurrent Liabilities		
Notes Payable		79,000
Total Liabilities		$100,300
Stockholders' Equity		
Capital Stock	$49,000	
Retained Earnings	50,600	99,600
Total Liabilities and Stockholders' Equity		$199,900

To keep this initial illustration reasonably simple, no attempt has been made to record all possible accounts or adjusting entries. For example, no accrued expenses have been recognized for either income taxes or interest expense owed in connection with the notes payable. One example of an accrued expense is sufficient in this early coverage because both income taxes and interest expense will be described in depth in a later chapter. Likewise, depreciation expense of noncurrent assets with finite lives (such as the truck shown on the company's trial balance) will be discussed subsequently. However, the creation of financial statements for the Lawndale Company should demonstrate the functioning of the accounting process as well as the basic structure of the income statement, statement of retained earnings, and balance sheet.

Several aspects of this process should be noted:

- The statements are properly identified by name of company, name of statement, and date. The balance sheet is for a particular day (December 31, Year Four) and the other statements cover a period of time (Year ending December 31, Year Four).

- Each account in the trial balance in Figure 5.7 appears within only one statement. Accounts receivable is an asset on the balance sheet. Cost of goods sold is an expense on the income statement. Dividends paid is a reduction shown on the statement of retained earnings. Each account serves one purpose and appears on only one financial statement.

- There is no T-account for net income. Net income is a composition of all revenues, gains, expenses, and losses for the year. The net income figure computed in the income statements is then used in the statement of retained earnings. In the same manner, there is no T-account for the ending retained earnings balance. Ending retained earnings is a composition of the beginning retained earnings balance, net income, and dividends paid. The ending retained earnings balance computed in the statement of retained earnings is then used in the balance sheet.

- The balance sheet does balance. The total of the assets is equal to the total of all liabilities and stockholders' equity (capital stock and retained earnings). Assets must always have a source.

The statement of cash flows for the Lawndale Company cannot be created based solely on the limited information available in this chapter concerning the changes in the cash account. Thus, it has been omitted. Complete coverage of the preparation of a statement of cash flows will be presented in Chapter 17.

3.2   The Purpose of Closing Entries

Question: Analyze, record, adjust, and report—the four basic steps in the accounting process. **Is the work year complete for the accountant after financial statements are prepared?**

closing entries

Entries made to reduce all temporary ledger accounts (revenues, expenses, gains, losses, and dividends paid) to zero at the end of an accounting period so that a new measurement for the subsequent period can begin; the net effect of this process is transferred into the retained earnings account to update the beginning balance to the year-end figure.

Answer: One last mechanical process needs to be mentioned. Whether a business is as big as **Microsoft** or as small as the local convenience store, the final action performed each year by the accountant is the preparation of **closing entries**. Five types of accounts—revenues, expenses, gains, losses, and dividends paid—reflect the various increases and decreases that occur in a company's net assets in the current period. These accounts are often deemed "temporary" because they only include changes for one year at a time. Consequently, the figure reported by **Microsoft** as its revenue for the year ended June 30, 2011, measures only sales during that year. T-accounts for rent expense, insurance expense, and the like reflect just the current decreases in net assets.

In order for the accounting system to start measuring the effects for each new year, these specific T-accounts must all be returned to a zero balance after annual financial statements are produced. Consequently, all of the revenue T-accounts maintained by **Microsoft** show a total at the end of its fiscal year (June 30, 2011) of $69.9 billion but contain a zero balance at the start of the very next day.

- Final credit totals existing in every revenue and gain account are closed out by recording equal and off-setting debits.

- Likewise, ending debit balances for expenses, losses, and dividends paid require a credit entry of the same amount to return each of these T-accounts to zero.

After these accounts are closed at year's end, the resulting single figure is the equivalent of net income reported for the year (revenues and gains less expenses and losses) reduced by any dividends paid. This net effect is recorded in the retained earnings T-account. The closing process effectively moves the balance for every revenue, expense, gain, loss, and dividend paid into retained earnings. In the same manner as journal entries and adjusting entries, closing entries are recorded initially in the journal and then posted to the ledger. As a result, the beginning retained earnings balance for the year is updated to arrive at the ending total reported on the balance sheet.

Assets, liabilities, capital stock, and retained earnings all start out each year with a balance that is the same as the ending figure reported on the previous balance sheet. Those accounts are permanent; they are not designed to report an impact occurring during the current year. In contrast, revenues, expenses, gains, losses, and dividends paid all begin the first day of each year with a zero balance—ready to record the events of this new period.

KEY TAKEAWAY

After all adjustments are prepared and recorded, an adjusted trial balance is created, and those figures are used to produce financial statements. The income statement is prepared first, followed by the statement of retained earnings and then the balance sheet. The statement of cash flows is constructed separately because its figures do not come from ending T-account balances. Net income is determined on the income statement and also reported on the statement of retained earnings. Ending retained earnings is computed there and carried over to provide a year-end figure for the balance sheet. Finally, closing entries are prepared for revenues, expenses, gains, losses, and dividends paid. Through this process, all of these T-accounts are returned to zero balances so that recording for the new year can begin. The various amounts in these temporary accounts are moved to retained earnings. In this way, the beginning retained earnings balance for the year is increased to equal the ending total reported on the company's balance sheet.

Talking with a Real Investing Pro (Continued)

Following is a continuation of our interview with Kevin G. Burns.

Question: Large business organizations such as **PepsiCo** and **IBM** have millions of transactions to analyze, classify, and record so that they can produce financial statements. That has to be a relatively expensive process that produces no revenue for the company. From your experience in analyzing financial statements and investment opportunities, do you think companies should spend more money on their accounting systems or would they be wise to spend less and save their resources?

Kevin Burns: Given the situations of the last decade ranging from the accounting scandals of **Enron** and **WorldCom** to recent troubles in the major investment banks, the credibility of financial statements and financial officers has eroded significantly. My view is that—particularly today—transparency is absolutely paramount and the more detail the better. Along those lines, I think any amounts spent by corporate officials to increase transparency in their financial reporting, and therefore improve investor confidence, is money well spent.

 ## Video Clip

Professor Joe Hoyle talks about the five most important points in Chapter 5.

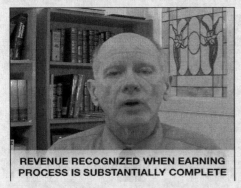

REVENUE RECOGNIZED WHEN EARNING PROCESS IS SUBSTANTIALLY COMPLETE

View the video online at: http://bit.ly/hoyle5-2

4. END-OF-CHAPTER EXERCISES

QUESTIONS

1. What is the purpose of adjusting entries?

2. Name the four general types of adjustments.

3. Give three examples of accrued expenses.

4. If a company's employees earn $2,000 each day, seven days per week, and they are last paid on December 25, what adjusting entry is required at the end of the period?

5. Briefly explain why accountants can find it difficult to determine whether revenue has been earned or not.

6. A company buys $9,000 in supplies on December 11, Year One. On the last day of that year, only $1,000 of these supplies remains with the company. The company's year-end trial balance shows a Supplies account of $9,000. What adjusting entry is needed?

7. A company buys $9,000 in supplies on December 11, Year One. On the last day of that year, only $1,000 of these supplies remains with the company. The company's year-end trial balance shows a Supplies Expense account of $9,000. What adjusting entry is needed?

8. A company owns a building that it rents for $3,000 per month. No payment was received for November or December although company officials do expect payment to be collected. If nothing has yet been recorded, what adjusting entry is needed at the end of the year?

9. Give an example of a business or industry where customers usually pay for the product or service in advance.

10. What type of account is unearned revenue? Why is that classification appropriate?

11. When should a company reclassify unearned revenue to revenue?

12. How often does a company produce a trial balance?

13. In preparing financial statements, what accounts are reported on the income statement, and what accounts are reported on the balance sheet?

14. Why do accountants prepare closing entries?

15. Into which account are revenues and expenses closed?

TRUE OR FALSE

1. ____ Determining when to recognize revenue can be difficult for accountants.

2. ____ Only permanent accounts are closed at the end of the financial accounting process each year.

3. ____ According to U.S. GAAP, revenue cannot be recorded until cash is collected.

4. ____ Some changes to account balances occur because of the passage of time.

5. ____ Accounting is a profession where judgment is rarely needed because so many rules exist that must be followed.

6. ____ Assets, liabilities and stockholders' equity accounts will all start each new accounting period with the same balance they had at the end of the previous period.

7. ____ An accrued revenue is one that is earned gradually over time.

8. ____ Companies have some discretion in how and when they record accruals such as rent expense or interest expense.

9. ____ The purpose of adjusting entries is to reduce the balance in temporary accounts to zero at the end of the reporting cycle.

10. ____ Only one trial balance is prepared during each separate accounting period.

11. ____ Employees for the Saginaw Corporation earn a salary of $8,000 per day, an amount that the accounting system recognizes automatically at the end of each day. If no salary is paid for the last nine days of the year, an adjusting entry is required before financial statements can be prepared.

12. ____ In producing financial statements for the Night Corporation, rent expense is accidentally reported as an asset rather than an expense. As a result, reported net income will be overstated for that period.

13. ____ In producing financial statements for the Day Corporation, rent expense is accidentally reported as an asset rather than an expense. As a result, the balance sheet will not balance.

14. ____ A company owes $9,000 in interest on a note payable at the end of the current year. The accountant accidentally overlooks that information and no adjusting entry is made. As a result, the balance sheet will not balance.

15. ____ A company owes $9,000 in interest on a note payable at the end of the current year. The accountant accidentally overlooks that information and no adjusting entry is made. As a result, reported net income will be overstated for that period.

MULTIPLE CHOICE

1. Which of the following accounts is closed at the end of the year after financial statements are produced?

    a. Accounts receivable

    b. Accounts payable

    c. Cost of goods sold

    d. Unearned revenue

2. Jenkins Company received $600 from a client in December for work to be performed by Jenkins over the following months. That cash collection was properly recorded at that time. The accountant for Jenkins believes that this work is really three separate jobs. What adjusting entry is recorded by this accountant on December 31 if one of these jobs is substantially completed by that time?

    a. **FIGURE 5.9**

    b. **FIGURE 5.10**

    c. **FIGURE 5.11**

    d. **FIGURE 5.12**

3. Which of the following accounts increases retained earnings when closing entries are prepared?

    a. Dividends

    b. Sales revenue

    c. Loss of sale of land

    d. Rent expense

4. Which of the following is the sequence of the accounting process?

    a. Analyze, Record, Adjust, Report

    b. Record, Report, Adjust, Analyze

    c. Adjust, Report, Record, Analyze

    d. Report, Analyze, Record, Adjust

5. On September 1, Year Three, the LaToya Corporation paid $42,000 for insurance for the next six months. The appropriate journal entry was made at that time. On December 31, LaToya's accountant forgot to make the adjusting entry that was needed. Which of the following is true about the Year Three financial statements?

    a. Assets are understated by $42,000.

    b. Net income is understated by $14,000.

    c. Expenses are overstated by $42,000.

    d. Net income is overstated by $28,000.

6. Starting on December 21, Year One, the Shakespeare Corporation begins to incur an expense of $1,000 per day. On January 21, Year Two, the company makes a payment of $31,000 for the previous thirty-one days. Assume the company failed to make an adjusting entry at December 31, Year One. Which of the following is true for the Year One financial statements?

    a. Net income is understated, and the total of the liabilities is understated.

    b. Net income is overstated, and the total of the liabilities is understated.

    c. Net income is understated, and the total of the liabilities is overstated.

    d. Net income is overstated, and the total of the liabilities is overstated.

7. Starting on December 21, Year One, the Shakespeare Corporation begins to incur an expense of $1,000 per day. On January 21, Year Two, the company makes a payment of $31,000. The company made the proper adjusting entry at December 31. When the payment was eventually made, what account or accounts were debited?

    a. Expense was debited for $31,000.

    b. A liability was debited for $31,000.

    c. Expense was debited for $11,000, and a liability was debited for $20,000.

    d. Expense was debited for $20,000, and a liability was debited for $11,000.

8. Starting on December 21, Year One, the Shakespeare Corporation begins to incur an expense of $1,000 per day. On January 21, Year Two, the company makes a payment of $31,000 for the previous thirty-one days. Assume the company failed to make the proper year-end adjusting entry. However, when payment was made, the journal entry was prepared as if the adjusting entry had been made (the accountant did not realize the adjusting entry was not made). After recording the erroneous journal entry, which of the following is true?

    a. Recorded expense in Year Two is too low.

    b. Recorded expense in Year Two is too high.

    c. Recorded liability balance is now too low.

    d. Recorded liability balance is now too high.

9. The Cone Company has prepared a trial balance that includes the following: accounts receivable—$19,000, inventory—$30,000, cost of goods sold—$72,000, sales revenue—$191,000, prepaid rent—$8,000, salary payable—$12,000, rent expense—$23,000, salary expense—$34,000, and dividends paid—$7,000. What should be reported as net income for the period?

    a. $50,000

    b. $55,000

    c. $62,000

    d. $70,000

10. A company pays $40,000 to rent a building for forty days. After nineteen days, financial statements are to be prepared. If the company originally recorded the $40,000 payment in rent expense, which of the following adjusting entries should be made prior to producing financial statements.

    a. Debit rent expense $19,000, and credit prepaid rent $19,000.

    b. Debit prepaid rent $21,000, and credit rent expense $21,000.

    c. Debit prepaid rent $19,000, and credit rent expense $19,000.

    d. Debit rent expense $21,000, and credit prepaid rent $21,000.

VIDEO PROBLEMS

Professor Joe Hoyle discusses the answers to these two problems at the links that are indicated. After formulating your answers, watch each video to see how Professor Hoyle answers these questions.

1. Your roommate is an English major. The roommate's parents own an ice cream shop in a resort community in Florida. One day, on the way to the local shopping center, your roommate blurts out this question: "My parents write down every penny they get and spend in their business. They are meticulous in their record keeping. However, at the end of each year, they pay money to hire an accountant. If they keep such perfect records every day, why could they possibly need an accountant after they have done all the work?" How would you respond?

View the video online at: http://bit.ly/hoyle5-3

2. Your uncle and two friends started a small office supply store at the beginning of the current year. Your uncle knows that you are taking a financial accounting class and asks you the following question: "We keep very careful records of all our transactions. At the end of the year, we will prepare financial statements to help us file our income taxes. We will also show the statements to the officers at the bank that gave us the loan that got us started. I know that we will need to make some changes in our records before we produce those financial statements, but I do not know what kinds of changes I should be making. Can you give me some suggestions on what kinds of changes I should think about making?" How would you respond?

View the video online at: http://bit.ly/hoyle5-4

PROBLEMS

1. Determine if the following adjusting entries involve the following:

   - Accrued expense (AE)
   - Prepaid expense (PE)
   - Accrued revenue (AR)
   - Unearned revenue (UR)

   a. _____ Atlas Magazine had previously collected $400,000 from its subscribers but has now delivered half of the magazines that were ordered.

   b. _____ Several weeks ago, the Hornsby Company agreed to provide 1,000 units of its product to Michaels Inc. and has now substantially completed that agreement with payment to be received in thirty days.

   c. _____ Nancy and Sons owes its employees $30,000 for work done over the past two weeks with payment to be made within the next ten days.

   d. _____ Replay Inc. advertised on television Channel 44 during the past month but has not yet made an entry to record the event because no payment has been made.

   e. _____ Four months ago, the Centurion Company paid Reliable Insurance Company $54,000 for insurance for the subsequent twelve months.

   f. _____ Four months ago, Reliable Insurance Company received a payment of $54,000 for insurance for the subsequent twelve months from Centurion Company.

2. For each of the following adjusting entries, describe what has probably taken place that necessitated these entries.

   a. **FIGURE 5.13**

   b. **FIGURE 5.14**

   c. **FIGURE 5.15**

d. **FIGURE 5.16**

e. **FIGURE 5.17**

f. **FIGURE 5.18**

3. For each of the following transactions of the Marlin Corporation determine if an adjusting entry is now needed. If an adjustment is required, provide that entry. Assume each journal entry was made properly.

   a. At the beginning of the month, Marlin agreed to perform services for the subsequent three months for Catsui Corporation for $30,000 per month. Catsui paid Marlin all $90,000 in advance. One month has now passed. Each month is viewed as an independent job.

   b. Marlin pays its employees every two weeks. At the end of the month, Marlin owes its employees $480,000, but will not pay them until the following week.

   c. Marlin paid $300,000 for rent at the beginning of the month by debiting prepaid rent and crediting cash. The $300,000 covered six months of occupancy, but only one month has passed.

   d. At the beginning of the month, Marlin agreed to perform services for Ryland Company for $16,000 per month for the next six months. Ryland has not yet paid any cash to Marlin, and no part of the work is yet viewed as being substantially complete.

4. Keating Inc. rents its headquarters from Starling Enterprises for $10,000 per month. On September 1, 20XX, Keating pays Starling $60,000 for six months worth of rent.

   a. Record the entry that Keating Inc. would make on September 1 when the payment is made to Starling.

   b. Record the entry that Starling Enterprises would make on September 1 when they receive the rent payment from Keating.

   c. Record the adjusting entry that Keating should make on December 31, when the company begins to prepare its annual financial statements.

   d. Record the adjusting entry that Starling should make on December 31, when the company begins to prepare its annual financial statements.

5. The accountant for the Osgood Company is preparing to produce financial statements for December 31, Year One, and the year then ended. The accountant has uncovered several interesting figures within the company's trial balance at the end of the year:

FIGURE 5.19 Financial Figures Reported by the Osgood Company

	Debit	Credit
Interest expense	16,000	
Interest payable	3,000	
Prepaid insurance	51,000	
Rent expense	56,000	
Revenue		411,000
Supplies	14,000	

Other information:

1. The company collected $32,000 from a customer during the early part of November. The amount was recorded as revenue at that time although very little of the work has yet to be accomplished.

2. The company paid $36,000 for nine months of rent on a building on January 1, Year One, and then paid $20,000 on October 1, Year One, for five additional months.

3. A count of all supplies at the end of the year showed $2,000 on hand.

4. An interest payment was made at the end of December. Although no previous recognition had been made of this amount, the accountant debited interest payable.

5. On January 1, Year One, the company paid $24,000 for insurance coverage for the following six months. On July 1, Year One, the company paid another $27,000 for an additional nine months of coverage.

6. The company did work for a customer throughout December and finished on December 30. Because it was so late in the year, no journal entry was recorded, and no part of the $17,000 payment has been received.

   Required:

   A. Prepare any necessary entries as of December 31, Year One.

   B. Provide the appropriate account balances for each account impacted by these adjusting entries.

6. The Warsaw Corporation began business operations on December 1, Year One. The company had the following transactions during the time when it was starting:

   1. An employee was hired on December 1 for $4,000 per month with the first payment to be made on January 1.

   2. The company made an $18,000 payment on December 1 to rent a building for the following six months.

   3. Supplies were bought on account for $10,000 on December 1. Supplies are counted at the end of the year and $3,600 is still on hand.

   4. The company receives $9,000 for a service that it had expected to provide immediately. However, a problem arises because of a series of delays and the parties agree that the service will be performed on January 9.

   5. A job was completed near the end of the year, and the customer will pay Warsaw all $8,000 early in the following year. Because of the late date, no entry was made at that time.

      Required:

      A. Prepare the proper journal entries for each of these transactions as well as the year-end adjustment (if needed) for each.

7. The Rohrbach Company has the following trial balance at the end of Year Four before adjusting entries are prepared. During the year, all cash transactions were recorded, but no other journal entries were made.

FIGURE 5.20 Rohrbach Company Unadjusted Trial Balance, December 31, Year Four

Account	Debit	Credit
Accounts payable		$ 33,400
Accounts receivable	$ 79,000	
Capital stock		90,000
Cash	41,000	
Cost of goods sold	180,000	
Dividends paid	20,000	
Insurance expense	7,400	
Inventory	98,000	
Land	320,000	
Notes payable		130,000
Prepaid rent	10,000	
Retained earnings, January 1, Year Four		200,000
Salary expense	88,000	
Sales revenue		400,000
Utilities expense	10,000	
Totals	$853,400	$853,400

Other Information:

1. Utilities were not paid for or recorded for the months of November and December at a total of $2,000.

2. On January 1, Year Four, insurance for six months was obtained for $2,000 in cash. On July 1, Year Four, insurance for another eighteen months was obtained for $5,400 in cash.

3. On January 1, Year Four, the company paid $2,000 to rent a building for four months. On May 1, Year Four, the company paid another $8,000 to rent the same building for an additional sixteen months.

4. Employees are paid $8,000 for each month with payments seven days after the end of the month.

   Required:

   A. Prepare the needed adjusting entries.

   B. Prepare an updated trial balance.

8. The following trial balance (at the end of Year Three) was produced by an accountant working for the Washburn Company. No adjusting entries have yet been made. During the year, all cash transactions were recorded, but no other journal entries were prepared.

FIGURE 5.21 Washburn Company Unadjusted Trial Balance, December 31, Year Three

Account	Debit	Credit
Accounts payable		$ 27,000
Accounts receivable	$ 65,000	
Capital stock		120,000
Cash	29,000	
Cost of goods sold	232,000	
Dividends paid	14,000	
Insurance expense	10,000	
Inventory	132,000	
Land	270,000	
Notes payable		170,000
Prepaid rent	10,000	
Retained earnings, January 1, Year Three		150,000
Salary expense	110,000	
Sales revenue		450,000
Supplies expense	8,000	
Utilities expense	37,000	
Totals	$917,000	$917,000

Other Information:

1. Income taxes of $9,000 will have to be paid for Year Three early in Year Four.

2. Supplies were bought for $8,000 early in the year, but $3,000 of that amount is still on hand at the end of the year.

3. On January 1, Year Three, insurance for eight months was obtained for $4,000 in cash. On September 1, Year Three, insurance for another fifteen months was obtained for $6,000 in cash.

4. During November, a payment of $5,000 was made for advertising during that month. By accident, the debit was made to utilities expense.

5. On January 1, Year Three, the company paid $2,000 to rent a building for four months. On May 1, Year Three, the company paid another $8,000 to rent the same building for an addition sixteen months.

6. Employees are paid $10,000 for each month with payments two weeks after the end of the month.

   Required:

   A. Prepare the needed adjusting entries.

   B. Prepare an income statement, statement of retained earnings, and a balance sheet for the Washburn Company.

9. Leon Jackson is an entrepreneur who plans to start a Web site design and maintenance business called Webworks. The First National Bank just approved a loan so he is now ready to purchase needed equipment, hire administrative help, and begin designing sites. During June, his first month of business, the following events occur.

   a. Webworks signs a note at the bank and is given $10,000 cash.

   b. Jackson deposits $2,000 of his own money into the company checking account as his capital contribution.

   c. Webworks purchases a new computer and other additional equipment for $3,000 in cash.

   d. Webworks purchases supplies worth $200 on account that should last Webworks two months.

   e. Webworks hires Nancy Po to assist with administrative tasks. She will charge $100 per Web site for her assistance.

   f. Webworks begins working on its first two Web sites, one for Juan Sanchez (a friend of Jackson's dad) and the other for Pauline Smith, a local businessperson.

   g. Webworks completes the site for Mr. Sanchez and sends him a bill for $600.

   h. Webworks completes the site for Ms. Smith and sends her a bill for $450.

   i. Webworks collects $600 in cash from Mr. Sanchez.

j. Webworks pays Nancy Po $100 for her work on Sanchez's Web site.

k. Webworks receives $500 in advance to work on a Web site for a local restaurant. Work on the site will not begin until July.

l. Webworks pays taxes of $200 in cash.

   Required:

   A. Prepare journal entries for the previous events if needed.

   B. Post the journal entries to T-accounts.

   C. Prepare an unadjusted trial balance for Webworks for June.

   D. Prepare adjusting entries for the following events and post them to the proper T-accounts, adding any additional T-accounts as necessary.

m. Webworks owes Nancy Po another $100 for her work on Smith's Web site.

n. The business is being operated in the house owned by Jackson's parents. They let him know that Webworks owes $80 toward the electricity bill for June. Webworks will pay them in July.

o. Webworks only used half of the supplies purchased in (d) above.

   E. Prepare an adjusted trial balance for Webworks for June.

10. Jan Haley owns and operates Haley's Dry Cleaners. The ledger for this company is presented in the next figure with balances as of December 1, Year Two. The following occurred during that month.

   a. On December 1, Haley prepaid rent on her store for December and January for $2,000 in cash.

   b. On December 1, Haley purchased insurance with cash in the amount of $2,400. The coverage will last for six months.

   c. Haley paid $900 of her accounts payable balance.

   d. Haley paid off all of her salaries payable balance.

   e. Haley purchased supplies on account in the amount of $2,400.

   f. Haley paid a salary to her assistant of $1,000 in cash for work done in the first two weeks of December.

   g. Haley dry-cleaned clothes for customers on account in the amount of $8,000.

   h. Haley collected $6,300 of her accounts receivable balance.

   i. Haley paid tax of $750 in cash.

      Required:

      A. Prepare the journal entry for each of these transactions.

      B. Prepare all necessary T-accounts with opening balances for the month of December.

FIGURE 5.22 Opening T-Account Balances for Haley's Dry Cleaners

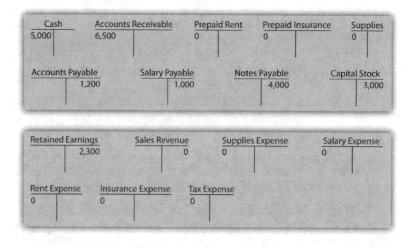

   C. Prepare a trial balance dated December 31, Year Two.

   D. Make the following adjusting entries for the month of December and post them to the T-accounts:

j. Rent expense:

k. Insurance expense:

  l. Haley owes her assistant $1,000 for work done during the last two weeks of December.

  m. An inventory of supplies shows $400 in supplies remaining on December 31.

   E. Prepare an adjusted trial balance dated December 31, Year Two.

   F. Prepare an income statement, statement of retained earnings, and balance sheet.

11. On January 1, Kevin Reynolds, a student at State U, decides to start a business. Kevin has noticed that various student organizations around campus are having more and more need for mass produced copies of programs on CDs. While a lot of students have a CD drive on their computers that can write to CDs, it is a slow process when a high volume of CDs is needed.

  Kevin believes that with a beginning investment in specialty equipment, he can provide a valuable product to the college community and earn some profit. On January 1, Year One, Kevin officially begins "Kevin's CD Kopies."

Part 1

The following occur during January:

  1. Kevin deposits $500 of his own money into the company's checking account as his capital contribution.

  2. As president of the company, Kevin signs a note payable in the amount of $1,000 from Neighborhood Bank. The note is due from the company in one year.

  3. KCDK (Kevin's CD Kopies) purchases a CD duplicator (a piece of equipment), which can copy seven CDs at one time. The cost is $1,300, and he pays cash.

  4. KCDK purchases 500 blank CDs for $150 on account.

  5. KCDK pays $20 cash for flyers that are used as advertising.

  6. KCDK quickly catches on with the student groups on campus. KCDK sells 400 CDs to various groups for $0.80 per CD. KCDK receives cash payment for 300 of the CDs, and the student groups owe for the other 100 CDs.

  7. KCDK pays $100 on its accounts payable.

  8. KCDK receives $40 in advance to copy 50 CDs for a student group. He will not begin work on the project until February.

  9. KCDK incurs $40 in tax expense. The taxes will be paid in February.

   Required:

   A. Prepare journal entries for the previous events as needed.

   B. Post the journal entries to T-accounts.

   C. Prepare an unadjusted trial balance for KCDK for January.

   D. Prepare adjusting entries for the following and post them to the company's T-accounts.

  10. Kevin's roommate, Mark, helps with copying and delivering the CDs. KCDK pays Mark a salary of $50 per month. Mark will get his first check on February 1.

  11. KCDK incurs $10 in interest expense. The interest will be paid with the note at the end of the year.

   E. Prepare an adjusted trial balance for KCDK for January.

   F. Prepare financial statements for KCDK for January.

   G. Prepare closing entries for the month of January.

Part 2

The following occur in February:

  12. Kevin decides to expand outside the college community. On the first day of the month, KCDK pays $20 in advance for advertising in the local newspaper. The advertisements will run during February and March.

  13. The student groups paid for the 100 CDs not paid for in January.

  14. KCDK paid off its remaining accounts payable, salaries payable, taxes payable and interest payable.

  15. KCDK purchases 450 CDs for $135 on account.

  16. KCDK sells 500 CDs during the month for $0.80 each. KCDK receives cash for 450 of them and is owed for the other 50.

  17. KCDK completes and delivers the advanced order of 50 CDs described in number 11.8.

  18. KCDK incurs $80 in tax expense. The taxes will be paid in March.

   Required:

   A. Prepare journal entries for the previous events if needed.

   B. Post the journal entries to the T-accounts.

      C. Prepare an unadjusted trial balance for KCDK for February.

      D. Prepare adjusting entries at the end of February for the following and post them to your T-accounts.

19. Mark continues to earn his salary of $50, and the next payment will be made on March 1.

20. An adjustment is made for advertising in number 11.12.

21. KCDK incurs $10 in interest expense. The interest will be paid with the note.

      E. Prepare an adjusted trial balance for KCDK for February.

      F. Prepare the financial statements for February.

RESEARCH ASSIGNMENT

A company places an ad in a newspaper late in Year Five. Is this an expense or an asset? When unsure, companies often investigate how other companies handle such costs.

Go to http://www.jnj.com/. At the **Johnson & Johnson** Web site, click on "Our Company" at the top right side. Scroll down and under "Company Publications," click on "2010 Annual Report On-Line." Click on "Financial Results" at the top of the next page.

Next, click on "Consolidated Balance Sheets." Under assets, what amount is reported by the company as "prepaid expenses and other receivables?"

Assume the question has been raised whether any amount of advertising is included in the prepaid expense figure reported by **Johnson & Johnson**. Close down the balance sheet page to get back to the "Financial Results" page. Click on "Notes to Consolidated Financial Statements." Scroll to page 47 and find the section for "Advertising." What does the first sentence tell decision makers about the handling of these costs?

CHAPTER 6
Why Should Decision Makers Trust Financial Statements?

 Video Clip

In this video, Professor Joe Hoyle introduces the essential points covered in Chapter 6.

View the video online at: http://bit.ly/hoyle6-1

1. THE NEED FOR THE SECURITIES AND EXCHANGE COMMISSION

LEARNING OBJECTIVES

At the end of this section, students should be able to meet the following objectives:

1. Understand the reasons that reported financial statements might not be presented fairly.
2. Describe the mission of the Securities and Exchange Commission (SEC).
3. Explain the purpose of the EDGAR (Electronic Data Gathering and Retrieval) system.
4. Discuss the times when state laws apply to corporate securities rather than the rules and regulations of the SEC.
5. Explain the relationship of the SEC and the Financial Accounting Standards Board (FASB).

1.1 Financial Reporting and the Need for Trust

Question: The importance of financial statements to any person who is analyzing a business or other organization appears rather obvious. The wide range of information provides a portrait of the reporting entity that reflects both its financial health and potential for future success. However, a degree of skepticism seems only natural when studying such statements because they are prepared by the company's own management, hardly an impartial group.

Decision makers are not naïve. They must harbor some concern about the validity of figures and other data that are self-reported. Company officials operate under pressure to present positive financial results consistently, period after period. What prevents less scrupulous members of management from producing fictitious numbers just to appear especially profitable and financially strong? Why should any investor or creditor be willing to risk money based on financial statements that the reporting organization itself has prepared?

Answer: The possible presence of material misstatements (created either accidentally or on purpose) is a fundamental concern that should occur to every individual who studies a set of financial statements. Throughout history, too many instances have arisen where information prepared by management ultimately proved to be fraudulent causing decision makers to lose fortunes. In fact, the colorful term "cooking the books" reflects the very real possibility of that practice. **Enron**, **WorldCom**, and **Madoff Investment Securities** are just a few examples of such scandals.

Although often viewed as a relatively recent linguistic creation, variations of the term "cooking the books" had already been in use for over one hundred years when Tobias Smollett included the following phrase in his book *The Adventures of Peregrine Pickle*, first published in 1751: "Some falsified printed accounts, artfully cooked up, on purpose to mislead and deceive." Even over 260 years later, those words aptly describe accounting fraud.

The potential for creating misleading financial statements that eventually cause damage to both investors and creditors is not limited to a particular time or place. Greed and human weakness have always rendered the likelihood of a perfect reporting environment virtually impossible. In addition, fraud is never the only cause for concern. Often a company's management is simply overly (or occasionally irrationally) optimistic about future possibilities. That is human nature. Therefore, financial information should never be accepted blindly, especially if monetary risk is involved.

Over the decades, numerous laws have been passed in hopes of creating a system to ensure that all distributed financial statements fairly present the underlying organization they profess to report. Because of the need for economic stability, this is an objective that governments take seriously. Under capitalism, the financial health of the entire economy depends on the ability of worthy businesses to gain external financing for both operations and expansion. Without trust in the reporting process, people simply will not invest so that the raising of large monetary amounts becomes difficult, if not impossible. As has been seen in recent times, hesitancy on the part of investors and creditors restricts the growth of businesses and undermines the strength of the entire economy.

Securities and Exchange Commission (SEC)

Federal government agency holding legal responsibility over the reporting made by companies that issue publicly traded securities in the United States; works to ensure that this entire reporting process functions as intended by the government; has opted to leave development of authoritative accounting principles to FASB, although a change to IFRS produced by the IASB may be required in the future.

In the United States, ultimate responsibility for the availability of complete and reliable information about every organization that issues publicly traded securities[1] lies with the **Securities and Exchange Commission (SEC)**. The SEC is an independent agency within the federal government established by the Securities Exchange Act of 1934. Its mission, as stated at its Web site (http://www.sec.gov), "is to protect investors, maintain fair, orderly, and efficient markets, and facilitate capital formation."

Virtually all U.S. companies of any significant size—as well as many foreign companies—fall under the jurisdiction of the SEC because their securities (either ownership shares or debt instruments such as bonds) are traded publicly within the United States. Financial statements and numerous other formal filings have to be submitted regularly to the SEC by these companies. A Form 10-K, which includes financial statements as well as a substantial amount of additional data, must be submitted each year. A Form 10-Q serves the same purpose each quarter. This information is then made available to the public through a system known as **EDGAR (Electronic Data Gathering and Retrieval)**.[2] All such statements and other released data must conform precisely to the extensive rules and regulations of the SEC.

EDGAR (Electronic Data Gathering and Retrieval)

SEC reporting system requiring companies to file their financial statements and other information electronically to allow current and potential investors access quickly and easily over the Internet.

Companies that do not issue even a minimum amount of securities to the public normally are required to comply with state laws rather than with the SEC and federal laws. Financial statements for such companies, although not as likely to be public information, are often required by financial institutions and other interested parties. For example, a bank might insist that a local convenience store include financial statements as part of a loan application. The form and distribution of that financial information must conform to state laws (often referred to as "blue sky laws").

1.2 The Relationship of the SEC to Official Accounting Standards

*Question: Companies such as **General Electric** or **Starbucks** that issue securities to the public are required to satisfy all applicable federal laws and regulations. The SEC has authority over the amount and nature of the information that must be provided and the actions that can be taken by both the buyer and the seller of the securities. **Does the SEC develop the specific accounting principles to be followed in the production of financial statements that are issued by public companies?***

Answer: Legally, the SEC has the ability to establish accounting rules for all companies under its jurisdiction simply by specifying that certain information must be presented in a particular manner in the public filings that it requires. However, for decades the SEC has opted to leave the development of authoritative accounting principles to the Financial Accounting Standards Board (FASB). As discussed in an earlier chapter, for nearly 40 years FASB has had the primary authority for producing U.S. GAAP. Because FASB is a private (rather than government) organization, this decision has, at times, been controversial. Some view it as an abdication of an important responsibility by the federal government so that the public is at risk. The assumption by the SEC is that the members of FASB can be trusted to study each reporting issue meticulously before arriving at a reasoned resolution.

The SEC does allow certain companies to follow International Financial Reporting Standards (IFRS) so that, in those cases, the same reliance is being placed on the work of the International Accounting Standards Board (IASB) in London. As indicated previously, movement to a single set of global standards over the next few years is constantly under debate. One of the arguments about the possible move by the SEC from U.S. GAAP to IFRS is whether the IASB as it is currently structured can be trusted as much in the future as FASB has been in the past.

At present, FASB produces accounting rules to be applied by all for-profit and not-for-profit organizations in the United States, while state and local governments follow accounting standards produced by a sister organization, the **Governmental Accounting Standards Board (GASB)**. In July, 2009, *FASB Accounting Standards Codification* was released to serve as the single source of authoritative nongovernmental U.S. GAAP. As a result, all the previous individual rules that had been created over several decades were reclassified into a logical framework. According to a FASB news release, "The Codification reorganizes the thousands of U.S. GAAP pronouncements into roughly 90 accounting topics and displays all topics using a consistent structure. It also includes relevant Securities and Exchange Commission (SEC) guidance that follows the same topical structure in separate sections in the Codification."[3]

Groups other than FASB also contribute to accounting standards but in a much less significant fashion. The most important of these is the **Emerging Issues Task Force (EITF)**, which was created in 1984 to assist FASB.[4] The EITF examines new problems when they initially arise in hopes of coming to quick agreement as to an appropriate method of reporting based on existing U.S. GAAP. Thus, the EITF is not forming U.S. GAAP as much as helping to apply it to newly emerging situations. If consensus is achieved (that is, no more than three members object), the conclusions rendered by the EITF are considered to be authoritative until such time—if ever—as FASB provides its own formal guidance. In this way, FASB does not have to issue hasty pronouncements to resolve every unique reporting concern when it first appears.

The SEC itself is not totally absent from the formation of U.S. GAAP. It occasionally issues guidelines to ensure that adequate information is being disclosed to the public through its own rules and interpretive releases. That is especially true in situations where reporting concerns have emerged and adequate official guidance does not exist. The SEC tends to restrict its own power over financial reporting to those areas where U.S. GAAP—for whatever reason—has not yet been well constructed. Assume, for example, that a new type of transaction arises and the EITF is unable to arrive at a consensus resolution. The SEC might specify relevant data to be included in the notes to financial statements to better describe these events or could prohibit certain methods of reporting until FASB has the opportunity to provide a studied ruling.

Governmental Accounting Standards Board (GASB)

Nonprofit organization that holds the authority for establishing accounting standards for state and local government units in the United States; sister organization to FASB.

Emerging Issues Task Force (EITF)

A group formed to assist FASB by examining new accounting issues as they arise in hopes of arriving at quick agreement as to the appropriate method of reporting based on existing U.S. GAAP.

TEST YOURSELF

Question:

The Barone Company is currently dealing with a unique set of transactions that took place recently. The company accountant has studied the appropriate accounting rules in preparing the information to be included in Barone's financial statements. These statements are being issued because the company's stock is publicly traded on a stock exchange. What is the most likely source of the accounting rules followed by the accountant?

a. The Securities and Exchange Commission (SEC)

b. The Financial Accounting Standards Board (FASB)

c. The Governmental Accounting Standards Board (GASB)

d. The Emerging Issues Task Force (EITF)

Answer:

The correct answer is choice b: The Financial Accounting Standards Board (FASB).

Explanation:

U.S. GAAP is produced primarily by FASB. The SEC has ultimate legal authority over the financial reporting of companies that issue securities to the public. However, the actual setting of accounting standards for businesses and other nongovernmental organizations has been left to FASB. The EITF only seeks to apply existing rules to new situations. GASB produces authoritative accounting standards, but only for the financial reporting of states, cities, and other nonfederal governmental units.

KEY TAKEAWAY

The U.S. economy depends on the willingness of investors and creditors to risk conveying their hard-earned financial resources to businesses and other organizations for operating and growth purposes. Financial statements play an essential role in this process by providing information that allows such decisions to be made based on proper analysis. However, accounting scandals periodically remind all parties that fraud can occur in the financial reporting process. In the United States, the Securities and Exchange Commission (SEC) is responsible for the fair distribution of information by those companies that issue publicly traded securities such as capital stock and debt instruments (such as bonds). The EDGAR system makes this information readily available to all interested parties. State laws apply to all other organizations. In hopes of creating a well-developed system of considered accounting principles, the SEC has chosen to allow FASB to set U.S. GAAP, although a movement to IFRS in the future is certainly possible. The SEC typically restricts its direct involvement in accounting to the creation of rules that specify required disclosure of information, but only in situations where current standards are found to be unclear or incomplete.

2. THE ROLE OF THE INDEPENDENT AUDITOR IN FINANCIAL REPORTING

LEARNING OBJECTIVES

At the end of this section, students should be able to meet the following objectives:

1. **Understand the purpose of an independent audit.**
2. **List the two primary components of an independent audit.**
3. **Explain the function of an independent audit firm.**
4. **Describe the steps required to become a Certified Public Accountant (CPA).**
5. **List the various types of services provided by many public accounting firms.**
6. **Discuss the necessity for the creation of the Public Company Accounting Oversight Board (PCAOB) and describe its function.**

2.1 The Need for an Independent Audit of Financial Statements

Question: The SEC allows FASB to set U.S. GAAP. **Does the SEC physically visit each company that issues securities to the public to ensure that periodic financial statements properly follow the rules and guidelines of U.S. GAAP?**

Answer: A detailed examination of the financial statements produced by thousands of publicly traded companies around the world would require a massive work force with an enormous cost. Therefore, this essential role in the financial reporting process has been left by the SEC to auditing (also known as public accounting) firms that operate both inside and outside the United States. Before submitting statements to the SEC and then to the public, reporting companies such as **IBM** and **Wells Fargo** must hire an independent auditing firm to do the following:

- Perform an **audit** (examination) of the company's financial statements
- Provide a report stating whether sufficient supporting evidence was obtained to enable the auditor to provide reasonable assurance that the statements are presented fairly because they contain no material misstatements according to U.S. GAAP

The independent auditor's written report is then attached to the financial statements for all to read. This expert opinion is essential to the integrity of the reporting process because it tells decision makers whether they should feel safe relying on the financial information. Even many companies that are not affected by the rules of the SEC have their statements audited by an independent firm to enhance credibility. For example, a convenience store seeking a bank loan could pay for an audit in hopes of increasing the chances that the application will be approved (or because bank officials have required the audit for the bank's own protection).

Not surprisingly, companies that have independent audits performed on their financial statements are able to get loans at lower interest rates than comparable organizations that do not have such examinations.[5] The audit and the related audit report serve to reduce the lender's risk of loss. Thus, banks and other institutions require a lower rate of interest to compensate for their risk of default.

audit

An examination carried out by an independent CPA of the evidence underlying the information presented in a set of financial statements followed by the issuance of a report as to whether the statements contain material misstatements in accordance with U.S. GAAP; this opinion is intended to provide reasonable assuranace that the statements are fairly presented, which adds credibility to the information provided.

In the United States, **independent auditing firms** can only be operated by individuals who have been formally recognized by a state government as **Certified Public Accountants (CPAs)**.[6] Such firms range in size from massive (**KPMG** employs 137,000 individuals working in 144 countries and generated revenues of approximately $20.6 billion for the year ended September 30, 2010[7]) to organizations comprised of only one or two people.

Obviously, for the financial statements of the biggest organizations (the **ExxonMobils** and **Walmarts** of the world), only a public accounting firm of truly significant size could effectively perform an audit engagement. Consequently, four firms (known collectively as the **Big Four**) have become huge global organizations:

- **Deloitte Touche Tohmatsu**
- **Ernst & Young**
- **KPMG**
- **PricewaterhouseCoopers**

However, thousands of smaller independent CPA firms exist providing numerous services, such as audit, **tax planning and preparation**, and **advisory work** for a wide range of clients. **Ernst & Young** indicates on its Web site (http://www.ey.com) that the following services are provided to its clients with each explained in detail: advisory, assurance, tax, transactions, strategic growth markets, and specialty services.

TEST YOURSELF

Question:

Financial statements have been produced by the management of the Southern Central Corporation. Unfortunately, a significant expense was accidentally recorded as an asset, so the company's net income was overstated by a large amount. Who is most likely to discover this mistake?

a. The board of directors for the company

b. Employees of the Securities and Exchange Commission

c. The company's independent CPA audit firm

d. Major investors in the company's stock

Answer:

The correct answer is choice c: The company's independent CPA audit firm.

Explanation:

The purpose of a financial statement audit performed by an independent CPA firm is to provide reasonable assurance that information is presented fairly according to U.S. Generally Accepted Accounting Principles because no material misstatements are present. While accumulating evidence to support this assertion, the independent auditor should discover that the expense has been improperly capitalized as an asset. Various testing techniques are designed to bring problems such as this to light.

2.2 Standards for a Proper Audit

Question: FASB creates U.S. GAAP, the official standards for the preparation of financial statements. What group sets the examination and reporting rules to be followed by independent auditors?

*The work performed by auditors is not in accordance with accounting principles. Instead, these experts are seeking to determine whether U.S. GAAP was applied properly when financial statements were created. Auditing firms provide a vital service by adding credibility to that reported information. How do independent auditors know what actions should be taken in assessing the data disclosed by a company such as **Xerox** or **Bank of America**?*

Answer: When an audit is performed on the financial statements of any organization that issues securities to the U.S. public, the examination and subsequent reporting is regulated by the **Public Company Accounting Oversight Board (PCAOB)**. The PCAOB was brought into existence by the U.S. Congress through the **Sarbanes-Oxley Act of 2002**, legislation passed in response to a number of massive accounting scandals, including **Enron** and **WorldCom**. Members of Congress apparently felt that the auditing profession had failed to provide adequate protection for decision makers who were relying on published financial information. Consequently, the federal government became more involved.

The PCAOB was established under the oversight and enforcement authority of the SEC. It holds wide-ranging powers that include the creation of official guidelines for the performance of a proper audit. Its vision is stated as follows: "Using innovative and cost-effective tools, the PCAOB aims to improve audit quality, reduce the risks of auditing failures in the U.S. public securities market, and promote public trust in both the financial reporting process and auditing profession."[8]

If an audit is performed on financial statements that are produced by an organization that does not issue securities to the public, the PCAOB holds no authority. For such smaller engagements, the **Auditing Standards Board (ASB)** officially sets the rules for an appropriate audit. The ASB is a technical committee within the **American Institute of Certified Public Accountants (AICPA)**, a national professional organization of CPAs.

A local convenience store, a medical practice, or a law firm (for example) might choose to have an audit on its financial statements. These audits fall under the guidelines provided by the ASB rather than the PCAOB because the organizations do not issue securities that are publicly traded. Thus, the rules for performing an audit on a large company can differ somewhat from those applied to a smaller private one.

2.3   The Role of the SEC

Question: FASB sets U.S. GAAP. The PCAOB (and the ASB) establishes rules for performing an audit. **What function does the SEC actually serve?**

Answer: The goal of the work done by the SEC is summed up in the following statement from its Web site: "The laws and rules that govern the securities industry in the United States derive from a simple and straightforward concept: all investors, whether large institutions or private individuals, should have access to certain basic facts about an investment prior to buying it, and so long as they hold it."[9]

Thus, the SEC strives to make certain that the organizations that fall under its jurisdiction are in total compliance with all laws so that decision makers have ready access to information that is viewed as relevant. It reviews the required filings submitted by each organization to ensure that the rules and regulations are followed. The SEC also has the power to enforce securities laws and punish companies and individuals who break them. For example, if a company fails to disclose a significant transaction or other event that the SEC believes is necessary, all trading of that company's securities can be halted until the matter is resolved. Such regulatory actions can cause a huge financial loss for a business. Thus, compliance is viewed as vital.

In addition, if corporate officials provide false or misleading data, fines and jail time are also possible: "L. Dennis Kozlowski, the former CEO of Tyco International, acquired hundreds of companies between 1996 and 2002 and created a conglomerate that made everything from fire suppression systems to health-care products, with worldwide sales of $40 billion. Now, while serving up to 25 years in jail for misleading investors and stealing money from Tyco, he's watching the breakup of all he built."[10]

Public Company Accounting Oversight Board (PCAOB)

Private sector, nonprofit corporation brought into existence by the U.S. Congress through the Sarbanes-Oxley Act of 2002 to oversee the audits of public companies in hopes of protecting and better serving investors.

Sarbanes-Oxley Act of 2002

Federal securities law passed by the U.S. Congress in response to the **Enron**, **WorldCom**, and other major accounting scandals; it brought about many changes in the audit process and in the relationship between reporting companies and their independent auditors.

Auditing Standards Board (ASB)

Technical body within the AICPA that holds the authority to set the rules for appropriate audits of organizations that do not issue securities to the public (often referred to as privately held organizations).

American Institute of Certified Public Accountants (AICPA)

A national professional organization of CPAs that sets ethical requirements, conducts research, and helps set a high standard for the profession.

3. PERFORMING AN AUDIT

LEARNING OBJECTIVES

At the end of this section, students should be able to meet the following objectives:

1. Describe the goal of an auditor in examining an account balance.
2. List the tests that might be performed in auditing a reported balance such as account receivable.
3. Understand the reason that an independent auditor only provides reasonable assurance and not absolute or perfect assurance.

3.1 Auditing a Reported Balance

*Question: A company creates a set of financial statements for the most recent year. It hires an independent firm of CPAs to audit those statements and prepare a report that will be attached to them. Perhaps this action is required of the company by the SEC or maybe by a local bank or other lender. **What work does an independent auditor perform in examining a set of financial statements?** The audit firm hopes to be able to provide reasonable assurance to decision makers that these statements are presented fairly and, thus, contain no material misstatements according to U.S. GAAP. How is the auditor able to gain sufficient evidence to make that assertion?*

Answer: An independent audit is a complicated activity that often requires scores of experienced CPAs many months to complete. Serious knowledge of the audit process is best achieved by taking upper-level college courses as well as through years of practical experience. However, a general under-standing of the process is important because of its relevance to almost all businesses as well as investors and creditors. For that reason, coverage here will include a limited overview of a financial audit.

The numbers found on a set of financial statements do not appear by magic. For example, if receivables are disclosed on a balance sheet as $12.7 million, a legitimate reason has to exist for reporting that particular figure. In preparing statements, company accountants should document the steps taken to arrive at each balance and the work performed to determine the appropriate method of reporting according to U.S. GAAP. The statements are the representation of the company; thus, the burden of proof is on that organization and its officials. The independent auditors then examine the available evidence to ascertain whether reliance on the reported information should be advised.

As an illustration, assume that a business presents a list of 1,000 customers and claims that the total amount due from them is $12.7 million. This figure is reported as "accounts receivable" under the asset section of the year-end balance sheet. The independent audit firm seeks to accumulate sufficient, competent evidence to substantiate that this reported balance is not materially misstated in accordance with U.S. GAAP.

For these receivables, the auditor carries out a number of possible testing procedures to gain the assurance needed. Such techniques might include the following:

- Add the individual account balances to ensure that the total really is $12.7 million.

- Examine sales documents for a sample of individual customers to determine that the amounts sold to them are equal to the figures listed within the receivable. For example, if the sales document indicates that Mr. A bought goods at a price of $1,544, is that same amount found in the company's receivable balance?

- Examine cash receipts documents for a sample of individual customers to ensure that no unrecorded payments were collected prior to the end of the year. If Mr. A paid cash of $1,544 on December 30, was the corresponding receivable balance reduced by that amount prior to the end of the year?

- Contact a sample of the customers directly to confirm that the balance shown is, indeed, appropriate. "Mr. A: Company records show that you owe $1,544 as of December 31. Is that amount correct?"

Through these and other testing procedures, the auditor hopes to ascertain that $12.7 million is a fairly presented amount for this asset. All other reported balances are also examined in a similar manner during the independent audit. The actual quantity and type of testing varies considerably based on the nature of the account. Auditing $12.7 million in receivables requires different steps than investigating a building bought for that same amount. Not surprisingly, large monetary balances often require especially extensive testing. In addition, certain accounts (such as cash or inventory) where the risk of misstatement is particularly high will draw particular attention from the independent auditors.

If the auditor eventually concludes that sufficient evidence has been obtained to reduce the risk of a material misstatement in the financial statements to an acceptably low level, an audit report can be issued with that opinion. Assuming no problems were encountered, reasonable assurance is provided by the independent auditor that the statements are presented fairly and, thus, contain no material misstatements according to U.S. GAAP.

As mentioned, the independent auditor's report is then attached to the financial statements. Upon reading this opinion, investors and creditors should feel confident relying on the information provided by those statements to make their financial decisions about the reporting organization.

TEST YOURSELF

Question:

The Aberton Corporation has recently produced financial statements for Year One. The CPA firm of Nash and Hill has been hired by the company to perform an independent audit. The firm is concerned because the accounts receivable balance seems unreasonably high and might contain a material misstatement. Members of the audit team are least likely to watch for which of the following?

    a. The accounts receivable contain fake account balances.

    b. The company has failed to record cash amounts collected on its accounts receivable near the end of the year.

    c. Credit sales made in Year Two were erroneously recorded in Year One.

    d. A large collection received on January 2, Year Two, was recorded on December 30, Year One.

Answer:

The correct answer is choice d: A large collection received on January 2, Year Two, was recorded on December 30, Year One.

Explanation:

The auditor suspects that the accounts receivable balance is inflated. Fake accounts cause that problem and might be fraudulently created to increase reported assets and revenues. Failure to record cash collections also inflates the receivable total because reductions were omitted. Adding Year Two sales into Year One causes the figures for the first period to be overstated. However, recording a cash collection in advance reduces the receivable balance prematurely so that it is understated.

3.2 Reasonable Assurance and not Perfect Assurance

Question: One aspect of the audit process seems particularly puzzling. The independent auditor merely provides reasonable assurance. The risk that a material misstatement is included in the accompanying financial statements is only reduced to a low level and not to zero. Why do decision makers who may be risking significant amounts of money not insist on absolute and complete assurance? Because of the potential for financial loss, investors and creditors surely want every possibility of incorrect reporting to be eliminated by the work of the independent auditor. Is reasonable assurance that no material misstatements are present truly adequate for decision makers who must rely on a set of financial statements for information?

Answer: As has been stated, independent auditors provide reasonable assurance but not absolute assurance that financial statements are presented fairly because they contain no material misstatements according to U.S. GAAP. A number of practical reasons exist as to why the level of assurance is limited in this manner.

First, many of the figures found on any set of financial statements are no more than estimations. Auditors do not possess reliable crystal balls that allow them to predict the future. The uncertainty inherent in these estimations immediately eliminates the possibility for absolute assurance. For example, reporting the amount of cash that will be collected from a large group of accounts receivable is simply a carefully considered guess. It is presented according to the rules of U.S. GAAP, but it is still an estimate. No one can provide absolute assurance about any estimation.

Second, organizations often take part in so many transactions during a period (millions for many large companies) that uncovering every potential problem or issue during an audit is impossible. Usually, in analyzing most account balances, the independent auditor only has time to test a sample of the entries and adjustments. Without examining every individual event, absolute assurance is not possible. Even with extreme vigilance, material misstatements can always be missed if less than 100 percent of the transactions are tested.

Third, an independent auditor visits a company for a few weeks or months each year to carry out testing procedures. Company officials who want to hide financial problems are sometimes successful at concealment. Auditors can never be completely certain that they have not been victimized by an elaborate camouflage scheme perpetrated by management. Thus, they are not comfortable providing absolute assurance.

Fourth, informed decision makers should understand that independent auditors can only provide reasonable assurance. Through appropriate testing procedures, risk of a material misstatement is reduced to an acceptably low level but not eliminated entirely for the reasons that have been named. Investors and creditors need to take that limitation into consideration when assessing the financial health and future well being of an organization as presented through a set of financial statements. Although the risk is small, their decisions should factor in the level of uncertainty that is always present.

TEST YOURSELF

Question:

The Osgood Company released its Year One financial statements after an audit by the independent audit firm of Hatley, Joyner, and Bostick. Subsequently, a material misstatement was found in these financial statements. If a proper audit was conducted, which of the following is least likely?

a. A large transaction took place early in Year Two but was reported by the company in Year One.

b. A large estimation was made in Year One that eventually proved to be materially incorrect.

c. A large liability was hidden by the management of the company.

d. The company eventually lost a large lawsuit that it had expected to win.

Answer:

The correct answer is choice a: A large transaction took place early in Year Two but was reported by the company in Year One.

Explanation:

Answers b and d relate to estimates. Auditors seek evidence that each estimate is reasonable, but absolute accuracy is impossible. In a proper audit, estimates can prove materially wrong. Answer c relates to the possibility that management can conceal events from the auditors. Auditors work to make sure they are not fooled, but again, absolute assurance is not possible. Answer a is correct; auditors should examine large transactions to determine proper reporting so that the timing error is found.

KEY TAKEAWAY

Financial statements are the product of company management. Independent auditors then seek to obtain sufficient evidence that these statements are presented fairly because no material misstatements are present according to U.S. GAAP. The auditing firm performs extensive testing of the balances and disclosures that are reported. When the risk of a material misstatement has been reduced to an acceptably low level, reasonable assurance can be provided. Thus, decision makers should feel safe using the information. Absolute assurance is not humanly possible because all statements contain numerous estimations and the auditors do not have time (or the need) to examine each individual transaction. Management can, in some cases, also conceal problems from the auditors. Thus, when examining a set of financial statements, decision makers need to understand that only reasonable assurance of no material misstatements is possible and take that into consideration.

---

4.   THE NEED FOR INTERNAL CONTROL

LEARNING OBJECTIVES

At the end of this section, students should be able to meet the following objectives:

1. **Define internal control.**
2. **Explain a company's need for internal control policies and procedures.**
3. **Describe the effect that a company's internal control has on the work of the independent auditor.**

4.1   Internal Controls Within an Organization

Question: In the previous discussions, the role of the independent auditor was described as the addition of credibility to financial statements. All reported figures, though, are still the responsibility of management. How can a company and its officials make certain that the information displayed in a set of financial statements is fairly presented?

*Businesses like **Barnes & Noble** and **RadioShack** participate in millions of transactions each year in geographically distant store locations as well as through their Web sites. Working with that enormous amount of data, gathered from around the world, must be a daunting technological challenge. Some organizations are able to accumulate and organize such massive quantities of information with few—if any—problems; others seem to be overwhelmed by the task. **How do companies ensure that their own information is free of material misstatements?***

Answer: The human body is made up of numerous systems that perform specific tasks, such as breathing air, circulating blood, and digesting food. Each system serves its own particular purpose that contributes to the good of the body as a whole. Organizations operate in much the same manner. Numerous systems are designed and set in place by management to carry out essential functions, such as paying employees, collecting cash from customers, managing inventory levels, and monitoring receivable balances. Within each system, individuals are charged with performing specific tasks, often in a preordained sequence. For example, a cash payment received in the mail from a customer should be handled in a set way every time that it occurs to ensure that the money is properly recorded and protected from theft.

To be efficient and effective, these systems must be carefully designed and maintained. They need to keep company assets secure and do so at a minimum cost. In addition, appropriate record keeping is a required aspect of virtually every system. For example, if the payroll system is designed properly, employees are paid when their salaries come due, and adequate documentation is maintained of the amounts distributed. The entire function is performed according to guidelines carefully established by company officials.

Well-designed systems generate information with fewer errors, which reduces the threat of material misstatements. However, simply having systems in place—even if they are properly designed and constructed—is not sufficient to guarantee both the effectiveness of the required actions and the reliability of the collected data.

Thus, extra procedures should be built into each system by management to help ensure that every operation is performed as intended and the resulting financial information is reliable. All the redundancies added to a system to make certain that it functions properly are known collectively as **internal control**. For example, a rule requiring two designated employees to sign any check for over $5,000 (or some other predetermined amount) is part of a company's internal control. There is no inherent necessity for having a second signature; it is an added safeguard included solely to minimize the chance of theft or error. All actions like this comprise a company's internal control.

Internal control policies and procedures can be found throughout the various systems of every company.

- One employee counts cash and a second verifies the figure.
- One employee requests the purchase of an asset and a second authorizes the request.

Internal control is made up of all the added procedures that are performed so that each system operates as intended. Systems cannot be considered well designed without the inclusion of adequate internal control. Management is responsible for the development of effective systems but also for all internal control rules and requirements created to ensure that these systems accomplish their stated objectives.

internal control

A group of policies and procedures within the accounting and other systems of a company to provide reasonable assurance that they are operating efficiently and effectively as intended by management.

4.2   Internal Control and the Independent Auditor

*Question: If a company creates and maintains good operating systems with appropriate internal control, the financial information that is produced is less likely to contain material misstatements. In performing an audit, is the work of the independent CPA affected by the company's internal control? **Does the quality of internal control policies and procedures impact the amount and type of audit testing that is performed?***

Answer: As one of the preliminary steps in an audit examination, the CPA gains an understanding of the internal control procedures included within each of these systems that relates to reported financial accounts and balances.[11] The auditor then makes an evaluation of the effectiveness of those policies and procedures. In cases where internal control is both well designed and appears to be functioning as intended, a reduction is possible in the amount of audit testing that is needed. There is less risk involved; the likelihood of a material misstatement is reduced by the company's own internal control.

To illustrate, assume that a company claims to hold accounts receivable totaling $12.7 million. The auditor plans to confirm 100 of the individual balances directly with the customers to substantiate the separate amounts listed in the accounting records. A letter will be written and mailed to each of these individuals asking whether the specified balance is correct. A stamped return envelope is included for the response.

This confirmation process is quite common in auditing financial statements. However, although effective, it is slow and expensive. During the year, assume that the reporting company consistently applied several internal control procedures within those systems that maintain the receivables balances. These controls are evaluated by the independent CPA and judged to be excellent. As a result of this assessment, the auditor might opt to confirm only 30 or 40 individual accounts rather than the 100 that had originally been planned. Because of the quality of internal control in the receivable area, the risk of a material misstatement is already low. Less audit testing is necessary. Both time and money are saved.

Thus, at the beginning of an independent audit, the design of the reporting company's internal control and the effectiveness of its procedures are assessed. Only then does the auditor determine the amount of evidence needed to substantiate that each account balance is presented fairly because no material misstatements are included according to U.S. GAAP.

TEST YOURSELF

Question:

Tomlinson and Partners is a local CPA firm that is in the process of auditing the financial statements of Agnew Corporation. Agnew reports both inventory and accounts receivable, and these accounts have approximately the same monetary balances. However, in doing the audit, the independent CPAs spent over twice as much time in testing inventory. Which of the following is the most likely reason for this allocation of effort?

a. Internal policies for handling accounts receivable are poorly designed.

b. The individuals within the company who monitor accounts receivable do not appear to follow appropriate guidelines.

c. Procedures have been established by management for monitoring the company's inventory, but they appear to be flawed.

d. Employees who maintain the inventory being held by the company are well trained.

Answer:

The correct answer is choice c: Procedures have been established by management for monitoring the company's inventory, but they appear to be flawed.

Explanation:

Here the auditors do more testing of inventory than accounts receivable. Several possible reasons exist. Internal control for inventory might be weaker than that for receivables. Thus, material misstatements are more likely present in inventory. To compensate, added audit testing is needed. In a and b, internal control is poor for the receivables rather than inventory. Answer d indicates that internal control over inventory is actually good. Only c has internal control for inventory as relatively weak.

KEY TAKEAWAY

All companies operate by means of numerous systems that carry out designated tasks, such as the collection of cash and the payment of purchases. These systems need to be well designed and function as intended to protect company assets and reduce the chance of material misstatements in the financial records. Additional policies and procedures are included at important junctures in these systems to ensure that they operate appropriately. All such safeguards make up the company's internal control system. The independent auditor evaluates the quality of the internal control that is found in the various systems. If the risk of material misstatement has been reduced as a result of the internal control in a particular system, less audit testing is required.

5. THE PURPOSE AND CONTENT OF AN INDEPENDENT AUDITOR'S REPORT

LEARNING OBJECTIVES

At the end of this section, students should be able to meet the following objectives:

1. Describe the purpose of the independent auditor's report.
2. Identify the intended beneficiaries of an independent auditor's report.
3. Discuss the contents of the introductory, scope, and opinion paragraphs in an independent auditor's report.
4. List problems that might require a change in the contents of an independent auditor's report.

5.1 The Structure of an Independent Auditor's Report

Question: At the conclusion of an audit, a report is issued by the CPA that will be attached to the financial statements for all to read. Much of this report is boilerplate: the words are virtually identical from one company to the next. **What information is conveyed by an independent auditor, and what should a decision maker look for when studying an audit report?**

Answer: The audit report accompanying the 2009 and 2010 financial statements for **The Procter & Gamble Company** is shown next.

> *To the Board of Directors and Shareholders of The Procter & Gamble Company*
>
> *We have audited the accompanying Consolidated Balance Sheets of The Procter & Gamble Company and subsidiaries (the "Company") as of June 30, 2010 and 2009, and the related Consolidated Statements of Earnings, Shareholders' Equity, and Cash Flows for each of the three years in the period ended June 30, 2010. These financial statements are the responsibility of the Company's management. Our responsibility is to express an opinion on these financial statements based on our audits.*
>
> *We conducted our audits in the accordance with the standards of the Public Company Accounting Oversight Board (United States). Those standards require that we plan and perform the audit to obtain reasonable assurance about whether the financial statements are free of material misstatements. An audit includes examining, on a test basis, evidence supporting the amounts and disclosures in the financial statements. An audit also includes assessing the accounting principles used and significant estimates made by management, as well as evaluating the overall financial statement presentation. We believe that our audits provide a reasonable basis for our opinion.*
>
> *In our opinion, such Consolidated Financial Statements present fairly, in all material respects, the financial position of the Company at June 30, 2010 and 2009, and the results of its operations and cash flows for each of the three years in the period ended June 30, 2010, in conformity with accounting principles generally accepted in the United States of America.*
>
> *We have also audited, in accordance with the standards of the Public Company Accounting Oversight Board (United States), the Company's internal control over financial reporting as of June 30, 2010, based on the criteria established in Internal Control—Integrated Framework issued by the Committee of Sponsoring Organizations of the Treadway Commission and our report dated August 13, 2010 expressed an unqualified opinion on the Company's internal control over financial reporting.*
>
> *Deloitte & Touche LLP*
>
> *Cincinnati, Ohio*
>
> *August 13, 2010*

To understand the role of the independent audit within the financial reporting process, a considerable amount of information should be noted in the **audit report** attached to the financial statements issued by **Procter & Gamble**.

1. The report is addressed to the board of directors (elected by the shareholders) and the shareholders. An audit is not performed for the direct benefit of the reporting company or its management but rather for any person or group studying the financial statements for decision-making purposes. The salutation stresses that external users (rather than the company itself) are the primary beneficiaries of the work carried out by the independent auditor.

    Interestingly, independent auditors are paid by the reporting company. The concern is raised periodically as to whether an auditor can remain properly independent of the organization that is providing payment for the services rendered. However, audit examinations can be quite expensive and no better method of remuneration has yet been devised.

2. To avoid any potential misunderstanding, the first (introductory) paragraph identifies the specific financial statements to which the report relates. In addition, both the responsibility of the management for those financial statements and the responsibility of the independent auditor for providing an opinion on those statements are clearly delineated. The statements are not created by the auditor; that is the job of management. The auditor examines the financial statements so that an expert opinion can be rendered.

3. The second (scope) paragraph provides information to explain the audit work. One key sentence in this paragraph is the second. It spells out the purpose of the audit by referring to the standards created by the PCAOB: "Those standards require that we plan and perform the audit to obtain reasonable assurance about whether the financial statements are free of material misstatements." This sentence clearly sets out the goal of an audit engagement and the level of assurance given by the auditor. No reader should expect absolute assurance.

    The remainder of the second paragraph describes in general terms the steps taken by the auditor, such as:

    - Examine evidence on a test basis to support reported amounts and disclosures.
    - Assess the accounting principles that were applied.
    - Assess significant estimations used in creating the statements.
    - Evaluate overall presentation.

4. The third (opinion) paragraph provides the auditor's opinion of the financial statements. In this illustration, an **unqualified opinion** is issued meaning that no problems worthy of note were discovered. The auditor provides the reader with reasonable assurance: "In our opinion, such consolidated financial statements present fairly, in all material respects…in conformity with accounting principles generally accepted in the United States of America." Through this sentence, the independent auditor is adding credibility to the financial statements. The auditor believes readers can rely on these statements in making their financial decisions.

5. The fourth (explanatory) paragraph provides an additional opinion by the auditor, this time in connection with the company's internal control. Such an assessment is required when an audit is performed on a company that is subject to the rules of the PCAOB. Not only is the auditor asserting that the financial statements are presented fairly in conformity with U.S. GAAP (paragraph 3) but also gives an unqualified opinion on the company's internal control over its financial reporting (paragraph 4). This additional assurance provides the reader with another reason to place reliance on the accompanying financial statements.

5.2   Qualified Audit Opinions

*Question: The audit report presented for **Procter & Gamble** is an unqualified opinion. The independent auditor is providing reasonable assurance to decision makers that the company's financial statements are presented fairly, in all material respects, in conformity with U.S. GAAP. **What can cause an independent auditor to issue an audit report that is less than an unqualified opinion and how is that report physically different?***

Answer: An independent auditor renders an opinion that is not unqualified in two general situations:

- Lack of evidence. The auditor was not able to obtain sufficient evidence during the audit to justify an unqualified opinion. Perhaps the amount reported for a building or a liability could simply not be substantiated to the auditor's satisfaction. The balance might well be fairly presented

---

audit report

Formal written opinion issued by an independent auditor to communicate findings at the conclusion of an audit as to indicate whether a specific set of financial statements contains any material misstatements according to U.S. GAAP; if not, the statements are viewed as fairly presented.

unqualified opinion

An audit opinion informing the reader that attached financial statements are presented fairly, in all material respects, in accordance with U.S. GAAP; thus, the auditor is providing reasonable assurance that the statements contain no material misstatements according to U.S. GAAP and can be relied on by the reader in making financial decisions.

according to U.S. GAAP but evidence was not available to allow the auditor to make that assertion with reasonable assurance.

- Presence of a material misstatement. The auditor discovered the existence of a material misstatement in the financial statements, a balance or disclosure that does not conform to U.S. GAAP. Because of the potential damage to the credibility of the financial statements, reporting companies usually make any adjustments necessary to eliminate such misstatements. If not, though, the auditor must clearly warn readers of the reporting problems.

The physical changes made in the report depend on the type of problem that is involved and its magnitude. The key method of warning is that a new paragraph is added between the scope and the opinion paragraphs to describe the auditor's concern. Decision makers often scan the audit report solely to see if such a paragraph is contained. If present, a careful reading of its contents (as well as related changes found in the wording of the opinion paragraph) should be made to determine the possible ramifications. Whether evidence was lacking or a material misstatement was uncovered, the auditor is responsible for letting the reader know. The presence of an added paragraph—prior to the opinion paragraph—always draws attention.

KEY TAKEAWAY

Upon completion of an audit, the independent auditor's report is attached to the financial statements. It is provided for the benefit of external decision makers. The financial statements are identified and the second (scope) paragraph provides an explanation of the audit process. If no problems are encountered, the report is said to be unqualified, and the opinion paragraph provides reasonable assurance to readers that the financial statements are presented fairly because no material misstatements are present according to U.S. GAAP. A qualification arises if the auditor is not able to obtain a satisfactory amount of evidence or if a material misstatement is found. Information about any such problem is then inserted into the audit report between the second (scope) paragraph and the third (opinion) paragraph.

Talking with a Real Investing Pro (Continued)

Following is a continuation of our interview with Kevin G. Burns.

Question: An independent audit is extremely expensive for any reporting company. As an investor, is the benefit gained from seeing the independent auditor's report attached to a set of financial statements actually worth the cost that must be incurred by the company?

Kevin Burns: I think the answer to this question is fairly obvious given the recent scandals, especially in the hedge fund world. An independent audit is absolutely critical for a corporation no matter what the expense. It is an exciting time to be in the accounting profession as investors are demanding additional transparency and independent oversight. Market confidence will be even more critical than usual for any business that wants to obtain money by issuing its equity shares and debt instruments. An internal audit would be perceived as self serving and untrustworthy and perception is 90 percent of reality, especially in today's cynical environment. Given the recent meltdown of financial institutions and stock prices, investors have a right to feel cynical and demand even more assurance before risking their money.

Video Clip

Professor Joe Hoyle talks about the five most important points in Chapter 6.

View the video online at: http://bit.ly/hoyle6-2

6. END-OF-CHAPTER EXERCISES

QUESTIONS

1. Why do people and organizations need to have trust in the financial reporting process?
2. What is the Securities and Exchange Commission (SEC)?
3. What types of companies fall under the jurisdiction of the SEC?
4. According to the SEC, who has the responsibility for setting generally accepted accounting principles in the United States (U.S. GAAP)?
5. What is the purpose of the *Accounting Standards Codification*?
6. What is a Form 10-K and a Form 10-Q?
7. Within the SEC, what is the purpose of EDGAR?
8. What role in the setting of financial accounting standards is played by the Emerging Issues Task Force (EITF)?
9. Why does the SEC not examine all the submitted financial statements to ensure their fair presentation?
10. Why must public companies hire an independent auditing firm before they submit their financial statements to the SEC?
11. Why do nonpublic companies often have their financial statements audited?
12. What is a CPA? How does a person become a CPA?
13. What organization regulates and sets the standards for the firms that audit public companies?
14. What legislation established the Public Company Accounting Oversight Board (PCAOB)?
15. What organization sets the standards for the firms that do not audit public companies?
16. An independent auditor examines the financial statements prepared by the management of Simon Corporation. Who is the primary beneficiary of the audit work?
17. An independent auditor examines the financial statements prepared by the management of Garfunkel Corporation. The auditor believes the financial information is fairly presented according to U. S. GAAP. What type of assurance does the auditor provide?
18. Why do auditors not provide absolute assurance that examined financial statements are presented fairly according to U.S. GAAP?
19. What are internal controls?
20. How is an auditor's work affected by the presence and quality of a company's internal controls?
21. What is an unqualified audit opinion?
22. Why might an auditor include an explanatory paragraph in an audit report between the scope paragraph and the opinion paragraph?
23. Under what conditions does an auditor not render an unqualified opinion?

TRUE OR FALSE

1. ____ The Howard Company has exceptionally good internal control. The quality of that internal control has no effect on the work of the company's independent auditor.

2. ____ An accountant becomes a CPA based on federal rules and regulations.

3. ____ A person who works as an accountant for a significant number of years becomes known as a CPA.

4. ____ The SEC is the current accounting standard-setting body in the United States.

5. ____ The inclusion of an added paragraph in an audit report after the scope (second) paragraph indicates that the financial statement contains a material misstatement.

6. ____ The PCAOB oversees the work of CPAs who audit companies that issue publicly traded securities.

7. ____ Nonpublic companies rarely have an audit performed on their financial statements because they do not issue publicly traded securities.

8. ____ The Auditing Standards Board works under FASB to resolve relatively simple issues.

9. ____ The Red Company creates a new type of transaction and is not sure how to apply current U.S. GAAP for its reporting. The EITF might be called on to provide guidance.

10. ____ Janice Hough serves as an investment analyst for a number of wealthy clients. She is likely to make use of EDGAR.

11. ____ The *Accounting Standards Codification* is one portion of U.S. GAAP.

12. ____ Audits are paid for by the creditors and investors of a company that receive the actual benefit of the CPA's work.

13. ____ A CPA firm rarely has more than 100 auditors in its employment.

14. ____ The term "presents fairly" means that the financial information contained in a set of financial statements is correct.

15. ____ FASB is a governmental agency that works under the jurisdiction of the SEC.

MULTIPLE CHOICE

1. Whittington and Company is a CPA firm that audits publicly traded companies in the state of Oregon. Which of the following is true concerning Whittington and Company?

    a. Whittington and Company is regulated by FASB.

    b. Whittington and Company is hired by the companies that the firm audits.

    c. Whittington and Company should follow the auditing standards set forth by the Auditing Standards Board (ASB).

    d. Whittington and Company prepares the financial statements for the companies that the firm audits.

2. Which of the following is **not** true about an audit report?

    a. An extra paragraph inserted after the scope paragraph indicates that the auditor has given something other than an unqualified opinion.

    b. If a material misstatement is discovered in the financial statements, the auditor should not issue an unqualified opinion.

    c. The report is addressed to the company's board of directors and shareholders.

    d. To ensure that the opinion is properly noted, it is provided in the very first sentence of the first paragraph.

3. Which of the following is true about the Financial Accounting Standards Board (FASB)?

    a. FASB sets standards that apply to companies throughout the world.

    b. FASB was created by the EITF to handle smaller issues in a timely manner.

    c. FASB produces accounting standards that apply to virtually all companies in the United States.

    d. FASB was created by the Securities Exchange Act of 1934.

4. Which organization is a governmental entity?

    a. SEC

    b. FASB

    c. EITF

    d. ASB

5. Which of the following is true about the Securities and Exchange Commission (SEC)?

    a. The SEC sets accounting standards in the United States.

    b. The SEC was not given any enforcement powers by the U.S. Congress.

    c. The SEC was charged with ensuring that adequate and fair information is made available about publicly traded companies.

    d. The SEC is an international agency that monitors financial reporting around the world.

6. Which of the following is true about the PCAOB?

    a. It regulates firms that audit companies that issue publicly traded securities.

    b. It sets accounting standards for smaller U.S. companies.

    c. It was created in 1934 during the Great Depression.

    d. Its standards apply to all companies within the United States.

7. An independent auditor provides an unqualified opinion on the financial statements of the O'Neil Corporation. Which of the following statements is true?

    a. The auditor must have followed the standards produced by the Auditing Standards Board (ASB).

    b. The first paragraph of the audit report indicates the auditor's responsibility and the company's responsibility.

    c. The SEC oversees the financial reporting by O'Neil.

    d. An added paragraph before the scope paragraph indicates that the auditor has not provided an unqualified audit opinion.

8. Which of the following is not a reason why an auditor only provides reasonable assurance in an audit report?

    a. Financial statements contain numerous estimations.

    b. The sheer volume of transactions means that the auditor cannot examine every transaction or other event.

    c. U.S. GAAP have only been produced since 2002 and do not cover all possible transactions.

    d. Fraud can be hidden from the independent auditor by the management of the reporting company.

9. Which of the following is not necessary to become a Certified Public Accountant (CPA)?

    a. A specified amount of education

    b. Two years of work with one of the Big Four firms

    c. A passing grade on every part of the CPA Exam

    d. Practical experience

VIDEO PROBLEMS

Professor Joe Hoyle discusses the answers to these two problems at the indicated links. After formulating your answers, watch each video to see how Professor Hoyle answers these questions.

1. Your roommate is an English major. The roommate's parents own a chain of ice cream shops throughout Florida. One day, on the way to a psychology class, your roommate poses this question: "Each year, my parents produce a set of financial statements for their business. The statements look great. Then, after all the work is finished, they go out and hire a CPA who charges them a hefty fee. That seems like such a waste of money. The financial statements have already been prepared before the CPA ever shows up. What are they getting for their money?" How would you respond?

View the video online at: http://bit.ly/hoyle6-3

2. Your uncle and two friends started a small office supply store several years ago. The company has expanded and now has several large locations. Your uncle knows that you are taking a financial accounting class and asks you the following question: "Our growth has been moving forward very nicely. We have an excellent business that is poised to continue getting bigger. Recently, our accountant came to us and indicated that we would need to start following the rules and regulations of the Securities and Exchange Commission. I realize that this can be time consuming and costly. Why do we need to worry about the SEC now when we have not had to do so in the past?" How would you respond?

View the video online at: http://bit.ly/hoyle6-4

PROBLEMS

1. Match the following organizations to their descriptions.

   - _____ FASB
   - _____ PCAOB
   - _____ SEC
   - _____ EITF
   - _____ ASB

   a. Sets auditing standards for auditors of publicly traded companies
   b. Sets U.S. Generally Accepted Accounting Principles
   c. Helps apply U.S. Generally Accepted Accounting Principles to new situations
   d. Sets auditing standards for auditors of private companies
   e. Created by the Securities Exchange Act of 1934 to protect investors

2. In an unqualified audit report, the first three paragraphs are the introductory paragraph, scope paragraph, and opinion paragraph. Describe the purpose of each and list several items included in each.

3. Explain the difference between the work of the PCAOB and the ASB.

4. Explain the difference between the work of the EITF and FASB.

5. Provide a short description of the role that each of the following plays in the financial reporting process.

   - FASB
   - Big Four
   - Unqualified audit opinion
   - EDGAR
   - Internal control

RESEARCH ASSIGNMENTS

1. The role of the CPA in the world of business is often misunderstood. Go to the Web site http://www.thisway2cpa.com. On the left side of the homepage, there are several links including "The Profession," "Education," "Career Tools," and "Exam & Licensure." Click on the link that seems most interesting. Make a list of four things that you learned by exploring the information provided through the chosen link.

2. Assume that you take a job as a summer employee for an investment advisory service. Your boss tells you that you need to learn to use the SEC Web site and EDGAR to locate information about various companies. For example, the boss wants to know whether the inventory held by **PepsiCo** increased or decreased between 2009 and 2010. That information will be found in the Form 10-K, which is the annual report filed by the company with the SEC. To get started, the boss jots down the following steps to find that desired piece of information. Follow the steps and determine the change. The boss also gives one more suggestion: "As you search through the Form 10-K for this company, start to notice all of the other types of information that are readily available to help us understand this company, its financial health and future prospects."

   a. Go to http://www.sec.gov.
   b. Scroll down to "Filings & Forms."
   c. Click on "Search for Company Filings."
   d. Click on "Company or fund name, ticker symbol, CIK (Central Index Key), file number, state, country, or SIC (Standard Industrial Classification)."
   e. Type in "**PepsiCo**" in the "Company Name" box and click on "Find Companies."
   f. On the "Filter Results" line, type "10-K" into the "Filing Type" box and type "20110701" into the "Prior to" box and click on "Search."
   g. The top line for the list of filings should be the 10-K that was filed by the company on 2011-02-18. Click on the "Documents" link for that 10-K.
   h. On the top line is listed the original 10-K filed on that date. Click on the link "d10k.htm."
   i. The original Form 10-K filed by **PepsiCo** for the fiscal year ended December 25, 2010, should appear.
   j. Scroll to page 75 and find the consolidated balance sheet for 2010 and 2009. Determine the amount of inventory reported by **PepsiCo** as of the end of both of these years and the increase or decrease that took place.

ENDNOTES

1. For this introductory textbook, a security will include ownership shares of a company as well as debt instruments such as bonds that can be sold from one party to another. A debt instrument is a promise to pay a stated amount plus a specified rate of interest at a particular point in time.

2. Considerable information on accessing the financial data filed with the SEC can be found at http://www.sec.gov/edgar.shtml. Any student considering a career in financial analysis or the like should visit this site to become familiar with its contents, especially the tutorial, so that the EDGAR system can be used to gain information provided by publicly traded companies.

3. News release by FASB, July 1, 2009.

4. In Chapter 2, http://www.fasb.org was mentioned as an excellent source of information about FASB. One of the tabs available at this Web site discusses the role of the EITF.

5. David W. Blackwell, Thomas R. Noland, and Drew B. Winters, "The Value of Auditor Assurance: Evidence from Loan Pricing," *Journal of Accounting Research*, Spring 1998, 57–70.

6. The rules for becoming a CPA vary by state but usually include a specific amount and level of education as well as a passing grade of at least 75 or above on the four parts of the uniform CPA Exam. Some states also require a defined length of practical experience such as one or two years. Considerable information about the auditing profession and the possibility of becoming a CPA can be found at http://www.thiswaytocpa.com.

7. See http://www.kpmg.com as of August 12, 2011.

8. See http://www.pcaob.org.

9. See http://www.sec.gov.

10. John Kostrzewa, "After the Scandal, a New Tyco," *The Providence Journal*, July 15, 2007, F-1.

11. Some internal controls have nothing to do with a company's financial statement accounts and are not of importance to the work of the independent auditor. For example, a company might establish a review procedure to ensure that only deserving employees receive promotions. This guideline is an important internal control for the operating effectiveness of the company. However, it does not relate to a reported account balance and is not evaluated by the independent auditor.

CHAPTER 7

In Financial Reporting, What Information Is Conveyed about Receivables?

 Video Clip

In this video, Professor Joe Hoyle introduces the essential points covered in Chapter 7.

View the video online at: http://bit.ly/hoyle7-1

1. ACCOUNTS RECEIVABLE AND NET REALIZABLE VALUE

LEARNING OBJECTIVES

At the end of this section, students should be able to meet the following objectives:

1. Understand that accounts receivable are reported at net realizable value.
2. Know that net realizable value is an estimation of the amount of cash to be collected from a particular asset.
3. Appreciate the challenge that uncertainty poses in the reporting of accounts receivable.
4. List the factors to be considered by officials when estimating the net realizable value of of a company's accounts receivable.

1.1 Reporting Accounts Receivable

Question: The goal of financial accounting is to paint a fairly presented portrait that enables decision makers to make a reasonable assessment of an organization's financial health and future prospects. This likeness should be communicated based on a set of generally accepted accounting principles (either U.S. GAAP or IFRS) with no material misstatements included. The success of the conveyance is dependent on the ability of the accountants to prepare financial statements that meet this rigorous standard.

Equally as important, every party analyzing the resulting statements must possess the knowledge necessary to understand the multitude of reported figures and explanations. If appropriate decisions are to result based on this information, both the preparer and the reader need an in-depth knowledge of the reporting standards.

*For example, the asset section of the balance sheet produced by **Dell Inc.** as of January 28, 2011, indicates that the company held "accounts receivable, net" amounting to $6.493 billion. What does this figure reflect? **What information is communicated to decision makers about a company and its accounts receivable when a single number such as $6.493 billion is reported?***

Answer: One of the most satisfying results of mastering the terminology, rules, and principles of financial accounting is the ability to understand the meaning of amounts and disclosures reported about an organization. Such information is presented and analyzed daily in magazines, newspapers, radio, television, and the Internet. As with any language, failure to comprehend elements of the discussion leaves the listener lost and feeling vulnerable. However, with a reasonable amount of study, the informational content begins to make sense and quickly becomes useful in arriving at logical decisions.

In previous chapters, the asset **accounts receivable** was introduced to report monetary amounts owed to a reporting entity by its customers. Individual balances are generated by sales made on credit. Businesses sell on credit, rather than demanding cash, as a way to increase the number of customers and the related revenue. According to U.S. GAAP, the figure presented on a balance sheet for accounts receivable is its **net realizable value**—the amount of cash the company estimates will be collected over time from these accounts.

Consequently, officials for **Dell Inc.** analyzed its accounts receivable as of January 28, 2011, and determined that $6.493 billion was the best guess as to the cash that would be collected. The actual total of receivables was higher than that figure but an estimated amount of doubtful accounts had been subtracted in recognition that a portion of these debts could never be collected. For this reason, the asset is identified on the balance sheet as "accounts receivable, net" or, sometimes, "accounts receivable, net of allowance for doubtful accounts" to explain that future losses have already been anticipated and removed.

accounts receivable

An asset that reports the amounts generated by credit sales that are still owed to an organization by its customers.

net realizable value

The amount of cash that is expected to be generated by an asset after costs necessary to obtain the cash are removed; as related to accounts receivable, it is the amount an organization estimates will ultimately be collected from customers.

TEST YOURSELF

Question:

Hawthorne Corporation operates a local hardware store in Townsville, Louisiana. The company's accountant recently prepared a set of financial statements to help justify a loan that is being sought from a bank. The balance sheet reports net accounts receivable of $27,342. What does that figure reflect?

a. Sales made to customers on account.

b. An estimation of the amount that will be collected from the debts now owed by customers.

c. The historical cost of the goods that were sold to customers who have not yet made payment.

d. The total amount owed by customers as of the balance sheet date.

Answer:

The correct answer is choice b: An estimation of the amount that will be collected from the debts now owed by customers.

Explanation:

According to U.S. GAAP, accounts receivable should be reported at net realizable value, the amount expected to be collected. This approach requires an estimation to be made of the amount of the present balances that will prove to be uncollectible so that the net receivable balance can be established for reporting purposes.

1.2 Lack of Exactness in Reporting Receivables

*Question: As discussed in previous chapters, many of the figures reported in financial accounting cannot be absolutely correct. Although $6.493 billion is the asset balance shown by **Dell**, the cash eventually collected will likely be somewhat higher or lower. **Should the lack of exactness in reporting receivables cause concern for decision makers?***

Answer: No one will ever be able to predict the precise amount of cash to be received from nearly $6.5 billion in accounts receivable. In fact, Note One to **Dell's** financial statements specifically states, "The preparation of financial statements in accordance with GAAP requires the use of management's estimates. These estimates are subjective in nature and involve judgments that affect the reported amounts of assets and liabilities, the disclosure of contingent assets and liabilities at fiscal year-end, and the reported amounts of revenues and expenses during the fiscal year. Actual results could differ from those estimates."

Knowledgeable decision makers understand that a degree of uncertainty exists in reporting all such balances. However, a very specific figure does appear on **Dell's** balance sheet for accounts receivable. By communicating this one amount, company officials are asserting that they believe sufficient evidence is available to provide reasonable assurance that the amount collected will not be a materially different figure.[1]

This is the meaning of any accounts receivable balance presented according to U.S. GAAP. All parties involved should understand what the figure represents. Actual receipts are expected to be so close to $6.493 billion that an interested party can rely on this number in arriving at decisions about the reporting company's financial health and future prospects. Officials believe that the discrepancy between this balance and the cash collected will be so small that the same decisions would have been made even if the exact outcome had been known. In other words, any difference between reported and actual figures will be inconsequential. Once again, though, absolute assurance is not given for the reported amount but merely reasonable assurance.

Clearly, the reporting of receivables moves the coverage of financial accounting into more complicated territory. In the transactions and events analyzed previously, uncertainty was rarely encountered. The financial impact of signing a bank loan or the payment of a salary can be described to the penny except in unusual situations. Here, the normal reporting of accounts receivable introduces the challenge of preparing statements where the ultimate outcome is literally unknown. The very nature of such uncertainty forces the accounting process to address such problems in some logical fashion.

1.3   Determining Net Realizable Value

Question: Inherent uncertainty is associated with the reporting of receivables. No one can know exactly how much cash will be collected. How do company officials obtain sufficient evidence to provide reasonable assurance that the balance is not materially misstated? **How does any business ever anticipate the amount of cash that will be collected from what can be a massive number of accounts receivable?**

Answer: In accounting, reported balances never represent random guesses. Considerable investigation and analysis goes into arriving at financial statement figures. To determine the net realizable value appropriate for accounts receivable, company officials consider the following relevant factors:

- Historical experience of the company in collecting its receivables
- Efficiency of the company's credit verification policy
- Current economic conditions
- Industry averages and trends
- Percentage of overdue accounts at present
- Efficiency of company's collection procedures

Dell Inc. explains this process within the notes to its financial statements by indicating that this estimation "is based on an analysis of historical bad debt experience, current receivables aging, and expected future write-offs, as well as an assessment of specific identifiable customer accounts considered at risk or uncollectible."

Additional information disclosed by **Dell** indicates that the company actually held $6.589 billion in accounts receivable, but—at the date of the balance sheet—$96 million of these accounts were anticipated to be uncollectible. Thus, the amount of cash estimated from the receivables is the reported $6.493 billion net balance ($6.589 billion total less $96 million expected to be uncollectible). Quite obviously, decision makers studying the company will be interested in comparing such data to figures disclosed by **Dell** in previous years as well as the information disseminated by competing organizations such as **Hewlett-Packard** and **Apple**. Just determining whether $96 million in uncollectible accounts is a relatively high or low figure is quite significant in evaluating the efficiency of **Dell's** current operations.

TEST YOURSELF

Question:

Gerwitz Corporation manufactures and sells shoes. At the end of the current year, the company holds $954,850 in accounts receivable and is presently assessing the amount of uncollectible accounts in that total. Which of the following is least likely to be relevant information in making this estimation?

  a. A current recession is taking place in the country.
  b. The company monitors its inventory levels very carefully.
  c. The company only sells to customers who have undergone an extensive credit check.
  d. Of the receivables held on the previous balance sheet date, 3 percent were never collected.

Answer:

The correct answer is choice b: The company monitors its inventory levels very carefully.

Explanation:

Companies study as much relevant information as possible in estimating uncollectible accounts. Economic conditions are considered (such as a recession, which might reduce payments) and previous collection trends. In addition, the methods by which the company extends credit and pushes for payment can impact the amount to be received. Although monitoring inventory levels is important because it can reduce theft and breakage, no information is provided as to the collectability of receivables.

KEY TAKEAWAY

Because of various uncertainties, many of the figures reported in a set of financial statements represent estimations. Therefore, as discussed previously, such figures cannot be exactly accurate. No one can predict the future with such precision. The accountant only holds that reported balances contain no material misstatements. Accounts receivable is shown at its net realizable value, the amount of cash expected to be collected. Losses from bad accounts are anticipated and removed based on historical trends and other relevant information. Thus, the figure reported in the asset section of the balance sheet is lower than the total amount of receivables held by the company on that date.

2. ACCOUNTING FOR UNCOLLECTIBLE ACCOUNTS

LEARNING OBJECTIVES

At the end of this section, students should be able to meet the following objectives:

1. **Understand the reason for reporting a separate allowance account on the balance sheet in connection with accounts receivable.**
2. **Know that bad debt expenses must be anticipated and recorded in the same time period as the related sales revenue to conform to the matching principle.**
3. **Prepare the adjusting entry to reduce accounts receivable to net realizable value and recognize the resulting bad debt expense.**

2.1 The Allowance for Doubtful Accounts

*Question: Based on the information provided by **Dell Inc.**, companies seem to maintain two separate ledger accounts in order to report accounts receivables at net realizable value. One is the sum of all accounts outstanding and the other is an estimation of the amount within the total that will never be collected. Interestingly, the first is a fact and the second is an opinion. The two are then combined to arrive at the net realizable value figure shown on the balance sheet. Is the amount reported for accounts receivable actually the net of the total due from customers less the anticipated doubtful accounts?*

  Answer: Yes, companies do maintain two separate T-accounts for accounts receivables, but that is solely because of the uncertainty involved. If the balance to be collected was known, one account would suffice for reporting purposes. However, that level of certainty is rarely possible.

- An accounts receivable T-account monitors the total due from all of a company's customers.

- A second account (often called the **allowance for doubtful accounts** or the allowance for uncollectible accounts) reflects the estimated amount that will eventually have to be written off as uncollectible.

Whenever a balance sheet is produced, these two accounts are netted to arrive at net realizable value, the figure to be reported for this particular asset.

The allowance for doubtful accounts is an example of a **contra account**, one that always appears with another account but as a direct reduction to lower the reported value. Here, the allowance decreases the receivable balance to its estimated net realizable value. As a contra asset account, debit and credit rules are applied that are opposite of the normal asset rules. Thus, the allowance increases with a credit (creating a decrease in the net receivable balance) and decreases with a debit. The more accounts receivable a company expects to be bad, the larger the allowance. This increase, in turn, reduces the net realizable value shown on the balance sheet.

By establishing two T-accounts, **Dell** can manage a total of $6.589 billion in accounts receivables while setting up a separate allowance balance of $96 million. As a result, the reported figure—as required by U.S. GAAP—is the estimated net realizable value of $6.493 billion.

2.2   Anticipating Bad Debt Expense

Question: Accounts receivable and the offsetting allowance for doubtful accounts are netted with the resulting figure reported as an asset on the balance sheet.[2] **How does the existence of doubtful accounts affect the income statement?** *Sales are made on account, but a portion of the resulting receivables must be reduced because collection is rarely expected to be 100 percent. Does the presence of bad accounts create an expense for the reporting company?*

Answer: Previously, an expense was defined as a measure of decreases in or outflows of net assets (assets minus liabilities) incurred in connection with the generation of revenues. If receivables are recorded that will eventually have to be decreased because they cannot be collected, an expense must be recognized. In financial reporting, terms such as **bad debt expense**, "doubtful accounts expense," or "the provision for uncollectible accounts" are often encountered for that purpose.

The inherent uncertainty as to the amount of cash that will be received affects the physical recording process. How is a reduction reported if the amount will not be known until sometime in the future?

To illustrate, assume that a company makes sales on account to one hundred different customers late in Year One for $1,000 each. The earning process is substantially complete at the time of sale and the amount of cash to be received can be reasonably estimated. According to the revenue realization principle within accrual accounting, the company should immediately recognize the $100,000 revenue generated by these transactions.[3]

FIGURE 7.1   Journal Entry—Year One—Sales Made on Credit

Accounts Receivable	100,000	(increase an asset—debit)
Sales	100,000	(increase a revenue—credit)

Assume further that the company's past history and other relevant information lead officials to estimate that approximately 7 percent of all credit sales will prove to be uncollectible. An expense of $7,000 (7 percent of $100,000) is anticipated because only $93,000 in cash is expected from these receivables rather than the full $100,000 that was recorded.

The specific identity and the actual amount of these bad accounts will probably not be known for many months. No physical evidence exists at the time of sale to indicate which will become worthless (buyers rarely make a purchase and then immediately declare bankruptcy or leave town). For convenience, accountants wait until financial statements are to be produced before making this estimation of net realizable value. The necessary reduction is then recorded by means of an adjusting entry.

In the adjustment, an expense is recognized. This method of presentation has a long history in financial accounting. However, recently FASB has been discussing whether a direct reduction in revenue might not be a more appropriate approach to portray bad debts. Financial accounting rules are under constant scrutiny, which leads to continual evolution.

---

allowance for doubtful accounts

A contra asset account reflecting the amount of accounts receivable that the reporting company estimates will eventually fail to be collected, also referred to as the allowance for uncollectible accounts.

contra account

An offset to a reported account that decreases the total balance to a net amount; in this chapter, the allowance for doubtful accounts reduces reported accounts receivable to the amount expected to be collected.

bad debt expense

Estimated expense from making sales on account to customers who will never pay; because of the matching principle, the expense is recorded in the same period as the sales revenue.

2.3 Bad Debts and the Matching Principle

Question: This company holds $100,000 in accounts receivable but only expects to collect $93,000 based on available evidence. The $7,000 reduction in the asset is an expense. When should the expense be recognized? These sales were made in Year One but the specific identity of the customers who fail to pay and the actual uncollectible amounts will not be determined until Year Two. **Should bad debt expense be recognized in the same year as the sales by relying on an estimate or delayed until the actual results are eventually finalized?** *How is the uncertainty addressed?*

Answer: This situation illustrates how accrual accounting plays such a key role within financial reporting. As discussed previously, the timing of expense recognition according to accrual accounting is based on the matching principle. Where possible, expenses are recorded in the same period as the revenues they helped generate. The guidance is clear. Thus, every company should handle uncollectible accounts in the same manner. The expected expense is the result of making sales to customers who ultimately will never pay. Because the revenue was reported at the time of sale in Year One, the related expense is also recognized in that year. This handling is appropriate according to accrual accounting even though the $7,000 is only an estimated figure.

Therefore, as shown in Figure 7.2, when the company produces financial statements at the end of Year One, an adjusting entry is made to (1) reduce the receivables balance to its net realizable value and (2) recognize the expense in the same period as the related revenue.

FIGURE 7.2 Adjusting Entry—End of Year One—Recognition of Bad Debt Expense for the Period

| Bad Debt Expense | 7,000 | | (increase an expense—debit) |
| Allowance for Doubtful Accounts | | 7,000 | (increase a contra asset—credit) |

After this entry is made and posted to the ledger, the Year One financial statements contain the information shown in Figure 7.3 based on the adjusted T-account balances (assuming for convenience that no other sales were made during the year):

FIGURE 7.3 Year One—Financial Statements

Income Statement (Partial) for Year One	
Revenue	
Sales	$100,000
Operating Expenses	
Bad Debt Expense	7,000
Balance Sheet (Partial) at End of Year One	
Current Assets	
Accounts Receivable	$100,000
Allowance for Doubtful Accounts	7,000
Accounts Receivable, Net	$93,000

From this information, anyone studying these financial statements should understand that an expense estimated at $7,000 was incurred this year because the company made sales of that amount that will never be collected. In addition, year-end accounts receivable total $100,000 but have an anticipated net realizable value of only $93,000. Neither the $7,000 nor the $93,000 figure is expected to be exact but the eventual amounts should not be materially different. With an understanding of financial accounting, the reported information is clear.

Question:

A company's general ledger includes a balance for bad debt expense and another for the allowance for doubtful accounts. Which of the following statements is true?

a. Both bad debt expense and the allowance for doubtful accounts are reported on the income statement.

b. Both bad debt expense and the allowance for doubtful accounts are reported on the balance sheet.

c. Bad debt expense is reported on the income statement; the allowance for doubtful accounts is reported on the balance sheet.

d. Bad debt expense is reported on the balance sheet; the allowance for doubtful accounts is reported on the income statement.

Answer:

The correct answer is choice c: Bad debt expense is reported on the income statement; the allowance for doubtful accounts is reported on the balance sheet.

Explanation:

Bad debt expense is reported on the income statement to show the amount of sales recognized this year that the company estimates will not be collected. The allowance for doubtful accounts is a contra asset account reported on the balance sheet to reduce accounts receivable to their estimated net realizable value.

2.4   The Need for a Separate Allowance Account

*Question: When financial statements are prepared, an expense must be recognized and the receivable balance reduced to net realizable value. However, in the previous adjusting entry, why was the accounts receivable account not directly decreased by $7,000 to the anticipated balance of $93,000? This approach is simpler as well as easier to understand. Why was the $7,000 added to this contra asset account? **In reporting receivables, why does the accountant go to the trouble of creating a separate allowance for reduction purposes?***

Answer: When the company prepares the adjustment in Figure 7.2 at the end of Year One, the actual accounts that will not be collected are unknown. Officials are only guessing that $7,000 will prove worthless. Plus, on the balance sheet date, the company does hold $100,000 in accounts receivable. That figure cannot be reduced directly until the specific identity of the accounts to be written off has been established. Utilizing a separate allowance allows the company to communicate the expected amount of cash while still maintaining a record of all balances in the accounts receivable T-account.

A sale on account and the eventual decision that the cash will never be collected can happen months, if not years, apart. During the interim, bad debts are estimated and recorded on the income statement as an expense and on the balance sheet by means of an allowance account, a contra asset. Through this process, the receivable balance is shown at net realizable value while expenses are recognized in the same period as the sale to correspond with the matching principle. When financial statements are prepared, an estimation of the uncollectible amounts is made and an adjusting entry recorded. Thus, the expense, the allowance account, and the accounts receivable are all presented according to financial accounting standards.

3. THE PROBLEM WITH ESTIMATIONS

3.1 The Write-Off of an Uncollectible Account

Question: The company in the above illustration expects to collect cash from its receivables that will not materially differ from $93,000. The $7,000 bad debt expense is recorded in the same period as the revenue through a Year One adjusting entry.

What happens when an actual account is determined to be uncollectible? For example, assume that on March 13, Year Two, a $1,000 balance is judged to be worthless. The customer dies, declares bankruptcy, disappears, or just refuses to make payment. This $1,000 is not a new expense. A total of $7,000 was already anticipated and recognized in Year One. It is merely the first discovery. **How does the subsequent write-off of an uncollectible receivable affect the various T-account balances?**

Answer: When an account proves to be uncollectible, the receivable T-account is decreased. The $1,000 balance is simply removed. It is not viewed as an asset because it has no future economic benefit. Furthermore, the amount of bad accounts within the receivables is no longer anticipated as $7,000. Because this first worthless receivable has been identified and eliminated, only $6,000 remains in the allowance for doubtful accounts.

In Figure 7.4, the journal entry is shown to write off this account. Throughout the year, this entry is repeated whenever a balance is found to be worthless. No additional expense is recognized. The expense was estimated and recorded in the previous period to comply with accrual accounting and the matching principle.

FIGURE 7.4 Journal Entry during Year Two—Write-Off of Specific Account as Uncollectible

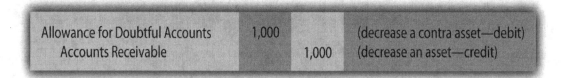

| Allowance for Doubtful Accounts | 1,000 | | (decrease a contra asset—debit) |
| Accounts Receivable | | 1,000 | (decrease an asset—credit) |

Two basic steps in the recording of doubtful accounts are shown here.

1. **Reporting of uncollectible accounts in the year of sale based on estimation.** The amount of bad accounts is estimated whenever financial statements are to be produced. An adjusting entry then recognizes the expense in the same period as the sales revenue. It also increases the allowance for doubtful accounts (to reduce the reported receivable balance to its anticipated net realizable value).

2. **Write-off of an account judged to be uncollectible.** Subsequently, whenever a specific account is deemed to be worthless, the balance is removed from both the accounts receivable and the allowance-for-doubtful-accounts T-accounts. The related expense has been recognized previously and is not affected by the removal of a specific uncollectible account.

These two steps are followed consistently throughout the reporting of sales made on account and the subsequent collection (or write-off) of the balances.

TEST YOURSELF

Question:

Near the end of Year One, a company is beginning to prepare financial statements. Accounts receivable total $320,000, but the net realizable value is only expected to be $290,000. On the last day of the year, the company realizes that a $3,000 receivable has become worthless and must be written off. The debtor had declared bankruptcy and will never be able to pay. What is the impact of this decision?

a. The net amount reported for receivables goes down.

b. The net amount reported for receivables stays the same.

c. The net amount reported for receivables goes up.

d. A company cannot write off an account at the end of the year in this manner.

Answer:

The correct answer is choice b: The net amount reported for receivables stays the same.

Explanation:

The allowance for doubtful accounts is $30,000 ($320,000 total less a net realizable value of $290,000). Writing off a $3,000 account reduces the receivable total from $320,000 to $317,000. In addition, the allowance drops from $30,000 to $27,000. The net balance to be reported remains $290,000 ($317,000 less $27,000). The company still expects to collect $290,000 from its receivables and reports that balance. Writing an account off as uncollectible does not impact the anticipated figure.

3.2   Collecting Accounts Previously Written Off

*Question: An account receivable is judged as a bad debt and an adjusting entry is prepared to remove it from the ledger accounts. What happens then? **After a receivable has been written off as uncollectible, does the company cease in its attempts to collect the amount due from the customer?***

Answer: Organizations always make every possible effort to recover money they are owed. Writing off an account simply means that the chances of collection are deemed to be slim. Efforts to force payment will continue, often with increasingly aggressive techniques. If money is ever received from a written off account, the company first reinstates the account by reversing the earlier entry (Figure 7.5). Then, the cash received is recorded in the normal fashion (Figure 7.6). The two entries shown here are appropriate if the above account is eventually collected from this customer. Some companies combine these entries by simply debiting cash and crediting the allowance. That single entry has the same overall impact as Figure 7.5 and Figure 7.6.

FIGURE 7.5 Journal Entry—Reinstate Account Previously Thought to Be Worthless

| Accounts Receivable | 1,000 | | (increase an asset—debit) |
| Allowance for Doubtful Accounts | | 1,000 | (increase a contra asset—credit) |

FIGURE 7.6 Journal Entry—Collection of Reinstated Account[4]

| Cash | 1,000 | | (increase an asset—debit) |
| Accounts Receivable | | 1,000 | (decrease an asset—credit) |

3.3   Reporting an Incorrect Estimation

Question: In this illustration, at the end of Year One, the company estimated that $7,000 of its accounts receivable will ultimately prove to be uncollectible. However, in Year Two, that figure is likely to be

proven wrong. It is merely a calculated guess. The actual amount might be $6,000 or $8,000 or many oth-er numbers. When the precise figure is known, does a company return to its Year One financial state-ments and adjust them to the correct balance? **Should a company continue reporting an estimated figure for a previous year even after it has been shown to be incorrect?**

Answer: According to U.S. GAAP, if a number in an earlier year is reported based on a reasonable estimation, any subsequent differences with actual amounts are not handled retroactively (by changing the previously released figures). For example, if uncollectible accounts here prove to be $8,000, the company does not adjust the balance reported as the Year One bad debt expense from $7,000 to $8,000. It continues to report $7,000 on the income statement for that period even though that number is now known to be wrong.

There are several practical reasons for the accountant's unwillingness to adjust previously reported estimations unless they were clearly unreasonable or fraudulent:

1. Most decision makers are well aware that many reported figures represent estimates. Discrepancies are expected and should be taken into consideration when making decisions based on numbers presented in a set of financial statements. In analyzing this company and its financial health, educated investors and creditors anticipate that the total of bad accounts will ultimately turn out to be an amount that is not materially different from $7,000 rather than exactly $7,000.

2. Because an extended period of time often exists between issuing statements and determining actual balances, most parties will have already used the original information to make their decisions. Knowing the exact number now does not allow them to undo those prior actions. There is no discernable benefit from having updated figures as long as the original estimate was reasonable.

3. Financial statements contain numerous estimations and nearly all will prove to be inaccurate to some degree. If exactness were required, correcting each of these previously reported figures would become virtually a never-ending task for a company and its accountants. Scores of updated statements might have to be issued before a "final" set of financial figures became available after several years. For example, the exact life of a building might not be known for 50 years or more. Decision makers want information that is usable as soon as possible. Speed in reporting is far more important than absolute precision.

4. At least theoretically, half of the differences between actual and anticipated results should make the reporting company look better and half make it look worse. If so, the corrections needed to rectify all previous estimation errors will tend to offset and have little overall impact on a company's reported income and financial condition.

Thus, no change is made in financial figures that have already been released whenever a reasonable es-timation proves to be wrong. However, differences that arise should be taken into consideration in cre-ating current and subsequent statements. For example, if the Year One bad debts were expected to be 7 percent, but 8 percent actually proved to be uncollectible, the accountant might well choose to use a higher percentage at the end of Year Two to reflect this new knowledge.

3.4 Recording Receivable Transactions in Subsequent Years

Question: To carry the previous illustration one step further, assume that $400,000 in new credit sales are made during Year Two while cash of $330,000 is collected. Uncollectible receivables totaling $10,000 are written off in that year. **What balances appear in the various T-accounts at the end of a subsequent year to reflect sales, collections, and the write-off of uncollectible receivables?**

Answer: Sales and bad debt expense were reported previously for Year One. However, as income statement accounts, both were closed out in order to begin Year Two with zero balances. They are tem-porary accounts. In contrast, accounts receivable and the allowance for doubtful accounts appear on the balance sheet and retain their ending figures going into each subsequent period. They are perman-ent accounts. Thus, these two T-accounts still show $100,000 and $7,000 respectively at the beginning of Year Two.

Assuming that no adjusting entries have yet been recorded, these four accounts hold the balances shown in Figure 7.7 at the end of Year Two. Notice that the bad debt expense account remains at zero until the end-of-year estimation is made and recorded.

FIGURE 7.7 End of Year Two—Sales, Receivables, and Bad Debt Balances

	Sales		
		0	Beginning Balance (Year Two)
		400,000	Credit Sales
		400,000	Ending Balance to Date

Bad Debt Expense	
Beginning Balance (Year Two)	0

Accounts Receivable			
Beginning Balance (Year Two)	100,000		
Credit Sales	400,000	330,000	Cash Collections
		10,000	Accounts Written Off
	500,000	340,000	
Ending Balance to Date	160,000		

Allowance for Doubtful Accounts			
		7,000	Beginning Balance (Year Two)
Accounts Written Off	10,000		
	10,000	7,000	
Ending Balance to Date	3,000		

3.5 Residual Balance in the Allowance for Doubtful Accounts

Question: In the T-accounts in Figure 7.7, the balances represent account totals for Year Two prior to year-end adjusting entries. Why does a debit balance of $3,000 appear in the allowance for doubtful accounts before recording the necessary adjustment for the current year? **When a debit balance is found in the allowance for doubtful accounts, what does this figure signify?**

Answer: When Year One financial statements were produced, $7,000 was estimated as the amount of receivables that would eventually be identified as uncollectible. In Year Two, the actual total written off turned out to be $10,000. The original figure was too low by $3,000. This difference is now reflected by the debit remaining in the allowance account. Until the estimation for the current year is determined and recorded, the balance residing in the allowance account indicates a previous underestimation (an ending debit balance) or overestimation (a credit) of the amount of worthless accounts.[5]

KEY TAKEAWAY

Bad debt expense is estimated and recorded in the period of sale to correspond with the matching principle. Subsequent write-offs of specific accounts do not affect the expense further. Rather, both the asset and the allowance for doubtful accounts are decreased at that time. If a written off account is subsequently collected, the allowance account is increased to reverse the previous impact. Estimation errors are anticipated in financial accounting; perfect predictions are rarely possible. When the amount of uncollectible accounts differs from the original figure recognized, no retroactive adjustment is made to restate earlier figures as long as a reasonable estimate was made. Decisions have already been made by investors and creditors based on the original data and cannot be reversed. These decision makers should have understood that the information they were using could not possibly reflect exact amounts.

4. THE ACTUAL ESTIMATION OF UNCOLLECTIBLE ACCOUNTS

LEARNING OBJECTIVES

At the end of this section, students should be able to meet the following objectives:

1. Estimate and record bad debts when the percentage of sales method is applied.
2. Estimate and record bad debts when the percentage of receivables method is applied.
3. Explain the reason that bad debt expense and the allowance for doubtful accounts normally report different figures.
4. Understand the reason for maintaining a subsidiary ledger.

4.1 Two Methods for Estimating Uncollectible Accounts

Question: The final step in reporting receivables for Year Two is the estimation of the bad accounts incurred during this period. This calculation enables the preparation of the year-end adjusting entry. According to the ledger balances in Figure 7.7, sales on credit for the year were $400,000, remaining accounts receivable amount to $160,000, and a $3,000 debit sits in the allowance for doubtful accounts. No recording has yet been made for the Year Two bad debt expense. **How does the accountant arrive at the estimation of uncollectible accounts each year?**

Answer: Much of financial accounting is quite standardized. However, estimations can be made by any method that is considered logical. After all, it is an estimate. Over the decades, two different approaches have come to predominate when predicting the amount of uncollectible receivables. As long as company officials obtain sufficient evidence to support the reported numbers, either way can be applied.

Percentage of sales method. This approach computes the current period expense by anticipating the percentage of sales (or credit sales) that will eventually fail to be collected. The percentage of sales method is sometimes referred to as an income statement approach because the only number being estimated (bad debt expense) appears on the income statement.

Percentage of receivables method. Here, the proper balance for the allowance for doubtful accounts is determined based on the percentage of ending accounts receivable that are presumed to be uncollectible. This method is identified as a balance sheet approach because the only figure being estimated (the allowance for doubtful accounts) is found on the balance sheet. A common variation applied by many companies is the **aging method**, which first classifies all receivable balances by age and then multiplies each of those individual totals by a different percentage. Normally, a higher rate is used for accounts that are older because they are considered more likely to become uncollectible.

4.2 Applying the Percentage of Sales Method

Question: Assume that this company chooses to use the percentage of sales method. All available evidence is studied by officials who come to believe that 8 percent of the credit sales made during Year Two will prove to be worthless. **In applying the percentage of sales method, what adjusting entry is made at the end of the year so that financial statements can be prepared and fairly presented?**

Answer: According to the ledger account in Figure 7.7, sales of $400,000 were made during Year Two. If uncollectible accounts are expected to be 8 percent of that amount, the expense for the period is $32,000 ($400,000 × 8 percent). Bad debt expense (the figure being estimated) must be raised from its present zero balance to $32,000. Bad debt expense must be reported as $32,000 when the process is completed.

---

percentage of sales method

An income statement approach for estimating uncollectible accounts that computes bad debt expense by multiplying sales (or just credit sales) by the percentage that are not expected to be collected.

percentage of receivables method

A balance sheet approach for estimating uncollectible accounts that computes the allowance for doubtful accounts by multiplying ending accounts receivable by the percentage that are not expected to be collected.

aging method

A variation of the percentage of receivables method where all receivables are first classified by age; the total of each category is then multiplied by an appropriate percentage and summed to determine the allowance balance to be reported.

FIGURE 7.8 Adjusting Entry for Year Two—Uncollectible Accounts Estimated as a Percentage of Sales

Bad Debt Expense	32,000		(increase an expense—debit)
Allowance for Doubtful Accounts		32,000	(increase a contra asset—credit)

The adjustment in Figure 7.8 does increase the expense to the $32,000 figure, the proper percentage of the sales figure. However, prior to adjustment, the allowance account held a residual $3,000 debit balance ($7,000 Year One estimation less $10,000 accounts written off). As can be seen in Figure 7.9, the $32,000 recorded expense for Year Two results in only a $29,000 balance for the allowance for doubtful accounts.

FIGURE 7.9 Resulting T-Accounts, Based on Percentage of Sales Method

Bad Debt Expense

Beginning Balance	0
Expense Adjustment	32,000
Ending Balance	32,000

Allowance for Doubtful Accounts

		7,000	Beginning Balance
Accounts Written Off	10,000	32,000	Expense Adjustment
	10,000	39,000	
		29,000	Ending Balance

After this adjustment, the figures appearing in the financial statements for Year Two are shown in Figure 7.10.

FIGURE 7.10 Uncollectible Accounts Estimated Based on 8 Percent of Sales

Income Statement (Partial) for Year Two	
Revenue	
Sales	$400,000
Operating Expenses	
Bad Debt Expense	32,000
Balance Sheet (Partial) at End of Year Two	
Current Assets	
Accounts Receivable	$160,000
Allowance for Doubtful Accounts	29,000
Accounts Receivable, Net	$131,000

TEST YOURSELF

Question:

The Travers Corporation starts operations in Year One and makes credit sales of $300,000 per year while collecting cash of only $200,000 per year. During each year, $15,000 in accounts are judged to be uncollectible. The company estimates that 8 percent of its credit sales will eventually prove to be worthless. What is reported as the allowance for doubtful accounts on the company's balance sheet at the end of Year Two?

a. $15,000

b. $18,000

c. $24,000

d. $30,000

Answer:

The correct answer is choice b: $18,000.

Explanation:

At the end of Year One, the allowance account will show a $15,000 debit for the accounts written off and a 24,000 credit for the estimated bad debt expense ($300,000 × 8 percent) for a reported total of $9,000. During Year Two, another $15,000 debit is recorded because of the accounts written off and a second $24,000 credit is recorded to recognize the current year's expense. The allowance balance is now $18,000 ($9,000 − $15,000 + $24,000).

4.3 The Difference Between Bad Debt Expense and the Allowance for Doubtful Accounts

Question: Figure 7.10 presents the financial statement figures for this company for Year Two. **How can bad debt expense be reported on the income statement as $32,000, whereas the allowance for doubtful accounts on the balance sheet shows only $29,000?** *Should those two numbers not be identical in every set of financial statements?*

Answer: The difference in these two accounts is caused by the failure of previous estimations to be accurate. In Year One, bad debt expense for this company was reported as $7,000 but accounts with balances totaling $10,000 actually proved to be uncollectible in Year Two. That caused an additional $3,000 reduction in the allowance as can be seen in Figure 7.7. This amount carries through and causes the allowance for doubtful account to be $3,000 lower at the end of Year Two. The reported expense is the estimated amount ($32,000), but the allowance ($29,000) is $3,000 less because of the difference in the actual and expected amounts for Year One.

Students are often concerned because these two reported numbers differ. However, both are merely estimates. The actual amount of worthless accounts is quite likely to be a number entirely different from either $29,000 or $32,000. Therefore, the lingering impact of the $3,000 Year One underestimation should not be an issue as long as company officials believe that neither of the two reported balances is materially misstated.

4.4 Applying the Percentage of Receivables Method

Question: The percentage of receivables method handles the calculation of bad debts a bit differently. Assume that the Year Two adjusting entry has not yet been made so that bad debt expense remains at zero and the allowance for doubtful accounts still holds a $3,000 debit balance as shown in Figure 7.7. Also assume that the company has now chosen to use the percentage of receivables method rather than the percentage of sales method. Officials have looked at all available evidence and come to the conclusion that 15 percent of ending accounts receivable ($160,000 × 15 percent or $24,000) are likely to prove uncollectible. **How does application of the percentage of receivables method affect the recording of doubtful accounts?**

Answer: The percentage of receivables method (or the aging method if that variation is used) views the estimated figure of $24,000 as the proper total for the allowance for doubtful accounts. Thus, the accountant must turn the $3,000 debit balance residing in that contra asset account into the proper $24,000 credit. That change can only be accomplished by recognizing an expense of $27,000 as shown in Figure 7.11. Under the percentage of receivables method, after the adjustment has been recorded, the allowance balance will equal the estimate ($24,000). The bad debt expense is not computed directly; it is the amount needed to arrive at this allowance figure.

FIGURE 7.11 Adjusting Entry for Year Two—Uncollectible Accounts Estimated as a Percentage of Receivables

Bad Debt Expense	27,000		(increase an expense—debit)
Allowance for Doubtful Accounts		27,000	(increase a contra asset—credit)

As shown in Figure 7.12, this entry successfully changes the allowance from a $3,000 debit balance to the desired $24,000 credit. Because bad debt expense had a zero balance prior to this entry, it now reports the $27,000 amount needed to establish the proper allowance.

FIGURE 7.12 Resulting T-Accounts, Based on Percentage of Receivables Method

Allowance for Doubtful Accounts

		7,000	Beginning Balance
Accounts Written Off	10,000	27,000	Expense Adjustment
	10,000	34,000	
		24,000	Ending Balance

Bad Debt Expense

Beginning Balance	0
Expense Adjustment	27,000
Ending Balance	27,000

After this adjusting entry has been posted, the balances appearing in Figure 7.13 appear in the financial statements for Year Two.

FIGURE 7.13 Uncollectible Accounts Estimated Based on 15 Percent of Receivables

Income Statement (Partial) for Year Two	
Revenue	
Sales	$400,000
Operating Expenses	
Bad Debt Expense	27,000
Balance Sheet (Partial) at End of Year Two	
Current Assets	
Accounts Receivable	$160,000
Allowance for Doubtful Accounts	24,000
Accounts Receivable, Net	$136,000

Once again, the reported expense ($27,000) is $3,000 higher than the allowance ($24,000). As before, the difference is the result of the estimation being too low in the prior year. The additional write-offs led to this lower balance in the allowance T-account.

Either approach can be used as long as adequate support is gathered for the numbers reported. They are just two alternatives to arrive at an estimate. However, financial accounting does stress the importance of consistency to help make numbers comparable from year to year. Once a method is selected, it normally must continue to be applied in all subsequent periods.

- Under the percentage of sales method, the expense account is aligned with the volume of sales.
- In applying the percentage of receivables method, the uncollectible portion of ending receivables is determined and reported as the allowance for doubtful accounts.

Regardless of the approach, both bad debt expense and the allowance for doubtful accounts are simply the result of estimating the final outcome of an uncertain event—the collection of accounts receivable.

TEST YOURSELF

Question:

The Yarrow Corporation starts operations in Year One and makes credit sales of $400,000 per year while collecting cash of only $300,000 per year. During each year, $12,000 in accounts are judged to be uncollectible. The company estimates that 10 percent of its ending accounts receivable each year will eventually prove to be worthless. What is reported as bad debt expense on the company's income statement for Year Two?

a. $17,600
b. $20,800
c. $28,800
d. $32,000

Answer:

The correct answer is choice b: $20,800.

Explanation:

In Year One, accounts receivable total $88,000 ($400,000 sales less $300,000 collections and $12,000 accounts written off). The allowance is $8,800 or 10 percent of the total. In Year Two, receivables rise to $176,000 ($88,000 plus $400,000 less $300,000 and $12,000). The allowance holds a debit of $3,200 ($8,800 beginning balance less $12,000 in write-offs). The allowance needs to be $17,600 (10 percent). To turn the $3,200 debit into a $17,600 credit, an expense of $20,800 is recognized.

4.5 The Purpose of a Subsidiary Ledger

*Question: A company such as **Dell Inc.** must have thousands or even hundreds of thousands of separate receivables. The accounts receivable T-account in the ledger maintains the total of all amounts owed to a company but does not indicate the balance due from each individual customer. **How does an accounting system monitor all the specific receivable amounts?** Those balances must be essential information for any organization for billing and collection purposes.*

subsidiary ledger

A group of individual accounts whose sum agrees with (and, therefore, explains) a general ledger account balance.

Answer: As indicated, a ledger account only reflects a single total at the present time. In many cases, as with accounts receivable, the composition of that balance is also essential information. For those T-accounts, the accounting system can be expanded to include a **subsidiary ledger** to maintain data about the various individual components making up the account total.

In the previous illustration, the company reports $160,000 as the total of its accounts receivable at the end of Year Two. A separate subsidiary ledger should also be in place to monitor the amounts owed by each customer (Mr. A, Ms. B, and so on). The general ledger figure is used whenever financial statements are to be produced. The subsidiary ledger allows the company to access individual balances so that appropriate action can be taken when collection is received or if specific receivables grow too large or become overdue.

When a subsidiary ledger is maintained, the accounting system can be programmed so that each entry into the general ledger T-account requires an immediate parallel increase or decrease to the appropriate individual account. Thus, a $75 sale on credit to Mr. A raises the accounts receivable T-account total by that amount while also increasing the balance listed specifically for Mr. A in the subsidiary ledger.

Subsidiary ledgers can be established in connection with any general ledger account where the availability of component information is helpful. Other than accounts receivable, subsidiary ledgers are commonly set up for inventory, equipment, and accounts payable. As might be imagined, large enterprises maintain additional records for virtually every T-account, whereas small companies are likely to limit use to accounts receivable and—possibly—a few other significant balances.

Before computer systems became common, manually keeping the total of thousands of individual accounts in a subsidiary ledger in agreement with the corresponding general ledger T-account balance was an arduous task. Mechanical errors (mathematical problems as well as debit and credit mistakes) tended to abound. However, current electronic systems are typically designed so that the totals reconcile automatically.

KEY TAKEAWAY

Each year, an estimation of uncollectible accounts must be made as a preliminary step in the preparation of financial statements. Some companies use the percentage of sales method, which calculates the reported expense, an amount that is also added to the allowance for doubtful accounts. Other companies use the percentage of receivable method (or a variation known as the aging method). It determines the ending balance for the allowance. Bad debt expense is the amount required to adjust the allowance balance to this ending total. Both methods provide no more than an approximation of net realizable value based on the validity of the numerical percentages that are applied. Because actual and expected uncollectible amounts will differ, the expense and the allowance almost always report different balances. Regardless of the method employed, virtually all companies maintain a subsidiary ledger to provide the individual balances that comprise the total found in the general ledger T-account.

5.   REPORTING FOREIGN CURRENCY BALANCES

LEARNING OBJECTIVES

At the end of this section, students should be able to meet the following objectives:

1. Recognize that transactions denominated in a foreign currency have become extremely common.
2. Understand the necessity of remeasuring the value of foreign currency balances into a company's functional currency prior to the preparation of financial statements.
3. Appreciate the problem that fluctuations in exchange rates cause when foreign currency balances are reported in a set of financial statements.
4. Know which foreign currency balances are reported using a historical exchange rate and which balances are reported using the currency exchange rate in effect on the date of the balance sheet.
5. Understand that gains and losses are reported on a company's income statement when foreign currency balances are remeasured using current exchange rates.

5.1   Reporting Balances Denominated in a Foreign Currency

Question: In today's global economy, many U.S. companies make a sizable portion of their sales internationally. **The Coca-Cola Company,** *for example, generated 69.7 percent of its revenues in 2010 outside of the United States. For* **McDonald's Corporation,** *foreign revenues were 66.4 percent of the reported total.*

In such cases, U.S. dollars might still be the currency received. However, U.S. companies frequently make sales that will be settled in a foreign currency such as the Mexican peso or the Japanese yen. For example, a sale made today might call for the transfer of 20,000 pesos in two months. **What reporting problems are created when a credit sale is denominated in a foreign currency?**

Answer: This situation is a perfect example of why authoritative standards, such as U.S. GAAP, are so important in financial accounting. Foreign currency balances are common in today's world. Although a company will have a functional currency in which it normally operates (probably the U.S. dollar for a U.S. company), transactions often involve a number of currencies. For many companies, sales, purchases, expenses, and the like can be denominated in dozens of different currencies. A company's financial statements may report U.S. dollars because that is its functional currency, but underlying amounts to be paid or received might be set in another currency such as the euro or the pound. Mechanically, many methods of reporting such foreign balances have been developed, each with a significantly different type of impact.

Without standardization, a decision maker would likely face a daunting task trying to analyze similar companies if they employed different approaches for reporting foreign currency figures. Assessing the comparative financial health and future prospects of organizations that do not use the same accounting always poses a difficult challenge for investors and creditors. That problem would be especially serious if optional approaches were allowed in connection with foreign currencies. Therefore, U.S. GAAP has long had an authoritative standard for this reporting.

The basic problem with reporting foreign currency balances is that exchange rates are constantly in flux. The price of one euro in terms of U.S. dollars changes many times each day. If these rates remained constant, a single conversion value could be determined at the time of the initial transaction and then used consistently for reporting purposes. However, currency exchange rates are rarely fixed; they often change moment by moment. For example, if a sale is made on account by a U.S. company with the money to be received in a foreign currency in 60 days, the relative worth of that balance in terms of U.S. dollars will probably move up and down countless times before collection. Because such values float, the reporting of these foreign currency amounts poses a challenge with no easy resolution.

5.2 Accounting for Changes in Currency Exchange Rates

Question: Exchange rates that vary over time create a reporting problem for companies operating in international markets. To illustrate, assume a U.S. company makes a sale of a service to a Mexican company on December 9, Year One, for 100,000 Mexican pesos that will be paid at a later date. Assume also that the exchange rate on the day when the sale was made was 1 peso equal to $0.08. However, by the end of Year One when financial statements are produced, the exchange rate is different: 1 peso is now worth $0.09. **What reporting does a U.S. company make of transactions that are denominated in a foreign currency if the exchange rate changes as time passes?**[6]

Answer: At the time of the sale, reporting is easy. The 100,000 pesos has an equivalent value of $8,000 (100,000 pesos × $0.08); thus, the journal entry in Figure 7.14 is appropriate. Even though 100,000 pesos will be received, $8,000 is reported so that all balances on the seller's financial statements are stated in terms of U.S. dollars.

FIGURE 7.14 Journal Entry—December 9, Year One—Sale of Services Made for 100,000 Pesos

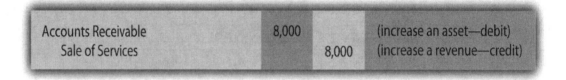

| Accounts Receivable | 8,000 | | (increase an asset—debit) |
| Sale of Services | | 8,000 | (increase a revenue—credit) |

By the end of the year, the exchange rate has changed so that 1 peso is equal to $0.09. The Mexican peso is worth a penny more in terms of the U.S. dollar. Thus, 100,000 pesos are more valuable and can now be exchanged for $9,000 (100,000 × $0.09). There are numerous reasons why the relative value of these two currencies might have changed, but the cause is not important from an accounting perspective.

When adjusting entries are prepared in connection with the production of financial statements at the end of Year One, one or both of the account balances (accounts receivable and sales of services) could remain at $8,000 or be updated to $9,000. The sale took place when the exchange rate was $0.08 but, now, before the money is collected, the peso has risen in value to $0.09. Accounting needs a standard rule as to whether the historical rate ($0.08) or the current rate ($0.09) is appropriate for reporting such foreign currency balances. Communication is difficult without that type of structure. Plus, the standard needs to be logical. It needs to make sense.

For over 25 years, U.S. GAAP has required that **monetary assets and liabilities** denominated in a foreign currency be reported at the current exchange rate as of the balance sheet date. All other balances continue to be shown at the historical exchange rate in effect on the date of the original transaction. That is the approach that all organizations adhering to U.S. GAAP follow. Both the individuals who produce financial statements as well as the decision makers who use this information should understand the rule that is applied to resolve this reporting issue.

Monetary assets and liabilities are amounts currently held as cash or that will require a future transfer of a specified amount of cash. In the coverage here, for convenience, such monetary accounts will be limited to cash, receivables, and payables. Because these balances reflect current or future cash amounts, the current exchange rate is viewed as most relevant. In this illustration, the value of the receivable (a monetary asset) has changed in terms of U.S. dollars. The 100,000 pesos that will be collected have an equivalent value now of $0.09 each rather than $0.08. The reported receivable is updated to a value of $9,000 (100,000 pesos × $0.09).

monetary assets and monetary liabilities

Amounts that are held by an organization as either cash or balances that will provide receipts or payments of a specified amount of cash in the future.

Cash, receivables, and payables denominated in a foreign currency must be adjusted for reporting purposes whenever exchange rates fluctuate. All other account balances (equipment, sales, rent expense, dividends, and the like) reflect historical events and not future cash flows. Thus, they retain the rate in effect at the time of the original transaction and no further changes are ever needed. Because the sales figure is not a monetary asset or liability, the $8,000 balance continues to be reported regardless of the relative value of the peso.

5.3   The Income Effect of a Change in Currency Exchange Rates

Question: Changes in exchange rates affect the reporting of monetary assets and liabilities. Those amounts are literally worth more or less U.S. dollars as the relative value of the currency fluctuates over time. For the two balances above, the account receivable has to be remeasured on the date of the balance sheet because it is a monetary asset whereas the sales balance remains reported as $8,000 permanently. How is this change in the receivable accomplished? **When monetary assets and liabilities denominated in a foreign currency are remeasured for reporting purposes, how is the increase or decrease in value reflected?**

Answer: In this example, the value of the 100,000-peso receivable is raised from $8,000 to $9,000. When the amount reported for monetary assets and liabilities increases or decreases because of changes in currency exchange rates, a gain or loss is recognized on the income statement. Here, the reported receivable is now $1,000 higher. The company's financial condition has improved and a gain is recognized. If the opposite occurs and the reported value of monetary assets declines (or the value of monetary liabilities increases), a loss is recognized. The adjusting entry shown in Figure 7.15 is appropriate to reflect this change.

FIGURE 7.15   Adjusting Entry at December 31, Year One—Remeasurement of 100,000 Pesos Receivable

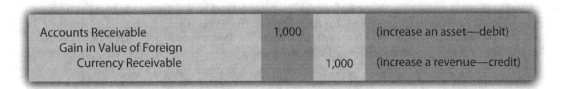

| Accounts Receivable | 1,000 | | (increase an asset—debit) |
| Gain in Value of Foreign Currency Receivable | | 1,000 | (increase a revenue—credit) |

On its balance sheet, this company now reports a receivable as of December 31, Year One, of $9,000 while its income statement for that year shows sales revenue of $8,000 as well as the above gain of $1,000. Although the transaction was actually for 100,000 Mexican pesos, the company records these events in terms of its functional currency (the U.S. dollar) according to the provisions of U.S. GAAP.

KEY TAKEAWAY

Foreign currency balances are prevalent because many companies buy and sell products and services internationally. Although these transactions are frequently denominated in foreign currencies, they are reported in U.S. dollars when financial statements are produced for distribution in this country. Because exchange rates often change rapidly, many equivalent values could be calculated for these balances. According to U.S. GAAP, monetary assets and liabilities (cash as well as receivables and payables to be settled in cash) are updated for reporting purposes using the exchange rate at the current date. Changes in these balances create gains or losses to be recognized on the income statement. All other foreign currency balances (land, buildings, sales, expenses, and the like) continue to be shown at the historical exchange rate in effect at the time of the original transaction.

6. A COMPANY'S VITAL SIGNS—ACCOUNTS RECEIVABLE

LEARNING OBJECTIVES

At the end of this section, students should be able to meet the following objectives:

1. Compute the current ratio, the amount of working capital, and other figures pertinent to the reporting of accounts receivable.

2. Describe the implications of a company's current ratio.

3. Describe the implications of a company's working capital balance.

4. Calculate the amount of time that passes before the average accounts receivable is collected and explain the importance of this information.

5. List techniques that a business can implement to speed up collection of its accounts receivable.

6.1 Current Ratio and Working Capital

Question: Individuals analyze financial statements to make logical and appropriate decisions about a company's financial health and well being. This process is somewhat similar to a medical doctor performing a physical examination on a patient. The doctor often begins by checking various vital signs, such as heart rate, blood pressure, weight, cholesterol level, and body temperature, looking for any signs of a serious change or problem. For example, if a person's heart rate is higher than expected or if blood pressure has increased significantly since the last visit, the doctor will investigate with special care. **In analyzing the financial statements of a business or other organization, are there vital signs that should be measured and studied by a decision maker?**

Answer: Financial statements are extremely complex and most analysts have certain preferred figures or ratios that they believe are especially significant when investigating a company. For example, in a previous chapter, both the **current ratio** and the amount of **working capital** were computed using the balances reported for current assets (those that will be used or consumed within one year) and current liabilities (those that will be paid within one year):

current ratio = current assets/current liabilities

working capital = current assets − current liabilities

These figures reflect a company's liquidity, or its ability to pay its debts as they come due and still have enough monetary resources available to generate profits in the near future. Both investors and creditors frequently calculate, study, and analyze these two amounts. They are vital signs that help indicate the financial health of a business and its future prospects.

For example, on December 31, 2010, **Avon Products** reported a current ratio of 1.42 to 1.00 (current assets of $4.184 billion divided by current liabilities of $2.956 billion), which was down from 1.84 to 1.00 at the end of 2009. On the same date at the end of 2010, **Caterpillar** disclosed working capital of $9.790 billion (current assets of $31.810 billion less current liabilities of $22.020 billion). **Caterpillar's** working capital increased by over $1.5 billion from the previous year when it was reported as $8.242 billion.

Whether these numbers are impressive or worrisome almost always depends on a careful comparison with other similar companies and results from prior years.

> **current ratio**
>
> Formula measuring an organization's liquidity (the ability to pay debts as they come due); calculated by dividing current assets by current liabilities.
>
> **working capital**
>
> Formula measuring an organization's liquidity (the ability to pay debts as they come due); calculated by subtracting current liabilities from current assets.

TEST YOURSELF

Question:

The Winsolie Corporation reports the following asset balances: cash—$4,000, accounts receivable, net—$17,000, inventory—$13,000, and land—$22,000. The company also has the following liabilities: salaries payable—$6,000, accounts payable—$4,000, note payable, due in seven months—$5,000, and note payable, due in five years—$14,000. What is the company's current ratio?

a. 1.400 to 1.000

b. 1.931 to 1.000

c. 2.267 to 1.000

d. 3.733 to 1.000

Answer:

The correct answer is choice c: 2.267 to 1.000.

Explanation:

Current assets are usually those that will be used or consumed within one year. For this company, that is cash, accounts receivable, and inventory that total to $34,000. Current liabilities are debts that will be paid within one year: salaries payable of $6,000, accounts payable of $4,000, and note payable due in seven months of $5,000. The current liability total for this company is $15,000. Thus, the current ratio is $34,000 divided by $15,000 or 2.267 to 1.000.

6.2 Computing the Age of Accounts Receivable

Question: This chapter deals with the financial reporting of accounts receivable. **What other vital signs might be studied in connection with a company's receivable balance?**

Answer: One indication of a company's financial health is its ability to collect receivables in a timely fashion. Money cannot be put to productive use until it is received. For that reason, companies work to encourage customers to make payments as quickly as possible. Furthermore, as stated previously in this chapter, the older a receivable becomes, the more likely it is to prove worthless.

Thus, interested parties (both inside a company as well as external) frequently monitor the time taken to collect receivables. Quick collection is normally viewed as desirable, whereas a slower rate can be a warning sign of possible problems. However, as with most generalizations, exceptions do exist so further investigation is always advised.

The age of a company's receivables is determined by dividing the receivable balance by the average sales made per day. Credit sales are used in this computation if known, but the total sales figure often has to serve as a substitute because of availability. The sales balance is first divided by 365 to derive the amount of sales per day. This daily balance is then divided into the reported receivable to arrive at the average number of days that the company waits to collect its money. A significant change in the age of receivables will be quickly noted by almost any interested party.

$$\text{age of receivables} = \text{receivables/sales per day}$$

For example, if a company reports sales for the current year of $7,665,000 and currently holds $609,000 in receivables, it requires 29 days on the average to collect a receivable.

$$\text{sales per day} = \$7,665,000/365 \text{ or } \$21,000$$

$$\text{age of receivables} = \$609,000/\$21,000 \text{ or } 29 \text{ days}$$

As a practical illustration, for the year ended January 28, 2011, **Dell Inc.** reported net revenue of $61.494 billion. The January 28, 2011, net accounts receivable balance for the company was $6.493 billion, which was up from $5.837 billion the year before. The daily sales figure is $168.5 million ($61.494 billion/365 days). Thus, the average age of **Dell's** ending receivable balance at this time was 38.5 days ($6.493 billion/$168.5 million). By itself, this figure is neither good nor bad. An assessment depends on the terms given to customers, the time of collection in other recent years, and comparable figures for companies in the same industry as **Dell**.

A similar figure is referred to as the **receivables turnover** and is computed by the following formula:

$$\text{receivables turnover} = \text{sales/average receivables.}$$

For **Dell Inc.**, the average receivable balance for this year was $6.165 billion ([$6.493 billion + $5.837]/2). The receivables turnover for **Dell** for this period of time was 9.97 times:

$$\text{receivables turnover} = \$61.494 \text{ billion/}\$6.165 \text{ billion} = 9.97.$$

The higher the receivable turnover, the faster collections are being received.

---

receivables turnover

Formula measuring speed of an organization's collection of its accounts receivable; calculated by dividing sales by the average accounts receivable balance for the period.

TEST YOURSELF

Question:

The Yang Corporation recently extended the time that customers are given to pay their accounts receivable. Investors are interested in the impact of that decision. In Year One, the company had $730,000 in sales with $58,000 in accounts receivable on hand at the end of the year. In Year Two, sales grew to $1,095,000 but accounts receivable also rose to $114,000. Which of the following statements is true?

a. The receivables turnover for Year Two was 9.61 times.

b. The age of the receivables at the end of Year Two was thirty-three days.

c. The receivables turnover for Year Two was 10.18 times.

d. The age of the receivables at the end of Year Two was thirty-eight days.

Answer:

The correct answer is choice d: The age of the receivables at the end of Year Two was thirty-eight days.

Explanation:

The receivables turnover for Year Two is the sales for the year ($1,095,000) divided by the average receivable balance of $86,000 ([$58,000 + $114,000] divided by 2). The receivables turnover is 12.73 ($1,095,000/$86,000). Computing the age of receivables begins by calculating the average sales per day as $3,000 ($1,095,000/365 days). That figure is divided into the ending receivable of $114,000 to arrive at thirty-eight days. On average, that is the time between a sale being made and cash collected.

6.3   Reducing the Time It Takes to Collect Receivables

Question: If members of management notice that the average age of accounts receivable *for their company is getting older, what type of remedial actions can be taken?* **How does a company reduce the average number of days that are required to collect receivables so that cash is available more quickly?**

Answer: A number of strategies can be used by astute officials to shorten the time between a sale being made and cash collected. The following are just a few common examples. Unfortunately, all such actions have a cost and can cause a negative impact on the volume of sales or create expenses that might outweigh the benefits of quicker cash inflows. Management should make such decisions with extreme care.

- Require a tighter review of credit worthiness before selling to a customer on credit. If sales on account are only made to individuals and companies with significant financial strength, the quantity of delayed payments should decline.
- Work to make the company's own accounting system more efficient so that bills (sales invoices) are sent to customers in a timely manner. Payments are rarely made—even by the best customers—before initial notification is received. If the billing system is not well designed and effectively operated, that process can be unnecessarily slow.
- Offer a discount if a customer pays quickly. This action has an obvious cost, but such reductions provide a strong incentive to the customer for fast action.
- Send out second bills more quickly. Customers often need reminding that a debt is due. An invoice marked "late" or "overdue" will often push the recipient into making payment. A company might decide to send out this notice after 30 days—as an example—rather than wait for 45 days.
- Instigate a more aggressive collection policy for accounts that are not paid on time. Companies use numerous strategies to "encourage" payment and begin applying these steps at an earlier point in time.

Most companies monitor the age of receivables very carefully and use some combination of these strategies whenever any sign of problem is noted.

average age of accounts receivable

Formula measuring the average length of time it takes to collect cash from sales; calculated by dividing either accounts receivable at a point in time or the average accounts receivable for the period by the average sales made per day.

KEY TAKEAWAY

Decision makers analyzing a particular company often look beyond reported balances in search of clues as to financial strengths or weaknesses. Both the current ratio and the amount of working capital provide an indication of short-term liquidity (ability to pay debts as they come due) and profitability. The age of receivables and the receivables turnover are measures of the speed of cash collections. Any change in the time needed to obtain payments from customers should be carefully considered when studying a company. Management can work to shorten the number of days it takes to receive cash by altering credit, billing, and collection policies or possibly by offering discounts or other incentives for quick payment.

Talking with a Real Investing Pro (Continued)

Following is a continuation of our interview with Kevin G. Burns.

Question: Let's say that you are analyzing a particular company and are presently looking at its current assets. When you are studying a company's accounts receivable, what types of information tend to catch your attention?

Kevin Burns: I look at three areas specifically. First, how long does it take for the company to collect its accounts receivable especially compared to previous periods? I really don't like to see radical changes in the age of receivables without some logical explanation. Second, how lenient is the company in offering credit? Are they owed money by weak customers or a small concentration of customers? Third, does the company depend on interest income and late charges on their accounts receivable for a significant part of their revenue? Some companies claim to be in business to sell products but they are really finance companies because they make their actual profits from finance charges that are added to the accounts receivable. It is always important to know how a company earns money.

Video Clip

Professor Joe Hoyle talks about the five most important points in Chapter 7.

View the video online at: http://bit.ly/hoyle7-2

7.   END-OF-CHAPTER EXERCISES

QUESTIONS

1. A company reports a balance of $3.6 million for its "accounts receivable." What is meant by accounts receivable? How are accounts receivable reported in a set of financial statements?

2. How is the net realizable value of a company's accounts receivable determined?

3. The Sylvester Corporation has accounts receivable that total $4.5 million. However, the company does not expect to collect that much cash. Identify several factors that a company might consider when trying to determine the amount of these accounts receivable that will ultimately be collected.

4. What does the account "allowance for doubtful accounts" represent?

5. In financial reporting, what is the purpose of a "contra account?"

6. According to the matching principle, when should bad debt expense be reported?

7. Why do companies set up an allowance for doubtful accounts instead of just decreasing accounts receivable for the expected amount of uncollectible balances?

8. The Abrahim Corporation discovered that one of its customers went into bankruptcy and will not be able to pay the $8,700 balance that it owes. What entry does a company like Abrahim make to write off a specific account receivable that has proven to be uncollectible?

9. A company writes off a $12,000 receivable as uncollectible. How does that entry change the amount reported by the company as its net receivable balance?

10. A company writes off a $2,200 receivable as uncollectible. How does that entry impact the reported net income of this company at that time?

11. In Year One, Jordan Company writes off nine accounts with a total balance of $11,675 as uncollectible. During Year Two, one of these accounts is paid because the debtor company has received financing and grown in strength. What entry does Jordan make when this cash is received?

12. In Year One, the Castagna Company reported bad debt expense of $37,000. However, in Year Two, the economy was weak and the company actually wrote off $43,000 in accounts as uncollectible. The $37,000 figure continued to be reported in the Year One financial statements. Why did Castagna not change the balance reported for Year One now that the actual number is known?

13. The Nagano Corporation is preparing financial statements for the latest year. The company sells on credit and, thus, must anticipate the amount of its bad accounts. What are the most common methods for making this estimation?

14. At the end of Year Two, before making adjusting entries and preparing financial statements, a company's allowance-for-doubtful-accounts T-account usually has a balance in it. What does that balance reflect?

15. In its Year Two financial statements, the Heather Company reported bad debt expense of $35,000 and an allowance for doubtful accounts of $34,000. Why are these figures not identical?

16. What is the purpose of a company maintaining an accounts receivable subsidiary ledger?

17. Why does the reporting of balances denominated in a foreign currency create challenges for the accountant when producing financial statements?

18. What are monetary assets and monetary liabilities?

19. The Lenoir Corporation has 47 T-accounts in its general ledger. Most of these balances are denominated in U.S. dollars, its functional currency. Some of the balances are dominated in a foreign currency. Which of these foreign currency balances are remeasured at historical exchange rates and which are remeasured at the current exchange rate for reporting purposes?

20. How is the current ratio calculated? How is the amount of working capital determined? What do these two computed amounts indicate about a company's financial health?

21. How do decision makers determine the average age of a reporting entity's accounts receivable?

22. How do decision makers determine the receivables turnover based on the information reported by a company?

23. The Pierce Company sells its merchandise on credit. At the end of Year One, company customers took an average of 23.3 days to pay for their goods. However, recently, that period has jumped to 27.5 days which concerns company officials. What actions could they take to reduce the number of days back to 23.3?

TRUE OR FALSE

1. _____ Companies use two separate T-accounts in order to monitor and report accounts receivable at its net realizable value.

2. _____ Bad debt expense is reported on the balance sheet as a contra account to reduce accounts receivable.

3. _____ Bad debt expense should be reported in the same period as related revenue regardless of when the receivable is determined to be uncollectible.

4. _____ A company has been in business for several years. In the current year, prior to preparing adjusting entries so that financial statements can be prepared, the bad expense T-account should report a zero balance.

5. _____ A company has been in business for several years. At the end of the current year, prior to any adjusting entries being prepared, the allowance for doubtful accounts holds a credit balance of $5,000. The previous year estimation of uncollectible accounts was too low.

6. _____ According to U.S. GAAP, all companies are required to perform their estimation of uncollectible accounts in the same manner.

7. _____ On a set of financial statements, the amount of bad debt expense and the ending balance in the allowance for doubtful accounts will frequently differ.

8. _____ A company ends the current year with sales of $600,000, accounts receivable of $100,000, and an allowance for doubtful accounts with a $1,000 debit balance. Bad debts are estimated to be 3 percent of sales. On financial statements, the allowance for doubtful accounts will be reported as having an $18,000 credit balance.

9. _____ A company ends the current year with sales of $600,000, accounts receivable of $100,000, and an allowance for doubtful accounts with a $1,000 credit balance. Bad debts are estimated to be 3 percent of sales. On financial statements, bad debt expense will be reported as having an $18,000 debit balance.

10. _____ A company ends the current year with sales of $600,000, accounts receivable of $100,000, and an allowance for doubtful accounts with a $1,000 debit balance. Uncollectible accounts at the end of the year are estimated to be 6 percent of receivables. Bad debt expense will be reported on the income statement as $7,000.

11. _____ A company ends the current year with sales of $600,000, accounts receivable of $100,000, and an allowance for doubtful accounts with a $1,000 credit balance. Uncollectible accounts at the end of the year are estimated to be 6 percent of receivables. Bad debt expense will be reported on the income statement as $5,000.

12. _____ A company ends Year Two with bad debt expense of $29,000 and an allowance for doubtful accounts of $27,000. On April 8, Year Three, a $1,900 receivable is written off as uncollectible. Net income is reduced by $1,900 on that date.

13. _____ A company ends Year Two with bad debt expense of $35,000 and an allowance for doubtful accounts of $34,000. On April 12, Year Three, a $2,300 receivable is written off as uncollectible. The net amount reported for accounts receivable is reduced by $2,300 on that date.

14. _____ A U.S. company with the U.S. dollar as its functional currency makes a sale in a foreign country and agrees to receive 20,000 vilsecks, the local currency. A vilseck is worth $0.42 on that date but is worth only $0.39 later on the balance sheet date. The company should report a loss on its income statement of $600 as a result of the change in the exchange rate.

15. _____ A U.S. company with the U.S. dollar as its functional currency makes a sale in a foreign country and agrees to receive 20,000 vilsecks, the local currency. A vilseck is worth $0.42 on that date but is worth only $0.39 later on the balance sheet date. On its income statement, the company should report a sale of $7,800.

16. _____ A company makes sales of $730,000 in Year Three. At the end of Year Three, the receivable balance is $48,000. The average customer at that time is taking 27 days to make payment to the company.

17. _____ A company has a current ratio of 3.0:1.0. An account receivable of $3,800 is collected. That transaction will cause an increase in the current ratio.

18. _____ A company has receivables of $300,000 on the first day of the year. During the year the company makes sales of $800,000 but only collects cash of $600,000. No bad debts were expected or uncovered during the year. The receivables turnover for the period was 2.

MULTIPLE CHOICE

1. Which of the following would **not** be used to help a company determine the net realizable value of its accounts receivable?

    a. Industry averages and trends

    b. The company's ability to pay its own debts

    c. Current economic conditions

    d. Efficiency of the company's collection procedures

2. Which accounting principle guides the timing of the reporting of bad debt expense?

    a. Matching principle

    b. Going concern principle

    c. Cost/benefit analysis

    d. Measurement principle

3. SunFun Company manufactures lawn furniture that is sold to retail stores. During October, Year One, SunFun sold furniture to Home Place on account in the amount of $40,000. At the end of Year One, the balance was still outstanding. In March, Year Two, SunFun decided to write off this particular account as it did not appear that the balance would ever be collected. Choose the correct journal entry for this write off.

    a. **FIGURE 7.16**

Allowance for Doubtful Accounts	40,000	
Accounts Receivable		40,000

    b. **FIGURE 7.17**

Bad Debt Expense	40,000	
Allowance for Doubtful Accounts		40,000

    c. **FIGURE 7.18**

Bad Debt Expense	40,000	
Accounts Receivable		40,000

    d. **FIGURE 7.19**

Cash	40,000	
Accounts Receivable		40,000

4. A company is preparing to produce a set of financial statements. The balance sheet being created shows a total for assets of $800,000 and a total for liabilities of $600,000. Just prior to the end of the year, one account receivable is determined to be uncollectible and is written off. Another receivable for $5,000 is collected. No other event or adjustment is made. What should the company now report as the total of its assets after recording these final two events?

     a. $784,000

     b. $789,000

     c. $800,000

     d. $805,000

5. Gladson Corporation reports bad debt expense using the percentage of sales method. At the end of the year, Gladson has $450,000 in accounts receivable and a $4,000 credit in its allowance for doubtful accounts before any entry is made for bad debts. Sales for the year were $1.9 million. The percentage that Gladson has historically used to calculate bad debts is 1 percent of sales. Which of the following is true?

     a. Gladson's bad debt expense for the year is $15,000.

     b. Gladson's bad debt expense for the year is $23,000.

     c. Gladson would report an allowance for doubtful accounts of $23,000.

     d. Gladson would report an allowance for doubtful accounts of $19,000.

6. On the first day of Year Two, the Raleigh Corporation holds accounts receivable of $500,000 and an allowance for doubtful accounts of $25,000 for a net realizable value of $475,000. During the year, credit sales were $520,000, and cash collections amounted to $440,000. In addition, $28,000 in receivables were written off as uncollectible. If 8 percent of sales is estimated as uncollectible each year, what is the net accounts receivable balance reported at the end of Year Two on Raleigh's balance sheet?

     a. $510,400

     b. $513,400

     c. $516,400

     d. $519,400

7. On the first day of Year Two, the Richmond Corporation holds accounts receivable of $400,000 and an allowance for doubtful accounts of $23,000 for a net realizable value of $377,000. During the year, credit sales were $450,000 and cash collections amounted to $380,000. In addition, $25,000 in receivables were written off as uncollectible. If 6 percent of ending accounts receivable is estimated as uncollectible, what bad debt expense is reported for Year Two on Richmond's income statement?

     a. $24,700

     b. $25,000

     c. $28,700

     d. $30,200

8. In Year One, the Simon Company wrote off a $14,000 receivable as uncollectible. However, on May 17, Year Two, the customer returned and paid Simon the entire amount. Which of the following is correct as a result of this payment?

     a. Accounts receivable goes down, but the allowance-for-doubtful-accounts account is not changed.

     b. Accounts receivable goes down, and the allowance-for-doubtful-accounts account also goes down.

     c. Accounts receivable stays the same, but the allowance for doubtful accounts goes up.

     d. Accounts receivable stays the same, and the allowance for doubtful accounts also stays the same.

9. A company ends Year Three with accounts receivable of $300,000, an allowance for doubtful accounts of $15,000, sales of $900,000, and bad debt expense of $27,000. In Year Four, sales of $1 million more are made. Cash collections are $800,000, and an additional $13,000 in receivables are written off as uncollectible. The company always estimates that 5 percent of its ending accounts receivable will prove to be bad. On December 31, Year Four, company officials find another $6,000 in receivables that might well be uncollectible. However, after further review, these receivables were not written off at this time. By how much did that decision not to write off these accounts change reported net income for Year Four?

     a. Reported net income was not affected.

     b. The decision made reported net income $300 higher.

     c. The decision made reported net income $5,700 higher.

     d. The decision made reported net income $6,000 higher.

10. A company ends Year Three with accounts receivable of $300,000, an allowance for doubtful accounts of $15,000, sales of $900,000, and bad debt expense of $27,000. In Year Four, sales of $1 million more are made. Cash collections are $800,000 and an additional $13,000 in receivables are written off as uncollectible. The company always estimates that 3 percent of its sales each year will eventually prove to be bad. On December 31, Year Four, company officials find another $6,000 in receivables that might well be uncollectible. However, after further review, these receivables were not written off at this time. By how much did that decision not to write off these accounts change reported net income for Year Four?

    a. Reported net income was not affected.
    b. The decision made reported net income $300 higher.
    c. The decision made reported net income $5,700 higher.
    d. The decision made reported net income $6,000 higher.

11. A U.S. company (with the U.S. dollar as its functional currency) buys inventory and immediately sells it to a customer in France on November 28, Year One, for 10,000 euros. The inventory had cost 6,000 euros several days before, an amount which had been paid on the day of purchase. This merchandise is sold on account with the money to be paid by the customer on January 19, Year Two. On November 28, Year One, 1 euro was worth $2.00 whereas on December 31, Year One, 1 euro is worth $1.90. What is the impact on net income of the change in the exchange rate?

    a. $600 gain
    b. $600 loss
    c. $1,000 gain
    d. $1,000 loss

12. On December 1, Year One, a company sells a service for 10,000 scoobies (the currency of the country where the sale was made) to be collected in six months. On that same day, the company pays 10,000 scoobies in cash for some inventory. This inventory was still held at year-end. On December 1, Year One, one scoobie is worth $0.61. By December 31, Year One, one scoobie is worth $0.73. The company is located in Ohio and is preparing to produce financial statements for Year One in terms of U.S. dollars. Which of the following will be reported on its balance sheet?

    a. Accounts receivable will be reported at $6,100, and inventory will also be reported as $6,100.
    b. Accounts receivable will be reported at $7,300, but inventory will be reported as $6,100.
    c. Accounts receivable will be reported at $6,100, but inventory will be reported as $7,300.
    d. Accounts receivable will be reported at $7,300, and inventory will also be reported as $7,300.

13. The New Orleans Company has more current assets than current liabilities. Near the end of the current year, the company pays off its rent payable for $5,000. What is the impact of this payment on the company current ratio?

    a. No change occurs in the current ratio
    b. Current ratio goes up
    c. Current ratio goes down
    d. The impact on the current ratio cannot be determined based on the information provided.

14. Darlene Corporation has $300,000 in assets, 30 percent of which are current, and $100,000 in liabilities, 40 percent of which are current. Which of the following is true?

    a. Darlene's current ratio is 3 to 1.
    b. Darlene's working capital is $200,000.
    c. Darlene's working capital is $50,000.
    d. The current ratio and working capital are measures of a company's profitability.

15. Fifer Inc. began the current year with $450,000 in accounts receivable and ended the year with $590,000 in accounts receivable and $4 million in sales. Last year Fifer's age of ending receivables was forty-six days and its receivables turnover was six times. Which of the following is **not** true?

    a. Fifer's age of ending receivables is 54 days.
    b. Fifer's receivables turnover is 7.69 times.
    c. Fifer's age of ending receivables is less than it was last year.
    d. External decision makers monitor the time it takes a company to collect its receivables.

16. Company A made sales this year of $400,000 and has ending accounts receivable of $120,000. Company Z made sales this year of $900,000 and has ending accounts receivable of $280,000. Which of the following is true?

    a. It takes Company Z approximately 4 days longer to collect its accounts receivable than it takes Company A.

b. It takes Company A approximately 4 days longer to collect its accounts receivable than it takes Company Z.

c. It takes Company Z approximately 13 days longer to collect its accounts receivable than it takes Company A.

d. It takes Company A approximately 13 days longer to collect its accounts receivable than it takes Company Z.

VIDEO PROBLEMS

Professor Joe Hoyle discusses the answers to these two problems at the links that are indicated. After formulating your answers, watch each video to see how Professor Hoyle answers these questions.

1. Your roommate is an English major. The roommate's parents own a chain of ice cream shops throughout Florida. One day, while sitting in a restaurant waiting for a pizza, your roommate poses this question: "This year, my parents began to furnish ice cream for a number of local restaurants. It was an easy way for them to expand their business. But, for the first time, they were making sales on credit. This seems to have caused some confusion when they started to produce financial statements. In the past, all sales were made for cash. However, this year they made $300,000 in sales to these restaurants on credit and they are still owed $90,000. I know they are worried about some of those accounts proving to be bad because of the economic times. In fact, one restaurant that owed them $2,000 filed for bankruptcy last fall and they didn't get a penny of what they were owed. How in the world do they report money that they have not received yet and might never receive?" How would you respond?

View the video online at: http://bit.ly/hoyle7-3

2. Your uncle and two friends started a small office supply store several years ago. The company has expanded and now has several large locations. All sales to other companies are made on credit. Your uncle knows that you are taking a financial accounting class and asks you the following question: "When we sell on credit, we give customers 30 days to pay. We monitor our customers very carefully and, consequently, we have very few bad debts. Our accountant came to us last week and said that our average customer used to pay us in 22 days but recently that has changed to 27 days. How did he figure that out? And, so what? As long as we get paid, why should I care? All I want is to make sure we get our money. But, if we do need to get paid faster, what am I supposed to do? The customers are still paying within the 30 days that we allow them so why should this make any difference?" How would you respond?

View the video online at: http://bit.ly/hoyle7-4

PROBLEMS

1. Nuance Company had net credit sales for the year of $500,000. Nuance estimates that 2 percent of its net credit sales will never be collected.

   a. Prepare the entry to record Nuance's bad debt expense for the year.

   b. Nuance had accounts receivable of $100,000 at the end of the year. Show how the net accounts receivable balance would be reported on the balance sheet. Assume that the allowance for doubtful accounts had an unadjusted credit balance at the end of the year of $1,000.

   c. Why is the accounts receivable balance shown at net rather than just showing the full amount?

2. Assume that Nuance in number 1 used the percentage of receivables method to estimate uncollectible accounts instead of the percentage of sales method. Nuance assumes that 5 percent of accounts receivable will never be collected.

   a. Prepare the entry to record Nuance's bad debt expense for the year.

   b. Show how the net accounts receivable balance would be reported on the balance sheet.

   c. Why are companies allowed to choose between the percentage of sales and the percentage of receivables method?

3. The Alfonso Corporation begins operations in Year One. The company makes credit sales of $800,000 each year while collecting cash of $430,000. Every year, receivables of $31,000 are written off as being doubtful. Company officials estimate that 5 percent of all credit sales will eventually prove to be uncollectible. What figures will be reported in the company's Year Two financial statements in connection with these credit sales?

4. The Fallston Corporation begins operations in Year One. The company makes credit sales of $1.2 million each year while collecting cash of $800,000. Every year, receivables of $30,000 are written off as being doubtful. Company officials estimate that 5 percent of ending accounts receivable will eventually prove to be uncollectible. What figures will be reported in the company's Year Two financial statements in connection with these credit sales?

5. Ray's GamePlace sells all the hottest gear and video games. On January 1, Year Three, Ray's had the following account balances:

FIGURE 7.20

Accounts Receivable	$27,000
Less Allowance for Doubtful Accounts	(4,000)
Net Accounts Receivable	$23,000

   a. During Year Three, Ray's wrote off $6,000 in uncollectible accounts. Make this journal entry.

   b. One account in the amount of $500 that had been written off in (a) above was later collected during the year. Make the journal entries to reinstate the account and show its collection.

   c. During Year Three, Ray's made credit sales of $145,000 and collected $115,000 of accounts receivable. Record these journal entries.

   d. At the end of the year, Ray's determines that approximately 7 percent of its ending accounts receivable balance will not be collected. Make the necessary journal entry.

6. The Lawndale Company starts the current year with the following T-account balances:

   ■ Accounts receivable = $300,000 debit
   ■ Allowance for doubtful accounts = $15,000 credit
        During the year, the following events take place:
   ■ $18,000 in receivables are written off as uncollectible.
   ■ Credit sales of $800,000 are made
   ■ Cash of $680,000 is collected from the receivables
   ■ A $2,000 receivable written off above is collected (amount is not included in the $680,000 figure).
        Company officials believe that 5 percent of the ending accounts receivable will eventually prove to be uncollectible.

   a. On its balance sheet, what is reported as the net accounts receivable balance?

   b. On its income statement, what is reported for bad debt expense?

7. Company A begins Year Two with accounts receivable of $200,000 and an allowance for doubtful accounts of $10,000 (credit balance). Company Z had the exact same balances. During Year Two, Company A made credit sales of $700,000 and cash collections on those accounts of $500,000. Uncollectible accounts of $19,000 were written off during the year. However, one of these accounts ($5,000) was actually collected later in the year (for convenience, that $5,000 collection was not included in the $500,000 figure above). Company Z has exactly the same transactions. In fact, the operations of these two companies are exactly the same. Officials for Company A anticipate that 2 percent of credit sales will prove uncollectible. As a result of this information (and other transactions), Company A reported net income of $100,000. Officials for Company Z believe that 5 percent of ending accounts receivable will prove to be uncollectible. What net income will Company Z report?

8. The Springs Corporation started Year Four with $200,000 in its accounts receivable T-account and an allowance for doubtful accounts of $10,000 (credit balance). During that year, the company made additional sales of $500,000 while collecting cash of $400,000. In addition, $7,000 in accounts were written off as uncollectible. Company officials for Springs estimated that 3 percent of sales would eventually prove to be uncollectible based on past history and current economic conditions. The adjusting entry was prepared and preliminary financial statements were created. These statements showed net income of $80,000 and a total for all reported assets of $460,000. At the last moment, on December 31, Year Four, company officials discovered another receivable of $1,000 that needed to be written off because the debtor went bankrupt and was liquidated. What should the company report as its net income for the year and as its total for all reported assets as of the end of that year?

9. The Wallace Corporation started Year Four with $500,000 in its accounts receivable T-account and an allowance for doubtful accounts of $20,000 (credit balance). During that year, the company made additional sales of $1.6 million while collecting cash of $1.3 million. In addition, $24,000 in accounts were written off as uncollectible. Company officials for Wallace estimated that 4 percent of ending receivables would eventually prove to be uncollectible based on past history and current economic conditions. The adjusting entry was prepared and preliminary financial statements were created. These statements showed net income of $220,000 and a total for all reported assets of $1.1 million. At the last moment, on December 31, Year Four, company officials discovered another receivable of $1,000 that needed to be written off because the debtor went bankrupt and was liquidated. What should the company report as its net income for the year and as its total for all reported assets as of the end of that year?

10. On November 1, Year One, a U.S. company acquires 1,000 widgets from a company in France for 8,000 euros on credit. The company still holds all of this inventory on December 31. The debt has not yet been paid. The company is getting ready to prepare its Year One financial statements in its functional currency, the U.S. dollar. On November 1, 1 euro was worth $1.72, but on December 31, 1 euro is worth only $1.61. What is reported on the company's Year One income statement? What is reported on the company's balance sheet as of December 31, Year One?

11. Medwear Corporation is a multinational dealer of uniforms for medical personnel. Medwear is headquartered in the United States and uses U.S. dollars as its functional currency. On March 17, Medwear sells a large quantity of uniforms to a hospital in Brussels, Belgium for exactly 267,000 euros to be paid in 45 days. On the date of the sale, the exchange rate was $1.32 for every euro.

    a. Record this transaction for Medwear on March 17 assuming that the uniforms are purchased on account.

    b. On March 31, Medwear prepares financial statements. On this date, the exchange rate is $1.27 per euro. Record the necessary adjusting entry for Medwear on this date.

12. The Boezi Corporation is beginning to report its financial statements at the end of Year Six. Preliminary information indicates that the company holds $90,000 in current assets and $210,000 in noncurrent assets. The company also plans to report current liabilities of $40,000 and noncurrent liabilities of $160,000. However, at the very end of the year, two final transactions take place. First, a $12,000 payment is made on an account payable. Second, a $21,000 collection is received from an account receivable.

    a. After recording these two transactions, what should the company report as the amount of its working capital?

    b. After recording these two transactions, what should the company report as its current ratio?

13. On January 1, Year Two, a company reports accounts receivable of $83,000. During Year Two, the company makes new credit sales of $511,000 while collecting cash of $437,000. No uncollectible accounts are expected or discovered. At the end of Year Two, how long does the average customer take to pay an account receivable balance?

14. On January 1, Year Two, a company reports accounts receivable of $83,000. During Year Two, the company makes new credit sales of $511,000 while collecting cash of $437,000. No uncollectible accounts are expected or discovered. What is the receivable turnover for Year Two?

15. In Chapter 4, Heather Miller started her own business, Sew Cool. The financial statements for December are shown next.

FIGURE 7.21

Sew Cool
Income Statement
As of December 31, 20X8

Revenue	$4,000
Cost of Goods	(2,000)
Gross Profit	2,000
Other Expenses	(1,695)
Earnings before Tax	305
Tax Expense	(107)
Net Income	$198

FIGURE 7.22

Sew Cool
Stmt. of Retained Earnings
As of December 31, 20X8

Retained Earnings, December 1, 20X8	$500
Net Income	198
Dividends	(158)
Retained Earnings, December 31, 20X8	$540

FIGURE 7.23

Sew Cool
Balance Sheet
December 31, 20X8

Assets		Liabilities	
Current		**Current**	
Cash	$940	Accounts Payable	$900
Accounts Receivable	500	Income Tax Payable	120
Less Allowance for		Total Current Liabilities	$1,020
Doubtful Accounts	(20)		
Net Accounts Receivable	480		
Inventory	700		
Total Current Assets	$2,120		
Noncurrent		**Noncurrent**	
Equipment	$1,000	Notes Payable	$1,060
		Owners' Equity	
		Capital Stock	$500
		Retained Earnings	540
		Total Owners' Equity	$1,040
		Total Liabilities & Owners'	
Total Assets	$3,120	Equity	$3,120

Based on the financial statements determine the following:

    a. Current ratio

    b. Working capital

    c. Age of receivables

    d. Receivables turnover—assuming that accounts receivable on January 1, 20X8 were $460.

COMPREHENSIVE PROBLEM

This problem will carry through over several chapters to enable students to build their accounting skills using knowledge gained in previous chapters.

In Chapter 5, Leon Jackson started Webworks, a Web site design and maintenance firm. At that time, an adjusted trial balance was prepared for June.

Here are Webworks financial statements as of June 30.

FIGURE 7.24

Webworks Income Statement As of June 30	
Revenue	$1,050
Expenses	(380)
Earnings before Tax	670
Tax Expense	(200)
Net Income	$ 470

FIGURE 7.25

Webworks Stmt. of Retained Earnings As of June 30	
Retained Earnings, June 1	$0
Net Income	470
Retained Earnings, June 30	$470

FIGURE 7.26

Webworks Balance Sheet June 30			
Assets		**Liabilities**	
Current		**Current**	
Cash	$9,800	Accounts Payable	$280
Accounts Receivable	450	Salaries Payable	100
Supplies Inventory	100	Unearned Revenue	500
Total Current Assets	$10,350	Total Current Liabilities	$880
Noncurrent		**Noncurrent**	
Equipment	$3,000	Notes Payable	$10,000
		Owners' Equity	
		Capital Stock	$2,000
		Retained Earnings	470
		Total Owners' Equity	$2,470
Total Assets	$13,350	Total Liabilities & Owners' Equity	$13,350

The following events occur during July:

a. Webworks purchases additional equipment for $4,000 cash.

b. Webworks purchases supplies worth $90 on account.

c. Webworks pays off accounts payable and salaries payable from June.

d. Webworks starts and completes four more sites and bills clients for $1,800.

e. In June, Webworks received $500 in advance to design a restaurant Web site. Webworks completes this site during July.

f. Webworks collects $1,200 in accounts receivable.

g. Webworks pays Nancy Po (the company employee hired in June) $500 for her work during the first three weeks of July.

h. Webworks receives $200 in advance to work on a Web site for a local dry cleaner and $300 in advance to work on a Web site for a local animal hospital. Work will not begin on these Web sites until August.

i. Leon's parents decide to charge rent after seeing how successful the business is and how much space it is taking up in their house. They all agree that rent will be $200 per month. Webworks pays $600 for July, August, and September.

j. Webworks pays taxes of $300 in cash.

> Required:
>
> A. Prepare journal entries for the previous events.
> B. Post the journal entries to T-accounts.
> C. Prepare an unadjusted trial balance for Webworks for July.
> D. Prepare adjusting entries for the following and post them to T-accounts.

k. Webworks owes Nancy Po $200 for her work during the last week of July.

l. Leon's parents let him know that Webworks owes $150 toward the electricity bill. Webworks will pay them in August.

m. Webworks determines that it has $50 worth of supplies remaining at the end of July.

n. Prepaid rent should be adjusted for July's rent.

o. Leon now believes that the company may not be able to collect all of its accounts receivable. A local CPA helps Leon determine that similar businesses report an allowance for bad debt at an average of 10 percent of their accounts receivable. Webworks will use this same approach.

> E. Prepare an adjusted trial balance.
> F. Prepare financial statements for July.

RESEARCH ASSIGNMENT

Assume that you take a job as a summer employee for an investment advisory service. One of the partners for that firm is currently looking at the possibility of investing in **eBay Inc.** The partner is a bit concerned about the impact of the recession on this company, especially its accounts receivable. The partner asks you to look at the 2010 financial statements for **eBay Inc.** by following this path:

- Go to http://www.ebay.com.
- At the bottom of this screen, click on "Company Info."
- On the left side of the next screen, click on "Investors."
- On the left side of the next screen, click on "Annual Reports & Proxy."
- In the center of the next screen, click on "2010 Annual Report" to download.
- Go to page 86 and find the December 31, 2009, and December 31, 2010, balance sheets.
- Go to page 87 and find the income statement for the year ended December 31, 2010.
- Go to page 94 and read the note about the composition of the allowance for doubtful accounts.

a. Using the figures found on the balance sheet and the income statement, determine the number of days **eBay** takes to collect its receivables at the end of 2010.

b. Using the figures found on the balance sheet and the income statement, determine the receivables turnover for **eBay** during 2010.

c. Using the figures found in the balance sheet and the information in the notes, determine the percentage of receivables as of December 31, 2010 that are expected to be uncollectible.

ENDNOTES

1. The independent auditors will also analyze the same available evidence and must agree that it is sufficient to serve as the basis for rendering reasonable assurance that the financial statements are presented fairly before an unqualified opinion can be released.

2. Some companies include both accounts on the balance sheet to indicate the origin of the reported balance. Others show only the single net figure with explanatory information provided in the notes to the financial statements.

3. Because the focus of the discussion here is on accounts receivable and their collectability, the recognition of cost of goods sold as well as the possible return of any merchandise will be omitted at this time.

4. Many companies combine these two entries for convenience. The debit to accounts receivable in the first entry exactly offsets the credit in the second. Thus, the same recording impact is achieved by simply debiting cash and crediting the allowance for doubtful accounts. However, the rationale for that single entry is not always as evident to a beginning student.

5. The $3,000 debit figure is assumed here for convenience to be solely the result of underestimating uncollectible accounts in Year One. Several other factors may also be present. For example, the balance in the allowance for doubtful accounts will be impacted by credit sales made in the current year that are discovered to be worthless before the end of the period. Such accounts actually reduce the allowance T-account prior to the recognition of an expense. The residual allowance balance is also affected by the collection of accounts that were written off as worthless in an earlier year. As described earlier, the allowance is actually increased by that event. However, the financial reporting is not altered by the actual cause of the final allowance figure.

6. As has been stated previously, this is an introductory textbook. Thus, a more in-depth examination of many important topics, such as foreign currency balances, can be found in upper-level accounting texts. The coverage here of foreign currency balances is only designed to introduce students to basic reporting problems and their resolutions.

CHAPTER 8

How Does a Company Gather Information about Its Inventory?

 Video Clip

In this video, Professor Joe Hoyle introduces the essential points covered in Chapter 8.

View the video online at: http://bit.ly/hoyle8-1

1. DETERMINING AND REPORTING THE COST OF INVENTORY

LEARNING OBJECTIVES

At the end of this section, students should be able to meet the following objectives:

1. Understand that inventory is recorded initially at historical cost.
2. Provide the guiding rule for identifying expenditures that are capitalized in the acquisition of inventory.
3. Explain the rationale for offering a discount for quick payments of cash as well as the accounting used to report such reductions.

1.1 The Reported Inventory Balance

*Question: The asset section of the February 26, 2011, balance sheet produced by **Best Buy Co. Inc.** reports net accounts receivable of $2.348 billion. Based on coverage provided in the previous chapter, savvy decision makers should know that this figure reflects net realizable value—the estimation by officials of the cash amount that will be collected from the receivables owed to the company by its customers. Knowledge of financial accounting allows any individual to understand the information conveyed in a set of financial statements.*

*As is common, the next account that appears on **Best Buy**'s balance sheet is "merchandise inventories." This asset includes all items held as of that date that were acquired for sales purposes—televisions,* *cameras, computers, and the like. The monetary figure disclosed by the company for this asset is $5.897 billion. Does this balance also indicate net realizable value—the cash expected to be generated from the company's merchandise—or is different information reflected?* **On a balance sheet, what does the amount reported for inventory represent?**

inventory

A current asset bought or manufactured for the purpose of selling in order to generate revenue.

Answer: The challenge of analyzing the various assets reported by an organization would be reduced substantially if all account balances disclosed the same basic information, such as net realizable value. However, over the decades, virtually every asset has come to have its own individualized method of reporting, one created to address the special peculiarities of that account. Thus, the term "presented fairly" is often reflected in a totally different way for each asset. Reporting accounts receivables, for example, at net realizable value has no impact on the approach that is generally accepted for **inventory**.

Accounting for inventory is more complicated because reporting is not as standardized as with accounts receivable. For example, under certain circumstances, the balance sheet amount shown for inventory actually does reflect net realizable value. However, several other meanings for that balance are more likely. The range of accounting alternatives emphasizes the need for a careful reading of financial statement notes rather than fixating on a few reported numbers alone. Without study of the available disclosures, a decision maker simply cannot know what **Best Buy** means by the $5.897 billion figure reported for its inventory.

For all cases, though, the reporting of inventory begins with its cost. In contrast, cost is never an issue even considered in the reporting of accounts receivable.

1.2   Determining the Cost of Inventory

Question: Every item bought for sales purposes has a definite cost. The accounting process for inventory begins with a calculation of that cost. **How does an accountant determine the cost of acquired inventory?**

Answer: The financial reporting for inventory starts by identifying the cost paid to obtain the item. In acquiring inventory, officials make the considered decision to allocate a certain amount of their scarce resources. The amount of that sacrifice is interesting information. What did the company expend to obtain this merchandise? That is a reasonable question to ask since this information can be valuable to decision makers.

To illustrate, assume that a sporting goods company (Rider Inc.) acquires a new bicycle (Model XY-7) to sell. Rider's accounting system should be designed to determine the cost of this piece of inventory, the price that the company willingly paid to obtain the asset. Assume that $250 was charged by the manufacturer (Builder Company) for the bicycle, and the purchase was made by Rider on credit. Rider spends $9 in cash to transport the item from the factory to one of its retail stores and another $6 to have the pieces assembled so that the bicycle can be displayed in the salesroom for customers to examine.

In accounting for the acquisition of inventory, cost is said to include all normal and necessary amounts incurred to get the item into condition and position to be sold. All such expenditures provide future value. Hence, as shown in Figure 8.1, by the time this bicycle has reached Rider's retail location and been readied for sale, the cost to the sporting goods company is $265.

FIGURE 8.1   Monitoring the Cost of an Inventory Item—Subsidiary Ledger

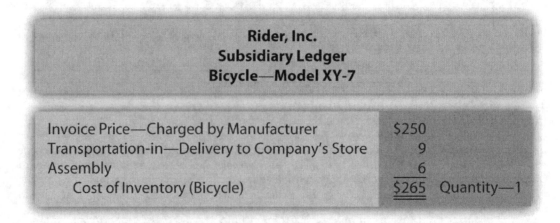

Charges for delivering this merchandise and assembling the parts were included in the asset account (the traditional term for adding a cost to an asset account, **capitalization**, was introduced previously). Both of these expenditures were properly viewed as normal and necessary to get the bicycle into condition and position to be sold. Interestingly, any amount later expended by the company to transport inventory from the store to a buying customer is recorded as an expense because that cost is incurred after the sale takes place. At that point, no further future value exists since the merchandise has already been sold.

Occasionally, costs arise where the "normal and necessary" standard may be difficult to apply. To illustrate, assume that the president of a store that sells antiques buys a 120-year-old table for resell purposes. When the table arrives at the store, another $300 must be spent to fix a scratch cut across its surface. Should this added cost be capitalized (added to the reported balance for inventory) or expensed? The answer to this question is not readily apparent and depends on ascertaining the relevant facts. Here are two possibilities.

Scenario one: The table was acquired by the president with the knowledge that the scratch already existed and needed to be fixed prior to offering the merchandise for sale. In that case, repair is a normal and necessary activity to bring the table into the condition necessary to be sold. The $300 is capitalized, recorded as an addition to the reported cost of the inventory.

Scenario two: The table was bought without the scratch but was damaged when first moved into the store through an act of employee carelessness. The table must be repaired, but the scratch was neither normal nor necessary. The cost could have been avoided. This $300 is not capitalized but rather reported as a repair expense by the store.

As discussed in an earlier chapter, if the accountant cannot make a reasonable determination as to whether a particular cost qualifies as normal and necessary, the practice of conservatism requires the $300 to be reported as an expense. When in doubt, the alternative that makes reported figures look best is avoided so that decision makers are not encouraged to be overly optimistic about the company's financial health and future prospects.

> **capitalization**
>
> The process of recording a cost as an asset rather than an expense; for inventory, it includes all normal and necessary costs associated with getting the asset into position and condition to be sold.

TEST YOURSELF

Question:

Near the end of Year One, the Morganton Hardware Company buys five lawn mowers for sale by paying $300 each. The delivery cost to transport these items to the store was another $40 in total. In January of the following year, $60 more was spent to assemble all the parts and then clean the finished products so they could be placed in the company's showroom. On February 3, Year Two, one of these lawn mowers was sold for $500 cash. The company paid a final $25 to have this item delivered to the buyer. If no other transactions take place, what net income does the company recognize for Year Two?

 a. $150
 b. $155
 c. $160
 d. $175

Answer:

The correct answer is choice b: $155.

Explanation:

The cost of the mowers ($1,500 or $300 × 5) along with transportation cost ($40) and assembling and cleaning costs ($60) are normal and necessary to get the items into position and condition to be sold. Total capitalized cost is $1,600 or $320 per unit. Gross profit on the first sale is $180 ($500 less $320). The $25 delivery charge is expensed; it is not capitalized because it occurred after the sale and had no future value. Net income is $155 ($180 gross profit minus $25 delivery expense).

1.3   Offering Discounts for Quick Payment

Question: When inventory is sold, some sellers are willing to accept a reduced amount to encourage fast payment—an offer that is called a cash discount (or sales discount or purchases discount depending on whether the seller or the buyer is making the entry). Cash becomes available sooner so that the seller can quickly put it back into circulation to make more profits. In addition, the possibility that a receivable will become uncollectible is reduced if the balance due is not allowed to get too old. Tempting buyers to make quick payments to reduce their cost is viewed as a smart business practice by many sellers.

To illustrate, assume the invoice received by the sporting goods company (Rider) for the above bicycle indicates the proper $250 balance but also includes the notation: 2/10, n/45. What message is being conveyed by the seller? **How do cash discounts impact the reporting of inventory?**

Answer: Sellers—such as Builder Company in this example—can offer a wide variety of discount terms to encourage speedy payment. One such as 2/10, n/45 is generally read "two ten, net 45." It informs the buyer that a 2 percent discount is available if the invoice is paid by the tenth day. The net amount that remains unpaid (after any merchandise returns or partial cash payments) is due on the forty-fifth day. Rider has the option to pay $245 for the bicycle within ten days of receiving the invoice by taking advantage of the $5 discount ($250 × 0.02). Or the sporting goods company can wait until the forty-fifth day but then is responsible for the entire $250. In practice, a variety of other discount terms are frequently encountered such as 1/10, n/30 or 2/10, n/30.

Many companies automatically take all cash discounts as a matter of policy because of the high rate of interest earned. If Rider does not submit the money after ten days, it must pay an extra $5 in order to hold onto $245 for an additional thirty-five days. This delay equates to a 2.04 percent interest rate over just that short period of time ($5/$245 = 2.04 percent [rounded]). There are over ten thirty-five-day periods in a year. Paying the extra $5 is the equivalent of an annual interest rate in excess of 21 percent.

365 days per year/35 days holding the money = 10.43 time periods per year

2.04% (for 35 days) × 10.43 time periods = 21.28% interest rate for a year

That substantial rate of interest expense is avoided by making early payment, a decision chosen by most companies unless they are experiencing serious cash flow difficulties.

Assuming that Rider avails itself of the discount offer, the capitalized cost of the inventory is reduced to $260.

FIGURE 8.2 Cost of Inventory Reduced by Cash Discount—Subsidiary Ledger

Rider, Inc.
Subsidiary Ledger
Bicycle—Model XY-7

Invoice Price—Charged by Manufacturer	$250
Discount Taken—2/10, n/45	(5)
Transportation-in from Seller to Store	9
Assembly	6
Cost of Inventory (Bicycle)	$260 Quantity—1

TEST YOURSELF

Question:

On March 1, a hardware store buys inventory for resale purposes at a cost of $300. The invoice is mailed on March 2, and the manufacturer offers cash terms of 3/10, n/30. Store officials choose to settle 60 percent of the invoice on March 10 and the remainder on March 30. What was the total amount paid for the inventory?

  a. $291.00
  b. $294.60
  c. $296.40
  d. $300.00

Answer:

The correct answer is choice b: $294.60.

Explanation:

Of the total amount charged, $180.00 (60 percent of $300.00) is settled in a timely fashion which allows the company to take a 3 percent discount or $5.40 ($180.00 × 3 percent). The company's first payment was $174.60 ($180.00 minus $5.40). The remaining $120.00 is paid at the end of thirty days, after the discount period has passed. No additional discount is available. The cost of the inventory to the company is $294.60 ($174.60 plus $120.00).

KEY TAKEAWAY

Any discussion of the reporting of inventory begins with the calculation of cost, the amount spent to obtain the merchandise. For inventory, cost encompasses all payments that are considered normal and necessary to get the items into condition and possession to be sold. All other expenditures are expensed as incurred. Cash discounts (such as 2/10, n/30) are often offered to buyers to encourage quick payment. The seller wants to get its money as quickly as possible to plow back into operations. For the buyer, taking advantage of such discounts is usually a wise business decision because they effectively provide interest at a relatively high rate.

2. PERPETUAL AND PERIODIC INVENTORY SYSTEMS

LEARNING OBJECTIVES

At the end of this section, students should be able to meet the following objectives:

1. **Identify the attributes as well as the advantages and disadvantages of a perpetual inventory system.**
2. **Identify the attributes as well as the advantages and disadvantages of a periodic inventory system.**
3. **Provide journal entries for a variety of transactions involved in the purchase of inventory using both a perpetual and a periodic inventory system.**

2.1 Maintaining Inventory Costs in a Perpetual System

*Question: In an earlier chapter, differences between a perpetual inventory system and a periodic inventory system were discussed briefly. Because of the availability of modern technology, most companies—but not all—maintain some type of perpetual inventory records. A perpetual system—which frequently relies on bar coding and computer scanning—provides an ongoing record of all items present, both in total and individually. **How is the recording of an inventory purchase carried out in a perpetual system?***

Answer: When a **perpetual inventory system** is in use, all additions and reductions are monitored in the inventory T-account. Thus, theoretically, the balance found in that general ledger account at any point in time is identical to the merchandise physically on hand. In actual practice, recording mistakes as well as losses such as theft and breakage create some (hopefully small) discrepancies. Consequently, even with a perpetual system, inventory records must be reconciled occasionally with the items actually present to reestablish accuracy.

In a perpetual inventory system, the maintenance of a separate subsidiary ledger showing data about the individual items on hand is essential. On February 26, 2011, **Best Buy** reported inventory totaling $5.897 billion. However, internally the company also needs specific information as to the quantity, type, and location of all televisions, cameras, computers, and the like that make up this sum. That is the significance of a perpetual system; it provides the ability to keep track of the various types of merchandise. The total cost is available in the inventory T-account but detailed data about the composition (the quantity and frequently the cost) of merchandise physically on hand is found in a subsidiary ledger where an individual file can be available for each item as is shown in Figure 8.2.

Assume that Rider Inc. (the sporting goods company) uses a perpetual inventory system. In Figure 8.3, journal entries are shown for the purchase of a bicycle to sell (Model XY-7). The bicycle is recorded at the $250 invoice amount and then reduced by $5 at the time the discount is taken. This approach is known as the "gross method of reporting discounts." As an alternative, companies can choose to anticipate taking the discount and simply make the initial entry for the $245 expected payment. This option is referred to as the "net method of reporting discounts." Under that approach, if the discount is not actually taken, the additional $5 cost is recorded as a loss or an expense rather than as a capitalized cost of the inventory because it is not normal or necessary to pay the extra amount.

FIGURE 8.3 Rider Inc.—Journal Entries—Perpetual Inventory System

Purchased Bicycle (Model XY-7)—Recorded Using Gross Method

Inventory	250		(increase an asset—debit)
Accounts Payable		250	(increase a liability—credit)

Paid for Bicycle after Taking 2 Percent Discount

Accounts Payable	250		(decrease a liability—debit)
Cash		245	(decrease an asset—credit)
Inventory		5	(decrease an asset—credit)

Payment Made to Transport Bicycle to Retail Store

Inventory	9		(increase an asset—debit)
Cash		9	(decrease an asset—credit)

Payment Made to Assemble Bicycle for Display Purposes

Inventory	6		(increase an asset—debit)
Cash		6	(decrease an asset—credit)

After posting these entries, the inventory T-account in the general ledger reports a net cost of $260 ($250 − $5 + $9 + $6) and the separate subsidiary ledger shown previously indicates that one Model XY-7 bicycle is on hand with a cost of $260.

TEST YOURSELF

Question:

A grocery store carries cans of tuna fish, salmon, and sardines. The company uses a perpetual inventory system with the general ledger inventory account backed up by a subsidiary ledger. Which of the following statements is most likely to not be true?

 a. The number of cans of salmon on hand can be found in the subsidiary ledger.
 b. The cost of all cans of fish can be found in the general ledger.
 c. The number of cans of tuna fish on hand can be found in the general ledger.
 d. The cost of the cans of sardines on hand can be found in the subsidiary ledger.

Answer:

The correct answer is choice c: The number of cans of tuna fish on hand can be found in the general ledger.

Explanation:

In a perpetual system, the total cost of all inventory on hand is recorded in the general ledger inventory T-account. The quantity (and frequently the cost) of the individual items is monitored in a subsidiary ledger. Here, the subsidiary ledger maintains the quantity and likely the cost for each type of fish: tuna fish, salmon, and sardines. No information is gained by recording the number of cans of fish in the general ledger since that figure will be available in the subsidiary ledger.

2.2   Recording Inventory Purchases in a Periodic System

Question: In a periodic system, no attempt is made to keep an ongoing record of a company's inventory. Instead, the quantity and cost of merchandise is only determined periodically as a preliminary step in preparing financial statements. **How is the actual recording of an inventory purchase carried out in a periodic system?**

Answer: If a company uses a **periodic inventory system**, neither the cost nor the quantity of the items on hand is monitored. Inventory amounts are unknown both in total and individually. These figures are not viewed by company officials as worth the cost and effort necessary to gather them. However, purchases are still made, and a record must be maintained of the costs incurred. This information is eventually used for financial reporting but also—more immediately—for control purposes. Regardless of the recording system, companies want to avoid spending unnecessary amounts on inventory as well as tangential expenditures such as transportation and assembly. If the accounting system indicates that a particular cost is growing too rapidly, alternatives can be investigated and implemented before the problem becomes serious. Periodic systems are designed to provide such information through the use of separate general ledger T-accounts for each cost incurred.

Assume that Rider uses a periodic inventory system. Its journal entries for the acquisition of the Model XY-7 bicycle are as shown in Figure 8.4. No separate subsidiary ledger is maintained. The overall cost of this inventory item is not readily available in the accounting records and the quantity (except by visual inspection) is unknown. At any point in time, company officials do have access to the amounts spent for each of the individual costs (such as transportation and assembly) for monitoring purposes.

Because these costs result from the acquisition of an asset that eventually becomes an expense when sold, they follow the same debit and credit rules as those accounts.

periodic inventory system

Accounting system that does not maintain an ongoing record of all inventory items; instead, ending inventory is determined by a physical count so that a formula (beginning inventory plus purchases less ending inventory) can be used to calculate cost of goods sold.

FIGURE 8.4 Rider Inc.—Journal Entries—Periodic Inventory System

Purchased Bicycle (Model XY-7)—Recorded Using Gross Method

Purchases of Inventory	250	(increase an asset—debit)
Accounts Payable	250	(increase a liability—credit)

Paid for Bicycle after Taking 2 Percent Discount

Accounts Payable	250	(decrease a liability—debit)
Cash	245	(decrease an asset—credit)
Purchases Discount	5	(decrease an asset—credit)

Payment Made to Transport Bicycle to Retail Stort

Transportation-in	9	(increase an asset—debit)
Cash	9	(decrease an asset—credit)

Payment Made to Assemble Bicycle for Display Purposes

Assembly of Inventory	6	(increase an asset—debit)
Cash	6	(decrease an asset—credit)

In a periodic system, when a sale occurs, the revenue entry is made as always. However, no journal entry is made for cost of goods sold. Because of the lack of information, the dollar amount of the cost is not known at this time so inventory is not reduced and cost of goods sold is not recognized. Instead, when a periodic system is in use, cost of goods sold is only determined and recorded when financial statements are prepared through the use of the following formula:

Cost of goods sold = Beginning inventory + Purchase costs for period − Ending inventory

Note that the choice between using a perpetual and periodic system impacts the following:

- Information available to company officials on a daily basis
- Journal entries to be made
- Cost necessary to operate the accounting system (the technology required by a perpetual system is more expensive)

Regardless of the system in use, Rider holds one piece of inventory with a cost of $260. The decision as to whether to utilize a perpetual or periodic system is based on the added cost of the perpetual system and the difference in the available information generated for use by company officials. The company's inventory is not physically affected by the method selected.

TEST YOURSELF

Question:

A company starts operations in Year One and buys ten units of inventory for $70 each. The transportation cost for the entire group of items was $110. A few days later, the president of the company checks out the balances in the general ledger. Which of the following is true?

   a. If a periodic inventory system is in use, no balances will be available in connection with this inventory.
   b. If a periodic inventory system is in use, an inventory account will be found with a balance of $810.
   c. If a perpetual inventory system is in use, a transportation-in account will be found with a balance of $110.
   d. If a perpetual inventory system is in use, an inventory account will be found with a balance of $810.

Answer:

The correct answer is choice d: If a perpetual inventory system is in use, an inventory account will be found with a balance of $810.

Explanation:

If a periodic system is used, a purchases account will report $700 (ten units at $70 each). Transportation-in will be $110. Until the end of the year, these balances are not adjusted to correspond with the inventory on hand or sold. In a perpetual system, the initial journal entries record $810 in the inventory account (invoice price of $700 plus transportation of $110) or $81 for each of the ten units. All costs are recorded within that one T-account and are not divided up by type.

TEST YOURSELF

Question:

A company is started in Year One, and the president and the accountant confer and opt to install a perpetual system to record and monitor inventory. Which of the following is not likely to have been a reason for this decision?

   a. The president knows that the perpetual system will cost more than the periodic system but did not consider it to be prohibitively expensive.
   b. The president fears that transportation charges may escalate quickly and wants to monitor that cost.
   c. The president wants to be aware when any inventory item is reduced to only five units so that the quantity can be replenished.
   d. The president wants to know the total cost of inventory because she plans to set sales price based on that figure.

Answer:

The correct answer is choice b: The president fears that transportation charges may escalate quickly and wants to monitor that cost.

Explanation:

Perpetual systems maintain updated records as to the cost and quantity of the inventory on hand so that decisions such as pricing and purchasing can be made. However, this benefit can be outweighed if the perpetual system is viewed as too costly. Although the information available in a periodic system is more limited, the various costs (such as transportation) are tracked so that company officials can take action if problems arise.

2.3   Actual Use of Periodic Inventory Systems

*Question: **Given the availability of sophisticated computers at moderate prices, do any companies still use periodic inventory systems?** With bar coding and the advanced state of technology, are periodic inventory procedures so antiquated that they are no longer found in actual practice?*

Answer: Obviously, in this computer age, perpetual inventory systems have come to dominate because they provide valuable and immediate information to company officials. However, some businesses are unlikely to ever change from the simplicity of a periodic system.

A beauty salon or barber shop, for example, where services are rendered but a small amount of inventory is kept on hand for occasional sales, would certainly not need to absorb the cost of a perpetual system. Visual inspection can alert employees as to the quantity of inventory on hand.

Restaurants, sandwich shops, ice cream stores, and the like might well choose to use a periodic system because customer purchases take place at a small establishment where quantities are easy to observe and manage. In such operations, the information provided by a perpetual system does not necessarily provide additional benefit.

"Dollar stores," which have become particularly prevalent in recent years, sell huge quantities of low-priced merchandise. Goods tend to be added to a store's inventory as they become available rather than based on a formal managed inventory strategy. Again, officials must decide whether keeping up with the amount of inventory on hand will improve their decision making. If not, the cost of a perpetual system is unnecessary.

Perhaps, most importantly, some companies use a hybrid system where the units on hand and sold are monitored carefully with a perpetual system. However, to reduce accounting costs, the dollar amounts for inventory and cost of goods sold are determined using a periodic system when financial statements are to be prepared. In that way, the company gains valuable information (the number of units on hand) but still utilizes a cheaper system.

KEY TAKEAWAY

Perpetual inventory systems are designed to maintain updated figures (quantity and cost) for inventory as a whole as well as for individual items. The general ledger account reports the total cost of all inventory. At the same time, separate subsidiary ledger accounts provide the balance for each type of inventory so that company officials can know the size, cost, and composition of the merchandise on hand. A periodic system is cheaper to operate because no attempt is made to monitor inventory balances (in total or individually) until financial statements are to be prepared. A periodic system does allow a company to control its costs by keeping track of the individual inventory expenditures as they occur. Small organizations often use a periodic inventory system because the added cost of a perpetual system cannot be justified.

3. THE CALCULATION OF COST OF GOODS SOLD

LEARNING OBJECTIVES

At the end of this section, students should be able to meet the following objectives:

1. Explain the meaning of the FOB point in connection with an inventory purchase and its impact on the recording of this transaction.
2. Identify the time at which cost of goods sold is computed in a perpetual inventory system as well as the recording made at the time of sale.
3. Identify the time at which cost of goods sold is computed in a periodic inventory system as well as the recording made at the time of sale.
4. Compute cost of goods sold in a periodic inventory system and prepare the adjustment to enter the appropriate balances into the accounting system.
5. Understand the necessity of taking a physical inventory count.

3.1 Recording Purchases Based on the FOB Point

Question: Rider Inc. (the sporting goods company) buys a bicycle for sales purposes. The company can record the transaction using either a perpetual system (debit Inventory) or periodic system (debit Purchases of Inventory). **When should an inventory purchase be recorded?** *Assume, for example, that Builder Company (the manufacturer of this bicycle) is located in Wisconsin, whereas the retail store operated by Rider is in Kentucky. Delivery takes several days at a minimum. The precise moment for recording the transaction is probably not critical except near the end of the year when the timing of journal entries will impact balances that are included on the financial statements.*

To illustrate, assume this bicycle is ordered by Rider Inc. on December 27 of Year One. It is shipped by Builder Company from Wisconsin on December 29 of Year One and arrives at the retail store on January 4 of Year Two. When Rider produces financial statements for Year One, should the inventory cost and related payable be included even though the bicycle was not physically received until Year Two?

Answer: Documents prepared in connection with inventory shipments are normally marked with an "FOB" point. FOB stands for "Free On Board" (a traditional maritime term that has gained a wider use over the years) and indicates when legal title to property is transferred from seller to buyer. At that moment, ownership of the bicycle is conveyed. The FOB point signifies the appropriate date for recording.

If Builder Company specifies that the sale of this bicycle is made **FOB shipping point** and Rider Inc. agrees to this condition, conveyance occurs on December 29, Year One, when the bicycle leaves the seller. Consequently, both the asset and the liability appear on the December 31, Year One, balance sheet prepared by the buyer. For the same reason, Builder records sales revenue in Year One.

However, if the contract states that the transaction is made **FOB destination**, the seller maintains ownership until the bicycle arrives at Rider's store on January 4, Year Two. Neither party records the transaction until that date. The date of recognition is based on the FOB point.

The FOB point can be important for two additional reasons.

- The party that holds legal title to merchandise during its delivery from seller to buyer normally incurs all transportation costs. If no other arrangements are negotiated, "FOB shipping point" means that Rider Inc. as the buyer is responsible for the delivery. "FOB destination" assigns this cost to Builder, as the seller.

- Any losses or damages that occur in route affect the party holding legal title (again, unless other arrangements are agreed upon by the parties). If shipment from Wisconsin to Kentucky was noted as FOB shipping point and the bicycle breaks as the result of an accident in Illinois, it is the buyer's inventory that was harmed. However, it is the seller's problem if the shipment is marked as FOB destination. The legal owner bears the cost of any damages that occur during the physical conveyance of property.

> **FOB shipping point**
>
> Terms of sale stipulating that legal title to shipped goods passes to the buyer at the time of shipment so that the buyer is responsible for transportation costs and any damages or losses in transit.

> **FOB destination**
>
> Terms of sale stipulating that legal title to shipped goods passes to the buyer when they arrive at the final destination so that the seller is responsible for transportation costs and any damages or losses in transit.

TEST YOURSELF

Question:

A company buys 144 inventory items at a total cost of $4,000. The shipment was made in Year One but did not arrive at the buyer's location until early in Year Two. Both the buyer and the seller believed the goods had been sold FOB destination so they each recorded the sale in that manner. However, a review of the documents indicates that the sale was actually made FOB shipping point. Which of the following is correct about the Year One financial statements?

a. The seller's sales account for Year One is overstated.

b. The seller's cost of goods sold account for Year One is overstated.

c. The buyer's inventory account at the end of Year One is overstated.

d. The buyer's accounts payable account at the end of Year One is understated.

Answer:

The correct answer is choice d: The buyer's accounts payable account at the end of Year One is understated.

Explanation:

Both companies believe the sale was FOB destination. The goods arrived at the buyer's business in Year Two. Thus, nothing was reported in Year One for accounts receivable, sales, and cost of goods sold (by the seller) or for inventory and accounts payable (by the buyer). It was actually FOB selling point. All five accounts are understated. Use of a periodic or perpetual system is not important because the question only asks about financial statements and not the method of recording.

3.2   Recording Cost Of Goods Sold: Perpetual and Periodic

*Question: When a sale of inventory is made, the seller recognizes an expense that has previously been identified as "cost of goods sold" or "cost of sales." For example, **Best Buy** reported "cost of goods sold," for the year ended February 26, 2011, as $37.611 billion. When should cost of goods sold be determined?*

To illustrate, assume that Rider Inc. begins the current year holding three Model XY-7 bicycles costing $260 each—$780 in total. During the period, another five units of this same model are acquired, again for $260 apiece or $1,300 in total. At this introductory stage, utilizing a single cost of $260 for all items eliminates a significant theoretical problem, one that will be discussed in detail in the following chapter.

*Eventually, a customer buys seven of these bicycles for her family and friends paying cash of $440 each or $3,080 in total. No further sales are made of this model during the current period so that only a single bicycle remains (3 + 5 − 7). One is still in stock while seven have been sold. **What is the proper method of recording the company's cost of goods sold?***

Answer: The answer here depends on whether a perpetual or a periodic system is used by the company.

Perpetual inventory system. The acquisition and subsequent sale of inventory when a perpetual system is in use was demonstrated briefly in an earlier chapter. The accounting records maintain current balances so that officials are cognizant of (a) the amount of merchandise on hand and (b) the cost of goods sold for the year to date. These figures are readily available in general ledger T-accounts. In addition, separate subsidiary ledger balances are usually established for the individual items in stock, showing the quantity on hand and the cost. When each sale is made, the applicable cost is reclassified from the inventory account on the balance sheet to cost of goods sold on the income statement. Simultaneously, the corresponding balance in the subsidiary ledger is lowered.

In this example, bicycles were acquired by Rider Inc. Seven of them, costing $260 each (a total of $1,820), are then sold to a customer for $440 apiece or $3,080. When a perpetual system is in use, two journal entries are prepared at the time of each sale: one for the sale and a second to shift the cost of the inventory from asset to expense.

FIGURE 8.5 Journal Entries for Sale of Seven Model XY-7 Bicycles—Perpetual Inventory System

Cash	3,080		(increase an asset—debit)
Sales Revenue—Merchandise		3,080	(increase a revenue—credit)
Cost of Goods Sold	1,820		(increase an expense—debit)
Inventory		1,820	(decrease an asset—credit)

gross profit

Difference between sales and cost of goods sold; also called gross margin or markup.

Removing $1,820 from inventory leaves a balance of $260 ($780 + $1,300 − $1,820) representing the cost of the one remaining unit. The $1,260 difference between revenue and cost of goods sold ($3,080 minus $1,820) is the markup (also known as **gross profit** or "gross margin") earned on the sale.

Periodic inventory system. In contrast, a periodic system monitors the various inventory expenditures but makes no attempt to maintain a record of the merchandise on hand or the cost of goods sold during the year. Although cheap to create and operate, the information available to company officials is extremely limited.

At the time the sale of these seven bicycles takes place, the first journal entry shown in Figure 8.5 is still made to recognize the revenue. Cash is debited for $3,080 and Sales Revenue-Merchandise is credited for $3,080. However, if a periodic system is in use, the second entry is omitted. Cost of goods sold is neither calculated nor recorded when a sale occurs. The available information is not sufficient to determine the amount. The inventory balance remains unadjusted throughout the year. Eventually, whenever financial statements are prepared, the figure to be reported for the asset (inventory) on that date must be determined along with the expense (cost of goods sold) for the entire period.

Because totals are not updated, the only accounts found in the general ledger relating to inventory show balances of $780 (beginning balance) and $1,300 (purchases of inventory).

General Ledger Balances—Periodic Inventory System	
Inventory (beginning balance remains unadjusted during the period):	3 units at $260 each or $780
Purchases of Inventory (total inventory costs incurred during the period; for this example, the balance includes the invoice price, sales discount, transportation-in, and assembly, although they would have been kept separate in the actual recording):	5 units at $260 each or $1,300

Based on this information, total inventory available to be sold by Rider Inc. during this period is eight units costing $2,080 ($780 plus $1,300).

physical inventory

A count of inventory on hand; necessary for reporting purposes when using a periodic system but also required for a perpetual system to ensure the accuracy of recorded information.

When using a periodic system, cost of goods sold is computed as a prerequisite step in preparing financial statements. Inventory on hand is counted (a process known as **physical inventory**), and all units that are no longer present are assumed to have been sold. The resulting figure is then reported as the company's cost of goods sold for the period. Because complete inventory records are not available, any units that are lost, stolen, or broken cannot be separately derived. All missing inventory is grouped into one expense—cost of goods sold.

In this example, a physical inventory count will be taken by the employees of Rider Inc. on or near the last day of the year so that financial statements can be produced. Because eight bicycles (Model XY-7) were available during the year but seven have now been sold, one unit—costing $260—remains (if no accident or theft has occurred). This amount is the inventory figure that appears in the asset section of the balance sheet.

Cost of goods sold is then computed by the following formula.

FIGURE 8.6 Computation of Cost of Goods Sold in a Periodic System[1]

Beginning Inventory	$780
Purchases for the Period	1,300
Goods Available for Sale	2,080
Ending Inventory (one unit at a cost of $260)	(260)
Cost of Goods Sold	$1,820

In a periodic system, three costs are used to arrive at the amount reported as cost of goods sold. It is important to understand how each of these figures is derived.

- *Beginning inventory* was derived by a count taken at the end of the previous year. After determining the number of units on hand (three bicycles), the accountant inserts the cost of these items based on the amount paid during the period ($260 each). The resulting monetary balance was recorded in the inventory T-account at the end of that year and has remained unchanged until the end of the current year. A periodic system only updates general ledger accounts when financial statements are prepared.

- The *purchases* figure has been maintained throughout the year in the general ledger to provide a record of the amounts expended ($1,300) for all normal and necessary costs (invoice price, discounts, transportation-in, assembly costs, and the like) needed to get the inventory into position and condition to be sold.

- *Ending inventory* is found by making a new physical count at the end of the current period. The number of units that are still held (one, in this case) is multiplied by the unit cost ($260) to arrive at the proper inventory total reported on the balance sheet.

TEST YOURSELF

Question:

Lincoln Corporation buys and sells widgets and uses a periodic system for accounting purposes. According to counts that were taken, the company started the year with 4,000 units and ended the year with 5,000. However, during the period, an additional 17,000 widgets were acquired. All inventory items are bought by the company for $7 each, a figure that includes all normal and necessary costs. What was cost of goods sold for this period?

- a. $112,000
- b. $118,000
- c. $119,000
- d. $125,000

Answer:

The correct answer is choice a: $112,000.

Explanation:

Beginning inventory cost $28,000 (4,000 units at $7 each) while purchases for the period totaled $119,000 (17,000 × $7). Thus, the total cost of the goods available for sale during the year was $147,000 ($28,000 plus $119,000). Ending inventory is $35,000 (5,000 units at $7 each). Thus, inventory with a cost of $112,000 is missing at year's end ($28,000 plus $119,000 less $35,000). In a periodic system, all missing inventory is assumed to make up the cost of the goods sold.

3.3   Periodic Inventory—Year-End Recording Process

Question: In a perpetual inventory system, cost of goods sold is determined at the time of each sale. Figures retained in a subsidiary ledger provide the cost of the specific item being surrendered so that an immediate reclassification from asset to expense is made.

With a periodic system, cost of goods sold is not calculated until financial statements are prepared. The beginning inventory balance (the ending amount from the previous year) is combined with the total acquisition costs for the current period. Merchandise still on hand is counted, and its cost is determined. All missing inventory is assumed to reflect the cost of goods sold. **When a periodic inventory system is used, how are ending inventory and cost of goods sold for the year physically entered into the accounting records?** *These figures have not been recorded on an ongoing basis; the general ledger must now be updated to agree with the reported balances.*

Answer: In the bicycle example, opening inventory for the period was three items costing $780. Another five were bought during the year for $1,300. The total cost of these eight units is $2,080. Because the financial impact of lost or broken units cannot be ascertained in a periodic system, the entire $2,080 is assigned to either ending inventory (one unit at a cost of $260) or cost of goods sold ($780 + $1,300 - $260 or $1,820). No other account exists in which to record inventory costs in a periodic system. The goods are assumed to be on hand or to have been sold.

For a periodic inventory system, a year-end adjusting entry is prepared so that these newly computed amounts are reflected as the final account balances. Transportation and assembly costs are included within the purchases figure in this entry for convenience.

FIGURE 8.7 Adjusting Entry—Recording Inventory and Cost of Goods Sold as Determined in Periodic Inventory System[2]

Inventory (ending—one unit at $260)	260		(increase an asset—debit)
Cost of Goods Sold (seven units missing at $260 each)	1,820		(increase an expense—debit)
Purchases of Inventory (five units at $260 each)		1,300	(decrease an asset—credit)
Inventory (beginning—three units at $260 each)		780	(decrease an asset—credit)

In this entry, the cost of the beginning inventory and the purchases for the period are basically switched to cost of goods sold and ending inventory.

Note that the reported costs on the financial statements ($260 for ending inventory and $1,820 for cost of goods sold) are identical under both perpetual and periodic systems. As will be demonstrated in another chapter, this agreement does not always exist when inventory items are acquired during the year at differing costs.

KEY TAKEAWAY

The legal conveyance of inventory from seller to buyer establishes the timing for recording the transaction and is based on the FOB point specified. This designation also identifies the party responsible for transportation costs and any items damaged while in transit. In contrast, the method of recording cost of goods sold depends on the inventory system in use. For a perpetual system, the reclassification of an item from inventory to expense occurs at the time of each sale. A periodic system makes no attempt to monitor inventory totals. Thus, cost of goods sold is unknown until the preparation of financial statements. The expense is calculated by adding beginning inventory to the purchase costs for the period and then subtracting ending inventory. The ending inventory figure comes from a year-end count of the merchandise on hand. A year-end adjusting entry updates the various general ledger accounts.

4. REPORTING INVENTORY AT LOWER OF COST OR MARKET

LEARNING OBJECTIVES

At the end of this section, students should be able to meet the following objectives:

1. Explain the need for reporting inventory at lower of cost or market.
2. Differentiate between a reporting problem caused by a drop in the purchase value of inventory and one resulting from the sales value of the merchandise.
3. Understand the difference in applying the lower-of-cost-or-market rule under U.S. GAAP and IFRS.

4.1 Inventory—The Reporting of Cost or Market Value

Question: In the example of Rider Inc., Model XY-7 bicycles have been bought and sold, and one unit remains in stock at year's end. The cost of this model has held steady at $260. However, its market value is likely to differ from that figure.

*Assume that, because of the sales made during the period, company officials believe that a buyer will soon be found to pay $440 for this last bicycle. **Is inventory always reported on a balance sheet at historical cost or is market (or fair) value ever taken into consideration?** Should this bicycle be shown as an asset at $260, $440, or some other pertinent figure?*

Answer: Under normal conditions, market value is rarely relevant in the reporting of inventory. For Rider Inc. this bicycle will likely appear as an asset at its cost of $260 until sold. Value is such a subjective figure that it is usually ignored in reporting inventory. The company has no reliable proof that the bicycle will bring in $440 until a sale actually occurs. The conservative nature of accounting resists the temptation to inflate reported inventory figures based purely on the anticipation of a profitable transaction at some future point in time.

An exception to this rule becomes relevant if the value of inventory falls below cost. Once again, the conservatism inherent in financial accounting is easily seen. If market value remains greater than cost, no change is made in the reported balance until a sale occurs. In contrast, if the value drops so that inventory is worth less than cost, a loss is recognized immediately. Accountants often say that losses are anticipated but gains are not.

As a note to the May 31, 2011, financial statements for **Nike Inc.** states, "inventories are stated at lower of cost or market." Whenever inventory appears to have lost value for any reason, the accountant compares the cost of the item to its market value and the lower figure then appears on the balance sheet.

4.2 Arriving at a Figure for Market Value

*Question: As mentioned, market value is a subjective figure. **When applying the lower-of-cost-or-market approach to inventory, how does the owner of the merchandise ascertain market value?***

Answer: The practical problem in applying the lower-of-cost-or-market approach arises from the difficulty in ascertaining an appropriate market value. There are several plausible ways to view the worth of any asset. For inventory, there is both a "purchase value" (replacement cost—the amount needed to acquire the same item again at the present time) and a "sales value" (net realizable value—the amount of cash expected from an eventual sale). When preparing financial statements, if either of these amounts is impaired, recognition of a loss is likely. Thus, the accountant must watch both values and be alert for potential problems.

Purchase Value. In some cases, often because of bad timing, a company finds that it has paid an excessive amount for inventory. Usually as the result of an increase in supply or a decrease in demand, replacement cost might drop after an item is acquired.

To illustrate, assume that Builder Company—the manufacturer of bicycle Model XY-7—has trouble selling the expected quantity of this particular style to retail stores because the design is not viewed as attractive. Near the end of the current year, Builder reduces the wholesale price offered for this model by $50 in hopes of stimulating sales. Rider Inc. bought a number of these bicycles earlier at a total cost of $260 each but now, before the last unit is sold, could obtain the same model for only $210.

The bicycle held in Rider's inventory is literally worth less than what the company paid for it. The purchase value, as demonstrated by replacement cost, has fallen to a figure lower than its historical cost.

When replacement cost for inventory drops below the amount paid, the lower (more conservative) figure is reported on the balance sheet, and the related loss is recognized on the income statement. In applying **lower of cost or market**, the remaining bicycle is now reported by Rider Inc. at its purchase value. A loss of $50 is created by the reduction in the inventory account from $260 to $210.

Sales value. Inventory also has a sales value that is, frequently, independent of replacement cost. The sales value of an item can fall for any number of reasons. For example, technological innovation will almost automatically reduce the amount that can be charged for earlier models. This phenomenon is typically seen whenever a new computer, camera, or phone is introduced to the market. Older items still in stock must be discounted significantly to attract buyers.

Similarly, changes in fashions and fads will hurt the sales value of certain types of inventory. Swim suits usually are offered at reduced prices in August and September as the summer season draws to a close. Damage can also impact an owner's ability to recoup the cost of inventory. Advertised sales tempt buyers by offering scratched and dented products, such as microwaves and refrigerators, at especially low prices.

For accounting purposes, the sales value of inventory is normally defined as estimated net realizable value. As discussed in the previous chapter, this figure is the amount of cash expected to be derived from an asset. For inventory, net realizable value is the anticipated sales price less any cost required to generate the sale. For example, the net realizable value of an older model digital camera might be the expected amount a customer will pay after money is spent to advertise the product. The net realizable value for a scratched refrigerator is likely to be the anticipated price of the item less the cost of any repairs that must be made prior to sale.

As with purchase value, if the sales value of an inventory item falls below its historical cost, the lower figure is reported along with a loss to mirror the impact of the asset reduction.

4.3 Applying Lower of Cost or Market

*Question: Inventory records are maintained at the historical cost of each item. For reporting purposes, this figure is utilized unless market value is lower. A reduction in value can result because of a drop in replacement cost (a purchase value) or in net realizable value (a sales value). **How is the comparison of cost and market value actually made when inventory is reported?***

Assume that Rider Inc. is currently preparing financial statements and holds two bicycles in ending inventory. Model XY-7 cost the company $260 while Model AB-9 cost $380. As mentioned, Model XY-7 now has a replacement cost of only $210. Because of market conditions, the exact sales value is uncertain. The other unit, Model AB-9, has been damaged and can only be sold for $400 after $50 is spent for necessary repairs. This inventory has a cost of $640 ($260 + $380). What should Rider report for its asset inventory?

Answer: As a preliminary step in preparing financial statements, a comparison of the cost and market value of the inventory is made. Although other alternatives exist, assume that Rider compares the cost to the market value for each separate item.[3] Market value used for the first item (XY-7) is its purchase value (replacement cost of $210) whereas the market value for the second item (AB-9) is the sales value of $350 (net realizable value of $400 minus $50). A problem with either value can lead to a reduction in the reported asset balance, which causes the recognition of a loss.

FIGURE 8.8 Recognition of a Loss on Impaired Inventory Value

Model	Cost	Impaired Market Value	Lower of Cost or Market Value
XY-7	$260	$210 (replacement cost)	$210
AB-9	380	350 (net realizable value)	350
Totals	$640		$560

Rider Inc. reports its inventory at the conservative $560 amount on its balance sheet with an $80 loss ($640 – $560) appearing in the income statement for this period. Such losses can be quite significant. **Mitsui & Co. (U.S.A.)** recognized a $25.3 million loss for the year ending March 31, 2011, that was attributed to applying the lower-of-cost-or-market approach to its inventory.

TEST YOURSELF

Question:

A company has three items of inventory: one is red, one is green, and one is blue. They cost $300 each and are usually sold for a profit of $50. The red and green units have a replacement cost of $310 each. The blue item has a replacement cost of $280. The red item can be sold for $340, the green item can be sold for $330, and the blue item can be sold for $320. It will cost $30 to sell the red one, $40 to sell the green one, and $10 to sell the blue one. If lower of cost or market value is applied on an item-by-item basis, what balance should be company report for its inventory?

a. $850

b. $860

c. $870

d. $880

Answer:

The correct answer is choice c: $870.

Explanation:

The red item has a replacement cost ($310) and a net realizable value (NRV) ($340 less $30 or $310) that are both above cost so the $300 figure continues to be reported. The green item has a replacement cost ($310) above cost ($300) but a NRV of only $290 ($330 less $40). That item is reported at this lower value. The blue item has a replacement cost ($280) that is below cost ($300) as well as NRV ($320 less $10 or $310) so the $280 is reported. The total is $870 ($300 + $290 + $280).

Talking with an Independent Auditor about International Financial Reporting Standards (Continued)

Following is a continuation of our interview with Robert A. Vallejo, partner with the accounting firm **PricewaterhouseCoopers**.

Question: When applying lower of cost or market to inventory, the determination of market value according to U.S. GAAP can be either net realizable value or replacement cost depending on whether a sales value or a purchase value is impaired. This process has been used in the United States for decades. How does International Financial Reporting Standards (IFRS) handle this issue? If a company begins to report its financial statements based on IFRS, how will the comparison of cost to market be made for inventory balances?

Rob Vallejo: International Accounting Standards 2, Inventories (IAS 2) states that inventories should be measured at the lower of cost and net realizable value. Net realizable value is defined as the anticipated sales price of the item (in the ordinary course of business) reduced by the estimated costs to complete the item and any estimated costs needed to make the sale. Replacement cost is not taken into consideration. In practice, because most U.S. companies determine net realizable value when considering whether or not to decrease the cost of their inventory, I do not expect any significant differences in this area of financial reporting (with the exception of some very industry specific circumstances) when a switch to IFRS is made. However, IFRS does allow reversals of previous write-downs if appropriate, whereas this is not allowed under U.S. GAAP.

KEY TAKEAWAY

Inventory is traditionally reported on a company's balance sheet at historical cost. However, reductions can be made based on applying the conservative lower-of-cost-or-market approach. In some cases, purchase value is in question if an item's replacement cost has dropped since the date of acquisition. For other inventory items, the problem is with the sales value if the net realizable value (expected sales price less any costs necessary to sale) falls below cost. Drops in sales value can occur because of changes in fads or technology or possibly as a result of damage. If either of these market values is below cost, the reported inventory figure should be reduced and a loss recognized.

5. DETERMINING INVENTORY ON HAND

LEARNING OBJECTIVES

At the end of this section, students should be able to meet the following objectives:

1. **Understand the necessity of taking a physical inventory count even in a perpetual inventory system.**
2. **Estimate the amount of inventory on hand using historic gross profit percentages and identify situations when this computation might be necessary.**

5.1 Counting Inventory in a Perpetual System

Question: In a periodic inventory system, a physical count is always taken at or near the end of the fiscal year. This procedure is essential in determining the final inventory figure and, hence, cost of goods sold for the period. **When a company uses a perpetual system, is a count of the goods on hand still needed since both the inventory balance and cost of goods sold are maintained and available in the accounting records?**

Answer: A physical inventory is necessary even if a company has invested the effort and cost to install a perpetual system. Merchandise can be lost, broken, or stolen. Errors can occur in the record keeping. Thus, a count is taken on a regular basis simply to ensure that subsidiary and general ledger balances are kept in alignment with the actual items held. Unless differences become material, this physical inventory can take place at a convenient time rather than at the end of the year. For example, assume that a company sells snow ski apparel. If an efficient perpetual system is in use, the merchandise could be inspected and counted by employees in May when quantities are low and damaged goods easier to spot.

An adjustment is necessary when the count does not agree with perpetual inventory figures. To illustrate, assume that company records indicate that 65 ski jackets are currently in stock costing $70 apiece. The physical inventory finds that only 63 items are actually on hand. The inventory account is reduced (credited) by $140 to mirror the shortfall (two missing units at $70 each).

The other half of the adjusting entry depends on the perceived cause of the shortage. For example, officials might have reason to believe that errors took place in the accounting process during the period. When merchandise is bought and sold, recording miscues do occur. Possibly two ski jackets were sold on a busy afternoon. The clerk got distracted and the cost of this merchandise was never reclassified to expense. This type of mistake means that the cost of goods sold figure is too low. The balance reported for these two jackets is moved to the expense account to rectify the mistake.

FIGURE 8.9 Adjusting Entry—To Bring Perpetual Inventory Records in Line with Physical Count, a Recording Error Is Assumed

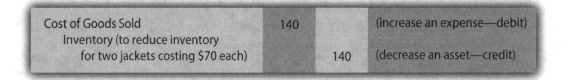

Conversely, if differences between actual and recorded inventory amounts occur because of damage, loss, or theft, the reported balance for cost of goods sold should not bear the cost of these items. The two jackets were not sold. Instead, a loss occurred.

If the assumption is made that the missing jackets were lost or stolen, rather than sold, the following alternative adjustment is appropriate.

FIGURE 8.10 Adjusting Entry—To Bring Perpetual Inventory Records in Line with Physical Count, Theft or Loss Is Assumed

Loss on Inventory Shortage	140		(increase an expense—debit)
Inventory (to reduce inventory for two jackets costing $70 each)		140	(decrease an asset—credit)

In practice, when an inventory count is made and the results differ from the amount of recorded merchandise, the exact cause is often impossible to identify. Whether a loss is reported or a change is made in reporting cost of goods sold, the impact on net income is the same. In such cases, construction of the adjustment is at the discretion of company officials. Normally, consistent application from year to year is the major objective.

5.2 Estimating the Amount of Inventory on Hand

Question: A periodic system is cheap and easy to operate. However, the lack of available information does present some practical problems. Assume that a company experiences a fire, flood, or other disaster and is attempting to gather evidence—for insurance or tax purposes—as to the amount of merchandise that was destroyed. If a periodic system has been used, how can the company support its claim? Or assume a company wants to produce interim financial statements for a single month or quarter (rather than a full year) without going to the cost and trouble of taking a complete physical inventory count. If the information is needed, how can a reasonable approximation of inventory on hand be derived when a periodic system is in use?

Answer: One entire branch of accounting—known as **forensic accounting**—specializes in investigations where information is limited or not available (or has even been purposely altered to be misleading). For example, assume that a hurricane floods a retail clothing store in Charleston, South Carolina. Only a portion of the merchandise costing $80,000 is salvaged.[4] In trying to determine the resulting loss, the amount of inventory in the building prior to the storm needs to be calculated. A forensic accountant might be hired, by either the owner of the store or the insurance company, to produce a reasonable estimate of the merchandise on hand at the time of the flood. Obviously, if the company had used a perpetual rather than a periodic system, the need to hire the services of an accounting expert would be less likely unless fraud was suspected.

In some cases, arriving at a probable inventory balance is not extremely complicated even if periodic inventory procedures are utilized. When historical trends can be determined with assurance, a valid estimation of the goods on hand is possible at any point in time without the benefit of perpetual records. To illustrate, assume that the general ledger for the Charleston store is located after the disaster. A periodic system was in use and the T-account balances provide the following information.

forensic accounting

A branch of accounting specializing in investigating and reporting on situations where important information is limited or unavailable.

FIGURE 8.11 Estimating Inventory—General Ledger Balances

Inventory available for sale:	
Inventory, beginning of year	$ 165,000
Purchases of inventory for current period	378,000
Cash discounts on purchases	(6,000)
Transportation-in	34,000
Cost to date	$571,000
Sales	$480,000

If no sales had taken place prior to the flood, the inventory on hand would have cost $571,000 as shown by these ledger accounts. However, sales had occurred, and a significant amount of merchandise was removed by customers as a result of those transactions. The $480,000 balance shown in the sales T-account does not reflect the cost of inventory items that were surrendered. It is a retail amount, the summation of the price charged for all sales during the year to date.

To determine the cost of inventory held at the time of the catastrophe, cost of goods sold for the current year has to be approximated and then removed from the $571,000 total. Many companies use a fairly standard markup percentage to set retail prices. By looking at previously reported balances, the forensic accountant is often able to make a reasonable determination of that markup. For example, assume that in the preceding year, this company reported sales revenue of $500,000 along with cost of goods sold of $300,000 and, hence, gross profit of $200,000. In this earlier period, cost of goods sold was 60 percent of sales revenue ($300,000/$500,000) while gross profit was 40 percent ($200,000/$500,000).

If available evidence does not indicate any significant changes this year in the method used to set retail prices, the accountant can assume that cost of goods sold during the period prior to the storm was about $288,000 ($480,000 sales revenue × 60 percent). Because the cost of all inventory was $571,000, approximately $283,000 of those goods were still in stock at the store when the hurricane hit Charleston ($571,000 total cost less $288,000 estimated cost of goods sold). This residual figure then serves as the basis for the insurance or tax claim. Only goods costing $80,000 were saved. Thus, the estimated loss was $203,000 ($283,000 inventory in stock less $80,000 inventory saved).

An identical set of procedures could also be used if the company was preparing financial statements for a period of time of less than a year (for example, a month or a quarter). For such interim reporting, companies often determine inventory and cost of goods sold based on estimations to avoid the cost of frequent physical counts.

The biggest obstacle in this type calculation is the validity of the cost and markup percentages. Many companies offer an eclectic variety of products, each with its own typical gross margin. Other companies change their markups frequently based on market conditions. In these cases, determining a reliable percentage can be difficult and the accuracy of the resulting estimation is much more questionable.

TEST YOURSELF

Question:

On January 1, Year One, the Wysocki Company holds inventory costing $230,000. During the first three months of the year, the company buys additional inventory for $290,000 and makes sales totaling $270,000. The company relies on a periodic inventory system for its record keeping. Typically, if the company buys a unit of inventory for $9, it will sell it for $15 although costs tend to vary a bit from product to product. The president of Wysocki wants to produce a balance sheet for the three months ending March 31, Year One, but prefers not to expend the time and money to take a physical inventory. What balance should be estimated and reported for the company's inventory on this balance sheet?

  a. $250,000

  b. $298,000

  c. $340,000

  d. $358,000

Answer:

The correct answer is choice d: $358,000.

Explanation:

If no goods are sold, the company holds inventory costing $520,000 ($230,000 plus $290,000). However, sales of $270,000 were made during these three months. Cost of goods sold has typically been 60 percent of the sales price ($9/$15). Therefore, the cost of the goods that were sold so far in this period can be estimated as $162,000 (60 percent × $270,000). After removing that amount, the inventory that remains has an estimated cost of $358,000 ($520,000 less $162,000).

KEY TAKEAWAY

Although perpetual inventory systems are designed to maintain current account balances, a physical count is still required periodically to update the records for errors, theft, and the like. In addition, knowledge of the amount of inventory on hand is sometimes needed in a periodic system even if complete records are not available. If a loss has occurred due to some type of disaster or if interim financial statements are to be prepared, the inventory balance can be estimated. This computation is based on determining the company's gross profit percentage using historical data. That allows cost of goods sold for the period to be estimated and then removed from the total inventory available for sale.

Talking with a Real Investing Pro (Continued)

Following is a continuation of our interview with Kevin G. Burns.

Question: Gross profit is the sales revenue generated by a company less cost of goods sold. In other words, it is the markup that a company is able to earn from the sale of its inventory. Goods are bought for a price and then sold at a higher value. In analyzing companies, gross profit is often stated as a percentage. A company's gross profit, for example, might be 37 percent of its sales. When you study a company, how much attention do you pay to changes in gross profit from year to year or differences that exist between one company and another?

Kevin Burns: Actually year to year differences only interest me if there is a significant change. If a company's gross profit margin increases significantly from one year to the next, my radar is activated. I want to know exactly why that happened. Is it temporary or something significant? If gross profit is especially volatile, it could easily go the other direction in the future. I prefer steady as she goes. Predictability and transparency are very important to me. As for gross profit margins between one company and another, the only way that is significant to me is if they are in the same industry and then only if there are big differences. Most companies in mature industries have similar margins, and large differences, again, tend to make me very suspicious.

 Video Clip

Professor Joe Hoyle talks about the five most important points in Chapter 8.

View the video online at: http://bit.ly/hoyle8-2

6. END-OF-CHAPTER EXERCISES

QUESTIONS

1. A company reports that it holds inventory with a cost of $397,000. What is meant here by the term "cost?"

2. At the end of the current year, the Waxhall Corporation paid $12,400 in connection with the acquisition of several pieces of inventory. This cost was capitalized when it should have been expensed. What is the impact of this misstatement on the company's financial statement totals?

3. What is a cash discount? Why does a company offer a cash discount?

4. What is meant by the term "3/10, n/30?"

5. When offered a cash discount, why is a buyer likely to take advantage of this opportunity?

6. How do cash discounts impact the reported value of inventory?

7. What is a perpetual inventory system? What is an advantage of using a perpetual system?

8. What is a periodic inventory system? What is an advantage of using a periodic system?

9. What is meant by the term "FOB point?"

10. The Allen Company sold $4,000 in inventory to the Gracie Company. Unfortunately, the goods were destroyed in a wreck while being delivered. Which company suffered this loss?

11. When does ownership transfer if transfer documents specify "FOB shipping point?"

12. When does ownership transfer if transfer documents specify "FOB destination?"

13. One company records its inventory using a perpetual system. Another company records its inventory using a periodic system. Other than the journal entries that are made, what differences are found between the two systems?

14. The Birgini Company buys one unit of inventory for $77 in cash. This item is later sold for $109 on credit. What journal entry or entries are made at the time of sale if a perpetual inventory system is used? What journal entry or entries are made at the time of sale if a periodic inventory system is used?

15. The Westmoreland Corporation uses a periodic system for its inventory. The company starts the current year with inventory costing $177,000. During the year, an additional $387,000 is paid for inventory purchases and $17,000 for transportation costs to get those items. A physical count at the end of the year finds $145,000 of ending inventory. How was each of these numbers derived? What is the company's cost of goods sold?

16. In question 15, what year-end adjusting entry is needed?

17. The Alberta Corporation maintains a perpetual inventory system but only keeps track of the number of units of inventory. The company actually makes its journal entries as is done in a periodic system. What is the reason for adopting this approach?

18. In accounting for inventory, what is meant by purchase value? How can a drop in the purchase value of inventory force the company to change the reported figure?

19. In accounting for inventory, what is meant by sales value? How can a drop in the sales value of inventory force the company to change the reported figure?

20. What types of companies would be most likely to have reductions to report in connection with the application of lower of cost or market?

21. Why would a company that uses a perpetual inventory system still perform a physical inventory count?

22. The Sharon Company recently estimated its inventory holdings. What are possible reasons for making this type of estimation?

TRUE OR FALSE

1. ____ A company should include the amount spent to transport an inventory item to its store when determining the reported cost of that item.

2. ____ In a periodic inventory system, an increase is made in the Inventory T-account if money is paid for the transportation to receive the items.

3. ____ In a perpetual inventory system, transportation costs to receive inventory is handled in the same manner by a company as delivery costs paid to get the item to a customer.

4. ____ Inventory is bought for $600 on terms of 2/10, n/60. Thus, if payment is made in 10 days, the buyer only has to pay $540.

5. ____ Buyers frequently choose not to take advantage of purchase (cash) discounts because the amount that is saved is so small.

6. ____ In a perpetual system, cost of goods sold is determined and recorded at the time of sale.

7. ____ Periodic inventory systems are, in general, less expensive to operate than perpetual systems.

8. ____ Periodic inventory systems are more common today because of the prevalence of computer systems.

9. ____ The Purchases of Inventory account is not used in a perpetual inventory system.

10. ____ If inventory is shipped FOB shipping point, the buyer takes title as soon as the inventory leaves the seller's warehouse.

11. ____ In a periodic system, cost of goods sold is the difference between what a company has available for sale (beginning inventory and purchases) and what they did not sell (ending inventory).

12. ____ In a periodic system, the Inventory T-account retains the beginning balance throughout the year.

13. ____ Ace Company reports Year One cost of goods sold as $324,000 using a periodic system. One inventory item was not recorded or counted. Ace had bought the item from Zebra for $6,000. Zebra shipped it on December 28, Year One, and Ace received it on January 5, Year Two. It was shipped FOB shipping point. Ace should have reported cost of goods sold as $330,000.

14. ____ Lower of cost or market is only used by companies that maintain a periodic inventory system.

15. ____ Lower of cost or market is only used by companies that maintain a perpetual inventory system.

16. ____ If the market value of a company's inventory increases after its acquisition, the company should record a gain.

17. ____ A company that uses a perpetual inventory system should still perform a physical inventory count.

18. ____ An estimation of inventory is most common in connection with companies that have a periodic inventory system.

19. ____ The Waynesboro Company always has gross profit equal to 30 percent of sales. This year, the company started with inventory costing $50,000 and made purchases of $100,000 and sales of $120,000. A fire destroyed all of the inventory on hand except for merchandise costing $6,000. The loss is estimated as $60,000.

20. ____ A forensic accountant attempts to generate financial information in situations where insufficient physical data might be available.

MULTIPLE CHOICE

1. Arne Company buys inventory for $400. The seller sends this merchandise to the company FOB destination. The transportation charge was $13. Arne received a discount of $9 for paying quickly. The inventory is sold to a customer for $670. Arne paid another $17 to have the item delivered to the customer's home. What did Arne report as cost of goods sold?

    a. $391

    b. $395

    c. $400

    d. $408

2. On February 13, NC Sofa Company purchases three sofas from a manufacturer for $300 each. The terms of the sale are 2/10, n/45. NC Sofa pays the invoice on February 21. How much did the company pay?

    a. $855

    b. $882

    c. $890

    d. $900

3. Crayson Inc. started the year with $490,000 in inventory. During the year, Crayson purchased an additional $1,060,000 in inventory and paid transportation costs of $30,000 to get this merchandise. At the end of the year, Crayson employees performed a physical count and determined that ending inventory amounted to $450,000. What was Crayson's cost of goods sold for the year?

    a. $1,050,000

    b. $1,060,000

    c. $1,100,000

    d. $1,130,000

4. The following account balances were found in the general ledger of the Applewhite Corporation: Purchases = $232,000, Sales = $458,000, Transportation-in = $15,000, Cash Discounts on Purchases = $23,000, Advertising Expense = $30,000. On January 1, a count of inventory showed $90,000, whereas on December 31, a count of inventory showed $123,000. What was cost of goods sold for the period?

    a. $176,000

    b. $191,000

    c. $214,000

    d. $221,000

5. Raceway Corporation manufactures miniature cars and racetracks for collectors and enthusiasts. Raceway placed an order for new auto supplies and other parts from Delta Inc. on December 1. The sales staff at Delta informed Raceway that the supplies would not be available to ship out until December 22. Raceway accepted this arrangement. The supplies actually shipped, FOB shipping point, on December 26 and arrived at Raceway's receiving dock on January 2. On which date should Raceway include the supplies in its inventory?

    a. December 1

    b. December 22

    c. December 26

    d. January 2

6. The Morning Company buys inventory and pays an additional $700 to have those goods shipped to its warehouse. How is the journal entry for this $700 cost recorded?

    a. In both a perpetual and a periodic system, inventory is debited for $700.

    b. In both a perpetual and a periodic system, purchases of inventory is debited for $700.

    c. In a perpetual system, inventory is debited for $700; in a periodic system, purchases of inventory is debited for $700.

    d. In a perpetual system, purchases of inventory is debited for $700; in a periodic system, inventory is debited for $700.

7. A company makes all of its purchases and sales using FOB shipping point. At the end of the year, the company had the following two transactions that were correctly recorded:

    ■ **Purchases.** Inventory costing $40,000 is shipped by the seller on December 28 and received by the company on January 4.

    ■ **Sales.** Inventory costing $30,000 is sold to a customer for $48,000. It is shipped on December 28 to the customer and arrives on January 4.

If this company had chosen to make these transactions FOB destination rather than FOB shipping point, how would that decision have impacted the reported amount of inventory on the year-end balance sheet?

    a. Reported inventory would have been $10,000 higher.

    b. Reported inventory would have been $10,000 lower.

    c. Reported inventory would have been $40,000 higher.

    d. Reported inventory would have been $40,000 lower.

8. The Charlotte Company made a $9,000 purchase near the end of the current year. The company also made a sale for $11,000 of inventory costing $6,000. Charlotte did not include either the inventory purchased or the inventory sold in its year-end inventory. Ending inventory was reported as $100,000. The purchase was FOB destination and shipped on December 29, Year One, and received by Charlotte on January 3, Year Two. The sale was FOB destination. It was shipped on December 30, Year One, and received by the customer on January 4, Year Two. What was the correct amount of inventory that Charlotte should have reported at the end of Year One?

    a. $94,000

    b. $97,000

    c. $106,000

    d. $109,000

9. At year-end, the Commonwealth Corporation holds 500 pieces of XY inventory costing $9 each and 700 pieces of AB inventory costing $11 each. XY inventory has flooded the market, and Commonwealth can now buy these same units for $6 each. AB inventory has not proven to be as popular as anticipated, and a unit can only be sold for $12 even after spending $2 extra on painting it a different color. In applying lower of cost or market, what should be reported for inventory by Commonwealth?

    a. $10,000

    b. $10,700

    c. $11,400

    d. $12,100

10. Which of the following concerning the "lower of cost or market" rule is **not** true?

    a. If the replacement cost of an inventory item falls below its historical cost, the value of the item should be written down.

    b. If the market value of an item exceeds its historical cost, it should be written up and a gain recorded.

    c. It is possible for an item's net realizable value to fall below its historical cost.

    d. Application of lower of cost or market is an example of the practice of conservatism in accounting.

11. Romulus Company sells maps. At the end of the current year, Romulus's inventory records indicated that it had 2,900 maps of Italy on hand that had originally cost $30 each but were being sold for $52 each. An inventory count showed that only 2,875 were actually present in ending inventory. What journal entry should Romulus make if management believes the discrepancy is due to errors in the accounting process?

    a. **FIGURE 8.12**

| Cost of Goods Sold | 750 | |
| Loss on Inventory Shortage | | 750 |

b. **FIGURE 8.13**

c. **FIGURE 8.14**

d. **FIGURE 8.15**

12. Real South Products holds $400,000 worth of inventory on January 1. Between January and March 13, Real South purchased an additional $190,000 in inventory. During that period, sales of $530,000 were made. On March 13, Real South's warehouse flooded and all but $15,000 worth of inventory was ruined. Historical records show that Real South has an average gross profit percentage of 25 percent. What was the approximate value of the inventory destroyed in the flood?

    a. $177,500

    b. $207,500

    c. $240,000

    d. $275,000

VIDEO PROBLEMS

Professor Joe Hoyle discusses the answers to these two problems at the links that are indicated. After formulating your answers, watch each video to see how Professor Hoyle answers these questions.

1. Your roommate is an English major. The roommate's parents own a chain of ice cream shops throughout Florida. One day, while driving over to the car wash, your roommate poses this question: "My parents are having a problem with their insurance company. As you know, we recently had a hurricane come through the Florida area. It knocked out the electricity at one of their stores for several hours. It was very hot that day, and all the ice cream at that store melted. Luckily, each store is insured. However, they are having a dispute with the insurance company as to the amount of ice cream that was destroyed. It all melted and ran down the drain so there is no proof. The insurance company argues that only half as much ice cream was destroyed as my parents claim. For a big store, that is a lot of money. How will they ever be able to sort out this mess? My parents only want a fair amount." How would you respond?

View the video online at: http://bit.ly/hoyle8-3

2. Your uncle and two friends started a small office supply store several years ago. The company has expanded and now has several large locations. Your uncle knows that you are taking a financial accounting class and asks you the following question: "When we first started, we did not spend much money on monitoring inventory. The stores were small, and a good manager could walk through and see where we needed to buy more goods. Now, however, every year we seem to have to spend more money in order to upgrade our inventory systems. Is this cost really worth what we continue to spend?" How would you respond?

View the video online at: http://bit.ly/hoyle8-4

PROBLEMS

1. Here are several T-account balances that the Absalom Company has in its ledger at the end of the current year before a physical inventory count is to be taken.

FIGURE 8.16

Advertising expense	$22,000
Rent expense	46,000
Purchases of inventory	332,000
Sales	696,000
Inventory, January 1	77,000
Transportation–in	8,000
Purchase Discounts	14,000

    a. What was the amount of goods available for sale for this company?

    b. If the company counts its ending inventory and finds merchandise costing $84,000, what should be reported as cost of goods sold for the year?

    c. What adjusting entry should Absalom make at the end of the current year to record cost of goods sold and ending inventory?

2. The Darth Corporation starts Year Two with 8,000 units of inventory. All inventory costs $1.00 per unit with an additional cost of $0.12 each for transportations costs. These costs continue to be consistent throughout Year Two. Inventory on January 1, Year Two, was reported as 8,000 units times $1.12 or $8,960.

    After these 8,000 units were sold, Darth Corporation buys an additional 20,000 units in Year Two. During that year, Darth sells 22,000 units for $2.00 each. No inventory was lost or stolen. During Year Two, the company accountant accidentally expensed all transportation costs incurred that period.

    a. What amount did the Darth Corporation report as its gross profit for Year Two?

    b. What amount should the Darth Corporation have reported as its gross profit for Year Two?

3. Overland Inc. starts buying and selling widgets this year. A box of 100 widgets can be bought for $600 on credit. Transportation to receive each box of widgets costs an additional $50 in cash. Overland uses a perpetual inventory system. Make journal entries for the following transactions.

    ■ January 15 – bought 4 boxes of widgets

    ■ February 19 – sold 3 boxes of widgets for cash of $1,100 each

    ■ April 3 – bought 5 boxes of widgets

    ■ June 15 – sold 3 boxes of widgets for cash of $1,200 each

    ■ September 4 – bought 6 boxes of widgets

    ■ October 5 – sold 4 boxes of widgets for cash of $1,250 each

4. Do problem 3 again but assume that Overland Inc. uses a periodic inventory system. Also assume that no widgets are lost, broken, or stolen. Include the needed year-end adjusting entry.

5. ConnecTech bought 400 computers in Year Two for $300 each on account. It paid $260 to have them delivered to its store. During January of Year Three, ConnecTech sold 220 of the computers for cash of $550 each. ConnecTech uses a perpetual inventory system.

    a. Prepare the journal entry or entries to record ConnecTech's purchase of the computers.

    b. Prepare the journal entry or entries to record the sale of the computers.

    c. Determine the balance in ConnecTech's ending inventory on January 31, Year Three.

6. Montez Muffins and More (MM&M) is a bakery located in New York City. MM&M purchases a great deal of flour in bulk from a wholesaler. The wholesaler offers purchase discounts for fast payment. MM&M purchased 600 pounds of flour for $0.20 per pound on May 1, under terms 2/10, n/30. Determine the amount MM&M should pay under the following scenarios.

    a. MM&M pays the full balance on May 25.

    b. MM&M pays the full balance on May 7.

    c. MM&M pays half the balance on May 7 and half on May 18.

7. Racer's ATVs sells many makes and models of all-terrain vehicles at its store in Indianapolis, Indiana. Racer's uses a periodic inventory system because its entire inventory is located in one large room and all employees know what is on hand and what new inventory is needed. On January 1, Racer's had beginning inventory costing $48,600. On January 14, Racer's received a new shipment of vehicles with a purchase price of $34,700 and additional transportation costs of $1,200. On May 19, Racers received a second shipment of vehicles with a purchase price of $36,900 and transportation costs of $950. On November 1, Racers received its pre-Christmas shipment of vehicles with a purchase price of $67,800 and transportation costs of $1,750. The company buys vehicles on account but pays cash for transportation.

    a. Make the necessary journal entries for January 14, May 19, and November 1 to show the purchase of this inventory.

    b. Assume that a physical inventory count on December 31 showed an ending inventory costing $35,800. Determine the cost of goods sold to be reported for the year.

    c. If sales for the year were reported as $296,700, what gross profit did Racer's make?

    d. Racer's is considering replacing its periodic inventory system with a perpetual one. Write a memo to Racer's management giving the pros and cons of this switch.

8. Ace Company counts inventory at the end of the current year and arrives at a cost of $300,000. Assume that each of the following four situations is independent of the others. In each case, assume that the inventory in question was not included in the count that was taken at the end of the year.

    a. Inventory costing $10,000 was sold by Ace for $16,000 on credit and shipped to the customer on December 29 and arrived on January 3. The shipment was marked FOB destination. If Ace reported $300,000 in inventory on its balance sheet, what amount should have been reported?

    b. Inventory costing $11,000 was shipped from the seller on December 29 and received by Ace on January 3. The shipment was marked FOB destination. If Ace reported $300,000 in inventory on its balance sheet, what amount should have been reported?

    c. Inventory costing $12,000 was sold by Ace for $17,000 on credit and shipped to the customer on December 30 and arrived on January 4. The shipment was marked FOB shipping point. If Ace reported $300,000 in inventory on its balance sheet, what amount should have been reported?

    d. Inventory costing $13,000 was shipped from the seller on December 30 and received by Ace on January 4. The shipment was marked FOB shipping point. If Ace reported $300,000 in inventory on its balance sheet, what amount should have been reported?

9. Magic Carpets Inc. sells a full line of area rugs, from top quality to bargain basement. Economic conditions have hit the textile industry, and the accountant for Magic Carpets is concerned that the rug inventory might not be worth the amount Magic paid. The following is information about three lines of rugs.

FIGURE 8.17

	Cost	Replacement Cost	Sales Price	Cost to Sell	Number in Inventory
High Flyers	$230	$240	$350	$40	80
Midflight	150	120	220	25	125
Under the Radar	100	100	110	20	165

    a. Determine lower of cost or market for each type of rug.

    b. Assume that Magic Carpets applies lower of cost or market to the individual types of rugs rather than to the entire stock of inventory as a whole. Determine if Magic Carpets has suffered a loss of value on its inventory, and if so, the amount of that loss.

10. Costello Corporation uses a perpetual inventory system. At the end of the year, the inventory balance reported by its system is $45,270. Costello performs an inventory count and determines that the actual ending inventory is $39,780.

    a. Discuss why a company that uses a perpetual inventory system would still go to the trouble to perform a physical inventory count.

    b. Why might the ending balance differ between the perpetual inventory system and physical inventory count?

    c. Assume that Costello determines that the difference between the perpetual records and the physical count is due to an accident that occurred during the year. What journal entry should Costello make?

    d. Assume that Costello believes the difference between the perpetual records and the physical count is due to errors made by the company's accounting staff. On occasion, the staff fail to transfer inventory to cost of goods sold when a sale were made. What journal entry should Costello make in this case?

11. Fabulous Fay's is a boutique clothing store in San Diego, California. Fay's uses a perpetual inventory system. In March, Fay's purchased a type of swimwear designed to be slimming to the wearer. The company purchased twenty suits of varying sizes for $40 each and priced them at $120 each. They sold out almost immediately, so Fay purchased forty more suits in April for $40 each and sold thirty-eight of them for $130 each. Again in July, Fay made one more purchase of twenty suits at $40 each and sold fifteen of them for $130 each. Fay decided not to put the rest of this inventory on sale at the end of the summer, but to hold onto the items until cruise season started the following winter. She believed she could sell the remainder of this merchandise without having to mark the items down.

    a. Make the journal entries for the purchases Fay made.

    b. Make the journal entries for the sales Fay made.

    c. Determine the balance in ending inventory on December 31.

    d. Fay performed a physical count on December 31 and determined that three of the swimsuits had been severely damaged due to a leaky pipe. They had to be thrown away. Make the journal entry to show the loss of this inventory.

12. Nakatobi Company has an inventory warehouse in Fargo, North Dakota. The company utilizes a periodic inventory system. At the beginning of the year, the warehouse contained $369,000 worth of inventory. During the first quarter of the year, Nakatobi purchased another $218,000 worth of inventory and made sales of $450,000. On April 1, a flood hit Fargo and destroyed 70 percent of the inventory housed in the warehouse. Nakatobi must estimate the cost of the destroyed inventory for insurance purposes. According to records kept for the past several years, Nakatobi has typically reported its cost of goods sold at 55 percent of sales.

    a. Determine the value of the inventory on March 31, before the flood hit.

    b. Determine Nakatobi's loss on April 1.

COMPREHENSIVE PROBLEM

This problem will carry through over several chapters to enable students to build their accounting skills using knowledge gained in previous chapters.

In Chapter 7, financial statements were prepared for Webworks for July 31 and the month then ended. Those financial statements are included here as a starting point for the financial reporting for August.

Here are Webworks financial statements as of July 31.

FIGURE 8.18

Webworks
Income Statement
As of July 31

Revenue	$2,300
Expenses	(1,295)
Earnings before Tax	1,005
Tax Expense	(300)
Net Income	$705

FIGURE 8.19

Webworks
Stmt. Of Retained Earnings
As of July 31

Retained Earnings, July 1	$470
Net Income	705
Retained Earnings, July 31	$1,175

FIGURE 8.20

Webworks
Balance Sheet
July 31

Assets		Liabilities	
Current		**Current**	
Cash	$5,720	Accounts Payable	$240
Accounts Receivable	1,050	Salaries Payable	200
Less Allowance for		Unearned Revenue	500
Doubtful Accounts	(105)	Total Current Liabilities	$940
Net Accounts Receivable	945		
Supplies Inventory	50		
Prepaid Rent	400		
Total Current Assets	$7,115		
Noncurrent		**Noncurrent**	
Equipment	$7,000	Notes Payable	$10,000
		Owners' Equity	
		Capital Stock	$2,000
		Retained Earnings	1,175
		Total Owners' Equity	$3,175
		Total Liabilities & Owners'	
Total Assets	$14,115	Equity	$14,115

The following events occur during August:

a. Webworks decides to begin selling a limited selection of inventory items related to its business. During August, Webworks purchases several specialty keyboards for $4,900 and flash drives for $3,200 both on account with the hopes of selling them to Web site customers or others who might be interested. Due to the limited quantity of inventory, Webworks will use a periodic system.

b. Webworks purchases supplies for $100 on account.

c. Webworks starts and completes six more Web sites and bills those clients a total of $2,700.

d. In July, Webworks received $500 in advance to design two Web sites. Webworks also completes both of these sites during August.

e. Webworks collects $2,400 in accounts receivable.

f. Webworks pays Nancy Po (the company employee hired in June) $600 for her work during the first three weeks of August.

g. In June, Webworks designed a Web site for Pauline Smith and billed her. Unfortunately, before she paid this bill completely, Ms. Smith's business folded. Webworks is not likely to collect any of the remaining money and writes off the $100 balance as uncollectible.

h. Webworks sells several keyboards for $4,500 and flash drives for $3,000. All of these transactions were for cash.

i. Webworks pays the salaries payable from July.

j. Webworks pays $6,000 of its accounts payable.

k. Webworks receives $100 in advance to work on a Web site for a local dentist. Work will not begin on the Web site until September.

l. Webworks pays Leon Jackson (owner of the company) a salary of $2,000 for his work.

m. Webworks pays taxes of $475 in cash.

Required:

    A. Prepare journal entries for the previous events.

    B. Post the journal entries to T-accounts.

    C. Prepare an unadjusted trial balance for Webworks at the end of August.

    D. Prepare adjusting entries for the following and post them to the appropriate T-accounts.

n. Webworks owes Nancy Po $250 for her work during the last week of August.

o. Leon's parents let him know that Webworks owes $250 toward the electricity bill. Webworks will pay them in September.

p. Webworks determines that it still has $60 worth of supplies remaining at the end of August.

q. Prepaid rent should be adjusted for August's portion.

r. Webworks assumes that 10 percent of its accounts receivable at the end of the month will prove to be uncollectible.

s. Webworks performs a count of ending inventory and determines that $1,900 in keyboards and $1,100 in flash drives remain. Cost of goods sold for the month should be recorded.

    E. Prepare an adjusted trial balance.

    F. Prepare financial statements for August 31 and the month then ended.

RESEARCH ASSIGNMENT

Assume that you take a job as a summer employee for an investment advisory service. One of the partners for that firm is currently looking at the possibility of investing in **Sears Holdings Corporations**. The partner is a bit concerned about the impact of the recession on this company. The partner is especially interested in what has happened to the company's ability to sell the merchandise inventory that it elects to buy. The partner asks you to look at the 2010 financial statements for **Sears** by following this path:

- Go to http://www.sears.com.
- At the bottom of this screen, click on "About **Sears**" and then on "Investor Relations."
- On the right side of the next screen, click on "Financial Information."
- On the left side of the next screen, click on "2010 Annual Report" to download.
- Go to page 49 and find the 2008, 2009, and 2010 income statements.
- Go to page 50 and find the balance sheets for the years ended January 30, 2010 and January 29, 2011.

a. Using the figures found on these three income statements, subtract the cost of sales, buying, and occupancy from merchandise sales and services to get an approximation of gross profit earned by **Sears** for each year. Divide that number by the merchandise sales and services figure to derive a gross profit percentage for each year. How has that percentage changed over these three years? What might that signal?

b. Using the figures found on the balance sheets, locate the amount reported for merchandise inventories for each year. Divide that figure by the amount reported each year by **Sears** as its total assets. How did the percentage change from the first year to the second? What might that signal?

ENDNOTES

1. The Purchases figure here could have also been shown by displaying the various cost components such as the invoice price, purchases discount, transportation-in, and assembly. That breakdown is important for internal decision making and control but probably of less interest to external parties.

2. As mentioned previously, if separate T-account balances are established for cost components such as transportation-in, assembly costs, and the like, they must be included in this entry rather than just a single Purchases figure.

3. In applying the lower-of-cost-or-market approach to inventory, the comparison can be made on an item-by-item basis. For example, XY-7 can be valued based on the lower of cost and market for that one item and then, separately, a similar determination can be made for AB-9. A company can also group its inventory (all bicycles, for example, might comprise a group that is separate from all motorcycles) and report the lower amount determined for each group. A third possibility is to sum the cost of all inventory items and make a single comparison of that figure to the total of all market values. U.S. GAAP does not specify a mechanical approach to use in applying lower of cost or market.

4. For a full description of forensic accounting, see Frank J. Grippo and J. W. (Ted) Ibex, "Introduction to Forensic Accounting," *The National Public Accountant*, June 2003.

CHAPTER 9
Why Does a Company Need a Cost Flow Assumption in Reporting Inventory?

 Video Clip

In this video, Professor Joe Hoyle introduces the essential points covered in Chapter 9.

View the video online at: http://bit.ly/hoyle9-1

1. THE NECESSITY OF ADOPTING A COST FLOW ASSUMPTION

LEARNING OBJECTIVES

At the end of this section, students should be able to meet the following objectives:

1. Understand that accounting rules tend to be standardized so that companies must often report events according to one set method.
2. Know that the selection of a particular cost flow assumption is necessary when inventory items are bought at more than one cost.
3. Apply each of the following cost flow assumptions to determine reported balances for ending inventory and cost of goods sold: specific identification, FIFO, LIFO, and averaging.

1.1 Accounting for Inventory When Costs Vary Over Time

Question: In the coverage of financial accounting to this point, general standardization has been evident. Most transactions are reported in an identical fashion by all companies. This defined structure (created by U.S. GAAP or IFRS) helps ensure understandable communication. It also enhances the ability of decision makers to compare results from one year to the next and from one company to another. For example, inventory—except in unusual circumstances—appears on a balance sheet at historical cost unless its value is lower. Consequently, experienced decision makers should be well aware of the normal meaning of a reported inventory figure.

However, an examination of the notes to financial statements for several well-known businesses shows an interesting inconsistency in the reporting of inventory (emphasis added).

__Mitsui & Co. (U.S.A.)__—as of March 31, 2011: "Commodities and materials for resale are stated at the lower of cost or market. Cost is determined using the __specific identification method__ or average cost."

__Johnson & Johnson__—as of January 2, 2011: "Inventories are stated at the lower of cost or market determined by the __first-in, first-out method__."

__Safeway Inc.__—as of January 1, 2011: "Merchandise inventory of $1,685 million at year-end 2010 and $1,629 million at year-end 2009 is valued at the lower of cost on a __last-in, first-out ("LIFO") basis__ or market value."

__Bristol-Myers Squibb__—as of December 31, 2010: "Inventories are stated at the lower of __average cost__ or market."

"Specific-identification method," "first-in, first-out method," "last-in, first-out basis," "average cost"—these are cost flow assumptions. What information do these terms provide about reported inventory balances? Why are such methods necessary? Why are all four of these businesses using different cost flow assumptions? __In the financial reporting of inventory, what is the significance of disclosing that a company applies "first-in, first-out," "last-in, first-out," or the like?__

Answer: In the previous chapter, the cost of all inventory items was kept constant over time. The first bicycle cost $260 and every bicycle purchased thereafter also had a cost of $260. This consistency helped simplify the introductory presentation of accounting issues in the coverage of inventory. However, such stability is hardly a realistic assumption. For example, the retail price of gasoline has moved up and down like a yo-yo in recent years. The costs of some commodities, such as bread and soft drinks, have increased gradually for many decades. In other industries, prices actually tend to fall over time. New technology products often start with a high price that drops as the manufacturing process ramps up and becomes more efficient. Several years ago, personal computers cost tens of thousands of dollars and now sell for hundreds.

A key event in accounting for inventory is the transfer of cost from the inventory T-account to cost of goods sold as the result of a sale. The inventory balance is reduced and the related expense is increased. For large organizations, such transactions take place thousands of times each day. If each item has an identical cost, no problem exists. This established amount is reclassified from asset to expense to reflect the sale (either at the time of sale in a perpetual system or when financial statements are produced in a periodic system).

However, if inventory items are acquired at different costs, a problem is created: Which of these costs is moved from asset to expense to reflect a sale? To resolve that question, a cost flow assumption must be selected by company officials to identify the cost that remains in inventory and the cost that moves to cost of goods sold. This choice can have a significant and ongoing impact on both income statement and balance sheet figures. Investors and creditors cannot properly analyze the reported net income and inventory balance of a company such as __ExxonMobil__ without knowing the cost flow assumption that has been utilized.

1.2   Applying Cost Flow Assumptions

Question: To illustrate, assume a men's retail clothing store holds $120 in cash. Numbers will be kept artificially low in this example so that the impact of the various cost flow assumptions is easier to visualize. On December 2, Year One, one blue dress shirt is bought for $50 in cash and added to inventory. Later, near the end of the year, this style of shirt suddenly becomes especially popular and prices skyrocket. On December 29, Year One, the store manager buys a second shirt exactly like the first but this time at a cost of $70. Cash on hand has been depleted ($120 less $50 and $70), but the company holds two shirts in its inventory.

On December 31, Year One, a customer buys one of these two shirts by paying cash of $110. Regardless of the cost flow assumption, the company retains one blue dress shirt in inventory at the end of the year and cash of $110. It also reports sales revenue of $110. Those facts are not in dispute.

From an accounting perspective, only two questions must be resolved: (1) what is the cost of goods sold reported for the one shirt that was sold, and (2) what is the cost remaining in inventory for the one item still on hand?

Should the $50 or $70 cost be reclassified to cost of goods sold? Should the $50 or $70 cost remain in ending inventory? In financial accounting, the importance of the answers to those questions cannot be overemphasized. If the shirts are truly identical, answers cannot be determined by any type of inspection; thus, a cost flow assumption is necessary. __What are the various cost flow assumptions, and how are they applied to inventory?__

Answer:

Specific Identification. In a literal sense, specific identification is not a cost flow assumption. Companies that use this method are not making an assumption because they know which item was sold. In some way, the inventory conveyed to the customer can be identified so that the actual cost is reclassified to expense to reflect the sale.

For some types of inventory, such as automobiles held by a car dealer, specific identification is relatively easy to apply. Each vehicle tends to be somewhat unique and can be tracked through identification numbers. Unfortunately, for many other types of inventory, no practical method exists for determining the physical flow of specific goods from seller to buyer.

Thus, if the men's retail store maintains a system where individual shirts are coded when acquired, it will be possible to know whether the $50 shirt or the $70 shirt was actually conveyed to the first customer. That cost can then be moved from inventory to cost of goods sold.

However, for identical items like shirts, cans of tuna fish, bags of coffee beans, hammers, packs of notebook paper and the like, the idea of maintaining such precise records is ludicrous. What informational benefit could be gained by knowing whether the first blue shirt was sold or the second? In most cases, unless merchandise items are both expensive and unique, the cost of creating such a meticulous record-keeping system far outweighs any potential advantages.

First-in, first-out (FIFO). The FIFO cost flow assumption is based on the premise that selling the oldest item first is most likely to mirror reality. Stores do not want inventory to lose freshness. The oldest items are often displayed on top in hopes that they will sell before becoming stale or damaged. Therefore, although the identity of the actual item sold is rarely known, the assumption is made in applying FIFO that the first (or oldest) cost is moved from inventory to cost of goods sold when a sale occurs.

Note that it is not the oldest item that is necessarily sold but rather the oldest cost that is reclassified first. No attempt is made to determine which shirt was purchased by the customer. Consequently, an assumption is necessary.

Here, because the first shirt cost $50, the entry in Figure 9.1 is made to reduce the inventory and record the expense.

FIGURE 9.1   Journal Entry—Reclassification of the Cost of One Piece of Inventory Using FIFO

Cost of Goods Sold	50	
Inventory		50

After the sale is recorded, the following financial information is reported by the retail story but only if FIFO is applied. Two shirts were bought for ($50 and $70), and one shirt was sold for $110.

FIFO	
Cost of Goods Sold (one unit sold—the cost of the first one)	$50
Gross Profit ($110 sales price less $50 cost)	$60
Ending Inventory (one unit remains—the cost of the last one)	$70

In a period of rising prices, the earliest (cheapest) cost moves to cost of goods sold and the latest (more expensive) cost remains in ending inventory. For this reason, in inflationary times, FIFO is associated with a higher reported net income as well as a higher reported inventory total on the company's balance sheet. Not surprisingly, these characteristics help make FIFO a popular choice.

specific identification

Inventory cost flow method in which a company physically identifies both its remaining inventory and the inventory that was sold to customers.

FIFO

Inventory cost flow assumption based on the oldest costs being transferred first from inventory to cost of goods sold so that the most recent costs remain in ending inventory.

TEST YOURSELF

Question:

A hardware store buys a lawn mower on Monday for $120, another identical model on Tuesday for $125, another on Wednesday for $132, and a final one on Thursday for $135. One is then sold on Friday for $180 in cash. The company uses the FIFO cost flow assumption for inventory. Because an identification number was left on the lawn mower bought on Tuesday, company officials know that this lawn mower was actually the one sold to the customer. In the accounting system, that specific cost is moved from inventory to cost of goods sold. Which of the following is true?

a. Reported inventory is too high by $5.

b. Gross profit is too high by $5.

c. Working capital is too low by $5.

d. Net income is correctly stated.

Answer:

The correct answer is choice c: Working capital is too low by $5.

Explanation:

Because FIFO is applied, the first cost ($120) should be moved from inventory to cost of goods sold instead of $125 (the cost of the Tuesday purchase). Cost of goods sold is too high by $5 and inventory is too low by the same amount. Working capital (current assets less current liabilities) is understated because the inventory balance within the current assets is too low. Because the expense is too high, both gross profit and net income are understated (too low).

LIFO (last in first out)

Inventory cost flow assumption based on the most recent costs being transferred first from inventory to cost of goods sold so that the oldest costs remain in ending inventory.

Last-in, first-out (LIFO). LIFO is the opposite of FIFO: The most recent costs are moved to expense as sales are made.

Theoretically, the LIFO assumption is often justified as more in line with the matching principle. Shirt One was bought on December 2 whereas Shirt Two was not acquired until December 29. The sales revenue was generated on December 31. Proponents of LIFO argue that matching the December 29 cost with the December 31 revenue is more appropriate than using a cost incurred several weeks earlier. According to this reasoning, income is more properly determined with LIFO because a relatively current cost is shown as cost of goods sold rather than a figure that is out-of-date.

The difference in reported figures is especially apparent in periods of high inflation which makes this accounting decision even more important. "By matching current costs against current sales, LIFO produces a truer picture of income; that is, the quality of income produced by the use of LIFO is higher because it more nearly approximates disposable income."[1] Note 1 to the 2010 financial statements for **ConocoPhillips** reiterates that point: "LIFO is used to better match current inventory costs with current revenues."

The last cost incurred in buying blue shirts was $70 so this amount is reclassified to expense at the time of the first sale as shown in Figure 9.2.

FIGURE 9.2 Journal Entry—Reclassification of the Cost of One Piece of Inventory Using LIFO

Although the physical results of these transaction are the same (one unit was sold, one unit was retained, and the company holds $110 in cash), the financial picture painted using the LIFO cost flow assumption is quite different from that shown previously in the FIFO example.

LIFO	
Cost of Goods Sold (one unit sold—the cost of the last one)	$70
Gross Profit ($110 sales price less $70 cost)	$40
Ending Inventory (one unit remains—the cost of the first one)	$50

Characteristics commonly associated with LIFO can be seen in this example. When prices rise, LIFO companies report lower net income (the most recent and, thus, the most costly purchases are moved to expense) and a lower inventory account on the balance sheet (the earlier, cheaper costs remain in the inventory T-account). As will be discussed in a subsequent section, LIFO is popular in the United States because it helps reduce the amount many companies must pay in income taxes.

TEST YOURSELF

Question:

A hardware store buys a lawn mower on Monday for $120, another identical model on Tuesday for $125, another on Wednesday for $132, and a final one on Thursday for $135. One is sold on Friday for $180 in cash. The company applied FIFO although company officials had originally argued for the use of LIFO. Which of the following statements are true?

  a. If the company had applied LIFO, its net income would have been $10 lower than is being reported.
  b. If the company had applied LIFO, gross profit would have been $15 lower than is being reported.
  c. If the company had applied LIFO, inventory on the balance sheet would have been $15 higher than is being reported.
  d. If the company had applied LIFO, cost of goods sold would have been $10 higher than is being reported.

Answer:

The correct answer is choice b: If the company had applied LIFO, gross profit would have been $15 lower than is being reported.

Explanation:

In FIFO, the $120 cost is removed from inventory and added to cost of goods sold because it is the first cost acquired. Under LIFO, the $135 cost of the last lawn mower would have been reclassified. Thus, in using LIFO, cost of goods sold is $15 higher so that both gross profit and net income are $15 lower. Because the higher (later) cost is removed from inventory, this asset balance will be $15 lower under LIFO.

Averaging. Because the identity of the items conveyed to buyers is unknown, this final cost flow assumption holds that **averaging** all costs is the most logical solution. Why choose any individual cost if no evidence exists of its validity? The first item received might have been sold or the last. Selecting either is an arbitrary decision. If items with varying costs are held, using an average provides a very appealing logic. In the shirt example, the two units cost a total of $120 ($50 plus $70) so the average is $60 ($120/2 units).

averaging

Inventory cost flow assumption based on the average cost being transferred from inventory to cost of goods sold so that this same average cost remains in ending inventory.

FIGURE 9.3 Journal Entry—Reclassification of the Cost of One Piece of Inventory Using Averaging

Cost of Goods Sold	60	
Inventory		60

Although no shirt actually cost $60, this average serves as the basis for reporting both cost of goods sold and the item still on hand. Therefore, all costs are included in arriving at each of these figures.

Averaging	
Cost of Goods Sold (one unit sold—the cost of the average one)	$60
Gross Profit ($110 sales price less $60 cost)	$50
Ending Inventory (one unit remains—the cost of the last one)	$60

Averaging has many supporters. However, it can be a rather complicated system to implement especially if inventory costs change frequently. In addition, it does not offer the benefits that make FIFO (higher reported income) and LIFO (lower taxes in the United States) so appealing. Company officials often arrive at practical accounting decisions based more on an evaluation of advantages and disadvantages rather than on theoretical merit.

TEST YOURSELF

Question:

A hardware store buys a lawn mower on Monday for $120, another identical model on Tuesday for $125, another on Wednesday for $132, and a final one on Thursday for $135. One is sold on Friday for $180 in cash. Company officials are trying to decide whether to select FIFO, LIFO, or averaging as the cost flow assumption. Which of the following statements is true?

a. Gross profit under FIFO is $7 higher than under averaging.

b. Gross profit under averaging is $7 higher than under LIFO.

c. Gross profit under averaging is $7 lower than under FIFO.

d. Gross profit under LIFO is $7 lower than under FIFO.

Answer:

The correct answer is choice b: Gross profit under averaging is $7 higher than under LIFO.

Explanation:

With FIFO, $120 (the first cost) is moved out of inventory and into cost of goods sold. Gross profit is $60 ($180 less $120). For LIFO, $135 (the last cost) is transferred to expense to gross profit is $45 ($180 less $135). In averaging, an average of $128 is calculated ([$120 + $125 + $132 + $135]/4 units). That cost is then reclassified from inventory to cost of goods sold so that gross profit is $52 ($180 less $128). FIFO is $8 higher than averaging; averaging is $7 higher than LIFO.

KEY TAKEAWAY

U.S. GAAP tends to apply standard reporting rules to many transactions to make resulting financial statements more easily understood by decision makers. The application of an inventory cost flow assumption is one area where significant variation does exist. A company can choose to use specific identification, first-in, first-out (FIFO), last-in, first-out (LIFO), or averaging. In each of these assumptions, a different cost is moved from inventory to cost of goods sold to reflect the sale of merchandise. The reported inventory balance as well as the expense on the income statement (and, hence, net income) are dependent on the cost flow assumption that is selected. In periods of inflation, FIFO reports a higher net income than LIFO and a larger inventory balance. Consequently, LIFO is popular because it is often used to reduce income tax costs.

---

2. THE SELECTION OF A COST FLOW ASSUMPTION FOR REPORTING PURPOSES

LEARNING OBJECTIVES

At the end of this section, students should be able to meet the following objectives:

1. **Appreciate that reported inventory and cost of goods sold balances are not intended to be right or wrong but rather in conformity with U.S. GAAP, which permits the use of several different cost flow assumptions.**

2. **Recognize that three cost flow assumptions (FIFO, LIFO, and averaging) are particularly popular in the United States.**

3. **Understand the meaning of the LIFO conformity rule and realize that use of LIFO in the United States largely stems from the presence of this tax law.**

4. **Know that U.S. companies prepare financial statements according to U.S. GAAP but their income tax returns are based on the Internal Revenue Code so that significant differences often exist.**

2.1 Presenting Inventory Balances Fairly

Question: FIFO, LIFO, and averaging can present radically different portraits of identical events. Is the gross profit for this men's clothing store really $60 (FIFO), $40 (LIFO), or $50 (averaging) following the sale of one blue dress shirt? Analyzing inventory numbers presented by most companies can be difficult if *not impossible without understanding the implications of the cost flow assumption that was applied. Which cost flow assumption is viewed as most appropriate in producing fairly presented financial statements?*

Answer: Because specific identification reclassifies the cost of the actual unit that was sold, finding theoretical fault with that approach is difficult. Unfortunately, specific identification is nearly impossible to apply unless easily distinguishable differences exist between similar inventory items. For a vast majority of companies, that leaves FIFO, LIFO, and averaging. Arguments over their merits and their problems have raged for decades. Ultimately, information in financial statements must be presented fairly based on the cost flow assumption that is utilized.

In a previous chapter, an important clarification was made about the report of the independent auditor. It never assures decision makers that financial statements are "presented fairly." That is a hopelessly abstract concept like truth and beauty. Instead, the auditor states that the statements "present fairly…in conformity with accounting principles generally accepted in the United States of America." That is a substantially more objective standard. Thus, for this men's clothing store, all the numbers in Figure 9.4 are presented fairly but only in conformity with the specific cost flow assumption that was applied.

FIGURE 9.4   Results of Possible Cost Flows Assumptions Used by Clothing Store

	Gross Profit	Ending Inventory	
Bought Two Units and Sold One	$60	$70	based on application of FIFO
Bought Two Units and Sold One	40	50	based on application of LIFO
Bought Two Units and Sold One	50	60	based on application of averaging

2.2 Most Popular Cost Flow Assumptions

Question: Since company officials are allowed to select a cost flow assumption, which of these methods is most typically found in the financial reporting of companies operating in the United States?

Answer: To help interested parties gauge the usage of various accounting methods and procedures, a survey is carried out annually of the financial statements of 500 large companies. The resulting information allows accountants, auditors, and decision makers to weigh the validity of a particular presentation. For 2009, this survey found the following frequency for the various cost flow assumptions. Some companies actually use multiple assumptions: one for a particular portion of its inventory and a different one for the remainder. Thus, the total here is above 500 even though 98 of the surveyed companies did not report having inventory or mention a cost flow assumption (inventory was probably an immaterial amount). As will be discussed later in this chapter, applying multiple assumptions is especially common when a U.S. company owns subsidiaries that are located internationally.

Inventory Cost Flow Assumptions—500 Companies Surveyed[2]	
First-in, First-out (FIFO)	325
Last-in, First-out (LIFO)	176
Averaging	147
Other	18

Interestingly, individual cost flow assumptions tend to be more prevalent in certain industries. In this same survey, 92 percent of the financial statements issued by food and drug stores made use of LIFO whereas only 11 percent of the companies labeled as "computers, office equipment" had adopted this same approach. This difference is likely caused by the presence of inflation or deflation in those industries. Prices of food and drugs tend to escalate consistently over time while computer prices often fall as technology advances.

2.3   The LIFO Conformity Rule

Question: In periods of inflation, FIFO reports a higher gross profit (and, hence, net income) and a higher inventory balance than does LIFO. Averaging presents figures that normally fall between these two extremes. Such results are widely expected by the readers of financial statements who understand the impact of the various cost flow assumptions.

In the United States, all of these methods are permitted for financial reporting. Why is FIFO not the obvious choice for every organization that anticipates inflation in its inventory costs? Officials must prefer to report figures that make the company look stronger and more profitable. With every rise in prices, FIFO shows a higher income because the earlier (cheaper) costs are transferred to cost of goods sold. Likewise, FIFO reports a higher total for ending inventory because the later (higher) cost figures are retained in the inventory T-account. The company is no different physically as a result of this decision but FIFO makes it look better. **Why does any company voluntarily choose LIFO, an approach that reduces reported income and total assets when prices rise?**

LIFO conformity rule

A United States income tax rule that requires LIFO to be used for financial reporting purposes if it is adopted for taxation purposes.

Answer: LIFO might well have faded into oblivion because of its negative impact on key reported figures (during inflationary periods) except for a U.S. income tax requirement known as the LIFO conformity rule. Although this tax regulation is not part of U.S. GAAP and looks rather innocuous, it has a huge impact on the way inventory and cost of goods sold are reported in this country.

If costs are increasing, companies prefer to apply LIFO for tax purposes because this assumption reduces reported income and, hence, required cash payments to the government. In the United States, LIFO has come to be universally equated with the saving of tax dollars. When LIFO was first proposed as a tax method in the 1930s, the United States Treasury Department appointed a panel of three experts to consider its validity. The members of this group were split over a final resolution. They eventually agreed to recommend that LIFO be allowed for income tax purposes but only if the company was also willing to use LIFO for financial reporting. At that point, tax rules bled over into U.S. GAAP.

The rationale behind this compromise was that companies were allowed the option but probably would not choose LIFO for their tax returns because of the potential negative effect on the figures reported to investors, creditors, and others. During inflationary periods, companies that apply LIFO do not look as financially healthy as those that adopt FIFO. Eventually this recommendation was put into law and the LIFO conformity rule was born. It is a federal law and not an accounting principle. If LIFO is used on a company's income tax return, it must also be applied on the financial statements.

However, as the previous statistics on usage point out, this requirement did not prove to be the deterrent that was anticipated. Actual use of LIFO has remained popular for decades. For many companies, the money saved in income tax dollars more than outweighs the problem of having to report numbers that make the company look weaker. Figure 9.5 shows that both methods have advantages and disadvantages. Company officials must weigh the options and make a decision.

As discussed later in this chapter, IFRS does not permit the use of LIFO. Therefore, if IFRS is ever mandated in the United States, a significant tax advantage will be lost unless the LIFO conformity rule is abolished.

FIGURE 9.5   Advantages and Disadvantages of FIFO and LIFO

*Assumes a rise in prices over time.

	Advantages*	Disadvantages*
FIFO	Company Looks Financially Stronger	Company Pays More Taxes
LIFO	Company Pays Less Taxes	Company Looks Financially Weaker

> ### TEST YOURSELF
>
> **Question:**
>
> The Cucina Company buys and sells widgets in a highly inflationary market. Prices tend to go up quickly. An analyst is studying the company and notes that LIFO has been selected as the company's cost flow assumption. Which of the following is not likely to be true?
>
>   a. Cost of goods sold will come closest to reflecting current costs.
>   b. The inventory balance will be below market value for the items being held.
>   c. The company will have more cash because tax payments will be lower.
>   d. Net income will be inflated.
>
> **Answer:**
>
> The correct answer is choice d: Net income will be inflated.
>
> **Explanation:**
>
> With LIFO, the latest costs are moved to cost of goods sold; thus, this expense is more reflective of current prices. These costs are high during inflation so the resulting gross profit and net income are lower. That allows the company to save tax dollars since payments are reduced. The earliest (cheapest) costs remain in inventory, which means this asset is reported at below its current value. LIFO, during inflation, is known for low inventory costs, low income, and low tax payments.

2.4   Two Sets of Books

Question: The LIFO conformity rule requires companies that apply LIFO for income tax purposes to also use that same cost flow assumption in conveying financial information to investors and creditors. **Are the balances submitted to the government for income tax purposes not always the same as that presented to decision makers in a set of financial statements?** *Reporting different numbers to different parties seems unethical.*

Answer: In both jokes and editorials, businesses are often derisively accused of "keeping two sets of books." The implication is that one is skewed toward making the company look good (for external reporting purposes) whereas the other makes the company look bad (for taxation purposes). However, the existence of separate accounting records is a practical necessity. One set is based on applicable tax laws while the other enables the company to prepare financial statements according to U.S. GAAP. With two different sets of rules, the outcomes have to look different.

In filing income taxes with the United States government, a company must follow the regulations of the Internal Revenue Code.[3] Those laws have several underlying objectives that influence their development.

First, income tax laws are designed to raise money for the operation of the federal government. Without adequate funding, the government could not provide hospitals, build roads, maintain a military and the like.

Second, income tax laws enable the government to help regulate the health of the economy. Simply by raising or lowering tax rates, the government can take money out of the economy (and slow public spending) or leave money in the economy (and increase public spending). For example, in a recent year, a significant tax break was passed by Congress to aid first-time home buyers. This move was designed to stimulate the housing market by encouraging individuals to consider making a purchase.

Third, income tax laws enable the government to assist certain members of society who are viewed as deserving help. For example, taxpayers who encounter high medical costs or casualty losses are entitled to a tax break. Donations conveyed to an approved charity can also reduce a taxpayer's tax bill. The rules and regulations were designed to provide assistance for specified needs.

In contrast, in the United States, external financial reporting is governed by U.S. GAAP, a system designed to achieve the fair presentation of accounting information. That is the reason U.S. GAAP exists. Because the goals are different, financial data reported according to U.S. GAAP will not necessarily correspond to the tax figures submitted by the same company to the Internal Revenue Service (IRS). At places, though, agreement can be found between the two sets of rules. For example, both normally recognize a cash sale of merchandise as revenue at the time of sale. However, many differences do exist between the two. A loss on the sale of an investment in equity securities is just one example of a transaction that is handled quite differently for taxes and financial reporting.

Although separately developed, financial statements and income tax returns are tied together at one significant spot: the LIFO conformity rule. If a company chooses to use LIFO in filing its United States income tax return, it must do the same for financial reporting. Without that legal requirement, many companies would likely use FIFO in creating their financial statements and LIFO for their income tax returns. Much of the popularity of LIFO is undoubtedly derived from this tax requirement rather than from any theoretical merit.

KEY TAKEAWAY

Information found in financial statements is required to be presented fairly in conformity with U.S. GAAP. Because several inventory cost flow assumptions are allowed, reported numbers can vary significantly from one company to another and still be appropriate. FIFO, LIFO, and averaging are all popular in the United States. Understanding and comparing financial statements is quite difficult without knowing the implications of the method selected. LIFO, for example, tends to produce low net income figures in a period of inflation. This cost flow assumption probably would not be used extensively except for the LIFO conformity rule. That tax law prohibits the use of LIFO for tax purposes unless also applied on the company's financial statements. Typically, financial reporting and the preparation of income tax returns are unrelated because two sets of rules are used with radically differing objectives. However, the LIFO conformity rule joins these two at this one key spot.

3. PROBLEMS WITH APPLYING LIFO

LEARNING OBJECTIVES

At the end of this section, students should be able to meet the following objectives:

1. Recognize that theoretical and practical problems with LIFO have led the creators of IFRS rules to prohibit its use.
2. Explain that the most obvious problem associated with LIFO is an inventory balance that can show costs from years (or even decades) earlier, costs that are totally irrelevant today.
3. Identify the cause of a LIFO liquidation and the reason that it is viewed as a theoretical concern by accountants.

3.1 Reporting Ending Inventory Using LIFO

Question: As a result of the LIFO conformity rule in the tax laws, this cost flow assumption is widely used in the United States. LIFO, though, is not allowed in many other areas of the world. It is not simply unpopular in those locations; its application is strictly forbidden by IFRS. Thus, international companies are often forced to resort to alternatives in reporting their foreign subsidiaries. For example, a note to the 2010 financial statements of **American Biltrite Inc.** *explains that "cost is determined by the last-in, first-out (LIFO) method for approximately 47% of the Company's domestic inventories. The use of LIFO results in a better matching of costs and revenues. Cost is determined by the first-in, first-out (FIFO) method for the Company's foreign inventories."*

Why is LIFO not accepted in most countries outside the United States?

Answer: Although LIFO can be supported as providing a better matching of expenses (cost of goods sold) with revenues, a number of serious problems arise from its application. The most common accusation made against LIFO is that it often presents a balance sheet figure that is out-of-date and completely useless. When applying this assumption, the latest costs are moved to cost of goods sold so that earlier costs remain in the inventory account—possibly for years and even decades. After some period of time, this asset balance is likely to report a number that has no relevance to today's prices.

For example, in its 2010 financial statements, **ExxonMobil** reported inventory on its balance sheet of approximately $13.0 billion based on applying the LIFO cost flow assumption. In the notes to those financial statements, the company disclosed that the current cost to acquire this same inventory was actually $21.3 billion higher than the number being reported. The asset was shown as $13.0 billion but the price to obtain that merchandise on the balance sheet date was $34.3 billion ($13.0 billion plus $21.3). What is the possible informational value of reporting an asset (one that is being held for sale) at an amount more than $21 billion below its current replacement cost?[4] That is the essential problem attributed to LIFO.

To illustrate, assume that a convenience store begins operations and has a tank that holds ten thousand gallons of gasoline. On January 1, 1972, the tank is filled at a cost of $1 per gallon. Almost immediately the price of gasoline jumps to $2 per gallon. During the remainder of 1972, the store buys and sells gas. The tank is filled one final time at the very end of the year bringing total purchases to one million gallons. The first 10,000 gallons were bought at $1.00 per gallon; the next one million gallons cost $2.00 per gallon.

LIFO and FIFO report these results as follows:

LIFO	
Cost of Goods Sold—1,000,000 gallons at last cost of $2 per gallon	$2,000,000
Ending Inventory—10,000 gallons at first cost of $1 per gallon	10,000

FIFO	
Cost of Goods Sold—first 10,000 gallons at $1 per gallon and next 990,000 gallons at $2 per gallon	$1,990,000
Ending Inventory—10,000 gallons at last cost of $2 per gallon	20,000

After just this initial period, the ending inventory balance shown for LIFO (10,000 gallons at $1 per gallon) already differs significantly from the current cost of $2 per gallon.

If this convenience store continues to finish each year with a full tank of 10,000 gallons (certainly not an unreasonable assumption), LIFO will report this inventory at $1 per gallon for the following decades regardless of current prices. The most recent costs get transferred to cost of goods sold every period leaving the first costs ($1 per gallon) in inventory. The tendency to report this asset at a cost expended years in the past is the single biggest reason that LIFO is viewed as an illegitimate cost flow assumption in many countries. That same sentiment would probably exist in the United States except for the LIFO conformity rule.

TEST YOURSELF

Question:

The Lenoir Corporation sells paperback books and boasts in its ads that it holds over one million volumes. Prices have risen over the years and, at the present time, books like those obtained by Lenoir cost between $4 and $5 each. Sandy Sanghvi is thinking about buying shares of the ownership stock of Lenoir and picks up a set of financial statements to help evaluate the company. The inventory figure on the company's balance sheet is reported as $832,000 based on the application of LIFO. Which of the following is Sanghvi most likely to assume?

a. Lenoir has many subsidiaries in countries outside of the United States.

b. Lenoir officials prefer to minimize tax payments rather than looking especially healthy in an economic sense.

c. Lenoir's net income is likely to be slightly inflated because of the impact of inflation.

d. Lenoir is likely to use different cost flow assumptions for financial reporting and income tax purposes.

Answer:

The correct answer is choice b: Lenoir officials prefer to minimize tax payments rather than looking especially healthy in an economic sense.

Explanation:

Knowledge of financial accounting provides a decision maker with an understanding of many aspects of the information reported by a company. Here, the inventory balance is significantly below current cost, which is common for LIFO, an assumption that often serves to reduce taxable income in order to decrease tax payments. Because of the LIFO conformity rule, use of that assumption for tax purposes requires that it also be adopted for financial reporting purposes. It is normally not used by foreign companies.

3.2 LIFO Liquidation

Question: In discussions of financial reporting, LIFO is also criticized because of the possibility of an event known as a LIFO *liquidation.* **What is a LIFO liquidation and why does it create a theoretical problem for accountants?**

Answer: As demonstrated above, costs from much earlier years often remain in the inventory T-account over a long period of time if LIFO is applied. With that cost flow assumption, a convenience store that opens in 1972 and ends each year with a full tank of 10,000 gallons of gasoline reports ending inventory at 1972 costs for years or even decades. Every balance sheet will show inventory as $10,000 (10,000 gallons in ending inventory at $1.00 per gallon).

However, if the quantity of inventory is ever allowed to decrease (accidentally or on purpose), some or all of those 1972 costs move to cost of goods sold. For example, if the convenience store ends 2012 with less than 10,000 gallons of gasoline, the reduction means that costs sitting in the inventory T-account since 1972 are recognized as an expense in the current year. Costs from 40 years earlier are matched with revenue in 2012. That is a LIFO liquidation and it can artificially inflate reported earnings if those earlier costs are especially low.

To illustrate, assume that this convenience store starts 2012 with 10,000 gallons of gasoline. LIFO has been applied over the years so that this inventory is reported at the 1972 cost of $1.00 per gallon. In 2012, gasoline costs the store $3.35 per gallon to buy and is then sold to the public for $3.50 per gallon creating a gross profit of $0.15 per gallon. That is the amount of income the store is making this year.

At the beginning of 2012, the convenience store sells its entire stock of 10,000 gallons of gasoline at the market price of $3.50 and then ceases to carry this product (perhaps the owners want to focus on groceries or automobile parts). Without any replacement of the inventory, the cost of the gasoline bought in 1972 for $1.00 per gallon is shifted from inventory to cost of goods sold in 2012. Instead of recognizing the normal profit margin of $0.15 per gallon or $1,500 for the 10,000 gallons, the store reports gross profit of $2.50 per gallon ($3.50 sales price minus $1.00 cost of goods sold) or $25,000 in total. The reported profit ($25,000) does not reflect the reality of current market conditions. This LIFO liquidation allows the store to look overly profitable.

In a LIFO liquidation, costs from an earlier period are matched with revenues of the present year. Revenue is measured in 2012 dollars but cost of goods sold is stated in 1972 prices. Although the reported figures are technically correct, the implication that this store earned a gross profit of $2.50 per gallon is misleading.

To warn decision makers of the impact that a LIFO liquidation has on reported net income, disclosure in the notes to the financial statements is needed whenever costs are mismatched in this manner. According to a note in the 2010 financial statements for **Alcoa Inc.** (all numbers in millions), "During the three-year period ended December 31, 2010, reductions in LIFO inventory quantities caused partial liquidations of the lower cost LIFO inventory base. These liquidations resulted in the recognition of income of $27 ($17 after-tax) in 2010, $175 ($114 after-tax) in 2009, and $38 ($25 after-tax) in 2008."

TEST YOURSELF

Question:

Margaret Besseler is studying the financial statements produced by Associated Chemicals of Rochester. Besseler notices that the footnotes indicate that a LIFO liquidation took place during the most recent year. Which of the following is least likely to be true?

a. Inventory quantities decreased during the year.

b. Reported net income was inflated by the LIFO liquidation.

c. The company converted from the use of LIFO to that of FIFO (or some other cost flow assumption).

d. Cost of goods sold was below the current cost of the inventory sold.

Answer:

The correct answer is choice c: The company converted from the use of LIFO to that of FIFO (or some other cost flow assumption).

Explanation:

A LIFO liquidation is a decrease in the quantity of inventory held by a company that applies LIFO so that a cost (often a much cheaper cost) from an earlier time period is moved from inventory to cost of goods sold. That artificially reduces this expense and, hence, increases both reported gross profit and net income. A LIFO liquidation is viewed unfavorably by accountants because an old, out-of-date (often much cheaper) cost is matched with current revenues.

Talking with an Independent Auditor about International Financial Reporting Standards (Continued)

Following is a continuation of our interview with Robert A. Vallejo, partner with the accounting firm **PricewaterhouseCoopers**.

Question: Companies in the United States are allowed to choose FIFO, LIFO, or averaging as an inventory cost flow assumption. Over the years, many U.S. companies have adopted LIFO, in part because of the possibility of reducing income taxes during a period of inflation. However, IFRS rules do not recognize LIFO as appropriate. Why does such strong resistance to LIFO exist outside the United States? If the United States adopts IFRS will all of these companies that now use LIFO have to switch their accounting systems to FIFO or averaging? How much trouble will that be?

Rob Vallejo: The International Accounting Standards Board revised International Accounting Standard No. 2, Inventories (IAS 2), in 2003. The issue of accounting for inventories using a LIFO costing method was debated and I would encourage anyone seeking additional information to read their basis for conclusion which accompanies IAS 2. The IASB did not believe that the LIFO costing method was a reliable representation of actual inventory flows. In other words, in most industries, older inventory is sold to customers before newer inventory. The standard specifically precludes the use of LIFO, but allows for the use of the FIFO or weighted average costing methods as the board members view these as better representations of actual inventory flows.

Therefore, when U.S. companies have to adopt IFRS, the inventory balances and the related impact on shareholders' equity will be restated as if FIFO or average costing had been used for all periods presented. Most companies keep their books on a FIFO or weighted average cost basis and then apply a LIFO adjustment, so the switch to an alternative method should not be a big issue in a mechanical sense. However, the reason most companies apply the LIFO costing method relates to U.S. tax law. Companies that want to apply LIFO for income tax purposes are required to also present their financial information under the LIFO method. The big question still being debated is whether or not U.S. tax law will change to accommodate the move to IFRS. This is very important to U.S. companies, as generally, applying LIFO has had a cumulative impact of deferring the payment of income taxes. If companies must change to FIFO or weighted average costing methods for tax purposes, that could mean substantial cash payments to the IRS. This continues to be a very hot topic for accountants and U.S. government officials, as the cash tax implications are significant for many companies.

4. MERGING PERIODIC AND PERPETUAL INVENTORY SYSTEMS WITH A COST FLOW ASSUMPTION

LEARNING OBJECTIVES

At the end of this section, students should be able to meet the following objectives:

1. Merge a cost flow assumption (FIFO, LIFO, and averaging) with a method of monitoring inventory (periodic or perpetual) to arrive at six different systems for determining reported inventory figures.
2. Understand that a cost flow assumption is only applied when determining the cost of ending inventory in a periodic system but is used for each reclassification from inventory to cost of goods sold in a perpetual system.
3. Calculate ending inventory and cost of goods sold using both a periodic and a perpetual FIFO system.
4. Recognize that periodic and perpetual FIFO systems will arrive at identical account balances.

4.1 Cost Flow Assumptions and Inventory Systems

Question: In the previous chapter, periodic and perpetual inventory systems were introduced. FIFO, LIFO, and averaging have now been presented. How does all of this material come together for reporting purposes? **How does the application of a cost flow assumption impact the operation of a periodic or a perpetual inventory system?**

Answer: Each company that holds inventory must develop a mechanism to both (a) monitor the balances and (b) allow for the creation of financial statements. If a periodic system is used, officials simply wait until financial statements are to be produced before taking a physical count. Then, a formula (beginning inventory plus all purchase costs less ending inventory) is applied to derive cost of goods sold.

In contrast, a perpetual system maintains an ongoing record of the goods that remain on hand and those that have been sold. As noted, both of these systems have advantages and disadvantages.

Companies also select a cost flow assumption to specify the cost that is transferred from inventory to cost of goods sold (and, hence, the cost that remains in the inventory T-account). For a periodic system, the cost flow assumption is only applied when the physical inventory count is taken and the cost of the ending inventory is determined. In a perpetual system, the cost flow assumption is used each time a sale is made to identify the cost to be reclassified to cost of goods sold. That can occur thousands of times each day.

Therefore, companies normally choose one of six systems to monitor their merchandise balances and determine the cost assignment between ending inventory and cost of goods sold:

- Periodic FIFO
- Perpetual FIFO
- Periodic LIFO
- Perpetual LIFO
- Periodic averaging (also called weighted averaging)
- Perpetual averaging (also called moving averaging)

4.2 Periodic and Perpetual FIFO

Question: To illustrate, assume that the Mayberry Home Improvement Store starts the new year with four bathtubs (Model WET-5) in its inventory, costing $110 each ($440 in total) when bought on December 9 of the previous period. The following events then take place during the current year.

- *On February 2, three of these bathtubs are sold for $200 each. (revenue $600)*
- *On February 6, three new bathtubs of this model are bought for $120 each. (cost $360)*
- *On June 8, three of these bathtubs are sold for $250 each. (revenue $750)*
- *On June 13, three new bathtubs of this model are bought for $130 each. (cost $390)*
- *On September 9, two of these bathtubs are sold for $300 each. (revenue $600)*
- *On September 22, two new bathtub of this model are bought for $149. (cost $298)*

At the end of the year, on December 31, a physical inventory is taken that finds that four bathtubs, Model WET-5, are in stock (4 – 3 + 3 – 3 + 3 – 2 + 2). None were stolen, lost, or damaged during the period. **How does a periodic FIFO system differ from a perpetual FIFO system in maintaining accounting records and reporting inventory totals?**

Answer: Regardless of the inventory system in use, several pieces of information are established in this example. These figures are factual, not impacted by accounting.

The Facts—Purchase and Sale of WET-5 Bathtubs

- Revenue: Eight units were sold for $1,950 ($600 + $750 + $600)
- Beginning Inventory: Four units costing $110 each or $440 in total
- Purchases: Eight units were bought during the year costing a total of $1,048 ($360 + $390 + $298)
- Ending Inventory: Four units are still held according to the physical inventory

Periodic FIFO. In a periodic system, the cost of all new purchases is the focus of the record keeping. Then, at the end of the period, the accountant must count and also determine the cost of the items held in ending inventory. When using FIFO, the first costs are transferred to cost of goods sold so the cost of the last four bathtubs remain in the inventory T-account. That is the FIFO assumption. The first costs are now in cost of goods sold while the most recent costs remain in the asset account.

In this illustration, the last four costs (starting at the end of the period and moving forward) are two units at $149 each and two units at $130 each for a total of $558. Only after that cost is assigned to the ending inventory units can cost of goods sold be calculated as shown in Figure 9.6.

FIGURE 9.6 Periodic FIFO—Bathtub Model WET-5

Beginning Inventory (carried over from previous year)—4 Units at $110 Each	$440
Purchases—8 Units	1,048
Goods Available for Sale (12 units in total)	$1,488
Ending Inventory (physical count)—2 Units at $149 Each and 2 Units at $130 Each	
Based on Applying FIFO	(558)
Cost of Goods Sold	$930

Under FIFO, the last costs for the period remain in ending inventory; the first costs have all been transferred to cost of goods sold. Based on the application of FIFO, Mayberry reports gross profit from the sale of bathtubs during this year of $1,020 (revenue of $1,950 minus the cost of goods sold figure of $930 calculated in Figure 9.6).

Perpetual FIFO. Perpetual accounting systems are constructed so that costs can be moved from inventory to cost of goods sold at the time of each new sale. With modern computer processing, that is a relatively simple task. In Figure 9.7, one format is shown that provides the information needed for this store about the cost and quantity of its inventory of bathtubs. In this figure, at points A, B, and C, costs are moved from inventory on hand to cost of goods sold based on FIFO. The cost of the first goods in the "inventory on hand" is reclassified to cost of goods sold at each of those three points in time.

FIGURE 9.7 Perpetual FIFO—Bathtub Model WET-5

	Inventory Acquired →	Inventory On Hand →	Cost of Goods Sold
1/1—Beginning Balance		4 Units @ $110	
2/2—3 Units Sold		1 Unit @ 110	(A) 3 Units @ $110 = $330
2/6—3 Units Bought	3 Units @ $120	1 Unit @ 110 3 Units @ 120	
6/8—3 Units Sold		1 Unit @ $120	(B) 1 Unit @ 110 2 Units @ 120 = 350
6/13—3 Units Bought	3 Units @ 130	1 Unit @ 120 3 Units @ 130	
9/9—2 Units Sold		2 Units @ 130	(C) 1 Unit @ 120 1 Unit @ $130 = 250
9/22—2 Units Bought	2 Units @ 149	2 Units @ 130 2 Units @ 149	
Totals		**$260 + $298 = $558**	**$330 + $350 + $250 = $930**

On this perpetual inventory spreadsheet, the final cell in the "inventory on hand" column ($558 or two units @ $130 and two units at $149) provides the cost of the ending inventory to be reported on the balance sheet. However, it is the summation of the entire "cost of goods sold" column that arrives at the expense for the period ($930 or $330 + $350 + $250).

One important characteristic of FIFO should be noted here. Under both periodic and perpetual FIFO, ending inventory is $558 and cost of goods sold is $930. The reported numbers are identical. The first cost for the period is always the first cost regardless of when the assignment to expense is made. Thus, the resulting amounts are the same when using either FIFO system.

For that reason, many companies that apply FIFO maintain perpetual records to track the units on hand throughout the period but ignore the costs. Later, when financial statements are prepared, a periodic computation is used to determine the cost of ending inventory in order to calculate cost of goods sold. That allows these companies to monitor their inventory quantities every day without the expense and effort of identifying the specific cost associated with each new sale.

Question:

The Hastings Widget Company starts the year with 27,000 widgets costing $2 each. During the year, the company bought another 450,000 widgets for a total of $1,243,000. Within these figures was the acquisition of 20,000 widgets for $3.10 each on December 26 and 15,000 widgets for $3.00 each on December 18. Those were the last two purchases of the year. On December 31, the company took a physical count and found 22,000 widgets still on hand. If a FIFO cost flow assumption is applied, what is cost of goods sold?

a. $1,229,000

b. $1,233,200

c. $1,243,000

d. $1,245,800

Answer:

The correct answer is choice a: $1,229,000.

Explanation:

Beginning inventory is $54,000 (27,000 units at $2 each) while purchases are $1,243,000, a total cost of $1,297,000. With FIFO, the remaining 22,000 units had the cost of the last purchases: 20,000 at $3.10 ($62,000) plus 2,000 bought for $3.00 each ($6,000). Ending inventory cost $68,000 ($62,000 + $6,000). Subtracting this cost from the goods available gives cost of goods sold of $1,229,000 ($1,297,000 less $68,000). The use of periodic or perpetual has no impact since FIFO was used.

KEY TAKEAWAY

Companies that sell inventory will choose a cost flow assumption such as FIFO, LIFO, or averaging. In addition, a monitoring system (either periodic or perpetual) must be installed to record inventory balances . Six combinations (periodic FIFO, perpetual FIFO, periodic LIFO, and the like) can result from these two decisions. With any periodic system, the cost flow assumption is only used to determine the cost of ending inventory units so that cost of goods sold for the period can be calculated. For a perpetual inventory system, the reclassification of costs from asset to expense is performed each time that a sale is made and is based on the selected cost flow assumption. Periodic FIFO and perpetual FIFO systems arrive at the same reported balances because the earliest cost is always the first to be transferred regardless of the method applied.

5. APPLYING LIFO AND AVERAGING TO DETERMINE REPORTED INVENTORY BALANCES

LEARNING OBJECTIVES

At the end of this section, students should be able to meet the following objectives:

1. **Determine ending inventory and cost of goods sold using a periodic LIFO system.**
2. **Monitor inventory on an ongoing basis through a perpetual LIFO system.**
3. **Understand the reason that periodic LIFO and perpetual LIFO usually arrive at different figures.**
4. **Use a weighted average system to determine the cost of ending inventory and cost of goods sold.**
5. **Calculate reported inventory balances by applying a moving average inventory system.**

5.1 Applying LIFO

*Question: LIFO reverses the FIFO cost flow assumption so that the last costs incurred are the first reclassified to cost of goods sold. **How is LIFO applied to the inventory of an actual business?** If the Mayberry Home Improvement Store adopted LIFO, how would the reported figures for its inventory have been affected by this decision?*

Answer: *Periodic LIFO.* In a periodic system, only the computation of the ending inventory is directly affected by the choice of a cost flow assumption.[5] Thus, for this illustration, beginning inventory remains $440 (4 units at $110 each), and the number of units purchased is still eight with a cost of $1,048. The figure that changes is the cost of the ending inventory. Four bathtubs remain in stock at the end of the year. According to LIFO, the last (most recent) costs are transferred to cost of goods sold. Only the cost of the first four units remains in ending inventory. That is $110 per unit or $440 in total.

FIGURE 9.8 Periodic LIFO—Bathtub Model WET-5

*If the number of units bought during a period equals the number of units sold (as is seen in this example), the quantity of inventory remains unchanged. In a periodic LIFO system, beginning inventory ($440) is then the same as ending inventory ($440) so that cost of goods sold ($1,048) equals the amount spent during the period to purchase inventory ($1,048). For that reason, company officials can easily keep track of gross profit during the year by subtracting purchases from revenues.

Beginning Inventory (carried over from previous year)—4 Units at $110 Each	$440
Purchases—8 Units	1,048
Goods Available for Sale (12 units in total)	$1,488
Ending Inventory (physical count)—4 Units at $110 Each Based on Applying LIFO	(440)
Cost of Goods Sold	$1,048*

If Mayberry Home Improvement Store uses a periodic LIFO system, gross profit for the year will be reported as $902 (revenue of $1,950 less cost of goods sold of $1,048).

Note here that the anticipated characteristics of LIFO are present. Ending inventory of $440 is lower than that reported by FIFO ($558). Cost of goods sold ($1,048) is higher than under FIFO ($930) so that reported gross profit (and, hence, net income) is lower by $118 ($1,020 for FIFO versus $902 for LIFO).

TEST YOURSELF

Question:

The Lowenstein Widget Company starts the year with 24,000 widgets costing $3 each. During the year, the company bought another 320,000 widgets for a total of $1,243,000. Within these figures was the acquisition of 20,000 widgets for $4.10 each on December 26 and 15,000 widgets for $4.00 each on December 18. Those were the last two purchases of the year. On December 31, the company took a physical count and found 21,000 widgets still on hand. If a periodic LIFO cost flow assumption is applied, what amount is reported on the income statement for cost of goods sold?

a. $1,249,000
b. $1,252,000
c. $1,256,000
d. $1,264,000

Answer:

The correct answer is choice b: $1,252,000.

Explanation:

Beginning inventory is $72,000 (24,000 units at $3 each) and purchases total $1,243,000. Cost of goods available is the total or $1,315,000. With LIFO, the 21,000 units on hand had the $3 cost of the first items. Total cost for ending inventory is $63,000. Subtracting this balance from goods of available for sale ($1,315,000 less $63,000) gives cost of goods sold of $1,252,000. A LIFO liquidation took place since the inventory declined. That has no impact on the answer but is disclosed.

Perpetual LIFO. The mechanical structure for a perpetual LIFO system is the same as that demonstrated previously for perpetual FIFO except that the most recent costs are moved into cost of goods sold at the time of each sale (points A, B, and C).

FIGURE 9.9 Perpetual LIFO—Bathtub Model WET-5

	Inventory Acquired →	Inventory On Hand →	Cost of Goods Sold
1/1—Beginning Balance		4 Units @ $110	
2/2—3 Units Sold		1 Unit @ 110	(A) 3 Units @ $110 = 330
2/6—3 Units Bought	3 Units @ $120	1 Unit @ 110 3 Units @ 120	
6/8—3 Units Sold		1 Unit @ 110	(B) 3 Units @ 120 = 360
6/13—3 Units Bought	3 Units @ 130	1 Unit @ 110 3 Units @ 130	
9/9—2 Units Sold		1 Unit @ 110 1 Unit @ 130	(C) 2 Units @ 130 = 260
9/22—2 Units Bought	2 Units @ 149	1 Unit @ 110 1 Unit @ 130 2 Units @ 149	
Totals		**$110 + $130 + $298 = $538**	**$330 + $360 + $260 = $950**

Once again, the last cell at the bottom of the "inventory on hand" column contains the asset figure to be reported on the balance sheet (a total of $538) while the summation of the "cost of goods sold" column provides the amount to be shown on the income statement ($950).

As can be seen here, periodic and perpetual LIFO do not necessarily produce identical numbers.

periodic LIFO: ending inventory $440 and cost of goods sold $1,048

perpetual LIFO: ending inventory $538 and cost of goods sold $950

Although periodic and perpetual FIFO always arrive at the same results, balances reported by periodic and perpetual LIFO frequently differ. The first cost incurred in a period (the cost transferred to expense under FIFO) is the same regardless of the date of sale. However, the identity of the last or most recent cost (expensed according to LIFO) depends on the perspective.

To illustrate, note that two bathtubs were sold on September 9 by the Mayberry Home Improvement Store. Perpetual LIFO immediately determines the cost of this sale and reclassifies the amount to expense. On that date, the cost of the most recent two units ($130 each) came from the June 13 purchase. In contrast, a periodic LIFO system makes this same determination but not until December 31. As viewed from year's end, the last bathtubs had a cost of $149 each. Although these items were bought on September 22, after the final sale, their costs are included in cost of goods sold when applying periodic LIFO.

Two bathtubs were sold on September 9, but the identity of the specific costs to be transferred (when using LIFO) depends on the date on which the determination is made. A periodic system views the costs from the perspective of the end of the year. A perpetual system determines the expense immediately when each sale is made.

TEST YOURSELF

Question:

A company starts the year with 100 units of inventory costing $9 each. Those units are all sold on June 23. Another 100 are bought on July 6 for $11 each. On November 18, 70 of these units are sold. On December 16, fifty units are bought for $15 each bringing the total to eighty (100 − 100 + 100 − 70 + 50). If a perpetual LIFO system is used, what is the cost of these eighty units in ending inventory?

  a. $720
  b. $960
  c. $1,080
  d. $1,200

Answer:

The correct answer is choice c: $1,080.

Explanation:

In a perpetual LIFO system, the entire opening cost is transferred to cost of goods sold on June 23. On November 18, the cost of seventy units bought on July 6 is also transferred. That leaves thirty units at $11 each ($330) plus the December 16 purchase of fifty units at $15 each or $750. Ending inventory then has a total of $1,080 ($330 plus $750). The reclassification takes place each time at the point of the sale.

In practice, many companies are unlikely to use perpetual LIFO inventory systems. They are costly to maintain and, as has been discussed previously, provide figures of dubious usefulness. For that reason, companies often choose to maintain a perpetual FIFO system for internal decision making and then use the periodic LIFO formula at the end of the year to convert the numbers for external reporting purposes.

For example, **The Kroger Co.** presented the following balances on its January 29, 2011, balance sheet:

- FIFO inventory: $5,793 million
- LIFO reserve: (827) million

Kroger apparently monitors its inventory on a daily basis using FIFO and arrived at a final cost of $5,793 million. However, at the end of that year, the company took a physical inventory and applied the LIFO cost flow assumption to arrive at a reported balance that was $827 million lower. The reduced figure was used for reporting purposes because of the LIFO conformity rule. However, investors and creditors could still see that ending inventory actually had a current cost of $5,793 million.

5.2 Applying Averaging as a Cost Flow Assumption

Question: Not surprisingly, averaging follows a path similar to that of the previous examples. Costs are either moved to cost of goods sold at the end of the year (periodic or weighted average) or at the time of each new sale (perpetual or moving average). The only added variable to this process is the calculation of average cost. In the operation of an averaging system, when and how is the average cost of inventory determined?

Answer: *Periodic (weighted) average.* In the problem being examined here, Mayberry Home Improvement Store eventually held twelve bathtubs. Four of these units were on hand at the start of the year and the other eight were acquired during the period. The beginning inventory cost $440 and the new purchases were bought for a total of $1,048.

These twelve units had a total cost of $1,488 ($440 + $1,048) or $124 per bathtub ($1,488/12 units). When applying a weighted average system, this single average for the entire period is the basis for both the ending inventory and cost of goods sold to be reported in the financial statements. No item actually cost $124 but that average is applied to all units.

FIGURE 9.10 Periodic (Weighted) Average—Bathtub Model WET-5

Beginning Inventory (carried over from previous year)—4 Units at $110 Each	$440
Purchases—8 Units	1,048
Goods Available for Sale (12 units in total)	$1,488
Ending Inventory (physical count)—4 Units at $124 Each	
Based on Applying Periodic Averaging	(496)
Cost of Goods Sold (can also be determined	
as 8 units at an average cost of $124 each)	$992

Perpetual (moving) average. In this final approach to maintaining and reporting inventory, each time that a company buys inventory at a new price, the average cost is recalculated. Therefore, a moving average system must be programmed to update the average whenever additional merchandise is acquired.

In Figure 9.11, a new average is computed at points D, E, and F. This figure is found by dividing the number of units on hand after the new purchase into the total cost of those items. For example, at point D, the company now has four bathtubs. One cost $110 while the other three were newly acquired for $120 each or $360 in total. Total cost was $470 ($110 + $360) for these four units for an updated average of $117.50 ($470/4 units). That average is used until the next purchase is made on June 13. The applicable average at the time of sale is transferred from inventory to cost of goods sold at points A ($110.00), B ($117.50), and C ($126.88).

FIGURE 9.11 Perpetual (Moving) Average—Bathtub Model WET-5

	Inventory Acquired →	Inventory on Hand	→	Cost of Goods Sold
1/1—Beginning Balance		4 Units @ $110 = $440		
2/2—3 Units Sold		1 Unit @ 110 = 110		(A) 3 Units @ $110 = $330
2/6 —3 Units Bought	3 Units @ $120	1 Unit @ 110 = 110		
		3 Units @ 120 = 360		
New Average		(D) 4 Units @ 117.50 = 470		
6/8—3 Units Sold		1 Unit @ 117.50		(B) 3 Units @ 117.50 = 352.50
6/13—3 Units Bought	3 Units @ 130	1 Unit @ 117.50 = 117.50		
		3 Units @ 130 = 390		
New Average		(E) 4 Units @ 126.88 = 507.50		
9/9—2 Units Sold		2 Units @ 126.88 = 253.76		(C) 2 Units @ 126.88 = 253.76
9/22—2 Units Bought	2 Units @ 149	2 Units @ 126.88 = 253.76		
		2 Units @ 149 = 298		
New Average		(F) 4 Units @ 137.94 = 551.76		
Totals		**$551.76**		**$330 + $352.50 + $253.76 = $936.26**

Summary. The six inventory systems shown here for Mayberry Home Improvement Store provide a number of distinct pictures of ending inventory and cost of goods sold. As stated earlier, these numbers are all fairly presented but only in conformity with the specified principles being applied. Interestingly, gross profit ranges from $902.00 to $1,020.00 based on the system applied by management.

FIGURE 9.12 Reported Balances for Six Inventory Systems

	Periodic FIFO	Perpetual FIFO	Periodic LIFO	Perpetual LIFO	Weighted Average	Moving Average
Ending Inventory (4 Units)	$558.00	$558.00	$440.00	$538.00	$496.00	$551.76
Cost of Goods Sold (8 Units)	930.00	930.00	1,048.00	950.00	992.00	936.26
Gross Profit (Sales Revenue of $1,950 Less Cost of Goods Sold)	$1,020.00	$1,020.00	$902.00	$1,000.00	$958.00	$1,013.74

TEST YOURSELF

Question:

A company begins the new year with twenty-five units of inventory costing $12 each. In February, fifteen of these units are sold. At the beginning of May, fifty new units are acquired at $15 each. Finally, in August, forty more units are sold. On December 31, a physical inventory count is taken and twenty units are still on hand. Thus, no units were lost or stolen (25 units − 15 sold + 50 bought − 40 sold = 20 units remaining). If a weighted average system is used, what is the cost to be reported for those twenty units of inventory?

a. $250

b. $260

c. $270

d. $280

Answer:

The correct answer is choice d: $280.

Explanation:

In a weighted (or periodic) averaging system, the average for the year is not determined until financial statements are to be produced. Beginning inventory was $300 (twenty-five units for $12 each) and purchases were $750 (fifty units for $15 each) for a total of seventy-five units costing $1,050 ($300 + $750). That gives an average of $14 per unit ($1,050 cost/75 units). With this assumption, the cost assigned to the ending inventory of 20 units is $280 (20 units at $14 each).

TEST YOURSELF

Question:

A company begins the new year with twenty-five units of inventory costing $12 each. In February, fifteen of these units are sold. At the beginning of May, fifty new units are acquired at $15 each. Finally, in August, forty more units are sold. On December 31, a physical inventory count is taken and twenty units are still on hand. Thus, no units were lost or stolen (25 units − 15 sold + 50 bought − 40 sold = 20 units remaining). If a moving average system is used, what is the cost to be reported for those twenty units?

a. $260

b. $270

c. $280

d. $290

Answer:

The correct answer is choice d: $290.

Explanation:

In a moving average system, a new average is determined at the time of each purchase. The company starts with twenty-five units and sells fifteen. That leaves ten with a unit cost of $12 or $120 in total. Then, fifty are bought (bringing the total to sixty) with a cost of $15 each or $750 (bringing total cost up to $120 + $750 or $870). The average has now "moved" to $14.50 ($870 cost for sixty units). Eventually, twenty units remain. The ending inventory is $290 (twenty units at $14.50 each).

6.   ANALYZING REPORTED INVENTORY FIGURES

6.1   Making Comparisons When LIFO Is Applied

Question: The point has been made several times in this chapter that LIFO provides a lower reported net income than does FIFO when prices are rising. In addition, the inventory figure shown on the balance sheet will be below current cost if LIFO is applied during inflation. Comparison between companies that are similar can become difficult, if not impossible, when one uses LIFO and the other FIFO.

*For example, **Rite Aid**, the drug store giant, applies LIFO while its rival **CVS Caremark** applies FIFO to the inventory held in its pharmacies. How can an investor or creditor possibly evaluate these two companies to assess which has the brightest financial future? In this situation, the utility of the available information seems limited.* ***How do experienced decision makers manage to compare companies that apply LIFO to other companies that do not?***

Answer: Significant variations in reported balances frequently result from the application of different cost flow assumptions. Because of the potential detrimental effects, companies that use LIFO often provide additional information to help interested parties understand the impact of this choice. For example, in discussing the use of LIFO, a note to the financial statements for **Rite Aid** explains (numbers are in thousands): "At February 26, 2011 and February 27, 2010, inventories were $875,012 and $831,113, respectively, lower than the amounts that would have been reported using the first-in, first-out ("FIFO") method."

Here, the reader is informed that the company's reported inventory balance would be nearly $900 million higher if FIFO was applied. That one sentence allows for a better comparison with a company like **CVS Caremark** that uses FIFO. The dampening impact of LIFO on reported assets can be removed by the reader as shown in Figure 9.13. Restatement of financial statements in this manner is a common technique relied on by investment analysts around the world to make available information more usable.

FIGURE 9.13 Adjusted Rite Aid's Inventory Balances from LIFO to FIFO

Inventory	February 26, 2011	February 27, 2010
Reported using LIFO	$3,158,145,000	$3,238,644,000
Adjustment to FIFO	875,012,000	831,113,000
Inventory if reported using FIFO	$4,033,157,000	$4,069,757,000

Adjusting **Rite Aid's** inventory balance from LIFO to FIFO is not difficult because the relevant information is available. However, restating the company's income statement to numbers in line with FIFO is a bit more challenging. **Rite Aid** reported an overall net loss for the year ended February 26, 2011, of $555,424,000. How would this number have been different with the application of FIFO?

As seen in the periodic inventory formula, beginning inventory is added to purchases in determining cost of goods sold while ending inventory is subtracted. With the LIFO figures reported by **Rite Aid**, $3,238,644,000 (beginning inventory) was added in arriving at this expense and then $3,158,145,000 (ending inventory) was subtracted. Together, the net effect is an addition of $80,499,000 in computing cost of goods sold for the year ended February 26, 2011. The resulting expense was $80,499,000 higher than the amount of inventory purchased.

If FIFO had been used by **Rite Aid**, $4,069,757,000 (beginning inventory) would have been added with $4,033,157,000 (ending inventory) subtracted. These two balances produce a net effect on cost of goods sold of adding $36,600,000.

LIFO: cost of goods sold = purchases + $80.499 million

FIFO: cost of goods sold = purchases + $36.600 million

Under LIFO, cost of goods sold is the purchases for the period plus $80,499,000. Using FIFO, cost of goods sold is the purchases plus only $36,600,000. The purchase figure is the same in both equations. Thus, cost of goods sold will be $43,899,000 lower according to FIFO ($80,499,000 less $36,600,000) so that net income is $43,899,000 higher. If FIFO had been used, **Rite Aid's** net loss for the period would have been $511,525,000 instead of $555,424,000. Knowledgeable decision makers can easily make this adjustment to help in evaluating a company. They can determine the amount of net income to be reported if FIFO had been selected and can use that figure for comparison purposes.

TEST YOURSELF

Question:

Two companies in the same industry each report sales of $1 million. Company F reports a gross profit of $400,000 while Company L reports a gross profit of only $300,000. A potential investor is looking at both companies and believes Company F is better because of the higher gross profit. However, according to the footnotes, Company F applied FIFO and Company L applied LIFO so that the two gross profit figures are not directly comparable. Company L reported inventory of $200,000 on January 1 and $208,000 at December 31. However, if FIFO had been used, those figures would have $450,000 (January 1) and $553,000 (December 31). Which of the following statements is true?

a. Under FIFO, Company L would still have a lower gross profit than Company F by $5,000.
b. Under FIFO, Company L would have a higher gross profit than Company F by $5,000.
c. Under FIFO, Company L would still have a lower gross profit than Company F by $3,000.
d. Under FIFO, Company L would have a higher gross profit than Company F by $3,000.

Answer:

The correct answer is choice a: Under FIFO, Company L would still have a lower gross profit than Company F by $5,000.

Explanation:

In computing cost of goods sold under LIFO, $200,000 (beginning inventory) is added and $208,000 (ending inventory) is subtracted for a net decrease of $8,000. Had FIFO been used, $450,000 (beginning inventory) is added and $553,000 (ending inventory) is subtracted for a net decrease of $103,000. In using FIFO, computation of this expense has a $95,000 ($103,000 less $8,000) larger decrease. Thus, cost of goods sold for Company L is smaller by $95,000. If that change is applied, gross profit reported by Company L goes up from $300,000 to $395,000. That adjusted figure is still $5,000 lower than the number reported by Company F.

6.2 Analyzing Vital Signs for Inventory

Question: When examining receivables in a previous chapter, the assertion was made that companies have vital signs that can be studied as an indication of financial well-being. These are ratios or other computed amounts considered to be of particular significance. In that coverage, the age of receivables and the receivable turnover were both calculated and explained. For inventory, do similar vital signs exist that decision makers should consider? **What vital signs should be determined in connection with inventory when analyzing the financial health and future prospects of a company?**

Answer: No definitive list of ratios and relevant amounts can be identified because different people tend to have their own personal preferences. However, several figures are widely computed and discussed in connection with inventory and cost of goods sold when the financial condition of a company and the likelihood of its prosperity are being evaluated.

Gross profit percentage. The first of these vital signs is the **gross profit percentage**, which is found by dividing the **gross profit** for the period by **net sales**.

$$\text{sales} - \text{sales returns and discounts} = \text{net sales}$$

$$\text{net sales} - \text{cost of goods sold} = \text{gross profit}$$

$$\text{gross profit}/\text{net sales} = \text{gross profit percentage}$$

As has been mentioned, gross profit is also commonly referred to as gross margin or markup. In simplest terms, it is the difference between the amount paid to buy (or manufacture) inventory and the amount received from an eventual sale. The gross profit percentage is often used to compare one company to another or one time period to the next. If one book store manages to earn a gross profit percentage of 35 percent and another only 25 percent, questions should be raised about this difference and which percentage is better? One company is making more profit on each sale but, possibly because of higher sales prices, it might be making significantly fewer sales.

For the year ended January 29, 2011, **Macy's Inc.** reported a gross profit percentage of 40.7 percent and reported net income for the year of $847 million on sales of approximately $25 billion. At the same time, **Walmart** earned a gross profit percentage of only 24.7 percent but managed to generate net income of nearly $17 billion on sales of just under $419 billion. With these companies, a clear difference in pricing strategy can be seen.

gross profit percentage

Formula measuring profitability calculated by dividing gross profit (sales less cost of goods sold) by sales.

gross profit

Difference between sales and cost of goods sold; also called gross margin or markup.

net sales

Sales less sales returns and discounts.

The gross profit percentage is also watched closely from one year to the next. For example, if this figure falls from 37 percent to 34 percent, analysts will be quite interested in the reason. A mere 1 percent drop in the gross profit percentage for **Walmart** in the previous year would have reduced gross profit by over $4 billion ($419 billion × 1 percent).

Such changes have a cause and any individual studying the company needs to consider the possibilities.

- Are costs rising more quickly than the sales price of the merchandise?
- Has a change occurred in the types of inventory being sold?
- Was the reduction in the gross profit offset by an increase in sales?

Amazon.com Inc., for example, reports that its gross profit was 22.6 percent in 2009 and 22.3 percent in 2010. That is certainly one piece of information to be included in a detailed investigation of this company.

Number of days inventory is held. A second vital sign is the **number of days inventory is held** on average. Companies want to turn their merchandise into cash as quickly as possible. Holding inventory for a length of time can lead to several unfortunate repercussions. The longer it sits in stock the more likely the goods are to get damaged, stolen, or go out of fashion. Such losses can be avoided through quick sales. Furthermore, as long as merchandise is sitting on the shelves, it is not earning any profit. Money is tied up with no return until a sale takes place.

Consequently, decision makers (both internal and external to the company) watch this figure closely. A change (especially any lengthening of the time required to sell merchandise) is often a warning of problems.

The number of days inventory is held is found in two steps. First, the cost of inventory that is sold each day on the average is determined.[6]

cost of goods sold/365 days = cost of inventory sold per day

Second, this daily cost figure is divided into the average amount of inventory held during the period. The average amount of inventory can be based on beginning and ending totals, monthly balances, or other available figures.

average inventory/cost of inventory sold per day = number of days inventory is held

If a company sells inventory costing $40,000 each day and holds an average inventory during the period of $520,000, the average item takes thirteen days ($520,000/$40,000) to be sold. Again, the significance of that figure depends on the type of inventory, a comparison to results reported by similar companies, and any change seen in recent periods of time.

Inventory turnover. A third vital sign that is often analyzed is the **inventory turnover**, which is simply another way to measure the speed by which a company sells inventory.

cost of goods sold/average inventory = inventory turnover

The resulting turnover figure indicates the number of times during the period that an amount equal to the average inventory was sold. The larger the turnover number, the faster inventory is selling. For example, **Best Buy Co. Inc.** recognized cost of goods sold for the year ending February 26, 2011, of $37,611 million. The company also reported beginning inventory for that period of $5,486 million and ending inventory of $5,897 million. Hence, the inventory turnover for this retail electronics giant was 6.61 times during that year.

($5,486 + $5,897)/2 = average inventory of $5,691.5 million

$37,611/$5,691.5 = inventory turnover of 6.61 times

number of days inventory is held

Measures the average number of days that a company takes to sell its inventory items; computed by dividing average inventory for the period by the cost of inventory sold per day.

inventory turnover

Ratio used to measure the speed at which a company sells inventory; computed by dividing cost of goods sold by average inventory for the period.

TEST YOURSELF

Question:

The Hayweather Company starts the year with inventory costing $130,000 and ends the year with inventory costing $150,000. During the period, purchases amounted to $695,250. What was the average number of days required to sell an item of the company's inventory?

a. 68.9 days

b. 72.4 days

c. 75.7 days

d. 80.8 days

Answer:

The correct answer is choice c: 75.7 days.

Explanation:

Cost of goods sold for Hayweather was $675,250 ($130,000 beginning inventory plus $695,250 in purchases less $150,000 ending inventory). That means the company sells inventory costing $1,850 ($675,250/365 days) on the average each day. Average inventory for the period is $140,000 ([$130,000 + $150,000]/2). The average age of the inventory is 75.7 days ($140,000/$1,850).

TEST YOURSELF

Question:

The Ostrich Company starts the year with inventory costing $150,000 and ends the year with inventory costing $130,000. During the period, purchases amounted to $1,030,000. What was the inventory turnover for this period?

a. 6.8 times

b. 7.1 times

c. 7.5 times

d. 7.9 times

Answer:

The correct answer is choice c: 7.5 times.

Explanation:

Inventory turnover is cost of goods sold divided by the average inventory (which is $140,000 here). Cost of goods sold for Ostrich was $1,050,000 ($150,000 beginning inventory plus $1,030,000 in purchases less $130,000 ending inventory). Therefore, inventory turnover for the period is 7.5 times ($1,050,000/$140,000).

KEY TAKEAWAY

Companies that apply LIFO (probably for income tax reasons) often hope decision makers will convert their reported numbers to FIFO for comparison purposes. Disclosure of FIFO figures can be included in the notes to the financial statements to make this conversion possible. In addition, analysts frequently determine several amounts and ratios to help illuminate trends and events happening inside a company. The gross profit percentage reflects the average markup on each sale. It demonstrates pricing policies and fluctuations often indicate policy changes or shifts in the market. The average number of days in inventory and the inventory turnover both help decision makers learn the length of time a company takes to sell its merchandise. Traditionally, a slowing down of sales is bad because inventory is more likely to become damaged, lost, or stolen. Plus, inventory generates no profit until sold.

Talking with a Real Investing Pro (Continued)

Following is a continuation of our interview with Kevin G. Burns.

Question: Companies that sell inventory instead of services must select a cost flow assumption for reporting purposes. Many companies use FIFO but a number of other companies use LIFO. What are your thoughts when you are analyzing two similar companies and discover that one has applied FIFO while the other LIFO?

Kevin Burns: Truthfully, it is easy to get distracted by issues such as FIFO and LIFO that probably make no difference in the long run. I rarely like to trade stocks quickly. For example, assume a company sells a commodity of some type (jewelry, for example). The commodity fluctuates dramatically in price so that when the price is falling you have paid more for the item than the market will now pay you for the finished good. When prices are rising, you reap the benefit by selling at an even greater price than you expected. So if you have two companies dealing with the same issues and one uses LIFO and the other FIFO, the reported results could be dramatically different. However, the underlying facts do not change. Over an extended period of time, the two companies probably end up in the same position regardless of whether they apply LIFO or FIFO. I am much more interested in how they are investing their cash inflows and the quality of the management. On the other hand, a person who trades stocks quickly could well be interested in reported results that might impact stock prices for a short period of time. For example, the trader may well wish to see a company use FIFO as reported profits will be higher for the short term if there is inflation and may believe that he can capitalize on that short-term phenomenon.

 Video Clip

Professor Joe Hoyle talks about the five most important points in Chapter 9.

DURING INFLATION, LIFO REPORTS LOWER NET INCOME AND ENDING INVENTORY

View the video online at: http://bit.ly/hoyle9-2

7. END-OF-CHAPTER EXERCISES

QUESTIONS

1. In the financial accounting for inventory, what is a cost flow assumption?

2. In calculating cost of goods sold for a company, under what condition is a cost flow assumption not needed?

3. A hardware store buys a refrigerator for $700. Later, the same store buys another refrigerator for $730 and then a final item for $790. Eventually, one of these refrigerators is sold for $1,200. If specific identification is used, how is cost of goods sold determined?

4. A hardware store buys a refrigerator for $700. Later, the same store buys another refrigerator for $730 and then a final item for $790. Eventually, one of these refrigerators is sold for $1,200. If FIFO is used, how is cost of goods sold determined?

5. A hardware store buys a refrigerator for $700. Later, the same store buys another refrigerator for $730 and then a final item for $790. Eventually, one of these refrigerators is sold for $1,200. If LIFO is used, how is cost of goods sold determined?

6. A hardware store buys a refrigerator for $700. Later, the same store buys another refrigerator for $730 and then a final item for $790. Eventually, one of these refrigerators is sold for $1,200. If averaging is used, how is cost of goods sold determined?

7. What characteristics are attributed to FIFO and to LIFO in a period of inflation?

8. Tax laws are designed to raise revenues so that a government can afford to operate. What are the other major uses made of income tax laws?

9. The Hawkins Company maintains one set of financial records for financial reporting purposes. Separate records are also kept for tax compliance purposes. Why is that necessary?

10. What is the LIFO conformity rule? What is the practical impact of the LIFO conformity rule?

11. IFRS does not permit the use of LIFO. What are the theoretical problems associated with the application of LIFO?

12. A grocery store has been in operation for several decades. One rack contains 100 loaves of bread. Each evening a local bakery restocks this rack so that the store always starts the next day with 100 loaves of bread. If the company uses LIFO, what is reported for this inventory?

13. Notes to the financial statements of the KaiKayle Corporation indicate that a LIFO liquidation occurred last year. What does this mean? What is the financial impact of that event?

14. The Petrakellon Company reports FIFO inventory of $900,000 but also reports a $300,000 negative figure labeled as a "LIFO reserve." What information do these balances convey to a decision maker?

15. In a periodic inventory system, when is the cost flow assumption applied? In a perpetual inventory system, when is the cost flow assumption applied?

16. A company maintains a perpetual FIFO inventory system and determines its cost of goods as $874,400. Why would cost of goods sold be the same if the company had used a periodic FIFO inventory system?

17. A company buys two units of inventory for $80 each. It sells one for $200. The company then buys three more units for $90 each. What is cost of goods sold if a periodic LIFO system is in use? What is cost of goods sold if a perpetual LIFO system is in use?

18. A company is using averaging to determine cost of goods sold. In a periodic (weighted) averaging system, when is the average cost determined? In a perpetual (moving) averaging system, when is the average cost determined?

19. The Pitt Corporation reports cost of goods sold as $300,000 using LIFO. Beginning inventory was $44,000 and ending inventory was $48,000. However, if FIFO had been used, beginning inventory would have been $76,000 and ending inventory would have been $114,000. What would cost of goods sold have been for the Pitt Corporation if FIFO had been used?

20. How is the gross profit percentage calculated and what does it tell a user about a company?

21. How is the number of days in inventory calculated and why would a decision maker want to know this number? What is the problem if the number begins to increase?

22. The Boston Company starts the current year with inventory of $300,000. During the year, purchases of $800,000 are made. A physical count at the end of the year finds that $400,000 is still on hand. What is the inventory turnover for this period?

23. The Ames Company has exactly $60 in cash. The company buys three pieces of inventory which are all exactly the same. Because it is a highly inflationary market, the first one cost $16, the second cost $19, and the third cost $25. Shortly thereafter, one of these three is sold for $40. Answer each of the following questions.

    a. If FIFO is applied, how many units are now on hand?

    b. If LIFO is applied, how many units are now on hand?

    c. If FIFO is applied, how much cash is the company holding?

    d. If LIFO is applied how much cash is the company holding?

e. If FIFO is applied, what appears on the income statement and the balance sheet?

f. If LIFO is applied, what appears on the income statement and the balance sheet?

TRUE OR FALSE

1. ____ Using the LIFO cost flow assumption will always result in a lower net income than using the FIFO cost flow assumption.

2. ____ LIFO tends to provide a better matching of expenses with revenues than does FIFO.

3. ____ The LIFO conformity rule states that if a company uses LIFO on its financial statements it must also use LIFO on its federal income tax return.

4. ____ It is impossible for decision makers to compare a company that uses LIFO with one that uses FIFO.

5. ____ A jewelry store or boat dealership would normally be able to use the specific identification method.

6. ____ The underlying rationale for FIFO is that the earliest inventory purchased would normally be sold first by a company.

7. ____ A company starts Year Two with 3,000 pieces of inventory costing $9 each. In Year Two, 1,000 units are sold and then 2,000 more units are bought for $12 each. Later, another 1,000 units are sold and 2,000 more units are bought for $14 each. On the last day of the year, one final unit is purchased for $16. If a perpetual LIFO system is used, this December 31 transaction has no impact on reported net income.

8. ____ A company starts Year Two with 3,000 pieces of inventory costing $9 each. In Year Two, 1,000 units are sold and then 2,000 more units are bought for $12 each. Later, another 1,000 units are sold and 2,000 more units are bought for $14 each. If a FIFO system is in use, the 5,000 units on hand at the end of the year have a reported cost of $58,000.

9. ____ A company starts Year Two with 3,000 pieces of inventory costing $9 each. In Year Two, 1,000 units are sold and then 2,000 more units are bought for $12 each. Later, another 1,000 units are sold and 2,000 more units are bought for $14 each. On the last day of the year, one final unit is bought for $16. If a periodic LIFO system is used, this December 31 transaction reduces reported gross profit by $2.

10. ____ A decision maker is analyzing a set of financial statements and finds a note about a LIFO liquidation that occurred during a long period of inflation. From this information, the decision maker knows that the company has manipulated its inventory balances to reduce the amount of income taxes to be paid in the current year.

11. ____ A company applies a periodic FIFO system and buys and sells inventory all during the year. Early in the year, the company bought some inventory and paid an additional $21,000 in connection with the purchase. The cost was recorded in the inventory account but should have been expensed. Despite this error, reported net income for that year does not require adjustment.

12. ____ The gross profit percentage can help decision makers determine how long it takes a company to sell inventory after the purchase date.

13. ____ A company starts Year Two with 3,000 pieces of inventory costing $9 each. In Year Two, 1,000 units are sold and then 2,000 more units are bought for $12 each. Later, another 3,000 units are sold and 2,000 more units are bought for $14 each. If a periodic FIFO system is used, the number of days that inventory is held on the average is 285.6.

14. ____ A company starts Year Two with 4,000 pieces of inventory costing $8 each. In Year Two, 1,000 units are sold and then 3,000 more units are bought for $10 each. Later, another 5,000 units are sold and 2,000 more units are bought for $14 each. If a periodic LIFO system is used, the number of days that inventory is held on the average is 136.8.

15. ____ A company starts Year Two with 10,000 pieces of inventory costing $10 each. During the year, the company buys 40,000 additional pieces of inventory for $15 each. At the end of the year, a physical inventory is taken and 11,000 units are still on hand. If periodic LIFO is used, the inventory turnover for Year Two is 6.44 times.

16. ____ A company starts Year Two with 10,000 pieces of inventory costing $10 each. During the year, the company buys 40,000 additional pieces of inventory for $15 each. At the end of the year, a physical inventory is taken and 11,000 units are still on hand. If periodic FIFO is used, the inventory turnover for Year Two is 4.04 times.

MULTIPLE CHOICE

1. Which of the following provides the best matching of expenses with related revenues?

   a. Specific Identification

   b. FIFO

   c. LIFO

   d. Averaging

2. Milby Corporation purchased three hats to sell during the year. The first, purchased in February, cost $5. The second, purchased in April, cost $6. The third, purchased in July, cost $8. If Milby sells two hats during the year and uses the FIFO method, what is cost of goods sold for the year?

   a. $11

   b. $13

   c. $14

   d. $19

3. Which of the following is not a typical reason that a company would choose to use LIFO for financial reporting when prices are rising?

   a. The company wishes to use LIFO for tax purposes.

   b. The company wants net income to be as high as possible to impress investors.

   c. The company would like to match the most current costs with current revenues.

   d. The company operates in an industry with a high rate of inflation.

4. Traylor Corporation began the year with three items in beginning inventory, each costing $4. During the year Traylor purchased five more items at a cost of $5 each and then two more items at a cost of $6.50 each. Traylor sold eight items for $9 each. If Traylor uses a periodic LIFO system, what would be Traylor's gross profit for this year?

   a. $30

   b. $35

   c. $42

   d. $72

5. The Greene Company uses a periodic LIFO system for its inventory and starts off the current year with 10 units costing $8 each. Seven units are sold for $16 each, followed by the purchase of 10 additional units at $10 each. Then, 7 more units are sold for $20 each. Finally, 10 units are bought for $13 each. On December 31 of that year, a customer offers to buy one of the units still in inventory but is only willing to pay $12. If Greene takes that offer, what is the impact of that sale on reported net income?

   a. Net income will not change.

   b. Net income will go down by $1.

   c. Net income will go up by $2.

   d. Net income will go up by $4.

6. The Bleu Company uses a perpetual LIFO system for its inventory and starts off the current year with 10 units costing $8 each. Seven units are sold for $16 each, followed by the purchase of 10 additional units at $10 each. Then, 7 more units are sold for $20 each. Finally, 10 units are bought for $13 each. On December 31 of that year, a customer offers to buy one of the units still in inventory but is only willing to pay $12. If Bleu takes that offer, what is the impact of that sale on reported net income?

   a. Net income will not change.

   b. Net income will go down by $1.

   c. Net income will go up by $2.

   d. Net income will go up by $4.

7. The Whyte Company uses a FIFO system for its inventory and starts off the current year with 10 units costing $8 each. Seven units are sold for $16 each, followed by the purchase of 10 additional units at $10 each. Then, 7 more units are sold for $20 each. Finally, 10 units are bought for $13 each. On December 31 of that year, a customer offers to buy one of the units still in inventory but is only willing to pay $12. If Whyte takes that offer, what is the impact of that sale on reported net income?

   a. Net income will not change.

   b. Net income will go down by $1.

   c. Net income will go up by $2.

   d. Net income will go up by $4.

8. The Osborne Company starts the current year with 30 units of inventory costing $20 each. A few weeks later, 20 of these units are sold for $40 each. Then, 20 units are bought to restock inventory at $24.50 each. Later, 20 more units are sold for $50 each and the company buys 20 new units but again at $24.50 each. Late in the year, 20 final units are sold for $60 each. What is the reported cost of the ending inventory if a moving average (perpetual) system is used?

   a. $220
   b. $226
   c. $230
   d. $240

9. A decision maker is studying a company that has applied LIFO for over 20 years during a period of inflation. The decision maker is looking at the most recent financial statements and notices a note that indicates that a LIFO liquidation occurred. What information is most likely being conveyed by this note?

   a. Inventory on the balance sheet is worth more than is reported.
   b. Inventory on the balance sheet is worth less than is reported.
   c. The company may be reporting an artificially high net income.
   d. The company has attempted to reduce its income tax payment by a significant amount this year.

10. Buffalo Inc. buys inventory items for $300 each and sells them for $400 each. During the year, the company bought and sold hundreds of these items. The company uses a perpetual system. One unit was sold near the end of the year. The recording was a debit to cash for $400, a credit to inventory for $300, and a credit to gain on sale of inventory for $100. No other entry or correction was made. Which of the following statements is true about Buffalo's reported information for the period?

   a. Gross profit was correct, net income was overstated, and inventory was understated.
   b. Gross profit was understated, net income was understated, and inventory was correct.
   c. Gross profit was understated, net income was correct, and inventory was correct.
   d. Gross profit was correct, net income was understated, and inventory was overstated.

   The following information pertains to multiple-choice questions 11, 12, 13, and 14: A company produces financial statements each year. It is started in Year One and has the following transactions:

   ### Year One
   - Bought 10 units of inventory for $12 each
   - Sold 8 units of inventory
   - Bought 10 units of inventory for $13 each

   ### Year Two
   - Sold 8 units of inventory
   - Bought 10 units of inventory for $15 each
   - Sold 8 units of inventory
   - Bought 10 units of inventory for $16 each

11. Based on the previous information, the company holds 16 units at the end of Year Two. What is reported for this inventory if a FIFO system is used?

   a. $206
   b. $230
   c. $240
   d. $250

12. Based on the previous information, the company holds 16 units at the end of Year Two. What is reported for this inventory if a periodic LIFO system is used?

   a. $206
   b. $230
   c. $240
   d. $250

13. Based on the previous information, the company holds 16 units at the end of Year Two. What is reported for this inventory if a perpetual LIFO system is used?

   a. $206
   b. $230

    c. $240

    d. $250

14. Based on the previous information, the company holds 16 units at the end of Year Two. What is reported for this inventory if a weighted average (periodic) system is used?

    a. $206

    b. $230

    c. $240

    d. $250

15. A company buys and sells inventory and ends each year with approximately 50 units kept in stock at all time. It pays $10 per unit in Year One, $8 per unit in Year Two, and $7 per unit in Year Three. Which of the following statements is true about the Year Three financial statements if LIFO is used rather than FIFO?

    a. Cost of goods sold will be lower

    b. Net income will be lower

    c. Income tax expense will be lower

    d. Ending inventory will be lower

16. During the year, Hostel Company had net sales of $4,300,000 and cost of goods sold of $2,800,000. Beginning inventory was $230,000 and ending inventory was $390,000. Which of the following would be Hostel's inventory turnover for the year?

    a. 4.84 times

    b. 7.18 times

    c. 9.03 times

    d. 13.87 times

17. During the year, the Brighton Corporation had net sales of $4,800,000 and inventory purchases of $3,600,000. Beginning inventory for the year was $280,000 and ending inventory was $320,000. Which of the following would be Brighton's inventory turnover for the year?

    a. 10.67 times

    b. 11.87 times

    c. 13.33 times

    d. 14.67 times

18. Ace Company starts the year with 30,000 units costing $8 each. During the year, Ace bought 100,000 more units at $12 each. A count of the ending inventory finds 40,000 units on hand. If the company uses periodic FIFO, what is the inventory turnover for the year?

    a. 2.67 times

    b. 3.00 times

    c. 3.20 times

    d. 3.67 times

19. During the year, the Trenton Company had net sales of $3,200,000 and cost of goods sold of $2,920,000. Beginning inventory was $250,000 and ending inventory was $390,000. What was the average number of days during the year that Trenton held its inventory items?

    a. 40 days

    b. 45 days

    c. 52 days

    d. 54 days

20. During the year, the Wyglio Corporation had net sales of $5,100,000 and inventory purchases of $4,340,000. Beginning inventory for the year was $320,000 and ending inventory was $280,000. What was the average number of days during the year that Wyglio held its inventory items?

    a. 22 days

    b. 24 days

    c. 25 days

    d. 28 days

VIDEO PROBLEMS

Professor Joe Hoyle discusses the answers to these two problems at the links that are indicated. After formulating your answers, watch each video to see how Professor Hoyle answers these questions.

1. Your roommate is an English major. The roommate's parents own a chain of ice cream shops throughout Florida. One day, while walking over to the science building for a general education class, your roommate poses this question: "Dairy prices have been going up over the last couple of years which has caused a steady rise in the price of the ice cream that my parents buy. I was talking with them recently and they were telling me that they use an accounting system called last-in, first-out in recording their inventory. This makes no sense to me. Everyone knows that all stores always sell their oldest ice cream first so it won't begin to melt and start losing flavor. I don't understand how they could possibly be using a last-in, first-out system. In this case, the accounting sounds like a work of fiction. What is going on?" How would you respond?

View the video online at: http://bit.ly/hoyle9-3

2. Your uncle and two friends started a small office supply store several years ago. The company has expanded and now has several large locations. Your uncle knows that you are taking a financial accounting class and asks you the following question: "When we first got started, our accountant told us to use LIFO for our inventory. We were paying her a lot of money so we followed that advice. One of our biggest customers is owned by a company located in Italy. Recently, the manager for that company was telling me that their accounting is based on IFRS rather than U.S. GAAP and that IFRS apparently believes that LIFO is theoretically flawed. Why are we using a flawed system? I don't even what impact LIFO has on our financial statements. I know that we started out this year with 100,000 units that cost $5 each and then we bought another 400,000 units for $8.00. At the end of the year, because of our sales during the period, we only had 100,000 units left. What difference did LIFO make?" How would you respond?

View the video online at: http://bit.ly/hoyle9-4

PROBLEMS

1. SuperDuper Company sells top of the line skateboards. SuperDuper is concerned about maintaining high earnings and has chosen to use the periodic FIFO method of inventory costing. At the beginning of the year, SuperDuper had 5,000 skateboards in inventory, each costing $20. In April, SuperDuper purchased 2,000 skateboards at a cost of $22 and in August, purchased 4,000 more at a cost of $23. During the year, SuperDuper sold 9,000 skateboards for $40 each.

   a. Record each purchase SuperDuper made.

   b. Assuming there is no breakage or theft, how many skateboards are on hand at the end of the year?

   c. Determine SuperDuper's cost of goods sold using FIFO.

2. Assume the same facts as problem 1, except that SuperDuper is more concerned with minimizing taxes and uses periodic LIFO. Determine SuperDuper's cost of goods sold.

3. Assume the same facts as problem 1, except that SuperDuper has decided to use averaging as a compromise between FIFO and LIFO. Determine SuperDuper's cost of goods sold.

4. Ulysses Company uses the LIFO cost flow assumption. This year, the company reported beginning inventory of $20,000,000 and ending inventory of $21,500,000. If FIFO were used to value inventory, beginning inventory would have been $23,000,000 (current cost at that time) and ending inventory would have been $28,700,000 (also current cost). Cost of goods sold using LIFO was $34,900,000. Determine the reported cost of goods sold if Ulysses had used FIFO.

5. A company starts operations on October 1, Year One, holding 400 units of inventory which fills its store. This inventory cost $10 per unit. After that, enough inventory is bought on the last day of each month to bring the quantity on hand back to exactly 400 units. In October, 140 units were sold; in November, 150 units were sold; and in December, 180 units were sold. On October 31, the company bought units for $12 each; on November 30, the company bought units for $13 each; on December 31, the company bought units for $15 each.

   a. What is the company's cost of goods sold if a periodic LIFO system is used?

   b. What is the company's cost of goods sold if a perpetual LIFO system is used?

6. Paula's Parkas sells NorthPlace jackets. At the beginning of the year, Paula's had 20 jackets in stock, each costing $35 and selling for $60. The following table details the purchases and sales made during January:

FIGURE 9.14

Date	Number of Items	Cost per Item
January 2	Purchased 12	$36.00
January 8	Purchased 10	36.50
January 10	Sold 15	
January 17	Sold 14	
January 22	Purchased 8	37.00
January 28	Sold 10	

Assume that Paula's Parkas uses the perpetual FIFO method to maintain its inventory records.

   a. Determine Paula's Parkas cost of goods sold and ending inventory for January.

   b. Determine Parka's gross profit for January.

7. Assume the same facts as in problem 6 except that Paula's Parkas uses the perpetual LIFO method.

   a. Determine Paula's Parkas cost of goods sold and ending inventory for January.

   b. Determine Parka's gross profit for January.

8. Assume the same facts as in problem 6 above except that Paula's Parkas uses the moving average method.

   a. Determine Paula's Parkas cost of goods sold and ending inventory for January.

   b. Determine Parka's gross profit for January.

9. In Year One, the Major Corporation had the following inventory transactions:

   - March 1: Buy 1,000 units at $7 each.
   - May 1: Sell 800 units for $12 each.
   - August 1: Buy 1,000 units at $8 each.
   - October 1: Sell 700 units for $14 each.
   - December 1: Buy 1,000 units for $10 each.

   In Year Two, the company had the following inventory transactions:

   - April 1: Sell 700 units for $17 each.
   - June 1: Buy 1,000 units for $11 each.
   - September 1: Sell 900 units for $20 each.
   - November 1: Buy 1,000 units for $12 each.
   - December 1: Sell 700 units for $22 each.

      a. What amount of gross profit should this company recognize in Year One and also in Year Two if a periodic LIFO system is in use?

      b. What amount of gross profit should this company recognize in Year One and also in Year Two if a perpetual LIFO system is in use?

10. A company starts the year with 20 units of inventory costing $20 each. In January, 10 of these units are sold for $40 each. Then, 10 new units are bought for $22 each. Shortly thereafter, 10 units are sold for $50 each. Then, 10 units are bought for $27 each. Finally, near the end of the year, 10 units are sold for $60 each.

    a. What is reported as the cost of ending inventory if a weighted average (periodic) system is in use?

    b. What is reported as the cost of ending inventory if a moving average (perpetual) system is in use?

11. The Quiqqley Company is started in Year One and buys 400 pieces of inventory for $4 each on June 1. The company sells 300 of these units on September 1 for $20 each. The company buys another 400 units for $7 each on November 1 and finishes Year One with 500 units in stock.

    In Year Two, on February 1, the company sells 300 units for $20 each. On July 1, Year Two, the company buys 200 more units for $9 each. On August 1, Year Two, the company sells 100 units for $25 each. Finally, on December 1, Year Two, the company buys another 100 units for $10 each.

    a. Assume the company uses a perpetual FIFO system. What is the cost of goods sold figure to be reported for Year Two?

    b. Assume the company uses a perpetual LIFO system. What is the cost of goods sold figure to be reported for Year Two?

12. A company applies LIFO and reports net income for Year Four of $328,000. Reported inventory at January 1 was $32,000 and at December 31 was $35,000. A note to the financial statements indicates that the beginning inventory would have been $52,000 and ending inventory would have been $78,000 if FIFO had been used. What would this company have reported as its net income for Year Four if FIFO has been applied as the cost flow assumption?

13. The Montana Company and the Florida Company are identical in every way. They have exactly the same transactions. In Year One, they both started with 10,000 units of inventory costing $6 per unit. During Year One, they both bought 20,000 additional units for $8 per unit and sold 20,000 units. During Year Two, they both bought 30,000 units for $9 per unit and sold 30,000 units. The Montana Company uses a periodic FIFO system and the Florida Company uses a periodic LIFO system. If the Montana Company reports net income in Year Two of $100,000, what will the Florida Company report as its net income?

14. The Furn Store sells home furnishings, including bean bag chairs. Furn currently uses the periodic FIFO method of inventory costing, but is considering implementing a perpetual system. It will cost a good deal of money to start and maintain, so Furn would like to see the difference, if any, between the two and is using its bean bag chair inventory to do so. Here is the first quarter information for bean bag chairs:

FIGURE 9.15

Date	Number of Items	Cost per Item
Beginning Balance:		
January 1	16	$19
January 17	Purchased 5	20
January 24	Sold 7	
February 10	Purchased 8	21
February 19	Sold 15	
March 1	Purchased 11	22
March 20	Sold 16	

Each bean bag chair sells for $40.

    a. Determine Furn's cost of goods sold and ending inventory under periodic FIFO.

    b. Determine Furn's cost of goods sold and ending inventory under perpetual FIFO.

15. Rollrbladz Inc. is trying to decide between a periodic or perpetual LIFO system. Management would like to see the effect of each on cost of goods sold and ending inventory for the year. The following is information concerning purchases and sales of its specialty line of rollerblades:

FIGURE 9.16

Date	Number of Items	Cost per Item	Sales Price
Beginning Balance:			
January 1	150	$34	
January 22	Purchased 120	35	
February 21	Sold 160		$75
April 8	Purchased 180	36	
June 10	Sold 190		80
August 19	Purchased 110	37	
September 28	Sold 50		82
October 14	Sold 60		82

    a. Determine Rollrbladz's cost of goods sold and ending inventory under periodic LIFO.

    b. Determine Rollrbladz's cost of goods sold and ending inventory under perpetual LIFO.

16. Highlander Corporation sells swords for decorative purposes. It would like to know the difference in cost of goods sold and ending inventory if it uses the weighted average method or the moving average method. Use the following information to help determine these amounts for the second quarter.

FIGURE 9.17

Date	Number of Items	Cost per Item
Beginning Balance:		
April 1	1,700	$70
April 13	Purchased 600	72
May 5	Sold 1,000	
May 25	Purchased 800	73
June 10	Sold 1,500	

Swords retail for $120 each.

    a. Determine Highlander's cost of goods sold and ending inventory under weighted average.

    b. Determine Highlander's cost of goods sold and ending inventory under moving average.

17. During the year, the California Corporation had net sales of $11,000,000 and inventory purchases of $7,500,000. Beginning inventory for the year was $1,030,000 but ending inventory was only $500,000 because the company wanted to reduce the amount of money tied up in inventory. What was the average number of days during the year that California held its inventory items before making a sale?

18. Deuce Company starts the year with 80,000 units costing $10 each. During the year, Deuce bought 100,000 more units at $12 each and then another 120,000 at $13 each. A count of the ending inventory finds 70,000 units on hand. If the company uses periodic FIFO, what is the inventory turnover for the year?

19. During the current year, the Decker Company had net sales of $15,700,000 and cost of goods sold of $9,200,000. Beginning inventory was $420,000 and ending inventory was $500,000. What was the inventory turnover for that year?

20. In Chapter 4, Heather Miller started her own business, Sew Cool. The financial statements for December were presented in Chapter 7 and are shown again below. For convenience, assume the business was started on January 1, 20X8 with no assets.

FIGURE 9.18

Sew Cool
Income Statement
As of December 31, 20X8

Revenue	$4,000
Cost of Goods	(2,000)
Gross Profit	2,000
Other Expenses	(1,695)
Earnings before Tax	305
Tax Expense	(107)
Net Income	$198

FIGURE 9.19

Sew Cool Stmt. of Retained Earnings As of December 31, 20X8	
Retained Earnings, December 1, 20X8	$500
Net Income	198
Dividends	(158)
Retained Earnings, December 31, 20X8	$540

FIGURE 9.20

Sew Cool Balance Sheet December 31, 20X8			
Assets		**Liabilities**	
Current		**Current**	
Cash	$940	Accounts Payable	$900
Accounts Receivable	500	Income Tax Payable	120
Less Allowance for		Total Current Liabilities	$1,020
Doubtful Accounts	(20)		
Net Accounts Receivable	480		
Inventory	700		
Total Current Assets	$2,120		
Noncurrent		**Noncurrent**	
Equipment	$1,000	Notes Payable	$1,060
		Owners' Equity	
		Capital Stock	$500
		Retained Earnings	540
		Total Owners' Equity	$1,040
		Total Liabilities & Owners'	
Total Assets	$3,120	Equity	$3,120

Based on the financial statements determine the following:

   a. Gross profit percentage
   b. Number of days inventory is held
   c. Inventory turnover

COMPREHENSIVE PROBLEM

This problem will carry through over several chapters to enable students to build their accounting skills using knowledge gained in previous chapters.

In Chapter 8, financial statements were prepared for Webworks for August 31 and the month then ended. Those financial statements are included here as a starting point for the financial reporting for September.

FIGURE 9.21

Webworks Stmt. of Retained Earnings As of August 31	
Retained Earnings, August 1	$1,175
Net Income	1,615
Retained Earnings, August 31	$2,790

FIGURE 9.22

Webworks Balance Sheet August 31				
Assets		**Liabilities**	
Current		**Current**	
Cash	$6,445	Accounts Payable	$2,690
Accounts Receivable	1,250	Salaries Payable	250
Less Allowance for Doubtful Accounts	(125)	Unearned Revenue	100
Net Accounts Receivable	1,125		
Merchandise Inventory	3,000		
Supplies Inventory	60		
Prepaid Rent	200		
Total Current Assets	$10,830	Total Current Liabilities	$3,040
Noncurrent		**Noncurrent**	
Equipment	$7,000	Notes Payable	$10,000
		Owners' Equity	
		Capital Stock	$2,000
		Retained Earnings	2,790
		Total Owners' Equity	$4,790
Total Assets	$17,830	Total Liabilities & Owners' Equity	$17,830

The following events occur during September:

a. Webworks purchases supplies worth $120 on account.

b. At the beginning of September, Webworks held 19 keyboards costing $100 each and 110 flash drives costing $10 each. Webworks has decided to use periodic FIFO to cost its inventory.

c. Webworks purchases 30 additional keyboards on account for $105 each and 50 flash drives for $11 each.

d. Webworks starts and completes five more Web sites and bills clients for $3,000.

e. Webworks pays Nancy Po (the company employee hired in June) $500 for her work during the first three weeks of September.

f. Webworks sells 40 keyboards for $6,000 and 120 flash drives for $2,400 cash.

g. Webworks collects $2,500 in accounts receivable.

h. Webworks pays off its salaries payable from August.

i. Webworks pays off $5,500 of its accounts payable.

j. Webworks pays off $5,000 of its outstanding note payable.

k. Webworks pays Leon Jackson (owner of the company) salary of $2,000.

l. Webworks pays taxes of $795 in cash.

  Required:

  A. Prepare journal entries for the previous events.

  B. Post the journal entries to T-accounts.

  C. Prepare an unadjusted trial balance for Webworks for September.

  D. Prepare adjusting entries for the following and post them to your T-accounts.

m. Webworks owes Nancy Po $300 for her work during the last week of September.

n. Leon's parents let him know that Webworks owes $275 toward the electricity bill. Webworks will pay them in October.

o. Webworks determines that it has $70 worth of supplies remaining at the end of September.

p. Prepaid rent should be adjusted for September's portion.

q. Webworks is continuing to accrue bad debts so that the allowance for doubtful accounts is 10 percent of accounts receivable.

r. Record cost of goods sold.

  E. Prepare an adjusted trial balance.

  F. Prepare financial statements for September.

RESEARCH ASSIGNMENT

Assume that you take a job as a summer employee for an investment advisory service. One of the partners for that firm is currently looking at the possibility of investing in **Deere & Company**. The partner is interested in the impact of the recession on a company that is so closely tied to the agriculture industry. The partner is especially interested in the speed with which the company is able to sell its inventory and also the impact of recording most inventory using LIFO. The partner asks you to look at the 2010 financial statements for **Deere & Company** by following this path:

- Go to http://www.deere.com.
- At the upper right side of the screen, click on "Our Company" and then on "Investor Relations." (If you're using a browser other than Internet Explorer, you may need to select your country before you can click on "Our Company.")
- On the left side of the next screen, click on "Annual Report."
- In the middle of the next screen, click on "2010 Annual Report" to download.
- Go to page 24 and find the 2008, 2009, and 2010 income statements.
- Go to page 25 and find the balance sheets for the years ended October 31, 2009 and 2010.
- Go to page 41 and read note 15 titled "Inventories."

a. Using the figures found on the 2010 income statement and the two balance sheets, determine the number of days that inventory was held by **Deere & Company** during 2010. Does the number seem particularly high or particularly low?

b. Using the figures found on the 2010 income statement and the information provided in note 15 of the financial statements, determine the change in cost of sales that would have occurred if the company had applied FIFO to all of its reported inventory. What was the monetary amount of the difference between this figure and the amount actually reported?

ENDNOTES

1. Clayton T. Rumble, "So You Still Have Not Adopted LIFO," *Management Accountant*, October 1983, 50.

2. Matthew C. Calderisi, senior editor, Doug Bowman, senior technical manager, and David Cohen, developmental editor, *Accounting Trends & Techniques*, 64th edition (New York: American Institute of Certified Public Accountants, 2010), 169.

3. Many states and some cities also charge a tax on income. Those governments have their own unique set of laws although they often resemble the tax laws applied by the federal government.

4. As will be seen in the next chapter, similar arguments are made in connection with property and equipment—the reported amount and the value can vary greatly. However, those assets are not normally held for resale purpose so that their current worth is of less interest to decision makers.

5. Because ending inventory for one period becomes the beginning inventory for the next, application of a cost flow assumption does change that figure also. However, the impact is only indirect because the number is simply carried forward from the previous period. No current computation of beginning inventory is made based on the cost flow assumption in use.

6. Some analysts prefer to use 360 instead of 365 days to make this computation simpler.

In a Set of Financial Statements, What Information Is Conveyed about Property and Equipment?

Video Clip

In this video, Professor Joe Hoyle introduces the essential points covered in Chapter 10.

View the video online at: http://bit.ly/hoyle10-1

1. THE REPORTING OF PROPERTY AND EQUIPMENT

LEARNING OBJECTIVES

At the end of this section, students should be able to meet the following objectives:

1. Recognize that tangible operating assets with lives of over one year (such as property and equipment) are initially reported at historical cost.
2. Understand the rationale for assigning the cost of these operating assets to expense over time if the item has a finite life.
3. Recognize that these assets are normally reported on the balance sheet at net book value, which is their cost less accumulated depreciation.
4. Explain the reason for not reporting property and equipment at fair value except in certain specified circumstances.

1.1 Initially Reporting Property and Equipment at Historical Cost

Question: The retail giant **Walmart** *owns thousands of huge outlets and supercenters located throughout the United States as well as in many foreign countries. These facilities contain a wide variety of machinery, fixtures, and the like such as cash registers and shelving. On its January 31, 2011, balance sheet,* **Walmart** *reports "property and equipment, net" of over $105 billion, a figure that made up almost 60 percent of the company's total assets. This monetary amount was more than twice as large as any other asset reported by this business. Based on sheer size, the information conveyed about this group of accounts is extremely significant to any decision maker analyzing* **Walmart** *or another similar company.* **In creating financial statements, what is the underlying meaning of the monetary figure reported for property, equipment, and the like?** *What information is conveyed by the $105 billion balance disclosed by* **Walmart***?*

Answer: Four accounts make up the property and equipment reported by **Walmart**:

- Land
- Buildings and improvements
- Fixtures and equipment
- Transportation equipment

historical cost

All the normal and necessary amounts incurred to get an asset into the position and condition to help generate revenues; it is the starting basis for the balance sheet presentation of assets such as inventory, land, and equipment.

These are common titles, but a variety of other names are also used to report similar asset groups such as property, plant, and equipment (PP&E), fixed assets, and plant assets. Regardless of the name that is applied, the starting basis in reporting property, equipment, and any other tangible operating assets with a life of over one year is **historical cost**.

This initial accounting is consistent with the recording process demonstrated previously for inventory. When available, accountants like historical cost because it is objective. Cost reflects the amount sacrificed to obtain land, machinery, buildings, furniture, and so forth. It can usually be determined when an arm's length acquisition takes place: a willing buyer and a willing seller, both acting in their own self-interests, agree on an exchange price.

Thus, the cost incurred to obtain property and equipment provides information to decision makers about management policy and decision making. Cost indicates the amount management chose to sacrifice in order to gain the use of a specific asset. Unless the seller was forced to dispose of the property in a hurry (because of an urgent need for funds, as an example), cost is likely to approximate fair value when purchased. However, after the date of acquisition, the figure reported on the balance sheet will probably never again reflect the actual value of the asset.

depreciation

A mechanically derived pattern allocating the cost of long-lived assets such as buildings and equipment to expense over the expected number of years that they will be used by a company to help generate revenues.

Subsequently, for each of these operating assets that has a finite life (and most pieces of property and equipment other than land do have finite lives), the matching principle necessitates that the historical cost be allocated to expense over the anticipated years of service. This **depreciation** expense is recognized systematically each period as the company utilizes the asset to generate revenue.

For example, if equipment has a life of ten years, all (or most) of its cost is assigned to expense over that period. This accounting resembles the handling of a prepaid expense such as rent. The cost is first recorded as an asset and then moved to expense over time in some logical fashion as the utility is consumed. At any point, the reported net book value for the asset is the original cost less the portion of that amount that has been reclassified to expense. For example, **Walmart** actually reported property and equipment costing $148 billion but then disclosed that $43 billion of that figure had been moved to expense leaving the $105 billion net asset balance. As the future value becomes a past value, the asset account shrinks to reflect the cost reclassified to expense.

1.2   The Reporting of Accumulated Depreciation

Question: The basic accounting for property and equipment resembles that utilized for prepaid expenses such as rent and insurance. **Do any significant differences exist between the method of reporting prepaid expenses and the handling of operating assets like machinery and equipment?**

Answer: One important mechanical distinction does exist when comparing the accounting for prepayments and that used for property and equipment having a finite life. With a prepaid expense (such as rent), the asset is directly reduced over time as the cost is assigned to expense. Prepaid rent balances get smaller each day as the period of usage passes. This reclassification creates the rent expense reported on the income statement.

In accounting for property and equipment, the asset does not physically shrink. A seven-story building does not become a six-story building and then a five-story building. As the utility is consumed, buildings and equipment do not get smaller; they only get older. To reflect that reality, a separate **accumulated depreciation** account[1] is created to represent the total amount of the asset's cost that has been reclassified to expense. Through this approach, information about the original cost continues to be available. For example, if equipment is reported as $30,000 and the related accumulated depreciation currently holds a balance of $10,000, the reader knows that the asset cost $30,000, but $10,000 of that amount has been expensed since the date of acquisition. If the asset has been used for two years to generate revenue, $6,000 might have been moved to expense in the first year and $4,000 in the second. The $20,000 **net book value** appearing on the balance sheet is the cost that has not yet been expensed because the asset still has future value.

As indicated previously, land does not have a finite life and, therefore, remains reported at historical cost with no assignment to expense and no accumulated depreciation balance.

> **accumulated depreciation**
>
> A contra-asset account created to measure the cost of a depreciable asset (such as buildings and equipment) that has been assigned to expense to date.
>
> **net book value**
>
> Original cost of a depreciable asset such as buildings and equipment less the total amount of accumulated depreciation to date; it is also called net book value or carrying value.

TEST YOURSELF

Question:

A company buys equipment for $100,000 with a ten-year life. Three years later, the company produces financial statements and prepares a balance sheet. The asset is not impaired in any way. What figure is reported for this equipment?

  a. The fair value on that date.

  b. The resale value at the end of the third year.

  c. $100,000 less the accumulated depreciation recorded for these three years.

  d. Fair value less accumulated depreciation for the most recent year.

Answer:

The correct answer is choice c: $100,000 less the accumulated depreciation recorded for these three years.

Explanation:

The historical cost ($100,000) serves as the beginning basis for the financial reporting of property and equipment. This monetary figure is then systematically transferred to expense over the life of the asset. The total amount of the expense recognized to date is recorded in an accumulated depreciation account. The book value to be shown on the balance sheet for this equipment is its historical cost less the accumulated depreciation to date.

1.3   Failure of Accounting to Reflect the Fair Value of Property and Equipment

Question: **Walmart** *reports property and equipment with a net book value of $105 billion. However, that figure has virtually nothing to do with the value of these assets. They might actually be worth hundreds of billions. Decision makers analyze financial statements in order to make decisions about an organization at the current moment. Are these decision makers not more interested in the fair value of these assets than in what remains of historical cost?* **Why are property and equipment not reported at fair value?** *Is fair value not a much more useful piece of information than cost minus accumulated depreciation when assessing the financial health and prospects of a business?*

Answer: The debate among accountants, company officials, investors, creditors, and others over whether various assets should be reported based on historical cost or fair value has raged for many years. There is no easy resolution. Good points can be made on each side of the argument. As financial accounting has evolved over the decades, rules for reporting certain assets (such as many types of stock and debt investments where exact market prices can be readily determined) have been changed to abandon historical cost in favor of reflecting fair value. However, no such radical changes in U.S. GAAP have taken place for property and equipment. Reporting has remained relatively unchanged for many decades. Unless the value of one of these assets has been impaired or it is going to be sold in the near future, historical cost less accumulated depreciation remains the basis for balance sheet presentation.

The fair value of property and equipment is a reporting alternative preferred by some decision makers, but only if the amount is objective and reliable. That is where the difficulty begins. Historical cost is both an objective and a reliable measure, determined through a transaction between a willing buyer and a willing seller. In contrast, any gathering of "experts" could assess the value of a large building or an acre of land at widely differing figures with equal certitude. No definitive value can possibly exist until sold. What is the informational benefit of a number that is so subjective? Furthermore, the asset's value might change radically on a daily basis rendering previous assessments useless. For that reason, historical cost, as adjusted for accumulated depreciation, remains the accepted method for reporting property and equipment on an owner's balance sheet.

Use of historical cost is supported by the going concern assumption that has long existed as part of the foundation of financial accounting. In simple terms, a long life is anticipated for virtually all organizations. Officials expect operations to continue for the years required to fulfill the goals that serve as the basis for their decisions. They do not plan to sell property and equipment prematurely but rather to utilize these assets for their entire lives. Consequently, financial statements are constructed assuming that the organization will function until all of its assets are consumed. Unless impaired or a sale is anticipated in the near future, the fair value of property and equipment is not truly of significance to the operations of a business. It might be interesting information but it is not directly relevant if no sale is contemplated.

market capitalization

Figure computed by multiplying a company's current stock price times the number of ownership shares outstanding in the hands of the public; it is used to gauge the fair value of a business as a whole.

However, the estimated fair value of a company's property and equipment is a factor that does influence the current price of ownership shares traded actively on a stock exchange. For example, the price of shares of **The Coca-Cola Company** is certainly impacted by the perceived value of its property and equipment. A widely discussed calculation known as **market capitalization** is one method used to gauge the fair value of a business as a whole. Market capitalization is determined by multiplying the current price of a company's stock times the number of ownership shares outstanding. For example, approximately 2.3 billion shares of **The Coca-Cola Company** were in the hands of investors at December 31, 2010. Because the stock was selling for $65.77 per share on that day, the company's market capitalization was about $151 billion. This figure does not provide a direct valuation for any specific asset but does give a general idea as to whether fair value approximates net book value or is radically different.

Talking with an Independent Auditor about International Financial Reporting Standards (Continued)

Following is a continuation of our interview with Robert A. Vallejo, partner with the accounting firm **PricewaterhouseCoopers**.

Question: In U.S. GAAP, land, buildings, and equipment have traditionally been reported at historical cost less the accumulated depreciation recognized to date. Adjustment to fair value is prohibited unless the asset's value has been impaired. Because of the conservative nature of accounting, increases in value are ignored completely until proven through a disposal. Thus, land might be worth $20 million but only shown on the balance sheet as $400,000 if that amount reflects cost. According to IFRS, can increases in the fair value of these assets be reported?

Rob Vallejo: Under IFRS, a company can elect to account for all or specific types of assets using fair value. In that instance, the designated assets are valued each reporting period, adjusted up or down accordingly. Based on my experience working with companies reporting under IFRS, companies do not elect to account for fixed assets using fair value. This decision is primarily due to the administrative challenges of determining fair value each and every reporting period (quarterly for US listed companies) and the volatility that would be created by such a policy. Financial officers and the financial investors that follow their stocks rarely like to see such swings, especially those swings that cannot be predicted. However, in the right circumstances, using fair value might be a reasonable decision for some companies.

KEY TAKEAWAY

Land, buildings, and equipment are reported on a company's balance sheet at net book value, which is historical cost less any portion of that figure that has been assigned to expense. Over time, the cost balance is not directly reduced. Instead, the expensed amount is maintained in a separate contra asset account known as accumulated depreciation. Thus, the asset's cost remains readily apparent as well as net book value. Land and any other asset that does not have a finite life continue to be reported at cost. Unless the value of specific items has been impaired or an asset is to be sold in the near future, fair value is never used in reporting land, buildings, and equipment. It is not viewed as an objective or reliable amount. In addition, because such assets are usually not expected to be sold, fair value is of limited informational benefit to decision makers.

2.   DETERMINING HISTORICAL COST AND DEPRECIATION EXPENSE

LEARNING OBJECTIVES

At the end of this section, students should be able to meet the following objectives:

1. Make use of the guiding accounting rule to ascertain which costs are capitalized and which are expensed when acquiring property and equipment.
2. List the variables that impact the amount of depreciation to be expensed each period in connection with the property and equipment owned by a company.
3. Recognize that the straight-line method for assigning depreciation predominates in practice but any system that provides a rational approach can be used to create a pattern for this cost allocation.

2.1   Assets Classified as Property and Equipment

Question: Businesses hold numerous types of assets, such as receivables, inventory, cash, investments, and patents. Proper classification is important for the clarity of the reported information. **In preparing a balance sheet, what requirements must be met for an asset to be included as part of a business's property and equipment?**

Answer: To be classified within the property and equipment category, an asset must have tangible physical substance and be expected to help generate revenues for longer than a single year. In addition, it must function within the normal operating activities of the business. However, it cannot be held for immediate resale, like inventory.

A building used as a warehouse and machinery operated in the production of inventory both meet these characteristics. Other examples include computers, furniture, fixtures, and equipment. Conversely, land acquired as a future plant site and a building held for speculative purposes are both classified as investments (or, possibly, "other assets") rather than as property and equipment. Neither of these assets is being used at the current time to help generate operating revenues.

2.2   Determining Historical Cost

Question: The accounting basis for reporting property and equipment is historical cost. What amounts are included in determining the cost of such assets? Assume, for example, that **Walmart** *purchases a parcel of land and then constructs a retail store on the site.* **Walmart** *also buys a new cash register to use at this outlet. Initially, such assets are reported at cost.* **For property and equipment, how is historical cost defined?**

Answer: In the previous chapter, the cost of a company's inventory was identified as the sum of all normal and necessary amounts paid to get the merchandise into condition and position to be sold. Property and equipment are not bought for resale, so this rule must be modified slightly. All expenditures are included within the cost of property and equipment if the amounts are normal and necessary to get the asset into condition and position to assist the company in generating revenues. That is the purpose of assets: to produce profits by helping to create the sale of goods and services.

Land can serve as an example. When purchased, the various normal and necessary expenditures made by the owner to ready the property for its intended use are capitalized to arrive at reported cost. These amounts include payments made to attain ownership as well as any fees required to obtain legal title. If the land is acquired as a building site, money spent for any needed grading and clearing is also included as a cost of the land rather than as a cost of the building or as an expense. These activities readied the land for its ultimate purpose.

Buildings, machinery, furniture, equipment and the like are all reported in a similar fashion. For example, the cost of constructing a retail store includes money spent for materials and labor as well as charges for permits and any fees paid to architects and engineers. These expenditures are all normal and necessary to get the structure into condition and position to help generate revenues.

As another example, the cost of a new cash register might well include shipping charges, installation fees, and training sessions to teach employees to use the asset. These costs all meet the criterion for capitalization. They are normal and necessary payments to permit use of the equipment for its intended purpose. Hence, a new cash register bought at a price of $4,100 might actually be reported as an asset by its owner at $5,300 as follows:

FIGURE 10.1 Capitalized Cost of Equipment

Invoice Price—Charged by Seller	$4,100
Shipping Costs from Manufacturer	300
Installation	400
Employee Training Sessions	500
Cost of Cash Register	$5,300

TEST YOURSELF

Question:

On January 1, Year One, a company buys a plot of land and proceeds to construct a warehouse on that spot. One specific cost of $10,000 was normal and necessary to the acquisition of the land. However, by accident, this charge was capitalized within the building account. Which of the following statements is not correct?

a. The building account will always be overstated by $10,000.

b. The land will be understated by $10,000 as long as the company owns it.

c. For the next few years, net income will be understated.

d. For the next few years, expenses will be overstated.

Answer:

The correct answer is choice a: The building account will always be overstated by $10,000.

Explanation:

A building has a finite life. During its use, the cost is systematically moved to expense. The $10,000 misstatement here overstates the building balance. However, the gradual expensing of that amount through depreciation reduces the overstatement over time. This error inflates the amount of expense reported each year understating net income. The land does not have a finite life. Therefore, its cost is not expensed, and the $10,000 understatement remains intact as long as the land is held.

2.3 Straight-Line Method of Determining Depreciation

Question: If a company pays $600,000 on January 1, Year One to rent a building to serve as a store for five years, a prepaid rent account (an asset) is established for that amount. Because the rented facility is used to generate revenues throughout this period, a portion of the cost is reclassified annually as expense to comply with the matching principle. At the end of Year One, $120,000 (or one-fifth) of the cost is moved from the asset balance into rent expense by means of an adjusting entry. Prepaid rent shown on the balance sheet drops to $480,000, the amount paid for the four remaining years. The same adjustment is required for each of the subsequent years as the time passes.

If, instead, the company buys a building with an expected five-year life[2] for $600,000, the accounting is quite similar. The initial cost is capitalized to reflect the future economic benefit. Once again, at the end of each year, a portion of this cost is assigned to expense to satisfy the matching principle. This *expense is referred to as depreciation. It is the cost of a long-lived asset that is recorded as expense each period. Should the Year One depreciation that is recognized in connection with this building also be $120,000 (one-fifth of the total cost)?* **How is the annual amount of depreciation expense determined for reporting purposes?**

Answer: Depreciation is based on a mathematically derived system that allocates the asset's cost to expense over the expected years of use. It does not mirror the actual loss of value over that period. The specific amount of depreciation expense recorded each year for buildings, machinery, furniture, and the like is determined using four variables:

1. The historical cost of the asset

2. Its expected useful life

3. Any residual (or salvage) value anticipated at the end of the expected useful life

4. An allocation pattern

After total cost is computed, officials estimate the useful life based on company experience with similar assets or on other sources of information such as guidelines provided by the manufacturer.[3] In a similar fashion, officials arrive at the expected residual value—an estimate of the likely worth of the asset at the end of its useful life. Both life expectancy and residual value can be no more than guesses.

To illustrate, assume a building is purchased by a company on January 1, Year One, for cash of $600,000. Based on experience with similar properties, officials believe that this structure will be worth only $30,000 at the end of an expected five-year life. U.S. GAAP does not require any specific computational method for determining the annual allocation of the asset's cost to expense. Over fifty years ago, the Committee on Accounting Procedure (the authoritative body at the time) issued Accounting Research Bulletin 43, which stated that any method could be used to determine annual depreciation if it provided an expense in a "systematic and rational manner." This guidance remains in effect today.

Consequently, a vast majority of reporting companies (including **Walmart**) have chosen to adopt the straight-line method to assign the cost of property and equipment to expense over their useful lives. The estimated residual value is subtracted from cost to arrive at the asset's depreciable base. This figure is then expensed evenly over the expected life. It is systematic and rational. **Straight-line depreciation** allocates an equal expense to each period in which the asset is used to generate revenue.

Straight-line method:

$$(\text{cost} - \text{estimated residual value}) = \text{depreciable base}$$

$$\text{depreciable base/expected useful life} = \text{annual depreciation}$$

$$(\$600{,}000 - \$30{,}000) = \$570{,}000/5 \text{ years} = \text{depreciation expense of } \$114{,}000 \text{ per year}$$

Straight-line depreciation

Method used to calculate the annual amount of depreciation expense by subtracting any estimated residual value from cost and then dividing this depreciable base by the asset's estimated useful life; a majority of companies in the United States use this method for financial reporting purposes.

2.4   Recording Depreciation Expense

Question: An accountant determines depreciation for the current year based on the asset's cost and estimated life and residual value. **After depreciation has been calculated, how is this allocation of the asset's cost to expense recorded within the company's accounting system?**

Answer: An adjusting entry is prepared at the end of each period to move the assigned cost from the asset account on the balance sheet to expense on the income statement. To reiterate, the building account is not directly reduced. A separate negative or contra account (accumulated depreciation) is created to reflect the total amount of the cost that has been expensed to date. Thus, the asset's net book value as well as its original historical cost are both still in evidence.

The entries to record the cost of acquiring this building and the annual depreciation expense over the five-year life are shown in Figure 10.2. The straight-line method is used here to determine each individual allocation to expense. Now that students are familiar with using debits and credits for recording, the number in parenthesis is included (where relevant to the discussion) to indicate the total account balance *after* the entry is posted. As has been indicated, revenues, expenses, and dividends are closed out each year. Thus, the depreciation expense reported on each income statement measures only the expense assigned to that period.

FIGURE 10.2 Building Acquisition and Straight-Line Depreciation

1/1/1	Building	$600,000 ($600,000)	
	Cash		$600,000
12/31/1	Depreciation Expense	114,000 (114,000)	
	Accumulated Depreciation		
	—Building		114,000 (114,000)
12/31/2	Depreciation Expense	114,000 (114,000)	
	Accumulated Depreciation		
	—Building		114,000 (228,000)
12/31/3	Depreciation Expense	114,000 (114,000)	
	Accumulated Depreciation		
	—Building		114,000 (342,000)
12/31/4	Depreciation Expense	114,000 (114,000)	
	Accumulated Depreciation		
	—Building		114,000 (456,000)
12/31/5	Depreciation Expense	114,000 (114,000)	
	Accumulated Depreciation		
	—Building		114,000 (570,000)

Because the straight-line method is applied, depreciation expense is a consistent $114,000 each year. As a result, the net book value reported on the balance sheet drops during the asset's useful life from $600,000 to $30,000. At the end of the first year, it is $486,000 ($600,000 cost minus accumulated depreciation $114,000). At the end of the second year, net book value is reduced to $372,000 ($600,000 cost minus accumulated depreciation of $228,000). This pattern continues over the entire five years until the net book value equals the expected residual value of $30,000.

TEST YOURSELF

Question:

On January 1, Year One, the Ramalda Corporation pays $600,000 for a piece of equipment that will produce widgets to be sold to the public. The company expects the asset to carry out this function for ten years and then be sold for $50,000. The straight-line method of depreciation is used. At the end of Year Two, company officials receive an offer to buy the equipment for $500,000. They reject this offer because they believe the asset is actually worth $525,000. What is the net reported balance for this equipment on the company's balance sheet as of December 31, Year Two?

a. $480,000
b. $490,000
c. $500,000
d. $525,000

Answer:

The correct answer is choice b: $490,000.

Explanation:

Unless the value of property or equipment is impaired or the asset will be sold in the near future, fair value is ignored. Cost is the reporting basis. This equipment has a depreciable base of $550,000 ($600,000 cost less $50,000 residual value). The asset is expected to generate revenues for ten years. Annual depreciation is $55,000 ($550,000/ten years). After two years, net book value is $490,000 ($600,000 cost less $55,000 and $55,000 or accumulated depreciation of $110,000).

KEY TAKEAWAY

Tangible operating assets with lives of over a year are initially reported at historical cost. All expenditures are capitalized if they are normal and necessary to put the property into the position and condition to assist the owner in generating revenue. If the asset has a finite life, this cost is then assigned to expense over the years of expected use by means of a systematic and rational pattern. Many companies apply the straight-line method, which assigns an equal amount of expense to every full year of use. In that approach, the expected residual value is subtracted from cost to get the depreciable base. This figure is allocated evenly over the anticipated years of use by the company.

3. RECORDING DEPRECIATION EXPENSE FOR A PARTIAL YEAR

LEARNING OBJECTIVES

At the end of this section, students should be able to meet the following objectives:

1. Understand the need to record depreciation for each period of use even when property and equipment are disposed of prior to the end of the year.
2. Construct the journal entry to record the disposal of property or equipment and the recognition of a gain or loss.
3. Explain the half-year convention and the reason that it is frequently used by companies for reporting purposes.

3.1 Recording the Disposal of Property or Equipment

Question: Property and equipment are occasionally sold before the end of their estimated lives. A company's operational needs might change or officials could want to gain the benefit of a newer or more efficient model. **What accounting is necessary in the event that a piece of property or equipment is sold prior to the conclusion of its useful life?** *In the example illustrated in Figure 10.2, assume that after the adjusting entry for depreciation is made on December 31, Year Two, the building is sold for $290,000 cash. How is that transaction recorded?*

Answer: Accounting for the disposal of property and equipment is relatively straightforward.

First, to establish account balances that are appropriate as of the date of sale, depreciation is recorded for the period of use during the current year. In this way, the expense is matched with the revenues earned in the current period.

Second, the amount received from the sale is recorded while the net book value of the asset (both its cost and accumulated depreciation) is removed. If the owner receives less for the asset than net book value, a loss is recognized for the difference. If more is received than net book value, the excess is recorded as a gain so that net income increases.

Because the building is sold for $290,000 on December 31, Year Two, when the net book value is $372,000 (cost of $600,000 less accumulated depreciation of $228,000), a loss of $82,000 is reported by the seller ($372,000 net book value less $290,000 proceeds). The journal entry shown in Figure 10.3 is recorded after the depreciation adjustment for the period is made.

FIGURE 10.3 Sale of Building at a Loss

12/31/2	Cash	290,000	
	Accumulated Depreciation—Building	228,000	
	Loss on Sale of Building	82,000	
	Building		600,000

Conversely, if this building is sold on that same date for $440,000 rather than $290,000, the company receives $68,000 more than net book value ($440,000 less $372,000) so that a gain of that amount is recognized. The entry under this second possibility is presented in Figure 10.4.

FIGURE 10.4 Sale of Building at a Gain

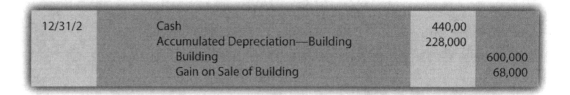

12/31/2	Cash	440,00	
	Accumulated Depreciation—Building	228,000	
	Building		600,000
	Gain on Sale of Building		68,000

Although gains and losses such as these appear on the income statement, they are often shown separately from revenues and expenses. In that way, a decision maker can determine both the income derived from primary operations (revenues less expenses) and the amount that resulted from tangential activities such as the sale of a building or other property (gains less losses).

TEST YOURSELF

Question:

The Lombardi Company buys equipment on January 1, Year One, for $2 million with an expected twenty-year life and a residual value of $100,000. Company officials apply the straight-line method to determine depreciation expense. On December 31, Year Three, this equipment is sold for $1.8 million. What gain is recognized on this sale?

a. $10,000

b. $85,000

c. $100,000

d. $185,000

Answer:

The correct answer is choice b: $85,000.

Explanation:

The depreciable basis for this asset is $1.9 million ($2 million cost less $100,000 estimated residual value). This amount is to be expensed over twenty years at a rate of $95,000 per year ($1.9 million/20 years). After three years, accumulated depreciation is $285,000 ($95,000 × 3) so net book value is $1,715,000 ($2 million cost less $285,000 accumulated depreciation). The sale was for $1.8 million. The company reports a gain of $85,000 ($1.8 million received less $1,715,000 book value).

3.2 Recognizing Depreciation When Asset Is Used for a Partial Year

Question: In the previous reporting, the building was bought on January 1 and later sold on December 31 so that depreciation was always determined and recorded for a full year. However, in reality, virtually all such assets are bought and sold at some point within the year so that a partial period of use is more likely. What amount of depreciation is appropriate if property or equipment is held for less than twelve months during a year?

Answer: The recording of depreciation follows the matching principle. If an asset is owned for less than a full year, it does not help generate revenues for all twelve months. The amount of expense should be reduced accordingly. For example, if the building from the previous reporting is purchased on April 1, Year One, depreciation expense of only $85,500 (9/12 of the full-year amount of $114,000) is recognized on December 31, Year One. Similarly, if the asset is sold on a day other than December 31, less than a full year's depreciation is assigned to expense in the year of sale. Revenue is not generated for the entire period; therefore, depreciation must also be recognized proportionally.

To illustrate, assume the building was purchased on April 1 of Year One for $600,000 and then sold for $350,000 on September 1 of Year Three. As just calculated, depreciation for Year One is $85,500 or 9/12 of the annual amount. In Year Three, depreciation for the final eight months that the property was used is $76,000 (8/12 of $114,000). The journal entries shown in Figure 10.5 reduce the asset's net book value to $324,500 (cost of $600,000 less accumulated depreciation of $275,500). Because cash of $350,000 is collected from the sale, a gain of $25,500 is recognized ($350,000 less $324,500).

FIGURE 10.5 Acquisition, Depreciation, and Sale of Building

4/1/1	Building	$600,000 ($600,000)	
	Cash		$600,000
12/31/1	Depreciation Expense	85,500 ($85,500)	
	Accumulated Depreciation —Building		85,500 (85,500)
12/31/2	Depreciation Expense	114,000 ($114,000)	
	Accumulated Depreciation —Building		114,000 (199,500)
9/1/3	Depreciation Expense	76,000 ($76,000)	
	Accumulated Depreciation —Building		76,000 (275,500)
9/1/3	Cash	350,000	
	Accumulated Depreciation —Building	275,500	
	Building		600,000
	Gain on Sale of Building		25,500

3.3   The Half-Year Convention

Question: Monitoring the specific days on which depreciable assets are bought and sold seems like a tedious process. For example, what happens when equipment is bought on August 8 or when a building is sold on April 24? **In practice, how do companies assign depreciation to expense when a piece of property or equipment is held for less than a full year?**

Answer: Most companies hold a great many depreciable assets, often thousands. Depreciation is nothing more than a mechanical cost allocation process. It is not an attempt to mirror current value. Cost is mathematically assigned to expense in a systematic and rational manner. Consequently, company officials often prefer not to invest the time and effort needed to keep track of the specific number of days or weeks of an asset's use during the years of purchase and sale.

As a result, depreciation can be calculated to the nearest month when one of these transactions is made. A full month of expense is recorded if an asset is held for fifteen days or more whereas no depreciation is recognized in a month where usage is less than fifteen days. No genuine informational value comes from calculating the depreciation of assets down to days, hours, and minutes. An automobile acquired on March 19, for example, is depreciated as if bought on April 1. A computer sold on November 11 is assumed to have been used until October 31.

As another accepted alternative, many companies apply the **half-year convention** (or some variation). When property or equipment is owned for any period less than a full year, a half year of depreciation is automatically assumed. The costly maintenance of exact records is not necessary. Long-lived assets are typically bought and sold at various times throughout each period so that, on the average, one-half year is a reasonable assumption. As long as such approaches are applied consistently, reported figures are viewed as fairly presented. Property and equipment bought on February 3 or sold on November 27 is depreciated for exactly one-half year in both situations.

half-year convention

Method of calculating depreciation for assets that are held for any period of time less than a year; automatically records one-half year of depreciation; it makes the maintenance of exact records as to the period of use unnecessary.

TEST YOURSELF

Question:

On August 12, Year One, the O'Connell Company buys a warehouse for $1.2 million with a ten-year expected life and an estimated residual value of $200,000. This building is eventually sold on March 18, Year Three, for $1,080,000 in cash. The straight-line method of depreciation is used for allocation purposes along with the half-year convention. What gain should O'Connell recognize on the sale of the warehouse?

a. $80,000

b. $84,000

c. $108,000

d. $120,000

Answer:

The correct answer is choice a: $80,000.

Explanation:

Annual depreciation is $100,000: the depreciable basis of $1 million ($1.2 million less $200,000) allocated over ten years. Because the half-year convention is used, $50,000 is recorded in Years One and Three. The asset was used less than twelve months in each of these periods. When sold, accumulated depreciation is $200,000 ($50,000 + $100,000 + $50,000) and net book value is $1 million (cost was $1.2 million). Cash of $1,080,000 was received so that a gain of $80,000 must be recognized.

KEY TAKEAWAY

Depreciation expense is recorded for property and equipment at the end of each fiscal year and also at the time of an asset's disposal. To record a disposal, cost and the accumulated depreciation as of that date are removed. Any proceeds are recorded and the difference between the amount received and the net book value surrendered is recognized as a gain (if more than net book value is collected) or a loss (if less is collected). Many companies automatically record depreciation for one-half year for any period of use of less than a full year. The process is much simpler and, as a mechanical allocation process, no need for absolute precision is warranted.

4. ALTERNATIVE DEPRECIATION PATTERNS AND THE RECORDING OF A WASTING ASSET

LEARNING OBJECTIVES

At the end of this section, students should be able to meet the following objectives:

1. Explain the justification for accelerated methods of depreciation.
2. Compute depreciation expense using the double-declining balance method.
3. Realize that the overall impact on net income is not affected by a particular cost allocation pattern.
4. Describe the units-of-production method, including its advantages and disadvantages.
5. Explain the purpose and characteristics of MACRS.
6. Compute depletion expense for a wasting asset such as an oil well or a forest of trees.
7. Explain the reason that depletion amounts are not directly recorded as an expense.

4.1 Accelerated Depreciation

*Question: Straight-line depreciation certainly qualifies as systematic and rational. The same amount of cost is assigned to expense during each period of an asset's use. **Because no specific method is required by U.S. GAAP, do companies ever use other approaches to create different allocation patterns for depreciation?** If so, how are these methods justified?*

Answer: The most common alternative to the straight-line method is **accelerated depreciation**, which records a larger expense in the initial years of an asset's service. The primary rationale for this pattern is that property and equipment frequently produce higher amounts of revenue earlier in their lives because they are newer. The matching principle would suggest that recognizing more depreciation in these periods is appropriate to better align the expense with the revenues earned.

A second justification for accelerated depreciation is that some types of property and equipment lose value more quickly in their first few years than they do in later years. Automobiles and other vehicles are a typical example of this pattern. Consequently, recording a greater expense in the initial years of use is said to better reflect reality.

Over the decades, a number of formulas have been invented to mathematically create an accelerated depreciation pattern—high expense at first with subsequent cost allocations falling each year throughout the life of the property. The most common is the **double-declining balance method (DDB)**. When using DDB, annual depreciation is determined by multiplying the current net book value of the asset times two divided by the expected years of life. As the net book value drops, the annual expense drops. This formula has no internal logic except that it creates the desired pattern, an expense that is higher in the first years of operation and less after that. Although residual value is not utilized in this computation, the final amount of depreciation recognized must be manipulated to arrive at this ending balance.

Depreciation for the building bought above for $600,000 with an expected five-year life and a residual value of $30,000 is calculated as follows if DDB is applied. Note how different this cost allocation pattern is than that shown in Figure 10.2 using the straight-line method.

(cost − accumulated depreciation) × 2/expected life = depreciation expense for period

Year One:

($600,000 − $0) = $600,000 × 2/5 = $240,000 depreciation expense

Year Two:

($600,000 − $240,000) = $360,000 × 2/5 = $144,000 depreciation expense

Year Three:

($600,000 − $384,000) = $216,000 × 2/5 = $86,400 depreciation expense

Year Four:

($600,000 − $470,400) = $129,600 × 2/5 = $51,840 depreciation expense

Year Five:

($600,000 − $522,240) = $77,760,

so depreciation for Year Five must be set at $47,760 to reduce the $77,760 net book value to the expected residual value of $30,000.

Note that the desired expense pattern for accelerated depreciation has resulted. The expense starts at $240,000 and becomes smaller in each subsequent period as can be seen in the adjusting entries prepared in Figure 10.6.

accelerated depreciation

Any method of determining depreciation that assigns larger expenses to the initial years of an asset's service and smaller expenses to the later years; it is often justified by the assumption that newer assets generate more revenues than older assets do.

double-declining balance method (DDB)

A common accelerated depreciation method that computes expense each year by multiplying the asset's net book value (cost less accumulated depreciation) times two divided by the expected useful life.

FIGURE 10.6 Building Acquisition and Double-Declining Balance Depreciation

1/1/1	Building	$600,000 ($600,000)	
	Cash		$600,000
12/31/1	Depreciation Expense	240,000 (240,000)	
	Accumulated Depreciation —Building		240,000 (240,000)
12/31/2	Depreciation Expense	144,000 (144,000)	
	Accumulated Depreciation —Building		144,000 (384,000)
12/31/3	Depreciation Expense	86,400 (86,400)	
	Accumulated Depreciation —Building		86,400 (470,400)
12/31/4	Depreciation Expense	51,840 (51,840)	
	Accumulated Depreciation —Building		51,840 (522,240)
12/31/5	Depreciation Expense	47,760 (47,760)	
	Accumulated Depreciation —Building		47,760 (570,000)

When applying an accelerated depreciation method, net book value falls quickly at first because of the high initial expense levels. Thus, if an asset is sold early in its life, a reported gain is more likely (the amount received will be greater than this lower net book value). For example, in Figure 10.3, the building was depreciated using the straight-line method and sold after two years for $290,000, creating a reported $82,000 loss because the net book value was $372,000. Net book value was high in comparison to the amount received.

With DDB, the accumulated depreciation will be $384,000 after two years as shown in Figure 10.6. If the building is then sold on December 31, Year Two for $290,000, a $74,000 gain is reported because net book value has dropped all the way to $216,000 ($600,000 cost less $384,000 accumulated depreciation). Accelerated depreciation creates a lower net book value, especially in the early years of ownership.

FIGURE 10.7 Building Sold after Two Years—Double-Declining Balance Method Used

12/31/2	Cash	290,000	
	Accumulated Depreciation—Building	384,000	
	Building		600,000
	Gain on Sale of Building		74,000

Although the annual amounts are quite different, the overall net income is never affected by the allocation pattern. In this example, a building was bought for $600,000 and later sold after two years for $290,000. Thus, net income for the entire period of use must be reduced by the $310,000 difference regardless of the approach applied.

FIGURE 10.8 Depreciation Methods—Overall Impact on Net Income

	Straight-Line Method	Double-Declining Balance Method
Year One Depreciation Expense	($114,000)	($240,000)
Year Two Depreciation Expense	(114,000)	(144,000)
Loss on Sale for $290,000	(82,000)	
Gain on Sale for $290,000		+74,000
Overall Impact on Net Income	($310,000)	($310,000)

TEST YOURSELF

Question:

On April 1, Year One, Hayden Corporation buys machinery for $30,000 and pays an additional $4,000 to have it delivered to its factory and then assembled. Company officials believe this machinery will last for ten years and then have a $2,000 remaining residual value. Depreciation is to be computed by applying the double-declining balance method. The half-year convention is utilized. The value of the asset actually declines at only a rate of 10 percent per year. On the company's balance sheet as of December 31, Year Three, what is reported as the net book value for this asset?

a. $18,432

b. $18,496

c. $19,584

d. $25,500

Answer:

The correct answer is choice c: $19,584.

Explanation:

Cost of the asset is $34,000, which is multiplied by 2/10 to get $6,800. Because of the half-year convention, $6,800 is multiplied by 1/2. Depreciation is $3,400. For Year Two, book value is $30,600 ($34,000 less $3,400). When multiplied by 2/10, depreciation is $6,120. The contra account rises to $9,520 and book value falls to $24,480. When multiplied by 2/10, expense for the third year is $4,896. Accumulated depreciation is now $14,416 and book value is $19,584 ($34,000 less $14,416).

4.2 Units-Of-Production Method

*Question: The two methods demonstrated so far for establishing a depreciation pattern are based on time, five years to be precise. In most cases, though, it is the physical use of the asset rather than the passage of time that is actually relevant to this process. Use is the action that generates revenues. **How is the depreciation of a long-lived tangible asset determined if usage can be measured?***

For example, assume that a limousine company buys a new vehicle for $90,000 to serve as an addition to its fleet. Company officials expect this limousine to be driven for 300,000 miles and then have no residual value. How is depreciation expense determined each period?

Answer: Depreciation does not have to be based on time; it only has to be computed in a systematic and rational manner. Thus, the **units-of-production method (UOP)** is another alternative that is occasionally encountered. UOP is justified because the periodic expense is matched with the work actually performed. In this illustration, the limousine's depreciation is based on the total number of miles expected. Then, the annual expense is computed using the number of miles driven in a year, an easy figure to determine.

units-of-production method (UOP)

A method of determining depreciation that is not based on the passage of time but rather on the level of actual usage during the period.

($90,000 less $0)/300,000 miles = $0.30 per mile

Depreciation is recorded at a rate of $0.30 per mile. The depreciable cost basis is allocated evenly over the miles that the vehicle is expected to be driven. UOP is a straight-line method but one that is based on usage (miles driven, in this example) rather than years. Because of the direct connection between the expense allocation and the work performed, UOP is a very appealing approach. It truly mirrors the matching principle. Unfortunately, measuring the physical use of most assets is rarely as easy as with a limousine.

To illustrate, assume this vehicle is driven 80,000 miles in Year One, 120,000 miles in Year Two, and 100,000 miles in Year Three, depreciation will be $24,000, $36,000, and $30,000 when the $0.30 per mile rate is applied. The annual adjusting entries are shown in Figure 10.9.

FIGURE 10.9 Depreciation—Units-of-Production Method

1/1/1	Vehicle	$90,000 ($90,000)	
	Cash		$90,000
12/31/1	Depreciation Expense	24,000 (24,000)	
	Accumulated Depreciation —Vehicle		24,000 (24,000)
12/31/2	Depreciation Expense	36,000 (36,000)	
	Accumulated Depreciation —Vehicle		36,000 (60,000)
12/31/3	Depreciation Expense	30,000 (30,000)	
	Accumulated Depreciation —Vehicle		30,000 (90,000)

Estimations rarely prove to be precise reflections of reality. This vehicle will not likely be driven exactly 300,000 miles. If used for less and then retired, both the cost and accumulated depreciation are removed. A loss is recorded equal to the remaining net book value unless some cash or other asset is received. If driven more than the anticipated number of miles, depreciation stops at 300,000 miles. At that point, the cost of the asset will have been depreciated completely.

Although alternative methods such as the double-declining balance method and the units-of-production method are interesting theoretically, they are not very widely used in practice. Probably only about 5–10 percent of companies apply a method other than straight-line depreciation. However, as indicated later, accelerated depreciation is an important method when computing a company's taxable income.

TEST YOURSELF

Question:

On March 1, Year One, the Good Eating Company buys a machine to make donuts so that it can expand its menu. The donut maker cost the company $22,000 but has an expected residual value of $4,000. Officials believe this machine should be able to produce 100,000 dozen donuts over a ten-year period. In Year One, 7,000 dozen donuts are prepared and sold while in Year Two, another 11,000 dozen are made. However, the company is not satisfied with the profits made from selling donuts. Thus, on April 1, Year Three, after making 3,000 more dozen, the company sells the machine for $19,000 in cash. If the units-of-production method is used to compute depreciation, what gain or loss should the company recognize on the sale of the donut maker?

a. Gain of $780

b. Gain of $320

c. Loss of $320

d. Loss of $780

Answer:

The correct answer is choice a: Gain of $780.

Explanation:

The company expects to recognize an expense of $18,000 ($22,000 less $4,000) as it makes 100,000 dozen. That is $0.18 per dozen ($18,000/100,000 dozen). While being used, 21,000 dozen donuts are prepared (7,000 + 11,000 + 3,000). At $0.18 per dozen, total depreciation of $3,780 is recognized (21,000 dozen at $0.18 each). This expense reduces book value to $18,220 ($22,000 less $3,780). If sold for $19,000, the company reports a gain of $780 based on the excess received ($19,000 less $18,220).

4.3 MACRS

Question: *Companies use straight-line depreciation, accelerated depreciation, or units-of-production depreciation for financial reporting.* **What method of determining depreciation is applied when a business files its federal income tax return?** *Can one of these methods be selected or is a specific approach required?*

Answer: In most cases, the government wants businesses to buy more machinery, equipment, and the like because such purchases help stimulate the economy and create jobs. Consequently, for federal income tax purposes, companies are required to use a designed method known as Modified Accelerated Cost Recovery System (MACRS). MACRS has several built-in tax incentives inserted to encourage businesses to acquire more depreciable assets. Greater depreciation expense is allowed, especially in the earlier years of use, so that the purchase reduces tax payments.

- Each depreciable asset must be placed into one of eight classes based upon its type and life. For example, a light truck goes into one class, but a typewriter is placed in another. Every asset within a class is depreciated by the same method and over the same life.

- For most of these classes, the number of years is relatively short so that the benefit of the expense is received quickly for tax purposes.

- Residual value is ignored completely. The entire cost can be expensed.

- For six of the eight classes, accelerated depreciation is required, which again creates more expense in the initial years.

4.4 Determining Depletion

Question: *The cost of land is not depreciated because it does not have a finite life. However, land is often acquired solely for the natural resources that it might contain such as oil, timber, gold or the like. As the oil is pumped, the timber harvested or the gold extracted, a portion of the value is physically separated from the land.* **How is the reported cost of land affected when its natural resources are removed?**

depletion

A method of allocating the cost of a wasting asset (such as a gold mine or an oil well) to expense over the periods during which the value is removed from the property.

Answer: Oil, timber, gold, and the like are known as "wasting assets." They are taken from land over time, a process referred to as **depletion**. Value is literally removed from the asset rather than being consumed through use as with the depreciation of property and equipment. The same mechanical calculation demonstrated above for the units-of-production (UOP) method is applied. The 2010 financial statements for **Alpha Natural Resources** state that "costs to obtain coal lands and leased mineral rights are capitalized and amortized to operations as depletion expense using the units-of-production method."

Because the value is separated rather than used up, depletion initially leads to the recording of inventory (such as oil or gold, for example). An expense is recognized only at the eventual point of sale.

As with other types of property and equipment, historical cost is the sum of all normal and necessary expenditures to get the wasting asset into condition and position to generate revenues. To illustrate, assume that at the beginning of Year One, land is acquired for $1.6 million cash while another $400,000 is spent to construct a mining operation. Total cost is $2 million. The land is estimated to hold ten thousand tons of ore to be mined and sold. The land will be worth an estimated amount of only $100,000 after all ore is removed. Depletion is $190 per ton ([$2,000,000 cost less $100,000 residual value]/10,000 tons). It is a straight-line approach based on tons and not years, an allocation that follows the procedures of the units-of-production method.

Assume that 3,000 tons of ore are extracted in Year One and sold in Year Two for $1 million cash. Another 3,600 tons are removed in the second year for sale at a later time. Depletion is $570,000 in Year One ($190 × 3,000 tons) and $684,000 in Year Two ($190 × 3,600 tons). Note in Figure 10.10 that the ore is initially recorded as inventory and only moved to expense (cost of goods sold) when sold in the subsequent period. For depreciation, expense is recognized immediately as the asset's utility is consumed. With depletion, no expense is recorded until the inventory is eventually sold.

FIGURE 10.10 Depletion of Wasting Asset

1/1/1	Land with Mineral Rights	$1,600,000	
	Cash		$1,600,000
1/1/1	Land with Mineral Rights	400,000 (2,000,000)	
	Cash		400,000
12/31/1	Inventory of Ore	570,000	
	Accumulated Depletion		570,000 (570,000)
Year Two	Cash	1,000,000	
	Revenue from Sale of Ore		1,000,000
	Cost of Goods Sold	570,000	
	Inventory of Ore		570,000
12/31/2	Inventory	684,000	
	Accumulated Depletion		684,000 (1,254,000)

After two years, this land is reported on the company's balance sheet at a net book value of $746,000 based on its historical cost of $2 million and accumulated depletion to date of $1,254,000 ($570,000 + $684,000). The remaining inventory of ore is reported as an asset at $684,000 because it has not yet been sold.

FIGURE 10.11 Net Book Value of Land with Mineral Rights After Depletion

Land with Mineral Rights	$2,000,000
Less: Accumulated Depletion	1,254,000
Net Book Value	$746,000

TEST YOURSELF

Question:

When crude oil is selling for $30 per barrel, the Ohio Oil Company buys an acre of land for $3.2 million because it believes that a reserve of oil lies under the ground. The company spends another $500,000 to set up the proper drilling apparatus. The company believes that 200,000 barrels of oil are in the ground at this location. Once the oil has been extracted, the land will have a resale value of only $100,000. In both Years One and Two, 70,000 barrels are pumped out but only 50,000 are sold in Year One and another 40,000 in Year Two. The price of crude oil stays steady in Year One but jumps to $39 per barrel during Year Two. What is the net book value of the land account at the end of Year Two?

a. $1,080,000

b. $1,180,000

c. $1,740,000

d. $2,340,000

Answer:

The correct answer is choice b: $1,180,000.

Explanation:

The cost of this property is $3.7 million ($3.2 million plus $500,000). Expected residual value is $100,000 so $3.6 million will be the total depletion ($3.7 million minus $100,000). The land holds an estimated 200,000 barrels; thus, the depletion rate is $18 per barrel ($3.6 million/200,000 barrels). Over the two years, 140,000 barrels are extracted so that total depletion is $2.52 million ($18 × 140,000). Net book value is reduced to $1.18 million ($3.7 million less $2.52 million).

KEY TAKEAWAY

Additional cost allocation patterns for determining depreciation exist beyond the straight-line method. Accelerated depreciation records more expense in the earlier years of use than in later periods. This pattern is sometimes considered a better matching of expenses with revenues and closer to actual drops in value. The double-declining balance method is the most common version of accelerated depreciation. Its formula was designed to create the appropriate allocation pattern. The units-of-production method can be used for property and equipment where the quantity of work performed is easily monitored. This approach is also used in recording the depletion of wasting assets such as oil wells and silver mines. For federal income tax purposes, the Modified Accelerated Cost Recovery System (MACRS) is required. It provides certain benefits for the acquisition of depreciable assets as a way of encouraging more purchases to help the economy grow. For example, residual values are ignored and the expense is computed for most assets using accelerated depreciation methods.

5. RECORDING ASSET EXCHANGES AND EXPENDITURES THAT AFFECT OLDER ASSETS

LEARNING OBJECTIVES

At the end of this section, students should be able to meet the following objectives:

1. Record the exchange of one asset for another and explain the rationale for this method of accounting.
2. Explain when the fair value of an asset received must be used for recording an exchange rather than the fair value of the property surrendered.
3. Compute the allocation of cost between assets when more than one is acquired in a single transaction.
4. Determine which costs are capitalized when incurred in connection with an asset that has already been in use for some time and explain the impact on future depreciation expense calculations.

5.1 Exchanging One Asset for Another

asset exchange

A trade of one asset for another in which the net book value of the old asset is removed from the records while the new asset is recorded at the fair value surrendered (if known); the difference between the recorded fair value and the previous net book value creates a gain or loss to be shown on the income statement.

*Question: Some items are acquired by a company through an asset **exchange** instead of as the result of a purchase. For example, the limousine discussed earlier might well be traded away after two years for a newer model. Such transactions are common, especially with vehicles. **How is the historical cost of a new asset measured if obtained through an exchange rather than an acquisition?***

To illustrate, assume that this limousine is traded to an automobile manufacturer for a new model on December 31, Year Two. By that time, as shown in Figure 10.9, the net book value had fallen to $30,000 (cost of $90,000 less accumulated depreciation of $60,000). However, because company employees have taken excellent care of the vehicle during its two years of use, its fair value is $45,000. As has been discussed, net book value rarely equals fair value during the life of property and equipment. Assume that the vehicle being acquired is worth $100,000 so the company also pays $55,000 in cash ($100,000 value received less $45,000 value surrendered) to complete the trade. How is such an exchange recorded?

Answer: In virtually all cases, fair value is the accounting basis used to record items received in an exchange. The net book value of the old asset is removed from the accounts and the new model is reported at fair value. Fair value is added; net book value is removed. A gain or loss is recognized for the difference.

In this example, the company surrenders two assets with a total fair value of $100,000 ($45,000 value for the old limousine plus $55,000 in cash) to obtain the new vehicle. However, the assets given up have a total net book value of only $85,000 ($30,000 and $55,000). A $15,000 gain is recognized on the exchange ($100,000 fair value less $85,000 net book value). The gain results because the old limousine had not lost as much value as the depreciation process had expensed. The net book value was reduced to $30,000 but the vehicle was worth $45,000.[4] Based on the actual decline in value, too much expense had been recognized.

The journal entry to record this exchange of assets is presented in Figure 10.12.

FIGURE 10.12 Recording Exchange of Assets

Vehicle (New)	100,000	
Accumulated Depreciation	60,000	
Vehicle (Old)		90,000
Cash		55,000
Gain on Exchange of Limousines		15,000

5.2 Determining the Fair Value to Record in an Exchange

Question: In the previous example, the value of the assets surrendered ($45,000 plus $55,000 or $100,000) equals the value of the new limousine received ($100,000). The trade was exactly even. Because one party *might have better negotiating skills or a serious need for a quick trade, the two values can differ, at least slightly. For example, the limousine company could give up its old vehicle (worth $45,000) and cash ($55,000) and manage to convince the automobile manufacturer to hand over a new asset worth $110,000. If the values are not equal in an exchange, which fair value is used for reporting the newly acquired asset? Should the new limousine be recorded at the $100,000 value given up or the $110,000 value received?*

Answer: To stay consistent with the historical cost principle, the new asset received in a trade is recorded at the fair value of the item or items surrendered. Giving up the previously owned property is the sacrifice made to obtain the new asset. That is the cost to the new buyer.

Generally, the fair value of the items sacrificed equals the fair value of the items received. Most exchanges involve properties of relatively equal worth; a value of $100,000 is surrendered to acquire a value of $100,000. However, that is not always the case. Thus, if known, the fair value of the assets given up always serves as the basis for recording the asset received. Only if the value of the property traded away cannot be readily determined is the new asset recorded at its own fair value.

TEST YOURSELF

Question:

On January 1, Year One, a company spends $39,000 to buy a new piece of machinery with an expected residual value of $3,000 and a useful life of ten years. The straight-line method of depreciation is applied but not the half-year convention. On October 1, Year Three, the company wants to exchange this asset (which is now worth $31,000) for a new machine worth $40,000. To finalize the exchange, the company also pays cash of $9,000. What is the gain or loss on the trade?

a. Loss of $600
b. Loss of $1,100
c. Gain of $1,300
d. Gain of $1,900

Answer:

The correct answer is choice d: Gain of $1,900.

Explanation:

The new asset is recorded at $40,000 ($31,000 fair value + $9,000 cash). Depreciation has been $3,600 per year—cost less residual value ($39,000 − $3,000 or $36,000) over a ten-year life. Depreciation in Year Three is $2,700 (9/12 of $3,600). Accumulated depreciation is $9,900 ($3,600 + $3,600 + $2,700); book value is $29,100 ($39,000 less $9,900). If new asset is $40,000 and book value surrendered is $38,100 ($29,100 plus $9,000), the increase in financial position creates a gain of $1,900.

5.3   Allocating a Purchase Price between Two Assets

Question: Occasionally, two or more assets are bought for a single purchase price. The most common example is the acquisition of a building along with the land on which it sits. As has been discussed, the portion of the cost assigned to the building is depreciated to expense over its useful life in some systematic and rational manner. However, land does not have a finite life. Its cost remains an asset so that this portion of the price has no impact on reported net income over time. How does an accountant separate the amount paid for land from the cost assigned to a building when the two assets are purchased together?

Assume a business pays $5.0 million for three acres of land along with a five-story building. What part of this cost is attributed to the land and what part to the building? Does management not have a bias to assign more of the $5.0 million to land and less to the building to reduce the future amounts reported as depreciation expense?

Answer: Companies commonly purchase more than one asset at a time. This is sometimes referred to as a **basket purchase**. For example, a manufacturer might buy several machines in a single transaction. The cost assigned to each should be based on their relative values.

For this illustration, assume that the land and building bought for $5.0 million have been appraised at $4.5 million and $1.5 million, respectively, for a total of $6.0 million. Perhaps the owner needed cash immediately and was willing to accept a price of only $5.0 million. For the buyer, the land makes up 75 percent of the value received ($4.5 million/$6.0 million) and the building the remaining 25 percent ($1.5 million/$6.0 million). The cost is simply assigned in those same proportions: $3.75

basket purchase

The acquisition of more than one asset at a single cost; the cost is then allocated among those assets based on their relative values.

million to the land ($5.0 million × 75 percent) and $1.25 million to the building ($5.0 million × 25 percent). This allocation enables the buyer to make the journal entry presented in Figure 10.13.

FIGURE 10.13 Allocation of Cost between Land and Building with Both Values Known

Occasionally, in a basket purchase, the value can be determined for one of the assets but not for all. As an example, the land might be worth $4.6 million, but no legitimate value is available for the building. Perhaps similar structures do not exist in this location for comparison purposes. In such cases, the known value is used for that asset with the remainder of the cost assigned to the other property. If the land is worth $4.6 million but no reasonable value can be ascribed to the building, the excess $400,000 ($5,000,000 cost less $4,600,000 assigned to the land) is arbitrarily assigned to the second asset.

FIGURE 10.14 Allocation of Cost Based on Known Value for Land Only

Does the possibility of bias exist in these allocations? Accounting is managed by human beings and they always face a variety of biases. That potential problem is one of the primary reasons that independent auditors play such an important role in the financial reporting process. These outside experts work to ensure that financial figures are presented fairly without bias. Obviously, if the buyer assigns more of the cost of a basket purchase to land, future depreciation will be less and reported net income higher. In contrast, if more of the cost is allocated to the building, depreciation expense is higher and taxable income and income tax payments are reduced. That is also a tempting choice.

Thus, the independent auditor gathers sufficient evidence to provide reasonable assurance that such allocations are based on reliable appraisal values so that both the land and the building figures are fairly presented. However, a decision maker is naïve not to realize that potential bias does exist in any reporting process.

5.4 Subsequent Expenditures for Property and Equipment

*Question: Assume that the building discussed earlier is assigned a cost of $1,250,000 as shown in Figure 10.13. Assume further that this asset has an expected life of twenty years and that straight-line depreciation is applied with no residual value. After eight years, accumulated depreciation is $500,000 ($1,250,000 × 8 years/20 years). At that point, when the building has a remaining life of 12 years, the owner spends an additional $150,000 on this asset. **Should a later expenditure made in connection with a piece of property or equipment that is already in use be capitalized (added to the asset account) or expensed immediately?***

Answer: The answer to this question depends on the impact that this later expenditure has on the building. In many cases, additional money is spent simply to keep the asset operating with no change in expected life or improvement in future productivity. As shown in Figure 10.15, such costs are recorded as maintenance expense if anticipated or repair expense if unexpected. For example, changing the oil in a truck at regular intervals is a maintenance expense whereas fixing a dent from an accident is a repair expense. However, this distinction has no impact on reported net income.

FIGURE 10.15 Recording of Cost to Maintain or Repair Asset

Other possibilities do exist. If the $150,000 expenditure increases the future operating capacity of the asset, the cost should be capitalized as shown in Figure 10.16. The building might have been made bigger, more efficient, more productive, or less expensive to operate. If the asset has been improved as a result of this expenditure, historical cost is raised.

FIGURE 10.16 Cost Capitalized Because of Increase in Operating Capacity

Assuming that no change in either the useful life of the building or its residual value occurs as a result of this work, depreciation expense will be $75,000 in each of the subsequent twelve years. The newly increased net book value is simply allocated over the useful life that remains.

$$(\$1,250,000 + \$150,000 - \$500,000)/12 \text{ remaining years} = \$75,000$$

Another possibility does exist. The $150,000 might extend the building's life without creating any other improvement. Because the building will now generate revenue for a longer period of time than previously expected, this cost is capitalized. A clear benefit has been gained from the amount spent. The asset is not physically bigger or improved but its estimated life has been extended. Consequently, the building is not increased directly, but instead, accumulated depreciation is reduced as shown in Figure 10.17. In effect, this expenditure has recaptured some of the previously expensed utility.

FIGURE 10.17 Cost Capitalized Because Expected Life Is Extended

| Accumulated Depreciation | 150,000 | |
| Cash | | 150,000 |

Assuming that the $150,000 payment extends the remaining useful life of the building from twelve to eighteen years with no accompanying change in residual value, depreciation expense will be $50,000 in each of these remaining eighteen years. Once again, net book value has increased by $150,000 but, in this situation, the life of the asset has also been lengthened.

reduced accumulated depreciation: $500,000 - $150,000 = $350,000

adjusted net book value: $1,250,000 - $350,000 = $900,000

annual depreciation: $900,000/18 years = $50,000

TEST YOURSELF

Question:

The Hatcher Company buys a building on January 1, Year One for $9 million. It has no anticipated residual value and should help generate revenues for thirty years. On December 31, Year Three, the company spends another $500,000 to cover the entire structure in a new type of plastic that will extend its useful life for an additional sixteen years. On December 31, Year Four, what will Hatcher report as accumulated depreciation for this building?

   a. $600,000
   b. $820,930
   c. $1,088,372
   d. $1,100,000

Answer:

The correct answer is choice a: $600,000.

Explanation:

Annual depreciation is $300,000 ($9 million/30 years) or $900,000 after three years. The $500,000 expenditure reduces that balance to $400,000 because it extends the life (from twenty-seven years to forty-three) with no other increase in productivity. Book value is now $8.6 million ($9 million cost less $400,000 accumulated depreciation), which is allocated over forty-three years at a rate of $200,000 per year. Depreciation for Year Four raises accumulated depreciation from $400,000 to $600,000.

KEY TAKEAWAY

Assets are occasionally obtained through exchange. The reported cost for the new acquisition is based on the fair value of the property surrendered because that figure reflects the company's sacrifice. The asset received is only recorded at its own fair value if the value of the asset given up cannot be determined. The difference between the net book value removed and the fair value recorded is recognized as a gain or loss. When more than one asset is acquired in a single transaction, the cost allocation is based on the relative fair values of the items received. Any subsequent costs incurred in connection with property and equipment are capitalized if the asset has been made bigger or better in some way or is just more efficient. If the length of the remaining useful life is extended, capitalization is established by reducing accumulated depreciation.

6. REPORTING LAND IMPROVEMENTS AND IMPAIRMENTS IN THE VALUE OF PROPERTY AND EQUIPMENT

LEARNING OBJECTIVES

At the end of this section, students should be able to meet the following objectives:

1. Identify assets that qualify as land improvements and understand that the distinction between land and land improvements is not always clear.
2. Perform the two tests used in financial accounting to determine the necessity of recognizing a loss because of an impairment in the value of a piece of property or equipment.
3. Explain the theoretical justification for capitalizing interest incurred during the construction of property and equipment.

6.1 Recognition of Land Improvements

*Question: Land is not subjected to the recording of depreciation expense because it has an infinite life. Often, though, a parking lot, fence, sidewalk, or the like will be attached to land. Those assets do have finite lives. **How are attachments to land—such as a sidewalk—reported in financial accounting?** Is that* *cost added to the land account or is some other reporting more appropriate? Should these assets be depreciated?*

Answer: Any asset that is attached to land but has a finite life is recorded in a separate account, frequently referred to as **land improvements**. This cost is then depreciated over the estimated life in the same way as equipment or machinery. The cost of a parking lot or sidewalk, for example, is capitalized and then reclassified to expense in a systematical and rational manner.

In some cases, a distinction between land and improvements is difficult to draw. Accounting rules do not always provide clear guidance for every possible situation. Judgment is occasionally necessary. For example, trees, shrubbery, and sewer systems might be viewed as normal and necessary costs to get land into the condition and position to generate revenues rather than serving as separate assets. Is a sewer system a cost incurred so that land can be utilized or is it truly a distinct asset? U.S. GAAP does not provide absolute rules. Such costs may be carried within the land account and not depreciated or reported as land improvements subject to depreciation. Such flexibility in accounting is more prevalent than might be imagined.

6.2   Property and Equipment with Impaired Value

Question: Property and equipment acquisitions are recorded at historical cost, a figure which is depreciated over the asset's anticipated useful life. Land is an exception because it will last forever. These assets are eventually sold, traded, consumed, or disposed of in some other manner. While in use, their value may decline rather rapidly if adverse conditions arise. The economy as a whole or the local business environment might suffer a recession that reduces the worth of a wide array of assets. Or, some unexpected action could create a drop in the value of a specific asset.

In financial reporting, increases in the fair value of property and equipment are ignored because of the conservative nature of accounting, but what about decreases? **If the value of property and equipment becomes impaired, is any accounting recognition made of that loss prior to disposal?** *Is historical cost always the basis for reporting such assets regardless of their worth? For example, as discussed previously, inventory is reported at the lower of cost or market whenever a decline in value has occurred. Is a similar treatment required in reporting property and equipment?*

To illustrate, assume that a company constructs a plant for $3 million to manufacture widgets. Shortly thereafter, the global market for widgets falls precipitously so that the owner of this structure has little use for it. Furthermore, no one else wants to own a manufacturing plant for widgets. Does historical cost continue to be reported for this asset even if the value has been damaged significantly?

Answer: Accounting is influenced by conservatism. Concern should always arise when any piece of property or equipment is thought to be worth less than its normal net book value. Because temporary swings in value can happen frequently and often have no long-term impact, they do not require accounting modification. Historical cost remains the reporting basis.

Permanent declines in the worth of an asset, though, are a problem for the owner that needs to be recognized in some appropriate manner. Consequently, two tests have been created by FASB to determine if the value of property or equipment has been impaired in such a serious fashion that a loss must be recognized.

If a possible impairment of the value of property or equipment is suspected, the owner must estimate the total amount of cash that will be generated by the asset during its remaining life. The resulting cash figure is then compared with the asset's current net book value (cost less accumulated depreciation). A reporting problem exists if the company does not anticipate receiving even enough cash to recover the net book value of the asset. At that point, the asset is a detriment to the company rather than a benefit. This **recoverability test** highlights situations that are so dire that immediate recognition of a loss must be considered.

If expected future cash flows exceed the current net book value of a piece of property or equipment, no reporting is necessary. The asset can still be used to recover its net book value. No permanent impairment has occurred according to the rules of U.S. GAAP.

---

land improvements

Assets attached to land with a finite life such as a parking lot or sidewalk.

recoverability test

A test used to determine whether the value of a long-lived asset has been impaired; if expected future cash flows are less than present net book value, a fair value test is then performed to determine the amount of impairment.

Conversely, if an asset cannot even generate sufficient cash to recover its own net book value, the accountant performs a second test (the fair value test) to determine the amount of loss, if any, to be reported. Net book value is compared to present fair value, the amount for which the asset could be sold. For property and equipment, the lower of these two figures is then reported on the balance sheet. Any reduction in the reported asset balance creates a loss to be recognized on the income statement.[5]

The recoverability test illustrated. Assume that the $3.0 million building in the previous example has been used for a short time so that it now has a net book value of $2.8 million. Also assume that because of the change in demand for its product, this building is now expected to generate a net positive cash flow of only $200,000 during each of the next five years or a total of $1.0 million. No amount of cash is expected after that time. This amount is far below the net book value of $2.8 million. The company will not be able to recover the asset's net book value through these cash flows. Thus, the building has failed the recoverability test. The fair value test must now be applied to see if a reported loss is necessary.

The fair value test illustrated. Assuming that a real estate appraiser believes this building could be sold for only $760,000, fair value is below net book value ($2.8 million is obviously greater than $760,000). Therefore, the asset account is reduced to this lower figure creating a reported loss of $2,040,000 ($2.8 million less $760,000).

FIGURE 10.18   Loss on Impaired Value of Building

Loss on Impaired Value of Building	2,040,000	
Building		2,040,000

In its 2010 financial statements, the **Ford Motor Company** describes this process as follows:

> *We monitor our asset groups for conditions that may indicate a potential impairment of long-lived assets. These conditions include current-period operating losses combined with a history of losses and a projection of continuing losses, and significant negative industry or economic trends. When these conditions exist, we test for impairment. An impairment charge is recognized for the amount by which the carrying value of the asset group exceeds its estimated fair value…. Based upon the financial impact of rapidly-changing U.S. market conditions during the second quarter of 2008, we projected a decline in net cash flows for the **Ford** North America segment. As a result, in the second quarter of 2008 we tested the long-lived assets for impairment and recorded in Automotive cost of sales a pretax charge of $5.3 billion.*

Talking with an Independent Auditor about International Financial Reporting Standards

Following is more of our interview with Robert A. Vallejo, partner with the accounting firm **PricewaterhouseCoopers**.

Question: The impairment of operational assets is an important reporting issue for many companies because acquired property does not always achieve anticipated levels of profitability. Buildings can be constructed and machinery purchased that simply fail to be as productive as forecasted. According to U.S. GAAP, an asset of this type is viewed as impaired when the total of all future cash flows generated by the asset are expected to be less than its current net book value. At that point, the owner cannot recover the net book value of the asset through continued usage. Consequently, the amount reported for the operational asset is reduced to fair value and a loss recognized. Does IFRS handle this type of problem in the same way as U.S. GAAP?

Rob Vallejo: The need to record impairment losses is the same under IFRS but the measurement process is different. The international standards require companies to identify an asset's fair value by calculating the present value of the future cash flows[6] or its net realizable value (anticipated sales price less costs required to sell) if that figure is higher. The asset's value is said to be impaired if this fair value (rather than total cash flows) is below net book value. If so, a loss is reported for the reduction from net book value to fair value. Also, under IFRS, companies return previously impaired assets to original net book value if fair value subsequently increases. In contrast, U.S. GAAP does not allow a write up in value once an impairment has been recorded.

TEST YOURSELF

Question:

Multi-Co. Company owns a small retail clothing store in a shopping center in Houston, Maine. This store has been reporting a loss in recent years because it is in a relatively remote location. The store cost $1.2 million but its book value has been reduced to $500,000 as the result of depreciation over the years. Cash flows remain positive at $40,000 per year. The store has several possible uses and it could be sold for $530,000. Or the company could continue to hold it for twelve additional years until its utility is consumed. What loss, if any, should the company report at the current time because of the impairment to the value of this asset?

a. Zero

b. $20,000

c. $30,000

d. $60,000

Answer:

The correct answer is choice a: Zero.

Explanation:

A possible impairment in the value of this store is indicated by the recoverability test. Book value is $500,000 but all future cash flows only amount to $480,000 ($40,000 per year for twelve years). The fair value test then becomes relevant. A reduction is required if the fair value of the asset is below book value. Fair value ($530,000) is above book value ($500,000) so no loss is reported. If fair value had been less than $500,000, the reported balance would be reduced and a loss recognized.

6.3   Capitalizing the Cost of Interest During Construction

Question: A company is considering buying a building for $1.0 million on January 1, Year One so that a retail store can be opened immediately. The company can borrow the money from a bank that requires payment of $100,000 in interest (an assumed annual rate of 10 percent) at the end of each year.

*As a second possibility, the company can borrow the same $1.0 million on the first day of the current year and use it to build a similar store to be completed and opened on December 31. Again, $100,000 in interest (10 percent annual rate) must be paid every year, starting at the end of Year One. In both cases, the same amount of money is expended to acquire the structure. **If money is borrowed and a building constructed, is the financial reporting the same as if the money had been spent to buy property that could be used immediately?***

Answer: A payment of $1 million is made in both cases for a building to serve as a retail store. Although the monetary cost is the same, the interest payments are handled differently from an accounting perspective. If a building is purchased, the structure can be used immediately to generate revenue. Borrowing the money and paying the $100,000 interest for Year One allows the company to open the store and start making sales at the beginning of that year. There is no waiting. The matching principle requires this cost to be reported as interest expense for Year One. Expense is matched with the revenue it helps to create.

capitalized interest

Interest cost incurred during the construction of a long-lived asset; the interest is added to the historical cost of the asset rather than being recorded as interest expense; it is viewed as a normal and necessary expenditure to get the asset into position and condition to generate revenues.

In contrast, if company officials choose to construct the building, no revenue is generated during Year One. Because of the decision to build rather than buy, revenues are postponed until Year Two. Without any corresponding revenues, expenses are not normally recognized. Choosing to build this structure means that the interest paid during Year One is a normal and necessary cost to get the building ready to use in Year Two. Thus, if the asset is constructed, all interest is **capitalized** rather than expensed until revenues are generated. The $100,000 is reported as part of the building's historical cost. The cost is then expensed over the useful life—as depreciation—in the years when revenues are earned.

The key distinction is that buying enables the company to generate revenue right away whereas constructing the building means that no revenue will be earned during Year One.

To illustrate, assume that this building is expected to generate revenues for twenty years with no expected residual value and that the straight-method is used for depreciation purposes. Notice the difference in many of the reported figures.

Store Bought on January 1, Year One—Revenues Generated Immediately

- Historical cost: $1 million
- Interest expense reported for Year One: $100,000
- Interest expense reported for Year Two: $100,000
- Depreciation expense reported for Year One: $50,000 ($1 million/20 years)
- Depreciation expense reported for Year Two: $50,000
- Net book value at end of Year Two: $900,000 ($1 million less $50,000 and $50,000)

Store Constructed during Year One—No Revenues Generated until Year Two

- Historical cost: $1.1 million (includes Year One interest)[7]
- Interest expense reported for Year One: -0- (no revenues earned)
- Interest expense reported for Year Two: $100,000
- Depreciation expense reported for Year One: Zero (no revenues earned)
- Depreciation expense reported for Year Two: $55,000 ($1.1 million/20 years)
- Net book value at end of Year Two: $1,045,000 ($1.1 million less $55,000)

6.4 Fixed Asset Turnover

*Question: In previous chapters, a number of vital signs were examined in analyzing receivables and inventory. These ratios and computations are computed by decision makers to help them evaluate the operations of a reporting entity. **Are there any vital signs normally studied in connection with property and equipment that a decision maker calculates in analyzing the financial health of a business?***

fixed asset turnover

Ratio calculated by dividing net sales by the average of the net fixed assets reported for the period; it indicates the efficiency by which property and equipment have been used to generate sales revenues.

Answer: Ratios and other computed amounts are not as common with noncurrent assets as has been seen with current assets. However, the **fixed asset turnover** indicates the efficiency by which a company uses its property and equipment to generate sales revenues. If a company holds large amounts of fixed assets but fails to generate an appropriate amount of revenue, the ability of management to make good use of those assets should be questioned.

This figure is calculated by taking net sales for a period and dividing it by the average net book value of the company's property and equipment (fixed assets). For example, assume a company reports $1 million in property and equipment on its balance sheet at the beginning of the year but $1.2 million at the end. During the year, the company generates $6.16 million in net sales. The average amount of the fixed assets for this period is $1.1 million and the fixed asset turnover is 5.6 times for the year.

net sales/average net fixed assets

$6,160,000/$1,100,000

5.6 times

KEY TAKEAWAY

"Land improvements" is an asset category that includes property attached to land (such as a fence, sidewalk, or sewer system) that has a finite life and should be depreciated. Unfortunately, the distinction between land and land improvements is sometimes difficult to draw. The accountant must determine whether the cost of property, such as shrubbery, is a separate asset or a cost to get the land into the condition to be used to generate revenues. Over time, property and equipment can lose a significant amount of value for many reasons. If impairment of that value is suspected, a recoverability test is applied to determine whether sufficient cash will be generated by the asset to recover its current net book value. If not, a fair value test is then applied and the asset's net book value is reduced to fair value if that number is lower. During construction of property and equipment, interest is capitalized rather than expensed because revenues are not being generated. The matching principle requires that recognition of this expense be deferred until revenue is earned. For that reason, interest incurred during construction is added to the cost of the asset.

Talking with a Real Investing Pro (Continued)

Following is a continuation of our interview with Kevin G. Burns.

Question: On a company's balance sheet, the reporting of land, buildings, and equipment is based on historical cost unless the value is impaired in some manner. Consequently, reported figures often represent expenditures that were made decades ago. However, the fair value of such assets is a very subjective and ever-changing number. The debate over the most relevant type of property and equipment information to provide decision makers is ongoing. Do you think a move should be made to report land, buildings, and equipment at current fair values?

Kevin Burns: I am a value investor. I look for companies that are worth more than is reflected in the current price of their ownership shares. Therefore, I always like "discovering" little nuggets—like hidden land values—that are still carried at cost after decades of ownership. However in the interest of full disclosure and transparency, I think it would be fairer to the average investor to have some sort of appraisal done to estimate fair market value. This information could be reported or just disclosed. The difficulty is, of course, how often to appraise? In a perfect world, a revaluation would be made at least every five years or if a major event occurs that changes the value of the land, building, and equipment by a significant amount.

 Video Clip

Professor Joe Hoyle talks about the five most important points in Chapter 10.

View the video online at: http://bit.ly/hoyle10-2

7. END-OF-CHAPTER EXERCISES

QUESTIONS

1. The Ames Corporation reports property and equipment as $19,300,000 on its balance sheet. What does that figure represent?

2. What is meant by the term "accumulated depreciation?"

3. In determining the historical cost of property and equipment, what amounts are included?

4. What is meant by the term "market capitalization?"

5. Why is property and equipment not reported on the balance sheet at fair value?

6. Why is the recording of depreciation expense necessary?

7. Why is the cost of land not subjected to depreciation?

8. A company is preparing to determine depreciation expense for a large piece of equipment. What information is needed to determine the amount to report in the current period?

9. Assume a machine is bought for $300,000, and depreciation each year is $25,000. What annual adjusting entry is recorded for this depreciation? What is reported as the net book value of the machine at the end of the second year? What expense is reported for the second year?

10. How does an asset qualify to be included as property and equipment on a company's balance sheet?

11. How is straight-line depreciation determined?

12. Equipment with a five-year expected life is bought during Year One but is later sold on November 8, Year Four. What journal entries are necessary to record the sale?

13. What is the half-year convention? Why is the half-year convention considered acceptable in financial accounting?

14. What is meant by accelerated depreciation? How is the use of accelerated depreciation methods justified theoretically?

15. How does the double-declining balance method determine depreciation expense for each year? What pattern is created by double-declining balance depreciation?

16. When is a company most likely to use the units-of-production method to determine depreciation expense? The units-of-production method is often referred to as a straight-line method. Why is that?

17. Why is the units-of-production method not more widely used?

18. What is meant by MACRS?

19. What are some characteristics commonly associated with MACRS? Why does the government allow those characteristics?

20. What is depletion? How is depletion different from depreciation?

21. A company buys a large building with four acres of land. Why is the allocation of the cost between the building and the land important?

22. A company buys a large building with four acres of land. How is the acquisition cost allocated between these two assets?

23. A company has been using a building for six years to generate revenues. In the current year, the company spends $900,000 on the building. How would the accountant determine whether this cost should be expensed or capitalized?

24. A company pays $6 million for a parcel of land and then spends another $500,000 to install a sewer system. The accountant is not sure whether this $500,000 cost should be reported within the land account or as a land improvement. Why is that decision important?

25. A company owns a piece of equipment and its value appears to have been impaired. What two tests should the accountant apply? Under what condition is loss reported on an asset impairment?

26. A company constructs a large warehouse. Why is the interest incurred during construction capitalized rather than being expensed? How is the impact of that capitalization reflected in the financial reporting?

27. How does a decision maker calculate the fixed asset turnover for a company?

TRUE OR FALSE

1. _____ A machine is bought, and the price agreed on with the seller is $13,250. The buyer must report this asset on its balance sheet on that date at $13,250.

2. _____ The depreciation process is designed to keep the net book value of property and equipment aligned with the asset's fair value.

3. _____ The depreciation for an asset is $10,000 in the first year, $20,000 in the second year, and $12,000 in the third year. On financial statements produced at the end of the third year, depreciation expense is $12,000, whereas accumulated depreciation is $42,000.

4. _____ Equipment is bought on October 9, Year One, for $75,000. It has a five -year life and expected residual value of $5,000. The half-year convention is used. If the straight-line method of depreciation is applied, accumulated depreciation at the end of Year Two is $21,000.

5. _____ The Osborne Company sells a piece of equipment that it held for several years. The sale results in a reported loss. This information indicates that the company is more likely to have used the double-declining balance method of depreciation rather than the straight-line method.

6. _____ On January 1, Year One, a company buys a large machine for $480,000. It has an expected life of eight years and residual value of $40,000. The double-declining balance method is applied but not the half-year convention. The machine is sold on April 1, Year Three, for cash of $280,000. The company should record a gain of $26,875 on the sale.

7. _____ Equipment is bought with an expected life of ten years and no residual value. After two years of use, the net book value will be higher if the straight-line method of depreciation is used rather than the double-declining balance method.

8. _____ A company buys machinery on October 1, Year One, for $500,000 with a $100,000 estimated residual value and an expected useful life of ten years. The double-declining balance method is applied along with the half-year convention. The machinery is destroyed on May 1, Year Three, in a flood. The insurance company pays $300,000 in cash to the company as settlement for the damages. The company will recognize a loss from the flood of $27,000.

9. _____ Equipment is acquired for $140,000 with a $20,000 residual value. The double-declining balance method is used. At the end of its useful life, the asset is sold for $19,000 in cash. A loss of $1,000 should be recognized.

10. _____ Equipment is acquired with a cost of $76,000 and an expected residual value of $20,000. In applying MACRS, the residual value is ignored. The primary reason that the government does not take residual value into consideration is to force businesses to pay more money in income taxes.

11. _____ Equipment is acquired for $78,000 with an expected residual value of $15,000. After the first year of use, depreciation recognized for financial reporting purposes will be larger than the figure expensed for federal income tax purposes.

12. _____ A company buys an oil well costing $8 million under the assumption that the well holds one million barrels of oil. The oil well has no residual value. During the first year of ownership, 220,000 barrels of oil are pumped out of the well. Cost of $1,760,000 must be expensed in that year.

13. _____ A piece of equipment with a cost of $40,000 and accumulated depreciation of $28,000 (and a fair value of $15,000) is traded along with $4,000 in cash for a similar piece of equipment valued at $20,000. This new equipment will be reported by the buyer on its financial records at a cost of $16,000.

14. _____ A piece of equipment with a cost of $40,000 and accumulated depreciation of $28,000 (and a fair value of $15,000) is traded along with $4,000 in cash for a similar piece of equipment valued at $20,000. This new equipment will be reported by the buyer on its financial records at a cost of $20,000.

15. _____ Equipment is bought by the Solomon Corporation for $360,000 on January 1, Year One. It has an expected life of 10 years with a $30,000 residual value. Straight-line depreciation is used, but the half-year convention is not applied. On January 1, Year Three, the equipment is traded for similar equipment with a value of $288,000. However, the value of the equipment surrendered is unknown. The Solomon Corporation should not recognize either a gain or a loss on this exchange.

16. _____ Poston Corporation buys equipment for $360,000 on January 1, Year One. It has an expected life of ten years and a residual value of $30,000. Straight-line depreciation is used but not the half-year convention. On January 1, Year Three, the company spends $39,000 on an improvement to this equipment that will enable it to last four years longer than originally expected. The expenditure has no impact on the estimated residual value. Depreciation expense for Year Three should be $28,000.

17. _____ On January 1, Year One, the Epstein Corporation buys a plot of land with a four-story office building. The company believes the building is worth $1.9 million and has an estimated life of twenty years (with no anticipated residual value). The straight-line method is used. The land has an assessed value of $100,000. Because the seller was interested in a quick sale, Epstein was able to buy this land and building for $1.7 million. Depreciation expense to be recognized in Year One is $80,750.

18. _____ A company buys a machine on October 1, Year One, for $500,000 with a $100,000 estimated residual value and an expected life of 10 years. The straight-line method of depreciation and the half-year convention are both used. On December 31, Year Three, company officials examine the machine and decide that it will only be able to generate $406,000 in future cash flows over its remaining life. It has a fair value at that date of $338,000. From an accounting perspective, the asset's value is not impaired, and no loss should be recognized.

19. _____ A company buys machinery for $320,000 in Year One. It has an expected residual value of $40,000 and a useful life of ten years. After three years, this machinery is sold for $210,000 in cash. Over the three-year period, the double-declining balance method will reduce net income more than the straight-line method will.

20. _____ A building is being constructed by a company to use in its operations. Interest of $55,000 is incurred during the construction process. This interest is not expensed but rather added to the capitalized cost of the building.

21. _____ A company has net sales in Year One of $10 million. The company starts the year with net property and equipment on its balance sheet of $1 million but ends the year with net property and equipment of $2.4 million. The fixed asset turnover for Year One is 5.9 times.

MULTIPLE CHOICE

1. On January 1, Year One, the Rhode Island Redbirds organization purchased new workout equipment for its athletes. The equipment had a cost of $15,600, transportation costs of $450, and set-up costs of $290. The Redbirds spent an additional $350 training their athletes on the proper use of this equipment. The expected useful life is five years. No residual value is anticipated. How much accumulated depreciation should the Redbirds report after two years if the straight-line method is used?

   a. $6,240

   b. $6,420

   c. $6,536

   d. $6,676

2. Refer to the information in number 1. Assume the Redbirds decide to use the double-declining balance depreciation method instead of the straight-line method. What amount of accumulated depreciation is reported on the balance sheet at the end of Year Two?

   a. $9,890

   b. $10,214

   c. $10,682

   d. $10,918

3. Ace Company buys a machine on April 1, Year One, for $50,000 in cash. It has a residual value of $10,000 and an expected useful life of ten years. The straight-line method and the half-year convention are applied. The asset is sold on September 1, Year Three, for $39,900. What loss should be reported on this sale?

   a. $100 loss

   b. $850 loss

   c. $1,767 loss

   d. $2,100 loss

4. The Timmons Company buys equipment on August 1, Year One, for a reported total amount of $60,000. It has a residual value of $10,000 and an expected useful life of five years. The straight-line method and the half-year convention are applied. The company reports net income in Year One of $70,000. However, an error was made. When this equipment was bought, a $5,000 cost was capitalized when it should have been expensed. What was the appropriate amount of net income that Timmons should have reported?

   a. $65,500

   b. $67,000

   c. $68,000

   d. $68,500

5. The Anna Corporation buys equipment on September 1, Year One, for $80,000 with a ten-year expected life and an estimated residual value of $10,000. The asset is depreciated using the double-declining balance method and the half-year convention. What is the net book value for this asset at the end of Year Three?

   a. $40,320

   b. $46,080

   c. $48,840

   d. $51,220

6. The Larisa Company buys machinery on April 1, Year One, for $50,000 with an expected life of ten years and residual value of $10,000. The double-declining balance method is applied along with the half-year convention. The machinery is sold on September 1, Year Three, for $32,400. What gain should be reported on this sale?

   a. $0

   b. $667

   c. $4,965

   d. $6,480

7. Which of the following is a characteristic of the MACRS system that is used in computing a company's taxable income for federal income tax purposes?

   a. Assets are assigned especially long lives for tax purposes.

   b. An automatic residual value of 10 percent of cost is always assumed.

    c. All assets are expensed by means of the straight-line method.

    d. Especially large amounts of expense are recognized in the first few years of an asset's life.

8. The Greenville Company starts operations in Year One and buys several pieces of equipment. All of this equipment is expected to last for ten years and have a residual value equal to 25 percent of cost. MACRS is properly used for tax purposes while straight-line depreciation is applied for financial reporting purposes. Based solely on the expensing of this equipment in Year One, which of the following statements is true?

    a. Reported net income for financial accounting purposes will be higher than taxable income.

    b. Reported net income for financial accounting purposes will be the same as taxable income.

    c. Reported net income for financial accounting purposes is likely to be lower than taxable income.

    d. Reported net income for financial accounting purposes must be lower than taxable income.

9. On January 3, Year One, Jewels Inc. purchases a South American mine (found to be rich in amethyst) for $560,000. After all of the amethyst has been removed, the land is estimated to be worth only $100,000. Experts predict that the mine contains 4,000 pounds of amethyst. Jewels plans on completing the extraction process in four years. In Year One, 400 pounds are dug from the mine. None of it has yet been sold. What should be reported as the net book value for the mine at the end of Year One?

    a. $420,000

    b. $445,000

    c. $514,000

    d. $560,000

10. Kite Corporation wishes to trade equipment it owns for a vehicle owned by the Runner Corporation. Kite's equipment has a net book value of $4,000 and a fair value of $4,500. Runner's vehicle has a net book value and fair value of $5,100. Kite agrees to pay Runner $600 in cash in addition to giving up the equipment. What is Kite's reported gain or loss on this exchange?

    a. $100

    b. $500

    c. $600

    d. $1,100

11. A company has equipment with a cost of $50,000 and a net book value at present of $15,000. The equipment is actually worth $18,000. It is traded along with cash of $12,000 for a truck that has a value of $30,400. What is the company's reported gain or loss on this exchange?

    a. $3,000 gain

    b. $3,000 loss

    c. $3,400 gain

    d. $3,400 loss

12. The Bristol Corporation buys equipment on January 1, Year One, for $50,000. It has a ten-year life and an expected residual value of $5,000. The double-declining balance method of determining depreciation is applied. The equipment actually loses exactly 10 percent of its initial value every year. On January 1, Year Three, this equipment is traded for some new machinery that has a fair value of $42,000. At what amount should this new machinery be recorded by Bristol?

    a. $28,800

    b. $32,000

    c. $40,000

    d. $42,000

13. At the beginning of Year Three, the Kelvin Company owned equipment that appeared on its balance sheet with a cost of $7 million and accumulated depreciation of $2 million. The equipment was purchased two years earlier and assigned a useful life of six years. The estimated residual value was $1 million. At the beginning of Year Three, Kelvin made several modifications to the equipment that increased its remaining useful life from four years to five years. No other changes occurred as a result of these modifications. Their cost was $50,000. What is the balance in the accumulated depreciation account on December 31, Year Three?

    a. $2,000,000

    b. $2,760,000

    c. $2,810,000

    d. $3,000,000

14. The Winslett Company buys a retail store on January 1, Year One, with a ten-year life and a cost of $800,000. No residual value is anticipated. Straight-line depreciation is used. The building was bought because the company believed that it could generate post-cash flows of $98,000 per year. On January 1, Year Four, a new road is opened in the area that takes much of the traffic away from the store. For the remainder of its life, the company only expects to generate a positive cash flow of $82,000 per year. An appraisal is made that indicates the building has a fair value of only $480,000. What recording should be made on that date for this building?

    a. No change should be made.

    b. A loss of $77,000 is recognized.

    c. A loss of $80,000 is recognized.

    d. A loss of $82,000 is recognized.

15. On January 1, Year One, the Capricorn Corporation borrows money on a loan paying 9 percent interest each year. The money is used to construct a new building, which takes exactly one year to complete. The building has a twenty-year expected life with no residual value. In determining net income for Year One, which of the following statements is true?

    a. Neither interest expense nor depreciation expense is recognized in Year One.

    b. Both interest expense and depreciation expense are recognized in Year One.

    c. Interest expense is recognized in Year One but not depreciation expense.

    d. Depreciation expense is recognized in Year One but not interest expense.

VIDEO PROBLEMS

Professor Joe Hoyle discusses the answers to these two problems at the links that are indicated. After formulating your answers, watch each video to see how Professor Hoyle answers these questions.

1. Your roommate is an English major. The roommate's parents own a chain of ice cream shops throughout Florida. One day, while packing to go home on spring break, your roommate poses this question: "My parents have always rented their store locations. However, last year, they built their first standalone shop in Orlando. It has been doing great business, but I know they spent a lot of money to build it. They have been talking recently about the depreciation making the first-year results look bad for that shop. I am not sure what they are talking about. The shop looks better than ever. It hasn't depreciated at all. In fact, the value of that facility has probably gone up. What is this depreciation, and why has it hurt the reported results for the shop in Orlando?" How would you respond?

View the video online at: http://bit.ly/hoyle10-3

2. Your uncle and two friends started a small office supply store several years ago. The company has expanded and now has several large locations. Your uncle knows that you are taking a financial accounting class and asks you the following question: "We bought one of our facilities too far from our other stores. We thought it was a good idea at the time. The store does well, but we have trouble managing it and keeping it stocked with merchandise because of the distance. It is a valuable asset, but it does not fit in with our future plans. Another company has come up to us and offered to trade a large warehouse near our headquarters for that store. The warehouse is actually worth slightly more than the store, but the other company would really like to have a store at that location. And, we could use the warehouse space. We are inclined to make the exchange, but we want to have a careful understanding of how this transaction might impact our financial statements. We don't want to do anything that would make us look bad. We don't want to scare our creditors. How would we record such a swap?" How would you respond?

View the video online at: http://bit.ly/hoyle10-4

PROBLEMS

1. Equipment was bought by a company on January 1, Year One, for $40,000. It had an expected useful life of five years and a $5,000 residual value. Unfortunately, at the time of purchase, an error was made. The accountant debited supplies expense for $40,000 and credited cash. No adjusting entry was ever made. At the end of Year One, the company reported net income of $100,000 and total assets of $300,000. What should those reported figures have been under each of the following situations?

   a. The company uses the straight-line method to depreciate all equipment.

   b. The company uses the double-declining balance method to depreciate all equipment.

2. Company X and Company Y are identical in every way except as follows. On August 1, Year One, both companies buy machinery with a cost of $80,000 and an estimated residual value of $10,000. The equipment has an expected useful life of ten years. Both companies use the half-year convention. Company X reported net income for Year One of $160,000. Company X used the straight-line method of determining depreciation expense. What would have been the reported net income for Company Y if it applied the double-declining balance method?

3. On January 1, Year One, the Sanborn Corporation buys a donut maker for $10,000 that has a ten-year estimated life and an estimated residual value of $1,000. The donut maker is expected to produce a total of 100,000 dozen donuts over its life. In Year One, 13,000 dozen are produced and, in Year Two, 11,000 dozen are produced.

   a. If the straight-line method of depreciation is applied, what appears in the Year One and in the Year Two financial statements in connection with this donut maker?

   b. If the double-declining balance method of depreciation is applied, what appears in the Year One and in the Year Two financial statements in connection with this donut maker?

   c. If the units-of-production method of depreciation is applied, what appears in the Year One and in the Year Two financial statements in connection with this donut maker?

   d. Based on the answers to the previous questions, what is the fair value of the donut maker at the end of Year Two?

   e. Which of these depreciation methods provides the fairest representation of the donut maker and its use?

   f. If the donut maker is sold on October 1, Year Three, depreciation must be recorded for the period from the beginning of the year until the sale. What are the two reasons that this recording is necessary?

   g. Assume the straight-line method is used, and the donut maker is sold on October 1, Year Three, for $7,100 in cash. What journal entry is recorded for the sale? Assume that the half-year convention is not in use.

   h. How is the journal entry in problem 3.g. impacted if the half-year convention is being used for any period of time of less than a full year?

4. Company A and Company Z both bought buildings on January 1, Year One, for $700,000 in cash. They each spent an additional $60,000 in connection with their buildings. Company A believed the $60,000 expenditure was normal and necessary to get the building into the condition to generate revenue. Company Z did not believe that cost was normal and necessary. Both companies use straight-line depreciation and believe the buildings have a ten-year life with a residual value of $50,000. What will be the difference in the reported net income of these two companies for Year One? What will be the difference in the reported net income of these two companies for Year Two?

5. On April 1, Year One, Chang and Chang Inc. invested in a new machine to manufacture soccer balls. The machine is expected to manufacture 1.4 million soccer balls over its life of three years and then be scrapped. The machine cost $50,000 including the normal and necessary costs of setting it up. The units-of-production method is used to depreciate the machine.

   a. Record depreciation for Year One and Year Two assuming that 450,000 soccer balls were manufactured and sold in Year One and 600,000 were manufactured and sold in Year Two.

   b. On January 1, Year Three, Chang and Chang decides to get out of the soccer ball production business and sells the machine for $15,000 in cash. Record this journal entry.

6. Springfield Corporation purchases a new machine on March 3, Year One, for $35,600 in cash. It pays an additional $3,400 to transport and set up the machine. Springfield's accountant determines that the equipment has no residual value and that the useful life is five years. It is expected to generate 2.4 million units during its life. If applicable, assume that Springfield employs the half-year convention.

   a. Record the purchase of the machine.

   b. Assume that Springfield uses the straight-line method of depreciation. Record depreciation expense for the first two years of the machine's life.

    c. Assume that Springfield uses the double-declining balance method of depreciation. Record depreciation expense for the first two years of the machine's life.

    d. Assume that Springfield uses the units-of-production method of depreciation. During Year One, the machine produces 600,000 units. During Year Two, the machine produces 578,000 units. Record depreciation expense for the first two years of the machine's life.

7. A company uses the half-year convention and buys equipment for $200,000 on December 1, Year One. The equipment has an expected life of ten years and a $40,000 anticipated residual value. The equipment is sold on March 1, Year Three, for $165,000 in cash.

    a. Make all the entries from December 1, Year One, to March 1, Year Three, for this equipment assuming that the double-declining balance method is in use.

    b. Make all the entries from December 1, Year One, to March 1, Year Three, for this equipment assuming that the straight-line method is in use.

8. The Huguenot Corporation buys equipment on October 1, Year One, for $120,000. It has an expected residual value of $30,000. The company expects to make use of it for ten years. The straight-line method of depreciation is applied but not the half-year convention. The equipment is sold on April 1, Year Three, for $107,000.

    What would have been the difference in reported net income for Year Three if the double-declining balance method had been used along with the half-year convention?

9. On January 1, Year One, the Oklahoma Corporation buys an oil well for $2 million in cash. The company believes that this well holds 400,000 barrels in crude oil. However, the oil well will have no residual value after the oil has been removed. In Year One, the company pumps out 100,000 barrels and sells 70,000 barrels for $19 per barrel. In Year Two, the company pumps out another 50,000 barrels but sells a total of 60,000 barrels for $20 per barrel.

    Make the necessary journal entries.

10. Markov Corporation owns forests that are harvested with the wood sold to papermaking companies. Markov purchases a new tract of forest on January 1, Year One, for $360,000. Company officials estimate that 4,000 tons of wood can be harvested from the forest and sold. After that, the land will be worth about $20,000.

    a. In Year One, 2,500 tons of wood are harvested, and 2,200 are sold for $120 per ton. Make any necessary journal entries.

    b. In Year Two, the remaining 1,500 tons of wood are harvested, and then 1,800 tons are sold for $120 per ton. Make any necessary journal entries.

11. The Watson Company buys a truck on February 3, Year One, for $53,000 with a six-year life and a $5,000 estimated residual value. The half-year convention is used along with straight-line depreciation. On May 23, Year Three, the truck is traded for a different style of truck. The old truck had a fair value of $40,000 at that time. The new truck had a fair value of $41,000. Because the dealer really wanted to make the trade, the $1,000 difference in the two fair values was ignored. What journal entry does the Watson Company make to record this trade?

12. The Ferrum Company acquired a large machine for $360,000 in cash on January 1, Year One. Straight-line depreciation is going to be recorded over an expected life of ten years. The asset has an estimated residual value of $20,000. In reality, this machine lost $60,000 of its value each year. On the first day of Year Three, the asset was traded for another machine with a fair value of $254,000. What journal entry does Ferrum prepare to record this exchange?

13. Gameplay Company operates in mall locations and sells videogame equipment and games. The company purchased furniture and fixtures to use in one of its stores for $440,000 on January 1, Year One. The furniture and fixtures were being depreciated using the straight-line method over ten years with a residual value of $10,000. Near the end of December, Year Five, Gameplay decided to close this location and entered into an exchange agreement with Allero Corporation. Allero agreed to give Gameplay vehicles with a fair value of $200,000 and cash of $50,000 in exchange for the furniture and fixtures from this store. The furniture and fixtures have an estimated fair value of $250,000 on the date of exchange.

    a. Make the depreciation entry for the furniture and fixtures necessary in December Year Five, assuming that no entries have been made during the year.

    b. Determine the net book value of the furniture and fixtures on the date of exchange.

    c. Record the journal entry Gameplay makes to record this exchange.

14. The Milan Corporation owns a building that it has used for a number of years. At the start of the current year, the building has a cost of $1.5 million and accumulated depreciation of $600,000. Straight line depreciation has been used with no expected residual value. The asset was originally assumed to have a thirty-year life, and twelve years have now passed.

Assume that each of the following situations is entirely independent. For each, prepare the appropriate journal entry and determine the amount of depreciation expense that should be reported for the current year.

    a. The company spends $22,000 in cash to paint the building. When the company bought the building originally, officials had anticipated that it would need to be painted periodically in order to last for thirty years.

    b. The company spends $80,000 to add a new room at the back of the building.

    c. The company spends $35,000 to fix a rotten space on the roof which was beginning to leak. Officials had not expected that the roof would rot.

    d. The company spends $30,000 on a new type of foundation improvement. Officials had not expected to do this but now believe the building will last for an additional five years because of this work.

15. The Monster Cookie Company buys a machine to make cookies on January 1, Year One. It costs $500,000 but has a $100,000 residual value and an expected life of ten years. Straight-line depreciation is to be applied. On January 1, Year Three, the company makes two changes to this machine. First, $30,000 is spent to add an attachment so that the company can make two types of cookies rather than just one. Second, the company spends $40,000 so that the machine will last five years longer than originally anticipated.

    In connection with this machine, what figures are reported on the company's financial statements for Year Three?

16. The Romo Corporation buys equipment for $190,000 on January 1, Year One. It has a twelve-year life and an expected residual value of $40,000. Straight-line depreciation is being applied. At the start of Year Three, the company spends $40,000 on this equipment to make it more effective at generating revenue (more widgets can be produced each period, and they will be of a better quality). This added cost did not extend the life of the asset or impact its residual value. Make all journal entries and adjusting entries for Year Three.

17. On June 30, Partyplace, a popular spot for receptions and other events, purchased a used limousine and a used Hummer from a car dealership. The company received a good deal because it was willing to buy both vehicles, paying a total of only $75,000. The market values were $45,000 for the limousine and $40,000 for the Hummer.

    a. Record the purchase of the vehicles.

    b. During the year, Partyplace performed maintenance on the vehicles (oil changes and the like) that amounted to $600. Record this expenditure.

    c. During the year, Partyplace made some modifications to the limo that should make it more appealing to its customers, thus, in effect, increasing its ability to generate revenues. These modifications cost $4,000. Record this expenditure.

18. An asset is bought for $360,000 on the first day of Year One. The life of this asset is ten years. There is no expected residual value. Straight-line depreciation is used for this asset but not the half-year convention. Subsequently, on the first day of Year Three, the asset is worth $240,000. On that day, company officials estimate that this asset will generate positive cash flows of $35,000 per year for the rest of its useful life. At what net book value should the asset be reported at that time?

19. The Randolph Corporation owns a building in Waynesboro, Arkansas, that originally cost $2 million. At the current time, this building has a net book value of $900,000 and a remaining useful life of ten years with no expected residual value. However, the company no longer uses the building for manufacturing purposes, so its fair value has fallen to only $576,000. To generate some revenue from the building, several rooms are rented out to other businesses as warehouse space. In each of the following questions, should the company recognize an impairment loss? If so, how much loss should be recognized?

    a. The cash received from the rental income is $86,000 per year and is expected to last for the remaining life of the building.

    b. The cash received from the rental income is $93,000 per year and is expected to last for the remaining life of the building.

20. Fairfield Inc. invested in a plant to manufacture "Jphones," thinking these devices would be the next "big thing." Unfortunately, things did not work out so well for the Jphone.

    a. Fairfield purchased the plant on March 1, Year One, for $46,790,000. Additional costs to get the facility up and running amounted to $3,780,000. Fairfield assigned a thirty-year useful life to the asset. The expected residual value is $4 million for the building. Fairfield uses the double-declining balance method. Record the acquisition of the plant and depreciation for the first three years, assuming that Fairfield does not use the half-year convention.

b. On December 31, Year Three, Fairfield's auditors raise concerns that the plant's market value might be below its net book value due to the failure of the Jphone to gain market share. The auditors believe this decline is permanent and decide to test for impairment. The accountants and auditors agree that the plant will generate net cash flows of approximately $2 million each year but only for the next fifteen years. Perform a test of recoverability on the plant.

c. Assume that the auditors determine that the plant's expected future cash flows are below its net book value. The company must now perform the fair value test. Several appraisers are called in, and the average fair value is $15,600,000. Determine if Fairfield must record an impairment loss and, if so, determine the amount.

21. Company A borrows $4 million on January 1, Year One, and uses the money to buy a retail store in Trenton, New Jersey. The store opens immediately and starts to make sales. The annual interest rate on the debt is 6 percent with payments made every December 31. The building has a twenty-year expected life and no residual value. Straight-line depreciation is used.

Company Z also borrows $4 million on January 1, Year One, but uses the money to construct a store in Reno, Nevada, that is exactly like the store owned by Company A. Construction takes one year, and the store is opened for business on January 1, Year Two. The annual interest rate is 6 percent, and the building is expected to last twenty years with no anticipated residual value. Straight-line depreciation is used.

On Year Two financial statements, how will the balances be different between the reporting by Company A and the reporting by Company Z?

COMPREHENSIVE PROBLEM

This problem will carry through over several chapters to enable students to build their accounting skills using knowledge gained in previous chapters.

In Chapter 9, financial statements were prepared for Webworks for September 30, and the month then ended. Those financial statements are included here as a starting point for the financial reporting for October.

FIGURE 10.19

Webworks Income Statement As of September 30	
Revenue	$11,400
Cost of Goods Sold	(5,315)
Gross Profit	6,085
Other Expenses	(3,435)
Earnings before Tax	2,650
Tax Expense	(795)
Net Income	$1,855

FIGURE 10.20

Webworks Stmt. of Retained Earnings As of September 30	
Retained Earnings, September 1	$2,790
Net Income	1,855
Retained Earnings, September 30	$4,645

FIGURE 10.21

Webworks
Balance Sheet
September 30

Assets			Liabilities		
Current			**Current**		
Cash		$3,300	Accounts Payable		$1,285
Accounts Receivable		1,750	Salaries Payable		300
Less Allowance for			Unearned Revenue		100
Doubtful Accounts		(175)			
Net Accounts Receivable		1,575			
Merchandise Inventory		1,385			
Supplies Inventory		70			
Total Current Assets		$6,330	Total Current Liabilities		$1,685
Noncurrent			**Noncurrent**		
Equipment		$7,000	Notes Payable		$5,000
			Owners' Equity		
			Capital Stock		$2,000
			Retained Earnings		4,645
			Total Owners' Equity		$6,645
			Total Liabilities & Owners'		
Total Assets		$13,330	Equity		$13,330

The following events occur during October:

a. Webworks purchases supplies worth $100 on account.

b. Webworks paid $600 in rent for October, November, and December.

c. At the beginning of October, Webworks had nine keyboards costing $105 each and forty flash drives costing $11 each. Webworks uses periodic FIFO to cost its inventory.

d. On account, Webworks purchases fifty keyboards for $110 each and 100 flash drives for $12 each.

e. Webworks starts and completes seven more sites and bills clients for $3,900.

f. Webworks pays Nancy Po $700 for her work during the first three weeks of October.

g. Webworks sells 50 keyboards for $7,500 and 110 flash drives for $2,200 cash.

h. The Web site paid for in August and started in September was completed. The client originally paid the entire $100 in advance.

i. Webworks paid off the remainder of its note payable.

j. Webworks collects $4,000 in accounts receivable.

k. Webworks pays off its salaries payable from September.

l. Webworks pays off $6,000 of its accounts payable.

m. One Web site client is dissatisfied with the work done and refuses to pay his bill. Rather than incur the expense of taking the client to court, Webworks writes off the $200 account as uncollectible.

n. Webworks pays Leon Jackson (the owner of this business) a salary of $2,000.

o. Webworks purchased office furniture on account for $1,000, including transportation and setup.

p. Webworks pays taxes of $868 in cash.

Required:

    A. Prepare journal entries for the previous events.

    B. Post the journal entries to T-accounts.

    C. Prepare an unadjusted trial balance for Webworks for October.

    D. Prepare adjusting entries for the following and post them to your T-accounts.

q. Webworks owes Nancy Po $100 for her work during the last week of October.

r. Leon's parents let him know that Webworks owes $300 toward the electricity bill. Webworks will pay them in November.

s. Webworks determines that it has $50 worth of supplies remaining at the end of October.

t. Prepaid rent should be adjusted for October's portion.

u. Webworks is continuing to accrue bad debts at 10 percent of accounts receivable.

v. A CPA tells Leon that Webworks should be depreciating its equipment and furniture. The CPA recommends that Webworks use the straight-line method with a four-year life for the equipment and a five-year life for the furniture. Since Webworks is only generating these monthly statements for internal information, the CPA recommends that Leon just "catch up" the prior month's depreciation on the equipment this month. So when Webworks records October's equipment depreciation, it will also record the deprecation that should have been taken in July, August and September. The depreciation on the furniture should just be for one month. Round to the nearest whole number.

w. Record cost of goods sold.

    E. Prepare an adjusted trial balance.

    F. Prepare financial statements for October.

RESEARCH ASSIGNMENT

Assume that you take a job as a summer employee for an investment advisory service. One of the partners for that firm is currently looking at the possibility of investing in **DuPont** (official name is **E. I. Du Pont de Nemours and Company**). The partner knows that this manufacturing company has been in business for many years and wonders about the age of its property and equipment. The partner asks you to look at the 2011 financial statements for **DuPont** by following this path:

- Go to investors.dupont.com.
- At the bottom of this screen, click on "SEC Filings."
- In the "Groupings Filter," click on "Annual Filings."
- Scroll through the document tables until you find the 10-K form for 2011 (issued early in 2012).
- Go to page F-5 and find the balance sheet for December 31, 2011.
- Go to page F-9 and read the note to the financial statements titled "Property, Plant and Equipment."

a. Using the amounts reported on the 2011 balance sheet for property, plant, and equipment and accumulated depreciation, divide the net book value by the cost of the asset. What does the resulting percentage tell about the current age and utility of the company's property, plant, and equipment?

b. Using the information disclosed on page F-9, what method of depreciation is being used by **DuPont**? What is the age used by the company for depreciation purposes?

c. Combine the information found in a. and b. to arrive at an estimation of the age of the property, plant, and equipment held by **DuPont**.

ENDNOTES

1. As discussed in the coverage of accounts receivable and the allowance for doubtful accounts, an account that appears with another but as a direct reduction is known as a contra account. Accumulated depreciation is a contra account that decreases the reported cost of property and equipment to reflect the portion of that cost that has now be assigned to expense.

2. The estimated lives of property and equipment will vary widely. For example, in notes to its financial statements as of January 31, 2011, and for the year then ended, **Walmart** disclosed that the expected lives of its buildings and improvements ranged from three years to forty.

3. As mentioned previously, land does not have a finite life and is, therefore, not subjected to the recording of depreciation expense.

4. Accounting rules are created through a slow and meticulous process to avoid unintended consequences. For example, assume that Company A and Company B buy identical antique limousines for $30,000 that then appreciate in value to $100,000 because of their scarcity. Based solely on the accounting rule described in this section, if the two companies exchange these assets, each reports a gain of $70,000 while still retaining possession of an identical vehicle. This reporting is not appropriate because nothing has changed for either party. In reality, there was no gain since the companies retain the same financial position as before the trade. Thus, in creating the official guidance described previously, FASB held that an exchange must have commercial substance to justify using fair value. In simple terms, the asset acquired has to be different from the asset surrendered as demonstrated by the amount and timing of future cash flows. Without a difference, no rationale exists for making the exchange. If a trade does not have commercial substance, net book value is retained for the newly received asset and no gain is recognized.

5. Mechanically, an impairment loss for property and equipment could be calculated in any one of several ways. FASB established these two tests. Thus, according to U.S. GAAP, the recoverability test and the fair value test must be used when impairment is suspected. Some might argue that this process is not the best method for determining an impairment loss. Standardization, though, helps to better ensure universal understanding of the figures being reported.

6. As will be demonstrated in Chapter 11, present value is a method used to compute the current worth of a future stream of cash flows by removing the amount of those payments that can be mathematically attributed to interest.

7. As discussed in intermediate accounting textbooks, the full amount of interest is not actually capitalized here because the borrowed money is only tied up during the construction gradually. Until added to the project, all remaining funds can be used to generate revenues. However, for this introductory textbook, focus is on the need to capitalize interest because the decision to build defers the earning of revenue until the project is completed. Complete coverage of the rules to be applied can be obtained in an intermediate accounting textbook.

CHAPTER 11

In a Set of Financial Statements, What Information Is Conveyed about Intangible Assets?

 Video Clip

In this video, Professor Joe Hoyle introduces the essential points covered in Chapter 11.

View the video online at: http://bit.ly/hoyle11-1

1. IDENTIFYING AND ACCOUNTING FOR INTANGIBLE ASSETS

LEARNING OBJECTIVES

At the end of this section, students should be able to meet the following objectives:

1. List the characteristics of intangible assets and provide several common examples.
2. Understand that intangible assets are becoming more important to businesses and, hence, are gaining increased attention in financial accounting.
3. Record the acquisition of an intangible asset.
4. Describe the amortization process for intangible assets.
5. Explain the accounting used to report an intangible asset that has increased in value since acquisition.

1.1 The Rise in the Importance of Intangible Assets

intangible asset

An asset lacking physical substance that is expected to help generate revenues for more than one year; common examples are patents, copyrights, and trademarks.

Question: Not so many years ago, the balance sheets of most large companies disclosed significant amounts of property and equipment but considerably smaller figures for intangible assets. *Businesses were often referred to as "bricks and mortar" operations because much of their money was invested in buildings and the long-lived tangible assets that were housed in those buildings.*

Today, the basic nature of many corporate operations has changed dramatically. As of June 30, 2011, **Microsoft Corporation** *reported a total of $13.3 billion for its "goodwill" and "intangible assets, net" versus only $8.2 billion in "property and equipment, net of accumulated depreciation." For* **Yahoo! Inc.,** *the difference is similarly striking. On December 31, 2010,* **Yahoo!** *disclosed $3.9 billion of "goodwill" and "intangible assets, net" but a mere $1.7 billion in "property and equipment, net."*

The rise in the number, value, and importance of intangible assets might well be the biggest change experienced in the reporting of businesses over the last ten to twenty years. The sudden growth of Internet and technology companies like **Microsoft** *and* **Yahoo!** *has focused attention on the significance of ideas and innovation (rather than bricks and mortar) for achieving profits.*

Financial accounting rules must evolve as the nature of business moves forward over time. Not surprisingly, considerable debate has taken place recently concerning the methods by which intangible assets are reported in a set of financial statements. A relatively minor topic in the past has gained a genuine level of importance in today's accounting conversations. Should an idea or an invention be reported in the same manner as a building or a machine? For financial accounting, that is a very important question. As a starting point for this discussion, the basic nature of an intangible asset needs to be understood. **What is an intangible asset and what are common examples?**

amortization

A mechanically derived pattern allocating the cost of an intangible asset to expense over the shorter of the legal life or estimated useful life; it is the equivalent of depreciation but relates to intangible assets.

copyright

An intangible asset that provides the owner with the right to use literary, dramatic, musical, artistic, and certain other intellectual works.

Answer: As the title implies, an intangible asset is one that lacks physical substance. It cannot be touched but is expected to provide future benefits for longer than one year. More specifically, it will assist the reporting company in generating revenues in the future. Except for a few slight variations, intangible assets are reported in the same manner as a building or equipment. For example, historical cost serves as the basis for reporting. If the intangible has a finite life, the depreciation process (although the term **amortization** is normally applied in reporting intangibles) reclassifies this cost from asset to expense over that estimated period.

U.S GAAP provides structure for the reporting process by placing all intangibles into six major categories:

1. Artistic-related (such as copyrights)
2. Technology-related (patents)
3. Marketing-related (trademarks)
4. Customer-related (a database of customer information)
5. Contract-related (franchises)
6. Goodwill

In all of these categories (except for goodwill, which will be explained later in this chapter), the intangible asset is actually an established right of usage. As an example, according to the Web site for the United States Copyright Office, a copyright provides its owner with the right to use "literary, dramatic, musical, artistic, and certain other intellectual works." Similarly, the United States Patent and

Trademark Office Web site explains that "a patent for an invention is the grant of a property right to the inventor." Thus, most intangible assets represent a legal right that helps the owner to generate revenues.

TEST YOURSELF

Question:

The Weddington Company reports a number of assets on its balance sheet. Which of the following should not be included as an intangible asset?

  a. Copyright

  b. Account receivable

  c. Patent

  d. Franchise

Answer:

The correct answer is choice b: Account receivable.

Explanation:

An intangible asset is one with no physical substance that provides a company with future benefit, usually a legal or contractual right, that helps to generate revenues for a period of over one year. Accounts receivable are not usually outstanding for that length of time and do not assist in the generation of future revenues. They help bring in cash that was earned in the past. Copyrights, patents, and franchises are rights that can be owned or controlled and are used to produce revenues.

1.2 The Acquisition of an Intangible

Question: Intangible assets are accounted for in a manner that is similar to property and equipment. To illustrate, assume that an automobile company is creating a series of television commercials for one of its new models. On January 1, Year One, the company pays $1 million cash to a famous musical group for the right to use a well-known song. The band holds the legal copyright on this piece of music and agrees to share that right with the automobile company so that the song can be played in one or more commercials. **What accounting is made by a company that acquires an intangible asset such as a copyright?**

Answer: The buyer of an intangible asset prepares a journal entry that is basically identical to the acquisition of inventory, land, or a machine. As with all those other assets, the intangible is recorded initially at historical cost.

FIGURE 11.1   January 1, Year One—Acquisition of Right to Use Copyrighted Song

| Copyright | 1,000,000 | |
| Cash | | 1,000,000 |

Many intangible assets have defined legal lives. For example, copyrights last for seventy years beyond the creator's life. Acquired intangibles (such as the copyright for this song) often have lives legally limited by contractual agreement. However, the true useful life of most intangibles is generally only a small number of years. Few intangibles manage to help a company generate revenues for decades. Amortization of the cost to expense should extend over the shorter of the asset's useful life or its legal life.

Assume that this piece of music is expected to be included by the automobile company in its television commercials for the next four years. After that, a different advertising campaign will likely be started. If the straight-line method is applied (which is normal for intangible assets), annual amortization of this copyright is $250,000 ($1 million cost/4 year life).

FIGURE 11.2 December 31, Year One—First Year Amortization of Copyright Cost

| Amortization Expense | 250,000 | |
| Copyright | | 250,000 |

At the end of the first year, the copyright appears on the automobile company's balance sheet as $750,000, the remainder of its historical cost. As can be seen in Figure 11.2, the credit in this adjusting entry is a direct decrease in the asset account. Although establishing a separate contra account (such as accumulated amortization) is permitted, most companies simply reduce the intangible asset balance because the utility is literally shrinking. Depreciation of a building or equipment does not mean that the asset is getting smaller. A four-story building remains a four-story building throughout its life. Reducing the building account directly is not a reflection of reality. In contrast, the right to use this song does get smaller over time. The automobile company went from holding a copyright to play this music in its commercials for an expected four years to a copyright that will likely only be used for three more years. A direct reduction of the cost is more appropriate.

1.3   Intangible Assets and Fair Value

*Question: In this example, the automobile company acquired the right to use this music for $1 million. That was historical cost, the figure to be reported for intangible assets on the company's balance sheet. The number was objectively determined and the accounting straightforward. However, the artist who originally created the music (or his or her recording company) still holds the original copyright. As indicated by the sale, the rights to this music are extremely valuable. **How does the creator report an intangible asset such as a copyright?** Should the copyright to this piece of music now be reported by the artist at its proven value of $1 million?*

Answer: Depending on the specific terms of the contract, the creator often continues to possess the copyright and maintains that asset on its own balance sheet. In many cases, the original artist only conveys permission to a buyer to use this music (or other intellectual work) for specific purposes or a set period of time. However, the copyright is not adjusted on the creator's books to this $1 million value; rather, it remains at historical cost less any amortization to date. That is the reporting basis for intangible assets according to U.S. GAAP in the same way as for land, buildings, and equipment. The figure shown on the balance sheet is not increased to reflect a rise in fair value.

The reported amount shown for copyrights and other similar intangibles contains all normal and necessary costs such as attorney fees and money spent for legal filings made with appropriate authorities. Subsequently, such intangible assets sometimes become the subject of lawsuits if other parties assert claims to the same ideas and creations. The cost of a successful defense is also capitalized and then amortized over the shorter of the remaining legal life or estimated useful life of the asset. If the defense proves unsuccessful, the remaining asset balance is written off as a loss.

TEST YOURSELF

Question:

John Doe successfully creates an invention and, on January 1, Year One, receives a patent that gives him the exclusive rights to that invention for twenty years. One year later, John Doe sells all of his rights to the patent to Nahquan Corporation for $3 million. Nahquan pays another $400,000 to a legal firm to help ensure that the right is properly transferred. Nahquan hopes to use the patent for five years and then sell it for $200,000. On December 31, Year Two, another company offers to pay Nahquan $4 million for this intangible asset but that amount is rejected as being too low. On its balance sheet at that time, what balance is reported by Nahquan for the patent?

a. $2,560,000

b. $2,760,000

c. $3,040,000

d. $3,221,053

Answer:

The correct answer is choice b: $2,760,000.

Explanation:

The capitalized cost of this asset is $3.4 million—the normal and necessary amount to acquire the patent so that it can be used to generate revenues. Annual amortization is $640,000 ([$3.4 million less $200,000 residual value] divided by five-year life). After one year, reported value is $2,760,000 ($3.4 million less $640,000). The $4 million offer does not affect the balance since it was not accepted. Amortized historical cost is the basis for financial reporting unless the value is impaired.

Talking With an Independent Auditor about International Financial Reporting Standards

Following is a continuation of our interview with Robert A. Vallejo, partner with the accounting firm **PricewaterhouseCoopers**.

Question: Under U.S. GAAP, intangible assets with a finite life are reported at historical cost less any accumulated amortization recognized to date. Except in impairment cases, fair value is ignored completely. How are intangible assets reported when IFRS standards are applied?

Robert Vallejo: Unless a company chooses to revalue its intangible assets regularly (an option that is available under IFRS but that is rarely chosen because the process must then be done every reporting period), the accounting under U.S. GAAP and IFRS is basically the same. After initial recognition under IFRS, intangible assets are carried at cost less accumulated amortization (as well as any impairment losses). If an active market is available, similar intangible assets can then be adjusted to fair value but, again, that value must be updated each reporting period. Per IAS 38, *Intangible Assets*, the method of amortization that is used should reflect the pattern in which the asset's future economic benefits are expected to be realized by the entity. If that pattern cannot be determined reliably, the straight-line method of amortization must be used.

KEY TAKEAWAY

The financial reporting of intangible assets has grown in significance in recent years because of the prevalence and success of businesses in industries such as technology and electronics. For the most part, intangible assets provide the owner with a legal right to use an idea, invention, artistic creation, or the like. Copyrights, patents, and trademarks are common examples. An intangible is recorded initially at historical cost. Most of these assets have a finite life, so the cost is then amortized to expense over the shorter of the legal life or estimated useful life. Consequently, intangible assets appear on the owner's balance sheet at net book value. Amortization is usually reflected as a direct reduction in the asset balance rather than indirectly through a separate contra account. Other than this difference, accounting for intangibles resembles that used with property and equipment so that, for example, increases in value are not reported.

2. BALANCE SHEET REPORTING OF INTANGIBLE ASSETS

2.1 Reporting Historical Cost for Intangible Assets Rather Than Fair Value

Question: Much was made in earlier chapters about the importance of painting a portrait that fairly presents the financial health and future prospects of an organization. Many companies develop copyrights and other intangible assets that have incredible value but little or no actual cost.

*Trademarks provide an excellent example. The golden arches that represent **McDonald's** must be worth many millions, but the original design cost was probably not significant and has likely been amortized entirely to expense by now. Could the balance sheet of **McDonald's** possibly be considered fairly presented if the value of its primary trademark is omitted?*

*Many other companies, such as **Walt Disney**, **UPS**, **Google**, **Apple**, **Coca-Cola**, and **Nike**, rely on trademarks to help create awareness and brand loyalty around the world. **Are a company's reported assets not understated if the value of a trademark is ignored despite serving as a recognizable symbol to millions of potential customers?** With property and equipment, this concern is not as pronounced because those assets tend to have significant costs whether bought or constructed. Internally developed trademarks and other intangibles often have little actual cost despite the possibility of gaining immense value.*

Answer: Figures reported for intangible assets such as trademarks may indeed be vastly understated on a company's balance sheet when compared to fair values. Decision makers who rely on financial statements need to understand what they are seeing. U.S. GAAP requires that companies follow the historical cost principle in reporting many assets. A few exceptions do exist, and several are examined at various points in this textbook. For example, historical cost may have to be abandoned when applying the lower-of-cost-or-market rule to inventory. The same is true when testing property and equipment for possible impairment losses. Those departures from historical cost were justified because the asset had lost value and financial accounting tends to be conservative. Reporting an asset at a balance in excess of its historical cost basis is much less common.

In financial accounting, what is the rationale for the prevalence of historical cost, which some might say was an obsession? As discussed in earlier chapters, cost can be reliably and objectively determined. It does not fluctuate from day to day throughout the year. It is based on an agreed-upon exchange price and reflects a resource allocation judgment made by management. Cost is not a guess, so it is less open to manipulation. Although fair value may appear to be more relevant, various parties might arrive at significantly different estimates of worth. What is the true value of the golden arches to **McDonald's** as a trademark? Is it $100 million or $10 billion? Six appraisals from six experts could suggest six largely different amounts.

Plus, if the asset is not going to be sold, is the fair value of much relevance at the current time?

Cost remains the basis for reporting many assets in financial accounting, though the use of fair value has gained considerable momentum. It is not that one way is right and one way is wrong. Instead, decision makers need to understand that historical cost is the generally accepted accounting principle normally used to report long-lived assets such as intangibles. The use of historical cost does have obvious flaws, primarily that it fails to report any appreciation in value no matter how significant. Unfortunately, any alternative number that can be put forth as a replacement also has its own set of problems.

At the present time, authoritative accounting literature holds that historical cost is the appropriate basis for reporting intangibles.

Even though fair value accounting seems quite appealing to many decision makers, accountants have proceeded slowly because of potential concerns. For example, the 2001 collapse of **Enron Corporation** was the most widely discussed accounting scandal to occur in recent decades. Many of **Enron's** reporting problems began when the company got special permission (due to the unusual nature of its business) to report a number of assets at fair value (a process referred to as "mark to market").[1] Because fair value was not easy to determine for many of those assets, **Enron** officials were able to manipulate reported figures to make the company appear especially strong and profitable.[2] Investors then flocked to the company only to lose billions when **Enron** eventually filed for bankruptcy. A troubling incident of this magnitude makes accountants less eager to embrace the reporting of fair value except in circumstances where very legitimate amounts can be determined. For intangible assets as well as property and equipment, fair value is rarely so objective that the possibility of manipulation can be eliminated.

TEST YOURSELF

Question:

The Consetti Company acquires a patent for $932,000 to be used in its daily operations. However, the value of this patent rises dramatically so that three years later, it is worth $3.2 million. Which of the following is not a reason that this fair value is ignored when the asset is reported on the Consetti's balance sheet?

a. Investors are not interested in the fair value of the patent or other intangible assets.

b. Fair value can change often so that any one figure is not necessarily relevant for a long period of time.

c. Different fair values might be estimated by different people.

d. Noncurrent assets are acquired to help generate revenues and not for resale purposes.

Answer:

The correct answer is choice a: Investors are not interested in the fair value of the patent or other intangible assets.

Explanation:

Investors are likely to be interested in the fair value of all company assets because that information helps to assess the worth of the company and, hence, the possible sales price of its stock. However, accounting rules shy away from use of fair value for property and equipment as well as intangible assets. That value is no more than a guess and it can swing radically over time. Plus, if the asset is not for sale, fair value is not particularly relevant to the operations of the company.

2.2 Acquiring a Company to Gain Control of Its Intangibles

*Question: Although a historical cost basis is used for intangible assets rather than fair value, **Microsoft Corporation** still reports $13.3 billion as "goodwill and intangible assets, net" while **Yahoo!** indicates similar balance sheet accounts totaling $3.9 billion. Even the size of these numbers is not particularly unusual for intangible assets in today's economic environment. As of June 30, 2011, for example, the balance sheet for **Procter & Gamble** listed goodwill of $57.6 billion and trademarks and other intangible assets, net of $32.6 billion. If historical cost is often insignificant, how do companies manage to report such immense monetary amounts for their intangible assets?*

Answer: Two possible reasons exist for a company's intangible asset figures to grow to incredible size. First, instead of being internally developed, assets such as copyrights and patents are often acquired from outside owners. Reported asset balances then represent the historical costs of these purchases which were based on fair value at the time of the transaction. Large payments may be necessary to acquire such rights if their value has already been firmly established.

Second, **Microsoft, Yahoo!**, and **Procter & Gamble** could have bought one or more entire companies so that title to a multitude of assets (including a possible plethora of intangibles) was obtained in a single transaction. In fact, such acquisitions often occur specifically because one company wants to gain valuable intangibles owned by another. In February 2008, **Microsoft** offered over $44 billion in hopes of purchasing **Yahoo!** for exactly that reason. **Yahoo!** certainly did not hold property and equipment worth $44 billion. **Microsoft** was primarily interested in acquiring a wide variety of intangibles owned by **Yahoo!** Although this proposed takeover was never completed, the sheer size of the bid demonstrates the staggering value of the intangible assets that companies often possess today.

If a company buys a single intangible asset directly from its owner, the financial reporting follows the pattern previously described. Whether the asset is a trademark, franchise, copyright, patent, or the like, it is reported at the amount paid. That cost is then amortized over the shorter of its estimated useful life or legal life. Intangible assets that do not have finite lives are not amortized and will be discussed later in this chapter.

Reporting the assigned cost of intangible assets acquired when one company (often referred to as "the parent") buys another company ("the subsidiary") is a complex issue discussed in more detail in Chapter 12. In simple terms, the subsidiary's assets (inventory, land, buildings, equipment and the like) are valued and recorded at that amount by the parent as the new owner. The subsidiary's assets and liabilities are consolidated with those of the parent. In this process, each intangible asset held by the subsidiary that meets certain requirements is identified and recorded by the parent at its fair value. The assumption is that a portion of the price conveyed to purchase the subsidiary is being paid to obtain these intangible assets.

To illustrate, assume Big Company pays $10 million in cash to buy all the capital stock of Little Company. Consolidated financial statements will now be necessary. Little owns three intangibles (perhaps a copyright, patent, and trademark) that are each worth $1 million. Little also holds land worth $7 million but has no liabilities. Little's previous net book value for these assets is not relevant to Big, the new owner.

Following the takeover of Little, Big reports each of the intangibles on its balance sheet at its cost of $1 million (and the land at $7 million). The acquisition price is assumed to be the historical cost paid by Big to obtain these assets. A parent that buys many subsidiaries will frequently report large intangible asset balances as a result. When Big purchases Little Company, it is really gaining control of all these assets and records the transaction as shown in Figure 11.3.

FIGURE 11.3 Big Company Buys Little Company, Which Holds Assets with These Values

Copyright	1,000,000	
Patents	1,000,000	
Trademarks	1,000,000	
Land	7,000,000	
Cash		10,000,000

TEST YOURSELF

Question:

The Tiny Company creates a logo for a product line and gets a copyright on it. The entire cost is $40,000, and the logo is expected to have a useful life of ten years. One year later, Gigantic Company buys all the ownership stock of Tiny Company. At that point in time, the logo has gained national prominence and is thought to be worth $400,000. If Gigantic prepares a consolidated balance sheet immediately after acquiring Tiny, what is reported for this logo?

a. $36,000

b. $400,000

c. $436,000

d. $440,000

Answer:

The correct answer is choice b: $400,000.

Explanation:

Because Gigantic bought Tiny, the assumption is made that a portion of the price that was paid for Tiny was made to acquire the logo at its fair value. Thus, to Gigantic, the historic cost of this asset is $400,000. The cost to Tiny is no longer relevant. The $400,000 will then be amortized to expense over the remaining life of the intangible.

3. RECOGNIZING INTANGIBLE ASSETS OWNED BY A SUBSIDIARY

LEARNING OBJECTIVES

At the end of this section, students should be able to meet the following objectives:

1. Understand that only subsidiary intangible assets that meet either of two specific criteria are recognized separately by a parent following an acquisition.
2. Explain the meaning of the asset goodwill.
3. Compute and record the amount to be reported as goodwill on a consolidated balance sheet when a parent acquires another company as a subsidiary.
4. Understand that amounts attributed to goodwill are not amortized to expense but rather are checked periodically for impairment of value.

3.1 Criteria for Recognizing Intangible Assets

Question: Most major businesses report some amount of intangible assets. These can be developed internally, bought individually, or obtained as part of the purchase of an entire company. Larger amounts usually come from the acquisition of a subsidiary by a parent. The accountant faces the challenge of determining which costs to capitalize and which costs to expense. Because of their very nature, identifying intangible assets is more difficult than identifying tangible assets. A computer is obviously an asset, but is a list of client names inside of that computer also an asset?

*For example, when one company buys another, the subsidiary is often holding rights to numerous intangibles. As mentioned previously, company acquisitions often take place to gain those rights. The parent then places the assets that qualify on its balance sheet at fair value to show that a portion of the amount paid for the subsidiary was the equivalent of an acquisition price for these items. That is a major reason why companies such as **Microsoft** and **Procter & Gamble** report billions of dollars in intangibles. They have probably gained ownership of many of these assets by acquiring entire companies.*

*However, according to U.S. GAAP, certain requirements have to be met before intangibles are recognized as assets. **What criteria must be satisfied for a company to record an intangible as an asset?** A business could very well spend millions of dollars for scores of intangibles: patents, copyrights, databases, smart employees, loyal customers, logos, and the like. Which of these intangibles should actually be recognized on a balance sheet as an asset?*

Answer: The rules for reporting intangible assets are best demonstrated through the acquisition of a subsidiary by a parent because large amounts are often spent for numerous items that might qualify as assets. In establishing rules for consolidated financial statements, FASB has stated that a parent company must identify all intangible assets held by a subsidiary on the date of acquisition. The fair value of each of these intangibles is recorded by the parent as an asset but only if contractual or other legal rights have been gained or the intangible can be separated and sold. This authoritative guideline serves as a minimum standard for recognition of intangible assets:

1. Contractual or other legal rights have been gained or
2. The intangible can be separated from the subsidiary and sold

Patents, copyrights, trademarks, and franchises clearly meet the first of these criteria. Legal rights are held for patents, copyrights, and trademarks while contractual rights allow the owner to operate franchises. By acquiring the subsidiary, the parent now controls these same rights and should record them on the consolidated balance sheet at fair value.

Other intangibles that can be separated from the subsidiary and sold should also be consolidated at fair value. For example, an acquired company might have a database containing extensive information about its customers. After purchasing the subsidiary, this information could be separated from that company and sold. Thus, on the date the subsidiary is purchased, the parent recognizes this database as an intangible asset at fair value to reflect the portion of the acquisition price paid to obtain it.

TEST YOURSELF

Question:

Tree Company buys all the ownership stock of Leaf Company. Leaf holds one intangible worth $10,000, but it is not separately consolidated by Tree after the purchase. What is the most likely reason that this intangible was not included by the new parent?

a. Leaf owned the intangible rather than Tree.

b. The intangible did not have a finite life and, therefore, could not be viewed as an asset.

c. Leaf must sell the intangible directly to Tree before it can be reported by the parent.

d. Leaf did not have contractual or legal rights to the intangible and it could not be separated from the company and sold.

Answer:

The correct answer is choice d: Leaf did not have contractual or legal rights to the intangible and it could not be separated from the company and sold.

Explanation:

To be recognized as an intangible asset after a corporate takeover, FASB has set guidelines. Either the company must have contractual or legal rights in the intangible asset or it must be an item that could be separated from Leaf and sold. Without meeting one of these criteria, it is uncertain as to whether the subsidiary actually possesses something that will have value to the consolidated company.

3.2 Recognition of Goodwill

Question: When one company buys another, payment amounts will likely be negotiated to compensate the seller for intangibles where contractual or legal rights are held or where the asset can be separated and then sold. Thus, parent companies who buy subsidiaries (especially in industries such as technology) will likely recognize significant intangible asset balances on a subsequently consolidated balance sheet.

However, some intangibles have significant value but fail to meet either of these two criteria. Customer loyalty, for example, is vitally important to the future profitability of a business, but neither contractual nor legal rights are present and loyalty cannot be separated from a company and sold. Hence, customer loyalty is not reported as an intangible asset regardless of its worth. Much the same can be said for brilliant and creative employees. A value exists but neither rule for recognition is met.

During negotiations, the owners of a company that is being acquired will argue for a higher price if attributes such as these are in place because they provide increased profitability in the future. The amount paid to obtain a subsidiary can be impacted although these intangibles do not meet the criteria for separate reporting as assets. **How is this additional acquisition cost reported by the parent in producing consolidated financial statements?**

To illustrate, assume Giant Corporation pays $16 million to acquire Tiny Corporation. The subsidiary owns property and equipment worth $4 million. It also holds patents worth $6 million, a database worth $2 million, and copyrights worth $3 million. The total value of these four assets is only $15 million. For convenience, assume Tiny has no liabilities. Assume that Giant agrees to pay the extra $1 million because the subsidiary has customer loyalty valued at $600,000 and a talented workforce worth $400,000. How is this additional $1 million reported on consolidated financial statements after the takeover? What recording is appropriate when a parent buys a subsidiary and pays an extra amount because valuable intangibles are present that do not meet the criteria for separate reporting?

Answer: Every subsidiary intangible (such as patents, copyrights, and databases) that meets either of the official criteria is consolidated by the parent as an asset at fair value. Any excess price paid over the total fair value of these recorded assets (the extra $1 million in this example) is also reported as an asset. It has a definite cost and an expected future value. The term that has long been used to report an amount paid to acquire a company that exceeded all the identified and recorded assets is **goodwill**. Some amount of goodwill is recognized as a result of virtually all corporate acquisitions. In this example, it specifically reflects the value of the customer loyalty and the quality of the subsidiary's workforce.

If Giant pays $16 million for the stock of Tiny when its reportable assets have a value of only $15 million, the entry shown in Figure 11.4 is made by Giant to consolidate the two companies. The additional payment of $1 million is labeled as goodwill, which will then be reported along with the other intangible assets.

> **goodwill**
>
> The price paid by one company to acquire another that is in excess of the fair value of net identifiable assets and liabilities; this cost is often associated with intangibles that do not meet the criteria for accounting recognition, such as employee expertise and customer loyalty.

FIGURE 11.4 Giant Company Buys Tiny Company—$1 Million Paid in Excess of Fair Value of Identifiable Assets

Property and Equipment	4,000,000	
Patents	6,000,000	
Database	2,000,000	
Copyrights	3,000,000	
Goodwill	1,000,000	
Cash		16,000,000

3.3 Excess Payment for a Subsidiary Not Identified with an Intangible

Question: In the previous illustration, Giant (the parent) paid an extra $1 million for specified intangibles. However, the subsidiary's customer loyalty and talented workforce could not be recognized separately as assets because they met neither of the required criteria. Instead, a goodwill balance was created.

*Will the reporting be any different if the parent simply paid this amount as a result of intense negotiations? Assume, for example, that Giant agreed to pay the additional $1 million to obtain Tiny solely because that company's owners refused to sell for less. That often happens in the business world. Giant believed that the $16 million price was still a good investment even though it required $1 million more than the value of the identified assets (tangible and intangible). **If a parent pays an additional amount to purchase a subsidiary without a specific rationale, is this cost still recorded as goodwill?***

Answer: The acquisition of one company by another can require months of bargaining between the parties. One company wants to collect as much as possible; the other wants to pay as little as possible. Compromise is frequently necessary to arrive at a figure that both parties are willing to accept. In most cases, the parent has to pay more than the sum of the value of all individual assets to entice the owners of the other company to sell.

Sometimes, as in the initial example, the reason for the added payment is apparent (customer loyalty and talented workforce). More likely, the increased amount is simply necessary in order to make the deal happen. Whenever an extra cost must be expended to gain control of a subsidiary, it is labeled by the parent as an asset known as goodwill. The rationale does not impact the accounting. Any additional acquisition price that was required to obtain a subsidiary appears in the parent's balance sheet as goodwill and is shown as an intangible asset.

TEST YOURSELF

Question:

Lance Company has three assets. The first is land with a cost of $700,000 and a fair value of $1 million. The second is a building with a net book value of $2 million but a fair value of $3 million. Finally, the company has a trademark that has no reported value (it has been fully depreciated) but is worth $400,000. The Empire Company offers $4.4 million for all the ownership shares of Lance. Lance owners counter with a price of $5.1 million. After nine days of negotiations, Empire pays $4.7 million to acquire Lance Company. When the financial statements of the two companies are consolidated, what amount will be reported as goodwill?

a. Zero

b. $300,000

c. $700,000

d. $2 million

Answer:

The correct answer is choice b: $300,000.

Explanation:

On consolidated statements after the takeover, Empire reports the land, building, and trademark at their fair values, which total $4.4 million. However, Empire paid an additional $300,000 ($4.7 million less $4.4 million) to convince the owners of Lance to sell. This payment is reported as the intangible asset goodwill. In this situation, it is not attributed to any specific value such as employee loyalty. It is the amount in excess of the individual fair values that the parent had to pay.

3.4 Accounting for Goodwill Over Time

*Question: Buildings, equipment, patents, databases, and the like are all assets. They have reported costs that will be assigned to expense over an expected life as they help generate revenues. Goodwill is a different type of asset. It represents either (a) a subsidiary attribute (such as customer loyalty) that is too nebulous to be recognized specifically as an asset or (b) an extra payment made by the parent to acquire the subsidiary as a result of the negotiation process. **What happens to a cost identified as the asset goodwill after the date a subsidiary is acquired?***

*How do **Microsoft**, **Yahoo!**, or **Procter & Gamble** account for their large goodwill balances over time? Is this asset like land that simply continues to be reported at historical cost potentially forever or, possibly, like equipment that is depreciated systematically over some anticipated useful life?*

Answer: Because goodwill is the one asset on a balance sheet that is not tied to an identifiable benefit, no attempt is ever made to determine an anticipated life. Consequently, the assigned cost is not amortized to expense. A goodwill balance can remain unchanged on a consolidated balance sheet for decades after a subsidiary is purchased. However, the reported figure is reduced immediately if its value is ever judged to be impaired. Attributes such as customer loyalty or a talented workforce might continue in place for years or disappear completely in a short period of time. If goodwill is merely a premium paid to acquire a subsidiary, the justification for that excess amount could vanish because of poor management decisions or environmental factors. The value of all assets is tentative but probably none is more so than goodwill.

Although a cost recorded as goodwill is not amortized over time, its ongoing worth is not assumed. Instead, a test to check for any loss of that value is performed periodically. This verification process is more complex than can be covered in an introductory course. The result, though, is important to understand. In the event that the goodwill associated with a subsidiary is ever found to be worth less than its reported balance, an impairment loss is recorded. Although not identical, the accounting is similar in some ways to the impairment test for land, buildings, and equipment demonstrated previously.

In 2000, **Time Warner** and **America Online (AOL)** merged. Because of the perceived benefit of combining these two companies, a huge premium was paid and reported as goodwill on the consolidated balance sheet. A mere two years later, it was obvious that the anticipated synergies from this transaction had not developed as expected. In simple terms, too much money had been paid by the owners to create the merger. The value of the combined companies had not managed to achieve overly optimistic projections. Consequently, goodwill was reduced in 2002 by nearly $100 billion. A loss of that amount was reported by the consolidated company. The goodwill account was not amortized to expense, but the impairment of its value had to be recognized.

TEST YOURSELF

Question:

Giant Company buys all the outstanding stock of Small Company on January 1, Year One. Subsequently, on the consolidated balance sheet as of December 31, Year Five, Giant and Consolidated Subsidiary reported a goodwill balance of $300,000. Which of the following is most likely to be true?

   a. $300,000 is the value of Small on this date in excess of the value of its assets minus its liabilities.

   b. $300,000 is the excess amount paid by Giant to acquire Small unless the value of that figure has become impaired since the purchase.

   c. $300,000 is the excess amount paid by Giant to acquire Small less any amortization since January 1, Year One.

   d. $300,000 is the fair value of the goodwill on December 31, Year Five.

Answer:

The correct answer is choice b: $300,000 is the excess amount paid by Giant to acquire Small unless the value of that figure has become impaired since the purchase.

Explanation:

Goodwill is initially recorded as the excess amount paid over the value of the identifiable assets and liabilities when a subsidiary is acquired. This figure stays unchanged because it is not subject to amortization unless the value is ever judged to have been impaired. If so, the recorded amount is reduced to recognize this loss of value.

KEY TAKEAWAY

When a parent acquires another company, all intangibles held by that subsidiary must be identified and consolidated at fair value if either of two criteria is met. Reporting these assets is necessary if legal or contractual rights are held or the intangible can be separated from the subsidiary and sold. Additional amounts are often included in the acquisition price of a subsidiary to compensate for intangibles (such as customer loyalty) that do not meet either of these criteria. An extra payment may also be necessary simply to entice the owner to sell. In either situation, this additional cost is reported as goodwill, an intangible asset that then appears on the consolidated balance sheet. Goodwill does not have an expected useful life. Consequently, the amount assigned to this intangible asset is not amortized to expense over time. Instead, the reported balance is checked periodically for impairment with a loss recognized if the value ever declines.

4.   ACCOUNTING FOR RESEARCH AND DEVELOPMENT

LEARNING OBJECTIVES

At the end of this section, students should be able to meet the following objectives:

1. **Define the terms "research" and "development."**
2. **Explain the problem that uncertainty creates for accountants in reporting research and development costs.**
3. **Understand the required method of reporting research and development costs according to U.S. GAAP.**
4. **Discuss the advantages of reporting research and development costs in the manner required by U.S. GAAP.**
5. **Recognize that many companies report asset totals that are vastly understated as a result of the authoritative handling of research and development costs.**

4.1   Reporting Research and Development Costs

Question: Many companies create internally developed intangibles such as copyrights and trademarks. One common intangible of this type is a patent, the right to make use of an invention. The creation and nurturing of an idea so that it can eventually earn a patent and be offered for sale often takes years. The monetary amounts spent in this way to arrive at new marketable products are often enormous. The risk of failure is always present.

Such expenditures are essential to the future success of a great many companies. In 2010 alone, **Intel** *reported spending $6.6 billion on* **research and development** *in hopes of discovering new products to patent and sell. During the same one-year period,* **Bristol-Myers Squibb** *incurred costs of $3.6 billion on research and development. Those are clearly not inconsequential amounts. What is meant by the term "research"? What is meant by the term "development"? If a company such as* **Intel** *or* **Bristol-Myers Squibb** *spends billions on research and development each year, what accounting is appropriate? Should an asset or expense be recognized or possibly some combination? The outcome is uncertain, but the money was spent under the assumption that future economic benefits would be derived.*

For example, assume that a technological company or a pharmaceutical company spends $1 million in Year One to do research on Future Product A. The company then spends another $1 million during the same period on development costs for Future Product A. At the end of this year, officials believe that a patent is 80 percent likely for Future Product A. If the patent is received, sales can be made.

Also during that time, the company spends another $1 million in research and $1 million in development in connection with Future Product B. However, at year's end, the same officials are less optimistic about these results. They believe that only a 30 percent chance exists that this second product will ever receive a patent so that it can be used to generate revenues. According to U.S. GAAP, what reporting is appropriate for the cost of these two projects?

Answer: Definitions are easy to recite.

- Research is any attempt made to find new knowledge with the hope that those results will eventually be useful in creating new products or services or significant improvements in existing products or services.

- Development is the natural next step. It is the translation of that new knowledge into actual products or services or into significant improvements in existing products or services.

In simple terms, research is the effort expended to create new ideas; development is the process of turning those new ideas into saleable products.

However, the reporting of research and development costs poses incredibly difficult challenges for the accountant. As can be seen with **Intel** and **Bristol-Myers Squibb**, the quantity of these expenditures is often massive because of the essential role that new ideas and products play in the future success of many organizations. Unfortunately, significant uncertainty is inherent in virtually all such endeavors. The probability that any research and development cost will eventually lead to a successful product can be impossible to determine for years. Furthermore, any estimation of the outcome of such work is open to manipulation. Often the only piece of information that is known with certainty is the amount that has been spent.

Thus, except for some relatively minor exceptions, all research and development costs are expensed as incurred according to U.S. GAAP. The probability for success is not viewed as relevant to this reporting. Standardization is very apparent. All companies provide the same information in the same manner. The total cost incurred each period for research and development appears on the income statement as an expense regardless of the chance for success.

Consequently, the accounting for Future Product A and Future Product B is identical. Although one is 80 percent likely to be successful whereas the other is only 30 percent likely, all research and development costs for both are expensed as incurred. No asset is reported despite the possibility of future benefits. The rigidity of this rule comes from the inherent uncertainty as to whether revenues will ever be generated and, if so, for how long. Rather than trying to anticipate success, the conservatism found in financial accounting simply expenses all such costs as incurred. The percentages associated with the likelihood of receiving a patent and generating future revenues are ignored.

Two major advantages are provided by this approach. First, the amount spent by a company on research and development each period is easy to determine and then compare with previous years and with other similar businesses. Most decision makers are interested in the amount invested in the search for new ideas and products and that information is readily apparent. Second, the possibility for manipulation is virtually eliminated. No distinction is drawn between a likely success and a probable failure. No reporting advantage is achieved by maneuvering the estimation of a profitable outcome.

research

The attempt to find new knowledge with the hope that the results will eventually be useful in creating new products or services or significant improvements in existing products or services; these costs are expensed as incurred according to U.S. GAAP.

development

The translation of new knowledge into actual products or services or into significant improvements in existing products or services; these costs are expensed as incurred according to U.S. GAAP.

TEST YOURSELF

Question:

On its income statement for the current year, the Acme Corporation reported an expense for research and development of $236 million. What information is conveyed by this balance?

- a. It is an amortization expense associated with patents, copyrights, and other intangible assets.
- b. It is the amount spent on projects that failed during the year.
- c. It is the amount spent on all research and development activities during the year.
- d. It is the amount spent on all projects during the year that did not become at least 50 percent likely of achieving status as an asset.

Answer:

The correct answer is choice c: It is the amount spent on all research and development activities during the year.

Explanation:

All research and development costs are expensed as incurred. No asset balances are recognized. In that way, the amount invested by a company each year in connection with this vital activity is evident to decision makers.

4.2   Research and Development Costs and the Impact on the Balance Sheet

Question: Billions of dollars are spent each year on research and development in hopes of creating new products that could be sold in the future. Company officials would never risk this money unless they believed that a reasonable chance existed for recouping such huge investments. However, whether success is 100 percent likely or only 2 percent, no assets are reported on the balance sheet for these costs. That is U.S. GAAP.

__Because all amounts spent on research and development are expensed automatically, are the assets reported by companies in industries such as technology and pharmaceuticals not omitting many of their most valuable future benefits?__ If a company spends $5 billion to develop a new drug or electronic device that becomes worth $11 billion, does the reporting of no asset make sense? Does that approach provide a fair portrait of the company?

Answer: Even a student in an introductory accounting course can quickly recognize the problems created by a rule requiring that all research and development costs be expensed as incurred. Companies in technology, pharmaceutical, and many other industries must exclude items of significant value from their balance sheets by following U.S. GAAP. While this approach is conservative, consistent, and allows for comparability, the rationale is confusing. The balance sheet hardly paints a fair portrait of the assets being held. Expensing research and development costs also violates the matching principle. These expenditures are made in the hopes of generating future revenues but the expense is recorded immediately before any revenues have been earned.

Capitalizing these costs so that they are reported as assets is logical but measuring the value of future benefits is extremely challenging. Without authoritative guidance, the extreme uncertainty of such projects would leave the accountant in a precarious position. The temptation would be to tailor the reporting to make the company look as good as possible. U.S. GAAP "solves" the problem by eliminating the need for any judgment by the accountant. All costs are expensed. No rule could be simpler to apply.

Consequently, any decision maker evaluating a company that invests heavily in research and development needs to recognize that the assets appearing on the balance sheet are incomplete. Such companies spend money to create future benefits that are not being reported. The wisdom of that approach has long been debated but it is the rule under U.S. GAAP. Difficult estimates are not needed and the possibility of manipulation is avoided.

Talking with an Independent Auditor about International Financial Reporting Standards

Following is a continuation of our interview with Robert A. Vallejo, partner with the accounting firm **PricewaterhouseCoopers**.

Question: Virtually without exception, U.S. GAAP requires that all research and development expenditures must be expensed as incurred. This requirement has existed for over thirty years. Does IFRS handle research and development costs in the same manner?

Robert Vallejo: This is one of the best examples of differences between IFRS and U.S. GAAP. If specified criteria are met, IFRS requires the capitalization of development costs. These guidelines help determine when a project moves from the research stage into the development stage. However, once the development stage commences, the costs are capitalized and amortized over the anticipated useful life. When companies first adopt IFRS, this change will require some effort, particularly if development costs are significant. Changing to IFRS will have a substantial impact on reported net income. This issue will need to be considered early in a conversion to IFRS, as recasting prior period information taking into account the capitalization of development costs will be difficult.

The difference between U.S. GAAP and IFRS is not a question of right or wrong but rather an example of differing yet valid viewpoints. U.S. GAAP prefers not to address the uncertainty inherent in research and development programs but rather to focus on comparability of amounts spent (between years and between companies). IFRS, on the other hand, takes a view that the expenses should be matched with the benefits to be obtained in future periods.

KEY TAKEAWAY

Research and development costs include all amounts spent to create new ideas and then turn them into products that can be sold to generate revenue. Because success in these endeavors is highly uncertain, accounting has long faced the challenge of determining whether such costs should be capitalized or expensed. U.S. GAAP requires that all research and development costs (with a few minor exceptions) be expensed as incurred. This official standard does prevent manipulation and provides decision makers with the monetary amount spent by management each year for this essential function. However, this method of accounting means that companies (especially in certain industries) often fail to show some of their most important assets on their balance sheets. Despite the obvious value of these assets, the cost is expensed entirely.

5. ACQUIRING AN ASSET WITH FUTURE CASH PAYMENTS

LEARNING OBJECTIVES

At the end of this section, students should be able to meet the following objectives:

1. Realize that if payments to acquire an asset are delayed into the future, part of the total cash amount is attributed to the purchase of the asset with the rest deemed to be interest.
2. Recognize that a reasonable rate of interest on a long-term debt can be stated explicitly in the contract and paid when due so that no present value computation is needed.
3. Record the acquisition of an intangible asset based on a present value computation whenever payments are made over a period of years and no explicit interest is included in those payments.
4. Define the term "compounding."
5. Compute interest to be recognized each period when a long-term debt was recorded using a present value computation.
6. Differentiate between an annuity due and an ordinary annuity.

5.1 Purchases Made with Future Cash Payments

Question: A company buys a patent from an inventor on January 1, Year One, for $1 million to be paid immediately. The accounting here is straightforward; the patent is recognized as an intangible asset and reported at the historical cost of $1 million. Accounting rules are clear on the handling of such acquisitions.

Assume, instead, that the company offers to pay this $1 million but not until five years have passed. The seller agrees to that proposal. The purchase is made now, but payment is delayed. Is the $1 million *still being paid solely for the patent? Does the entire $1 million reflect the historical cost of this intangible?* **What reporting is appropriate if an asset such as a patent, building, or land is bought but payment will not take place for several years?** *In such cases, how is historical cost determined?*

Answer: More than forty years ago, the accounting body that was viewed as authoritative at the time ruled that when cash is paid for a purchase[3] over an extended period of time, two distinct reasons for the payments always exist.[4]

- The first is obviously the acquisition of the property such as the patent in this example.
- The second is **interest**. Interest is the charge for the use of money over time.

This rule assumes that no reasonable seller would allow cash payments to be spread over several years without some interest charge being factored into the negotiated amounts. In other words, interest (the charge for the use of the money over time) is included whether it can be seen or not. The accounting demonstrated here is the result of that assertion.

In many purchases where payments are made over time, interest payments are explicitly included. For example, the contract to buy this patent could have required payment of the $1 million after five years plus interest at a 7 percent rate to be paid each year. With those terms, the accounting process is not complicated. The $1 million is the historical cost of the patent while the annual $70,000 payments ($1 million × 7 percent) are recorded each year by the buyer as interest expense. The two amounts are clearly differentiated based on the terms of the agreement.

A theoretical problem arises if interest is not identified in the contract. In the current illustration, assume that the company agrees to make a single $1 million payment in five years with no mention of interest. According to U.S. GAAP, interest is still present and must be recognized because the conveyance of cash has been delayed. This means that only part of the $1 million is actually paid for the patent with the rest serving as interest. Authoritative accounting rules hold that an interest charge is always present when payment is put off into the future. Payment has been deferred for five years; some part of that amount serves to compensate the seller for having to wait to receive the money.

However, the specific allocation of the $1 million between patent and interest is not readily apparent. To calculate the interest included within the price, an introduction to **present value** computations is necessary.

In simple terms, the present value of future cash flows is the amount left after all future interest is removed (hence the term "present value"). The present value is the portion within the $1 million that is being paid for the patent. The remainder will be recognized as interest expense over the five-year period until payment is made.

To determine the present value of future cash flows, a reasonable interest rate is needed. Then, the amount of interest for these five years can be mathematically calculated and removed. An appropriate interest rate is often viewed as the one the buyer would be charged if the money were borrowed from a local bank.

Assume here that 10 percent is a reasonable annual interest rate. Fortunately, present value conversion factors have already been mechanically computed. They can serve to remove the future amount of interest so that only the present value (the amount paid for the patent) is left. The formula to determine the present value of $1 at a designated point in the future is $1 divided by $(1 + i)$ raised to the nth power with "n" being the number of periods and "i" the appropriate interest rate. In this case, because payment is due in five years, the present value $1 is $1/(1.10)^5$, or 0.62092. This factor can then be multiplied by the actual cash payment to determine its present value.

In an Excel spreadsheet, the present value of $1 at 10 percent for five years is derived by entering the following formula into one of the cells: =PV(.10,5,0,1). Thus, the present value of $1,000,000 is found in Excel by entering =PV(.10,5,0,1000000).

Regardless of the method being applied, if $1 is paid in five years for an asset and a reasonable rate of interest is 10 percent per year, then the $0.62 (rounded) present value is the portion being paid for the asset with the remaining $0.38 representing interest for those years. The present value computation mathematically determines the interest and then removes it to leave the cost of the asset.

Predetermined present value tables are available as well as calculators and computer spreadsheets that make this computation relatively easy. Present value tables can be found at the end of this book as well as through Internet links provided at appropriate spots throughout the chapters.

On a table created to provide the present value of a single amount of $1, the factor is found by looking under the specific interest rate column (10 percent) at the line for the number of applicable time periods (five).

---

interest

The charge for using money over time, often associated with long-term loans; even if not specifically mentioned in the debt agreement, financial accounting rules require it to be computed and reported based on a reasonable rate.

present value

The amount associated with cash flows after all future interest—computed at a reasonable rate—has been mathematically removed; this figure is the principal of those future cash flows.

Present Value of Single Amount of $1

http://www.principlesofaccounting.com/ART/fv.pv.tables/pvof1.htm

The present value today of paying $1 million in five years assuming a 10 percent annual interest rate is $1 million times 0.62092 or $620,920. This is the cost before any future interest is accrued over time. Mathematically, the interest for these five years has been computed and removed to arrive at this figure. The remainder of the payment ($379,080) will be reported as interest expense by the buyer over the subsequent five years using a 10 percent annual rate. The total ($620,920 for the patent plus $379,080 in interest) equals the $1 million payment.

The journal entries for Year One are shown in Figure 11.5. On January 1, the patent and the liability are reported at present value. No time has passed so no interest is recognized. However, at the end of that first year, interest expense of $62,092 should be reported. That amount is 10 percent of the liability's principal balance for that year ($620,920).[5]

FIGURE 11.5 Present Value—Acquisition of Patent with Future Payment of Cash and Recognition of Year One Interest

1/1/1	Patent	$620,920		($1,000,000 × .620920)
	Note Payable		$620,920	
12/31/1	Interest Expense	62,092		(620,920 × .10)
	Note Payable		62,092	

Notice in the December 31 entry that no interest is paid on that date. Payment of this additional charge actually occurs in five years when $1 million is paid and not just $620,920. Because interest was recognized in Year One but not paid, the amount of the liability (the principal) has grown. Increasing a debt to reflect the accrual of interest is referred to as "compounding." Whenever interest is recognized but not paid, it is compounded which means that it is added to the principal of the liability.

In the second year, the expense to be recognized is higher because the principal has increased from $620,920 to $683,012 ($620,920 plus $62,092) as a result of compounding the Year One interest. The ongoing compounding raises the principal each year so that the interest expense also increases as can be seen in the series of entries in Figure 11.6.

FIGURE 11.6 Present Value—Recognition and Compounding of Interest[6]

12/31/2	Interest Expense	$68,301		(($620,920 + $62,092) × .10)
	Note Payable		$68,301	
12/31/3	Interest Expense	75,131		((683,012 + 68,301) × .10)
	Note Payable		75,131	
12/31/4	Interest Expense	82,644		((751,313 + 75,131) × .10)
	Note Payable		82,644	
12/31/5	Interest Expense	90,912		((826,444 + 82,644) × .10)
	Note Payable		90,912	
12/31/5	Note Payable	1,000,000		
	Cash		1,000,000	

These journal entries show that three goals are achieved by this reporting process.

- The patent is recorded at its historical cost of $620,920, the total amount to be paid less a reasonable interest rate for the five year delay until payment is made.
- The compounding process adds the interest back into the liability that was removed in determining the present value so that the reported balance returns to $1 million as of the due date.
- Interest expense of $379,080 is recognized over the five-year period ($62,092 + $68,301 + $75,131 + $82,644 + $90,912). Although interest was not mentioned in the contract, U.S. GAAP requires it to be computed and reported over these five years.

TEST YOURSELF

Question:

Osgood Company buys an intangible asset on January 1, Year One, for $300,000. The company will make this payment at the end of Year Three. In the interim, interest payments of $27,000 will be made each year based on a reasonable rate. On January 1, Year One, what amount is reported for the intangible and the liability?

a. $300,000

b. The present value of $300,000

c. The present value of $327,000

d. The present value of $381,000

Answer:

The correct answer is choice a: $300,000.

Explanation:

A reasonable interest rate is being paid, so although payment to acquire the intangible has been delayed for three years, there is no reason to compute the present value of the cash flows. Present value is only used when a reasonable interest is not explicitly stated and paid. The $300,000 amount is the principal amount and the $27,000 annual payments are the interest.

TEST YOURSELF

Question:

Weisz Company buys an intangible asset on January 1, Year One, for $300,000 to be paid in exactly three years. No additional amounts are mentioned in the contract although a reasonable interest rate is 8 percent per year. The present value of $1 at an 8 percent rate to be paid at the end of a three-year period is $0.79383. What does the company report on the date of acquisition?

a. Asset of $238,149 and liability of $238,149

b. Asset of $300,000 and liability of $238,149

c. Asset of $238,149 and liability of $300,000

d. Asset of $300,000 and liability of $300,000

Answer:

The correct answer is choice a: Asset of $238,149 and liability of $238,149.

Explanation:

Because a reasonable interest rate is not being paid, the initial acquisition (both the cost of the asset and the principal of the liability) is recorded at the present value of the future cash flows ($238,149 or $300,000 × 0.79383). Present value computes the interest for three years at an 8 percent rate and then removes it to leave the amount paid, here, for the intangible asset.

TEST YOURSELF

Question:

Tylo Company buys an intangible asset on January 1, Year One, for a single $400,000 payment in exactly four years with no additional cash being paid in the interim. A reasonable interest rate is 10 percent per year. The present value of $1 at a 10 percent rate to be paid at the end of a four-year period is $0.68301. How does the annual recognition of interest over those four years impact the recorded amount of the intangible asset?

   a. It has no effect.

   b. It increases the reported asset by $6,830.10 per year.

   c. It increases the reported asset by $27,320.40 per year.

   d. It increases the reported asset by $40,000.00 per year.

Answer:

The correct answer is choice a: It has no effect.

Explanation:

Interest will be recognized each year based on the reasonable rate of 10 percent. However, that impacts the liability balance and has no impact on the asset. The asset is recorded initially at present value and that cost is then amortized to expense over the useful life of the asset (unless the asset does not have a finite life). The interest is recorded each year as an expense and compounded to increase the liability.

TEST YOURSELF

Question:

Guthrie Company buys an intangible asset on January 1, Year One, for a single $500,000 payment in exactly five years with no additional cash being paid in the interim. A reasonable interest rate is 10 percent per year. The present value of $1 at a 10 percent rate to be paid at the end of a five-year period is $0.62092. What interest is recognized in each of the first two years?

   a. Zero in Year One and Zero in Year Two

   b. $31,046 in Year One and $31,046 in Year Two

   c. $31,046 in Year One and $34,150.60 in Year Two

   d. $50,000 in Year One and $50,000 in Year Two

Answer:

The correct answer is choice c: $31,046 in Year One and $34,150.60 in Year Two.

Explanation:

Because a reasonable interest rate is not paid, the liability for this $500,000 payment is recorded initially at its present value of $310,460 ($500,000 × 0.62092). Interest for the first year is 10 percent of this principal or $31,046 ($310,460 × 10 percent). No interest is paid at that time so this entire amount is compounded raising the principal to $341,506 ($310,460 plus $31,046). Interest expense for the second year is $34,150.60 based on the reasonable 10 percent annual rate.

TEST YOURSELF

Question:

Laettner Company buys an intangible asset on January 1, Year One, for $200,000 to be paid in exactly five years with no additional cash being paid in the interim. A reasonable interest rate is 10 percent per year. The present value of $1 at 10 percent rate to be paid at the end of a five-year period is $0.62092. What does Laettner Company report on its December 31, Year Two balance sheet for this liability?

   a. $124,184.00

   b. $136,602.40

   c. $150,262.64

   d. $200,000.00

Answer:

The correct answer is choice c: $150,262.64.

Explanation:

Because reasonable interest is not paid, the liability is recorded at present value ($200,000 × 0.62092 or $124,184). After one year, interest of $12,418.40 ($124,184 × 10 percent) is recognized. It is not paid but compounded raising the principal to $136,602.40 ($124,184.00 plus $12,418.40). After the second year, interest is again computed. It is $13,660.24 ($136,602.40 × 10 percent). It is compounded raising the principal to $150,262.64 ($136,602.40 plus $13,660.24).

5.2 The Present Value of Cash Flows Paid as an Annuity

Question: Does the application of present value change substantially if cash is paid each year rather than as a lump sum at the end of the term? **What reporting is appropriate if an intangible asset is purchased by making a down payment today followed by a series of equal payments in the future?**

To illustrate, assume a company acquires a copyright from an artist by paying $10,000 on January 1, Year One, and agreeing to pay an additional $10,000 at the beginning of each subsequent year until January 1, Year Five. The total cash amount is $50,000. As with the previous example, no separate interest is paid so that a present value computation is required. What is the historical cost to be reported for this intangible asset and what interest should be recorded on the liability over these future years?

Answer: Cash is conveyed over an extended period of time in this purchase. However, a reasonable rate of interest is not being explicitly paid to compensate for the delay in payments. Once again, accounting believes that interest exists within the cash amounts. A present value computation is necessary to pull out the appropriate amount of interest and leave just the cost of the newly acquired asset. As before, the present value of the payments is the cash paid after all future interest is mathematically removed. The idea behind the process has not changed. Here, though, cash is not conveyed as a single amount but rather as an **annuity**—an equal amount paid at equal time intervals. An annuity can be either of the following:

annuity
A series of equal payments made at equal time intervals.

- An **ordinary annuity** with payments made at the end of each period
- An **annuity due** with payments starting immediately at the beginning of each period

The specific series of payments in this question is an annuity due pattern because the first $10,000 is conveyed immediately when the contract is signed. As before, the applicable present value factor to remove the interest can be determined by a calculator[7] or computer spreadsheet.[8] Tables are also available at the end of this book or through the following Internet link.

ordinary annuity
An annuity with payments made at the end of each period; it is also referred to as an annuity in arrears.

annuity due
An annuity with payments made at the beginning of each period; it is also referred to as an annuity in advance.

Present Value of an Annuity Due of $1 per Period

http://www.principlesofaccounting.com/ART/fv.pv.tables/pvforannuitydue.htm

Regardless of the approach applied, if a reasonable rate is assumed to be 12 percent per year, the present value of a $1 per year annuity due for five periods is 4.0374. Thus, the present value of paying $10,000 annually for five years beginning immediately is $10,000 times 4.0374 or $40,374. For annuities, the computation is constructed so that a single payment ($10,000) is multiplied rather than the total cash amount ($50,000).

Of the total cash to be paid, $40,374 (the present value) is the cost of the copyright with the remaining $9,626 ($50,000 total less $40,374) representing the interest expense over this period. The initial journal entry to record this acquisition is shown in Figure 11.7. No interest is reported because no time has yet passed.

FIGURE 11.7 Acquisition of Intangible Asset—Present Value of an Annuity Due

1/1/1	Copyright	40,374	
	Cash		10,000
	Note Payable		30,374

At the end of the first year, amortization of the cost of the copyright must be recognized along with interest expense on the liability. Assuming a life of ten years and no residual value, annual amortization is $40,374 divided by ten years, or $4,037. Interest for the period is the $30,374 principal of the liability times the 12 percent reasonable rate, or $3,645 (rounded). Because no interest is explicitly paid in this contract, all of this interest is compounded (added to the liability). The year-end adjusting entries are shown in Figure 11.8.

FIGURE 11.8 Intangible Asset—Recognition of Interest and Amortization for Year One

12/31/1	Interest Expense	3,645	
	Note Payable		3,645
	Amortization Expense	4,037	
	Copyright		4,037

The second scheduled payment is made on January 1, Year Two, and reduces the amount of the liability.

FIGURE 11.9 Second Payment for Copyright—Start of Year Two

| 1/1/2 | Note Payable | 10,000 | |
| | Cash | | 10,000 |

At the end of Year Two, both amortization of the asset's cost and interest expense on the liability must be recognized again to reflect the passage of another period. The amortization figure remains the same (assuming application of the straight-line method) but interest must be recomputed. The principal of the liability was $30,374 for the first year, but interest of $3,645 was then compounded at the end of that period followed by another $10,000 payment. As shown in Figure 11.10, these changes result in a liability principal throughout Year Two of $24,019.

FIGURE 11.10 Computation of Liability Principal Throughout Year Two

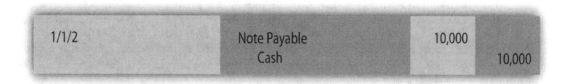

Liability Principal—January 1, Year Two	
($30,374 plus Year One interest of $3,645)	$34,019
Payment on January 1, Year Two	(10,000)
Liability Principal—Throughout Year Two	$24,019

Thus, during the second year, the principal amount of the liability is $24,019 and the interest, at the reasonable rate of 12 percent, is $2,882 (rounded).

FIGURE 11.11 Intangible Asset—Recognition of Interest and Amortization for Year Two

12/31/2	Interest Expense	2,882	
	Note Payable		2,882
	Amortization Expense	4,037	
	Copyright		4,037

This pattern of entries will continue until the liability has been extinguished and the capitalized cost of the asset amortized to expense.

KEY TAKEAWAY

In making purchases, companies often delay making cash payments for years. If interest is calculated and paid in the interim, the purchase price and the interest are easy to differentiate and record. The accounting is straightforward. However, if no interest payments are specified, a present value computation is made to separate the amount paid for the asset from the interest. The resulting amount (the present value) is recognized initially for both the asset and liability. Present value can be determined using a table, a mathematical formula, or an Excel spreadsheet. Thereafter, interest is recognized each period and compounded (added to the principal of the liability) since it is not paid at the time. Future cash payments can be a single amount or an annuity (a stream of equal payments made at equal time intervals). Payments constitute an ordinary annuity if made at the end of each period or an annuity due if started immediately.

Talking with a Real Investing Pro (Continued)

Following is a continuation of our interview with Kevin G. Burns.

Question: Goodwill is one of the most misunderstood balances on any set of financial statements. For example, at June 30, 2011, **Procter & Gamble** reported goodwill of nearly $58 billion. Many investors (even serious investors) probably are unsure of what to make of that number. How do you factor the reported balance for goodwill into your decision making?

Kevin Burns: I am not a big fan of goodwill. As a reported asset, it is way too subjective and frankly I am not sure that it provides credible information. How do you value something from an accounting standpoint that you cannot really measure or touch or feel? You cannot borrow against it. The goodwill balance is irrelevant for the kind of investing I do where I am more interested in asset values and what the real market values are for those assets. My feeling about goodwill is a bit like my feeling for financial footnotes. I prefer companies that can explain how they have value and make money without relying too much on either one.

Video Clip

Professor Joe Hoyle talks about the five most important points in Chapter 11.

View the video online at: http://bit.ly/hoyle11-2

6.   END-OF-CHAPTER EXERCISES

QUESTIONS

1. Define "intangible asset" and give three common examples.

2. For accounting purposes, at what amount are intangible assets typically reported?

3. What are the six general types of intangibles that are reported as assets?

4. In connection with intangible assets, what is the purpose of amortization?

5. A company owns an intangible asset that is being amortized to expense over fifteen years. How was this fifteen-year period determined?

6. The Ladorne Company owns a patent with a historical cost of $130,000 and a net book value of $82,000. The patent has become extremely valuable and is now worth $2.2 million. What does Ladorne report on its balance sheet for this intangible asset? Explain the reason for that method of accounting.

7. The Bailor Company has a copyright with a cost of $200,000 and annual amortization of $40,000. In recording amortization, why might the company reduce the copyright's cost directly rather than set up a separate accumulated amortization account?

8. The Winston Corporation holds a patent with a cost of $2.1 million and a net book value of $1.5 million. Winston has to defend its right to this patent in court at a cost of $212,000. In what ways can this legal cost be reported?

9. Large Corporation purchases all of the outstanding capital stock of Small Corporation. Large paid an especially large amount because Small had a certain attribute that was valued at over $3 million. Under what condition will Large be able to recognize this attribute as an identifiable intangible asset after the purchase has been finalized?

10. Large Corporation purchases all of the outstanding capital stock of Small Corporation. Large paid an especially large amount because Small had a certain attribute that was valued at over $3 million. Assume that this attribute does not qualify for separate recognition as an identifiable intangible asset. What reporting will Large make of this $3 million on consolidated financial statements after the acquisition is finalized?

11. A decision maker looks at the financial statements produced by the Rotolo Corporation for the current year. On the balance sheet, an account titled "goodwill" is reported with a balance of $13.8 million. What does the decision maker know from this information?

12. Goodwill is recognized on a consolidated balance sheet on January 1, Year One. What happens to that asset balance over subsequent years?

13. Giant Corporation acquires all of the outstanding capital stock of Little Corporation on January 1, Year One. As a result, goodwill of $15 million is reported. On a balance sheet produced 5 years later, will the goodwill balance still be reported and, if so, will $15 million be the figure that appears?

14. Hammerstine Corporation pays $3 million for research and $5 million for development in connection with the creation of a new product that the company believes will generate over $19 million in revenue. How are the research and development costs reported under U.S. GAAP?

15. How does U.S. GAAP differ in its method of reporting research and development costs from the rules established by IFRS?

16. The Albright Corporation spends millions each year on research and development and, as a result, has been able to create a number of valuable patents and copyrights. Because of the handling required by U.S. GAAP, what can a decision maker say about a balance sheet reported by the Albright Corporation?

17. What are the advantages of reporting research and development costs in the method required by U.S. GAAP?

18. A company pays $2 million to acquire a patent. Under two different conditions, no determination of present value is required. What are those two conditions?

19. The NortonRidge Corporation buys an intangible asset for $11 million to be paid in five years. No other payment is to be made. The present value of this cash payment is computed as $7.6 million using a reasonable interest rate. Mechanically, what does a present value computation accomplish?

20. An intangible asset with a five-year useful life and no residual value is bought on January 1, Year One, for $4 million. However, the purchase is made with a future cash payment that has a present value of only $3 million based on a reasonable annual interest rate of 10 percent. What is the total amount of expense to be reported by the acquiring company in Year One?

21. An intangible asset with a five-year useful life and no residual value is bought on January 1, Year One, for $4 million. However, the purchase is made with a future cash payment that has a present value of only $3 million based on a reasonable annual interest rate of 10 percent. What is the total amount of expense to be reported by the acquiring company in Year Two?

22. A company has agreed to pay $6 million in the future and needs to determine the present value of that cash flow. What three pieces of information are needed to calculate present value?

23. What is meant by the term "compounding"?

24. What is the difference between an ordinary annuity and an annuity due?

TRUE OR FALSE

1. ____ On December 31, Year One, a company acquires a trademark and reports the intangible asset on its balance sheet at that date at $1.3 million. This figure represents the historical cost of this asset.

2. ____ A company has a technology-related asset. It also has a marketing-related asset. These two assets cannot both be reported as intangible assets at the same time.

3. ____ Amortization of intangibles is usually done over the asset's legal life.

4. ____ If an intangible asset is successfully defended from a legal challenge, the incurred legal costs are capitalized to the asset account.

5. ____ Typically, intangible assets are shown on a company's balance sheet at fair value.

6. ____ One company acquires another. Subsequently, the acquiring company continues to report any intangible assets owned by the acquired company at the same historical cost basis that had been used by the acquired company.

7. ____ A company has bought another company and is in the process of identifying the acquired intangible assets. To be reported as an intangible asset on a consolidated balance sheet, the parent company must be able to separate the item from the subsidiary and sell it.

8. ____ A balance sheet reports goodwill as an intangible asset at $745,000. This figure indicates that the reporting company has an especially talented workforce.

9. ____ A balance sheet reports goodwill as an intangible asset at $745,000. This figure indicates that the reporting company has given an extensive amount of money to charities.

10. ____ Goodwill is an intangible asset that is usually written off to expense over forty years, although its actual life is likely to be much shorter than that.

11. ____ After a company records goodwill, it will remain on the company's balance sheet forever because it is not amortized.

12. ____ A company must be able to connect goodwill with a specific intangible (such as the quality of a company's workforce) before the asset can be recognized on a balance sheet.

13. ____ Research and development costs that help a company to develop successful products are capitalized under U.S. GAAP.

14. ____ Because of the handling of research and development costs required by U.S. GAAP, companies that spend significant amounts to develop new products will normally have exceptionally high amounts reported as assets on their balance sheets.

15. ____ U.S. GAAP and IFRS handle research and development costs in the same manner.

16. ____ A company agrees to pay $2 million for a patent in six years plus interest at an annual rate of 5 percent, which is considered a reasonable rate. A present value calculation must be carried out to determine the amount to be reported for the asset and the related liability.

17. ____ A company buys a copyright for $400,000 on January 1, Year One. If four payments are to be made annually on each January 1, starting on January 1, Year One, the asset balance is determined by finding the present value of an annuity due.

18. ____ On January 1, Year One, a company buys an intangible asset by agreeing to make a single payment of $300,000 in five years. Assume that, at a 10 percent annual interest rate which is viewed as reasonable, the present value is $170,000. On December 31, Year One, the liability is reported as $187,000.

19. ____ On January 1, Year One, a company buys an intangible asset by agreeing to make a single payment of $500,000 in five years. Assume that, at a 10 percent annual interest rate which is viewed as reasonable, the present value is $310,000. Interest expense to be recognized in Year Two is $34,100.

20. ____ On January 1, Year One, a company buys an intangible asset by agreeing to make a single payment of $700,000 in five years. Assume that, at a 10 percent annual interest rate which is viewed as reasonable, the present value is $400,000. The asset is expected to last for eight years and have no residual value. Amortization expense recognized on the asset for Year One is $50,000.

MULTIPLE CHOICE

1. A company spends $600,000 on research and $800,000 on development to earn a patent on a new invention. All of the legal costs to establish the patent amounted to $50,000. The company also had to spend an additional $90,000 to defend the patent (successfully) against a law suit. What is the capitalized cost of this patent?

    a. $50,000

    b. $90,000

    c. $140,000

    d. $1,540,000

2. On January 1, Year One, a company acquires the rights to an intangible asset for $300,000 with no residual value. The intangible has a legal life of ten years but is only expected to help generate revenues for six years. The straight-line method is always used. What is the net book value of this intangible asset at the end of Year Two?

    a. Zero

    b. $200,000

    c. $240,000

    d. $300,000

3. Which of the following intangible assets would not be subject to amortization?

    a. Goodwill

    b. Patent

    c. Copyright

    d. All intangible assets are subject to amortization

4. The Birmingham Corporation buys a patent from an inventor on January 1, Year One, for $350,000. The company expects the patent to help generate revenues for ten years. It has no residual value, and the straight-line method is always used. On December 31, Year Two, the patent has a fair value of $500,000. What is reported for this asset on the company's balance sheet on that date?

    a. $280,000

    b. $350,000

    c. $400,000

    d. $500,000

5. Krypton Corporation offers Earth Company $800,000 for a patent held by Earth Company. The patent is currently recorded by Earth Company at $14,000, the legal cost required to register the patent. Krypton had appraisers examine the patent before making an offer to purchase it, and those experts determined that it was worth between $459,000 and $1,090,000. If the purchase falls through, at what amount should Earth Company now report the patent?

    a. $14,000

    b. $459,000

    c. $800,000

    d. $1,090,000

6. Mitchell Inc. developed a product, spending $4,000,000 in research and $1,100,000 in development to do so. Mitchell applied for and received a patent for the product on January 1, Year One, spending $34,000 in legal and filing fees. The patent is valid for twenty years and is expected to generate revenue for that period of time. The patent has no expected residual value after that date. The straight-line method is always applied. What would be the net book value of the patent at the end of Year One?

    a. $32,300

    b. $34,000

    c. $4,832,000

    d. $5,134,000

7. The Goodin Corporation purchases all of the outstanding stock of the Winslow Corporation for $62 million. In buying Winslow, Goodin acquired several items that might qualify to be reported as identifiable intangible assets. Which of the following criteria are applied to determine whether Goodin can report an intangible?

    a. Goodin must have obtained contractual or other legal rights or the item can be separated from Winslow and sold.

    b. The item must have a life of over one year and generate revenue that the parent company can assess.

    c. The item must have a tangible element to it or be legally valid in nature.

    d. The item must improve the operations of Goodin or have a value that can be objectively determined.

8. A decision maker picks up a set of financial statements for the Barnes Corporation. On the balance sheet, the largest asset is titled "Goodwill." Which of the following statements is most likely to be true about this company?

    a. The company has donated significant amounts of money to charities in the local area.

    b. The company has bought other companies and paid more for those companies than the fair value of their identifiable net assets.

    c. The company has a large workforce of well-trained employees.

    d. The company has a superior management team in place.

9. On January 1, Year One, the Curry Corporation pays $7 million for all of the outstanding capital stock of a company that holds three assets and no liabilities. It has a building with a net book value of $2.3 million and a fair value of $2.8 million. It has equipment with a net book value of $1.1 and a fair value of $900,000. It holds several patents with no book value but a fair value of $1.3 million. Curry believes that this new subsidiary will be especially profitable for at least ten years. On a consolidated balance sheet as of December 31, Year One, what will Curry report as its goodwill balance?

    a. $1.3 million

    b. $1.8 million

    c. $2.0 million

    d. $3.6 million

10. Kremlin Company pays $2,900,000 for all of the outstanding common stock of Reticular Corporation. Reticular has assets on its balance sheet with a net book value of $1,500,000 and a fair value of $2,500,000. Reticular had no liabilities at this time. What is goodwill in this purchase?

    a. $0

    b. $400,000

    c. $1,000,000

    d. $1,400,000

11. Which of the following statements concerning research and development costs is not true?

    a. According to U.S. GAAP, research and development costs must be expensed as incurred.

    b. Current U.S. GAAP rules for reporting research and development costs violate the matching principle.

    c. International Financial Reporting Standards allow some development costs to be capitalized.

    d. U.S. GAAP reporting for research and development costs creates exceptionally large asset balances.

12. The Barcelona Company is a technology company and spends an enormous amount on research and development. The company has been successful in the past on a very high percentage of these projects. In connection with financial reporting, which of the following statements is true?

    a. Company officials must evaluate each project each year to estimate the possibility of success.

    b. All research and development costs will be capitalized and then amortized to expense over a reasonable period of time.

    c. Any project where the possibility of success is more than 50 percent must be capitalized.

    d. The company's total assets are probably worth more than shown on the balance sheet.

13. Lincoln Company has an accounting policy for internal reporting purposes whereby the costs of any research and development projects that are over 70 percent likely to succeed are capitalized and then depreciated over a five-year period with a full year of depreciation in the year of capitalization. In the current year, $400,000 was spent on Project One, and it was 55 percent likely to succeed, $600,000 was spent on Project Two, and it was 65 percent likely to succeed, and $900,000 was spent on Project Three, and it was 75 percent likely to succeed. In converting the internal financial statements to external financial statements, by how much will net income for the current year have to be reduced?

    a. $180,000

    b. $380,000

    c. $720,000

    d. $900,000

14. The El Paso Corporation buys a significant intangible asset for $900,000, an amount that will be paid in six years. If a reasonable annual interest rate is 5 percent, what is the capitalized cost of the asset?

    a. $522,743

    b. $671,594

    c. $754,090

    d. $900,000

15. The Vaska Company buys a patent on January 1, Year One, and agrees to pay $100,000 per year for the next five years. The first payment is made immediately, and the payments are made on each January 1 thereafter. If a reasonable annual interest rate is 8 percent, what is the recorded value of the patent?

    a. $378,425

    b. $431,213

    c. $468,950

    d. $500,000

16. On January 1, Year One, the Anderson Corporation buys a copyright and agrees to make a single payment of $700,000 in exactly four years. A reasonable annual interest rate is viewed as 10 percent, and a present value of $478,107 was determined. What amount of interest expense should Anderson recognize for Year One?

    a. Zero

    b. $47,811

    c. $70,000

    d. Cannot be determined from the information provided.

17. On January 1, Year One, the Maroni Corporation buys an intangible asset and agrees to make a single payment of $800,000 in exactly six years. A reasonable annual interest rate is viewed as 10 percent, and a present value of $451,580 was determined. What amount of interest expense should Maroni recognize for Year Two?

    a. Zero

    b. $45,158

    c. $49,674

    d. $80,000

18. The Heinline Company buys a patent on January 1, Year One, and agrees to pay exactly $100,000 per year for the next eight years (or $800,000 in total). The first payment is made immediately, and the payments are made on each January 1 thereafter. A reasonable annual interest rate is 10 percent, which gives an assumed present value of $586,840. What amount of interest expense should Heinline recognize for Year Two?

    a. Zero

    b. $43,552

    c. $58,684

    d. $60,000

VIDEO PROBLEMS

Professor Joe Hoyle discusses the answers to these two problems at the links that are indicated. After formulating your answers, watch each video to see how Professor Hoyle answers these questions.

1. Your roommate is an English major. The roommate's parents own a chain of ice cream shops located throughout Florida. One day, while reading a play by Shakespeare, your roommate poses this question: "My parents recently bought a new shop in Tallahassee. They bought it from an elderly couple who wanted to retire. It is in a great location and already has a huge number of regular customers. However, I don't understand why they paid so much. The building and land were worth $1 million, and the equipment and ice cream on hand couldn't have been worth more than $25,000. So, I expected them to pay around $1,025,000. But they paid $1.5 million. Why in the world did they pay so much? How are they ever going to report that shop in the future since they clearly overpaid?" How would you respond?

View the video online at: http://bit.ly/hoyle11-3

2. Your uncle and two friends started a small office supply store several years ago. The company has expanded and now has several large locations. Your uncle knows that you are taking a financial accounting class and asks you the following question: "In the office supply business, the North Lakeside Company is the best known name in the world. They manufacture great products, and everyone has heard of their high quality. We started selling their merchandise recently. We wanted to let people know of this relationship. We want to put the North Lakeside logo on each of our stores so that our customers would associate us with that same level of quality. It is good for our business, and it will bring us more customers who will buy more goods. We contacted North Lakeside about using their logo. They told us they would give us that right for $400,000. Well, we don't have that type of cash available at this time just for a logo. We tried to negotiate with them, and they said they still wanted exactly $400,000, but we could wait for four years before making the payment. By that time, the logo should have produced a lot of extra profits for us. We've certainly never done something like this before. When we sign the contract, how do we report this transaction?" How would you respond?

View the video online at: http://bit.ly/hoyle11-4

PROBLEMS

1. At the beginning of Year One, Jaguar Corporation purchased a license from Angel Corporation that gives Jaguar the legal right to use a process Angel developed. The purchase price of the license was $1,500,000, including legal fees. According to the agreement, Jaguar will be able to use the process for five years.

    a. Record Jaguar's purchase of the license.

    b. Record amortization of the license at the end of Year One assuming the straight-line method is used and there is no expected residual value.

    c. What is the net book value of the license reported on Jaguar's balance sheet at the end of Year Three?

2. Yolanda Company created a product for which it was able to obtain a patent. Yolanda sold this patent to Christiana Inc. for $4 million at the beginning of Year One. Christiana paid an additional $200,000 in legal fees to properly record the patent. On that date, Christiana determined that the patent had a remaining legal life of ten years but a useful life of only seven years. The straight-line method is to be applied with no expected residual value.

    a. Record Christiana's purchase of the patent.

    b. Record amortization of the patent at the end of Year One and Year Two.

    c. What is the book value of the patent reported on Christiana's balance sheet at the end of Year Three?

    d. During Year Four, Christiana is sued by Bushnell Corporation. Bushnell claims that it has a patent on a product very similar to the one held by Christiana and that Bushnell's patent was registered first. Christiana spends $600,000 during Year Four and successfully defends the patent. What entry is made for these expenditures?

    e. Use the same facts as in 2.d. except assume that Christiana is not able to successfully defend its right to this patent. What journal entry is made?

3. As of January 1, Year One, Company Z has no liabilities and only two assets: a donut maker with a net book value of $300,000 (and a fair value of $360,000) and a cookie machine with a net book value of $400,000 (and a fair value of $440,000). Each of these assets has a remaining useful life of ten years and no expected residual value. Company A offers $1 million to acquire all of the ownership of Company Z. The owners of Company Z hold out and manage to get $1.2 million in cash.

    a. Make the journal entry to be recorded by Company A for this acquisition.

    b. What depreciation/amortization expense will Company A recognize in connection with these acquired assets at the end of Year One?

    c. What is the appropriate handling of any goodwill resulting from this transaction?

4. On January 1, Year One, a pharmaceutical company starts work on creating three new medicines that could lead to valuable products. The company will spend millions on each project and would not undertake this endeavor if it did not believe that it has a reasonable chance of recovering its investment. Historically for this company, one out of every three new projects actually became a successful product on the market. If that happens, the company expects to generate over $10 million in revenue at a minimum. By the end of Year One, the company spent exactly $1 million in research and development for each of three projects. Based on a careful evaluation, company officials believe the first project has a 30 percent chance of success, the second project has a 60 percent chance of success, and the third project has a 90 percent chance of success.

    a. Assume U.S. GAAP does not have an official standard in this area of accounting. Provide as many viable methods as possible to record the $3 million cost that has been incurred to date. For each, provide at least one reason the method could be appropriate.

    b. How does U.S. GAAP account for the $3 million in costs incurred here for research and development?

    c. How does IFRS account for the $3 million in costs incurred here for research and development?

5. The Wisconsin Corporation spends $100,000 in research and $200,000 in development during Year One. The company spends the same amounts in Year Two. For its internal reporting, the company has a policy whereby all research costs are expensed as incurred but all development costs are capitalized. These capitalized costs are then amortized to expense over five full years beginning with the year after the cost is incurred.

    a. What change is necessary to reduce the internally reported net income figure for Year One to the amount that should be shown for external reporting purposes according to U.S. GAAP?

    b. What change is necessary to reduce the internally reported net income figure for Year Two to the amount that should be shown for external reporting purposes according to U.S. GAAP?

6. The Baltimore Corporation reported net income in Year One of $90,000 and in Year Two of $140,000. The company spent $16,000 for research and development in Year One and another $24,000 for research and development in Year Two. The company follows the policy of capitalizing its research and development costs and then amortizing them over four years (using the half-year convention for the initial year). The straight-line method is used for amortization with no expected residual value.

    a. If U.S. GAAP is to be applied, what was the correctly reported net income for Year One?

    b. If U.S. GAAP is to be applied, what was the correctly reported net income for Year Two?

7. The American Corporation and the French Corporation are identical in every way. Both companies spend $200,000 for research costs in Year One as well as $100,000 in development costs during that same year. The American Corporation follows U.S. GAAP. The French Corporation follows IFRS and believes these development costs meet the criteria for capitalization. The capitalized costs are amortized over four years using the straight-line method and the half-year convention.

    a. What is the difference in reported net income between these two companies for Year One?

    b. Assuming no further amounts were spent for research and development in Year Two, what is the difference in reported net income between these two companies in that second year?

8. Star Corporation purchases Trek Inc. Through this acquisition, Star Corporation is gaining the following assets and liabilities:

	Value on Trek's Books	Current Market Value
Inventory	$480,000	$480,000
Land	$1,050,000	$50,000,000
Trademarks	$64,000	$20,000,000
Patent	$15,000	$1,850,000
Accounts Payable	$650,000	$650,000

    a. Assume Star pays cash of exactly $71,680,000 to acquire all of the outstanding ownership shares of Trek Inc. Prepare the appropriate journal entry for Star.

    b. Assume the negotiations between Star and Trek are fierce and, eventually, Star agrees to pay $83 million for all of the outstanding ownership shares of Trek Inc. Prepare the appropriate journal entry for Star.

    c. What subsequent accounting is applied in reporting any goodwill that results from this acquisition?

9. Calculate the present value of each of the following single payment amounts based on the indicated reasonable rate of annual interest and the number of time periods until the payment is made.

Future Cash Flow	Annual Interest Rate	Number of Periods	Present Value
$400,000	4%	7 years	
$400,000	6%	7 years	
$400,000	4%	12 years	
$400,000	6%	12 years	

    a. Does the present value of the future cash flows increase or decrease when the interest rate increases? What causes that effect?

    b. Does the present value of the future cash flows increase or decrease as the number of time periods increases? What causes that effect?

10. On January 1, Year One, Fred Corporation purchases a patent from Barney Company for $10 million, payable at the end of three years. The patent itself has an expected life of ten years and no anticipated residual value. No interest rate is stated in the contract, but Fred could borrow that amount of money from a bank at 6 percent interest. Amortization is recorded using the straight-line method.

    a. Record the journal entry for the patent acquisition on January 1, Year One.

    b. Record the year-end adjusting entries to recognize both interest expense and amortization expense for each of these three years.

    c. Record the journal entry for Fred's payment on December 31, Year Three.

11. Calculate the present value of each of the following annuity amounts based on the reasonable interest rate that is specified and the number of time periods. Assume that the first payment is made immediately so that the cash payments create an annuity due.

Payment per Period	Annual Interest Rate	Number of Periods	Present Value
$30,000	5%	8 years	
$60,000	4%	7 years	
$25,000	8%	10 years	
$56,000	6%	4 years	

12. Highlight Company purchases the right to use a piece of music from the original musician who created it. Officials hope to make this music the company's "signature song." Therefore, the contract (which is signed on January 1, Year One) is for four years. The agreed upon price is $800,000, with no stated interest rate to be paid. Highlight could borrow this amount of money at a 5 percent annual interest rate at the current time. The arrangement states that Highlight will make this $800,000 payment on December 31, Year Four.

   a. Record the journal entry for Highlight for the acquisition of this copyright on January 1, Year One.

   b. Record the adjusting entries to recognize interest expense and amortization expense on December 31 of each of the subsequent four years.

   c. Record the journal entry for the payment of the $800,000 on December 31, Year Four.

13. Moonbeam Company purchases the right to use a piece of music from the original musician who created it. Officials hope to make this music the company's "signature song." Therefore, the contract (which is signed on January 1, Year One) is for four years. The agreed upon price is $800,000, with no stated interest rate. Moonbeam could borrow this amount of money at an 8 percent annual interest at the current time. The arrangement states that Moonbeam will actually make an annual payment of $200,000 for four years on each January 1 starting on January 1, Year One.

   a. Record the journal entry for Moonbeam for the acquisition of this copyright on January 1, Year One.

   b. Record the adjusting entries for Moonbeam to recognize amortization expense on December 31, Year One. Assume the straight-line method is applied.

   c. Record the journal entries and the adjusting entries for Moonbeam for these payments and to recognize interest expense from December 31, Year One through January 1, Year Four.

COMPREHENSIVE PROBLEM

This problem will carry through several chapters, building in difficulty. It allows students to continually practice skills and knowledge learned in previous chapters.

In Chapter 10, you prepared Webworks statements for October. They are included here as a starting point for November.

FIGURE 11.12 Webworks Financial Statements

Webworks
Income Statement
As of October 31

Revenue	$13,700
Cost of Goods Sold	(6,615)
Gross Profit	7,085
Depreciation Expense	(601)
Other Expenses	(3,590)
Earnings before Tax	2,894
Tax Expense	(868)
Net Income	$2,026

FIGURE 11.13

Webworks
Stmt. of Retained Earnings
As of October 31

Retained Earnings, October 1	$4,645
Net Income	2,026
Retained Earnings, October 31	$6,671

FIGURE 11.14

	Webworks Balance Sheet October 31			
Assets		**Liabilities**		
Current		**Current**		
Cash	$1,532	Accounts Payable	$3,385	
Accounts Receivable	1,450	Salaries Payable	100	
Less Allowance for				
Doubtful Accounts	(145)			
Net Accounts Receivable	1,305			
Merchandise Inventory	1,470			
Supplies Inventory	50			
Prepaid Rent	400			
Total Current Assets	$4,757	Total Current Liabilities	$3,485	
Noncurrent				
Equipment				
Less Accumulated				
Depreciation	$7,000			
Furniture	(584)			
Less Accumulated	1,000			
Depreciation	(17)			
Total Noncurrent Assets	$7,399			
		Owners' Equity		
		Capital Stock	$2,000	
		Retained Earnings	6,671	
		Total Owners' Equity	$8,671	
		Total Liabilities & Owners'		
Total Assets	$12,156	Equity	$12,156	

The following events occur during November:

a. Webworks starts and completes eight more sites and bills clients for $4,600.

b. Webworks purchases supplies worth $80 on account.

c. At the beginning of November, Webworks had nine keyboards in stock costing $110 each and forty flash drives costing $12 each. Webworks uses periodic FIFO to monitor the cost of its inventory.

d. Webworks purchases sixty keyboards for $111 each and ninety flash drives for $13 each. These purchases were on account.

e. Webworks pays Nancy Po (an employee) $800 for her work during the first three weeks of October.

f. Webworks sells 60 keyboards for $9,000 and 120 flash drives for $2,400 cash.

g. A local realtor pays $400 in advance for a Web site. It will not be completed until December.

h. Leon Jackson (the owner of the business) read in a trade publication about a new software program that could enhance the Web sites Webworks is developing for clients. He purchases a license to use this program for one year by paying $2,400 cash.

i. Webworks collects $5,000 in accounts receivable.

    j. Webworks pays off its salaries payable from November.

    k. Webworks pays off $8,500 of its accounts payable.

    l. Webworks pays Leon Jackson a salary of $2,000.

   m. Webworks wrote off an uncollectible account in the amount of $100.

    n. Webworks pays taxes of $1,304 in cash.

       Required:

         A. Prepare journal entries for the previous events.

         B. Post the journal entries to T-accounts.

         C. Prepare an unadjusted trial balance for Webworks for November.

         D. Prepare adjusting entries for the following and post them to your T-accounts.

    o. Webworks owes Nancy Po $150 for her work during the last week of November.

    p. Leon's parents let him know that Webworks owes $290 toward the electricity bill. Webworks will pay them this amount in December.

    q. Webworks determines that it has $20 worth of supplies remaining at the end of November.

    r. Prepaid rent should be adjusted for November's portion.

    s. Webworks is continuing to accrue bad debts at 10 percent of accounts receivable.

    t. Webworks continues to depreciate its equipment over four years and its furniture over five years, using the straight-line method.

    u. The license agreement should be amortized over its one-year life.

    v. Record cost of goods sold.

         E. Prepare an adjusted trial balance.

         F. Prepare financial statements for November.

RESEARCH ASSIGNMENT

Assume that you take a job as a summer employee for an investment advisory service. One of the partners for that firm is currently looking at the possibility of investing in **Amazon.com**. The partner believes that the company's assets increased by a rather large amount during 2010. The partner is curious as to how much of that increase is from intangible assets that were acquired through the purchase of other companies. The partner asks you to look at the 2010 financial statements for Amazon by following this path:

- Go to http://www.amazon.com.
- At the very bottom of this screen, click on "Investor Relations."
- On the left side of the next screen, click on "Annual Reports and Proxies."
- On the next screen, click on "2010 Annual Report" to download.
- Go to page 39 and find the balance sheet for December 31, 2010.
- Go to page 51 and read the first part of "Note 4 – Acquisitions, Goodwill, and Acquired Intangible Assets" that is titled "2010 Acquisition Activity."

    a. Using the balance sheet information above, determine the amount of goodwill reported at the end of 2009 and also at the end of 2010. What does that indicate?

    b. Using the balance sheet information above, determine the amount of goodwill as percentage of total assets at the end of 2009 and also at the end of 2010. Has goodwill become a larger percentage of assets in 2010 than it was in 2009?

    c. What information is found in the first part of Note 4 that will be of interest to the partner who is looking at this company?

ENDNOTES

1. Unique accounting rules have long existed in certain industries to address unusual circumstances. College accounting textbooks such as this one tend to focus on general rules rather than delve into the specifics of accounting as it applies to a particular industry.

2. For a complete coverage of the history and ramifications of the **Enron** scandal, both the movie and the book *The Smartest Guys in the Room* are quite informative and fascinating.

3. Similar rules apply when an asset is sold and the money is to be collected over a period of future years. For convenience, the illustrations in this chapter will focus solely on cash payments made in an acquisition.

4. The Accounting Principles Board (APB) was the primary group in charge of creating U.S. GAAP from 1962 until 1973 when it was replaced by the Financial Accounting Standards Board (FASB). During those years, the APB produced thirty-one opinions. Its Opinion 21, "Interest of Receivables and Payables" was issued in August 1971 and established the rules described here. Within the new *Accounting Standards Codification*, information on the reporting of interest can be found at FASB ASC 835-30.

5. The effective rate method of computing interest is demonstrated here. The principal balance is multiplied by the reasonable interest rate to get the amount of interest to be recorded each period. The effective rate method is the preferred approach according to U.S. GAAP. In Chapter 14, an alternative method known as the straight-line method is also demonstrated. It is also allowed by U.S. GAAP if the differences are not viewed as material.

6. If the computations and entries are all correct, the liability balance will grow to $1 million at the end of five years. In the present value computation, the interest was removed at a 10 percent annual rate and then put back into the liability each year through compounding at the same rate. Because figures are rounded in these computations, the final interest journal entry may have to be adjusted by a few dollars to arrive at the $1 million total.

7. The mathematical formula to determine the present value of an annuity due of $1 per period is present value of an annuity due = $[(1 - 1/[1 + i]^n)/i] \times (1 + i)$, where i is the appropriate interest rate and n is the number of payment periods.

   The mathematical formula to determine the present value of an ordinary annuity of $1 per period is present value of an ordinary annuity = $(1 - 1/[1 + i]^n)/i$, where *i* is the appropriate interest rate and *n* is the number of payment periods.

8. On an Excel spreadsheet, the present value of a $1 per year annuity due for five periods at a reasonable rate of 12 percent is computed by typing the following data into a cell: =PV(.12,5,1,,1). Therefore, the present value of seven annual payments of $25,000 made as annuity due with a reasonable interest rate of 9 percent would be found by entering =PV(.09,7,25000,,1)

   If this had been an ordinary annuity because the initial payment was delayed until the end of the first period, present value of that $1 per year ordinary annuity is =PV(.12,5,1,,0). The present value of seven annual payments of $25,000 made as an ordinary annuity with a reasonable interest rate of 9 percent would be found by entering =PV(.09,7,25000,,0)

In a Set of Financial Statements, What Information Is Conveyed about Equity Investments?

 Video Clip

In this video, Professor Joe Hoyle introduces the essential points covered in Chapter 12.

View the video online at: http://bit.ly/hoyle12-1

1. ACCOUNTING FOR INVESTMENTS IN TRADING SECURITIES

LEARNING OBJECTIVES

At the end of this section, students should be able to meet the following objectives:

1. Realize that the financial reporting of investments in the ownership shares of another company depends on the purpose of the acquisition.
2. Explain the characteristics of investments that are classified as trading securities.
3. Account for changes in the value of investments in trading securities and understand the rationale for this handling.
4. Record dividends received from investments that are classified as trading securities.
5. Determine the gain or loss to be recorded on the sale of a trading security.

1.1 The Reasons Why One Company Buys Ownership Shares of Another

*Question: Businesses frequently acquire ownership shares (often referred to as equity or capital shares) of other companies. On September 30, 2011, **Microsoft** disclosed that it held "equity and other investments" reported at nearly $8.6 billion. Many such investments are only made to acquire a small percentage of the ownership. However, that is not always the case. In April, 2011, **Johnson & Johnson** announced the $21.3 billion purchase of Swiss medical device maker **Synthes Inc.** Whether a few shares are bought, or the entire company is bought, such investments offer many potential benefits. **What are the most common reasons for one company to buy the ownership shares of another company?***

Answer: Potentially, many benefits can accrue from obtaining shares of the capital stock issued by another business. Interestingly, the specific method of financial reporting depends on the owner's purpose for holding such investments. Thus, the accounting process here is quite unique. The reporting of most assets (such as inventory and equipment) does not vary because of the rationale for making the purchase and then retaining the property. In contrast, the accounting process used to report the ownership of stock in another company falls within one of several methods based solely on the reason for the investment.

Companies frequently find that they are holding excess cash not needed at the moment for operating purposes. Such money can be temporarily invested to increase net income. Traditional savings accounts or money market funds offer only very low returns. Company officials often seek greater profit by using surplus money to buy the ownership shares of other organizations. The hope is that the market price of these shares will appreciate in value and/or dividends will be received before the cash is needed for operations. Such investments can be held for a few days (or even hours) or many years. Although earnings can improve through this strategy, the buyer does face additional risk. Share prices do not always go up. They can also decline in value, resulting in losses for the investor.

When equity shares are bought solely as a way to store cash and increase profits, the investor has no desire to influence or control the decisions of the other company. That is not the reason for the purchase; the ownership interest is much too small.

control

According to U.S. GAAP, it exists when one company owns more than 50 percent of the outstanding common shares of another company so that the parent can direct all decision making; for external reporting purposes, the financial information of both companies must be consolidated to form a single set of financial statements.

Investors, though, may also embrace a strategy of acquiring enough shares to gain some degree of influence over the other organization. Often, profitable synergies can be developed by having two companies connected in this way. For example, as of October 3, 2010, **Starbucks Corporation** held 39.9 percent of the outstanding stock of **Starbucks Coffee Japan Ltd. Starbucks** does not own a sufficient number of shares to control the operations of the Japanese company, but it certainly can apply significant influence if it so chooses.

Finally, as in the acquisition of **Synthes** by **Johnson & Johnson**, the investor may seek to obtain a controlling interest in the other company (in U.S. GAAP that is viewed as being over 50 percent of the outstanding capital stock). In many cases, the parent company chooses to buy 100 percent ownership of the other business to gain complete control. Such acquisitions are common as large companies attempt to (a) move into new industries or geographical areas, (b) become bigger players in their current markets, (c) gain access to valuable assets, or (d) eliminate competitors. Many smaller companies are started by entrepreneurs with the specific hope that success will attract acquisition interest from a larger organization. Often, significant fortunes are earned by the original owners as a result of the sale of their company to a bigger business.

1.2 Trading Securities

Question: As can be seen in the previous answer, several different reasons exist for buying capital stock. Applicable accounting rules can best be demonstrated by focusing on one of these types of investments at a time.

Assume that Valente Corporation is holding $25,000 in cash that it will not need for several weeks. This money is currently in a money market fund earning only a 1 percent annual rate of return. In hopes of generating a higher profit, the president of Valente has studied the financial statements of Bayless Corporation, a company with capital stock trading on the New York Stock Exchange for $25 per share. By November 30, Year One, the president has come to believe that Bayless stock will make a rather significant jump in market price in the near future. Consequently, Valente uses the $25,000 to acquire one thousand shares of stock in Bayless that will be held for only a few weeks or months. How does a company report an equity investment that is bought with the expectation that the shares will be sold shortly after the purchase is made?

Answer: If management intends to sell the equity shares of another company shortly after buying them, the purchase is classified on the balance sheet as an investment in **trading securities**. On the acquisition date, as shown in Figure 12.1, the asset is recorded by Valente at historical cost.

trading securities

Classification of investments in stocks and bonds when management's intentions are to sell them quickly in the near term; they are reported as assets on the balance sheet at fair value with all changes in value affecting net income.

FIGURE 12.1 Purchase of Ownership Shares Classified as Trading Securities

As an owner, even if the shares are only held for a short time, Valente might receive a cash dividend from Bayless. Many companies distribute dividends to their stockholders periodically as a way of sharing a portion of any income that has been earned.

Assume that Bayless has been profitable and, as a result, a $0.20 per share cash dividend is declared by its board of directors and paid in December, Year One. Valente receives $200 of this dividend ($0.20 per share × 1,000 shares), which is reported as revenue on the owner's Year One income statement. The journal entry is presented in Figure 12.2.

FIGURE 12.2 Receipt of Dividend from Investment in Stock

Because of the short-term nature of this investment, Valente might sell these shares prior to the end of Year One. The purchase of Bayless stock was made anticipating a quick sale. Consequently, a gain is reported if more than $25,000 is received, whereas a loss results if the shares are sold for less than $25,000. Such gains and losses appear on the owner's income statement when created by the sale of a trading security.

1.3 The Value of Trading Securities at Year's End

Question: The accounting process for trading securities becomes more complicated if Valente continues to own this investment in Bayless at year end. Should equity shares held as a trading security be reported on the owner's balance sheet at historical cost or current fair value? Which reporting provides the most helpful information to outside decision makers?

Answer: U.S. GAAP requires investments in trading securities to be reported on the owner's balance sheet at fair value. Therefore, if the shares of Bayless are worth $28,000 at December 31, Year One, Valente must adjust the reported value from $25,000 to $28,000 by reporting a gain as shown in Figure 12.3.

FIGURE 12.3 Shares of Bayless (a Trading Security) Adjusted to Fair Value at End of Year One

Investment in Trading Securities	3,000	
Unrealized Gain—Trading Securities		3,000

unrealized gain or loss

A gain or loss created by an increase or decrease in the value of an asset although not yet finalized by a sale.

The gain here is labeled as **unrealized** to indicate that the value of the asset has appreciated but no final sale has yet taken place. Therefore, the gain is not guaranteed; the value might go back down before the shares are sold. However, the $3,000 unrealized gain is reported on Valente's Year One income statement so that net income is affected.

TEST YOURSELF

Question:

James Attenborough is studying the financial statements published for the Hawthorne Roberts Corporation. This company owns shares in **Microsoft** and several other companies. Consequently, it reports an investment in trading securities account on its year-end balance sheet as an asset with a balance of $18,765. What does that figure represent?

    a. It is impossible to tell without reading the notes to the financial statements.

    b. The $18,765 was the historical cost of these shares.

    c. The $18,765 is the fair value of the shares on the balance sheet date.

    d. The $18,765 is the lower of the cost or market value of these shares at the end of the year.

Answer:

The correct answer is choice c: The $18,765 is the fair value of the shares on the balance sheet date.

Explanation:

Investments in trading securities are held for a relatively quick sale. They are always reported at fair value regardless of whether that figure is above or below the cost of acquisition. Fair value is easy to determine and the company knows that it can get that amount on the balance sheet date.

1.4 Reporting Trading Securities at Fair Value

*Question: The reporting demonstrated above for an investment in a trading security raises a theoretical question that has long been debated in financial accounting. Is recognizing a gain in the value of a trading security (or a loss if the stock price has declined) on the owner's income statement appropriate before an actual sale takes place? In this illustration, for example, a $3,000 gain is reported, but the value of these shares might suddenly plummet and eliminate that gain prior to a sale. The gain might never be received. In previous chapters, assets such as buildings and inventory were never adjusted to fair value unless impairment had taken place. **Why is an investment in a trading security always reported at fair value regardless of whether that value is above or below historical cost?***

    Answer: Changes in the value of trading securities are recognized and the resulting gains or losses are included within current net income for several reasons:

- The Bayless shares sell on a stock exchange. Thus, the reported value of $28,000 can be objectively determined. It is not an estimated amount subject to manipulation as is the fair value of assets such as buildings and inventory.

- The stock can be sold immediately; Valente does not even have to find a buyer. The stock exchange provides a workable mechanism to create a sale whenever the owner wants to liquidate the investment. No question exists that these shares can be sold at any time. Once again, the same assertion cannot be made for assets such as buildings and inventory.

- As a trading security, a sale is anticipated in the near term. The owner does not plan to hold the stock for a long period of time. Further changes in value can certainly take place but are less likely to be severe. The shortness of time limits the chance of radical fluctuations in value after the balance sheet date.

For these reasons, U.S. GAAP requires that investments in trading securities be reported on the owner's balance sheet at fair value ($28,000 in this example). Therefore, Valente will report both the dividend revenue of $200 and the unrealized gain of $3,000 on its Year One income statement.

If, instead, the fair value at year-end had been only $21,000, a $4,000 unrealized loss appears on Valente's income statement to reflect the decline in value ($25,000 historical cost dropping to $21,000 fair value).

TEST YOURSELF

Question:

During Year One, Hancock Corporation buys 2,000 shares of Waltz Inc. for $34 per share. Hancock appropriately records this acquisition as an investment in trading securities because it plans to make a sale in the near future. In December of Year One, Waltz pays a $1 per share cash dividend to its owners. On the last day of December, the stock is selling on a stock exchange for $39 per share. What is the impact of these events on the income reported by Hancock for Year One?

a. No effect

b. Increase of $2,000

c. Increase of $10,000

d. Increase of $12,000

Answer:

The correct answer is choice d: Increase of $12,000.

Explanation:

The dividend that is received ($2,000 or $1.00 per share × 2,000 shares) is reported as revenue by the recipient (Hancock). In addition, because these shares are classified as trading securities, the change in value this year also impacts net income. The price of the stock went up $5 per share ($39 less $34) so that Hancock reports a gain of $10,000 ($5 per share × 2,000 shares). Total increase in income reported by Hancock is $12,000 ($2,000 plus $10,000).

1.5 The Sale of a Trading Security

Question: In this ongoing illustration, Valente Corporation bought one thousand shares of Bayless Corporation which it planned to sell in a relatively short period of time. At the end of Year One, this trading security was adjusted from the historical cost of $25,000 to its fair value of $28,000. The $3,000 unrealized gain was reported within net income on the Year One income statement.

Assume that these shares are sold by Valente on February 3, Year Two, for $27,000 in cash. **What financial reporting is appropriate when an investment in trading securities is sold in a subsequent period?** *What effect does this final transaction have on reported income?*

Answer: Following the Year One adjustment, this investment is recorded in the general ledger at the fair value of $28,000 rather than historical cost. When eventually sold, any difference between the sales price and this carrying amount is recorded as a gain or a loss on the Year Two income statement.

Because the sales price of these shares ($27,000) is less than the balance now being reported ($28,000), recognition of a $1,000 loss is appropriate, as can be seen in Figure 12.4. This loss reflects the drop in value of the shares that took place during Year Two.

FIGURE 12.4 Sale of Shares of Bayless (a Trading Security) for $27,000 in Year Two

Cash	27,000	
Loss on Sale of Trading Investment	1,000	
Investment in Trading Securities		28,000

This investment was originally bought for $25,000 and later sold for $27,000 so an overall gain of $2,000 was earned. For reporting purposes, this income effect is spread between the two years of ownership. A gain of $3,000 was recognized in Year One to reflect the appreciation in value during that period of time. Then, in Year Two, a loss of $1,000 is reported because the stock price fell by that amount prior to being sold.

Investments in trading securities are always shown on the owner's balance sheet at fair value. The gains and losses reported in the income statement will parallel the movement in value that took place each period.

TEST YOURSELF

Question:

Late in Year One, a company buys one share of a publicly traded company for $75. This investment is reported as a trading security because the owner plans to sell the stock in the near future. At the end of Year One, this share is only worth $62. However, early in Year Two, the stock price soars to $80 and the stock is sold. A $2 cash dividend is also received by the owner in January of Year Two. What is the reported income effect of this ownership?

a. No change in income in Year One but a $5 increase in Year Two.
b. No change in income in Year One but a $7 increase in Year Two.
c. Net income is reduced $13 in Year One but an $18 increase in Year Two.
d. Net income is reduced $13 in Year One but a $20 increase in Year Two.

Answer:

The correct answer is choice d: Net income is reduced $13 in Year One but a $20 increase in Year Two.

Explanation:

As a trading security, the $13 drop in value in Year One ($75 less $62) is reported as a loss on the owner's income statement. Then, the $18 rise in value in Year Two ($80 less $62) increases net income. In addition, the $2 dividend increases the Year Two income reported by the owner bringing it up to $20.

KEY TAKEAWAY

Many companies acquire the equity shares of other companies as investments. The applicable accounting procedures depend on the purpose for the ownership. If the stock is only to be held for a short period of time, it is labeled a trading security. The investment is then adjusted to fair value whenever financial statements are to be produced. Any change in value creates a gain or loss that is reported within net income because fair value is objectively determined, the shares can be liquidated easily, and a quick sale is anticipated before a significant change in fair value is likely to occur. Dividends received by the owner are recorded as revenue. Whenever trading securities are sold, only the increase or decrease in value during the current year is reported within net income since earlier changes have already been reported in that manner.

2. ACCOUNTING FOR INVESTMENTS IN SECURITIES THAT ARE CLASSIFIED AS AVAILABLE-FOR-SALE

LEARNING OBJECTIVES

At the end of this section, students should be able to meet the following objectives:

1. Identify the types of investments classified as available-for-sale.
2. Record the receipt of dividends from an investment that is viewed as available-for-sale.
3. Explain the financial reporting of changes in the fair value of investments in available-for-sale securities.
4. Calculate the gain or loss to be reported when available-for-sale securities are eventually sold.
5. Understand the need for reporting comprehensive income as well as net income.
6. Explain the adjustment made to net income in order to arrive at comprehensive income.

2.1 Reporting Available-For-Sale Investments

Question: Not all investments in stock are bought for quick sale. Assume that Valente Corporation bought one thousand shares of Bayless Corporation for $25 each in Year One but does not anticipate selling this investment in the near term. Company officials intend to hold these shares for the foreseeable future until the money is clearly needed. Although the stock could be sold at any time, the president of Valente believes the investment might well be retained for years. During Year One, a $200 cash dividend is received from the Bayless shares. At the end of that period, the stock is selling for $28 per share. **How does the decision to hold equity shares for an extended period of time impact the financial reporting process?**

Answer: Valente does not anticipate a quick sale of its investment in Bayless. Because Valente's intention is to retain these shares for an indefinite period, they will be classified on the company's balance sheet as an investment in **available-for-sale securities** rather than as trading securities. Despite the difference in the plan for holding these shares, they are—once again—recorded at historical cost when acquired, as shown in Figure 12.5.

available-for-sale securities

Accounting classification for investments in stocks and bonds when management's intentions are to retain them for an indefinite period; they are reported on the balance sheet at fair value although unrealized gains and losses are included in stockholders' equity and not within net income.

FIGURE 12.5 Purchase of Ownership Shares Classified as Available-for-Sale Securities

| Investment in Available-for-Sale Securities | 25,000 | |
| Cash | | 25,000 |

The receipt of the dividend is also reported in the same manner as before with the dividend revenue increasing Valente's net income. No difference is created between the accounting for trading securities and accounting for available-for-sale securities as a result of a dividend.

FIGURE 12.6 Receipt of Dividend from Investment in Available-for-Sale Securities

| Cash | 200 | |
| Dividend Revenue | | 200 |

The difference in reporting begins at the end of the year. U.S. GAAP requires available-for-sale investments to be included on the investor's balance sheet at fair value (in the same manner as trading securities). As before, this adjustment to fair value creates an unrealized gain of $3,000, as is reflected in Figure 12.7. However, reported net income is not affected as it was with the investment in the trading security.

FIGURE 12.7 Shares of Bayless (an Available-for-Sale Security) Are Adjusted to Fair Value at End of Year One

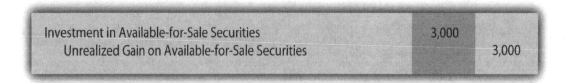

| Investment in Available-for-Sale Securities | 3,000 | |
| Unrealized Gain on Available-for-Sale Securities | | 3,000 |

2.2 Accumulated Other Comprehensive Income

Question: Based on the previous discussion, an immediate question is obvious: If the $3,000 unrealized gain shown in Figure 12.7 is not presented on the income statement, where is that amount reported by the owner? **How are changes in the fair value of available-for-sale securities reported?**

Answer: Because no sale is anticipated in the near term, the fair value of available-for-sale shares will possibly go up and down numerous times before being sold. Hence, the current gain is not viewed as "sure enough." As a result of this uncertainty, a change in the owner's reported net income is not considered appropriate.

Instead, any unrealized gain (or loss) in the value of an investment that is classified as available-for-sale is reported within the stockholders' equity section of the balance sheet. The figure is listed either just above or below the retained earnings account. A few other unrealized gains and losses are handled in this manner and are combined and reported as **accumulated other comprehensive income** as shown in Figure 12.8.

accumulated other comprehensive income

A section of the stockholders' equity of a balance sheet where unrealized gains and losses on available-for-sale securities (as well as a few other specified gains and losses) are shown rather than being presented on the reporting company's income statement.

FIGURE 12.8 Stockholders' Equity Including Accumulated Other Comprehensive Income

Contributed Capital (or Capital Stock)	XXX
Retained Earnings	XXX
Accumulated Other Comprehensive Income:	
Unrealized Gain on Available-for-Sale Securities	3,000

Consequently, the primary difference in the financial accounting for trading securities and available-for-sale securities is in the placement of unrealized gains and losses from changes in value:

- Changes in the value of trading securities are reported in the income statement.
- Changes in the value of available-for-sale securities are shown in stockholders' equity and not net income.

The described procedures were first created in 1993 and have been used since that time. Interestingly, in 2007, FASB passed a rule that allows companies to elect to report available-for-sale investments as trading securities. This option must be selected when the investment is purchased. Thus, if that election is made, the $3,000 unrealized gain is reported on the income statement despite the intention to hold the securities for an indefinite period. This is another example of accounting rules that are not as rigid as sometimes perceived.

TEST YOURSELF

Question:

Company A buys shares of a well-known company in Year One for $130,000. Company officials plan to hold this investment for only a short period of time so that it is classified as a trading security. Coincidentally, Company B makes the same investment at the same time for the same cost. However, Company B officials expect to hold these shares indefinitely. Company B reports this investment as available-for-sale and does not elect to report it in the same manner as a trading security. Both companies continue to hold their investments at the end of the year when they are each worth $144,000. Which of the following is not true?

a. Both companies will report their investment at $144,000.

b. Net income will increase more for Company A than for Company B because of these investments.

c. Company A reports other accumulated comprehensive income on the December 31, Year One, balance sheet of $14,000.

d. Company B reports other accumulated comprehensive income on the December 31, Year One, balance sheet of $14,000.

Answer:

The correct answer is choice c: Company A reports other accumulated comprehensive income on the December 31, Year One, balance sheet of $14,000.

Explanation:

Both companies report the asset as $144,000, its fair value at the end of the year. Company A views these shares as trading securities so that the increase in value of $14,000 is reported as an unrealized gain in net income. However, Company B has classified the investment as available-for-sale. Thus, the $14,000 unrealized gain is not shown within net income but, rather, in stockholders' equity as "other accumulated comprehensive income."

2.3 The Sale of Available-For-Sale Securities

Question: Assume that Valente did not choose to report the available-for-sale investment as a trading security but rather by means of the traditional approach. Thus, the $3,000 unrealized gain created by the appreciation of value is reported within stockholders' equity at the end of Year One. In Year Two, these shares are sold on the stock exchange for $27,000. What reporting is made at that time? **How is the eventual sale of investments that are classified as available-for-sale securities reported?**

Answer: When available-for-sale securities are sold, the difference between the original cost ($25,000) and the selling price ($27,000) appears as a realized gain (or loss) on the owner's income statement. Because no change in net income was reported in the previous year, this entire amount has to be recognized at the date of sale. Having presented the unrealized gain within stockholders' equity in Year One, the change in value only touches net income when sold.

However, mechanical complexities now exist. The investment has been adjusted to a $28,000 carrying amount, and a $3,000 unrealized gain still remains within stockholders' equity. As a balance sheet account, this $3,000 figure is not closed out at the end of Year One. Therefore, when the investment is sold, both the $28,000 asset and the $3,000 unrealized gain must be removed. The net amount mirrors the $25,000 historical cost of these shares. By eliminating the previous gain in this manner, the asset is brought back to the original $25,000. Thus, as shown in Figure 12.9, the appropriate realized gain of $2,000 is recognized. The shares were bought for $25,000 and sold for $27,000, and the previous unrealized gain is removed.

FIGURE 12.9 Sale of Available-for-Sale Security in Year Two

Cash	27,000	
Unrealized Gain on Available-for-Sale Securities	3,000	
Investment in Available-for-Sale Securities		28,000
Gain on Sale of Available-for-Sale Investment		2,000

TEST YOURSELF

Question:

Company A buys ownership shares of a well-known company for $68,000 in Year One and classifies the asset as an investment in trading securities. Company B also buys shares of this company on the same date for $68,000. However, the investment is reported by this owner as available-for-sale. Company B does not elect to report this investment in the same manner as a trading security. Both investments are worth $70,000 at the end of Year One. Both investments are sold in Year Two for $60,000. Which of the following is true?

a. Company B reports a bigger gain on its income statement in Year One than does Company A.

b. Company B reports a bigger loss on its income statement in Year Two than does Company A.

c. Company A reports a bigger loss on its income statement in Year One than does Company B.

d. Company A reports a bigger loss on its income statement in Year Two than does Company B.

Answer:

The correct answer is choice d: Company A reports a bigger loss on its income statement in Year Two than does Company B.

Explanation:

Company A reports a trading security; the $2,000 increase in value is an income statement gain in Year One. The $10,000 drop in value is an income statement loss in Year Two. Because Company B reports these shares as available-for-sale, no income effect is recognized in Year One. In Year Two, the $8,000 difference between cost and amount received is a loss on the income statement. The gain reported by Company A is larger in Year One but the loss reported by Company A is larger in Year Two.

2.4   The Reporting of Comprehensive Income

Question: In Year One, Valente's investment in the shares of Bayless Corporation rose in value by $3,000. As discussed earlier, if those securities are classified as available-for-sale, the unrealized gain does not impact reported net income but, rather, stockholders' equity. This handling is justified because a number of additional changes in value (both increases and decreases) are likely to take place prior to the eventual sale of the investment.

As a result, the net income figure reported by Valente seems a bit misleading. It does not include the increase in the reported worth of this asset. Are decision makers well-served by an income figure that omits certain gains and losses? Assume, for example, that Valente reports total net income for Year One of $80,000. This figure includes no part of the $3,000 unrealized gain. **What reporting is necessary to help investors and creditors understand the impact on income of a change in value when investments are labeled as available-for-sale?**

Answer: As noted, changes in the value of available-for-sale securities create unrealized gains or losses that appear in the stockholders' equity section of the balance sheet but not in net income. The completeness of reported net income in such situations can be questioned.

To help decision makers better evaluate reporting companies with such unrealized items, a second income figure is presented that does include these gains or losses. The resulting balance, known as **comprehensive income**, is shown within a company's financial statements. In Figure 12.10, by adding in the $3,000 change in fair value, Valente's net income figure is adjusted to the more complete total.

comprehensive income

Net income plus any unrealized gains and less any unrealized losses that appear in stockholders' equity rather than within net income.

FIGURE 12.10 Net Income Converted to Comprehensive Income

Net Income	$80,000
Unrealized Gain in Available-for-Sale Securities	3,000
Comprehensive Income	$83,000

Decision makers can choose to emphasize one figure (net income) or another (comprehensive income) in their analysis of a reporting company. More appropriately, they can view these two figures as simply different ways to portray the results of the current year and make use of both.

Comprehensive income includes all changes in stockholders' equity other than (a) amounts contributed by stockholders and (b) dividend distributions made to stockholders. Unrealized gains and losses on available-for-sale securities are common but several other unrealized gains and losses are also included in moving from net income to comprehensive income.

Sometimes comprehensive income makes a company appear more successful, sometimes less so. For example, for the year ended December 31, 2010, **Yahoo! Inc.** reported its net income as $1.245 billion. However, the financial picture seems improved by disclosure of comprehensive income for the period of $1.367 billion. Conversely, **The Dow Chemical Company** reported net income for the same year of $2.321 billion but comprehensive income of only $1.803 billion.

TEST YOURSELF

Question:

The Jelanizada Company reports revenue of $800,000 in Year One along with expenses of $700,000. In addition, the company bought shares of a publicly held company for $50,000 that was worth $70,000 by year's end. This investment was reported as available-for-sale. Which of the following is true?

a. Jelanizada should report net income for Year One of $80,000.

b. Jelanizada should report net income for Year One of $120,000.

c. Jelanizada should report comprehensive income for Year One of $100,000.

d. Jelanizada should report comprehensive income for Year One of $120,000.

Answer:

The correct answer is choice d: Jelanizada should report comprehensive income for Year One of $120,000.

Explanation:

As an investment in an available-for-sale security, the $20,000 increase in value is reported as a gain in other accumulated comprehensive income in the stockholders' equity section of the balance sheet. Net income is revenue minus expenses or $100,000 ($800,000 less $700,000). The gain, though, must then be included in arriving at a more inclusive comprehensive income figure of $120,000 (net income of $100,000 plus gain of $20,000).

KEY TAKEAWAY

Investments in equity securities are often held by the owner for an indefinite period of time. As such, the asset is classified as available-for-sale and shown at fair value each period. Any change in the reported amount is not included in net income but is rather listed within accumulated other comprehensive income in the stockholders' equity section of the balance sheet. However, dividends that are received from the investment are reported as revenue and do impact the computation of net income. When eventually sold, the difference between the original cost of the securities and the proceeds received is reported as a gain or loss shown within net income. Because the periodic changes in value are not factored into the calculation of net income, they are included in the calculation of comprehensive income. Thus, both net income and comprehensive income are reported to decision makers to provide them with a better understanding of the impact of these unrealized gains and losses.

3.   ACCOUNTING FOR INVESTMENTS BY MEANS OF THE EQUITY METHOD

LEARNING OBJECTIVES

At the end of this section, students should be able to meet the following objectives:

1. Describe the theoretical criterion for applying the equity method to an investment in stock and explain the practical standard that is often used.
2. Compute the amount of income to be recognized when using the equity method and make the journal entry for its recording.
3. Understand the handling of dividends that are received when the equity method is applied and make the journal entry.
4. Indicate the impact that a change in fair value has on the reporting of an equity method investment.
5. Prepare the journal entry to record the sale of an equity method security.

3.1   The Need to Apply the Equity Method

*Question: Not all investments in capital stock are made solely for the possibility of gaining dividends and share price appreciation. As mentioned earlier, **Starbucks** holds 39.9 percent ownership of **Starbucks Coffee Japan Ltd**. The relationship between those two companies is different. The investor has real power; it can exert some amount of authority over the investee. **Starbucks** owns a large enough stake in Starbucks Coffee Japan Ltd. so that operating and financing decisions can be influenced. **When one company holds a sizable portion of another company, is accounting for the investment as either an available-for-sale or trading security a reasonable approach?***

equity method

A method of reporting an investment in stock that is applied when the owner has the ability to exert significant influence on the decisions of an investee; in practice, it is used to report investments where 20 percent or more and less than or equal to 50 percent of the shares are held, unless evidence exists that significant influence does not exist.

Answer: The answer to this question depends on the size of ownership. As the percentage of shares being held grows, the investor gradually moves from having little or no authority over the investee to a position where significant influence can be exerted. At that point, for financial reporting purposes, the investment no longer qualifies as a trading security or an available-for-sale security. Instead, the shares are reported by means of the **equity method**. The owner's rationale for holding the investment has changed. The equity method views the connection between the two companies in an entirely different fashion. The accounting process applied by the investor is altered to more closely mirror this relationship.

The equity method is applied when the investor has the ability to apply significant influence to the operating and financing decisions of the investee. Unfortunately, the precise point at which one company gains that ability is impossible to ascertain. A bright line distinction simply does not exist. Although certain clues such as membership on the board of directors and the comparative size of other ownership interests can be helpful, the degree of influence is a nebulous criterion. When a question arises as to whether the ability to apply significant influence exists, the percentage of ownership can be used to provide an arbitrary standard.

According to U.S. GAAP, unless signs of significant influence are present, an investor owning less than 20 percent of the outstanding shares of another company reports the investment as either a trading security or available-for-sale security. In contrast, an investor holding 20 percent or more but less than or equal to 50 percent of the shares of another company is assumed to possess the ability to exert significant influence. Consequently, unless evidence is present that significant influence does not exist, the equity method is applied by the investor to report all investments in this 20–50 percent range of ownership.

TEST YOURSELF

Question:

Howard Company acquires 26 percent of the outstanding stock of Birmington Bottling Company. Unfortunately, the Larito Company holds the other 74 percent of Birmington and pays no attention to the ideas and suggestions put forth by Howard. Which of the following is true about Howard's reporting of this investment?

a. The equity method should be applied because Howard holds 20–50 percent of the shares of Birmington Bottling.

b. The equity method should not be applied because Howard only holds 26 percent of the shares of Birmington Bottling.

c. The equity method should be applied because Howard has significant influence over Birmington Bottling.

d. The equity method should not be applied because Howard does not have significant influence over Birmington Bottling.

Answer:

The correct answer is choice d: The equity method should not be applied because Howard does not have significant influence over Birmington Bottling.

Explanation:

Normally, if one company holds 20–50 percent of the outstanding stock of another company, significant influence is assumed and the equity method is applied. However, in this situation, Howard Company has virtually no influence because Larito Company holds a majority of the stock and does not pay any attention to Howard Company. Without the ability to apply significant influence, the equity method should not be adopted regardless of the amount of stock that is held.

3.2   The Reporting of Investments When Applying the Equity Method

Question: One company holds shares of another and has the ability to apply significant influence. Thus, the equity method of accounting is appropriate. **What financial reporting is made of an investment when the equity method is used?** *What asset value is reported on the owner's balance sheet and when is income recognized from the investment under this approach?*

Answer: When applying the equity method, the investor does not wait until dividends are received to recognize profit from its investment. Because of the close relationship between the two companies, the investor reports income as it is earned by the investee. That is a key element of using the equity method. If, for example, a company reports net income of $100,000 in the current year, an investor holding a 40 percent ownership interest immediately records an increase in its own income of $40,000 ($100,000 × 40 percent). The appropriate percentage of the investee's income is recognized by the investor. The investor also increases its investment account by $40,000 to reflect the growth in the size of the investee company.

Because income is recognized by the investor as earned by the investee, it cannot be reported again when a subsequent dividend is collected. That would double-count the impact. Income must be recognized either when earned by the investee or when later distributed to the investor in the form of a dividend, but not at both times. The equity method uses the earlier date rather than the latter.

Eventual payment of a dividend actually shrinks the size of the investee company because it has fewer assets. To reflect that change in size, the investor decreases the investment account when a dividend is received if the equity method is applied. No additional income is recorded because it was recorded by the investor when earned by the investee.

Because of the fair value option, companies are also allowed to report equity investments as if they were trading securities. However, few investors seem to have opted to make this election. If chosen, the investment is reported at fair value despite the degree of ownership with gains and losses in the change of fair value reported within net income.

3.3   Application of the Equity Method Illustrated

Question: In applying the equity method, income is recognized by the investor when earned by the investee. Subsequent dividend collections are not reported as revenue by the investor but rather as a reduction in the size of the investment account to avoid including the income twice.

To illustrate, assume that Big Company buys 40 percent of the outstanding stock of Little Company on January 1, Year One, for $900,000. No evidence is present to indicate that Big lacks the ability to exert significant influence over the financing and operating decisions of Little. Thus, application of the equity *method is appropriate. During Year One, Little reports net income of $200,000 and distributes a total cash dividend to its stockholders of $30,000. **What journal entries are appropriate for an investor when the equity method is applied to an investment?***

Answer: The purchase of 40 percent of Little Company for cash is merely the exchange of one asset for another. Thus, the investment is recorded initially by Big at its historical cost, as shown in Figure 12.11.

FIGURE 12.11 Acquisition of Shares of Little to Be Reported Using the Equity Method

Ownership here is in the 20 to 50 percent range and no evidence is presented to indicate that the ability to apply significant influence is missing. Thus, according to U.S. GAAP, the equity method should be applied. That means Big recognizes its portion of Little's $200,000 net income as soon as it is earned by the investee. As a 40 percent owner, Big accrues income of $80,000 ($200,000 × 40%). Because earning this income caused Little Company to grow, Big increases its investment account to reflect the change in the size of the investee. Big's journal entry is shown in Figure 12.12.

FIGURE 12.12 Income of Investee Recognized by Investor Using the Equity Method

Big recognized its share of the income from this investee as it was earned. Consequently, any eventual dividend received from Little is a reduction in the investment rather than a new revenue. The investee company is smaller as a result of the cash payout. The balance in this investment account rises when the investee reports income but falls (by $12,000 or 40 percent of the dividend distribution of $30,000) when that income is later passed through to the stockholders.

FIGURE 12.13 Dividend Received from Investment Accounted for by the Equity Method

At the end of Year One, the investment account appearing on Big's balance sheet reports a total of $968,000 ($900,000 + 80,000 − 12,000). This balance does not reflect fair value as was appropriate with investments in trading securities and available-for-sale securities. Unless impaired, fair value is ignored in reporting an equity method investment.

The reported amount also does not disclose historical cost. Rather, the asset figure determined under the equity method is an unusual mixture. It is the original cost of the shares plus the investor's share of the investee's subsequent income less any dividends received since the date of acquisition. Under the equity method, the investment balance is a conglomerate of amounts.

TEST YOURSELF

Question:

Giant Company buys 30 percent of the outstanding stock of Tiny Company on January 1, Year One for $300,000. This ownership provides Giant with the ability to significantly influence the operating and financing decisions of Tiny. Subsequently, Tiny reports net income of $70,000 each year and pays an annual cash dividend of $20,000. Giant does not elect to report this investment as a trading security. Which of the following statements is true?

  a. Giant will report this investment at $342,000 on December 31, Year Two.

  b. Giant will report this investment at $363,000 on December 31, Year Three.

  c. Giant will report income from this investment of $27,000 in Year Two.

  d. Giant will report income from this investment of $21,000 in Year Three.

Answer:

The correct answer is choice d: Giant will report income from this investment of $21,000 in Year Three.

Explanation:

Because the ability to apply significant influence is held, Giant uses the equity method. Each year, income of $21,000 is recognized ($70,000 × 30 percent) with an increase in the investment. Dividends are reported by Giant as a $6,000 reduction in the investment and not as income. The investment balance grows at a rate of $15,000 per year ($21,000 increase less $6,000 decrease) so that it is reported as $315,000 at the end of Year One, $330,000 (Year Two), and $345,000 (Year Three).

3.4   Selling an Investment Reported by Means of the Equity Method

Question: Assume, at the end of Year One, after the above journal entries have been made, Big sells all of its shares in Little Company for $950,000 in cash. **When the equity method is applied to an investment, what is the appropriate recording of an eventual sale?**

Answer: Any investment reported using the equity method quickly moves away from historical cost as income is earned and dividends received. After just one year in this illustration, the asset balance reported by Big has risen from $900,000 to $968,000 (income of $80,000 was added and $12,000 in dividends were subtracted). If these shares are then sold for $950,000, a loss of $18,000 is recognized, as shown in Figure 12.14.

FIGURE 12.14   Sale of Investment Reported Using the Equity Method

Cash	950,000	
Loss on Sale of Equity Method Securities	18,000	
Investment in Little		968,000

If the shares of Little had been sold for more than their $968,000 carrying value, a gain on the sale is recorded.

Summary. All investments in the stock of another company—where ownership is no more than 50 percent—must be accounted for in one of three ways depending on the degree of ownership and the intention of the investor: as trading securities, as available-for-sale securities, or according to the equity method. Figure 12.15 provides an overview of the essential differences in these three accounting approaches. Note here that the available-for-sale securities and the investment using the equity method will have the same accounting as the trading securities if the fair value option is chosen.

FIGURE 12.15 Comparison of Three Methods to Account for Investments

	Investment in Trading Securities	Investment in Available for Sale Securities	Investment—Equity Method
Primary Characteristic	Expected to be sold in near term	Will be sold when cash is eventually needed	Investor has ability to apply significant influence (usually shown by 20% to 50% ownership)
Reported Investment Balance	Fair value	Fair value	Cost plus portion of income less portion of dividends
Changes in Fair Value	Included in net income	Included within stockholders' equity and then within comprehensive income	Ignored unless permanent drop in value occurs
Amounts Reported within Investor's Net Income	Dividends received plus change in fair value	Dividends received	Portion of income as earned by Investee
Dividends Received	Included in net income	Included in net income	Reduces investment balance

TEST YOURSELF

Question:

A company holds many investments in the stock of other companies. A dividend is received from one of these investments. Which of the following is true?

a. If the equity method is applied, the investment balance is increased.

b. If the investment is a trading security, the investment balance is reduced.

c. If the investment is available-for-sale, net income is increased.

d. If the equity method is applied, net income is increased.

Answer:

The correct answer is choice c: If the investment is available-for-sale, net income is increased.

Explanation:

For trading securities and available-for-sale securities, dividends are recorded as income and have no impact on the investment balance. For an equity method investment, dividends are recorded as a reduction in the investment account with no change reported in net income.

Question:

A company holds many investments in the stock of other companies. One of these investments goes up in value by $10,000. Which of the following is true?

a. Net income increases if the investment is available-for-sale.

b. Net income increases if the investment is a trading security.

c. Net income increases if the equity method is applied.

d. Comprehensive income increases if the equity method is applied.

Answer:

The correct answer is choice b: Net income increases if the investment is a trading security.

Explanation:

Increases in value are not recorded when the equity method is in use. For trading securities, they increase net income. For available-for-sale securities, they do not increase net income but are recorded as other accumulated comprehensive income in the stockholders' equity section of the balance sheet. They are then used in adjusting net income to arrive at comprehensive income.

KEY TAKEAWAY

An investor can gain enough equity shares of another company to have the ability to apply significant influence to its operating and financing decisions. For accounting purposes, use of the equity method then becomes appropriate. The point where significant influence is achieved can be difficult to gauge, so ownership of 20–50 percent of the stock is the normal standard applied in practice. However, if specific evidence is found indicating that significant influence is either present or does not exist, that information takes precedence regardless of the degree of ownership. According to the equity method, income is recognized by the investor as soon as earned by the investee. The investment account also increases as a result of this income recognition. Conversely, dividends are not reported as income but rather as reductions in the investment balance. Unless an impairment occurs, fair value is not taken into consideration in accounting for an equity method investment. When sold, the book value of the asset is removed, and any difference with the amount received is recognized as a gain or loss.

4. REPORTING CONSOLIDATED FINANCIAL STATEMENTS

LEARNING OBJECTIVES

At the end of this section, students should be able to meet the following objectives:

1. **List various reasons for one company to seek to gain control over another.**

2. **Recognize that consolidated financial statements must be prepared if one company has control over another which is normally assumed at the point when ownership is over 50 percent of the other company's outstanding stock.**

3. **Explain the reporting of a subsidiary's revenues and expenses when consolidated financial statements are prepared at the date of acquisition.**

4. **Explain the reporting of a subsidiary's assets and liabilities when consolidated financial statements are prepared at the date of acquisition.**

4.1 Accounting for Mergers and Acquisitions

Question: Companies frequently buy more than 50 percent of the stock of other companies in order to gain control. In a large number of these transactions, one company obtains all the outstanding shares of the other so that ownership is complete. If two companies are brought together to form a third, a merger has taken place. If one company simply buys another, the transaction is referred to as an acquisition. These corporate purchases can be monetarily huge and have a long-lasting impact on an industry or the *economy as a whole. "Global dollar volume in announced mergers and acquisitions rose 23.1 percent in 2010, to $2.4 trillion, according to Thomson Reuters data. In the United States, merger volume rose 14.2 percent, to $822 billion."*[1]

- *Such investments are often made to expand operations into new markets or new industries. **Google**, for example, acquired **YouTube** for $1.65 billion to provide an entrance into online videos.*

- *As discussed earlier in the coverage of intangible assets, one company might buy another to obtain valuable assets such as patents, real estate, trademarks, technology, and the like. The purchase by **Walt Disney** of **Pixar** and its digital animation expertise certainly falls into this category.*

- *A takeover can also be made to eliminate competition or in hopes of gaining economies of scale. The $35 billion merger of **Sprint** with **Nextel** was projected to increase profits for the combined companies by lowering operating expenses while also reducing the number of competitors in the wireless communication industry.*

*To help demonstrate the appropriate method of accounting for such investments, assume that Giant Company acquires 100 percent of Tiny Company. Obviously, Giant has gained control of Tiny. How is the reporting by Giant affected? Because over 50 percent of the stock was purchased, none of the previously described accounting methods are applicable. **How does a company report the acquisition of another company where control is established?***

consolidated financial statements

Statements that are prepared when one company holds control over another company so that all assets, liabilities, revenues, and expenses must be combined in a method stipulated by U.S. GAAP; control is assumed to exist when more than 50 percent of the ownership shares are owned.

Answer: The stockholders of Giant now control both Giant and Tiny. As a result, a business combination has been formed from the two previously independent companies. For external reporting purposes, consolidated financial statements are required. Giant does not report an investment in Tiny on its balance sheet as with the other accounting methods described previously. Instead, the individual account balances from each organization are put together in a prescribed fashion to represent the single economic entity that has been created. In simple terms, the assets, liabilities, revenues, and expenses of Tiny (the subsidiary) are consolidated with those of Giant (the parent) to reflect the united business.

Because such acquisitions are common, the financial statements reported by most well-known corporations actually include consolidated financial data from dozens, if not hundreds, of different subsidiaries where control has been gained over a number of years. As just one example, **Cisco Systems** made over 40 acquisitions of other companies between 2006 and 2011. Consolidated financial statements published today by **Cisco Systems** will include the revenues, expenses, assets, and liabilities of each of those subsidiaries along with those same accounts for the parent.

Consolidation of financial statements is one of the most complex topics in all of financial accounting. However, the basic process is quite straightforward.

Subsidiary revenues and expenses. The revenues and expenses reported by each subsidiary are included in consolidated figures but only for the period of time after control is obtained. Consequently, if Giant obtains Tiny by buying 100 percent of its stock on April 1, Year One, a consolidated income statement will contain no revenues and expenses recognized by Tiny prior to that date. Income statement balances accrued under previous owners have no financial impact on the new owner (Giant). Only the revenues earned and expenses incurred by this subsidiary after April 1 are included in consolidated totals.

Subsidiary assets and liabilities. Consolidation of subsidiary assets and liabilities is a more complicated process. On the date of the takeover, a total acquisition price is determined based on the fair value surrendered by the parent to gain control. A search is then made to identify all of the individual assets and liabilities held by the subsidiary at that time. As discussed previously, the parent recognizes subsidiary assets (1) that provide contractual or legal rights or (2) that can be separated from the subsidiary and then sold. Fair value is established and recorded for each of these assets as if the parent were acquiring them individually. A transaction has taken place that brings all of the subsidiary properties under the control of the parent.

Also, as explained previously, if the acquisition price is more than the total fair value of these identifiable assets and liabilities, the intangible asset goodwill is reported for the excess. As a going concern, a total value is usually attributed to a company that exceeds the individual values of its assets and liabilities. Having loyal customers and trained employees, for example, helps a company generate more profits than its assets could otherwise earn. When a company is being bought, such anticipated profitability usually leads to an increase in the negotiated price. This excess amount necessitates the recognition of goodwill on the consolidated balance sheet.

Question:

Tall Company buys all the outstanding stock of Small Company on November 1, Year One for $500,000 and is now preparing consolidated financial statements at the end of Year One. Small earned revenues of $10,000 per month during Year One along with expenses of $8,000 per month. On November 1, Year One, Small had one asset—a piece of land with a cost of $300,000 and a fair value of $450,000—and no liabilities. The land continues to appreciate in value and is worth $470,000 at the end of Year One. Which of the following statements is true about the consolidated financial statements at the end of Year One?

a. Consolidated net income will include $4,000 earned by Small.

b. Goodwill at the end of Year One is reported as $30,000.

c. The land owned by Small is reported at the end of Year One at $470,000.

d. On consolidated financial statements, a $150,000 gain is reported on the land that was owned by Small.

Answer:

The correct answer is choice a: Consolidated net income will include $4,000 earned by Small.

Explanation:

In consolidation, only revenues and expenses recognized by Small after the purchase are included. Revenues of $20,000 ($10,000 × 2 months) for November and December are recorded this year as well as expenses of $16,000 ($8,000 × two months). The value of subsidiary assets and liabilities at the date of acquisition serves as the basis for reporting so the land will be shown in consolidation at $450,000. Because $500,000 was paid by the parent, goodwill is the excess $50,000.

4.2   The Consolidation of Financial Information

Question: To illustrate the consolidation process, assume that Tiny has earned revenues of $800,000 and incurred expenses of $500,000 during the year to date. In addition, the company reports a single asset, land costing $400,000 but with a $720,000 fair value. The only liability is a $300,000 note payable. Thus, the company's reported net book value is $100,000 ($400,000 land less $300,000 note payable). Tiny also owns the rights to a well-known trademark that has no book value because it was developed many years ago at little or no cost. However, it is now estimated to be worth $210,000.

The assets and liabilities held by Tiny have a net fair value of $630,000 ($720,000 land plus $210,000 trademark less $300,000 note payable). Over the years, the company has been extremely popular and developed a large customer base. Therefore, after extensive negotiations, Giant agrees to pay $900,000 in cash to acquire all the outstanding stock of Tiny. If consolidated financial statements are created at the time of a corporate acquisition, what figures are reported by the business combination?

Answer: In consolidating Giant and its subsidiary Tiny at the date of this acquisition, neither the subsidiary revenues of $800,000 nor its expenses of $500,000 are included. Their financial impact occurred prior to the takeover by Giant. Those profits benefited the previous owners. Therefore, only revenues and expenses reported by Giant make up the consolidated income statement totals determined on the day the parent acquires this subsidiary.

At the same time, consolidated balance sheet totals will not show any "investment in Tiny Company" as in the other methods demonstrated earlier. Instead, Tiny's land is added to Giant's own totals at its $720,000 fair value, and the trademark is consolidated at its $210,000 fair value. These balances reflect the amounts paid by Giant to acquire ownership of the subsidiary. The note payable is included in the consolidated figures at $300,000, which was its fair value as well as its book value. Subsidiary assets and liabilities are consolidated as if purchased by the parent on an open market.

The acquisition price of $900,000 paid by Giant exceeds the net value of the subsidiary's identifiable assets and liabilities ($630,000 or $720,000 + $210,000 − $300,000) by $270,000. In consolidation of a parent and subsidiary, any excess acquisition payment is assumed to represent goodwill and is reported as an intangible asset.

FIGURE 12.16 Consolidated Totals—Date of Acquisition

Revenues	Parent total only
Expenses	Parent total only
Net income	Parent total only
Reported Assets and Liabilities	Parent book value plus fair value of subsidiary accounts
Trademark (previously unreported)	Fair value of subsidiary account
Investment in Tiny	Not reported for consolidation—actual assets and liabilities are included instead
Goodwill	Excess payment made to acquire subsidiary
Liabilities	Parent book value plus fair value of subsidiary figures
Stockholders' Equity	Parent total only

TEST YOURSELF

Question:

Large Company produces a balance sheet that shows patents with a book value of $200,000. The next day, Large Company buys all of Short Company for $3 million. Consolidated financial statements are then produced that show patents with a book value of $300,000. What does the reader of these financial statements know about the patents held by Large and its consolidated subsidiary?

a. Acquiring Short made the patents held by Large more valuable.

b. At the date of acquisition, Short held patents with a fair value of $100,000.

c. At the date of acquisition, Short held patents with a historical cost of $100,000.

d. At the date of acquisition, Short held patents with a net book value (cost minus accumulated amortization) of $100,000.

Answer:

The correct answer is choice b: At the date of acquisition, Short held patents with a fair value of $100,000.

Explanation:

On the date that a business combination is formed, the fair value of all identifiable assets and liabilities of the subsidiary are added to those same accounts of the parent. Because the patent account balance went up by $100,000 as a result of the purchase, that figure was the apparent fair value of any patents held by Short Company at that time.

4.3 Analyzing a Company's Use of Its Assets

Question: This chapter completes coverage of the assets reported by an organization on its balance sheet. In earlier chapters, vital signs were computed and explained in connection with receivables, inventory, and property and equipment. Figures and ratios were presented that are often used in evaluating a business—especially its financial health and future prospects. Do any similar vital signs exist for assets as a whole that decision makers will typically determine as part of an overall examination of an organization such as PepsiCo or The Coca-Cola Company?

Answer: A company controls a specific amount of assets. Investors and other decision makers are interested in how effectively management is able to make use of these resources. Individuals who study specific companies search for signs that an appropriate level of income was generated from the assets on hand.

Total asset turnover. **Total asset turnover** is one such figure. It indicates management's efficiency at generating sales revenue. Sales must occur before profits can be earned from normal operations. If assets are not well used to create sales, profits are unlikely to arise.

total asset turnover

A ratio used to measure the efficient use of assets; it is computed by dividing sales revenue by average total assets for the period.

$$\text{total asset turnover} = \text{sales revenue/average total assets}$$

To illustrate, here is information reported for 2010 by **PepsiCo Inc.** and **The Coca-Cola Company**. Based on these figures, the total asset turnover can be computed for each company for comparison purposes as shown in Figure 12.17.

FIGURE 12.17   2010 Comparison of PepsiCo Inc. and The Coca-Cola Company

	PepsiCo	**Coca-Cola**
Total Assets		
Beginning of Year	$39.8 billion	$48.7 billion
End of Year	$68.2 billion	$72.9 billion
Average for Year	$54.0 billion	$60.8 billion
Net Sales Revenue	$57.8 billion	$35.1 billion
Total Asset Turnover	1.07 times	.58 times

Return on assets. Probably one of the most commonly used vital signs employed in studying the financial health of a company is its **return on assets**, often known as ROA. It is computed by taking net income and then dividing that figure by the average total assets for the period. It is viewed by many as an appropriate means of measuring management's efficiency in using company resources.

return on assets (ROA) = net income/average total assets

Variations of this formula do exist. For example, some analysts modify the income figure by removing interest expense to eliminate the impact of different financing strategies so that the computation focuses on operations.

For 2010, **PepsiCo** reported net income of $6.3 billion so that its ROA for the year was 11.7 percent ($6.3 billion net income/$54.0 billion as the average total assets). For the same period, **The Coca-Cola Company** reported net income of $11.8 billion for an ROA of 19.4 percent ($11.8 billion net income/$60.8 billion in average total assets).

KEY TAKEAWAY

Companies attempt to obtain control of other companies for many reasons including obtaining access to valuable assets, gaining entry into new industries, and eliminating competition. According to U.S. GAAP, control is established over another company by acquiring 50 percent or more of its ownership shares. At that point, consolidated financial statements must be prepared bringing together the financial accounts from both companies. For the subsidiary, only revenues and expenses since the takeover are included. In consolidating the assets and liabilities of the subsidiary, the fair value at the date of acquisition is assumed to represent the cost incurred by the parent. The intangible asset goodwill is reported for any unexplained excess payment made by the parent in acquiring control over the subsidiary. To evaluate the efficiency of management's use of company assets, many analysts compute total asset turnover and return on assets (ROA).

Talking with a Real Investing Pro (Continued)

Following is a continuation of our interview with Kevin G. Burns.

Question: For the year ended December 31, 2010, **The Dow Chemical Company** reported its net income as approximately $2.321 billion. The company also disclosed comprehensive income for the same period of only $1.803 billion. That's a 22 percent reduction. Are you disturbed that a company can report two separate income figures that are so significantly different? Or, do you find disclosing income in two distinct ways to be helpful when you analyze a business?

Kevin Burns: Actually I think the idea of disclosing income in two different ways makes sense. Having said that, if I were a shareholder of **Dow Chemical**, I would want to know why these numbers are so far apart? What exactly is included in (or excluded from) each of these income figures? Is the company's core business sound? This question is probably best answered by net income. The reduction in arriving at comprehensive income is likely to have come from losses in the value of available-for-sale investments and from holding foreign currency balances. That can provide interesting information. Perhaps the management is distracted by trying to manage a large stock investment portfolio. How much of the difference comes from currency rate changes, and is there a way to hedge this volatility to reduce the impact? If there is a way to hedge that risk, why did company officials choose not to do so?

In sum, the reason I like including both income numbers is that anything that increases disclosure is a positive, especially when investing money. The more transparency the better is my feeling. Then, investors can make up their own minds as to management's competence and the future success of the overall business operations.

 Video Clip

Professor Joe Hoyle talks about the five most important points in Chapter 12.

FINANCIAL STATEMENTS FOR MOST MAJOR COMPANIES ARE ACTUALLY CONSOLIDATED

View the video online at: http://bit.ly/hoyle12-2

5. END-OF-CHAPTER EXERCISES

QUESTIONS

1. On January 1, Year One, the Lawrence Company acquires 10,000 shares of the Memphis Company for $39 per share. What are possible reasons why Lawrence chose to use its cash to make this acquisition?

2. Wilson Company buys 200 shares of Pepitone Corporation for $17 per share, an asset that is classified as an investment in trading securities. Why is an investment classified in this manner?

3. An investor owns equity shares of a number of companies. Some of these investments are reported as trading securities while others are shown as available-for-sale securities. The investor receives a cash dividend of $1,000. How is that receipt reported by the investor?

4. The Amos Corporation bought 1,000 shares of Jones Company during Year One for $18 per share. The investment is labeled as a trading security. Amos plans to sell these shares on the stock market for $27 each and is trying to decide whether to make the sell on December 30, Year One, or January 2, Year Two. How will reported net income differ in Year One and in Year Two based on the timing of this sale?

5. Unless value is impaired, equipment and inventory are reported based on historical cost. Why is the financial accounting of an investment in trading securities handled differently from these other assets?

6. StampCo Corporation bought 1,000 shares of Bates Corporation on December 1, Year One. Company officials are trying to decide whether to report this asset as an investment in trading securities or as an investment in available-for-sale securities. How is this decision made?

7. Company A bought 1,000 shares of Company Y for $13 per share and 2,000 shares of Company Z for $18 per share. At the end of the year, the stock of Company Y is worth $15 per share and the stock of Company Z is worth $14 per share. What is reported at year-end if these investments are both classified as investments in trading securities? What is reported at year-end if these investments are both classified as investments in available-for-sale securities?

8. An investment is bought during Year One for a total of $9,000. At the end of Year One, these shares are worth $10,000. However, they are sold on February 11, Year Two, for only $6,000. What is the income effect for these two years if this stock is viewed by company officials as a trading security? What is the income effect for these two years if this stock is viewed by company officials as available-for-sale?

9. A company acquires an investment in available-for-sale securities during Year one for $23,000. At the end of the year, this investment was worth $19,000. Reported net income was $200,000. What should the company report as its comprehensive income?

10. The Lincoln Corporation bought 1,000 shares of Illinois Company during Year One for $21 per share. The investment is labeled as available-for-sale. Lincoln plans to sell these shares on the stock market for $26 each and is trying to decide whether to make the sell on December 30, Year One, or January 2, Year Two. How will reported net income differ in Year One and in Year Two based on the timing of this sale?

11. Big Company acquired enough shares of Little Company so that it has gained the ability to exert significant influence over its operating and financing decisions. How should Big report this investment?

12. Mama Corporation acquired a rather large block of the capital shares of Child Corporation. Currently, company officials for Mama are trying to decide whether application of the equity method is appropriate. In theory, how is that decision made? In practice, how is that decision made?

13. Archibald Corporation owns 30 percent of Saratoga Corporation and will apply the equity method to this investment. During the current year, Saratoga reported net income of $150,000 and paid a total cash dividend of $60,000. What reporting is required of Archibald in connection with this investment?

14. Why are dividends that are received from an investment that is being accounted for by means of the equity method not reported as revenue?

15. The Walters Company acquired 40 percent of the Ameston Company on January 1, Year One, for $388,000. Ameston reported net income of $100,000 for Year One and paid a total cash dividend of $40,000. At the end of Year One, this investment was worth $460,000. What is reported on the owner's balance sheet for this investment, and what does that figure represent?

16. Giant Corporation buys 54 percent of the outstanding stock of Small Corporation. Under normal conditions, how will this investment be reported?

17. Lauderdale Corporation has two assets. The land cost $100,000 and is worth $220,000. A building has a net book value of $650,000 and a fair value of $730,000. Yarrow Corporation buys 100 percent of the outstanding stock of Lauderdale for cash of $1 million. What journal entry does Yarrow make to consolidate Lauderdale's assets within its own financial records?

18. Donnelly Corporation generated revenues of $900,000 during Year One while Nelson Company generated revenues of $600,000 during the same period. On the last day of the year, Donnelly buys all of the ownership shares of Nelson. In consolidated financial statements for December 31, Year One, and the year then ended, what is the reported amount of revenues?

19. Financial analysts determine the total asset turnover for the Paquet Corporation as 2.3. How did these decision makers arrive at this figure?

20. Financial analysts study the financial statements reported by Williamston Corporation and calculate a return on assets of 11.3 percent. How did they arrive at that figure?

TRUE OR FALSE

1. ____ To keep the information relatively simple for financial statement users, all investments in the ownership shares of other companies are accounted for in the same way according to U.S. GAAP.

2. ____ If the owner of trading securities receives a cash dividend, it should be recorded as revenue at that time and shown on the income statement.

3. ____ All investments in other companies should be reported at the historical cost of the investment.

4. ____ A company buys trading securities in Year One for $11,000. They increase in value by $2,000 in Year One and are then sold in Year Two for $14,000. A gain of $3,000 is recognized on the company's income statement in Year Two.

5. ____ The Argentina Company buys shares of another company and is currently attempting to determine whether this ownership qualifies as an investment in trading securities or available-for-sale securities. The total amount of assets reported by Argentina will vary depending on which approach is selected.

6. ____ Changes in the value of available-for-sale securities do not affect the reported net income of the investor until the securities are sold.

7. ____ The Nile Company buys 100 shares of a company for $7,000 in cash in Year One. The shares increase in value by $1,000 in Year One and then by $2,000 in Year Two and are then sold. In addition, a dividend is received from this investment of $300. In Year Two, the Nile Company will increase its net income by $3,300 if this investment is judged to be a trading security.

8. ____ At the beginning of Year One, the Barksdale Corporation buys shares of another company for $7,000. The stock goes up in value during Year One by $5,000. Dividends of $1,000 are also collected. Company officials view this as an investment in available-for-sale securities. If net income is reported as $40,000, then comprehensive income will be $45,000.

9. ____ Accumulated other comprehensive income is included by a company on its income statement within the computation of net income.

10. ____ If one company owns 25 percent of another company, it must use the equity method to account for this investment.

11. ____ Equity method investments are reported at current fair value on the owner's balance sheet.

12. ____ On January 1, Year One, Ajax Company spends $200,000 on an investment. In this purchase, the company gains 30 percent ownership of another company and the ability to apply significant influence. During Year One, the other company reports net income of $50,000 and distributes a cash dividend of $10,000. Ajax should report dividend revenue of $3,000.

13. ____ On January 1, Year One, Dylan Company spends $300,000 on an investment. The company buys 30 percent of another company and gains the ability to apply significant influence. During Year One, the other company reports net income of $70,000 and distributes a cash dividend of $20,000. At the end of the year, these shares have a fair value of $400,000. Ajax should report the investment on its balance sheet at $315,000.

14. ____ Big Company has held 30 percent of Little Company's ownership for several years and uses the equity method for financial reporting. Little reports net income in the current year of $40,000 while paying no dividends. Big reports its share of Little's net income in the current year.

15. ____ Consolidated financial statements are only created when one company acquires 100 percent ownership over another company.

16. ____ Bismarck Company buys control over another company late in Year One. One of the likely reasons for this acquisition is so that the revenues earned throughout the year can be added to those of Bismarck on consolidated statements to make that company's financial situation look better.

17. ____ Reinstein Company has net assets with a net book value of $600,000 but a fair value of $740,000. If a company buys control over Reinstein for $740,000, no goodwill is recognized.

18. ____ The NYork Company has only one asset and no liabilities. It owns a building that it rents out. The building has a net book value of $800,000 but is worth $960,000. Another company paid exactly $1 million to gain all of the outstanding stock of NYork. The building will be added to consolidated financial statements on that date at $960,000.

19. ____ The higher a company's ROA, the more efficiently the company is using its assets.

MULTIPLE CHOICE

1. On November 5, Year One, Maxwell Corporation purchased seventy shares of Tyrone Company for $30 per share, planning to hold the investment for a short time and then sell these shares. At the end of Year One, Tyrone is selling for $32 per share on a stock exchange. What unrealized gain will Maxwell report for Year One, and where should that balance be reported?

   a. $140 unrealized gain, stockholders' equity section of balance sheet

   b. $140 unrealized gain, income statement

   c. $2,240 unrealized gain, income statement

   d. $2,240 unrealized gain, stockholders' equity section of balance sheet

2. Which of the following is **not** a reason investments in trading securities are shown at fair value on the balance sheet?

   a. The fair values of publicly-traded securities are readily available.

   b. Fair value is considered relevant information to financial statement users.

   c. The fair value is an objective amount determined by the stock market.

   d. Fair value is easier to determine than historical cost.

3. Hope Corporation buys shares of Lonesome Corporation for $14,000 during Year One. By year-end, the stock has a total market value of $18,000. Which of the following is **not** true?

   a. If viewed as a trading security, the asset is reported on the balance sheet at $18,000.

   b. If viewed as a trading security, Hope's net income will increase in Year One by $4,000.

   c. If viewed as an available-for-sale security, the asset is reported on the balance sheet at $18,000.

   d. If viewed as an available-for-sale security, Hope's net income will increase in Year One by $4,000.

4. An investor spends $23,000 for shares of another company late in Year One. The shares are worth $24,000 at the end of that year. Early in Year Two, a $1,200 dividend is received from this investment. Shortly thereafter, the shares are sold for $26,000. If this asset is an investment in trading securities, what is the impact on net income in Year Two?

   a. Increase by $1,200.

   b. Increase by $2,000.

   c. Increase by $3,200.

   d. Increase by $4,200.

5. The Andre Corporation spends $35,000 for shares of another company late in Year One. The shares are worth $34,000 at the end of that year. Early in Year Two, a $900 dividend is received from this investment. Shortly thereafter, the shares are sold for $38,000. If this asset is viewed as an investment in trading securities, what is the impact on net income in Year Two?

   a. Increase by $3,000

   b. Increase by $3,900

   c. Increase by $4,000

   d. Increase by $4,900

6. Early in Year One, Jackson Corporation purchased 150 shares of Riley Corporation for $46 per share. The investment is classified as available-for-sale. At the end of Year One, Riley's stock is selling on a stock exchange for $43 per share. Jackson's reported net income for the year was $235,000. What should Jackson report as its comprehensive income for Year One?

   a. $228,100

   b. $228,550

   c. $234,550

   d. $235,000

7. In Year One, Jeremiah Corporation purchased shares of Lauren Corporation for $9,000. The investment is classified as a trading security. At the end of Year One, Lauren's stock has a value on a stock exchange equal to $13,000. Jeremiah's reported net income for the year was $180,000. What should Jeremiah report as its comprehensive income for Year One?

   a. $180,000

   b. $184,000

   c. $189,000

   d. $193,000

8. The Monroe Corporation owns the capital stock of several corporations and receives a cash dividend of $7,000 this year. Which of the following statements is true?

   a. For both trading securities and available-for-sale securities, the dividend is a reduction in the investment account.

   b. For trading securities, the dividend is included in net income; for available-for-sale securities, the dividend is a reduction in the investment account.

   c. For trading securities, the dividend is a reduction in the investment account; for available-for-sale securities, the dividend is included in net income.

   d. For both trading securities and available-for-sale securities, the dividend is included in net income.

9. Wisconsin Corporation makes an investment in Badger Corporation for $38,000 at the beginning of Year One. At the end of the year, the shares are selling at an amount equal to $34,000. The drop in value is viewed as temporary. During the period, Badger earned $30,000 in income and Wisconsin received a dividend of $1,800. Which of the following is **not** true?

   a. If this investment is viewed as a trading security, it should be reported on a year-end balance sheet at $34,000.

   b. If this this investment is viewed as available-for-sale, dividend revenue is recognized for $1,800.

   c. If this investment is viewed as a trading security, dividend revenue is recognized for $1,800.

   d. If this investment is accounted for by means of the equity method, it should be reported on a year-end balance sheet at $34,000.

10. Anton Company owns shares of Charlotte Corporation. Which of the following is true about the reporting for this investment?

    a. If Anton owns 15 percent of Charlotte and has significant influence, the investment must be reported by the equity method.

    b. If Anton owns 25 percent of Charlotte and does not have significant influence, the investment must be reported by the equity method.

    c. If Anton owns 4 percent of Charlotte and does not have significant influence, the investment must be reported as a trading security.

    d. If Anton owns 56 percent of Charlotte and has control, the investment must be reported by the equity method.

11. Rocko Corporation acquires 40 percent of Hailey Corporation on January 1, Year One, for $400,000. By this purchase, Rocko has gained the ability to exert significant influence over Hailey. Hailey reports net income of $80,000 in Year One and $100,000 in Year Two. Hailey pays a total dividend of $30,000 each year. These shares have a value of $460,000 at the end of Year One and $500,000 at the end of Year Two. On a December 31, Year Two, balance sheet, what does Rocko report for this investment?

    a. $448,000
    b. $472,000
    c. $500,000
    d. $520,000

12. Lancaster Inc. purchases all the outstanding stock of Lucy Company for $4,500,000. The net assets of Lucy have a total fair value of $2,900,000. These assets include a patent with a net book value of $4,700 and a fair value of $159,000. At what amount should the patent and any goodwill from this purchase be shown on consolidated financial statements produced on the date of purchase?

    a. Patent—$4,700; Goodwill—$0
    b. Patent—$159,000; Goodwill—$0
    c. Patent—$159,000; Goodwill—$1,600,000
    d. Patent—$4,700; Goodwill—$1,600,000

13. On December 31, Year One, Brenda Corporation purchased 100 percent of Kyle Inc. for $3,400,000. The net assets of Kyle had a net book value of $3 million. Kyle had a trademark with a fair value ($45,000) that exceeded its book value ($15,000) by $30,000. For all other assets and liabilities reported by Kyle, net book value was the same as fair value. At what amounts should the trademark and goodwill be shown on Brenda's consolidated balance sheet on December 31, Year One?

    a. Trademark—$15,000; Goodwill—$370,000
    b. Trademark—$15,000; Goodwill—$400,000
    c. Trademark—$45,000; Goodwill—$370,000
    d. Trademark—$45,000; Goodwill—$400,000

14. On December 31, Year One, the Bolger Corporation purchases all of the capital stock of Osbourne Corporation for $200,000 more than the fair value of the subsidiary's identifiable assets and liability. During Year One, Bolger reported revenues of $900,000 and expenses of $600,000. In the same period, Osbourne reported revenues of $700,000 and expenses of $500,000. On a consolidated income statement for Year One, what is reported for revenues and expenses?

    a. Revenues—$900,000; Expenses—$600,000
    b. Revenues—$1.6 million; Expenses—$600,000
    c. Revenues—$900,000; Expenses—$1.1 million
    d. Revenues—$1.6 million, Expenses—$1.1 million

15. Hydro Company and Aqua Corporation are in the same industry. During Year One, Hydro had average total assets of $35,000 and sales of $47,800. Aqua had average total assets of $49,000 and sales of $56,900. Which of the following is true?

    a. Aqua Corporation has a total asset turnover of 0.86 times.
    b. Hydro Company is not using its assets as efficiently as Aqua Corporation.
    c. Aqua Corporation has a higher ROA than Hydro Company.
    d. Hydro Corporation has a total asset turnover of 1.37 times.

16. Tried Company began the year with $450,000 in total assets and ended the year with $530,000 in total assets. Sales for the year were $560,000 while net income for the year was $46,000. What was Tried Company's return on assets (ROA) for the year?

    a. 8.2%
    b. 9.4%
    c. 10.2%
    d. 14.0%

VIDEO PROBLEMS

Professor Joe Hoyle discusses the answers to these two problems at the links that are indicated. After formulating your answers, watch each video to see how Professor Hoyle answers these questions.

1. Your roommate is an English major. The roommate's parents own a chain of ice cream shops located throughout Florida. One day, while waiting for a bus to go across campus, your roommate poses this question: "As you can imagine, my parent's business is very seasonal. They do great during the summer but not nearly as well in the winter. So, the business has to save up enough cash by the end of summer to support operations over the colder months. This year the business bought shares of several well-known companies in September that will be sold in February when cash reserves begin to run low. Unfortunately, the stock market went down, and now my parents are telling me that they have to report a loss at the end of December. I don't understand. If they are not going to sell this stock until February, why do they have to report a loss in December? The stock market price may well go way up by the time they sell those shares in February. They have plenty of time to recoup the lost value." How would you respond?

View the video online at: http://bit.ly/hoyle12-3

2. Your uncle and two friends started a small office supply store several years ago. The company has expanded and now has several large locations. Your uncle knows that you are taking a financial accounting class and asks you the following question: "We have some friends who own an office supply service in the next state. They had been having some trouble, so at the beginning of the current year, our company bought 35 percent of their company for a considerable amount of money. We have plans to help them get their operations turned around. We believe, in the long run, that this investment will be very profitable as they begin to make the changes we suggest. This year, that other company only made a profit of $40,000 and paid a total cash dividend of $10,000. However, in the future, we believe that they will do much better. We've never owned a portion of a business like this before. How do we go about accounting for our ownership interest in this other company?" How would you respond?

View the video online at: http://bit.ly/hoyle12-4

PROBLEMS

1. The Kansas Company buys 1,000 shares of Topeka Inc. on August 1, Year One, for $19 per share. Topeka paid a $1 per share cash dividend on December 12, Year One. The shares are worth $23 per share on December 31, Year One. Kansas sells this entire investment on April 7, Year Two, for $25 per share.

   a. If this asset is viewed as an investment in trading securities, what is reported in the Year One financial statements for Kansas?

   b. If this asset is viewed as an investment in trading securities, what is reported in the Year Two financial statements for Kansas?

   c. If this asset is viewed as an investment in available-for-sale securities, what is reported in the Year One financial statements for Kansas?

   d. If this asset is viewed as an investment in available-for-sale securities, what is reported in the Year Two financial statements for Kansas?

2. Record Investor Corporation's journal entry for each of the following events.

   a. Investor Corporation purchases 600 shares of stock in Company A for $60 per share on December 6, Year One. This investment is considered a trading security.

   b. At the end of Year One, Company A shares are selling for $63 each.

   c. On January 31, Year Two, Company A pays a cash dividend of $2 per share.

   d. At the end of Year Two, Company A shares are selling for $59 each.

   e. On January 22, Year Three, Investor sells all of the shares of Company A for $62 each.

3. On September 9, Year One, Johnson Inc. purchased 500 shares of Thomas Company stock when this stock was selling for $20 per share. Johnson plans to hold these shares for a short time and hopefully sell the investment for a gain. Shortly thereafter, Thomas paid a cash dividend of $0.32 per share.

   On December 31, Year One, Johnson prepares its financial statements. At that time, this stock is selling for $18 per share.

   a. Determine all balances that Johnson will report on its Year One income statement in connection with this investment.

   b. Determine all balances that Johnson will report on its December 31, Year One, balance sheet in connection with this investment.

   c. If Johnson reports net income of $79,000 for Year One, what should be disclosed as comprehensive income?

4. In Year One, Waterloo Corporation makes an investment in the equity securities of another company for $53,000. The company then collects a cash dividend of $2,000. At the end of Year One, this investment is valued at $58,000. In March of Year Two, the entire investment is sold for cash of $54,000.

   Waterloo reported this investment as being in available-for-sale securities. How would Waterloo's reported net income have been different in each of these two years if the investment had been reported as a trading security?

5. Record Christopher Corporation's journal entry for each of the following events. After each entry, indicate the balances that will be reported on Christopher Corporation's balance sheet at that date.

   a. Christopher Corporation purchases 1,000 shares of stock in Alpha Company for $30 per share on July 7, Year Two. This investment is considered an available-for-sale security.

   b. At the end of Year Two, Alpha Company's stock is selling for $25 per share.

   c. At the end of Year Three, Alpha Company's stock is selling for $28 per share.

   d. On February 16, Year Four, Alpha Company pays a $0.60 per share cash dividend to its stockholders.

   e. On March 27, Year Four, Christopher sells all of these shares for $36 per share in cash.

6. On April 16, Youngstown Inc. purchased 900 shares of Cool Company stock when Cool's stock was selling for $15 per share. Youngstown plans to hold this stock indefinitely until the company has a need for cash.

   a. On December 31, Cool's stock is selling for $20 per share. What appears on the financial statements for Youngstown?

   b. If Youngstown reports net income of $190,000, what should the company report as its comprehensive income?

   c. Assume that Youngstown sells this investment three months later when Cool's shares are selling for $24 per share. Make the journal entry to record the sale.

7. Ordello Company buys 20 percent of the capital stock of Pottsboro Corporation on January 1, Year One, for $370,000. Ordello plans to hold these shares for an indefinite period of time. Pottsboro reports net income of $80,000 in Year One and $100,000 in Year Two. The company pays a total cash dividend of $30,000 in each year. Ordello's investment is worth $420,000 at the end of Year One and $470,000 at the end of Year Two. Ordello sells this investment on the first day of Year Three for $470,000 in cash.

   a. Assume that the ownership of these shares does not give Ordello the ability to apply significant influence over Pottsboro. Make all journal entries for Ordello for Years One, Two, and Three.

   b. Assume that the ownership of these shares does give Ordello the ability to apply significant influence over Pottsboro. Make all journal entries for Ordello for Years One, Two, and Three.

8. Oregon Company, a paper products manufacturer, wishes to enter the Canadian market. The company purchased 30 percent of the outstanding stock of Canadian Paper Inc. on January 1, Year One, for $6,000,000. The CEO of Oregon will sit on the board of directors of Canadian, and other evidence of significant influence does exist.

   a. Canadian reported net income of $760,000 for the year. Record the journal entry (if any) to be prepared by Oregon.

   b. Canadian paid a cash dividend of $80,000. Record the journal entry for Oregon.

   c. What amount would Oregon report on its balance sheet as its investment in Canadian as of the end of Year One?

9. At the beginning of Year One, Current Properties paid $1,000,000 for 25 percent of the shares of Nealy Enterprises. Current immediately begins to exert significant influence over the operating decisions of Nealy.

   a. Nealy reported earnings of $400,000 during Year One. Record the appropriate journal entry for Current.

   b. Nealy paid a total cash dividend of $50,000 during October of Year One. Record the appropriate journal entry for Current when the company receives this dividend.

   c. At the end of Year One, what amount does Current report on its balance sheet as its investment in Nealy? What does Current report on its income statement as its investment income from Nealy?

   d. Nealy reported earnings of $440,000 during Year Two. Nealy paid dividends of $60,000 during Year Two. What is the balance of the Investment in Nealy at the end of Year Two?

   e. At the end of Year Two, Current sells its entire investment in Nealy for $1,200,000 in cash. Record the appropriate journal entry for Current.

10. Teckla Corporation purchases all the outstanding stock of Feather Company on January 1, 20X3 for $5,000,000. Teckla's balance sheet on that date **before the purchase** is shown in the following:

FIGURE 12.18   Assets and Liabilities of Teckla

Teckla Corporation
Balance Sheet
January 1, 20X3

Assets		Liabilities	
Cash	$9,400,000	Accounts Payable	$1,950,000
Inventory	700,000	Notes Payable	4,895,000
Land	5,000,000		
		Owners' Equity	
		Capital Stock	$5,000,000
		Retained Earnings	3,255,000
		Total Liabilities &	
Total Assets	$15,100,000	Owners' Equity	$15,100,000

On January 1, 20X3, Feather has assets and liabilities as shown in the following:

FIGURE 12.19 Assets and Liabilities of Feather

	Value on Feather's Books	Current Market Value
Cash	$456,000	$456,000
Inventory	873,000	873,000
Land	50,000	760,000
Patent	5,000	1,000,000
Accounts Payable	500,000	500,000

a. Determine the amount of goodwill (if any) that Teckla will show on its consolidated balance sheet at January 1, 20X3.

b. Prepare a consolidated balance sheet for Teckla after it purchases Feather on January 1, 20X3.

11. In several past chapters, we have met Heather Miller, who started her own business, Sew Cool. The following are the financial statements for December. To calculate average total assets, assume that total assets on June 1, 20X8, when Sew Cool first started in business, were zero.

FIGURE 12.20 Sew Cool Financial Statements

Sew Cool
Income Statement
As of December 31, 20X8

Revenue	$4,000
Cost of Goods	(2,000)
Gross Profit	2,000
Other Expenses	(1,695)
Earnings before Tax	305
Tax Expense	(107)
Net Income	$198

FIGURE 12.21

Sew Cool
Stmt. of Retained Earnings
As of December 31, 20X8

Retained Earnings, December 1, 20X8	$500
Net Income	198
Dividends	(158)
Retained Earnings, December 31, 20X8	$540

FIGURE 12.22

Sew Cool
Balance Sheet
December 31, 20X8

Assets		Liabilities	
Current		**Current**	
Cash	$940	Accounts Payable	$900
Accounts Receivable	500	Income Tax Payable	120
Less Allowance for		Total Current Liabilities	$1,020
Doubtful Accounts	(20)		
Net Accounts Receivable	480		
Inventory	700		
Total Current Assets	$2,120		
Noncurrent		**Noncurrent**	
Equipment	$1,000	Notes Payable	$1,060
		Owners' Equity	
		Capital Stock	$500
		Retained Earnings	540
		Total Owners' Equity	$1,040
		Total Liabilities & Owners'	
Total Assets	$3,120	Equity	$3,120

Based on the financial statements determine the following:

a. Total asset turnover
b. Return on assets

COMPREHENSIVE PROBLEM

This problem will carry through several chapters, building in difficulty. It allows students to continually practice skills and knowledge learned in previous chapters.

In Chapter 11, financial statements for November were prepared for Webworks. They are included here as a starting point for the required recording for December.

FIGURE 12.23 Webworks Financial Statements

Webworks Income Statement As of November 30	
Revenue	$16,000
Cost of Goods Sold	(8,171)
Gross Profit	7,829
Deprec. and Amort. Expense	(363)
Other Expenses	(3,680)
Earnings before Tax	3,786
Tax Expense	(1,135)
Net Income	$2,651

FIGURE 12.24

Webworks Stmt. of Retained Earnings As of November 30	
Retained Earnings, November 1	$6,671
Net Income	2,651
Retained Earnings, November 30	$9,322

FIGURE 12.25

Webworks Balance Sheet November 30			
Assets		**Liabilities**	
Current		**Current**	
Cash	$ 2,097	Accounts Payable	$ 2,585
Accounts Receivable	1,750	Salaries Payable	$ 150
Less Allowance for Doubtful Accounts	(175)	Unearned Revenue	400
Net Accounts Receivable	1,575		
Merchandise Inventory	1,129		
Supplies Inventory	20		
Prepaid Rent	200		
Total Current Assets	$ 5,021	Total Current Liabilities	$ 3,135
Property, Plant, and Equipment			
Equipment	$ 7,000		
Less Accumulated Depreciation	(730)		
Furniture	1,000		
Less Accumulated Depreciation	(34)		
Total P, P, and E	$ 7,236		
Other Noncurrent Assets			
Licensing Agreement, Net	$ 2,200		
		Owners' Equity	
		Capital Stock	$ 2,000
		Retained Earnings	9,322
		Total Owners' Equity	$11,322
Total Assets	$14,457	Total Liabilities & Owners' Equity	$14,457

The following events occur during December:

a. Webworks starts and completes nine more Web sites and bills clients for $5,000.

b. Webworks purchases supplies worth $130 on account.

c. At the beginning of December, Webworks had nine keyboards costing $111 each and ten flash drives costing $13 each. Webworks uses periodic FIFO to cost its inventory.

d. Webworks purchases seventy keyboards for $113 each and one hundred flash drives for $15 each, all on account.

e. Webworks decides to invest a small amount of its excess cash in the stock market in the hopes of making a quick gain. Webworks purchases sixty shares of stock in XYZ Corporation for $5 per share in cash.

f. Webworks pays Nancy Po $750 for her work during the first three weeks of December.

g. Webworks sells sixty-five keyboards for $9,750 and ninety flash drives for $1,800 cash.

h. The Web site for the realtor started in November is completed.

i. Webworks collects $4,500 in accounts receivable.

j. Webworks pays off its salaries payable from November.

k. Webworks pays off $10,500 of its accounts payable.

l. XYZ Corporation pays Webworks a dividend of $40.

m. Webworks pays Leon Jackson (the owner of the business) a salary of $2,000.

n. Webworks pays taxes of $1,272 in cash.

> *Required:*
>
> A. Prepare journal entries for the previous events.
> B. Post the journal entries to T-accounts.
> C. Prepare an unadjusted trial balance for Webworks for December.
> D. Prepare adjusting entries for the following and post them to your T-accounts.

o. Webworks owes Nancy Po $200 for her work during the last week of December.

p. Leon's parents let him know that Webworks owes $300 toward the electricity bill. Webworks will pay them in January.

q. Webworks determines that it has $60 worth of supplies remaining at the end of December.

r. Prepaid rent should be adjusted for December's portion.

s. Webworks is continuing to accrue bad debts at 10 percent of accounts receivable.

t. Webworks continues to depreciate its equipment over four years and its furniture over five years, using the straight-line method.

u. The license agreement should continue to be amortized over its one-year life.

v. On December 31, XYZ stock is selling for $6 per share.

w. Record cost of goods sold.

x. Near the end of December, a new flash drive appears on the market that makes the ones Webworks has been selling virtually obsolete. Leon believes that it might be able to sell the rest of its inventory (twenty flash drives) for $5 each.

> E. Prepare an adjusted trial balance.
> F. Prepare financial statements for December.

RESEARCH ASSIGNMENT

Assume that you take a job as a summer employee for an investment advisory service. One of the partners for that firm is currently looking at the possibility of investing in **Google**. The partner is aware that **Google** holds an enormous amount of marketable securities. The partner is curious as to the actual size of that balance. The partner is also interested in knowing whether these marketable securities are reported as trading securities or as available-for-sale securities. The partner asks you to look at the 2010 financial statements for **Google** by following this path:

- Go to http://www.google.com.
- At the very bottom of this screen, click on "About Google."
- Near the top of the next screen, click on "Investor Relations."
- On the next screen, scroll to the bottom and click on "View 2011 Proxy Materials."
- On the next screen, in the center, click on "December 31, 2010 Annual Report" to download.
- Go to page 49 and find the balance sheet for December 31, 2010.
- Go to page 56 and read the second paragraph under "Cash, Cash Equivalents, and Marketable Securities" shown within Note One.

a. Using the balance sheet information located on **Google**'s website, what is the dollar amount reported by **Google** as of December 31, 2010, for its "marketable securities?" What percentage does this asset comprise of the company's total assets?

b. Using the information found in the section of Note One describing "Cash, Cash Equivalents, and Marketable Securities," determine whether these marketable securities are reported as trading securities or available-for-sale securities.

ENDNOTES

1. Michael J. de la Merced and Jeffrey Cane, "Confident Deal Makers Pulled Out Check-books in 2010," *DealB%k* (January 3, 2011), http://dealbook.nytimes.com/2011/01/03/confident-deal-makers-pulled-out-checkbooks-in-2010/.

In a Set of Financial Statements, What Information Is Conveyed about Current and Contingent Liabilities?

Video Clip

In this video, Professor Joe Hoyle introduces the essential points covered in Chapter 13.

View the video online at: http://bit.ly/hoyle13-1

1.   THE BASIC REPORTING OF LIABILITIES

L E A R N I N G   O B J E C T I V E S

At the end of this section students should be able to meet the following objectives:

1. Define a liability by listing its essential characteristics.
2. Differentiate a current liability from a noncurrent liability.
3. Explain the significance that current liabilities have for investors and creditors who are studying the financial health and future prospects of an organization.
4. Compute the current ratio.
5. Identify the appropriate timing for the recognition of a liability.

1.1   Current and Noncurrent Liabilities

liabilities

Probable future sacrifices of economic benefits arising from present obligations; the debts of an organization.

Question: The June 30, 2011, consolidated balance sheet for **The Procter & Gamble Company** *reports total* **liabilities** *of over $70 billion, including current liabilities of approximately $27 billion. In contrast, the business held only $2.8 billion in cash and cash equivalents.*

For reporting purposes, **Procter & Gamble** *divided its* current liabilities *into several specific categories:*

- *Accounts payable ($8.0 billion)*
- *Accrued and other liabilities ($9.3 billion)*
- *Debt due within one year ($10.0 billion)*

current liabilities

Debts that will be satisfied within one year from the date of a balance sheet.

When creating a balance sheet, what is reported as a liability? Why are some of these liabilities shown as current whereas others are not? **How does an accountant draw a distinction between liabilities that are labeled as current and those that are reported as noncurrent?**

Answer: A liability is an obligation owed to a party outside the reporting organization—a debt that can be stated in monetary terms. Liabilities normally require the payment of cash but might at times be settled by the conveyance of other assets or the delivery of services. Some reported liabilities are for definite amounts, although a significant number are no more than estimations.

noncurrent liabilities

Debts that will not be satisfied within one year from the date of a balance sheet.

The distinction between current and **noncurrent liabilities** is a function of time. A debt that is expected to be satisfied within one year from the balance sheet date is normally classified as a current liability.[1] Amounts owed for rent, insurance, utilities, inventory purchases, and the like usually fall into this category. If payment will not be made until after that one-year interval, the liability is reported as noncurrent. Bonds and notes payable are common examples of noncurrent debts as are liabilities for employee pensions, long-term leases, and deferred income taxes. Current liabilities are listed before noncurrent liabilities on a balance sheet.

1.2   The Importance of Information about Liabilities

Question: Figure 13.1 is the liability section of the balance sheet reported by **Johnson & Johnson** *as of January 2, 2011. Note that additional information about many of these liabilities is available in the notes to the company's financial statements.*

FIGURE 13.1   Liability Section of Balance Sheet, Johnson & Johnson as of January 2, 2011

All figures in millions	
Current liabilities	
Loans and notes payable (Note 7)	$ 7,617
Accounts payable	5,623
Accrued liabilities	4,100
Accrued rebates, returns and promotions	2,512
Accrued compensation and employee related obligations	2,642
Accrued taxes on income	578
Total current liabilities	23,072
Long-term debt (Note 7)	9,156
Deferred taxes on income (Note 8)	1,447
Employee related obligations (Notes 9 and 10)	6,087
Other liabilities	6,567
Total liabilities	46,329

*Investors and creditors (and other interested parties) who analyze an organization such as **Johnson &
Johnson** usually spend considerable time studying the data that is provided about liabilities, often focusing on current liabilities. **Why is information about liabilities, especially the size and composition of
current liabilities, considered so important when assessing the financial position and economic health
of a business?***

Answer: Liabilities represent claims to a company's assets. Debts must be paid as they come due or
the entity risks serious consequences. Missed payments might damage a company's ability to obtain additional credit in the future. Unfortunately, even bankruptcy can quickly become a possibility if obligations are not met.

To stay viable, organizations have to manage their liabilities carefully. They must be able to generate sufficient cash on an ongoing basis to meet all required payments. Virtually no other goal can be
more important, both to company officials and external decision makers.

In general, the larger a liability total is in comparison to the reported amount of assets, the riskier
the financial position. The future is always cloudy for a business when the size of its debts begins to approach the total of its assets. The amount reported as current liabilities is especially significant because
those debts must be satisfied in the near future. Cash has to be available quickly, often within weeks or
months.

Not surprisingly, decision makers become concerned when the reported total for current liabilities
is high in comparison with current assets. The essential question is obvious: will the organization be
able to meet those obligations as they come due? In a newspaper account about the financial difficulties
of **Advanced Cell Technology**, the following warning was issued: "It reported $17 million in current li-
abilities, but only $1 million in cash and other current assets, an indication it could be forced to file for
bankruptcy protection."[2]

As mentioned in an earlier chapter, one vital sign monitored by decision makers in judging the
present level of risk posed by a company's liability requirements is the **current ratio**: current assets divided by current liabilities. The current ratio is a simple benchmark that can be easily computed using
available balance sheet information. Although many theories exist as to an appropriate standard, any
current ratio below 1.00 to 1.00 signals that the company's current liabilities exceed its current assets.
Figure 13.2 presents recent current ratios for three well-known companies: **Target**, **Dillard's**, and
Aeropostale.

current ratio

Formula measuring an
organization's liquidity (the
ability to pay debts as they
come due); calculated by
dividing current assets by
current liabilities.

FIGURE 13.2   Sample of Recent Current Ratios as of January 29, 2011

Target	1.71 to 1.00 (at 12/31/10)
Dillard's	2.05 to 1.00 (at 1/29/11)
Aeropostale	2.17 to 1.00 (at 1/31/11)

Question:

The Petersen Company currently holds $500,000 in current assets and $200,000 in current liabilities. The company borrows $60,000 cash. However, a question arises as to whether this debt is a current or noncurrent liability. Which of the following statements is true?

a. If the liability is noncurrent, the transaction has no impact on the current ratio.

b. If the liability is noncurrent, the transaction causes the current ratio to increase.

c. If the liability is current, the transaction has no impact on the current ratio.

d. If the liability is current, the transaction causes the current ratio to increase.

Answer:

The correct answer is choice b: If the liability is noncurrent, the transaction causes the current ratio to increase.

Explanation:

If the liability incurred here is noncurrent, the transaction causes current assets to go up by $60,000, but there is no change in current liabilities. Thus, the current ratio (current assets divided by current liabilities) will be higher. If the liability is current, the transaction causes both the current asset total and the current liability total to increase by $60,000. The current ratio is no longer 2.50 to 1.00 ($500,000/$200,000) but will fall to 2.15 to 1.00 ($560,000/$260,000).

1.3   Characteristics of a Liability

Question: In the real world of business, organizations are not inclined to report more liabilities than necessary because of potential damage to the image being portrayed. The inclusion of debts usually makes a company look riskier to creditors and investors. Thus, the danger that officials will report an excessive amount of liabilities seems slight. Balance sheets look better to decision makers if fewer obligations are present to drain off financial resources. Consequently, where possible, officials probably have a tendency to limit the debts that are reported. **At what point does an entity have to recognize a liability?** *How does U.S. GAAP ensure that all liabilities are appropriately included on a balance sheet?*

Answer: FASB *Statement of Financial Accounting Concepts No. 6* defines many of the elements found in a set of financial statements. According to this guideline, a liability should be recognized when all of the following characteristics exist:

1. There is a probable future sacrifice

2. This sacrifice involves the reporting entity's assets or services.

3. The sacrifice arises from a present obligation that is the result of a past transaction or event.

To understand the reporting of liabilities, several aspects of these characteristics are especially important to note. First, the obligation does not have to be absolute before recognition is required. A future sacrifice only has to be "probable." This standard leaves open a degree of uncertainty. As might be expected, determination as to whether a potential payment is probable or not can be a point of close scrutiny when independent CPAs audit a set of financial statements. The line between "probable" and "not quite probable" is hardly an easily defined benchmark.

Second, for reporting to be required, a debt must result from a past transaction or event.

- An employee works for a company and is owed a salary. The work previously performed is the past event that creates the obligation.

- A vendor delivers merchandise to a business. Receipt of these purchased goods is the past event that creates the obligation.

Third, the past transaction or event must create a present obligation. In other words, an actual debt must exist and not just a potential debt. Ordering a piece of equipment is a past event but, in most cases, no liability has yet been incurred. In contrast, the delivery of this equipment probably does obligate the buyer and, thus, necessitates the reporting of a debt. Often, in deciding whether a liability should be recognized, the accountant must address two key questions: what event actually obligates the company, and when did that event occur?

Determining all of the liabilities to be included on a balance sheet often takes considerable thought and analysis. Accountants for the reporting company produce a list of debts that meet the characteristics listed above. The independent auditor then spends considerable time and energy searching for any other obligations that might have been omitted, either accidentally or on purpose.

2.   REPORTING CURRENT LIABILITIES SUCH AS GIFT CARDS

LEARNING OBJECTIVES

At the end of this section students should be able to meet the following objectives:

1. **Define and record accrued liabilities.**
2. **Report the sale and redemption of gift cards.**
3. **Account for gift cards that are not expected to be redeemed.**

2.1   Recognizing All of a Company's Current Liabilities

Question: Current liabilities often include rent payable, salary payable, insurance payable, and the like. These debts are incurred in connection with day-to-day operations. The amounts are known and payment will be made within a relatively short period of time.

Liabilities that result from physical events such as the purchase of inventory or supplies are often reported under the generic title "accounts payable." Other current debts (interest payable or rent payable, for example) are sometimes grouped together as **accrued liabilities** *because they grow gradually in size over time rather than through a specific transaction.* **How does an organization determine the amount of current liabilities to be reported on its balance sheet?**

> **accrued liabilities**
>
> Liabilities that grow gradually because of the passage of time; common examples include salaries, rent, and interest.

Answer: As discussed in a previous chapter, the timing for the recognition of a purchase is guided by the FOB point specified by the seller or negotiated by the parties. If marked "FOB shipping point," the liability is reported by the buyer when the goods leave the seller's place of business. "FOB destination" delays recording until the merchandise is received by the buyer. Unless goods are damaged during transit or a dispute arises over payment for transportation charges, the FOB point is only relevant near the end of the fiscal year as the accountant attempts to separate transactions between one period and the next.

Many other liabilities are not created by a specific event but rather grow gradually day by day. Interest and rent are common examples but salaries, payroll taxes, and utilities also accrue in the same manner. They increase based on the passage of time. Interest on a loan or the amount due to an employee gets larger on a continual basis until paid. Adjusting entries are required at the end of a period to recognize any accrued liabilities that have been omitted from the general ledger.

To illustrate, assume a large group of employees earns total wages of $10,000 per day. They work Monday through Friday with payment made on the final day of each week. If the company's fiscal year ends on a Wednesday, an adjustment is necessary so that both the expense on the income statement and the liability on the balance sheet are presented fairly for the three days that passed without payment. The adjustment shown in Figure 13.3 is made for $30,000 ($10,000 per day for three days) so that the debt incurred for salaries prior to the end of the year is reported. The expense is recognized in this period to match the cost with the revenues that were earned during these three days by the employees.

FIGURE 13.3 Year-End Adjusting Entry to Recognize Debt to Employees for Three Days' Work

| Wages Expense | 30,000 | |
| Wages Payable | | 30,000 |

As a second example, assume a company borrows $100,000 from a bank on December 1 with payment to be made in six months. The bank has to earn a profit and charges a 6 percent annual interest rate. By the end of that year, the company owes interest but only for the one month that has passed. As of December 31, interest expense has grown to $500 ($100,000 principal × 6 percent × 1/12 year). This accrued liability is recognized through the adjusting entry shown in Figure 13.4.

FIGURE 13.4 Year-End Adjusting Entry to Recognize Interest for One Month

| Interest Expense | 500 | |
| Interest Payable | | 500 |

TEST YOURSELF

Question:

An organization rents a warehouse for $8,000 per week. Cash payments are made to the owner of the building at the end of every six weeks. No payments were made for the last four weeks of Year One but the company accountant forgot to accrue this liability. Which of the following statements is not true concerning the Year One financial statements?

a. The current ratio is overstated.

b. Total liabilities are understated.

c. Net income is understated.

d. Rent expense is understated.

Answer:

The correct answer is choice c: Net income is understated.

Explanation:

Rent expense and rent payable for these four weeks ($32,000) have been omitted. Current liabilities (and, hence, total liabilities) are understated because of the debt was never recorded. If current liabilities are too low, the current ratio (current assets/current liabilities) is too high. Rent for this period has not been recorded so the expense on the income statement is understated, which makes the reported net income too high.

2.2 Reporting the Sale of Gift Cards as a Liability

gift card liability

An obligation arising when a business accepts cash and issues a card that can be redeemed in the future for a specified amount of assets or services.

Question: The February 26, 2011, balance sheet for **Best Buy Co. Inc.** *shows several typical current liability accounts such as accounts payable and accrued liabilities. However, a $474 million figure also appears titled "Unredeemed* **Gift Card Liabilities.**"

Over the last decade or so, the importance of gift cards has escalated dramatically as a source of revenue for many businesses. By purchasing such cards, customers obtain the right to a specified amount of goods or services. From **Starbucks** *to* **McDonald's** *to* **Amazon.com**, *these cards are sold to serve as gifts or merely as a convenient method for handling future payments.* **How does a company such as** **Best Buy** **account for the thousands of gift cards that it sells each year?**

Answer: As stated previously, a liability represents a probable future sacrifice of an asset or service. By selling a gift card, a company has created an obligation to the customer that must be reported. Businesses such as **Best Buy** or **Barnes & Noble** accept cash but then have to be willing to hand over inventory items such as cameras or books whenever the gift card is presented. Or, perhaps, some service is due to the cardholder such as the repair of a computer or a massage. To the seller, a gift card reflects a liability but one that is not normally settled with cash. Undoubtedly, the most common type of gift card in the world is a postal stamp. When bought, the stamp provides a person with the right to receive a particular service, the mailing of a letter or package.

To illustrate, assume that a company sells ten thousand gift cards with a redemption value of $50 each. Revenue cannot be reported at the time of sale; the earning process is not yet substantially complete. No asset or service has been conveyed to the customer. Rather, as shown in Figure 13.5, a liability (labeled as "unearned revenue" or "gift card liability") is recognized to indicate that the company has an obligation to the holder of the card.

FIGURE 13.5 Sale of Ten Thousand $50 Gift Cards for Cash

| Cash | 500,000 | |
| Unearned Revenue | | 500,000 |

Over time, customers will present their gift cards for selected merchandise. To complete this illustration, assume that a person uses one of the $50 cards to acquire goods that had originally cost the company $32. Upon redemption, the liability is satisfied and the revenue is recognized. This exchange is reported in Figure 13.6. A perpetual inventory system is used in this example to demonstrate the impact on inventory and cost of goods sold.

FIGURE 13.6 Redemption of Gift Card

Unearned Revenue	50	
Revenue		50
Cost of Goods Sold	32	
Inventory		32

2.3   Accounting for Gift Cards That Are Never Redeemed

*Question: Some gift cards are never redeemed. They might be lost or just forgotten by their owners. **Does the liability for a gift card remain on a company's balance sheet indefinitely if it is unlikely that redemption will ever occur?***

Answer: One reason that gift cards have become so popular with businesses is that some percentage will never be redeemed. They will be misplaced, stolen, or the holder will move away or die. Perhaps the person simply does not want the merchandise that is available. In such cases, the seller received money but has never had to fulfill the obligation. The entire amount of cash from the sale of the gift card is profit.

For the accountant, a question arises as to the appropriate timing of revenue recognition from such anticipated defaults. The earning process is never substantially completed by a redemption. In theory, a company recognizes this revenue when reasonable evidence exists that the card will never be used by the customer. Practically, though, determining this precise point is a matter of speculation.

Companies typically report the revenue from unused gift cards at one of three possible times:

1. When the cards expire if a time limit is imposed.

2. After the passage of a specified period of time such as eighteen months or two years.

3. In proportion to the cards that are actually redeemed. To illustrate this final option, assume that a company sells thousands of cards. Based on historical trends, company officials believe that $8,000 of these gift cards will never be turned in by their owners. If 10 percent of the expected gift cards are redeemed this month, the company can also reclassify $800 (10 percent of $8,000) from unearned revenue to revenue to reflect the estimated portion of those cards that will never be presented.

Because of this accounting issue, a note to the financial statements produced by **Best Buy** explains, "We recognize revenue from gift cards when: (i) the gift card is redeemed by the customer, or (ii) the likelihood of the gift card being redeemed by the customer is remote ('gift card breakage'), and we determine that we do not have a legal obligation to remit the value of unredeemed gift cards to the relevant jurisdictions. We determine our gift card breakage rate based upon historical redemption patterns."

TEST YOURSELF

Question:

The Boston Book Company (BBC) sells $700,000 of gift cards during Year One. Of this amount, 60 percent are redeemed before the end of the year and properly recorded. Another 4 percent expired because of time limitations. The others remain outstanding at the end of the year. The accountant for BBC did not realize that the time limitations had been reached so made no entry for the 4 percent. What is the result of the accountant's failure to make an entry?

a. Revenues are overstated.

b. Net income is overstated.

c. Liabilities are overstated.

d. There is an impact on liabilities but not on net income.

Answer:

The correct answer is choice c: Liabilities are overstated.

Explanation:

When the gift cards were sold, the total amount was recorded as a liability to indicate that the company owed a service or an asset to the customer. At the time of redemption or expiration, this liability should have been reclassified as revenue. That adjustment was not made for the cards that had expired. The liability was not properly reduced. It remains too high while revenue (and, hence, net income) is understated because of the failure to recognize this amount.

KEY TAKEAWAY

Companies report a wide variety of current liabilities. Accounts payable are normally created by the purchase of inventory or supplies. Accrued liabilities such as rent and interest are those debts that grow gradually over time. All such liabilities must be found and recorded prior to the preparation of financial statements. One common liability is created by the sale of gift cards. In today's retail world, many companies offer these cards in hopes of increasing profits. Because a product or service must be provided when the card is presented, the company has an obligation so that a liability is reported. This liability is later reclassified as revenue when the card is redeemed because the earning process is substantially complete at that point. Revenue should also be recorded for a gift card when it becomes likely that redemption will never occur. Cards can be lost, stolen, or the customer might die or leave the area. The revenue associated with unredeemed gift cards must be reported at an appropriate point in time such as on the date of expiration or in proportion to the redemption of other cards.

3. ACCOUNTING FOR CONTINGENCIES

LEARNING OBJECTIVES

At the end of this section students should be able to meet the following objectives:

1. Define a commitment and explain the method by which it is reported.
2. Define a contingency and explain the method by which it is reported.
3. Explain the criteria that guide the reporting of a contingent loss.
4. Describe the appropriate accounting for contingent losses that do not qualify for recognition at the present time.
5. Describe the handling of a contingent loss that ultimately proves to be different from the originally estimated and recorded balance.
6. Compare the reporting of contingent losses and contingent gains.

3.1 Commitments and Contingencies

*Question: The December 31, 2010, balance sheet for **E. I. du Pont de Nemours and Company** (better known as **DuPont**) shows total liabilities of approximately $30.7 billion. Immediately following the liability section, a separate category titled "Commitments and Contingent Liabilities" is included but no monetary figure is presented. Note 19 to the company's financial statements provides further details. In several pages of explanatory material, a number of future matters facing the company are described such as product warranties, environmental actions, litigation, and operating leases. **In financial reporting, what is meant by the terms "commitments" and "contingencies?"***

Answer:

Commitments. Commitments represent unexecuted contracts. A contract has been created (either orally or in writing) and all parties have agreed to the terms. However, the listed actions have not yet been performed.

For example, assume that a business places an order with a truck company for the purchase of a large truck. The business has made a **commitment** to pay for this new vehicle but only after delivery has been received. Although a cash payment will be required in the future, the specified event (conveyance of the truck) has not occurred. No transaction has taken place, so no journal entry is needed. The liability does not yet exist.

Information about such commitments is still of importance to decision makers because future cash payments will be required of the reporting company. However, events have not reached the point where all the characteristics of a liability are present. Thus, an extensive explanation about such commitments (as found in the notes for **DuPont**) is included in the notes to financial statements but no amounts are reported on either the income statement or the balance sheet. When a commitment is described, investors and creditors know that a step has been taken that will likely lead to a liability.

Contingencies. A **contingency** poses a different reporting quandary for the accountant. A past event has already occurred but the amount of the present obligation (if any) cannot yet be determined.

With a contingency, the uncertainty is about the ultimate outcome of an action that took place in the past. The accountant is not a fortune teller who can predict the future. To illustrate, assume Wysocki Corporation commits an act that is detrimental to the environment so that the federal government files a lawsuit for damages. The original action against the environment is the past event that creates the contingency. However, both the chance of losing the lawsuit and the possible amount of any penalties might not be known for several years. What, if anything, should be recognized in the interim?

Because companies prefer to avoid (or at least minimize) the recognition of losses and liabilities, authoritative guidelines are necessary to guide the appropriate reporting of contingencies. Otherwise, few if any contingencies would ever be reported.

According to U.S. GAAP, the recognition of a **loss contingency** is required if the following are true:

1. The loss is deemed to be probable.
2. The amount of that loss can be reasonably estimated.

As soon as both of these criteria are met, the expected impact of the loss contingency must be recorded.

To illustrate, assume that the previous lawsuit for environmental damages was filed in Year One. Wysocki officials assess the situation. They believe that a loss is probable and that $800,000 is a

commitment

An unexecuted contract such as for the future purchase of inventory at a set price; amounts are not reported on the balance sheet or income statement because no transaction has yet occurred; disclosure of information within the financial statement notes is necessary.

contingency

A potential gain or loss that might eventually arise as a result of a past event; uncertainty exists as to the likelihood that a gain or loss will occur and the actual amount, if any, that will result.

loss contingency

A potential loss resulting from a past event that must be recognized on an entity's financial statements if it is deemed probable and the amount can be reasonably estimated.

reasonable estimation of the amount that will eventually have to be paid as a result of this litigation. Although this balance is only an estimate and the case may not be finalized for some time, the contingent loss is recognized, as can be seen in Figure 13.7.

FIGURE 13.7 Year One—Expected Loss from Lawsuit (Contingency)

| Loss from Lawsuit—Estimated | 800,000 | |
| Estimated Liability from Lawsuit | | 800,000 |

FASB has identified a number of examples of loss contingencies that are evaluated and reported in this same manner including:

- Collectability of receivables
- Obligations related to product warranties and product defects
- Risk of loss or damage of enterprise property by fire, explosion, or other hazards
- Threat of expropriation of assets
- Pending or threatened litigation
- Actual or possible claims and assessments
- Guarantees of indebtedness of others

3.2   Accounting Rules Used to Record Contingent Losses

Question: The likelihood of loss in connection with contingencies is not always going to be probable or subject to a reasonable estimation. These two criteria will be met in some but certainly not in all cases. **What reporting is appropriate for a loss contingency that does not qualify for recording at the present time?**

Answer: If a contingent loss is only reasonably possible (rather than probable) or if the amount of a probable loss does not lend itself to a reasonable estimation, only disclosure in the notes to the financial statements is necessary rather than actual recognition. Furthermore, a contingency where the chance of loss is viewed as merely remote can be omitted entirely from the financial statements.

Unfortunately, as discussed previously, official guidance provides little specific detail about what constitutes a probable, reasonably possible, or remote loss. At best, each of those terms seems vague. For example, within U.S. GAAP, "probable" is described as "likely to occur." Thus, the professional judgment of the accountants and auditors must be relied on to determine the exact point in time when a contingent loss moves from reasonably possible to probable.

Not surprisingly, many companies contend that any future adverse effects from loss contingencies are only reasonably possible so that no actual amounts are reported on the balance sheet. Practical application of official accounting standards is not always theoretically pure, especially when the guidelines are nebulous.

3.3   Fixing an Incorrect Estimate

Question: Assume that a company recognizes a contingent loss because it is judged as probable and subject to a reasonable estimation. Eventually, most such guesses are likely to prove to be wrong, at least in some small amount. **What happens when an estimate is reported in a set of financial statements and the actual total is later found to be different?**

For example, as shown in Figure 13.7, Wysocki Corporation recognized a loss of $800,000 in Year One because of a lawsuit involving environmental damage. Assume the case is eventually settled in Year Two for $900,000. How is the additional loss of $100,000 reported? It relates to an action taken in Year One but the actual amount is not finalized until Year Two. The difference is not apparent until the later date.

Answer: In Year One, because both criteria for reporting were met, an $800,000 loss was recognized on the income statement along with a corresponding liability. In addition, notes to the company's financial statement will explain the nature of this lawsuit as well as the range of any reasonably possible losses. Decision makers analyzing the Wysocki Corporation should realize that the amount reported is not meant as a precise measure of the eventual loss. The same is true of all contingencies and other estimations. By the time that the exact amount of loss is determined, investors and creditors have already incorporated the original information into their decisions, including the uncertainty of the outcome. Restating the Year One loss to $900,000 does not allow them to undo and change decisions that were made in the past.

Consequently, no alteration is made in the $800,000 figure reported for Year One. The additional $100,000 loss is recorded in Year Two. The adjustment is recognized as soon as a better estimation (or final figure) is available. This approach is required to correct any reasonable estimate. Wysocki recognizes the updated balances through the journal entry shown in Figure 13.8 that removes the liability and records the remainder of the loss that has now been incurred.

FIGURE 13.8   Year Two—Settlement of Lawsuit at an Amount $100,000 More than Originally Reported

Estimated Liability from Lawsuit	800,000	
Additional Loss on Lawsuit	100,000	
Cash		900,000

One important exception to this handling does exist. If the initial estimate is viewed as fraudulent—an attempt to deceive decision makers—the $800,000 figure reported in Year One is physically restated. It simply cannot continue to appear. All amounts in a set of financial statements have to be presented in good faith. Any reported balance that fails this essential test cannot be allowed to remain. Furthermore, even if company officials made no overt attempt to deceive, restatement is still required if they should have known that a reported figure was materially wrong. Such amounts were not reported in good faith; officials have been grossly negligent in reporting the financial information.

From a journal entry perspective, restatement of a previously reported income statement balance is accomplished by adjusting retained earnings. Revenues and expenses (as well as gains, losses, and any dividends paid figures) are closed into retained earnings at the end of each year. Thus, this account is where the previous year error now resides.

Upon discovery that the actual loss from the lawsuit is $900,000, this amount is reported by one of the two approaches presented in Figure 13.9. However, use of the second method is rare because accounting mistakes do not often reach this level of deceit or incompetence. An announcement that a company has had to "restate its earnings" is never a good sign.

FIGURE 13.9   Two Ways to Correct an Estimate

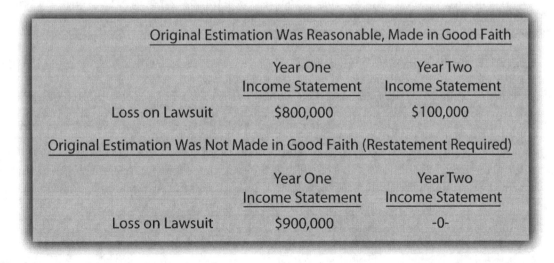

Original Estimation Was Reasonable, Made in Good Faith		
	Year One Income Statement	Year Two Income Statement
Loss on Lawsuit	$800,000	$100,000
Original Estimation Was Not Made in Good Faith (Restatement Required)		
	Year One Income Statement	Year Two Income Statement
Loss on Lawsuit	$900,000	-0-

Question:

The Red Company incurs a contingency in Year One. At that time, the company's accountants believe that a loss of $200,000 is probable but a loss of $290,000 is reasonably possible. Nothing is settled by the end of Year Two. On that date, the accountants believe that a loss of $240,000 is probable but a loss of $330,000 is reasonably possible. All these estimations are viewed as reasonable. The contingency ends in Year Three when Red Company pays the other party $170,000 to settle the problem. What does Red Company recognize on its Year Three income statement?

a. Gain (or Loss Recovery) of $30,000

b. Gain (or Loss Recovery) of $70,000

c. Gain (or Loss Recovery) of $120,000

d. Gain (or Loss Recovery) of $160,000

Answer:

The correct answer is choice b: Gain (or Loss Recovery) of $70,000.

Explanation:

A loss of $200,000 is recognized in Year One because that amount is viewed as probable. An additional $40,000 loss is recognized in Year Two so that the total loss reported to date corresponds to the estimated $240,000 probable amount. However, the company does not lose all $240,000 that has now been recognized but only $170,000. The reduction in the reported loss increases net income by the $70,000 difference and is shown as either a gain or a loss recovery.

3.4 Gain Contingencies

gain contingency

A potential gain resulting from a past event that is not recognized in an entity's financial statements until it actually occurs due to the conservatism inherent in financial accounting.

Question: The previous discussion focused entirely on the accounting that is required for loss contingencies. Companies obviously can also have **gain** *contingencies. In a lawsuit, for example, one party might anticipate winning $800,000 but eventually collect $900,000.* **Are the rules for reporting gain contingencies the same as those applied to loss contingencies?**

Answer: As a result of the conservatism inherent in financial accounting, the timing used in the recognition of gains does not follow the same rules applied to losses. Losses are anticipated when they become probable; that has long been a fundamental rule of financial reporting. The recognition of gains is delayed until they actually occur (or, at least until they reach the point of being substantially complete). Disclosure in the notes is still important but the decision as to whether the outcome is probable or reasonably possible is irrelevant in reporting a gain. As reflected in Figure 13.10, gains are not anticipated for reporting purposes.

FIGURE 13.10 Reporting a Gain Contingency

	Year One Income Statement	Year Two Income Statement
Gain on Lawsuit	-0-	$900,000

TEST YOURSELF

Question:

The Blue Company files a lawsuit against another company in Year One and thinks there is a good chance for a win. At that time, the company's accountants believe that a gain of $200,000 is probable but a gain of $290,000 is reasonably possible. Nothing is settled by the end of Year Two. On that date, the accountants believe that a gain of $240,000 is probable but a gain of $330,000 is reasonably possible. The contingency is settled in Year Three when Blue Company collects $170,000. What does Blue Company recognize on its Year Three income statement?

a. Decrease in income of $30,000

b. Decrease in income of $70,000

c. Decrease in income of $120,000

d. Increase in income of $170,000

Answer:

The correct answer is choice d: Increase in income of $170,000.

Explanation:

As a gain contingency, no amount will be recognized until the point where substantial completion is reached. Consequently, no gain or loss is reported in either Year One or Year Two despite the optimism that a gain will be achieved. Thus, the entire amount of the gain is recorded when the case is settled in Year Three. That final event increases net income by $170,000.

Talking with an Independent Auditor about International Financial Reporting Standards

Following is a continuation of our interview with Robert A. Vallejo, partner with the accounting firm **PricewaterhouseCoopers**.

Question: According to U.S. GAAP, a contingent loss must be recognized when it is probable and a reasonable estimation of the amount can be made. That rule has been in place now for over thirty years and is well understood in this country. Are contingent losses handled in the same way by IFRS?

Robert Vallejo: The theory is the same under IFRS but some interesting and subtle differences do exist. If there is a probable future outflow of economic benefits and the company can form a reliable estimate, then that amount must be recognized. However, the term "probable" is defined as "more likely than not" which is easier to reach than the U.S. GAAP equivalent. Thus, the reporting of more contingent losses is likely under IFRS than currently under U.S. GAAP.

IAS 37, *Provisions, Contingent Liabilities and Contingent Assets*, states that the amount recorded should be the best estimate of the expenditure that would be required to settle the present obligation at the balance sheet date. That is the best estimate of the amount that an entity would rationally pay to settle the obligation at the balance sheet date or to transfer it to a third party. Under U.S. GAAP, if there is a range of possible losses but no best estimate exists within that range, the entity records the low end of the range. Under IFRS, the entity records the midpoint of the range. That is a subtle difference in wording, but it is one that could have a significant impact on financial reporting for organizations where expected losses exist within a very wide range.

In July 2010, the FASB published an exposure draft, *Disclosure of Certain Loss Contingencies*, as investors and other users of financial reporting had expressed concerns that disclosures about loss contingencies. Many felt that existing guidance does not provide adequate and timely information to assist them in assessing the likelihood, timing, and magnitude of future cash outflows associated with loss contingencies. After receiving comments from constituents, the FASB is re-deliberating the need to update existing U.S. GAAP.

K E Y   T A K E A W A Y

Entities often enter into contractual arrangements. Prior to performing the requirements of the contract, financial commitments frequently exist. They are future obligations that do not yet qualify as liabilities. For accounting purposes, they are only described in the notes to the financial statements. In contrast, contingencies are potential liabilities that might result because of a past event. The likelihood of loss or the actual amount of the loss both remain uncertain. Loss contingencies are recognized when their likelihood is probable and this loss is subject to a reasonable estimation. Reasonably possible contingent losses are only described in the notes whereas potential losses that are only remote can be omitted entirely from a company's financial statements. Eventually, such estimates often prove to be incorrect and are normally fixed when first discovered. However, if fraud, either purposely or through gross negligence, has occurred, the amounts reported in prior years are restated. Contingent gains are only reported to decision makers through disclosure within the notes to the financial statements.

---

4.   ACCOUNTING FOR PRODUCT WARRANTIES

L E A R N I N G   O B J E C T I V E S

At the end of this section students should be able to meet the following objectives:

1. Explain the difference between an embedded and an extended product warranty.
2. Account for the liability and expense incurred by a company that provides customers with an embedded warranty on a purchased product.
3. Account for the amount received on the sale of an extended warranty and any subsequent costs incurred as a result of this warranty.
4. Compute the average age of accounts payable.

4.1   Accounting for Embedded Product Warranties

embedded product warranty

An obligation established by the sale of a product where the seller promises to fix or replace the product if it proves to be defective.

*Question: U.S. GAAP includes an **embedded product warranty** as one type of loss contingency. A company sells merchandise such as a car or a microwave and agrees to fix certain problems if they arise within a specified period of time. The seller might promise, for example, to replace a car's transmission if it breaks. Making the sale with this warranty attached is the past event that creates the contingency. However, the item acquired by the customer must break before the company has an actual loss. That outcome is uncertain.*

In accounting for an embedded product warranty, several estimates are required:

- *The approximate number of claims that can be expected*
- *The percentage of these claims will meet the requirements of the warranty*
- *The eventual cost from the average approved claim*

*As an example, **General Electric** reported on its December 31, 2010, balance sheet a liability for product warranties totaling over $1.5 billion. That is certainly not a minor obligation. In the notes to the financial statements, the company explains, "We provide for estimated product warranty expenses when we sell the related products. Because warranty estimates are forecasts that are based on the best available information—mostly historical claims experience—claims costs may differ from amounts provided." **How does a company record and report contingencies such as embedded product warranties?***

Answer: In accounting for warranties, cash rebates, the collectability of receivables and other similar contingencies, the likelihood of loss is rarely an issue. These losses are almost always probable. For the accountant, the challenge is in arriving at a reasonable estimate of that loss. How many microwaves will break and have to be repaired? What percentage of cash rebate coupons will be presented by customers in the allotted time? How often will a car's transmission need to be replaced?

Many companies utilize such programs on an ongoing basis so that data from previous offers will be available to help determine the amount of the expected loss. However, historical trends cannot be followed blindly. Officials still have to be alert for any changes that could impact previous patterns. For example, in bad economic periods, customers are more likely to take the time to complete the paperwork required to receive a cash rebate. Or, the terms may vary from one warranty program to the next. Even small changes in the wording of an offer can alter the expected number of claims.

To illustrate, assume that a retail store sells ten thousand compact refrigerators during Year One for $400 cash each. The product is covered by a warranty that extends until the end of Year Three. No claims are made in Year One but similar programs in the past have resulted in repairs having to be made on 3 percent of the refrigerators at an average cost of $90. Thus, the warranty on the Year One sales is expected to cost a total of $27,000 (10,000 units × 3 percent = 300 claims; 300 claims × $90 each = $27,000).

Although no repairs are made in Year One, the $27,000 liability is reported in that period. Immediate recognition is appropriate because the loss is both probable and subject to reasonable estimation. In addition, the matching principle states that expenses should be reported in the same period as the revenues they help generate. Because the revenue from the sale of the refrigerators is recognized in Year One (Figure 13.11), the warranty expense resulting from those revenues is included at that time (Figure 13.12).

FIGURE 13.11 Year One—Sale of Ten Thousand Compact Refrigerators for $400 Each

FIGURE 13.12 Year One—Recognize Expected Cost of Warranty Claims

This warranty is in effect until the end of Year Three. Assume that repairs made in the year following the sale (Year Two) cost the company $13,000 but are made for these customers at no charge. When a refrigerator breaks, it is fixed as promised by the warranty. Because the expense has already been recognized in the year of sale (Figure 13.12), these payments reduce the recorded liability as is shown in Figure 13.13. The actual costs create no additional impact on net income.

FIGURE 13.13 Year Two—Payment for Repair Work Covered by Embedded Warranty

At the end of Year Two, the liability balance in the general ledger holds a balance of $14,000 to reflect the expected warranty costs for Year Three ($27,000 original estimation less the $13,000 payout made for repairs to date). Because the warranty has not expired, company officials need to evaluate whether this $14,000 liability is still a reasonable estimation of the remaining costs to be incurred. If so, no further adjustment is made.

However, the original $27,000 was merely an estimate. More information is now available, some of which might suggest that $14,000 is no longer the best number to be utilized for the final year of the warranty. To illustrate, assume that a flaw has been found in the refrigerator's design and that $20,000 (rather than $14,000) is now a better estimate of the costs to be incurred in the final year of the warranty.

The $14,000 balance is no longer appropriate. The reported figure is updated in Figure 13.14 to provide a fair presentation of the data that is now available. Estimates should be changed at the point where new information provides a clearer vision of future events.

FIGURE 13.14 December 31, Year Two—Adjust Warranty Liability from $14,000 to Newly Expected $20,000

In this adjusting entry, the change in the expense is not recorded in the period of the sale. As discussed earlier, no retroactive restatements are made to figures previously reported unless fraud occurred or an estimate was held to be so unreasonable that it was not made in good faith.

4.2 Accounting for Extended Product Warranties

extended product warranty

An obligation whereby the buyer of a product pays the seller for the equivalent of an insurance policy to protect against breakage or other harm to the product for a specified period of time.

Question: Not all warranties are built into a sales transaction. Many retailers also offer **extended product warranties** *for an additional fee. For example, assume a business sells a high-definition television with an automatic one-year warranty. The buyer receives this warranty as part of the purchase agreement. The accounting for that first year is the same as just demonstrated; an estimated expense and liability are recognized at the time of sale.*

However, an additional warranty for three more years is also offered at a price of $50. If on January 1, Year One, a customer buys a new television and also chooses to acquire this additional three-year coverage, what recording is made by the seller? **Is an extended warranty purchased by a customer reported in the same manner as an automatic product warranty embedded within a sales contract?**

Answer: Extended warranties, which are quite popular in many industries, are simply insurance policies. If the customer buys the coverage, the product is insured against breakage or other harm for the specified period of time. In most cases, the company is making the offer in an attempt to earn an extra profit. The seller hopes that the money received for the extended warranty will outweigh the eventual repair costs. Therefore, the accounting differs here from the process demonstrated previously for an embedded warranty that was provided to encourage the sale of the product. In that earlier example, all of the revenue as well as the related (but estimated) expense were recorded immediately.

By accepting money for an extended warranty, the seller agrees to provide services in the future. This contract is much like a gift card. The revenue cannot be recognized until the earning process is substantially complete. Thus, as shown in Figure 13.15, the $50 received for the extended warranty on this television is initially recorded as "unearned revenue." This balance is a liability because the company owes a specified service to the customer. As indicated previously, liabilities do not always represent future cash payments.

FIGURE 13.15 January 1, Year One—Sale of Extended Warranty Covering Years Two through Four

Note in Figure 13.15 that no expense was estimated and recorded in connection with this warranty. As explained by the matching principle, expenses are not recognized until the related revenue is reported.

Because of the terms specified, this extended warranty does not become active until January 1, Year Two. The television is then covered for a three-year period. The revenue is recognized, most likely on a straight-line basis, over that time. Consequently, the $50 is reported at the rate of 1/3 per year or $16.66.

FIGURE 13.16 December 31, Year Two (as well as Three and Four)—Recognition of Revenue from Extended Warranty

| Unearned Revenue | 16.66 | |
| Revenue from Extended Warranty | | 16.66 |

In any period in which a repair must be made, the expense is recognized as incurred because revenue from this warranty contract is also being reported. For example, assume that on August 8, Year Two, a slight adjustment must be made to the television at a cost of $9. The product is under warranty so the customer is not charged for this service. The Year Two expense shown in Figure 13.17 is being matched with the Year Two revenue recognized in Figure 13.16.

FIGURE 13.17 August 8, Year Two—Repair of Television under Warranty Contract

| Warranty Expense | 9 | |
| Cash | | 9 |

TEST YOURSELF

Question:

A company sells a product late in Year One. The customer holds a one-year warranty on that product. The company believes the product will break in Year Two and have to be repaired at a cost of $16. Which of the following statements is true?

a. If this is an embedded warranty that the customer received automatically when the product was acquired, the $16 expense is reported in Year One.

b. If this is an extended warranty that the customer bought when the product was acquired, the $16 expense is reported in Year One.

c. If this is an extended warranty that cost the customer $20, the company recognizes a $4 profit in Year One.

d. If this is an embedded warranty that the customer received automatically when the product was acquired, revenue is recognized by the company in Year Two.

Answer:

The correct answer is choice a: If this is an embedded warranty that the customer received automatically when the product was acquired, the $16 expense is reported in Year One.

Explanation:

For an embedded warranty that comes with the purchase of a product, the expense (and related liability) is recognized immediately and no revenue is recorded for the warranty. For an extended warranty acquired by the customer, revenue is recognized over the period of coverage (like an insurance policy), and the expense is recognized as incurred. If an extended warranty was sold for $20, the expense and virtually all the revenue are reported in Year Two.

4.3   Computing the Age of Accounts Payable

Question: Previously, the current ratio (current assets divided by current liabilities) and the amount of **working capital** *(current assets minus current liabilities) were discussed. Do investors and creditors analyze any other vital signs when analyzing the current liabilities reported by a business or other organization? Should decision makers be aware of any specific ratios or amounts in connection with current liabilities that provide especially insightful information about a company's financial health and operations?*

working capital

Formula measuring an organization's liquidity (the ability to pay debts as they come due); calculated by subtracting current liabilities from current assets.

Answer: In studying current liabilities, the number of days a business takes to pay its accounts payable is usually a figure of interest. If a business begins to struggle, the time of payment tends to lengthen because of the difficulty in generating sufficient cash amounts. Therefore, an unexpected jump in this number is often one of the first signs of financial distress and warrants concern.

To determine the **age of accounts payable** (or the number of days in accounts payable), the amount of inventory purchased during the year is first calculated:

age of accounts payable

A determination of the number of days that a company takes to pay for the inventory that it buys; computed by dividing accounts payable by the average inventory purchases made per day during the period.

$$\text{cost of goods sold} = \text{beginning inventory} + \text{purchases} - \text{ending inventory}.$$

Thus,

$$\text{purchases} = \text{cost of goods sold} - \text{beginning inventory} + \text{ending inventory}.$$

Using this computed purchases figure, the number of days that a company takes to pay its accounts payable on the average can be determined. Either the average accounts payable for the year can be used or just the ending balance.

$$\text{purchases}/365 = \text{average purchases per day}$$

$$\text{accounts payable}/\text{average purchases per day} = \text{average age of accounts payable}$$

As an illustration, the information presented in Figure 13.18 comes from the 2010 financial statements for **Safeway Inc.**

FIGURE 13.18 Information from 2010 Financial Statements for Safeway Inc.

Beginning Inventory	$2.509 billion
Ending Inventory	$2.623 billion
Cost of Goods Sold	$29.443 billion
Ending Accounts Payable	$2.533 billion

The total amount of inventory purchased by Safeway during 2010 was over $29 billion:

$$\text{purchases} = \text{cost of goods sold} - \text{beginning inventory} + \text{ending inventory}$$

$$\text{purchases} = \$29.443 \text{ billion} - \$2.509 \text{ billion} + \$2.623 \text{ billion}$$

$$\text{purchases} = \$29.557 \text{ billion}.$$

The average purchases amount made each day during 2010 by **Safeway** was nearly $81 million:

$$\text{purchases}/365$$

$$\$29.557/365 = \$80.978 \text{ million}.$$

The average age of the reported accounts payable for **Safeway** at the end of 2010 was between thirty-one and thirty-two days:

$$\text{accounts payable}/\text{average daily purchases}$$

$$\$2.533 \text{ billion}/\$80.978 \text{ million} = 31.28 \text{ days}.$$

To evaluate that number, a decision maker needs to compare it to (a) previous time periods for that company, (b) the typical payment terms for a business in that particular industry, and (c) comparable figures from other similar corporations. Interestingly, the same computation for 2008 showed that **Safeway** was taking 28.48 days to pay its accounts payable during that earlier period.

KEY TAKEAWAY

Many companies incur contingent liabilities as a result of product warranties. If the warranty is given to a customer along with a purchased item, an anticipated expense should be recognized at that time along with the related liability. If the reported cost of this type of embedded warranty eventually proves to be wrong, a correction is made when discovered assuming that the original estimate was made in good faith. Companies also sell extended warranties, primarily as a means of increasing profits. These warranties are recorded initially as liabilities (unearned revenue) with that amount reclassified to revenue over the time of the obligation. Subsequent costs are expensed as incurred to be in alignment with the matching principle. Thus, for extended warranties, expenses are not estimated and recorded in advance. Analysts often calculate the average age of accounts payable to determine how quickly liabilities are being paid as a vital sign used to indicate an entity's financial health.

Talking with a Real Investing Pro (Continued)

Following is a continuation of our interview with Kevin G. Burns.

Question: Analysts often look closely at current liabilities when evaluating the future prospects of a company. Is there anything in particular that you look for when examining a company and the reported balances for its current liabilities?

Kevin Burns: For almost any company, there are a number of things that I look at in connection with current liabilities. I always have several questions where possible answers can concern me. I am interested in the terms of the current liabilities as well as the age of those liabilities. In other words, is the company current with its payments to vendors? Does the company have a significant amount of current liabilities but only a small amount of current assets? Or, stated more directly, can these liabilities be paid on time? Have current liabilities been growing while business has remained flat or grown much more slowly? Are any of the current liabilities to organizations controlled by corporate insiders? That always makes me suspicious so that, at the very least, I want more information. In sum, I like balance sheets where there are no potential conflicts of interest and the company is a reasonably fast payer of its debts.

 Video Clip

Professor Joe Hoyle talks about the five most important points in Chapter 13.

View the video online at: http://bit.ly/hoyle13-2

5. END-OF-CHAPTER EXERCISES

QUESTIONS

1. The Saint Louis Corporation is trying to determine whether a liability needs to be recognized in connection with an event that recently took place. What characteristics must be present before a liability has to be reported?

2. The Topeka Company has a liability for $1.3 million. Company officials are trying to decide whether the debt should be shown as a current or noncurrent liability. How is that decision made?

3. Why are most decision makers particularly concerned about the amount of current liabilities reported by a company?

4. The Ames Company reports $300,000 in current assets and $100,000 in current liabilities. At the very end of the year, the company pays a $20,000 account payable. What was the current ratio before the payment? What was the current ratio after the payment?

5. What are several examples of accrued liabilities? Why do they often require adjusting entries prior to the production of financial statements?

6. How do companies account for gift cards that they sold?

7. How do companies account for gift cards that are redeemed?

8. How do companies account for gift cards that are unlikely to be redeemed?

9. In financial reporting, what is a commitment, and how is it shown within a set of financial statements? Why is that reporting considered appropriate?

10. The Atkinson Company has a contingent loss at December 31, Year One. It will not be completely settled for at least two years. Under what condition, should the company report a liability at the present time?

11. Give three examples of possible contingencies that a company might have to report in its financial statements.

12. The Salem Corporation has been sued for $2 million. Company lawyers believe that the chances of a loss are only reasonably possible. If a loss is incurred, the expected amount is $775,000. What does Salem report in connection with this contingency?

13. The Oregon Company has been sued for $3 million. Company lawyers believe that a loss of $500,000 might result, but the chances of such a loss are really remote. How does Oregon report this contingent loss?

14. The Randolph Corporation is being sued for $2 million. How does the reporting under U.S. GAAP differ from the reporting required under IFRS?

15. The Remshaw Corporation has filed suit against a competitor for patent infringement. Company lawyers are confident of a positive outcome. They believe that an award of $1.2 million is probable. How does Remshaw report this contingent gain?

16. A landscaping company sells live plants (such as azaleas) and promises to replace any plants that die within one year of purchase. At the end of the current fiscal year, how does the company determine the amount that must be reported as its liability?

17. A company sells computers and promises to fix any problems that the customer encounters within two years of a purchase. When does the company recognize expense from this warranty program?

18. A company sells computers and also sells an extended warranty that obligates the company to fix any problems that are encountered within two years from the purchase date. When does the company recognize expense from this warranty program?

19. How is the age of accounts payable calculated?

TRUE OR FALSE

1. ____ A company has a liability, and company officials are not sure if it should be reported as a current liability or as a noncurrent liability. They are likely to prefer to report the balance as a current liability.

2. ____ A current ratio of less than 1.0 to 1.0 means that a company has more current assets than current liabilities.

3. ____ A company signs a contract on December 29, Year One, to buy 1,000 barrels of crude oil on January 24, Year Two, at $82 per barrel. The likelihood of this contingency is probable and, therefore, should be reported as a liability at the end of Year One.

4. ____ Contingent liabilities should be reported on the balance sheet if they are both probable and can be reasonably estimated.

5. ____ Because of conservatism, a contingent liability should be disclosed in a company's financial statements even if the chance of loss is only remote.

6. ____ Contingent gains should only be recorded if they are probable.

7. ____ Liabilities for gift cards must remain on the balance sheet until they are redeemed, regardless of how long that takes.

8. ____ If a gift card is redeemed, a liability is reduced for reporting purposes.

9. ____ Restatement of previously issued financial statements will occur if a company attempts to mislead investors by understating liabilities.

10. ____ A company has a contingent loss of $1 million. If a liability is reported using IFRS, the same monetary liability will also have to be reported according to U.S. GAAP.

11. ____ A company has both embedded product warranties and extended product warranties. These warranties will be reported in the same way by this company.

12. ____ A company gives customers an embedded warranty with each purchase. During the past several years, 4 percent of these products have been returned under the warranty program. Thus, the company should anticipate that 4 percent of the items sold this year will have to be fixed.

13. ____ Company A takes twenty-two days to pay its accounts payable. Company Z takes thirty-one days to pay its accounts payable. Company A is a more financially healthy company than Company Z.

MULTIPLE CHOICE

1. Which of the following is **not** a criterion that must be met for an item to be classified as a liability?

    a. A certain cash payment will occur in the future.

    b. A sacrifice will require the entity's assets or services.

    c. There is a probable future sacrifice.

    d. There is a present obligation that results from a past transaction.

2. Watkins Inc. has the following assets at the end of Year One:

Cash	$400
Inventory	$730
Prepaid Rent	$460
Equipment (net book value)	$4,000

    Watkins also has the following liabilities at the end of Year One:

Accounts Payable	$560
Rent Payable	$200
Note Payable, due on June 1, Year Four	$3,500

    At the end of Year One, what is Watkins's current ratio?

    a. 1.14 to 1.0

    b. 1.31 to 1.0

    c. 1.49 to 1.0

    d. 2.09 to 1.0

3. Which of the following is the least likely to be an accrued liability?

    a. Accounts payable

    b. Interest payable

    c. Rent payable

    d. Salary payable

4. The Taylor Company sells music systems. Each music system costs the company $100 and will be sold to the public for $250. In Year One, the company sells 100 gift cards to customers for $250 each ($25,000 in total). These cards are valid for just one year, and company officials expect them to all be redeemed. In Year Two, only 96 of the cards are returned. What amount of net income does the company report for Year Two in connection with these cards?

    a. $15,000

    b. $15,400

    c. $15,500

    d. $15,800

5. Osgood sells music systems. Each system costs the company $100 and is sold for $250. During Year One, the company sells 1,000 of these systems ($250,000 in total). Each system comes with a free one-year warranty. The company expects 5 percent of the music systems to break and cost $40 each to fix. None break in Year One, but unfortunately, the systems were not well-manufactured, and 300 break in Year Two and cost $70 each to fix. What is the impact of this embedded warranty on Osgood's reported net income for Year Two?

    a. Decrease of $15,000

    b. Decrease of $17,000

    c. Decrease of $19,000

    d. Decrease of $21,000

6. The James Corporation sells music systems. Each system costs the company $100 and is sold for $250. During Year One, the company sold 1,000 music systems ($250,000 in total). Every customer also paid $10 each ($10,000 in total) for a one-year warranty. The company expects 5 percent of the music systems to break and cost $40 each to fix. None break in Year One, but unfortunately, the systems were not well-manufactured, and 300 break in Year Two and cost $70 each to fix. What is the impact of this extended warranty on James's reported net income for Year Two?

    a. Decrease of $10,000

    b. Decrease of $11,000

   c. Decrease of $18,000

   d. Decrease of $21,000

7. In Year One, Company A was allegedly damaged by Company Z and has filed suit for $300,000. At the end of Year One, Company A thinks it is probable that it will win $130,000 but reasonably possible that it will win $200,000. On that same day, Company Z thinks it is probable that it will lose $80,000 but reasonably possible that it will lose $180,000. On June 14, Year Two, the suit is settled when Company Z pays $97,000 in cash to Company A. Which of the following is true about the financial reporting for Year Two?

   a. Company A increases net income by $97,000; Company Z decreases net income by $17,000.

   b. Company A increases net income by $97,000; Company Z increases net income by $83,000.

   c. Company A decreases net income by $33,000; Company Z decreases net income by $17,000.

   d. Company A decreases net income by $33,000; Company Z increases net income by $83,000.

8. Stimpson Corporation buys cameras for $500 apiece and then sells each one for $1,200. During Year One, 9,000 units were sold. Each sale includes a one-year warranty. Stimpson estimates that 6 percent of the cameras will break (all during Year Two) and have to be fixed at an estimated cost of $190 each. In Year Two, no additional cameras are sold, but 590 cameras actually break but only cost $180 each to fix. What expense should Stimpson recognize for Year Two?

   a. $3,600

   b. $5,900

   c. $9,000

   d. $9,500

9. The Greene Company sells appliances along with an embedded warranty. In Year One, the company recognizes a warranty expense of $54,000. In Year Two, the company has an actual expense that is different than $54,000. Under what condition will the company restate the number reported for Year One?

   a. Under no condition.

   b. If the original estimate was discovered to be too low.

   c. If the original estimate was not made by company officials in good faith.

   d. If the original estimate was discovered to be too high.

10. The Knafo Company sells toaster ovens for $50 apiece. The company also planned to sell a one-year warranty with each purchase for $3. Company officials believe that 10 percent of all toaster ovens will break during Year Two and cost $7 each to fix. The company expects 40 percent of its customers to buy this extended warranty. At the last moment, company officials decide to give all customers a free one-year warranty to create customer loyalty. During Year One, the company sells 1,000 units. In Year Two, 11 percent of all toasters broke. Each repair cost $7. Because of the decision to give the warranty to all customers for free, the company will report a lower net income in Year One. How much lower will the net income figure be for Year One because of this decision?

   a. $298

   b. $400

   c. $700

   d. $1,200

11. Use the information in problem 10 again. Because of the decision to give the warranty to all customers for free, the company will report a lower liability at the end of Year One. How much lower will the liability be at the end of Year One because of this decision?

   a. $500

   b. $700

   c. $900

   d. $1,200

12. Use the information in problem 10 again. Because of the decision to give the warranty to all customers for free, the company will report a lower net income in Year Two. How much lower will the net income figure be in Year Two because of this decision?

   a. $320

   b. $468

   c. $648

   d. $962

13. On January 1, Year One, Purple Company sues Yellow Company for $6 million. At the end of Year One, both companies think that the probable outcome of this lawsuit is a settlement for $170,000. They also believe that a settlement of $290,000 is reasonably possible while a settlement of $540,000 is possible but remote. In Year Two, the lawsuit is settled with Purple winning exactly $120,000. Which of the following is correct about the reporting for Year Two?

    a. Purple recognizes a loss of $50,000; Yellow recognizes a gain (a recovery) of $50,000.

    b. Purple recognizes a gain of $120,000; Yellow recognizes a gain (a recovery) of $50,000.

    c. Purple recognizes a gain of $120,000; Yellow recognizes a loss of $120,000.

    d. Purple recognizes a loss of $50,000; Yellow recognizes a loss of $120,000.

14. Langston Corporation is being sued by a competitor for $1 million. At the end of the year, company officials believe that there is a 51 percent chance of a loss of $420,000 from this lawsuit. Which of the following statements is true?

    a. Under both U.S. GAAP and IFRS, a liability of $420,000 is recognized.

    b. Under U.S.GAAP (but not under IFRS), a liability of $420,000 is recognized.

    c. Under IFRS (but not under U.S. GAAP), a liability of $420,000 is recognized.

    d. Under both U.S. GAAP and IFRS, no liability is recognized at this time.

15. Maxout Company sells computers. Customers have the option to buy an extended warranty that covers their computer for two years. To get the extended warranty, the customer must pay $200. Maxout expects every computer will have to be fixed during the warranty period at a cost of $100. What journal entry will Maxout make at the time the computer is purchased, assuming the customer buys the extended warranty?

    a. **FIGURE 13.19**

Warranty Expense	100	
Warranty Liability		100

    b. **FIGURE 13.20**

Cash	200	
Unearned Revenue		200

c. **FIGURE 13.21**

d. **FIGURE 13.22**

16. Sierra Inc. manufactures environmentally friendly appliances. It provides a four-year warranty as a standard part of each purchase. In Year One, Sierra sold 450,000 toasters. Past experience has shown that 4 percent of the toasters usually require repair at an average cost of $10 each. During Year One, Sierra actually spends $38,000 on repairs and during Year Two, Sierra spends another $65,000. What is the balance in the warranty liability account at the end of Year Two?

    a. $67,000

    b. $77,000

    c. $84,000

    d. $94,000

17. The following figures appear on LaGrange's financial statements for the most recent fiscal year:

Cost of goods sold	$1,960,000
Beginning inventory	238,000
Ending inventory	278,000
Accounts payable	182,000

What is the age of this company's accounts payable?

    a. 33.2 days

    b. 33.9 days

    c. 34.7 days

    d. 35.3 days

VIDEO PROBLEMS

Professor Joe Hoyle discusses the answers to these two problems at the links that are indicated. After formulating your answers, watch each video to see how Professor Hoyle answers these questions.

1. Your roommate is an English major. The roommate's parents own a chain of ice cream shops located throughout Florida. One day, while returning a book at the library, your roommate poses this question: "My parents came up with this great idea. They started selling gift cards this year right before Christmas. A lot of our older customers bought bunches of these cards to give to their children and grandchildren as presents. This was one of my parent's best ideas ever; the money really poured into each of the shops. However, when I asked my parents about their net income for the year, they said that these sales had not affected net income. That makes absolutely no sense. They sold thousands of gift cards for ice cream and got real money. How could their net income have not gone up through the roof?" How would you respond?

View the video online at: http://bit.ly/hoyle13-3

2. Your uncle and two friends started a small office supply store several years ago. The company has expanded and now has several large locations. Your uncle knows that you are taking a financial accounting class and asks you the following question: "We are about to start selling a new line of office equipment. We really want to get our customers to consider this merchandise. We have been thinking about giving a free two-year warranty with each purchase. That eliminates risk and makes people feel more comfortable about the purchase. However, one of the other owners wants to charge a small amount for this warranty just so that we can make a small profit. We still take away the risk, but we also increase our net income. The decision is important, so I want to understand: how will each of these two alternatives affect the way our company looks on its balance sheet and income statement?" How would you respond?

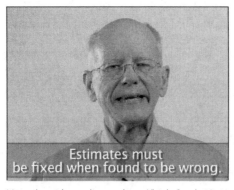

View the video online at: http://bit.ly/hoyle13-4

PROBLEMS

1. Knockoff Corporation sells a videogame unit known as the Gii. During the month of December, the following events occur. Prepare any necessary journal entries and adjusting entries that Knockoff should record.

    a. Knockoff purchased $300,000 of inventory on account.

    b. The company incurs salary expense of $45,000, although employees will not be paid until the beginning of January. The company also owes an additional $7,000 to the government for payroll taxes.

    c. Knockoff determines that it owes the IRS $120,000 in income taxes for this year.

    d. A retail customer places an advance order for Giis and pays Knockoff $23,000. The Giis will be shipped in January.

    e. Knockoff owes a local bank $4,000 in interest on a loan.

    f. Knockoff rents a warehouse of $3,000 per week. No payments were made for the last three weeks of the year.

2. OK Corporation sells gift cards in various denominations. The company likes to sell these cards because cash is collected immediately, but a certain percentage will never be redeemed for merchandise. On December 1, Year One, OK reported a balance in unearned revenue of $728,000 from the sale of gift cards.

    a. During December, OK sold an additional $578,000 in gift cards. Prepare this journal entry.

    b. During December, gift cards totaling $327,000 were redeemed to purchase inventory that had originally cost OK $190,000. Prepare these journal entries. Assume OK uses a perpetual inventory system.

    c. On December 31, OK's accountant determines that 3 percent of the outstanding gift cards will never be redeemed because they have expired. Prepare a journal entry if necessary.

    d. What is the amount reported by OK on its December 31, Year One, balance sheet for unearned revenues?

3. In Year One, the Yankee Corporation allegedly damaged the Sox Corporation. The Sox Corporation sued the Yankee Corporation for $1 million. At the end of Year One, both companies believed that an eventual payment of $300,000 by Yankee was probable, but a payment of $480,000 was reasonably possible. The case moved through the court system rather slowly, and at the end of Year Two, both companies had come to believe that an eventual payment of $340,000 by Yankee was now probable, but a payment of $700,000 was reasonably possible. In Year Three, this lawsuit is settled for $275,000 in cash.

    a. Determine the income effect to be reported by each company for each of these three years.

    b. Discuss how the financial reporting might be different if these companies were reporting according to IFRS instead of U.S. GAAP.

4. Whalens Corporation buys large screen televisions for $500 each and sells them for $1,200 each. During Year One, 8,000 sets were bought and sold for cash. Whalens estimates that 1 percent of all sets will break during Year Two. Company officials believe they will cost $150 to fix. Whalens offers a one-year warranty for $40. A total of only 700 customers choose to buy the warranty. In Year Two, nine of the televisions under warranty break but cost only $140 to repair.

    a. At the end of Year One, what revenue and expense should Whalens report in connection with this warranty?

    b. At the end of Year Two, what revenue and expense should Whalens report in connection with this warranty?

5. The Haynesworth Corporation is sued for $10 million in Year One. At the end of Year One, company officials believe a loss is only remote. However, the case drags on so that by the end of Year Two, company officials believe it is reasonably possible that a loss of $2 million could be incurred. The case goes to trial during Year Three, and company officials now believe that a loss of $3 million is probable. The case ends on April 23, Year Four, when the Haynesworth Corporation agrees to pay $2.6 million in cash to settle all claims.

    Indicate the amount of loss that will be reported by the Haynesworth Corporation in each of these four years.

6. On January 1, Year One, the Atlanta Company sues the Seattle Company for $100 million for patent infringement. The case is expected to take years to settle. For each of the following independent situations, indicate the financial reporting to be made by each company.

    a. Both companies believe that Atlanta will probably win this case. However, both feel that estimating the amount of this loss is virtually impossible.

    b. Both companies believe that Atlanta will probably win this case. Both feel that Atlanta will probably win approximately $9 million, but a win as high as $46 million is reasonably possible.

c. Both companies believe that a loss by Seattle of $53 million is reasonably possible.

d. Atlanta officials believe that their company will probably win $44 million whereas Seattle officials believe that their company will probably lose $8 million.

7. Ingalls Company is a jeweler located in a shopping mall in a midsize city in Ohio. During December of Year One, an unfortunate accident occurs. Mrs. Rita Yeargin trips over a giant, singing Rudolph set up by the mall management and goes sprawling into Ingalls's store where she cracked her head on a display case. She spent several days in the hospital with a sprained ankle, severely bruised elbow, and a concussion. Prior to the end of the year, Mrs. Yeargin's lawyer files papers to sue both the mall management company and Ingalls for $1,000,000. Ingalls's insurance company informs the jeweler that the store policy does not cover accidents involving giant, singing Rudolphs. Ingalls's attorney is unsure as to what a jury might do in this case because of the unusual nature of the event. He estimates that a loss of $800,000 is probable but that Ingalls will only be liable for 20 percent of that amount since the Rudolph actually belonged to the mall.

a. Determine if Ingalls needs to record a journal entry on December 31, Year One, and if so, prepare that entry.

b. Ingalls pays Mrs. Yeargin $97,000 on July 11, Year Two, to settle this claim. Make the journal entry for Ingalls at that time.

8. Sadler Corporation produces lawnmowers. The lawnmowers are sold with a free three-year warranty. During Year One, Sadler sold 20,000 lawnmowers for $10 million in cash. These lawnmowers cost $5,800,000. Sadler's accountant estimates that 10 percent of the units will need to be repaired at some point over the next three years at an average cost of $37 per lawnmower.

a. Make the journal entry to record the sale of the lawnmowers in Year One if a perpetual inventory system is used.

b. Make the journal entry (if any is needed) to record the warranty.

c. During Year Two, Sadler spends $24,000 to repair a number of these lawnmowers. Prepare the necessary journal entry.

d. At the end of Year Two, Sadler's accountant reevaluates the warranty. The accountant suspects that the actual warranty liability will be higher than her original estimate. She now believes that 12 percent of the original sales will eventually result in a repair (but still at $37 each). Make the necessary adjusting entry.

9. The Eyes Have It sells custom eyewear during Year One that come with an embedded warranty. If the glasses break during Year Two, they will be fixed for free. Customers may also purchase an extended warranty that covers Year Three. During Year One, the company sold 55,000 pairs of eyeglasses for $1,000,000. Customers who purchased 40,000 of those pairs also purchased the Year Three extended warranty. The extended warranty brought in additional cash of $200,000. The company expects that 6 percent of the glasses will break during Year Two, and another 8 percent will break during Year Three. Each repair will cost $20 to fix.

a. Record the embedded warranty in Year One.

b. Record the sale of the extended warranties in Year One.

c. Assume that during Year Two the company spends $70,000 to repair glasses for these customers. Prepare the necessary journal entry.

d. Assume that during Year Three the company spends another $102,000 to repair glasses that are covered under the extended warranty. Prepare the necessary journal entry.

10. During Year One, Company A and Company Z both sell 1,000 computers for $1,000 each in cash. Company A provides a one-year warranty to its customers for free. Company Z sells a one-year warranty to all of its customers for $50 each. Both companies expect 5 percent of the computers to break and cost $600 each to repair. In Year Two, both companies actually have 6 percent of these computers break. However, the required cost to fix each one was only $550.

a. In financial reporting for Year One, which company will report the highest amount of net income? What will be the difference in the two reported amounts?

b. In financial reporting for Year Two, which company will report the highest amount of net income? What will be the difference in the two reported amounts?

11. In several past chapters, we have met Heather Miller, who started her own business, Sew Cool. The following are the financial statements for December. To calculate age of accounts payable, assume that beginning inventory on 6/1/20X8, when Sew Cool started business, was zero. *Also, assume that Sew Cool was only in business for 210 days.*

FIGURE 13.23 Sew Cool Financial Statements

Sew Cool
Income Statement
As of December 31, 20X8

Revenue	$4,000
Cost of Goods	(2,000)
Gross Profit	2,000
Other Expenses	(1,695)
Earnings before Tax	305
Tax Expense	(107)
Net Income	$198

FIGURE 13.24

Sew Cool
Stmt. of Retained Earnings
As of December 31, 20X8

Retained Earnings, December 1, 20X8	$500
Net Income	198
Dividends	(158)
Retained Earnings, December 31, 20X8	$540

FIGURE 13.25

Sew Cool
Balance Sheet
December 31, 20X8

Assets		Liabilities	
Current		**Current**	
Cash	$940	Accounts Payable	$900
Accounts Receivable	500	Income Tax Payable	120
Less Allowance for		Total Current Liabilities	$1,020
Doubtful Accounts	(20)		
Net Accounts Receivable	480		
Inventory	700		
Total Current Assets	$2,120		
Noncurrent		**Noncurrent**	
Equipment	$1,000	Notes Payable	$1,060
		Owners' Equity	
		Capital Stock	$500
		Retained Earnings	540
		Total Owners' Equity	$1,040
		Total Liabilities & Owners'	
Total Assets	$3,120	Equity	$3,120

Based on the financial statements determine the following:

    a. Current ratio

    b. Age of accounts payable

This problem will carry through several chapters, building in difficulty. It allows students to continually practice skills and knowledge learned in previous chapters.

In Chapter 12, financial statements for December were prepared for Webworks. They are included here as a starting point for the required recording for January.

FIGURE 13.26 Webworks Financial Statements

Webworks Income Statement As of December 31	
Revenue	$16,950
Cost of Goods Sold	(8,657)
Gross Profit	8,293
Deprec. and Amort. Expense	(363)
Other Expenses and Losses	(3,790)
Investment Income	100
Earnings before Tax	4,240
Tax Expense	(1,272)
Net Income	$ 2,968

FIGURE 13.27

Webworks Stmt. of Retained Earnings As of December 31	
Retained Earnings, December 1	$9,322
Net Income	2,968
Retained Earnings, December 31	$12,290

FIGURE 13.28

Webworks
Balance Sheet
December 31

Assets			Liabilities		
Current			**Current**		
Cash	$ 3,215		Accounts Payable	$ 1,925	
Accounts Receivable	2,250		Salaries Payable	200	
Less Allowance for					
Doubtful Accounts	(225)				
Net Accounts Receivable	2,025				
Trading Securities, Net	360				
Merchandise Inventory	1,682				
Supplies Inventory	60				
Total Current Assets	$ 7,342		Total Current Liabilities	$ 2,125	
Property, Plant, and Equipment					
Equipment	$ 7,000				
Less Accumulated Depreciation	(876)				
Furniture	1,000				
Less Accumulated Depreciation	(51)				
Total P, P, and E	$ 7,073				
Other Noncurrent Assets					
Licensing Agreement, Net	$ 2,000				
			Owners' Equity		
			Capital Stock	$2,000	
			Retained Earnings	12,290	
			Total Owners' Equity	$14,290	
Total Assets	$16,415		Total Liabilities & Owners' Equity	$16,415	

The following events occur during January:

a. Webworks starts and completes seven more sites and bills clients for $4,500.

b. Webworks purchases supplies worth $100 on account.

c. At the beginning of January, Webworks had fourteen keyboards costing $113 each and twenty flash drives that had been written down to $5 each in December due to obsolescence. Webworks uses periodic FIFO to cost its inventory.

d. On account, Webworks purchases sixty-five keyboards for $117 each and ninety of the new flash drives for $20 each.

e. Webworks pays Nancy Po (company employee) $775 for her work during the first three weeks of January.

f. Webworks writes off an account receivable from October in the amount of $150 because collection appears unlikely.

g. Webworks receives $450 in advance to design a Web site for a local salon. Work will not begin on the Web site until February.

h. Webworks sells sixty keyboards for $9,000, all twenty of the old flash drives for $100 and eighty of the new flash drives for $2,400 cash.

i. During January, Webworks receives notice that one of its former clients is not happy with the work performed. When Webworks refuses to refund the client's money, the client decides to sue for what he paid plus damages for his "pain and suffering," which comes to $5,000. An attorney friend of Leon Jackson's (the owner of the business) mother believes that the suit is without merit and that Webworks probably will not have to pay anything.

j. Webworks collects $5,000 in accounts receivable.

k. During January, Webworks sells all of its stock in XYZ Company for $8 per share. Webworks had originally purchased sixty shares for $5 and they were selling for $6 per share on the last balance sheet date.

l. Webworks pays $200 for advertising that will run over the next two months.

m. Webworks pays off its salaries payable from December.

n. Webworks purchased 175 shares of QRS Company for $10 per share. Webworks considers this an available-for-sale security.

o. Webworks pays off $9,000 of its accounts payable.

p. Webworks pays Leon Jackson a salary of $2,000.

q. Webworks prepays $600 for rent for the months of January, February, and March.

r. QRS Company pays Webworks a dividend of $30.

s. Webworks pays taxes of $1,000 in cash.

> *Required:*
>
> A. Prepare journal entries for the previous events.
> B. Post the journal entries to T-accounts.
> C. Prepare an unadjusted trial balance for Webworks for January.
> D. Prepare adjusting entries for the following and post them to your T-accounts.

t. Webworks owes Nancy Po $200 for her work during the last week of January.

u. Leon's parents let him know that Webworks owes $320 toward the electricity bill. Webworks will pay them in February.

v. Webworks determines that it has $40 worth of supplies remaining at the end of January.

w. Prepaid rent should be adjusted for January's portion.

x. Prepaid advertising should be adjusted for January's portion.

y. Webworks is continuing to accrue bad debts at 10 percent of accounts receivable.

z. Webworks continues to depreciate its equipment over four years and its furniture over five years, using the straight-line method.

aa. The license agreement should be amortized over its one-year life.

ab. QRS Company is selling for $9 per share on January 31.

ac. Record cost of goods sold.

> E. Prepare an adjusted trial balance.
> F. Prepare financial statements for January.

RESEARCH ASSIGNMENT

Assume that you take a job as a summer employee for an investment advisory service. One of the partners for that firm is currently looking at the possibility of investing in **Barnes & Noble**. The partner is aware that **Barnes & Noble** sells a lot of gift cards. The partner is curious as to the size of the changes in that liability balance because the partner feels that increases and decreases will signal similar changes in revenue balances for the following year. The partner is also interested in knowing how much profit **Barnes & Noble** makes from breakage (gift cards that are never redeemed). The partner asks you to look at the 2011 financial statements for **Barnes & Noble** by following this path:

- Go to http://www.barnesandnoble.com.
- At the very bottom of this screen, click on "Investor Relations."
- On the next screen, scroll to the bottom and click on "Annual Reports."
- On the next screen, in the center, click on "2011 Annual Report" to download.
- Go to page 38 and read the paragraph under "Gift Cards."

a. What was the amount of gift card liability at the end of the previous year and at the end of the current year? What was the percentage change?

b. What was the amount of net income reported for the most recent year as a result of breakage (gift cards that were not redeemed)?

ENDNOTES

1. In upper-level accounting courses, the definition of a current liability is refined a bit. It refers to any liability that will require the use of a current asset or the creation of another current liability. However, the one-year standard presented in this textbook is sufficient in a vast majority of cases.

2. Todd Wallack, "Fame-courting biotech running short of cash," *The Boston Globe*, July 17, 2008, A-1.

In a Set of Financial Statements, What Information Is Conveyed about Noncurrent Liabilities Such as Bonds?

 Video Clip

In this video, Professor Joe Hoyle introduces the essential points covered in Chapter 14.

View the video online at: http://bit.ly/hoyle14-1

1. DEBT FINANCING

LEARNING OBJECTIVES

At the end of this section, students should be able to meet the following objectives:

1. List and explain the advantages of debt financing.
2. List and explain the disadvantages of debt financing.
3. Describe and illustrate the use of financial leverage.
4. Define notes and bonds as used in debt financing.

1.1 The Cost and Risk of Debt

Question: Businesses and other organizations need monetary funds to finance their operations and possible expansions. Such amounts can be quite significant. A portion of these resources normally come from investors who choose to become owners through the purchase of shares of capital stock directly from the company. Monetary amounts can also be generated internally by means of profitable operations. If net income each period exceeds the dividends that are paid to stockholders, a company has an ongoing source of financing.

*However, many companies obtain a large part of the funding needed to support themselves and their growth through borrowing. If those debts will not be paid within the following year, they are listed on the balance sheet as noncurrent liabilities. The **Xerox Corporation**, for example, listed noncurrent liabilities on its December 31, 2010, balance sheet of $11.7 billion.*

*Creditors expect their entire loan balance to be repaid plus **interest** at the specified due date. The money has to be available. Consequently, incurring debts of such large amounts exposes the organization to risks. **What problems and potential dangers does an entity face when liabilities—especially those of significant size—are owed?***

<aside>
interest

The charge for using money over time, often associated with long-term loans; even if not specifically mentioned in the debt agreement, financial accounting rules require it to be computed and reported based on a reasonable rate.
</aside>

Answer: Few things in life are free. The most obvious problem with financing an organization through debt is that it has a cost. A bank or other creditor will demand interest in exchange for the use of its money. For example, **Xerox Corporation** reported interest expense for the year ending December 31, 2010, of approximately $592 million. The rate of interest charged on debt will vary based on economic conditions and the perceived financial health of the debtor. As should be expected, strong companies are able to borrow money at a lower rate than weaker ones.

In addition, debt brings risk. A business must be able to generate enough surplus cash to satisfy creditors as liabilities come due. **Xerox** owes noncurrent liabilities of $11.7 billion. Eventually, company officials will have to find sufficient money to satisfy these obligations. Those funds might well be generated by profitable operations or contributed by investors. Or **Xerox** may simply borrow more money to pay off debts as they mature. This type of rollover financing is common but only as long as the debtor remains economically strong. Whatever the approach, the company has to manage its financial resources in such a way that all debts are settled in a timely manner.

<aside>
bankruptcy

A formal court process that often results in the liquidation of a debtor's assets when it cannot pay liabilities as they come due; in some cases, bankrupt companies are allowed to reorganize their finances and continue operations so that liquidation is not necessary.
</aside>

The most serious risk associated with debt financing is the possibility of bankruptcy. As has become unfortunately commonplace during the recent economic crisis, organizations that are unable to pay their liabilities can be forced into legal bankruptcy.[1] The end result of **bankruptcy** is frequently the liquidation of company assets with the distribution of those proceeds to creditors. However, under U.S. law, financial reorganization and continued existence is also a possibility. When **Circuit City** entered bankruptcy, company officials tried to reorganize to save the company. Eventually, **Circuit City** sold its assets and went out of business. In contrast, **Delta Air Lines** was able to leave bankruptcy protection in 2007 as a business that had been completely reorganized in hopes of remaining a viable entity.[2]

Given the cost and risk associated with owing large amounts of debt, the desire of decision makers to receive adequate and clear information is understandable. Few areas of financial accounting have been more discussed over the decades than the reporting of noncurrent liabilities.

1.2   The Benefits of Debt Financing

*Question: Debt is a costly and possibly risky method of financing a company's operations and growth. Some advantages must exist or no company would ever incur any noncurrent liabilities. **What are the advantages to an organization of using debt to generate funding for operations and other vital activities?***

Answer: One advantage of borrowing money is that interest expense is tax deductible. A company will essentially recoup a significant portion of all interest costs from the government. As mentioned above, **Xerox** incurred interest expense of $592 million. This interest reduced the company's taxable income by that amount. If the assumption is made that **Xerox** has an effective income tax rate of 35 percent, the total amount paid to the government is lowered by $207.2 million (35 percent times $592 million). **Xerox** pays interest of $592 million, which reduces its income taxes by $207.2 million so that the net cost of borrowing for the period was $384.8 million.

Another advantage associated with debt financing is that it can be eliminated. Liabilities are not permanent. If the economic situation changes, a company can rid itself of all debt by making payments as each balance comes due. In contrast, if money is raised by issuing capital stock, the new shareholders can maintain their ownership indefinitely.

However, the biggest advantage commonly linked to debt is the benefit provided by **financial leverage**. This term refers to an organization's ability to increase its reported net income by earning more money on borrowed funds than the associated cost of interest. For example, if a company borrows $1 million on a debt that charges interest of 5 percent per year, annual interest is $50,000. If the $1 million that is received can be used to generate profit of $80,000 (added revenue minus added operating expenses), net income has gone up $30,000 ($80,000 - $50,000) using funds provided solely by creditors. The owners did not have to contribute any additional funds to increase profits by $30,000.

Over the decades, many companies have adopted a strategy of being highly leveraged, meaning that most of their funds come from debt financing. If profitable, the owners can earn huge profits with little or no investment of their own. Unfortunately, companies that take this approach face a much greater risk of falling into bankruptcy because of the large amounts of interest that have to be paid at regular intervals.

> **financial leverage**
>
> A company's ability to earn more on borrowed money than the associated interest cost so that net income increases; often viewed as a wise business strategy although risks (such as possible bankruptcy) are elevated.

TEST YOURSELF

Question:

James Thorpe invests $100,000 to start a new business. He immediately borrows another $400,000 at a 6 percent annual interest rate. The business earns a profit on its assets of 10 percent per year. At the end of one year, Thorpe liquidates all assets at book value and closes the business. What rate of return did he earn on this investment during this year of operations? Ignore income taxes.

a. 10 percent

b. 14 percent

c. 15 percent

d. 26 percent

Answer:

The correct answer is choice d: 26 percent.

Explanation:

The business is heavily debt financed; 80 percent of assets came from debt. Assets of $500,000 earn a profit of 10 percent, or $50,000. Interest cost is only $24,000 ($400,000 × 6 percent). The profit is $26,000 ($50,000 less $24,000). A profit of $26,000 is earned from the owner's investment of $100,000, a return of 26 percent in one year. A profit of 10 percent was made from borrowed funds that cost 6 percent to obtain. The residual profit goes to the owners. This is financial leverage.

1.3 Raising Funds by Issuing Notes and Bonds

Question: Long-term financing typically comes from the issuance of notes or bonds. **What are notes and bonds and how do they differ from each other?**

Answer: Both notes and bonds are written contracts (often referred to as indentures) that specify the payment of designated amounts of cash by the debtor on stated dates. The two terms have become somewhat interchangeable over the years and clear distinctions are not likely to be found in practice.

- In this textbook, for convenience, the term "note" is used when a contract is negotiated directly between two parties. For example, assume officials from Jones Company go to City Street Bank and borrow $1.2 million to construct a new warehouse. The contract between these parties to establish the specific requirements of this loan agreement will be referred to as a note.

- The term "bond" will be used to describe a contract or group of contracts created by a debtor and then issued for money, often to members of the general public. Jones Company could opt to raise the $1.2 million needed for its new warehouse by printing 1,200 $1,000 bonds that it then sells to a wide array of creditors around the world. Such bonds are prepared in a wide variety of denominations.

Typically, the issuance of debt to multiple parties enables a company to raise extremely large amounts of money. A news story from the end of 2010 confirms the magnitude of these transactions: "Corporate bond sales worldwide topped $3 trillion for a second straight year."[3] If securities are being issued to the public in this way, the legal rules and regulations of the U.S. Securities and Exchange Commission must be followed, which adds another layer of cost to the raising of funds.

Most companies have a periodic need to raise money for operations and capital improvements. Debt financing is common for this purpose, although it leads to an interest charge and increased risk, even the possibility of bankruptcy. The cost of debt is offset somewhat because interest expense is tax deductible. Incurring liabilities also allows a business to use financial leverage to boost reported profits but only if the proceeds received generate more income than the cost of the related interest. Notes and bonds are debt contracts that spell out the specific legal rights and responsibilities of both parties. In this textbook, notes will indicate that loans have been negotiated between two parties whereas bonds will refer to debt instruments that are issued, often to the public.

2.　ISSUANCE OF NOTES AND BONDS

LEARNING OBJECTIVES

At the end of this section, students should be able to meet the following objectives:

1. **Identify common terms found in a note or bond contract such as face value, stated cash interest rate, and various types of security agreements or covenants.**
2. **Record notes and bonds that are issued at face value where periodic interest payments are made on dates other than the year-end.**
3. **Explain the handling of notes and bonds that are sold between interest dates and make the journal entries for both the issuance and the first interest payment.**

2.1　Debt Contracts

Question: Notes and bonds are contracts that facilitate the borrowing of money. They are produced with great care by attorneys who are knowledgeable in contract law. **What legal terms are typically included in a debt instrument?**

Answer: The specific terms written into a loan indenture vary considerably depending on what a debtor is willing to promise in hopes of enticing a creditor to turn over needed financial resources. Some of the most common are as follows.

Face value *(or maturity value).* The note or bond will specify the amount to be repaid at the end of the contract term. A $1,000 bond, for example, has a face value of $1,000—the payment to be made on a designated maturity date. The face value can be set at any figure of the debtor's choosing.

face value

Monetary amount of a note or bond to be repaid at the end of the contract; it serves as the basis for computing interest payments and is also known as the maturity value.

note

A written contract to convey money as a loan at a specified interest rate and repayment schedule between two parties.

bond

A written contract created by a debtor that is issued (to specific parties or to the members of the general public) to raise money; the contract specifies the amount and time of repayment as well as other terms and covenants promised by the debtor.

Payment pattern. With some debts, no part of the face value is scheduled for repayment until the conclusion of the contract period. These loans are often referred to as **term notes or term bonds**. The entire amount of the face value is paid when the contract reaches the end of its term (sometimes referred to as a balloon payment). For many debtors, accumulating this amount of cash at one time might pose a significant financial burden.

Other loans, known as **serial debts**, require many individual payments of the face value to be made periodically over time. Home mortgages, for example, are commonly structured as serial notes. Part of each scheduled payment reduces the face value of the obligation so that no large amount remains to be paid on the maturity date.

Notes and bonds can also be set up to allow the debtor the choice of repaying part or all of the face value prior to the due date. Such debts are referred to as "callable." This feature is popular because it permits refinancing if interest rates fall. If a new loan can be obtained at a cheaper interest rate, the money is used to pay off any callable debt that charges a higher interest rate. Sometimes a penalty payment is required if a note or bond is paid prematurely.

Interest rate. Creditors require the promise of interest before they are willing to risk loaning money to a debtor. Therefore, within the debt contract, a stated cash interest rate[4] is normally included. A loan that is identified as having a $100,000 face value with a stated annual interest rate of 5 percent informs both parties that $5,000 in interest ($100,000 × 5 percent) will be conveyed from debtor to creditor each year.

For example, the 2010 financial statements for the **Intel Corporation** indicated that the company had issued over $1 billion in bonds during 2009 that paid a **stated annual interest rate** of 3.25 percent with a maturity date in 2039.

Interest payment dates. The stated amount of interest is paid at the times identified in the contract. Payments can range from monthly to quarterly to semiannually to annually to the final day of the debt term.

Security. Many companies are not able to borrow money (or cannot borrow money without paying a steep rate of interest) unless some additional security is provided for the creditor. Any reduction of risk makes a note or bond instrument more appealing to potential lenders.

For example, some loans (often dealing with the purchase of real estate) are mortgage agreements that provide the creditor with an interest in identified property. Although specific rights can vary based on state law and the wording of the contract, this type of security usually allows the creditor to repossess the property or force its liquidation if the debtor fails to make payments in a timely manner. The recent downturn in the housing market has seen many debtor defaults that have led to bank foreclosures on homes across the country because of such mortgage agreements.

A **debenture** is a debt contract that does not contain any security. The debtor is viewed as so financially strong that money can be obtained at a reasonable interest rate without having to add extra security agreements to the contract.

Covenants *and other terms.* Notes and bonds can contain an almost infinite list of other agreements. In legal terms, a covenant is a promise to do a certain action or a promise not to do a certain action. Most loan covenants are promises made by the debtor to help ensure that adequate money will be available to make required payments when they come due. For example, the debtor might agree to limit the size of any dividend payments, keep its current ratio above a minimum standard, or not exceed a maximum amount of debt.

Debts can also be convertible so that the creditor can swap them for something else of value (often the capital stock of the debtor) if that seems a prudent move. The notes to the financial statements for the **Ford Motor Company** as of December 31, 2010, and the year then ended describe one such noncurrent liability. "At December 31, 2010, we had outstanding $883 million principal of 4.25% Senior Convertible Notes due December 15, 2016 ('2016 Convertible Notes'). The 2016 Convertible Notes pay interest semiannually at a rate of 4.25% per annum. The 2016 Convertible Notes are convertible into shares of **Ford** Common Stock, based on a conversion rate (subject to adjustment) of 107.5269 shares per $1,000 principal amount."

2.2   Recording a Note Issued at Face Value

*Question: The financial reporting of a debt contract appears to be fairly straightforward. Assume, for example, that Brisbane Company borrows $400,000 in cash from a local bank on May 1, Year One. The face value of this loan is to be repaid in exactly five years. In the interim, interest payments at an annual rate of 6 percent will be made every six months beginning on November 1, Year One. **What journal entries are appropriate to record a debt issued for a cash amount equal to the face value of the contract?***

---

term notes or term bonds

A type of debt instrument where interest is paid at regular time intervals with the entire face value due at the end of the contract period.

serial debts

A type of debt instrument where a set repayment is to be made each period to cover both interest and a portion of the face value; home mortgages and automobile loans are common examples.

stated interest rate

Percentage rate established in a debt contract to be paid by the debtor in addition to the face value usually at specified time intervals; it is also called the cash rate, contract rate or coupon rate.

debenture

A debt contract that does not contain any type of security for the creditor; these contracts are usually offered by debtors that are considered financially strong so that no additional security is required by creditors to reduce their chance of loss.

covenants

Promises made by the issuer of a debt contract to help ensure that sufficient money will be available to make required payments at their scheduled times.

Answer: Brisbane receives $400,000 in cash but also accepts a noncurrent liability for the same amount. The resulting journal entry is shown in Figure 14.1.

FIGURE 14.1 May 1, Year One—Cash of $400,000 Borrowed on Long-term Note Payable

| Cash | 400,000 | |
| Note Payable | | 400,000 |

The first semiannual interest payment will be made on November 1, Year One. Because the 6 percent interest rate stated in the contract is for a full year, it must be adjusted to calculate the payment that covers each six-month interval. These payments will be for $12,000 ($400,000 face value × 6 percent annual stated interest rate × 6/12 year). The recording of the first payment is presented in Figure 14.2.

FIGURE 14.2 November 1, Year One—Payment of Interest for Six Months

| Interest Expense | 12,000 | |
| Cash | | 12,000 |

By December 31, Year One, when financial statements are to be prepared, interest for two additional months (November and December) has accrued. This amount ($4,000 or $400,000 × 6 percent × 2/12 year) is recognized at that time so (a) the amount due on the balance sheet date will be presented fairly and (b) the cost of the debt for these two months is included on the Year One income statement. No transaction occurs on that date but the adjusting entry in Figure 14.3 brings all reported figures up to date.

FIGURE 14.3 December 31, Year One—Accrual of Interest for Two Months

| Interest Expense | 4,000 | |
| Interest Payable | | 4,000 |

When the next $12,000 interest payment is made by Brisbane on May 1, Year Two, the recorded $4,000 liability is extinguished and interest for four additional months (January through April) is recognized. The appropriate expense for this period is $8,000 ($400,000 × 6 percent × 4/12 year). Mechanically, this payment could be recorded in more than one way but the journal entry shown in Figure 14.4 is probably the easiest to follow. Interest expense for the first two months was recorded in Year One with interest for the next four months recorded here in Year Two.

FIGURE 14.4 May 1, Year Two—Payment of Interest for Six Months

Interest Expense	8,000	
Interest Payable	4,000	
Cash		12,000

Interest payments and the recording process will continue in this same way until all five years have passed and the face value is paid.

Except for the initial entry, these events are recorded in an identical fashion if Brisbane had signed this same note to acquire an asset—such as a piece of machinery—directly from the seller. The only reporting difference is that the asset replaces cash in Figure 14.1 above.

TEST YOURSELF

Question:

On January 1, Year One, the Leaver Company signs a nine-year note payable with a face value of $800,000 and a stated annual cash interest rate of 7 percent. Interest will be paid annually beginning on January 1, Year Two. Which of the following statements is true?

a. Interest expense of $56,000 is recognized on January 1, Year Two.

b. Interest payable of $56,000 is reduced on January 1, Year Two.

c. No interest expense is reported for Year One because no interest was paid in that year.

d. No interest liability is recorded at the end of Year One because payment is not due until Year Two.

Answer:

The correct answer is choice b: Interest payable of $56,000 is reduced on January 1, Year Two.

Explanation:

Interest was incurred throughout Year One on the borrowed funds and is recognized through a year-end adjusting entry. Both the interest expense and the interest payable for the period are reported in that way. On the following day, when payment is made, the liability is removed and cash is reduced. No additional interest expense is recognized on January 1, Year Two, because no time has yet passed since the interest was recognized at the end of Year One.

2.3 Issuance of Bonds between Interest Dates

Question: Bonds can be issued to a group of known investors or to the public in general. Often, companies will print bond indentures but not offer them to buyers until monetary levels run low. Thus, bonds are frequently issued on a day that falls between two interest dates. Payment must still be made to creditors as specified by the contract regardless of the length of time that the debt has been outstanding. If an interest payment is required, the debtor is legally obligated.

To illustrate, assume that the Brisbane Company plans to issue bonds with a face value of $400,000 to a consortium of twenty wealthy individuals. As in the previous example, these bonds pay a 6 percent annual interest rate with payments every May 1 and November 1. However, this transaction is not finalized until October 1, Year One, when Brisbane has need for the cash.

*The first six-month interest payment must still be made on November 1 as stated in the contract. After just one month, the debtor is forced to pay interest for six months. That is not fair, and Brisbane would be foolish to agree to this arrangement. **How does a company that issues a bond between interest payment dates ensure that the transaction is fair to both parties?***

Answer: As indicated in this question, the issuance of a bond between interest dates is common. Thus, a standard system of aligning the first interest payment with the time that the debt has been outstanding is necessary. Because of the terms of the contract, Brisbane must pay interest for six months on November 1 even though the cash proceeds have been held for only one month. In this first payment, the creditor receives interest for an extra five months.

Consequently, such bonds are normally issued for a stated amount plus accrued interest. The accrued interest is measured from the previous interest payment date to the present and is charged to the buyer. Later, when the first payment is made, the net effect reflects just the time that the bond has been outstanding. If issued on October 1, Year One, the creditors should pay for the bonds plus five months of accrued interest. Later, when Brisbane makes the first required interest payment on November 1 for six months, the net effect is interest for one month—the period that has passed since the date of issuance (six months minus five months).

Assume that the creditors buy these bonds on October 1, Year One, for face value plus accrued interest. Because five months have passed since the previous interest date (May 1), interest on the bonds as of the issuance date is $10,000 ($400,000 × 6 percent × 5/12 year). Thus, the creditors pay $400,000 for the bond and an additional $10,000 for the interest that has accrued to that date. Once again, the actual recording can be made in more than one way but the entry presented in Figure 14.5 seems easiest.

FIGURE 14.5 Issuance of Bond on October 1 at Face Value plus Accrued Interest Recognized for Five Months

Cash	410,000	
Bonds Payable		400,000
Interest Payable		10,000

One month later, Brisbane makes the first interest payment of $12,000. However, interest expense of only $2,000 is actually recognized in the entry in Figure 14.6. That amount is the appropriate interest for the month of October ($400,000 × 6 percent × 1/12 year). This expense reflects the cost associated with the period that the bond has been outstanding. Interest of $10,000 for five months was collected initially by Brisbane. Interest of $12,000 was later paid by Brisbane for the entire six month period. Interest expense of $2,000 is the net result for that one month.

FIGURE 14.6 November 1, Year One—Payment of First Interest Payment

Interest Payable	10,000	
Interest Expense	2,000	
Cash		12,000

After this entry, the recording of interest follows the process demonstrated previously in Figure 14.3 and Figure 14.4.

TEST YOURSELF

Question:

On January 1, Year One, the Halenstein Corporation creates bond indentures with a total face value of $1.5 million that pay annual interest of 10 percent every December 31. The company had expected to sell the bonds on that date. However, the company's monetary needs changed and the bonds were not issued until August 1. On that date they were sold for face value plus accrued interest. Thereafter, the bonds were serviced normally until their maturity on December 31, Year Four. Which of the following statements is true in connection with the Year One transactions?

  a. Halenstein receives $1,587,500 (August 1) and pays $150,000 (December 31).
  b. Halenstein receives $1,562,500 (August 1) and pays $150,000 (December 31).
  c. Halenstein receives $1,650,000 (August 1) and pays $62,500 (December 31).
  d. Halenstein receives $1,650,000 (August 1) and pays $87,500 (December 31).

Answer:

The correct answer is choice a: Halenstein receives $1,587,500 (August 1) and pays $150,000 (December 31).

Explanation:

Seven months pass before the bond is issued (January 1 to August 1). The interest that has accrued on this bond by that date is $87,500 ($1.5 million × 10 percent interest × 7/12 year). Thus, the buyers pay $1.5 million for the bond and $87,500 to cover the accrued interest. On the last day of the year, the contract calls for the payment of interest for a full year or $150,000 ($1.5 million face value × 10 percent stated interest rate).

3.   ACCOUNTING FOR ZERO-COUPON BONDS

LEARNING OBJECTIVES

At the end of this section, students should be able to meet the following objectives:

1. **Identify the characteristics of a zero-coupon bond.**
2. **Explain how interest is earned by a creditor on a zero-coupon bond.**
3. **Understand the method of arriving at an effective interest rate for a bond.**
4. **Calculate the price of a zero-coupon bond and list the variables that affect this computation.**
5. **Prepare journal entries for a zero-coupon bond using the effective rate method.**
6. **Explain the term "compounding."**
7. **Describe the theoretical problems associated with the straight-line method, and identify the situation in which this method can be applied.**

3.1   The Issuance of a Zero-Coupon Bond

Question: A wide array of bonds and other types of financial instruments can be issued by parties (businesses and other organizations) seeking money. A zero-coupon bond is one that is popular because of its ease. The face value of a zero-coupon bond is paid to the creditor after a specified period of time, but no further cash is ever exchanged. Thus, no stated cash interest rate is paid. Money is received when the bond is issued and money is paid at the end of the term but no other payments are made. **Why does any investor choose to purchase a zero-coupon bond if no interest is paid?**

Answer: No investor would buy a note or bond that did not pay interest. That makes no economic sense. Because zero-coupon bonds are widely issued, some form of interest must be included.

These bonds are sold at a discount below face value with that reduction serving as interest. If a bond is issued for $37,000 and the company eventually repays its face value of $40,000, the $3,000 difference is the interest on the debt. That additional payment is the charge paid for the use of the money that was borrowed. The price reduction below face value can be so significant that zero-coupon bonds are sometimes referred to as deep discount bonds.

To illustrate, assume that on January 1, Year One, a company offers a $20,000 two-year **zero-coupon bond** to the public. A single payment of $20,000 will be made to the holder of this bond on December 31, Year Two. According to the contract, no other cash will be paid. An investor who wishes to earn 7 percent annual interest can mathematically compute the exact amount to bid for this contract. The debtor must then decide whether to accept this offer.

zero-coupon bond

A debt instrument that includes no interest payments; these bonds are issued at a discount with the difference between the cash received at the beginning and the cash paid on the maturity date serving as interest for that period of time.

effective rate

The interest rate determined by negotiation and market forces that is used to set the price of a bond; it is also called the yield rate and often varies from the interest rate stated on the indenture that is used to establish cash interest payments.

Often, the actual exchange price for a bond is the result of a serious negotiation process to establish the interest rate to be earned. The potential creditor might initially offer an amount that equates to interest at an annual rate of 7 percent. The debtor could then counter by suggesting that an annual rate of 5 percent is more reasonable. After some discussion, the two parties might compromise by settling on a price that provides an annual interest rate of 6 percent. In the bond market, interest rates are the subject of intense negotiations. After the **effective rate** (also called the yield or negotiated rate) has been agreed on by both parties, the actual price of the bond is simply a mathematical computation.

3.2 Agreeing on a Price for a Bond

Question: A $20,000 zero-coupon bond is being issued by a company. According to the indenture, it comes due in exactly two years. The parties have negotiated an annual interest rate to be earned of 6 percent. **How is the actual price to be paid for a bond mathematically determined after an effective rate of interest has been established?**

Answer: Calculation of the price of a bond is based on the present value of the cash payments in the same manner as demonstrated previously in the coverage of intangible assets. Future cash payments are first identified and then valued by the mathematical removal of interest (the present value computation).

Here, a single cash payment of $20,000 is to be made by the debtor in two years. The parties have negotiated an annual 6 percent effective interest rate. Thus, a portion of the future cash ($20,000) serves as interest at an annual rate of 6 percent for this two-year period of time. In a present value computation, interest at the designated rate is calculated and subtracted to leave the principal amount of those payments. That is the price of the bond. Interest at a 6 percent annual rate for two years is removed. The remainder is the amount paid for the bond.

Present Value of $1

http://www.principlesofaccounting.com/ART/fv.pv.tables/pvof1.htm

The present value of $1 in two years at an annual rate of interest of 6 percent is $0.8900. This can be found in a chart (through the link presented or in the tables at the end of this book), by formula, or by use of an Excel spreadsheet.[5] Because the actual payment is $20,000 and not $1, the present value of the cash flows from this bond (its price) can be found as follows:

$$\text{present value} = \text{future cash payment} \times \$0.8900$$

$$\text{present value} = \$20,000 \times \$0.8900$$

$$\text{present value} = \$17,800$$

Bond prices are often stated as a percentage of face value. Thus, this bond is sold to the investor at "89" ($17,800/$20,000), which indicates that the price is 89 percent of the $20,000 face value. The price is the future cash payments with the negotiated rate of interest removed. If the investor pays $17,800 today and the debtor returns $20,000 in two years, the additional $2,200 is the interest. Mathematically, this extra $2,200 is equal to interest at 6 percent per year.

The issuance is recorded through the entry presented in Figure 14.7.[6]

FIGURE 14.7 January 1, Year One—Zero-Coupon Bond Issued at Effective Annual Interest Rate of 6 Percent

Cash	17,800	
Bond Payable		17,800

TEST YOURSELF

Question:

On January 1, Year One, the Leisinger Company offers a ten-year zero-coupon bond with a face value of $80,000 to an investor. Leisinger hopes to issue this bond at an annual interest rate of 4 percent. The investor wants 7 percent and they finally agree on 5 percent. The present value of $1 at 4 percent annual interest for 10 years is $0.6756 and at 5 percent for ten years is $0.6139. The present value of an ordinary annuity of $1 for ten years at 4 percent annual interest is $8.1109 and at 5 percent is $7.7217. What amount does Leisinger Company receive (rounded)?

a. $49,112

b. $54,048

c. $61,774

d. $64,887

Answer:

The correct answer is choice a: $49,112.

Explanation:

The negotiated effective (or yield) interest rate is 5 percent per year. A single payment will be made in ten years. Using the rate for $1 (a single amount) in ten years at 5 percent interest per year, the present value is the cash of $80,000 times $0.6139 or $49,112. The present value factors have been mathematically determined to compute the appropriate interest which is then removed to leave the principal. At an annual rate of 5 percent, $49,112 will grow to be exactly $80,000 in ten years.

3.3 Recognizing Interest on a Zero-Coupon Bond

Question: The $20,000 zero-coupon bond discussed above is issued for $17,800 so that a 6 percent annual interest rate will be earned. As shown in Figure 14.7, the bond is initially recorded at this principal amount.

Subsequently, two problems must be addressed by the accountant.

- *First, the company actually has to pay $20,000. Over time, the $17,800 principal balance must be raised to that face value. At the end of Year Two, the liability should be reported as $20,000.*

- *Second, the $2,200 difference between the amount received and the eventual repayment ($20,000 less $17,800) has to be recognized as interest expense over these two years. The additional payment is the cost of the debt for this period, the interest.*

To arrive at fairly presented figures, both of these problems must be resolved. **How is a zero-coupon bond reported in the period after its issuance?**

Answer: In the earlier discussion of present value and the purchase of assets (such as a patent), the effective rate method was demonstrated. It solves the two accounting problems mentioned here. The reported debt balance is raised gradually to the face value and interest expense equal to 6 percent is reported each year until maturity.

Interest recognized for Year One should be the $17,800 principal balance multiplied by the effective interest rate of 6 percent or $1,068. However, no cash interest payment is made for this zero-coupon bond. Thus, as is shown in Figure 14.8, this interest is compounded—added to the principal of the debt. Interest that is recognized but not paid at that time is compounded, included in the balance of the liability.

FIGURE 14.8 December 31, Year One—Interest on Zero-Coupon Bond at 6 Percent Rate Is Recognized and Compounded[7]

| Interest Expense | 1,068 | |
| Bond Payable | | 1,068 |

The compounding of this interest raises the principal by $1,068 from $17,800 to $18,868. The balances to be reported in the financial statements at the end of Year One are as follows:

| Year One—Interest Expense (Income Statement) | $1,068 |
| December 31, Year One—Bond Payable (Balance Sheet) | $18,868 |

The principal is higher in Year Two because of the compounding (addition) of the first year interest. As the principal increases, interest for subsequent periods must also go up. As reflected in Figure 14.9, interest for Year Two is 6 percent of the new liability balance of $18,868 or $1,132 (rounded).

FIGURE 14.9 December 31, Year Two—Interest on Zero-Coupon Bond at 6 Percent Rate Is Recognized and Compounded

Note that the bond payable balance has now been raised to $20,000 as of the date of payment ($17,800 + $1,068 + $1,132). In addition, interest expense of $2,200 ($1,068 + $1,132) has been recognized over the two years. Reported interest was exactly 6 percent of the principal in each year. Total interest reported for this zero-coupon bond is equal to the difference between the amount received by the debtor and the face value eventually repaid. Both of the accounting problems have been resolved through the application of the effective rate method.

The $17,800 price of the bond was computed mathematically based on the following:

- The cash payment ($20,000)
- The time periods (two)
- The effective rate of interest (the 6 percent negotiated rate)
- The pattern of cash flows (a single payment in the future)

Interest is then recognized each period based on this same set of variables. Thus, the resulting numbers will reconcile. Interest expense reported for the two years is $2,200 and the final liability balance comes back to $20,000.

TEST YOURSELF

Question:

The O'Neil Company issues a six-year $40,000 zero-coupon bond on January 1, Year One. At that time, most companies are able to borrow money at an annual rate of 10 percent. O'Neil is in such good financial health that the bond is sold for $25,207 to yield a negotiated rate of 8 percent per year. What is reported in O'Neil's financial statements at the end of Year One if the effective rate method is applied? (All numbers are rounded.)

a. Interest expense of $2,017 and a bond payable of $27,224.

b. Interest expense of $2,112 and a bond payable of $27,319.

c. Interest expense of $2,215 and a bond payable of $27,422.

d. Interest expense of $2,521 and a bond payable of $27,728.

Answer:

The correct answer is choice a: Interest expense of $2,017 and a bond payable of $27,224.

Explanation:

Interest to be reported for the first year is the 8 percent negotiated rate times the principal of $25,207 or $2,017 (rounded). This is a zero-coupon bond so no interest is paid as time passes. Because no cash interest is actually paid, this entire amount of interest for the first year is compounded to raise the principal by $2,017 from $25,207 to $27,224. In this manner, the principal balance should reach $40,000 after six years.

TEST YOURSELF

Question:

Johnson Company issues an eight-year $50,000 zero-coupon bond on January 1, Year One. After serious negotiations between the company and the investor, this bond is sold for $31,371 to yield an effective annual rate of 6 percent. What is reported in Johnson's financial statements at the end of Year Two if the effective rate method is applied? (All numbers are rounded.)

  a. Interest expense of $1,882 and a bond payable of $33,253.
  b. Interest expense of $1,882 and a bond payable of $35,135.
  c. Interest expense of $1,995 and a bond payable of $35,248.
  d. Interest expense of $2,015 and a bond payable of $35,285.

Answer:

The correct answer is choice c: Interest expense of $1,995 and a bond payable of $35,248.

Explanation:

Interest for the first year is the $31,371 principal times the effective annual rate of 6 percent or $1,882. As a zero-coupon bond, no interest is paid. The entire $1,882 is compounded by adding it to the principal so that the balance is $33,253. For Year Two, interest expense is now recognized as $1,995 or 6 percent times the updated principal of $33,253. Again, the interest is compounded so the liability is reported at $35,248. In this manner, the balance will be $50,000 after 8 years.

3.4 Recognizing Interest Using the Straight-Line Method

Question: The previous zero-coupon bond was sold at the present value of its future cash flows based on a rate of interest negotiated by the parties involved. Interest was then recognized each year by applying the effective rate method. Is the effective rate method the only acceptable technique that can be used to compute and report interest when the face value of a debt differs from its issue price?

Answer: When a zero-coupon bond is issued at a discount, interest to be reported each year can also be calculated by a simpler approach known as the straight-line method. According to this technique, an equal amount of the discount is assigned to interest each period over the life of the bond. This zero-coupon bond was issued for $2,200 below face value to provide interest to the buyer. Payment of the face value will be made in two years. As is shown in Figure 14.10, the straight-line method recognizes interest of $1,100 annually ($2,200/2 years).

FIGURE 14.10 December 31, Years One and Two—Interest on Zero-Coupon Bond at 6 Percent Rate—Straight-Line Method

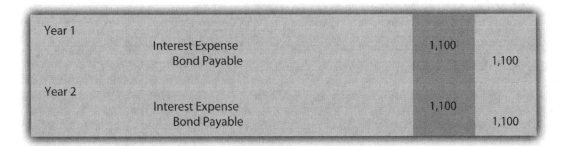

Year 1		
Interest Expense	1,100	
Bond Payable		1,100
Year 2		
Interest Expense	1,100	
Bond Payable		1,100

Once again, the bond payable balance has been raised to $20,000 by the end of the second year ($17,800 + $1,100 + $1,100) and total interest expense over the life of the bond equals the $2,200 discount ($1,100 + $1,100). However, a theoretical question should be raised as to whether the information reported under this method is a fairly presented portrait of the events that took place. Although the bond was sold to earn 6 percent annual interest, this rate is not reported for either period.

  Year One: $1,100 interest/$17,800 principal = 6.2 percent
  Compounding of the interest raises the principal by $1,100 to $18,900
  Year Two: $1,100 interest/$18,900 principal = 5.8 percent
  The debtor and creditor agreed on an annual rate of exactly 6 percent for the entire two-year period. When applying the straight-line method, this rate is not reported for either year. Furthermore, the interest rate appears to float (6.2 percent to 5.8 percent) as if a different rate was negotiated for each

year. That change does not reflect reality. A single 6 percent annual interest rate was established by these two parties.

Although the straight-line method creates some theoretical concerns, it can still be applied according to U.S. GAAP but only if the reported results are not materially different from those derived using the effective rate method.

TEST YOURSELF

Question:

The Reynolda Company issues an eight-year $80,000 zero-coupon bond on January 1, Year One. After serious negotiations, this bond is sold for $54,144 to yield an effective annual rate of 5 percent. What is reported in Reynolda's financial statements at the end of Year Two if the straight-line method is applied to this discount? (All numbers are rounded.)

  a. Interest expense of $3,198 and a bond payable of $60,540.

  b. Interest expense of $3,232 and a bond payable of $60,608.

  c. Interest expense of $3,268 and a bond payable of $60,680.

  d. Interest expense of $3,304 and a bond payable of $60,752.

Answer:

The correct answer is choice b: Interest expense of $3,232 and a bond payable of $60,608.

Explanation:

This bond was sold at a discount of $25,856 ($80,000 less $54,144) to provide interest over the eight-year life of this bond. If the straight-line method is used, this discount is allocated equally to interest each period. That annual amount is $3,232 ($25,856/8 years). No cash interest is being paid during the life of this bond. Thus, the recognized interest each period is compounded to arrive at a principal balance of $60,608 after two years ($54,144 plus $3,232 plus $3,232).

KEY TAKEAWAY

Zero-coupon bonds pay no explicitly-stated cash interest. Instead, they are issued at a discount with the difference between the price and face value serving as interest. The price of the bond is determined by computing the present value of the required cash flows based on the effective interest rate negotiated by the two parties. The present value figure represents the principal of the debt with all future interest mathematically removed. The bond is issued for this amount. Interest is subsequently determined each period using the effective (or yield) rate. Because no interest is paid, the entire amount recognized must be compounded (added) to the principal. The straight-line method can also be used to record interest if the resulting numbers are not materially different from the effective rate method. This alternative assigns an equal amount of the discount to interest each period over the bond's life.

4. PRICING AND REPORTING TERM BONDS

LEARNING OBJECTIVES

At the end of this section, students should be able to meet the following objectives:

1. Understand the difference between a stated cash interest rate in a debt contract and an effective interest rate negotiated by the debtor and creditor.
2. Compute the price of a term bond when the stated cash interest rate is different from the effective interest rate.
3. Determine the amount of interest to be compounded each period when the stated cash interest rate specified on a bond contract is different from the effective interest rate established by the parties.
4. Prepare all journal entries for a term bond when the stated cash interest rate is different from the effective interest rate.

4.1 Determining the Price of a Term Bond

Question: Although zero-coupon bonds are popular, most bonds actually do pay a stated rate of cash interest, one that is specified in the contract. If the buyer and seller negotiate an effective rate of interest that is the same as this stated rate, an amount equal to face value is paid for the bond. For example, if the stated interest is 7 percent per year and a negotiated annual rate of 7 percent is accepted by the parties, the bond is issued at its face value. No discount or premium results; the debtor and creditor are both satisfied with the interest being paid. The effective rate method is not needed because the cash interest and the effective interest are the same—7 percent is paid each period and recognized as interest.

However, the negotiated rate often differs from the cash rate stated in the bond contract. Market interest rate conditions change quickly. The interest that creditors demand will often shift between the printing of the indenture and the actual issuance day. Or the financial reputation of the company might move up or down during this time. Information travels so quickly in this technology age that news about companies—both good and bad—spreads rapidly.

To illustrate, assume that Smith Corporation decides to issue $1 million in term bonds to the public on January 1, Year One. The face value of these bonds comes due in four years. During the interim, annual interest at a stated rate of 5 percent will be paid starting on December 31, Year One.

No investors can be found who want to purchase Smith Corporation bonds with only a 5 percent annual return. Therefore, in setting an issuance price, annual interest of 6 percent is negotiated. Possibly, interest offered by other similar companies is 6 percent so that Smith had to match this rate to entice investors to buy its bonds. Or some recent event has made Smith seem slightly more risky causing potential creditors to demand a higher rate of return. A list of market conditions that can impact the price of a bond would be almost unlimited. How is the price of a bond calculated when the stated cash interest rate differs from the effective rate negotiated by the two parties involved?

Answer: The pricing of a bond always begins by identifying the cash flows specified by the contract. These amounts are set and will not be affected by the eventual sales price. The debtor is legally obligated to make these payments regardless of whether the bond is sold for $1 or $10 million.

Here, Smith Corporation must pay $50,000 per year in interest ($1 million × 5 percent) for four years and then the $1 million face value:

Future Cash Flows Set by Bond Contract
$50,000 annually for four years (5 percent stated rate)
$1,000,000 in four years (face value of term bond)

After the cash flows are identified, the present value of each is calculated based on the negotiated yield rate. These two present values are then summed to arrive at the price to be paid for the bond. The $50,000 annual interest payments form an annuity—equal amounts are paid at equal time intervals. Because interest is paid at the end of each period starting on December 31, Year One, these payments constitute an ordinary annuity.[8]

As determined by table, formula, or Excel spreadsheet, the present value of an ordinary annuity of $1 at an effective annual interest rate of 6 percent over four years is $3.46511.[9] Thus, the present value of the four interest payments is $50,000 times $3.46511 or $173,256 (rounded). Note that the present value computation requires the multiplication of one annuity payment ($50,000) rather than the total amount of all interest payments ($200,000).

Present Value of an Ordinary Annuity of $1

http://www.principlesofaccounting.com/ART/fv.pv.tables/pvofordinaryannuity.htm

The second part of the cash flows promised by this bond is a single payment of $1 million in four years. The present value of a payment of $1 in four years at a 6 percent annual rate is $0.79209 so the present value of the entire $1 million is $792,090.

Present Value of $1

http://www.principlesofaccounting.com/ART/fv.pv.tables/pvof1.htm

Based on an annual interest rate of 6 percent for four years, the present value of the cash flows required by this term bond contract is $173,256 (cash interest) plus $792,090 (face value) or a total of $965,346. Smith receives this amount on January 1, Year One, but must pay back $50,000 per year for four years followed by a single payment of $1 million. Mathematically, that is equivalent to a 6 percent rate of interest each year for four years. The journal entry to record the issuance is shown in Figure 14.11.

FIGURE 14.11 January 1, Year One—Term Bonds Issued at an Effective Rate of 6 Percent

Cash	965,346	
Bonds Payable		965,346

TEST YOURSELF

Question:

The Venture Company issues a twenty-year bond with a face value of $500,000 on January 1, Year One. According to the bond contract, cash interest at a stated rate of 2 percent will be paid each year beginning on December 31, Year One. The Manhattan Investment Company wants to buy this bond but demands an effective annual interest rate of 9 percent. After some discussion, both parties agree that the bond will be sold to earn an annual interest rate of 8 percent. The present value of $1 in twenty years at a rate of 8 percent is $0.21455. The present value of an ordinary annuity of $1 per year for twenty years at a rate of 8 percent per year is $9.81815. The present value of an annuity due of $1 per year for twenty years at a rate of 8 percent per year is $10.60360. How much does Manhattan Investment Company pay the Venture Company for this bond (rounded)?

a. $205,457

b. $209,145

c. $213,311

d. $217,445

Answer:

The correct answer is choice a: $205,457.

Explanation:

Cash interest of $10,000 is paid annually for twenty years ($500,000 × 2 percent). This is an ordinary annuity, since payments are made at each year's end. A single payment of $500,000 is also due in twenty years. Present value of the interest is $10,000 times $9.81815, or $98,182. Present value of the face value is $500,000 times $0.21455, or $107,275. Total present value is $205,457. That amount is offered by the creditor and accepted by the debtor because it equals 8 percent per year.

4.2   Calculating Interest When a Term Bond Is Issued at a Discount

Question: After the previously described term bond was issued at a discount, the debtor has the same two accounting problems that were discussed previously for zero-coupon bonds.

- *First, the recorded principal must be raised gradually over four years from $965,346 (as shown in Figure 14.11) to the $1 million face value.*
- *Second, the cash interest of 5 percent paid each year has to be adjusted to the annual 6 percent effective rate negotiated by the two parties.*

How does a debtor report a bond payable over its life if the stated cash interest rate and the effective rate differ?

Answer: At the end of Year One, Smith Corporation pays $50,000 cash interest to the bondholders as specified in the contract ($1 million face value × 5 percent annual stated rate). However, interest expense must be reported on the income statement based on the agreed upon rate of 6 percent. That was the negotiated rate that led to the initial payment of $965,346. This discounted price was accepted by Smith (the debtor) as a means of increasing the actual rate of return from 5 percent per year to 6 percent.

The effective rate is reflected in the financial statements by recognizing interest in Year One of $57,921 (rounded), which is the $965,346 principal balance times 6 percent. The $7,921 difference between the effective interest expense of $57,921 and the cash interest payment of $50,000 will eventually be paid at the end of the four-year term when $1 million rather than $965,346 is conveyed to the bondholders. Therefore, at the current time, this extra $7,921 is compounded (increasing the liability balance). Note that only the portion of this interest that is not paid is added to the principal. Earlier, with the zero-coupon bond, the entire amount of interest each year was compounded, but that was because no cash interest payment was made.

The cash interest payment is recorded in Figure 14.12 with the compounding entry shown in Figure 14.13. These two entries can be recorded separately or combined.

FIGURE 14.12 December 31, Year One—Payment of Cash Interest at 5 Percent Rate

| Interest Expense | 50,000 | |
| Cash | | 50,000 |

FIGURE 14.13 December 31, Year One—Compounding Entry to Adjust Interest to Effective Annual Rate of 6 Percent

| Interest Expense | 7,921 | |
| Bond Payable | | 7,921 |

The interest expense reported on the income statement for Year One of $57,921 ($50,000 + $7,921) equals the 6 percent effective rate times the principal of the debt for that period. The liability on the balance sheet at the end of Year One has begun to move closer to the $1 million face value. The reported figure is now $973,267 ($965,346 + $7,921) as a result of the compounding.

As shown in Figure 14.14, reported figures for the remaining three years of this bond contract can be calculated to verify that the ending balance does grow to $1 million by the time of payment.

FIGURE 14.14 Reported Bond Figures for Remaining Three Years until Maturity[10]

	Year Two	Year Three	Year Four
Beginning Bond Principal	$973,267	$981,663	$990,563
Effective Rate	6%	6%	6%
Interest Expense (rounded)	58,396	58,900	59,437
Stated Cash Interest	50,000	50,000	50,000
Interest Compounded (added to principal)	8,396	8,900	9,437
Ending Bond Principal	981,663	990,563	1,000,000

Through the use of the effective rate method, interest expense of 6 percent is recognized each period and the principal balance reported for the liability does gradually grow to equal the face value of the bond on the maturity date.

TEST YOURSELF

Question:

On June 30, Year One, a company issues ten-year term bonds with a total face value of $600,000. Only interest at a 4 percent annual rate is paid each June 30 and December 31 beginning at the end of Year One. These bonds were issued for $375,680 to earn a negotiated rate of 10 percent per year over the ten-year term. What does the company report on its December 31, Year One, balance sheet for this liability?

a. $380,775
b. $381,225
c. $382,464
d. $383,646

Answer:

The correct answer is choice c: $382,464.

Explanation:

After six months, the company pays interest to the creditors of $12,000 ($600,000 × 4% × 1/2 year). Interest for the same period—based on an annual yield rate of 10 percent—is $18,784 ($375,680 × 10% × 1/2). The extra interest recognized over the amount paid ($6,784 or $18,784 less $12,000) is compounded to begin moving the principal to the $600,000 face value. At the end of Year One, the bond payable has been raised to $382,464, the original principal of $375,680 plus the compound interest of $6,784.

KEY TAKEAWAY

The stated cash interest rate for a term bond is often different from the effective interest rate negotiated between the creditor and the debtor. To compute the amount of money to be exchanged for the bond, the cash flows are determined based on the terms of the contract. The present value of these payments is then calculated. The resulting total is the amount initially paid so that the agreed upon rate of interest is earned over the life of the bond. Cash interest payments are conveyed thereafter with the interest balance adjusted each period based on the effective rate. The interest rate stated in the contract times the face value provides the amount of each cash payment. The principal of the debt times the effective rate gives the interest expense to be recognized for the period. The difference in the effective interest and the cash payment is compounded (added to the principal of the debt). On the maturity date, the liability balance should be equal to the face value of the debt instrument.

5.   ISSUING AND ACCOUNTING FOR SERIAL BONDS

LEARNING OBJECTIVES

At the end of this section, students should be able to meet the following objectives:

1. Define a serial bond.
2. Identify the steps to calculate the price of a serial bond and provide the proper accounting for the issuance.
3. Record the interest and payments on a serial bond over its life.
4. Explain the determination of interest expense for a serial bond and the amount that must be compounded each period.

5.1   Recording the Issuance of a Serial Bond

Question: The previous section examined the recording of term bonds. Interest was paid each period but no payment was made on the face value until the maturity date. How do these procedures differ for a serial bond where both interest and a portion of the face value are paid periodically?

To demonstrate this process, assume that Smith Corporation issues a four-year, $1 million serial bond on January 1, Year One. This bond will pay a 5 percent stated interest rate at the end of each year on the unpaid face value for the period. The indenture further specifies that $250,000 of the face value is to be paid annually at the same time as the interest. Smith officials negotiate with potential investors and finally agree on a 6 percent annual effective rate. **What accounting is appropriate for a serial bond?**

Answer: From the previous coverage, the reporting of a term bond where the stated cash interest and the effective rate are different can be divided into five steps:

1. The cash flows required by the bond contract are identified.
2. The total present value of these cash flows is determined using the effective rate of interest negotiated by the parties. Present value mathematically removes all future interest at the appropriate rate leaving only the principal of the debt. Thus, this resulting figure is the exact amount to be paid so that the agreed-upon interest rate is earned over the life of the bond.
3. The bond is recorded at the principal (present value) amount paid by the investors.
4. The debtor pays the stated rate of interest periodically on the dates indicated in the contract.
5. The effective rate method is applied. Interest to be reported for each period is determined by multiplying the liability's principal balance times the effective interest rate. The cash interest figure is adjusted to this calculated amount with the difference compounded (added to the principal).[11]

This same process is applied when a serial bond is issued. The sole difference is that regular payments are also made to reduce the face value of the debt over time. To account for the Smith Corporation serial bond described above, the following five steps are required.

Identify cash flows specified in the bond contract. As shown in Figure 14.15, Smith is required to make an annual $250,000 payment to reduce the face value of this serial bond. In addition, interest must be paid each year. During Year One, the unpaid face value is the original $1 million. The stated rate is 5 percent necessitating a $50,000 year-end interest payment ($1,000,000 × 5 percent).

Following the $250,000 payment on December 31, Year One, the face value of the bond drops to $750,000 throughout the second year. Consequently, the interest payment at the end of Year Two is only $37,500 ($750,000 × 5 percent). As a serial bond, the annual payments cause the face value to get smaller so that the interest payments are less each year.

Based on the terms of the contract, the cash flows required by this bond are identified in Figure 14.15.

FIGURE 14.15 Cash Payments Required by Serial Bond Contract

Year	Beginning Face Value	Cash Interest Rate	Cash Interest	Principal Payment	Ending Face Value
One	$1,000,000	5%	$50,000	$250,000	$750,000
Two	750,000	5%	37,500	250,000	500,000
Three	500,000	5%	25,000	250,000	250,000
Four	250,000	5%	12,500	250,000	-0-

Determine present value of the cash flows. These required cash flows can be organized in either of two ways.

- First, they can be viewed as an ordinary annuity of $250,000 per year for four years plus four separate single amounts of $50,000 (one year), $37,500 (two years), $25,000 (three years) and $12,500 (four years). The pattern is that of an ordinary annuity rather than an annuity due because the payments are at the end of each period. The present value computation for this version of the cash flows is shown in Figure 14.16.

- Second, the payments of the face value and interest can be combined into four separate single amounts of $300,000 (one year), $287,500 (two years), $275,000 (three years), and $262,500 (four years). The present value computation for this version of the cash flows is shown in Figure 14.17.

The same cash flows are described in both cases. Thus, as proven by a comparison of Figure 14.16 and Figure 14.17, the resulting present value will be identical ($977,714) regardless of the approach that is followed. A link to the tables for the present value of an ordinary annuity of $1 and the present value of $1 are provided here but those tables are also included at the end of this textbook.

Present Value of an Ordinary Annuity of $1

http://www.principlesofaccounting.com/ART/fv.pv.tables/pvofordinaryannuity.htm

Present Value of $1

http://www.principlesofaccounting.com/ART/fv.pv.tables/pvof1.htm

FIGURE 14.16 Computation of Present Value of Serial Bond—First Pattern of Cash Flows

---

Computation of Present Value of Serial Bond—First Pattern of Cash Flows

Present value of an ordinary annuity of $250,000 at a 6 percent annual interest rate for four years:
$250,000 (for four years) ×   3.46511 = $866,278 (rounded)

Present value of four different single amounts at a 6 percent annual interest rate in each of the next four years:

$50,000 (in one year)	× .94340 =	$47,170	
$37,500 (in two years)	× .89000 =	33,375	
$25,000 (in three years)	× .83962 =	20,990	(rounded)
$12,500 (in four years)	× .79209 =	9,901	(rounded)
Total present value of single payments		$111,436	

Total present value of these cash flows: $866,278 for the ordinary annuity plus $111,436 for the four single payments provides a total present value for all required cash flows of $977,714.

FIGURE 14.17 Computation of Present Value of Serial Bond—Second Pattern of Cash Flows

---

Computation of Present Value of Serial Bond—Second Pattern of Cash Flows

Present value of four different single amounts at a 6 percent annual interest rate in each of the next four years:

$300,000 (in one year)	× .94340 =	$283,020	
287,500 (in two years)	× .89000 =	255,875	
275,000 (in three years)	× .83962 =	230,895	(rounded)
262,500 (in four years)	× .79209 =	207,924	(rounded)
Total present value of cash flows		$977,714	

Record the principal amount received in the issuance of the bond. Based on either of these computations, $977,714 in cash is exchanged for this four-year $1 million serial bond with an annual stated rate of 5 percent. That payment amount creates an effective rate of interest of 6 percent per year. The issuance of the bond is recorded through the journal entry shown in Figure 14.18.

FIGURE 14.18 January 1, Year One—Issuance of $1 Million Serial Bonds Paying 5 Percent Annual Interest with an Effective Rate of 6 Percent

Cash	977,714	
Bonds Payable		977,714

Payment of stated cash interest at 5 percent annual rate. Because of the terms specified in the bond contract, interest of $50,000 will be paid at the end of Year One, $37,500 at the end of Year Two, and so on. The Year One interest payment is recorded in Figure 14.19. To better illustrate the handling of interest in a serial bond, the $250,000 payments on the face value are shown separately in Figure 14.21.

FIGURE 14.19 December 31, Year One—Payment of 5 Percent Interest on Serial Bond

Effective rate method is applied to recognize the interest rate that was negotiated by the two parties. For the first year, the principal balance of this debt is the original issuance price of $977,714. The yield rate agreed on by the two parties was 6 percent. Thus, the interest to be recognized for Year One is $58,663 ($977,714 × 6 percent).

As shown in Figure 14.19, the cash interest paid is only 5 percent of the face value or $50,000. The $8,663 in extra interest for the period ($58,663 less $50,000) is compounded—added to the principal of the bond payable. The interest to be compounded is added to the principal in Figure 14.20.

The journal entries shown in Figure 14.19 and Figure 14.20 are often combined in practice. They are separated here for discussion purposes.

FIGURE 14.20 December 31, Year One—Adjustment of Interest from Cash Rate to Effective Rate

In addition, as a serial bond, the first payment of the face value is made at the end of Year One and shown in Figure 14.21.

FIGURE 14.21 December 31, Year One—Payment on Face Value of Serial Bond

Whether a long-term liability is a term bond or a serial bond, the accounting process is the same. It follows the five steps that have been listed above and demonstrated here. All the amounts to be recorded over the four-year life of this bond can be computed to verify that the final payment does appropriately remove the remainder of the debt. Those figures are presented in Figure 14.22.

FIGURE 14.22 Balances to be Reported Over the Four-year Life of Serial Bond[12]

	Year One	Year Two	Year Three	Year Four
Beginning Principal Balance	$977,714	$736,377	$493,060	$247,644
Effective Annual Interest Rate	6%	6%	6%	6%
Interest to Be Recognized (principal times effective rate)	58,396	44,183	29,584	14,856
Cash Interest (face value times stated cash rate)	50,000	37,500	25,000	12,500
Compound Interest (difference)	8,663	6,683	4,584	2,356
Face Value Payment	250,000	250,000	250,000	250,000
Ending Principal Balance (beginning balance plus compound interest less face value payment)	736,377	493,060	247,644	-0-

Question:

The Heyman Company issues a $500,000 serial bond on January 1, Year One. At the end of each year, the bond pays $100,000 of the face value plus interest at a 4 percent rate on the unpaid balance for the period. The bond was sold at an effective yield rate of 5 percent per year. The present value of $1 at a 5 percent annual rate in one year is $0.95238, in two years is $0.90703, in three years is $0.86384, in four years is $0.82270, and in five years is $0.78353. The present value of an ordinary annuity at a 5 percent annual rate for five years is $4.32948. What amount did Heyman Company receive when the bond was issued (rounded)?

  a. $483,865
  b. $486,590
  c. $490,130
  d. $492,545

Answer:

The correct answer is choice b: $486,590.

Explanation:

As a serial bond, cash payments of $100,000 are made each year. In addition, interest payments for each year are as follows.

Year	Unpaid Face Value	Stated Cash Interest Rate	Interest Payments
One	$500,000	4%	$20,000
Two	$400,000	4%	$16,000
Three	$300,000	4%	$12,000
Four	$200,000	4%	$ 8,000
Five	$100,000	4%	$ 4,000

By combining the face value payments with the interest, the present value at an annual rate of 5 percent can be calculated.

Year (rounded)	Face Value plus Interest Payments	PV of $1	Present Value
One	$120,000	.95238	$114,286
Two	$116,000	.90703	$105,215
Three	$112,000	.86384	$ 96,750
Four	$108,000	.82270	$ 88,852
Five	$104,000	.78353	$ 81,487
Total			$486,590

TEST YOURSELF

Question:

The Mullins Company issues a $500,000 serial bond on January 1, Year One. At the end of each year, the bond pays $100,000 of the face value plus interest at a 3 percent rate on the unpaid balance for the period. The bond was sold for $473,200 to yield an effective rate of 5 percent per year. What will Mullins report for this bond on its December 31, Year Two, balance sheet?

a. $288,953

b. $292,875

c. $295,445

d. $297,905

Answer:

The correct answer is choice a: $288,953.

Explanation:

Effective interest for Year One is $473,200 × the yield rate of 5 percent or $23,660. Because only $15,000 ($500,000 times 3 percent) is paid, the extra $8,660 is compounded. The $473,200 goes up by this $8,660 but down by the $100,000 payment to $381,860. Interest for Year Two is $19,093 ($381,860 × 5 percent). Only $12,000 ($400,000 × 3 percent) is paid so the $7,093 difference is compounded. The $381,860 plus $7,093 but less the next $100,000 payment leaves a balance of $288,953.

KEY TAKEAWAY

The issuance price for bonds (whether serial bonds or term bonds) can be computed and the subsequent accounting outlined in five general steps: (1) determine the cash payments required by the bond contract, (2) calculate the present value of those cash flows based on the negotiated effective rate of interest, a computation that sets the price to be paid for the bond, (3) record the bond at this exchange price (the present value amount), (4) over time, record each periodic cash interest payment, and (5) adjust the stated cash interest amounts to the effective interest rate through a compounding entry. A serial bond extends this process slightly because a portion of the face value is also paid periodically. The debt principal goes up each year as a result of interest compounding. However, in recording a serial bond, the principal also goes down because of the periodic payments of the face value.

6. BONDS WITH OTHER THAN ANNUAL INTEREST PAYMENTS

LEARNING OBJECTIVES

At the end of this section, students should be able to meet the following objectives:

1. Realize that cash interest payments are often made more frequently than once a year, such as each quarter or semiannually.
2. Determine the stated interest rate, the effective interest rate, and the number of time periods to be used in a present value computation when interest payments cover a period of time of less than a year.
3. Compute the stated cash interest payments and the effective interest rate when interest is paid on a bond more frequently than once each year.
4. Prepare journal entries for a bond when the interest payments are made for a period of time shorter than a year.

Question: In the previous examples, both the interest rates and payments always covered a full year. How is this process affected if interest payments are made at other time intervals such as each quarter or semiannually?

As an illustration, assume that on January 1, Year One, an entity issues term bonds with a face value of $500,000 that will come due in six years. Cash interest payments at a 6 percent annual rate are required by the contract. However, the actual disbursements are made every six months on June 30 and

December 31. In setting a price for these bonds, the debtor and the creditor negotiate an effective interest rate of 8 percent per year. **How is the price of a bond determined and the debt reported if interest payments occur more often than once each year?**

Answer: None of the five basic steps for issuing and reporting a bond is affected by a change in the frequency of interest payments. However, both the stated cash rate and the effective rate must be set to agree with the time interval between payment dates. The number of time periods used in the present value computation also varies based on the time that passes from one payment to the next.

In this current example, interest is paid semiannually, so each time period is only six months in length. The stated cash interest rate to be paid during that period is 3 percent or 6/12 of the annual 6 percent rate listed in the bond contract. Similarly, the effective interest rate is 4 percent or 6/12 of the annual 8 percent negotiated rate. Both of these interest rates must align with the specific amount of time between payments. Over the six years until maturity, the bond is outstanding for twelve of these six-month periods of time.

Thus, for this bond, the cash flows will be the interest payments followed by settlement of the face value.

- *Interest Payments*: $500,000 face value times 3 percent stated rate for a $15,000 interest payment every six months during these twelve periods. Equal payments are made at equal time intervals making this an annuity. Because payments are made at the end of each period, these payments constitute an ordinary annuity.

- *Face value*: $500,000 is paid at the end of these same twelve periods. This cash payment is a single amount.

As indicated, the effective rate to be used in determining the present value of these cash payments is 4 percent per period or 6/12 times 8 percent.

Present Value of Annuity Due of $1

http://www.principlesofaccounting.com/ART/fv.pv.tables/pvof1.htm

Present Value of Ordinary Annuity of $1

http://www.principlesofaccounting.com/ART/fv.pv.tables/pvofordinaryannuity.htm

- The present value of $1 in twelve periods at an effective rate of 4 percent per period is $0.62460.
- The present value of an ordinary annuity of $1 for twelve periods at an effective rate of 4 percent per period is $9.38507.
- The present value of the face value cash payment is $500,000 times $0.62460 or $312,300.
- The present value of the cash interest payments every six months is $15,000 times $9.38507 or $140,776 (rounded).
- The total present value of the cash flows established by this contract is $312,300 plus $140,776 or $453,076. As shown in Figure 14.23, the bond is issued for this present value amount. With this payment, the agreed-upon effective rate of interest (8 percent for a full year or 4 percent for each six-month period) will be earned by the investor over the entire life of the bond.

FIGURE 14.23 January 1, Year One—Issuance of $500,000 Bond with a 3 Percent Stated Rate to Yield Effective Rate of 4 Percent Semiannually

Cash	453,076	
Bonds Payable		453,076

On June 30, Year One, the first $15,000 interest payment is made as reported in Figure 14.24. However, the effective interest rate for that period is the principal of $453,076 times the six-month negotiated rate of 4 percent or $18,123 (rounded). Therefore, the interest to be compounded for this first six-month period is $3,123 ($18,123 interest less $15,000 payment). That is the amount of interest recognized but not yet paid that is added to the liability as shown in Figure 14.25.

FIGURE 14.24 June 30, Year One—Cash Interest Paid on Bond for Six-Month Period

FIGURE 14.25 June 30, Year One—Interest on Bond Adjusted to Effective Rate

The compound interest recorded previously raises the bond's principal to $456,199 ($453,076 principal plus $3,123 in compound interest). The principal is gradually moving to the $500,000 face value. Another $15,000 in cash interest is paid on December 31, Year One (Figure 14.26). The effective interest for this second six-month period is $18,248 (rounded) or $456,199 times 4 percent interest. The compound interest recognized on December 31, Year One, is $3,248 ($18,248 less $15,000), a balance that is recognized by the entry presented in Figure 14.27.

FIGURE 14.26 December 31, Year One—Cash Interest Paid on Bond for Six-Month Period

FIGURE 14.27 December 31, Year One—Interest on Bond Adjusted to Effective Rate

The Year One income statement will report interest expense of $18,123 for the first six months and $18,248 for the second, giving a total for that year of $36,371. The second amount is larger than the first because of compounding.

The December 31, Year One, balance sheet reports the bond payable as a noncurrent liability of $459,447. That is the original principal (present value) of $453,076 plus compound interest of $3,123 (first six months) and $3,248 (second six months). Once again, interest each period has been adjusted from the cash rate stated in the bond contract to the effective rate negotiated by the two parties. Here, the annual rates had to be halved because payments were made semiannually.

TEST YOURSELF

Question:

Friday Corporation issues a two-year bond on January 1, Year One, with a $300,000 face value and a stated annual cash rate of 8 percent. The bond was sold to earn an effective annual rate of 12 percent. Interest payments are made quarterly beginning on April 1, Year One. The present value of $1 at a 3 percent rate in eight periods is $0.78941. The present value of $1 at a 12 percent rate in two periods is $0.79719. The present value of an ordinary annuity of $1 at a 3 percent rate for eight periods is $7.01969. The present value of an ordinary annuity of $1 at a 12 percent rate for two periods is $1.69005. What amount will Friday receive for this bond?

a. $276,055

b. $278,941

c. $284,785

d. $285,179

Answer:

The correct answer is choice b: $278,941.

Explanation:

This bond pays interest of $6,000 every three months ($300,000 × 8 percent × 3/12) and $300,000 in two years. Based on quarterly payments, effective interest is 3 percent (12 percent × 3/12 year) and cash flows are for eight periods (every three months for two years). Present value of the interest is $6,000 × $7.01969, or $42,118. Present value of the face value is $300,000 × $0.78941, or $236,823. Total present value (price of the bond) is $42,118 + $236,823, or $278,941.

KEY TAKEAWAY

Bonds often pay interest more frequently than once a year—for example, at an interval such as every three months or six months. If the stated cash rate and the effective rate differ, determination of present value is still required to arrive at the principal amount to be paid when the bond is issued. However, the present value computation must be adjusted to reflect the change in the length of a time period. The amount of time between payments is considered one period. The stated cash interest rate, the effective rate negotiated by the parties, and the number of time periods until maturity are all set for that particular time. The actual accounting and reporting are not affected, merely the method by which the interest rates and the number of periods are calculated.

Talking With a Real Investing Pro (Continued)

Following is a continuation of our interview with Kevin G. Burns.

Question: Assume that you are investigating two similar companies. You are thinking about recommending one of them to your clients as an investment possibility. The financial statements look much the same except that one of these companies has an especially low amount of noncurrent liabilities whereas the other has a noncurrent liability total that seems quite high. How does that difference impact your thinking? Long-term liabilities are a great way to gain financing because a company can make use of someone else's money. However, debt does increase risk.

Kevin Burns: I have managed to do well now for many years by being a conservative investor. My preference is always for the company that is debt free or as close to debt free as possible. I do not like financial leverage, never have. I even paid off my own home mortgage more than ten years ago.

On the other hand, long-term liabilities have to be analyzed as they are so very common. Is any of the debt convertible into capital stock so that it could potentially dilute everyone's ownership in the company? Is the company forced to pay a high rate of interest? Why was the debt issued? In other words, how did the company use all that cash that it received? As with virtually every area of financial reporting, you have to look behind the numbers to see what is actually happening. That is why transparency is important. If the debt was issued at a low interest rate in order to make a smart acquisition, I am impressed. If the debt has a high rate of interest and the money was not well used, that is not attractive to me at all.

Video Clip

Professor Joe Hoyle talks about the five most important points in Chapter 14.

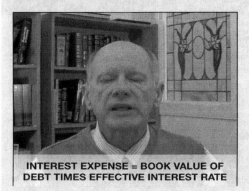

INTEREST EXPENSE = BOOK VALUE OF
DEBT TIMES EFFECTIVE INTEREST RATE

View the video online at: http://bit.ly/hoyle14-2

7.   END-OF-CHAPTER EXERCISES

QUESTIONS

1. The Lohr Company needs $40 million in cash to expand several of its facilities. Company officials chose to issue bonds to raise this money rather than capital stock. What are some of the possible reasons for this decision?

2. Officials for the Bohannon Corporation have always avoided incurring noncurrent liabilities as a company policy. Over the years, they have raised long-term financing through operations or from the issuance of capital stock. Why might these officials have preferred that money be raised by means other than noncurrent liabilities?

3. The president of the Nelson Company is a fan of financial leverage. He wants to expand operations into California and Oregon and borrows $70 million on 8 percent term bonds to finance this decision. How does he hope to make financial leveraging work for the Nelson Company in this expansion?

4. What is a term bond?

5. What is a serial bond?

6. What is an indenture?

7. A company is forced into bankruptcy. Assuming that the bankruptcy petition is not dismissed by the court, what are the two possible outcomes of a bankruptcy?

8. The Arapo Corporation issued $10 million in term bonds that are callable. What information does the term "callable" indicate to decision makers?

9. On January 1, Year One, the Rexal Company issues term bonds with a face value of $30 million that pay a stated cash interest rate of 6 percent. The bonds are actually issued for $27 million to yield an effective interest rate of 8 percent. If the first payment is made on December 31, Year One, how much cash is paid?

10. What is a mortgage agreement?

11. The Philadelphia Corporation issues $17 million in debentures. What is a debenture?

12. A company issues $12 million in term bonds on March 1, Year One, for face value. The bonds pay a stated cash interest rate of 10 percent per year. Interest payments are made every February 28 and August 31. On financial statements for Year One, what is recognized as interest expense on the income statements? What interest payable is reported on the December 31, Year One, balance sheet?

13. A company issues $18 million in term bonds on March 1, Year One, for face value plus accrued interest. The bonds pay a stated cash interest rate of 10 percent per year. Interest payments are made every January 31 and July 31. Prepare journal entries on March 1, Year One, July 31, Year One, and December 31, Year One?

14. The Shelby Corporation issues $10 million in zero-coupon bonds. What is a zero-coupon bond? Why would an investor be willing to acquire a zero-coupon bond? How is the price of a zero-coupon bond determined?

15. What is meant by the term "compounding"?

16. On January 1, Year One, a zero-coupon bond with a face value of $12 million is issued for $7.8 million to create an effective annual interest rate of 9 percent. The bond will be paid in exactly five years. If the effective rate method is applied, what liability balance is reported on December 31, Year One, and also on December 31, Year Two?

17. Do Problem 16 again but assume that the straight-line method is used rather than the effective rate method.

18. Why is the straight-line method of recognizing interest on a bond that is issued at a discount not viewed as theoretically appropriate? When can the straight-line method be used in connection with the reporting of bond interest?

19. On January 1, Year One, a company issues term bonds with a face value of $20 million and an annual stated cash interest rate of 6 percent. Assume the bonds are issued for $18 million to earn an effective yield rate of 8 percent per year. If the first interest payment is made on December 31, Year One, what is the liability balance reported on the balance sheet at the end of that day?

20. On January 1, Year One, the Vallee Corporation issues a five-year $10 million serial bond paying a stated annual cash interest rate each December 31 of 5 percent. What are the cash payments specified by this bond contract?

TRUE OR FALSE

1. ____ A company borrows $1 million on a term bond that pays 8 percent cash interest each year. The money is used by the company to create additional profits of $93,000 per year. This company is using financial leverage.

2. ____ One advantage of debt financing is that the payments made on the liability are tax deductible.

3. ____ Companies that are forced into bankruptcy will have their assets liquidated with the resulting money going to pay the creditors.

4. ____ Banks typically charge stronger companies higher interest rates than weaker ones because a financially healthy company can better afford to pay the extra amounts each period.

5. ____ All bonds are issued for cash amounts equal to their face value.

6. ____ A callable bond can be exchanged by the creditor for the capital stock of the debtor company.

7. ____ A serial bond is a debt that pays interest more frequently than just once each year.

8. ____ A debenture is a debt that is not secured.

9. ____ The term "indenture" refers to a bond contract.

10. ____ A term bond pays interest each February 1 and August 1. It is issued on February 1, Year One. The company will report interest expense on its Year One income statement for 11 months.

11. ____ When a company issues a bond between interest dates, the first interest payment will be reduced.

12. ____ A zero-coupon bond is issued for a price determined by computing the present value of the stated cash interest payments.

13. ____ A company recognizes interest expense for the current year of $23,000 but pays cash interest of only $18,000. The $5,000 difference is compounded.

14. ____ On January 1, Year One, a company issues a $1 million term bond that pays a stated cash interest rate of 8 percent per year at the end of each year. To determine the price of this bond, the present value of a single amount of $1 million must be determined along with the present value of an annuity due of $80,000.

15. ____ A company issues a $1 million term bond for $700,000. The $300,000 discount can never be recognized as interest expense through the use of the straight-line method.

16. ____ A serial bond is issued on December 31, Year One, for $885,000. Interest of $17,000 is compounded at the end of Year Two, and the first principal payment of $50,000 is made on that date. The liability balance to be reported on the December 31, Year Two, balance sheet is $818,000.

MULTIPLE CHOICE

1. A company needs to raise $9 million and issues bonds for that amount rather than additional capital stock. Which of the following is not a likely reason the company chose debt financing?

    a. Management hopes to increase profits by using financial leveraging.

    b. The cost of borrowing is reduced because interest expense is tax deductible.

    c. Adding new owners increases the possibility of bankruptcy if economic conditions get worse.

    d. If money becomes available, the company can rid itself of debts.

2. A company issues bonds with a face value of $12 million on June 1, Year One, for the face value plus accrued interest. The bonds pay an annual cash interest rate of 10 percent with payments made on April 1 and October 1 of each year. On financial statements as of December 31, Year One, and the year then ended, which of the following balances will appear?

    a. Interest expense: $400,000; interest payable: -0-

    b. Interest expense: $600,000; interest payable: -0-

    c. Interest expense: $700,000; interest payable: $300,000

    d. Interest expense: $900,000; interest payable: $300,000

3. The Akimbo Company issues bonds with a face value of $12 million on June 1, Year One, for 93 percent of face value plus accrued interest. The bonds pay an annual cash interest rate of 10 percent with payments made on April 1 and October 1 of each year. The bonds were sold at a discount to create an effective interest rate of 12 percent per year. What amount of cash interest will Akimbo actually pay during Year One?

    a. $400,000

    b. $600,000

    c. $700,000

    d. $900,000

4. Kitten Inc. issued $105,000 in bonds on September 1 for face value plus any accrued interest. The annual interest rate is 6 percent, and interest is paid on the bonds every June 30 and December 31. When the bonds are issued on September 1, how much cash will the company collect?

    a. $105,000

    b. $106,050

    c. $106,575

    d. $108,150

5. The Alexander Company issues a fifteen-year, zero-coupon bond with a face value of $500,000. The effective interest negotiated by the parties to the exchange was an annual rate of 7 percent. The present value of $1 in 15 periods at an annual interest rate of 7 percent is $0.36245. The present value of an ordinary annuity of $1 for 15 periods at an annual interest rate of 7 percent is $9.10791. The present value of an annuity due of $1 for 15 periods at an annual interest rate of 7 percent is $9.74547. What was the exchange price for the bond (rounded)?

    a. $181,225

    b. $192,687

    c. $318,777

    d. $341,091

6. A zero coupon bond with a face value of $900,000 is issued on January 1, Year One. It will mature in ten years and was issued for $502,550 to earn an annual effective rate of 6 percent. If the effective rate method is used, what interest expense does the company recognize for Year Two (rounded)?

    a. $30,153

    b. $31,962

    c. $38,128

    d. $39,745

7. A zero coupon bond with a face value of $600,000 is issued on January 1, Year One. It will mature in five years and was issued for $408,350 to earn an annual effective rate of 8 percent. If the effective rate method is used, what liability balance does the company report at the end of Year Two (rounded)?

    a. $476,299

    b. $478,821

    c. $482,678

    d. $485,010

8. A zero coupon bond with a face value of $800,000 is issued on January 1, Year One. It will mature in eight years and was issued for $541,470 to earn an annual effective rate of 5 percent. If the straight-line method is used, what liability balance does the company report at the end of Year Two (rounded)?

    a. $601,350

    b. $602,974

    c. $604,755

    d. $606,102

9. On January 1, Krystal Corporation issued bonds with a face value of $100,000 and a 4 percent annual stated interest rate. The effective annual rate of interest negotiated by the parties was 6 percent. Interest is paid semiannually on June 30 and December 31. The bonds mature in ten years. The present value of $1 in 10 periods at a 4 percent interest rate is $0.67556, in 10 periods at 6 percent interest is $0.55839, in 20 periods at a 2 percent interest rate is $0.67297, and in 20 periods at a 3 percent interest rate is $0.55368. The present value of an ordinary annuity of $1 for 10 periods at a 4 percent interest rate is $8.11090, for 10 periods at 6 percent interest is $7.36009, for 20 periods at a 2 percent interest rate is $16.35143, and in 20 periods at a 3 percent interest rate is $14.87747. What will be the price of the bonds on January 1 (rounded)?

    a. $85,123

    b. $85,279

    c. $86,054

    d. $86,311

10. On January 1, Year One, Giant Company decides to issue term bonds with a total face value of $1 million. The bonds come due in ten years and pay cash interest of 4 percent each year on December 31. An investor is found for these bonds, but that person wants to earn an annual effective rate of 8 percent. After some serious negotiations, Giant agrees to a 7 percent annual rate, and the bonds are issued for a total of $789,292. The effective rate method is applied to recognize interest. What amount of interest expense should be recognized by Giant on its Year Two income statement (rounded)?

    a. $48,515

    b. $50,375

    c. $52,936

    d. $56,318

11. On January 1, Year One, Super Company decides to issue term bonds with a total face value of $600,000. The bonds come due in six years and pay cash interest of 3 percent each year on December 31. An investor is found and an effective annual interest rate of 8 percent is agreed to by all parties. As a result, the bond is issued for $461,315. The effective rate method is applied. What was the reported balance of this liability at the end of Year One (rounded)?

    a. $473,018

    b. $476,550

    c. $477,105

    d. $480,220

12. On January 1, Year One, the Elizabeth Corporation issues a $1 million serial bond. Beginning on December 31, Year One, the company will pay $100,000 per year plus interest at an 8 percent rate on the unpaid balance during that year. The bond will be issued at an effective rate of 9 percent per year. How much cash will the company pay on December 31, Year Two?

    a. $162,000

    b. $172,000

    c. $180,000

    d. $184,000

13. On January 1, Year One, the Benson Company issues a $400,000 serial bond. Beginning on December 31, Year One, the company will pay $100,000 per year plus interest at a 4 percent rate on the unpaid balance during that year. The bond is issued for $373,740 to earn an effective annual interest rate of 7 percent. What is the liability balance reported on this company's balance sheet as of December 31, Year One (rounded)?

    a. $278,750

    b. $281,865

    c. $283,902

    d. $285,776

VIDEO PROBLEMS

Professor Joe Hoyle discusses the answers to these two problems at the links that are indicated. After formulating your answers, watch each video to see how Professor Hoyle answers these questions.

1. Your roommate is an English major. The roommate's parents own a chain of ice cream shops located throughout Florida. One day, while warming up to go jogging, your roommate poses this question: "My parents plan to build four new shops in the next year or so. They will need several million dollars to construct these facilities and add the necessary equipment and furniture. I thought they were going to obtain this money by adding one or two new owners. Instead, they borrowed the money by issuing bonds to a number of investors throughout the state. I don't like debt; it scares me. I don't understand why they would have taken on so much debt when they could simply have gotten new ownership involved. Why would they have made this decision? How will this affect their financial statements in the future?" How would you respond?

View the video online at: http://bit.ly/hoyle14-3

2. Your uncle and two friends started a small office supply store several years ago. The company has grown and now has several large locations. Your uncle knows that you are taking a financial accounting class and asks you the following question: "We are beginning a major expansion project that will cost us about $10 million. We plan to raise the needed money by issuing bonds. One of my partners wants to issue zero-coupon bonds. Our lawyer tells us that we really should issue serial bonds. Our financial advisor suggests term bonds. I am not even sure I know the difference. Can you explain how these three types of bonds differ? How do those differences impact the financial reporting?" How would you respond?

View the video online at: http://bit.ly/hoyle14-4

PROBLEMS

1. Joni Corporation borrows $500,000 from Friendly Bank on February 1, Year One. The principal will not be repaid until the end of six years, but interest payments are due every February 1 and August 1 beginning on August 1, Year One. The interest rate is 4 percent annually. Record the journal entry or adjusting entry necessary for each of the following.

   a. The signing of the loan on February 1, Year One.

   b. The payment of interest on August 1, Year One.

   c. The recognition of accrued interest on December 31, Year One.

   d. The payment of interest on February 1, Year Two.

2. Colson Corporation produces women's clothing. Company officials decide to issue $50,000 in long-term bonds to finance an expansion of its swimwear line. These bonds are issued for face value on April 1, Year One and pay interest in the amount of 5 percent annually. Interest payments are made semiannually, every April 1 and October 1. Record the journal entry or the adjusting necessary for each of the following.

   a. The issuance of the bonds.

   b. The first payment of interest on October 1, Year One.

   c. The accrual of interest on December 31, Year One, so that financial statements can be prepared.

   d. The payment of interest on April 1, Year Two.

3. Assume the same facts as in problem 2, but instead of April 1, Year One, the bonds are issued on July 1, Year One. The bonds are issued for face value plus accrued interest. Record the journal entry or adjusting entry necessary for each of the following.

   a. The issuance of the bonds on July 1, Year One.

   b. The first payment of interest on October 1, Year One.

   c. The accrual of interest on December 31, Year One, so that financial statements can be prepared.

   d. The payment of interest on April 1, Year Two.

4. Keller Corporation offers to issue zero-coupon bonds of $80,000 on January 1, Year One. The bonds will come due on December 31, Year Three. Keller and several potential creditors negotiate an annual interest rate of 7 percent on the bonds. The present value of $1 in 3 periods at an annual interest rate of 7 percent is $0.81630. The present value of an ordinary annuity of $1 for 3 periods at an annual interest rate of 7 percent is $2.62432. The present value of an annuity due of $1 for 3 periods at an annual interest rate of 7 percent is $2.80802.

   a. Determine the amount the creditors will pay on January 1, Year One, for these bonds.

   b. Record the issuance of the bonds on January 1, Year One.

   c. Make the necessary adjusting entry at the end of Year One. What is the liability balance at the end of Year One?

   d. Make the necessary adjusting entry at the end of Year Two. What is the liability balance at the end of Year Two?

5. The Rangaletta Company issues a five-year, zero-coupon bond on January 1, Year One. The bond has a face value of $200,000 and is issued to yield an effective interest rate of 9 percent. Rangaletta receives $129,986. On January 1, Year Three, Rangaletta pays off the bond early by making a payment of $155,000 to the bondholder. Make all journal entries from January 1, Year One, through January 1, Year Three assuming the effective rate method is applied.

6. Do problem 5 again but assume that the straight-line method is used.

7. A company issues $600,000 in zero-coupon bonds on January 1, Year One. They come due in exactly six years and are sold to yield an effective interest rate of 4 percent per year. They are issued for $474,186. The effective rate method is applied.

   a. What interest expense was recognized for Year One and for Year Two?

   b. How would the company's net income have been affected in each of the first two years if the straight-line method had been used rather than the effective rate method?

8. On January 1, Year One, Gijulka Corporation offers to issue a $100,000 bond coming due in exactly ten years. This bond pays a stated cash interest rate of 6 percent per year on December 31. A buyer is found. After some negotiations, the parties agree on an effective annual yield rate of 7 percent. Consequently, the bond is issued for $92,974. The effective rate method is applied.

   a. What figures will be reported for this bond in Gijulka's Year One financial statements?

   b. What figures will be reported for this bond in Gijulka's Year Two financial statements?

9. Jaguar Corporation issues term bonds with a face value of $300,000 on January 1, Year One. The bonds have a stated rate of interest of 7 percent per year and a life of four years. They pay this interest annually on December 31. Because the market rate of interest at that time was 9 percent, the bonds were issued at a discount to create an effective annual rate of 9 percent. The present value of $1 in 4 periods at an annual interest rate of 9 percent is $0.70843. The present value of an ordinary annuity of $1 for 4 periods at an annual interest rate of 9 percent is $3.23972.

   a. What amount will Jaguar receive when the bonds are issued?
   b. What journal entry does the company make on January 1, Year One, when the bonds are issued?
   c. What journal entry or entries does the company make on December 31, Year One?
   d. What is the liability balance reported on the December 31, Year One, balance sheet?
   e. What journal entry or entries does the company make on December 31, Year Two?
   f. What is the liability balance reported on the December 31, Year Two, balance sheet?

10. Arizona Corporation issues term bonds with a face value of $800,000 on January 1, Year One. The bonds have a stated rate of interest of 7 percent per year and a life of six years. They pay interest annually on December 31. These bonds were issued at $695,470 to create an effective annual rate of 10 percent.

   a. What journal entry does the company make on January 1, Year One, when the bonds are issued?
   b. What journal entry or entries does the company make on December 31, Year One?
   c. What is the liability balance reported on the December 31, Year One, balance sheet?
   d. What journal entry or entries does the company make on December 31, Year Two?
   e. What is the liability balance reported on the December 31, Year Two, balance sheet?

11. Collins Company issues term bonds with a face value of $100,000 on January 1, Year One. The bonds have an annual stated rate of interest of 4 percent and a life of ten years. They pay interest semiannually on June 30 and December 31. The bonds were issued to yield an effective annual interest rate of 6 percent.

   The present value of $1 in 10 periods at a 4 percent interest rate is $0.67556, in 10 periods at 6 percent interest is $0.55839, in 20 periods at a 2 percent interest rate is $0.67297, and in 20 periods at a 3 percent interest rate is $0.55368.

   The present value of an ordinary annuity of $1 for 10 periods at a 4 percent interest rate is $8.11090, for 10 periods at 6 percent interest is $7.36009, for 20 periods at a 2 percent interest rate is $16.35143, and in 20 periods at a 3 percent interest rate is $14.87747.

   a. Prepare the journal entry to record the issuance of the bonds on January 1, Year One.
   b. Prepare the journal entry to record the first payment of interest on June 30, Year One.
   c. Prepare the journal entry to record the second payment of interest on December 31, Year One.
   d. What amount of interest expense is reported on the Year One income statement?
   e. What is the liability balance to be reported for this bond on a December 31, Year One, balance sheet?

12. Chyrsalys Corporation issues $4,000,000 in serial bonds on January 1, Year One, with a stated cash interest rate of 4 percent. The bonds are issued at face value. The bond terms specify that interest and $2,000,000 in principal will be paid on December 31, Year One and December 31, Year Two.

   a. What journal entry, or entries, is recorded on December 31, Year One?
   b. What journal entry, or entries, is recorded on December 31, Year Two?

13. The Empire Company issues $3 million in bonds on January 1, Year One. The bonds are for three years with $1 million paid at the end of each year plus interest of 6 percent on the unpaid balance for that period. These bonds are sold to yield an effective rate of 8 percent per year. The present value of $1 at an 8 percent interest rate in one year is $0.92593, in two years is $0.85734, and in three years is $0.79383. The present value of an ordinary annuity of $1 at an 8 percent interest rate over three years is $2.57710.

   a. What amount of cash will Empire pay on December 31 of each of these three years?
   b. What is the present value of these cash payments at an 8 percent effective annual interest rate?
   c. What journal entry or entries is recorded on December 31, Year One?
   d. What journal entry or entries is recorded on December 31, Year Two?

14. The Althenon Corporation issues bonds with a $1 million face value on January 1, Year One. The bonds pay a stated interest rate of 5 percent each year on December 31. They come due in eight years. The Zephyr Corporation also issues bonds with a $1 million face value on January 1, Year One. These bonds pay a stated interest rate of 8 percent each year on December 31. They come due in eight years. Both companies actually issue their bonds to yield an effective annual interest rate of 10 percent. Both companies use the effective rate method. The present value of $1 at a 10 percent interest rate in eight years is $0.46651. The present value of an ordinary annuity of $1 at a 10 percent interest rate over eight years is $5.33493.

    a. What interest expense does Althenon report for Year One and also for Year Two?

    b. What interest expense does Zephyr report for Year One and also for Year Two?

15. On January 1, Year One, the Pulaski Corporation issues bonds with a face value of $1 million. These bonds come due in twenty years and pay an annual stated interest rate (each December 31) of 5 percent. An investor offers to buy the entire group of bonds for an amount that will yield an effective interest rate of 10 percent per year. Company officials negotiate and are able to reduce the effective rate by 2 percent to 8 percent per year. The present value of $1 at a 10 percent interest rate in twenty years is $0.14864. The present value of an ordinary annuity of $1 at a 10 percent interest rate over twenty years is $8.51356. The present value of $1 at an 8 percent interest rate in twenty years is $0.21455. The present value of an ordinary annuity of $1 at an 8 percent interest rate over twenty years is $9.81815.

    a. As a result of the 2 percent reduction in the annual effective interest for this bond, what is the decrease in the amount of interest expense that Pulaski recognizes in Year One?

    b. As a result of the 2 percent reduction in the annual effective interest for this bond, what is the decrease in the amount of interest expense that Pulaski recognizes in Year Two?

This problem will carry through several chapters, building in difficulty. It allows students to continually practice skills and knowledge learned in previous chapters.

In Chapter 13, financial statements for January were prepared for Webworks. They are included here as a starting point for the required recording for February.

FIGURE 14.28 Webworks Financial Statements

Webworks Income Statement As of January 31	
Revenue	$16,000
Cost of Goods Sold	(8,664)
Gross Profit	7,336
Deprec. and Amort. Expense	(363)
Other Expenses and Losses	(3,800)
Investment Income	150
Earnings before Tax	3,323
Tax Expense	(1,000)
Net Income	$2,323

FIGURE 14.29

Webworks Stmt. of Retained Earnings As of January 31	
Retained Earnings, January 1	$12,290
Net Income	2,323
Retained Earnings, January 31	$14,613

FIGURE 14.30

Webworks
Balance Sheet
January 31

Assets		Liabilities	
Current		**Current**	
Cash	$5,150	Accounts Payable	$2,750
Accounts Receivable	1,600	Salaries Payable	200
Less Allowance for		Unearned Revenue	450
Doubtful Accounts	(160)		
Net Accounts Receivable	1,440		
Merchandise Inventory	2,423		
Supplies Inventory	40		
Prepaid Rent	400		
Prepaid Advertising	100		
Total Current Assets	$9,553	Total Current Liabilities	$ 3,400
Property, Plant, and Equipment			
Equipment	$7,000		
Less Accumulated Depreciation	(1,022)		
Furniture	1,000		
Less Accumulated Depreciation	(68)		
Total P, P, and E	$6,910		
Other Noncurrent Assets		**Owners' Equity**	
Available for Sale Securities	$1,575	Capital Stock	$2,000
Licensing Agreement, Net	1,800	Retained Earnings	14,613
		Other Accumulated Comprehensive Income:	
		Unrealized Loss on Available for Sale Securities	(175)
		Total Owners' Equity	$16,438
Total Assets	$19,838	Total Liabilities & Owners' Equity	$19,838

The following events occur during February:

a. Webworks starts and completes nine more sites and bills clients for $5,400.

b. Webworks purchases supplies worth $150 on account.

c. At the beginning of February, Webworks had nineteen keyboards costing $117 each and ten flash drives costing $20 each. Webworks uses periodic FIFO to cost its inventory.

d. On account, Webworks purchases seventy keyboards for $118 each and one hundred of the new flash drives for $22 each.

e. On February 1, Webworks borrows $3,000 from Local Area Bank. The loan plus accrued interest will be repaid at the end of two years. The interest rate is 6 percent.

f. Webworks purchases new computer equipment for use in designing Web sites. The equipment costs $5,500 and was paid for in cash.

g. Webworks pays Nancy Po (company employee) $800 for her work during the first three weeks of February.

h. Webworks sells seventy keyboards for $11,250 and ninety of the new flash drives for $2,700 cash.

i. Webworks collects $5,200 in accounts receivable.

j. Webworks purchases one hundred shares of RST Company for $18 per share in cash. This is considered a trading security.

k. Webworks pays off its salaries payable from January.

l. Webworks is hired to design Web sites for a local photographer and bakery. It is paid $600 in advance.

m. Webworks pays off $11,300 of its accounts payable.

n. Webworks pays Leon Jackson (company owner) a salary of $2,000.

o. Webworks completes the salon Web site and earns the $450 paid in January.

p. RST Company pays Webworks a dividend of $25.

q. Webworks pays taxes of $1,558 in cash.

> *Required:*
>
> A. Prepare journal entries for the previous events.
>
> B. Post the journal entries to T-accounts.
>
> C. Prepare an unadjusted trial balance for Webworks for February.
>
> D. Prepare adjusting entries for the following and post them to your T-accounts.

r. Webworks owes Nancy Po $220 for her work during the last week of February.

s. Leon's parents let him know that Webworks owes $300 toward the electricity bill. Webworks will pay them in March.

t. Webworks determines that it has $70 worth of supplies remaining at the end of January.

u. Prepaid rent should be adjusted for February's portion.

v. Prepaid advertising should be adjusted for February's portion.

w. Webworks is continuing to accrue bad debts at 10 percent of accounts receivable.

x. Webworks continues to depreciate its equipment over four years and its furniture over five years, using the straight-line method. The new equipment will also be depreciated over five years using the straight-line method.

y. The license agreement should be amortized over its one-year life.

z. QRS Company is selling for $12 per share and RST is selling for $16 per share on February 28.

aa. Interest should be accrued for February.

ab. Record cost of goods sold.

> E. Prepare an adjusted trial balance.
>
> F. Prepare financial statements for February.

RESEARCH ASSIGNMENT

Assume that you take a job as a summer employee for an investment advisory service. One of the partners for that firm is currently looking at the possibility of investing in **Marriott International**. The partner is aware that **Marriott** builds a lot of hotels and, therefore, probably has to borrow a significant amount of money. The partner is curious as to the cost of the interest on the money that **Marriott** borrows. The partner asks you to look at the 2010 financial statements for **Marriott** by following this path:

- Go to http://www.marriott.com.
- At the bottom of this screen, click on "About Marriott."
- At the top of the next screen, on the right, click on "Investors."
- On the next screen, on the right side, click on "2010 Annual Report" to download.
- On the next screen, click on "Financials" at the top right side.
- On the next screen, click on "Financial Statements" on the left side.
- The company's income statement should appear. Review the contents of that statement.
- Click the number 2 at the top of the screen to see the balance sheet. Review the contents of that statement.
- On the left side of the screen, click on "Notes to Financial Statements."
- Go to note 13 "Long-term debt." A schedule of the company's senior notes can be found in that note.

a. What was the amount of interest expense the company recognized on its 2010 income statement? How did that number compare with the interest expense recognized in 2009?

b. What was the amount of long-term debt reported by the company on its balance sheet at the end of 2010? How did that number compare with the long-term debt at the end of 2009?

c. According to the information in note 13, what was the stated cash interest rate for the various senior notes that the company has outstanding? What was the effective interest rate on each of these senior notes?

ENDNOTES

1. A company can seek protection from its creditors by voluntarily asking the court to allow it to enter bankruptcy. Or, three creditors holding a minimum amount of debt can push a company into bankruptcy, an event known as an involuntary bankruptcy filing.

2. Information on the bankruptcy and subsequent legal reorganization of Delta Air Lines can be found at http://money.cnn.com/2007/04/30/news/companies/delta_bankruptcy/index.htm.

3. Tim Catts and Sapna Maheshwari, "GE Leads $3.19 Trillion in Corporate Bond Sales: Credit Markets," December 30, 2010, http://www.bloomberg.com/news/2010-12-30/ge-leads-3-trillion-in-company-bond-sales-as-yields-fall-credit-markets.html.

4. The rate for interest on a debt can be identified by any of several terms. Cash rate, stated rate, contract rate, and coupon rate are all examples of the same information: the rate of interest to be paid by the debtor at specified times.

5. As explained in the chapter on acquiring intangible assets, the present value of $1 can be mathematically determined using the formula $1/(1 + i)^n$. Here, i is 0.06 and n is two periods. Present value can also be determined using an Excel spreadsheet. If a spreadsheet is used, the present value of $1 at 6 percent in two periods is found by typing the following formula into a cell: =PV(.06,2,,1,0).

6. The entry shown in Figure 14.7 can also be recorded in a slightly different manner. Under this alternative, the liability is entered into the records at its face value of $20,000 along with a separate discount of $2,200. The discount serves as a contra account to reduce the net liability balance to its principal amount. Although visually different, the liability is still reported as $17,800.

Cash	17,800	
Discount on Bond Payable	2,200	
Bond Payable		20,000

7. If a discount is recorded in the initial entry, as is shown in endnote 6, the credit shown in Figure 14.8 is to the Discount account and not directly to the bond payable. Because the contra account is reduced, the net liability balance increases by $1,068. Thus, overall reporting of the interest and the liability is not impacted by the method used in recording the issuance of the bond.

8. As mentioned in earlier discussions about the acquisition of intangible assets, an annuity with payments made at the beginning of each period is known as an annuity due. If the interest had been paid starting on January 1, Year One, the payments here would form an annuity due rather than an ordinary annuity. The cash flow pattern for notes and bonds is more likely to be in the form of an ordinary annuity since interest is not typically paid in advance.

9. The mathematical formula to determine the present value of an ordinary annuity of $1 is $(1 - 1/[1 + i]^n)/i$, where i is the appropriate interest rate (6 percent in this illustration) and n is the number of payment periods (four). If using an Excel spreadsheet, the present value of a $1 per period ordinary annuity for four periods at an annual rate of interest of 6 percent can be found by typing the following data into a cell: =PV(.06,4,1,,0).

10. Interest expense for the final year has been increased by $3 so that the final bond payable balance is exactly equal to the $1 million debt that must be paid. Slight adjustments of this type are common to compensate for numbers having been rounded.

11. The series of steps shown here is also used when a bond is issued at a premium above face value. If the effective interest rate negotiated by the parties is below the stated cash rate, the amount paid for the bond (the present value) will be above face value rather than below. In effect, the high rate of cash interest makes the bond more valuable. Thereafter, the effective interest recognized each period will be below the cash interest. Adjustment is made to lower the cash interest rate to the effective rate, which also reduces the reported principal balance moving it toward face value. Thus, when the negotiated rate is below the stated cash rate, a premium is created rather than a discount. The subsequent accounting process is not affected except that the increases and decreases are reversed from the examples shown here for a discount.

12. The interest recognized in the final year has been adjusted by $3 to compensate for the rounding of several computations so that the liability balance drops precisely to zero at the end of the four years.

In a Set of Financial Statements, What Information Is Conveyed about Other Noncurrent Liabilities?

 Video Clip

In this video, Professor Joe Hoyle introduces the essential points covered in Chapter 15.

View the video online at: http://bit.ly/hoyle15-1

1. ACCOUNTING FOR LEASES

1.1 Reporting a Liability for Leased Property

Question: Notes and bonds payable serve as the predominant source of long-term financing in the United States. Virtually all companies raise significant sums of money by incurring debts of this type. However, a quick perusal of the balance sheets of most well-known companies finds a broad array of other noncurrent liabilities, some of staggering size.

- *Sears Holdings Corporation disclosed long-term capital lease obligations of $597 million as of January 29, 2011.*
- *Southwest Airlines Co. reported deferred income tax liabilities of approximately $2.5 billion on December 31, 2010.*
- *Alcoa Inc. at December 31, 2010, lists $2.6 billion in liabilities (slightly under 12 percent of the company's total) labeled as accrued* **postretirement benefits** *(other than pensions).*

These noncurrent liabilities represent large amounts of debts that are different from traditional notes and bonds. Some understanding of these balances is necessary to comprehend the information being conveyed in a set of financial statements. The reporting of liabilities such as those above is explored in depth in upper-level financial accounting courses. However, a basic level of knowledge is essential for every potential decision maker, not just those individuals who chose to major in accounting in college.

Lease liabilities will be explored first in this chapter. To illustrate, assume that the Abilene Company needs an airplane to use in its daily operations. Rather than buy this asset, Abilene leases one from a business that owns a variety of aircraft. The lease is for seven years at an annual cost of $100,000. A number of reasons might exist for choosing to lease rather than buy. Perhaps Abilene is able to negotiate especially good terms for the airplane because of the company's willingness to commit to such a long period of time.

On the day that the lease is signed, should Abilene report a liability and, if so, is the amount just the first $100,000 installment, the $700,000 total of all payments, or some other figure? **When a company leases an asset, how is the related liability reported?**

Answer: The liability balance to be reported by the Abilene Company cannot be determined based purely on the information that is provided. When a **lessee** (the party that will make use of the asset) signs a lease agreement, the transaction is recorded in one of two ways based on the terms of the contract.

Possibility One—An Operating Lease. Abilene might have obtained the use of this airplane through an operating lease, a rental arrangement. If so, the liability recognized when the contract is signed is $100,000, only the amount due immediately. Upon payment, the reported debt is reduced to zero despite the requirement that six more installments have to be paid. In financial accounting, the future payments on an operating lease are viewed as a commitment rather than a liability. Thus, information about those payments is disclosed in the notes to the financial statements but not formally reported.

---

postretirement benefits

Promises such as pension payments, health care insurance coverage, and life insurance benefits made by employers to eligible employees to be received after the individuals reach a specified retirement age.

---

lessee

A party that pays cash for the use of an asset in a lease contract.

---

operating lease

A rental agreement where the benefits and risks of ownership are not conveyed from the lessor to the lessee.

Possibility Two—A Capital Lease. This transaction could also have met specific criteria for classification as a capital lease. That type of lease is viewed as the equivalent of Abilene buying the airplane. The initial liability recognized by Abilene is the present value of the $700,000, the entire amount of cash to be paid over these seven years. The present value is determined by the mathematical removal of a reasonable rate of interest.

capital lease

A rental agreement where the benefits and risks of ownership are conveyed from the lessor to the lessee so that both the asset and liability are reported initially by the lessee at the present value of the cash payments; for accounting purposes, it exists when one of four established criteria are met.

TEST YOURSELF

Question:

A lessee signs a lease agreement so that a piece of property can be used for the specified period of time. From an accounting perspective, what are the two types of leases?

a. Fixed leases and variable leases

b. Operating leases and capital leases

c. Income leases and expenditure-based leases

d. Noncontractual leases and contractual leases

Answer:

The correct answer is choice b: Operating leases and capital leases.

Explanation:

For the lessee, all leases are classified for financial reporting purposes as either a rental (an operating lease) or the equivalent of a purchase (a capital lease).

1.2   Does a Lessee Prefer to Report an Operating or Capital Lease?

Question: The previous answer raises a number of immediate questions about lease accounting. Probably the first of these relates to the practical goal of officials who want to produce financial statements that make their company look as financially healthy as possible. A lease agreement can be reported as (a) an operating lease with only the initial payment recorded as a liability or (b) a capital lease where the present value of all payments (a much larger number) is shown as the liability.

Officials for the lessee must surely prefer to classify all leases as operating leases to reduce the reported debt total. **In financial accounting, does a lessee not have a bias to report operating leases rather than capital leases?**

Answer: The answer to this question is obviously "Yes." If an option exists between reporting a larger liability (capital lease) or a smaller one (operating lease), officials for the lessee are inclined to take whatever measures necessary to classify each contract as an operating lease. This is not a choice such as applying FIFO or LIFO. The reporting classification is based on the nature of the agreement.

Thus, Abilene Company will likely attempt to structure the contract for this airplane to meet any designated criteria for an operating lease. Financial accounting is supposed to report events and not influence them. However, at times, authoritative reporting standards impact the method by which companies design the transactions in which they engage.

off-balance sheet financing

Description used for an obligation where an amount of money must be paid that is larger than the figure reported on the balance sheet; for a lessee, an operating lease provides an example of off-balance sheet financing.

If the previous example is judged to be an operating lease, Abilene only reports an initial liability of $100,000 although legally bound by the agreement to pay a much larger amount. The term off-balance sheet financing is commonly used when a company is obligated for more money than the reported debt. Operating leases are one of the primary examples of "off-balance sheet financing."

As mentioned at the start of this chapter, **Sears Holdings Corporation** reports noncurrent liabilities of about $597 million on January 29, 2011, in connection with capital leases. However, that obligation seems small in comparison to the amount to be paid by the company on its operating leases. As the notes to those financial statements explain, **Sears** has numerous operating leases (for the use of stores, office facilities, warehouses, computers and transportation equipment) that will require payment of over $5.3 billion in the next few years. Most of the debt for this additional $5.3 billion is "off the balance sheet." In other words, the obligation is not included in the liability section of the company's balance sheet. For an operating lease, the reported liability balance does not reflect the total obligation, just the current amount that is due.

TEST YOURSELF

Question:

A lessee is negotiating a new lease for a large piece of property. Which of the following is most likely to be true?

a. The lessee will try to structure this contract as an operating lease to take advantage of off-balance sheet financing.

b. The lessee will not care whether the contract is viewed as an operating lease or a capital lease.

c. The lessee will try to structure this contract as a capital lease to avoid the implications of off-balance sheet financing.

d. The lessee will structure the contract in whatever way is most convenient for the lessor (the actual owner of the property).

Answer:

The correct answer is choice a: The lessee will try to structure this contract as an operating lease to take advantage of off-balance sheet financing.

Explanation:

The liability balance reported for an operating lease is only the amount currently due. For most leases, that is a relatively small amount. A lessee will typically prefer to create this type of lease so that the reported liability total is lower. The remainder of the obligation will not be recognized until it comes due. The ability to use accounting rules to omit some amount of debt is commonly known as off-balance sheet financing.

1.3 Differentiating an Operating Lease from a Capital Lease

Question: For a lessee, a radical difference in reporting exists between operating leases and capital leases. Company officials prefer to report operating leases so that the amount of liabilities appearing on the balance sheet is lower. **What is the distinction between an operating lease and a capital lease?**

Answer: In form, all lease agreements are rental arrangements. One party (the lessor) owns legal title to property while the other (the lessee) rents the use of that property for a specified period of time. However, in substance, a lease agreement may go beyond a pure rental agreement. Financial accounting has long held that a fairly presented portrait of an entity's financial operations and economic health is only achieved by looking past the form of a transaction to report the actual substance of what is taking place. "Substance over form" is a mantra often heard in financial accounting.

Over thirty years ago, U.S. GAAP was created (by FASB) to provide authoritative guidance for the financial reporting of leases. An official pronouncement released at that time states that "a lease that transfers substantially all of the benefits and risks incident to the ownership of property should be accounted for as the acquisition of an asset and the incurrence of an obligation by the lessee." In simple terms, this standard means that a lessee can obtain such a significant stake in leased property that the transaction more resembles a purchase than it does a rental. If the transaction looks like a purchase, the accounting should be that of a purchase.

When the transaction is more like a purchase, it is recorded as a capital lease. When the transaction is more like a rental, it is recorded as an operating lease.

- *Capital lease.* The lessee gains substantially all the benefits and risks of ownership. Although legal form is still that of a lease arrangement, the transaction is reported as a purchase at the present value of the future cash flows.

- *Operating lease.* The lessee does not obtain substantially all the benefits and risks of ownership. The transaction is reported as a rental arrangement.

TEST YOURSELF

Question:

A lessee signs a contract with the word "LEASE" typed across the top. Which of the following statements is true?

a. Rental expense will be recognized over the life of this contract.

b. If this contract is accounted for as a capital lease, that is an example of reporting substance over form.

c. If this contract is accounted for as an operating lease, that is an example of reporting form over substance.

d. Because a formal legal document has been created, this lease must be reported as a capital lease.

Answer:

The correct answer is choice b: If this contract is accounted for as a capital lease, that is an example of reporting substance over form.

Explanation:

Although this contract is in the form of a rental arrangement, it must be accounted for as a capital lease if it has the substance of a purchase. Accountants always want to record the substance of a transaction rather than its mere form. Without knowing the information provided in the contract, the accountant cannot determine whether rent expense is appropriate here (an operating lease) or if the arrangement is the equivalent of a purchase (a capital lease).

1.4   Criteria for a Capital Lease

*Question: A capital lease is accounted for as a purchase because it so closely resembles the acquisition of the asset. An operating lease is more like a rent. The lessee normally prefers to report all such transactions as operating leases to reduce the amount of debt shown on its balance sheet. **How does an accountant determine whether a contract qualifies as a capital lease or an operating lease?***

Answer: In establishing reporting guidelines in this area, FASB created four specific criteria to serve as the line of demarcation between the two types of leases. Such rules set a standard that all companies must follow. If any one of these criteria is met, the lease is automatically recorded by the lessee as a capital lease. In that case, both the asset and liability are reported as if an actual purchase took place.

Not surprisingly, accountants and other company officials study these four criteria carefully. They hope to determine how the rules can be avoided so that most of their new contracts are viewed as operating leases. Interestingly, in recent years, official groups here and abroad have been examining these rules to decide whether U.S. GAAP and IFRS will be revised so that virtually all leases are reported as capital leases. At this time, the final outcome of those deliberations remains uncertain. However, a serious limitation on the use of the operating lease category seems likely in the next few years.

Criteria to Qualify as a Capital Lease (only one must be met):

1. If the lease contract specifies that title to the property will be conveyed to the lessee by the end of the lease term, it is a capital lease. If legal ownership is to be transferred from **lessor** to lessee, the entire series of payments is simply a method devised to purchase the asset. From the beginning, the property was being acquired.

2. If the contract allows the lessee to buy the property at a specified time at an amount sufficiently below expected fair value (so that a purchase is reasonably assured), it is a capital lease. The availability of this bargain purchase option indicates, once again, that the true intention of the contract is the conveyance of ownership. The transaction is the equivalent of a purchase if the option price is so low that purchase by the lessee can be anticipated.

3. If the lease contract is for a term that is equal to 75 percent or more of the estimated life of the property, it is a capital lease. This criterion is different from the first two where the transaction was just a disguised purchased. Here, the lessee will never gain ownership. However, the lease is for such an extensive portion of the asset's life that the lessee obtains a vast majority of its utility. Although the 75 percent standard is an arbitrary benchmark, no doubt can exist that the lessee will be the primary beneficiary of the property.

4. The fourth criterion is too complicated to cover in an introductory textbook. The general idea is that the lessee is paying approximately the same amount as would have been charged to buy the asset. Paying the equivalent of the purchase price (or close to it) indicates that no real difference exists between the nature of the lease transaction and an acquisition.

lessor

A party that receives cash for granting the use of owned property to a lessee through a lease contract.

TEST YOURSELF

Question:

A lessee signs a three-year lease for $79,000 per year to gain use of a machine. The machine has an expected useful life of five years. At the end of this three-year period, the machine is expected to be worth $60,000. The lessee has the right to buy it at that time for $50,000. The required payments are not the equivalent of the acquisition value of this asset. Which of the following is true for the lessee?

a. The lease is a capital lease.

b. The lease is an operating lease.

c. The lease might be a capital lease but not enough information is available.

d. The lease will be an operating lease if one of the four criteria is met.

Answer:

The correct answer is choice c: The lease might be a capital lease but not enough information is available.

Explanation:

If one of the four criteria established by FASB is met, this lease is reported as a capital lease. One of the criteria is still in question. Is a $50,000 purchase option viewed as a bargain if the expected fair value is $60,000? Is the $10,000 discount sufficient so that purchase is reasonably assured? Although the rules are clear, those judgments can be extremely difficult to make in practice. Not enough information is provided here to determine whether this purchase option is a bargain.

KEY TAKEAWAY

A lessee accounts for a lease contract as either an operating lease or a capital lease depending on the specific terms of the agreement. Officials working for the lessee will likely prefer the contract to qualify as an operating lease because a smaller liability is reported. Thus, the reporting of an operating lease is a common example of off-balance sheet financing because a significant portion of the contractual payments are not included as liabilities on the balance sheet. In contrast, for a capital lease, the present value of all future cash flows must be reported as a liability. To differentiate operating leases from capital leases, four criteria have been established within U.S. GAAP. If any one of these criteria is met, the lessee accounts for the transaction as a capital lease. Although still a lease in legal form, the contract is viewed as a purchase in substance and reported in that manner.

2. OPERATING LEASES VERSUS CAPITAL LEASES

LEARNING OBJECTIVES

At the end of this section, students should be able to meet the following objectives:

1. **Account for an operating lease, realizing that the only liability to be reported is the amount that is currently due.**

2. **Understand that the only asset reported in connection with an operating lease is prepaid rent if payments are made in advance.**

3. **Record the initial entry for a capital lease with both the asset and the liability calculated at the present value of the future cash flows.**

4. **Explain the interest rate to be used by the lessee in determining the present value of a capital lease and the amount of interest expense to be recognized each period.**

5. **Determine and recognize the depreciation of an asset recorded as the result of a capital lease.**

2.1 The Financial Reporting of an Operating Lease

Question: The Abilene Company has agreed to pay $100,000 per year for seven years to lease an airplane. Assume that legal title will not be received by Abilene and no purchase option is mentioned in the contract. Assume also that the life of the airplane is judged to be ten years and the payments do not approximate the fair value of the item.

The contract is signed on December 31, Year One, with the first annual payment made immediately. Based on the description of the agreement, none of the four criteria for a capital lease have been met. Thus, Abilene has an operating lease. **What financial accounting is appropriate for an operating lease?**

Answer: None of the four criteria for a capital lease is met in this transaction:

1. Legal ownership is not conveyed to the lessee.

2. No bargain purchase option is included in the contract.

3. The life of the lease is less than 75 percent of the life of asset (seven years out of ten years or 70 percent).

4. Payments do not approximate the acquisition value of the asset.

Thus, Abilene is just renting the airplane and agrees on an operating lease. The first annual payment was made immediately to cover the subsequent year.

FIGURE 15.1   December 31, Year One—Payment of First Installment of Operating Lease

Because the first payment has been made, no liability is reported on Abilene's balance sheet although the contract specifies that an additional $600,000 in payments will be required over the subsequent six years. In addition, the airplane itself is not shown as an asset by the lessee. The operating lease is viewed as the equivalent of a rent and not a purchase.

During Year Two, as time passes, the future value provided by the first prepayment gradually becomes a past value. The asset balance is reclassified as an expense. At the end of that period, the second payment will also be made.

FIGURE 15.2   December 31, Year Two—Adjustment to Record Rent Expense for Year Two

FIGURE 15.3   December 31, Year Two—Payment of Second Installment of Operating Lease

2.2   Initial Recording of a Capital Lease

Question: One slight change can move this contract from an operating lease to a capital lease. Assume all the information remains the same in the previous example except that the airplane has an expected life of only nine years rather than ten. With that minor alteration, the life of the lease is 77.8 percent of the life of the asset (seven years out of nine years). The contract is now 75 percent or more of the life of the asset. Because one of the criteria is now met, this contract must be viewed as a capital lease. The change in that one estimation creates a major impact on the reporting process. **How is a capital lease reported initially by the lessee?**

Answer: As a capital lease, the transaction is reported in the same manner as a purchase. Abilene has agreed to pay $100,000 per year for seven years, but no part of this amount is specifically identified as interest. According to U.S. GAAP, if a reasonable rate of interest is not explicitly paid each period, a present value computation is required to split the contractual payments between principal (the amount paid for the airplane) and interest (the amount paid to extend payment over this seven-year period). This accounting is not only appropriate for an actual purchase when payments are made over time but also for a capital lease.

Before the lessee computes the present value of the future cash flows, one issue must be resolved. A determination is needed of the appropriate rate of interest to be applied. In the previous discussion of bonds, a negotiated rate was established between the investor and the issuing company. No such bargained rate exists in connection with a lease. According to U.S. GAAP, the lessee should use its own incremental borrowing rate. That is the interest rate the lessee would be forced to pay to borrow this same amount of money from a bank or other lending institution.[1] Assume here that the incremental borrowing rate for Abilene is 10 percent per year. If the company had signed a loan to buy this airplane instead of lease it, the assumption is that the lender would have demanded an annual interest rate of 10 percent.

Abilene will pay $100,000 annually over these seven years. Because the first payment is made immediately, these payments form an annuity due. As always, the present value calculation computes the interest at the appropriate rate and then removes it to leave the principal: the amount of the debt incurred to obtain the airplane. Once again, present value can be found by table (in the following link or included at the end of this book), by formula, or by Excel spreadsheet.[2]

Present Value of an Annuity Due of $1

http://www.principlesofaccounting.com/ART/fv.pv.tables/pvforannuitydue.htm

Present value of an annuity due of $1 per year for seven years at a 10 percent annual interest rate is $5.35526. The present value of seven payments of $100,000 is $535,526.

$$\text{present value} = \$100,000 \times 5.35526$$

$$\text{present value} = \$535,526$$

After the present value has been determined, the recording of the capital lease proceeds very much like a purchase made by signing a long-term liability.

FIGURE 15.4 December 31, Year One—Capital Lease Recorded at Present Value

| Leased Airplane | 535,526 | |
| Lease Liability | | 535,526 |

FIGURE 15.5 December 31, Year One—Initial Payment on Capital Lease

| Lease Liability | 100,000 | |
| Cash | | 100,000 |

A comparison at this point between the reporting of an operating lease and a capital lease is striking. The differences are not inconsequential. For the lessee, good reasons exist for seeking an operating lease rather than a capital lease.

FIGURE 15.6 Comparison of Initially Reported Amounts for an Operating Lease and for a Capital Lease

	Operating Lease	Capital Lease
December 31, Year One		
Asset	Prepaid Rent—$100,000	Leased Airplane—$535,526
Liability (first payment made immediately)	Liability—0	Lease Liability—$435,526

TEST YOURSELF

Question:

A company signs a lease on January 1, Year One, to lease a machine for eight years. Payments are $10,000 per year with the first payment made immediately. The company has an incremental borrowing rate of 6 percent. This lease qualifies as a capital lease. The present value of an ordinary annuity of $1 for eight periods at an annual interest rate of 6 percent is $6.20979. The present value of an annuity due of $1 for eight periods at an annual interest rate of 6 percent is $6.58238. If financial statements are produced after this lease has been signed and settled, which of the following balances will be reported (rounded)?

a. Leased asset of $62,098 and lease liability of $52,098
b. Leased asset of $52,098 and lease liability of $62,098
c. Leased asset of $65,824 and lease liability of $55,824
d. Leased asset of $55,824 and lease liability of $65,824

Answer:

The correct answer is choice c: Leased asset of $65,824 and lease liability of $55,824.

Explanation:

Because the first payment is made immediately, this contract is classified as an annuity due. As a capital lease, both the asset and the liability are initially reported at the present value of these cash flows at the lessee's incremental borrowing rate or $65,824 ($10,000 × $6.5824). However, the first $10,000 payment is also made at that time so the liability balance is reduced by that amount.

2.3   Accounting for a Capital Lease over Time

Question: In a capital lease, property is not bought but is accounted for as if it had been purchased. When the contract is signed in the previous example, Abilene records both the leased airplane and the liability at the present value of the required cash payments. **What reporting takes place subsequent to the initial recording of a capital lease transaction?**

Answer: As with any purchase of an asset having a finite life where payments extend into the future, the cost of the asset is depreciated, and interest is recognized in connection with the liability. This process remains the same whether the asset is bought or obtained by capital lease.

Depreciation. The airplane will be used by Abilene for the seven-year life of the lease. The recorded cost of the asset is depreciated over this period to match the expense recognition with the revenue that the airplane helps generate. Assuming the straight-line method is applied, annual depreciation is $76,504 (rounded) or $535,526/seven years.

Interest. The principal of the lease liability during Year Two is $435,526. That balance is the initial $535,526 present value less the first payment of $100,000. The annual interest rate used in determining present value was 10 percent so interest expense of $43,553 (rounded) is recognized for this period of time—the liability principal of $435,526 times this 10 percent annual rate. As in the chapter on bonds and notes, the effective rate method is applied here.

FIGURE 15.7 December 31, Year Two—Depreciation of Airplane Obtained in Capital Lease

| Depreciation Expense | 76,504 | |
| Accumulated Depreciation | | 76,504 |

FIGURE 15.8 December 31, Year Two—Interest on Lease Liability from Capital Lease

| Interest Expense | 43,553 | |
| Lease Liability | | 43,553 |

FIGURE 15.9 December 31, Year Two—Second Payment on Capital Lease

| Lease Liability | 100,000 | |
| Cash | | 100,000 |

TEST YOURSELF

Question:

A company leases a truck for its operations. The accountant is attempting to determine if this lease is a capital lease or an operating lease. Which of the following statements is true?

a. The reported liability balance is likely to be higher in an operating lease.
b. A prepaid rental account is likely to be reported in a capital lease.
c. The leased asset will appear in the financial statements if this is an operating lease.
d. Both depreciation expense and interest expense are recognized for a capital lease.

Answer:

The correct answer is choice d: Both depreciation expense and interest expense are recognized for a capital lease.

Explanation:

In an operating lease, a prepaid rent account is established by the cash payments with that amount then reclassified to rent expense as time passes. Little or no liability is reported. In a capital lease, both the asset and the liability are reported at the present value of the future cash payments. The cost attributed to the asset is depreciated while interest expense must be recognized on the liability balance each period.

Talking with an Independent Auditor about International Financial Reporting Standards

Following is a continuation of our interview with Robert A. Vallejo, partner with the accounting firm **PricewaterhouseCoopers**.

Question: In U.S. GAAP, if a lease arrangement meets any one of four criteria, the transaction is reported as a capital lease. Companies often design transactions to either avoid or meet these criteria based on the desired method of accounting. Do IFRS requirements utilize the same set of criteria to determine whether a capital lease or an operating lease has been created?

Rob Vallejo: This is difficult to answer based on the current status of the FASB and IASB's joint project on "Leases" that began with a discussion paper in 2009. After receiving a large number of comments on a draft version of a new standard, the FASB and IASB are currently making revisions and will release a new draft version in the first half of 2012. Regardless of the outcome, after the new standard is issued (effective date could be as early as 2014), the distinction between operating and capital leases will be eliminated, as all leases will be treated as finance leases and included on the balance sheet at inception. For organizations that have structured leases to meet the definition of an operating lease, the new standard will have a significant impact. Officials should already be considering the implications to their financial statements and ongoing financial reporting. To check the latest status of the FASB and IASB's joint project on leases, check the FASB's web-site, http://www.FASB.org. Currently, a leasing arrangement may well be classified differently under IFRS than under U.S. GAAP. This is an example of where existing U.S. GAAP has rules and IFRS has principles. Under today's U.S. GAAP, guidance is very specific based on the four rigid criteria established by FASB. However, under IFRS, the guidance focuses on the substance of the transaction and there are no quantitative breakpoints or bright lines to apply. For example, there is no definitive rule such as the "75 percent of the asset's life" criterion found in U.S. GAAP. IFRS simply asks the question: have all the risks and rewards of ownership been substantially transferred?

KEY TAKEAWAY

Operating leases record payment amounts as they come due and are paid. Therefore, the only reported asset is a prepaid rent, and the liability is the current amount due. For a capital lease, the present value of all future cash payments is determined using the incremental borrowing rate of the lessee. The resulting amount is recorded as both the leased asset and the lease liability. The asset is then depreciated over the time that the lessee will make use of it. Interest expense is recorded (along with periodic payments) in connection with the liability as time passes using the effective rate method.

3.   RECOGNITION OF DEFERRED INCOME TAXES

LEARNING OBJECTIVES

At the end of this section, students should be able to meet the following objectives:

1. **Understand that the recognition of revenues and expenses under U.S. GAAP differs at many critical points from the taxation rules established by the Internal Revenue Code.**
2. **Explain the desire by corporate officials to defer the payment of income taxes.**
3. **Determine the timing for the reporting of a deferred income tax liability and explain the connection of this process to the matching principle.**
4. **Calculate taxable income as well as the related deferred income tax liability when the installment sales method is used.**

3.1   The Reporting of Deferred Tax Liabilities

Question: At the beginning of this chapter, mention was made that **Southwest Airlines** *reported deferred income taxes at the end of 2010 as a noncurrent liability of $2.5 billion. Such an account balance is not unusual. The* **Dow Chemical Company** *listed a similar debt of almost $1.3 billion on its December 31, 2010, balance sheet while* **Marathon Oil Corporation** *showed approximately $3.6 billion. What information is conveyed by these huge account balances?* **How is a deferred income tax liability created?**

deferred tax liability

A balance sheet account indicating that the current payment of an income tax amount has been delayed until a future date; companies often seek to create this deferral so that tax dollars can be used in the interim to increase net income.

Answer: The reporting of **deferred income tax liabilities** is, indeed, quite prevalent. One recent survey found that approximately 70 percent of businesses included a deferred tax balance within their noncurrent liabilities.[3] Decision makers need to have a basic understanding of any account that is so commonly encountered in a set of financial statements.

In the earlier discussion of LIFO, the disparity between financial accounting principles and income tax rules was described. In the United States, financial information is presented based on the requirements of U.S. GAAP (created by FASB) whereas income tax reporting is determined according to the Internal Revenue Code (written by Congress). At many places, these two sets of guidelines converge. If a grocery store sells a can of tuna fish for $6 in cash, the revenue is $6 on both the reported financial statements and the income tax return. However, at a number of critical junctures, the recognized amounts can be quite different.

Where legal, companies frequently exploit these differences for their own benefit by delaying tax payments. The deferral of income taxes is usually considered a wise business strategy because the organization is able to use its cash for a longer period of time and, hence, generate additional revenues. When paid, the money is gone, but until then, it can be used to raise net income. For example, if an entity earns a 10 percent return on assets and manages to defer a tax payment of $700 million for one year, the increased profit is $70 million ($700 million × 10 percent).

Businesses commonly attempt to reduce their current taxable income by moving reported gains and revenue into the future. That is one prevalent method for deferring tax payments. **Southwest**, **Dow Chemical**, and **Marathon** likely used this approach to create a portion of the deferred tax liabilities they are reporting. Revenue or a gain might be recognized this year for financial reporting purposes although deferred until an upcoming time period for tax purposes. Consequently, the payment of tax on this income is pushed into that future year. As long as the tax laws are obeyed, such deferral is legal.

temporary tax difference

A revenue or expense reported for both financial accounting and income tax purposes but in two different time periods; leads to the recognition of deferred income taxes.

Taxable income is reduced in the current period (revenue is moved out) but increased at a later time (the revenue is moved back into taxable income). Because a larger tax will have to be paid in the subsequent period, a deferred income tax liability is created. To illustrate, assume that a business reports revenue of $10,000 on its Year One income statement. Because of tax rules and regulations, assume that this amount will not be subject to income taxation until Year Six. The $10,000 is referred to as a **temporary tax difference**. It is reported for both financial accounting and tax purposes but in two different time periods.

If the effective tax rate for this business is 40 percent, it reports a $4,000 ($10,000 × 40 percent) deferred income tax liability on its December 31, Year One, balance sheet. The revenue was earned in Year One, so the related expense and liability are also recorded in Year One. This amount will be paid to the government but not until Year Six when the revenue becomes taxable. The revenue is recognized now according to U.S. GAAP but in a later year for income tax purposes. Although, net income is higher in the current year than taxable income, taxable income will be higher in the future by $10,000. Most important, payment of the $4,000 income tax is delayed until Year Six.

Simply put, a deferred income tax liability[4] is created when an event occurs now that will lead to a higher amount of income tax payment in the future.

TEST YOURSELF

Question:

A company earns $60,000 late in Year One. The tax rate is 25 percent so the tax payment on this income will be $15,000. Because of a specific rule in the Internal Revenue Code, this $60,000 is not taxable until Year Two. Thus, the $15,000 will be paid on March 15, Year Three when the company files its Year Two income tax return. Which of the following statements is true?

a. The liability is first recognized in Year One even though payment is not made until Year Three.

b. The liability is first recognized in Year Two even though payment is not made until Year Three.

c. The liability is not recognized until Year Three when the tax return is filed.

d. There is not enough information presented here to determine when the liability should first be recognized.

Answer:

The correct answer is choice a: The liability is first recognized in Year One even though payment is not made until Year Three.

Explanation:

The income is recognized in Year One so the related income tax expense should be recognized in that same period to conform to the matching principle. Because recognition of the income has been delayed for tax purposes, a deferred income tax liability is also reported in Year One to disclose the future payment. The income was earned in Year One according to U.S. GAAP so the related liability must be reported then as well.

3.2   The Installment Sales Method and Deferred Income Taxes

Question: Assume that the Hill Company buys an asset (land, for example) for $150,000. Later, this asset is sold for $250,000 during Year One. The earning process is substantially complete at that point. Hill reports a gain on its Year One income statement of $100,000 ($250,000 less $150,000). Because of the terms of the sales contract, this money will not be collected from the buyer until Year Five. The buyer is financially strong and should be able to pay at the required times. Hill's effective tax rate for this transaction is 30 percent.

Officials for Hill are pleased to recognize the $100,000 gain on this sale in Year One because it makes the company looks better. However, they prefer to wait as long as possible to pay the income tax especially since no cash has yet been collected. **How can the recognition of income for tax purposes be delayed, thereby creating the need to report a deferred income tax liability?**

Answer: According to U.S. GAAP, this $100,000 gain is recognized on Hill Company's income statement in Year One based on accrual accounting. The earning process is substantially complete and the amount to be collected can be reasonably estimated. However, if certain conditions are met, income tax laws permit taxpayers to report such gains using the installment sales method.[5] In simple terms, the installment sales method allows a seller to delay reporting a gain for tax purposes until cash is collected. In this illustration, no cash is received in Year One, so no taxable income is reported. The tax will be paid in Year Five when Hill collects the cash. Thus, as shown in Figure 15.10, the income is reported now on the financial statements but not until Year Five for tax purposes.

FIGURE 15.10 Year One—Comparison of Financial Reporting and Tax Reporting

Year One	Financial Accounting	Income Tax Return
Gain on Sale of Asset	$100,000 (accrual accounting)	0 (installment sales method)

The eventual tax to be paid on the gain will be $30,000 ($100,000 × 30 percent). How is this $30,000 reported in Year One if payment to the government is not required until Year Five?

- First, because of the matching principle, the income tax expense of $30,000 must be recorded in Year One. The $100,000 gain is reported on the income statement in that year; therefore, any related expense is recognized in the same period. That is the basic premise of the matching principle.

- Second, the $100,000 gain creates a temporary difference. The amount will become taxable when the cash is collected in Year Five. At that time, a tax payment of $30,000 is required. Accountants have long debated whether this liability is created when the income is earned (Year One) or when the payment is to be made (Year Five). Legally, the company does not owe any money to the government until the Year Five income tax return is filed. However, reporting guidance provided by U.S. GAAP holds that recognition of the gain in Year One is the event that creates the probable future sacrifice. Thus, the liability is recognized immediately; a deferred income tax liability must be reported.

Consequently, the adjusting entry shown in Figure 15.11 is prepared at the end of Year One so that both the expense and the liability are properly reported.

FIGURE 15.11   December 31, Year One—Recognition of Deferred Income Tax on Gain

| Income Tax Expense—Deferred | 30,000 | |
| Deferred Income Tax Liability | | 30,000 |

In Year Five, when the cash is received from the sale, Hill will report the $100,000 gain on its income tax return. The resulting $30,000 payment to the government eliminates the deferred income tax liability. However, as shown in Figure 15.11, the income tax expense was reported back in Year One when the original sale was recognized for financial reporting purposes.

TEST YOURSELF

Question:

A local business buys property for $80,000 and later sells it for $200,000. Payments will be collected equally over this year and the following three. The profit is recognized immediately for financial reporting purposes. For tax purposes, assume that this transaction qualified for use of the installment sales method. The business's effective tax rate is 20 percent. What amount of deferred income tax liability should this entity recognize as of December 31, Year One?

a. Zero

b. $18,000

c. $24,000

d. $30,000

Answer:

The correct answer is choice b: $18,000.

Explanation:

The company makes a profit of $120,000 ($200,000-$80,000). Using the installment sales method, the gain is taxed when cash is collected. Because 25 percent of the cash is collected in the first year, $30,000 of that profit (25 percent × $120,000) is recognized immediately for tax purposes. Only the remaining $90,000 ($120,000 less $30,000) is deferred until later years for tax purposes. At a rate of 20 percent, the deferred tax liability is $18,000 ($90,000 × 20 percent).

KEY TAKEAWAY

U.S. GAAP and the Internal Revenue Code are created by separate groups with different goals in mind. Consequently, many differences exist as to amounts and timing of income recognition. The management of a business will try to use these differences to postpone payment of income taxes so that the money can remain in use and generate additional profits. Although payment is not made immediately, the matching principle requires the income tax expense to be reported in the same time period as the related revenue. If payment is delayed, a deferred income tax liability is created that remains in the financial records until the income becomes taxable. One of the most common methods for deferring income tax payments is application of the installment sales method. For financial reporting purposes, any gain is recorded immediately as is the related income tax expense. However, according to tax laws, recognition of the profit can be delayed until cash is collected. In the interim, a deferred tax liability is reported to alert decision makers to the eventual payment that will be required.

4. REPORTING POSTRETIREMENT BENEFITS

LEARNING OBJECTIVES

At the end of this section, students should be able to meet the following objectives:

1. Define the term "postretirement benefits."
2. Explain the accounting problems associated with the recognition of accrued postretirement benefits.
3. List the steps that are followed to determine a company's reported obligation for postretirement benefits.
4. Identify the role of the actuary in accounting for postretirement benefits.
5. Calculate a company's debt-to-equity ratio and explain its meaning.
6. Calculate the times interest earned ratio and explain its meaning.

4.1 Liability for Postretirement Benefits

Question: *According to the information provided at the beginning of this chapter,* **Alcoa** *reported a $2.6 billion liability at the end of 2010 for accrued postretirement benefits.* **What constitutes a postretirement benefit?**

Answer: In a note to the 2010 financial statements, **Alcoa** explains part of this liability as follows:
"**Alcoa** also maintains health care and life insurance benefit plans covering eligible U.S. retired employees and certain retirees from foreign locations. Generally, the medical plans pay a percentage of medical expenses, reduced by deductibles and other coverages. These plans are generally unfunded, except for certain benefits funded through a trust. Life benefits are generally provided by insurance contracts. **Alcoa** retains the right, subject to existing agreements, to change or eliminate these benefits."

Postretirement benefits cover a broad array of promises that companies make to their employees to boost morale and keep them from seeking other jobs. According to this note disclosure, **Alcoa** provides two of the most common: health care insurance and life insurance. Based on stipulations as to eligibility, **Alcoa** helps its employees by paying a portion of these insurance costs even after they have retired. **Alcoa** apparently continues to provide these payments as a reward for years of employee service.

4.2 Determining a Liability for Postretirement Benefits

Question: *Assume that one of the employees for the Michigan Company is currently thirty-four years old and is entitled to certain postretirement benefits starting at the age of sixty-five. The company has promised to continue paying health care and life insurance premiums for all retirees as long as they live.[6] For this employee, no postretirement benefits will be paid for the next thirty-one years (65 less 34). After that, an unknown payment amount will begin and continue for an unknown period of time. In one of the opening chapters of this book, the challenge presented to accountants as a result of future uncertainty was discussed. Probably no better example of uncertainty can be found than postretirement benefits. Payments may continue for decades and neither their amount nor their duration is more than a guess.*

The employee is helping the company generate revenues currently so that, as always, the related expense should be recognized now according to the matching principle. Although this obligation might not be paid for many years, both the expense and related liability are recorded when the person is actually working for the company and earning these benefits.

How is the amount of this liability possibly determined? An employee might retire at sixty-five and then die at sixty-six or live to be ninety-nine. Plus, estimating the cost of insurance (especially medical insurance) over several decades into the future seems to be a virtually impossible challenge. The skyrocketing cost of health care is difficult to anticipate months in advance, let alone decades. The dollar amount of the company's obligation for these future costs appears to be a nebulous figure at best. In this textbook, previous liabilities have been contractual or at least subject to a reasonable estimation prior to recognition. **How is the liability calculated that will be reported by a company for the postretirement benefits promised to its employees?**

Answer: As shown by the **Alcoa** example, postretirement benefits are estimated and reported according to U.S. GAAP while employees work. Because of the length of time involved and the large number of variables (some of which, such as future health care costs, are quite volatile), a precise determination of this liability is impossible. In fact, this liability might be the most uncertain number found on any set of financial statements. Apparently, reporting a dollar amount for postretirement benefits, despite its inexactness, is more helpful than omitting the expense and liability entirely. However, decision makers need to understand that these reported balances are no more than approximations.

The actual computation and reporting of postretirement benefits is more complicated than can be covered adequately in an introductory financial accounting textbook. An overview of the basic steps, though, is useful in helping decision makers understand the information that is provided.

actuary

An individual who mathematically computes the likelihood of future events.

To arrive at the liability to be reported for postretirement benefits that are earned now but only paid after retirement, the Michigan Company takes two primary steps. First, an **actuary** calculates an estimation of the cash amounts that will eventually have to be paid as a result of the terms promised to employees. "An actuary is a business professional who analyzes the financial consequences of risk. Actuaries use mathematics, statistics, and financial theory to study uncertain future events, especially those of concern to insurance and pension programs."[7] In simpler terms, an actuary is a mathematical expert who computes the likelihood of future events.

To make a reasonable guess at the amount of postretirement benefits, the actuary has to make a number of difficult estimations such as the average length of time employees will live and the future costs of health care and life insurance (and any other benefits provided to retirees). For example, an actuary's calculations might indicate that these costs will average $10,000 per year for the twenty years that an employee is expected to live following retirement.

The future payments to be made by the company are estimated by an actuary, but they are projected decades into the future. Thus, as the second step in this process, the present value of these amounts is calculated to derive the figure to be reported currently on the balance sheet. Once again, as in previous chapters, interest for this period of time is determined mathematically and removed to leave just the principal of the obligation as of the balance sheet date. That is the amount reported by the employer within noncurrent liabilities.

Determining Accrued Postretirement Benefits
Step One: Estimate Future Payments
Step Two: Calculate Present Value of Estimated Future Payments

---

TEST YOURSELF

Question:

The Johnson Corporation hires 100 employees in Year One. At that time, the organization makes a promise to each of its employees. If they will work for Johnson for twenty years, the company will pay for the college education of all their children. At that time, none of the employees has a child who will start college until after the next six years. Which of the following statements is true?

a. The company should report an expense and a liability at the end of Year One.

b. The company should start reporting an expense and a liability after six years.

c. The company should start reporting an expense in Year One but no liability.

d. The company will never report this promise as an expense and a liability.

Answer:

The correct answer is choice a: The company should report an expense and a liability at the end of Year One.

Explanation:

Johnson Corporation has begun to incur an expected cost in connection with future benefits for its employees. The related expense should be recognized beginning in Year One because these employees are working to generate revenues. An actuary can estimate the eventual cost of this promise based on the amount of work performed to date. A present value computation will then be made to determine the amount of this expense and liability that are applicable to the first year.

4.3   The Consequences of Having to Report a Liability

Question: Alcoa recognizes an accrued postretirement benefit liability on its balance sheet of $2.6 billion. This number is the present value of the estimated amounts that the company will have to pay starting when each employee retires. Except for the inherent level of uncertainty, this accounting seems reasonable. At one time decades ago, companies were not required to recognize this obligation. The liability was ignored and costs were simply expensed as paid. Only after advanced computer technology and sophisticated mathematical formulas became available was the reporting of this liability mandated. **What is the impact of reporting postretirement benefits if the numbers can only be approximated?**

Answer: Organizations typically prefer not to report balances that appear to weaken the portrait of their economic health and vitality. However, better decisions are made by all parties when relevant information is readily available. Transparency is a primary goal of financial accounting. Arguments can be made that some part of the problems that many businesses currently face are the result of promises that were made over past decades where the eventual costs were not properly understood.

As the result of the evolution of U.S. GAAP, decision makers (both inside and outside the company) can now better see the costs associated with postretirement benefits. Not surprisingly, once disclosed, some companies opted to cut back on the amounts promised to retirees. The note disclosure quoted previously for **Alcoa** goes on further to say, "All U.S. salaried and certain hourly employees hired after January 1, 2002 are **not** eligible for postretirement health care benefits. All U.S. salaried and certain hourly employees that retire on or after April 1, 2008 are **not** eligible for postretirement life insurance benefits" (emphasis added).

For the employees directly impacted, these decisions may have been understandably alarming. However, by forcing the company to recognize this liability, U.S. GAAP has helped draw attention to the costs of making such promises.

TEST YOURSELF

Question:

On its most recent balance sheet, the Randle Company reports a noncurrent liability of $30 million as an accrued postretirement benefit obligation. Which of the following statements is least likely to be true?

a. The amount to be paid will be more than $30 million.

b. The company will have the $30 million in cash payments scheduled out at set times.

c. The $30 million figure is a culmination of a number of difficult estimations.

d. This liability could extend into the future for several decades.

Answer:

The correct answer is choice b: The company will have the $30 million in cash payments scheduled out at set times.

Explanation:

Postretirement benefits are amounts that a company will pay years into the future, often based on the life expectancy of retirees. After amounts are determined based on several estimates, cash payments are reduced to present value for reporting purposes. Because of the length of time involved, present value is often much less than the anticipated cash payments. Determination of the exact amount and timing of payments is subject to many variables that are not yet known such as life expectancy.

4.4 Vital Signs Studied in Connection with Liabilities

Question: In previous chapters, various vital signs have been examined—numbers, ratios, and the like—that assist decision makers in evaluating an entity's financial condition and future prospects. In connection with liabilities, do specific vital signs exist that are frequently relied on to help assess the economic health of a business or other organization?

debt-to-equity ratio

A measure of a company's use of debt for financing purposes; it is computed by dividing total liabilities by total stockholders' equity.

Answer: One vital sign that is often studied by decision makers is the **debt-to-equity ratio**. This figure is simply the total liabilities reported by a company divided by total stockholders' equity. The resulting number indicates whether most of a company's assets have come from borrowing and other debt or from its own operations and owners. A high debt-to-equity ratio indicates that a company is highly leveraged. As discussed previously, that raises the level of risk but also increases the possible profits earned by stockholders. Relying on debt financing makes a company more vulnerable to bankruptcy and other financial problems but also provides owners with the chance for higher financial rewards.

Recent debt-to-equity ratios presented in Figure 15.12 for several prominent companies show a wide range of results. No single financing strategy is evident here. The debt-to-equity ratio indicates a company's policy toward debt, but other factors are involved. For example, in some industries, debt levels tend to be higher than in others. Also, individual responses to the recent economic recession might have impacted some companies more than others.

FIGURE 15.12 Recent Debt-to-Equity Ratios for Several Prominent Companies

Company	Debt-to-Equity Ratio
Kellogg Company	4.50 to 1.00 (as of January 1, 2011)
J. C. Penney Company	1.39 to 1.00 (as of January 29, 2011)
Monsanto Company	0.76 to 1.00 (as of August 31, 2010)
The Walt Disney Company	0.76 to 1.00 (as of October 2, 2010)

Another method to evaluate the potential problem posed by a company's debts is to compute the **times interest earned (TIE)** ratio. Normally, debt only becomes a risk if interest cannot be paid when due. This calculation helps measure how easily a company has been able to meet its interest obligations through current operations.

Times interest earned begins with the company's net income before both interest expense and income taxes are removed (a number commonly referred to as "EBIT" or "earnings before interest and taxes"). Interest expense for the period is then divided into this income figure. For example, if EBIT is $500,000 and interest expense is $100,000, the reporting company earned enough during the year to cover the required interest obligations five times.

times interest earned (TIE)

A measure of a company's ability to meet obligations as they come due; it is computed by taking EBIT (earnings before interest and taxes) and dividing that number by interest expense for the period.

FIGURE 15.13   Recent Times Interest Earned for Several Prominent Companies

Company	Times Interest Earned
Kellogg Company	8.1 times (year ended January 1, 2011)
J. C. Penney Company	3.6 times (year ended January 29, 2011)
Monsanto Company	10.1 times (year ended August 31, 2010)
The Walt Disney Company	16.3 times (year ended October 2 , 2010)

TEST YOURSELF

Question:

The owners of a company contribute $100,000 to acquire its capital stock. Another $200,000 is borrowed from a bank. In its first year, the company earns a reported net income of $50,000. If the company then pays a cash dividend of $10,000, what is the impact of this distribution on the debt-to-equity ratio?

a. There is no effect on the debt-to-equity ratio.

b. It goes up. It was 1.33 to 1.00 and now is 1.43 to 1.00.

c. It goes down. It was 1.33 to 1.00 and now is 1.25 to 1.00.

d. It goes down. It was 1.43 to 1.00 and now is 1.33 to 1.00.

Answer:

The correct answer is choice b: It goes up. It was 1.33 to 1.00 and now is 1.43 to 1.00.

Explanation:

The company has one debt of $200,000. Before the dividend, stockholders' equity is $150,000 ($100,000 in contributed capital and $50,000 in retained earnings). The debt-to-equity ratio is $200,000/$150,000 or 1.33 to 1.00. The dividend reduces retained earnings (this portion of net income is distributed to stockholders rather than leaving the assets in the business) to $40,000. Stockholders' equity has dropped to $140,000. The debt-to-equity ratio is $200,000/$140,000 or 1.43 to 1.00.

KEY TAKEAWAY

Businesses and other organizations often promise benefits (such as health care and life insurance) to eligible employees to cover the years after they reach retirement age. Determining the liability balance to be reported at the current time poses a significant challenge for accountants because eventual payment amounts are so uncertain. An actuary uses historical data, computer programs, and statistical models to estimate these amounts. The present value of the projected cash payments is then calculated and recognized by the company as a noncurrent liability. The size of this debt can be quite large but the numbers are no more than approximations. Decision makers often analyze the level of a company's debt by computing the debt-to-equity ratio and the times interest earned ratio. Both of these calculations help decision makers evaluate the risk and possible advantage of the current degree of debt financing.

Talking with a Real Investing Pro (Continued)

Following is a continuation of our interview with Kevin G. Burns.

Question: Lease arrangements are quite common in today's business environment. For a capital lease, the present value of the future payments is reported by the lessee as a liability. In contrast, for an operating lease, only the amount currently due is included on the balance sheet as a liability. The reporting of such off-balance sheet financing has been criticized because businesses often go out of their way to create operating leases to minimize the total shown for their debts. However, information about these operating leases must be clearly disclosed in the notes to the financial statements. Are you concerned when you see a company with a lot of off-balance sheet financing? Would you prefer a system where companies had to report more of their debts from leasing arrangements? Do you believe off-balance sheet financing is a problem for the users of financial accounting information?

Kevin Burns: I hate off balance sheet financing. It is trickery in my opinion. As usual, I prefer full or even too much disclosure. A lease is a liability. It should be categorized as such. It is really quite simple—show the liability. Having information in the notes helps but liabilities should be reported on the balance sheet for all to see easily. Anything that reduces transparency is bad for the accounting industry and the people relying on reported financial information.

Obviously, I prefer for companies to have less debt. But, there are exceptions. I own a stake in a company that has a large building that has had a significant appreciation in value. Because they use that building, they cannot take advantage of that increase in value. I suggested to the management that they sell the building to get all of that money and then lease the building back so they could still use it. They would have to report the liability for the lease, but they get their money in a usable form right now, and they can remain in the building.

 ### Video Clip

Professor Joe Hoyle talks about the five most important points in Chapter 15.

View the video online at: http://bit.ly/hoyle15-2

5. END-OF-CHAPTER EXERCISES

1. The Ace Company buys a large piece of equipment, which it immediately leases to Zebra Corporation for five years. Which company is the lessor and which company is the lessee?

2. In simplest terms, what is an operating lease? In simplest terms, what is a capital lease?

3. On December 31, Year One, a company agrees to pay $100,000 per year for the next nine years to lease a large piece of machinery. The first payment is made when the contract is signed. If the contract qualifies as an operating lease, what appears on this company's balance sheet at December 31, Year One?

4. Use the information in question 3 to explain the term "off-balance sheet financing."

5. On December 31, Year One, a company agrees to pay a set amount each year for six years to lease a large truck for hauling purposes. The first payment is made when the contract is signed. If this contract qualifies as a capital lease, what appears on this company's balance sheet at December 31, Year One?

6. A five-year lease is signed. At the end of that time, the lessee can buy the leased asset for an amount of money that is viewed as a bargain. Why does this option make the contract a capital lease?

7. A lease is signed for property that has an expected life of ten years. The lease is for only eight years. Why does the length of this lease require the parties to record it as a capital lease?

8. How many of the four official criteria must be met to require capital lease accounting?

9. A company believes that its incremental borrowing rate is 7 percent. What is meant by the term "incremental borrowing rate?"

10. A company is negotiating to lease an asset for use in its business operations. Why will company officials attempt to structure the agreement as an operating lease rather than as a capital lease?

11. On January 1, Year One, the Atkins Corporation signs a four-year lease with the first payment made immediately. If this contract is an operating lease, what type of expense or expenses will be recognized at the end of Year One?

12. On January 1, Year One, the Carleton Company signs a five-year lease with the first payment made immediately. If this contract is a capital lease, what type of expense or expenses will be recognized at the end of Year One?

13. A company leases a building for eighteen years and records it as a capital lease. Why does the handling of this lease illustrate the desire of accountants to report substance over form?

14. The Marlento Company reports net income in Year One for financial reporting purposes of $983,000. However, when the company prepares its income tax return for Year One, taxable income is shown as only $536,000. In general, why are these two income totals different?

15. What is meant by the term "temporary tax difference?"

16. The Wyndsoki Corporation reports a gain of $3 million in Year One. For income tax purposes, the gain is not taxable until Year Four. Will company officials be happy with this delay? Why or why not?

17. The Lendmor Corporation earns income of $1.2 million in Year One before income taxes. However, by careful planning, all of this income has been deferred for tax purposes until Year Four. Assume that the tax rate is 30 percent. What adjusting entry, if any, is made for income taxes at the end of Year One?

18. The Astomori Corporation buys land for $300,000 in Year One and sells it for $400,000 in Year Two. The company collects half of this money in Year Three and the other half in Year Four. Assume that the tax rate is 30 percent. In what year is the income tax expense recognized on this gain? What journal entry or adjusting entry is used to record the income tax expense at the end of Year Two?

19. Jane Buenti-Jones is hired by the Cleveland Corporation. She is thirty years old. The company promises to pay her medical insurance while she works for the company and also after she retires. What is the accounting problem that the company faces here?

20. The Abraham Company informs all employees that their life insurance will be paid by the company each year after they retire. What must be done to determine the amounts to be reported on the company's financial statements in the current year?

21. What role does an actuary play in accounting for postretirement benefits?

22. What impact can the reporting of postretirement benefits have on company employees?

23. A financial analyst mentions that a certain company reports EBIT of $1.4 million. What does EBIT represent?

24. The James Company reports liabilities of $3.5 million and stockholders' equity of $2.0 million. Then, just before the end of the current year, the company pays off a long-term liability with $500,000 in cash. What was the impact of that payment on James Company's debt-to-equity ratio?

25. A company reports a number of figures on its income statement including rent expense of $600,000, interest expense of $500,000, and income tax expense of $400,000. The company's net income was shown as $1.8 million. Compute the times interest earned ratio for this company.

TRUE OR FALSE

1. _____ A lessee that is reporting the effects of a capital lease will record depreciation expense on the leased property.

2. _____ A capital lease is a common example of off-balance sheet financing.

3. _____ A lessee negotiates the lease of a piece of equipment. The lessee will likely attempt to structure the lease as an operating lease.

4. _____ A lease has been signed that meets only two of the four criteria for a capital lease. Thus, this transaction will be recorded as an operating lease.

5. _____ Lessees usually prefer to record leases as operating leases rather than capital leases.

6. _____ Depreciation and interest are both recorded by a lessee in connection with a capital lease, but not an operating lease.

7. _____ A lease is signed on December 31, Year One, that calls for annual payments of $20,000. The present value of these payments is $73,000. The lease is an operating lease. On its December 31, Year One, balance sheet, the company will record a liability of $53,000.

8. _____ A lease contract is for six years although the asset has an expected life of twelve years. The lessee can buy the asset at the end of six years for $14,000. The lease has to be recorded as a capital asset.

9. _____ On January 1, Year One, a lease is signed that is a capital lease. The cash payments are $10,000 per year starting on January 1, Year One. The present value of the cash flows before the first payment is $65,860. If the incremental borrowing rate is 10 percent, the lessee recognizes interest of $6,586 for the first year.

10. _____ A company's Year One income statement reports net income of $348,000. The company's taxable income for that same year will also be $348,000.

11. _____ If a gain is earned in Year One but taxed in Year Three, the related expense is reported in Year One.

12. _____ If a gain is earned in Year One but taxed in Year Three, a deferred tax liability is reported at the end of Year One.

13. _____ The deferral of income tax payments is viewed as a strategy for increasing reported net income.

14. _____ When using the installment sales method for tax purposes, gains are generally taxed when the sale is made.

15. _____ Postretirement benefits are not expensed until they are paid.

16. _____ The liability recorded for postretirement benefits reflects a factual number that is known by company officials.

17. _____ Because Melody Stuart works for a company this year, an expense will be recorded in connection with benefits that she will receive after her retirement in 2020.

18. _____ Companies work to reduce their debt-to-equity ratio because of the risk that this figure reflects.

19. _____ The computation of times interest earned is found by dividing interest expense for the period by the total amount of noncurrent liabilities.

MULTIPLE CHOICE

1. Wichita Corporation leases a large machine with a life of twenty years. Which of the following does not necessitate reporting this contract as a capital lease?

    a. The lease is only for sixteen years.

    b. At the end of the lease, Wichita can (but doesn't have to) buy the machine at an amount significantly below expected fair value.

    c. At the end of twelve years, title to the machine goes to Wichita.

    d. Wichita will pay a smaller amount each year over a lease life of fourteen years.

2. Sizemore Corporation leases a building to use for the next twenty years. Which of the following is true about Sizemore's reporting?

    a. If this contract is a capital lease, rent expense is recognized each period.

    b. If this contract is an operating lease, depreciation expense is recognized each period.

    c. If this contract is an operating lease, interest expense and rent expense are recognized each period.

    d. If this contract is a capital lease, depreciation expense and interest expense are recognized each period.

3. Albemarle Corporation leases a truck for six years and is trying to determine whether the contract qualifies as an operating lease or a capital lease. Which of the following is true?

    a. Albemarle will want the lease to be a capital lease because less interest is reported.

    b. Albemarle will want the lease to be a capital lease because less depreciation is reported.

    c. Albemarle will want the lease to be an operating lease because the reported liability will be lower.

    d. Albemarle will want the lease to be an operating lease because the reported asset balance will be larger.

4. Myers Company leases a boat on January 1, Year One. The lease does qualify as a capital lease. The lease covers four years, with payments of $20,000 annually, beginning on January 1, Year One. The expected life of the boat is six years. Myers annual incremental borrowing rate is 5 percent. The present value of an ordinary annuity for four years at a 5 percent rate is $3.54595. The present value of an annuity due for four years at a 5 percent rate is $3.72325. What amount of depreciation (rounded) should Myers recognize on the boat for Year One if Myers chooses to use the straight-line method?

    a. $12,411

    b. $13,616

    c. $17,730

    d. $18,616

5. Charlotte Company leases a piece of equipment on February 1. The lease covers two years although the life of the equipment is four years. The contract contains no bargain purchase option, the equipment does not transfer to Charlotte at the end of the lease, and the payments do not approximate the fair value of the equipment. The annual payments are $4,000 due each February 1, starting with the current one. Charlotte's incremental borrow rate is 5 percent. The present value of an annuity due of $1 at a 5 percent interest rate for two years is $1.95238. What journal entry or entries should Charlotte make on February 1?

    a. **FIGURE 15.14**

Leased Equipment	8,000	
Lease Liability		8,000
Lease Liability	4,000	
Cash		4,000

b. **FIGURE 15.15**

c. **FIGURE 15.16**

d. **FIGURE 15.17**

6. On December 31, Year One, the Brangdon Corporation leases a truck to use in its operations. The truck has a life of ten years, although the lease is only for six years. Payments are $10,000 per year with the first payment made immediately. No interest payments are made but Brangsdon has an incremental borrowing rate of 9 percent. The present value of an annuity due at a 9 percent rate for six periods is $4.88965. The present value of an ordinary annuity at a 9 percent rate for six periods is $4.48592. If this is an operating lease, what figure is recorded initially as the capitalized cost of the truck?

     a. Zero

     b. $38,897

     c. $44,859

     d. $48,897

7. On December 31, Year One, the Sliyvoid Corporation leases a large machine for five years, its entire expected life. Depreciation is recorded using the straight-line method. Payments are $12,000 per year starting on December 31, Year One, and every December 31 thereafter. The incremental borrowing rate is 10 percent per year. The present value of an annuity due at a 10 percent rate for five periods is $4.16987. The present value of an ordinary annuity at a 10 percent rate for five periods is $3.79079. What is the net book value of the leased asset on December 31, Year Two?

     a. $30,431

     b. $36,392

     c. $37,875

     d. $40,030

8. Use the same information as in problem 7. Determine the interest expense to be recognized in Year Two.

     a. $3,349

     b. $3,804

     c. $4,549

     d. $5,004

9. Use the same information as in problem 7. Determine the lease liability to be reported on the company's balance sheet at the end of Year Two.

     a. $24,838

    b. $29,842

    c. $38,038

    d. $43,042

10. On December 31, Year One, Company A leases a car for four years and pays $10,000 per year with the first payment made immediately. Company A believes the asset has a life of six years and records it as an operating lease. On December 31, Year One, Company B leases an identical car for four years and pays $10,000 per year with the first payment made immediately. Company B believes the asset has a life of five years and records it as a capital lease. The straight-line method of depreciation is used. Both companies have an annual incremental borrowing rate of 5 percent. The present value of an annuity due of $1 over four years at a 5 percent interest rate is $3.7232. Which of the following is true?

    a. Company B will report more expense in Year Two than Company A by $670.

    b. Company B will report more expense in Year Two than Company A by $1,120.

    c. Company A will report more expense in Year Two than Company B by $840.

    d. Company A will report more expense in Year Two than Company B by $1,250.

11. Potslitini Corporation has a large amount of income that is earned in Year One but will not be subject to income taxes until Year Three. Which of the following statements is true for financial reporting purposes?

    a. The income tax expense is reported when the income appears on the company's income tax return.

    b. The income tax expense is reported when the tax money is physically paid to the government.

    c. The income tax expense is reported in Year One when the income is earned.

    d. The income tax expense can only be reported in this problem in Year Three.

12. Fargo Corporation earns revenue in Year One that will be reported on its Year One income statement but will not be reported on its tax return until Year Three. This revenue amounts to $800,000, and Fargo's tax rate is 40 percent. Which of the following statements is true?

    a. Fargo should report a deferred tax liability of $800,000 at the end of Year One.

    b. Fargo should not recognize any deferred tax liability until Year Three.

    c. Fargo should report a deferred tax liability of $320,000 at the end of Year One.

    d. Fargo should recognize a deferred tax liability when the payment is eventually paid.

13. The Sinson Company buys land in Year One for $90,000 and then sells it in Year Two for $200,000. The company will collect this money in Year Four. For income tax purposes, Sinson will use the installment sales method. Sinson has a tax rate of 40 percent. Which of the following statements is true?

    a. Sinson records an income tax expense of $36,000 in Year Two.

    b. Sinson records an income tax expense of $80,000 in Year Four.

    c. Sinson records a deferred income tax liability of $44,000 at the end of Year Two.

    d. Sinson records a deferred income tax liability of $80,000 at the beginning of Year Four.

14. Which of the following is **not** a true statement about postretirement benefits?

    a. A company's liability for postretirement benefits is quite difficult to estimate.

    b. An expense for an employee's future postretirement benefits should be recognized during the period the employee helps generate revenue.

    c. The liability for postretirement benefits is reported at its present value.

    d. The liability reported for postretirement benefits represents the actual amount that will have to be paid.

15. At the start of Year One, the Arkansas Company promises all employees that it will pay their medical insurance after they retire. As a result, company officials realize that a liability will have to be reported. This promise is expected to cost the company a total cash amount of $3.3 million over the next 30 years. Who most likely determined this figure?

    a. An attorney.

    b. An insurance agent.

    c. An actuary.

    d. The head of the employee group.

16. Use the information in problem 15. What liability does Arkansas have to report at the end of Year One?

    a. $3.3 million

    b. $110,000

c. The present value of $3.3 million

d. Zero

17. On its latest balance sheet, the Sellers Corporation reports assets of $450,000 and liabilities of $200,000. What is Sellers' debt-to-equity ratio?

   a. 0.44 to 1.00

   b. 0.80 to 1.00

   c. 1.25 to 1.00

   d. 2.25 to 1.00

18. The Xi Company is started at the beginning of Year One when its owners contribute $120,000 in cash. The company reports net income of $70,000 and pays cash dividends of $10,000 every year thereafter. At the end of Year Three, the company reports total assets of $900,000. On that date, what is the debt-to-equity ratio?

   a. 1.00 to 1.00

   b. 2.00 to 1.00

   c. 3.00 to 1.00

   d. 3.33 to 1.00

19. A company has a debt-to-equity ratio of 3.00 to 1.00. The company pays a cash dividend of $62,000. What is the impact on the debt-to-equity ratio?

   a. The debt-to-equity ratio will increase.

   b. The debt-to-equity ratio will decrease.

   c. The debt-to-equity ratio will not be affected.

   d. No determination of the impact on the debt-to-equity ratio can be made with the information provided.

20. Hyde Corporation has long-term liabilities, such as bonds, notes and leases, for which interest expense must be accrued. During Year One, Hyde reported net income of $65,000 after income taxes of $15,000 and interest expense of $10,000. Which of the following is Hyde's times interest earned?

   a. 6.5 times

   b. 7.5 times

   c. 8.0 times

   d. 9.0 times

VIDEO PROBLEMS

Professor Joe Hoyle discusses the answers to these two problems at the links that are indicated. After formulating your answers, watch each video to see how Professor Hoyle answers these questions.

1. Your roommate is an English major. The roommate's parents own a chain of ice cream shops located throughout Florida. One day, while walking over to the computer lab your roommate poses this question: "My parents just signed a contract to lease a new shop in Tampa. It is in a great location so they are going to pay $120,000 each year to lease this facility for 10 years. That's $1.2 million. However, they were telling me that they will not have to report this liability on their financial statements. That makes no sense to me. They have a contract that requires them to pay over $1 million in the future. How could they possibly not have to report that as a liability?" How would you respond?

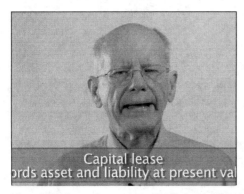

View the video online at: http://bit.ly/hoyle15-3

2. Your uncle and two friends started a small office supply store several years ago. The company has grown and now has several large locations. Your uncle knows that you are taking a financial accounting class and asks you the following question: "We always want to make sure that our financial statements and our tax returns are done properly. Several years ago we bought some land and built a store on it. However, we didn't use all the land, so this year we sold several extra acres. The land had really appreciated in value, and we made a very large gain. We made the sale this year, but the payments will not start for a couple of years. Our accountant tells us that we have to report the related income tax expense this year, but we don't have to pay the government anything until we start getting the money. That doesn't sound right. It seems to me that the expense and the payment should be at the same time. Can you explain what is going on here because I really don't want to get into any trouble?" How would you respond?

View the video online at: http://bit.ly/hoyle15-4

PROBLEMS

1. On October 1, Year One, United Company leases an office space in a downtown building. This contract qualifies as an operating lease. United pays $30,000 in advance for rent every year. Record journal entries and adjusting entries for United for the following dates in connection with this property.

    a. October 1, Year One.

    b. December 31, Year One.

    c. September 30, Year Two.

2. Ralph Corporation agreed to lease a piece of equipment to Amy Company on January 1, Year One. The following information relates to this lease:

    ■ The lease term is five years, at the end of which time the equipment will revert back to Ralph. The life of the equipment is expected to be six years.

    ■ Payments of $90,000 will be due at the beginning of each year, with the first payment to be made at the signing of the lease.

    ■ Amy's incremental borrowing rate is 8 percent. The present value of a single payment of $1 in five years at an annual interest rate of 8 percent is $0.68058. The present value of an ordinary annuity of $1 for five years at an annual interest rate of 8 percent is $3.99271. The present value of an annuity due of $1 for five years at an annual interest rate of 8 percent is $4.31213.

        Prepare the following journal entries for Amy.

        a. Record the signing of the lease on January 1, Year One.

        b. Record the first payment on January 1, Year One.

        c. Record depreciation on the equipment on December 31, Year One.

        d. Record interest on the liability on December 31, Year One.

        e. Record the second payment on January 1, Year Two.

3. On January 1, Year One, Landon Corporation decides to lease a truck for $20,000 per year for three years. The annual incremental borrowing rate for Landon is 10 percent. The truck has a life of five years. Landon cannot buy or obtain title to the truck. The present value of an annuity due of $1 for three years at an annual interest rate of 10 percent is $2.73554. At the last moment, Landon changes the contract to four years instead of three. No other changes are made. The present value of an annuity due of $1 for four years at an annual interest rate of 10 percent is $3.48685.

    a. How did the change from three years to four years affect the expense to be reported by Landon in Year One?

    b. How did the change from three years to four years affect the expense to be reported by Landon in Year Two?

    c. After changing the contract to four years, what net book value will be shown for the leased truck at the end of Year One?

    d. After changing the contract to four years, what lease liability balance will be shown at the end of Year One?

4. On December 31, Year One, the Abertion Company decides to lease a piece of equipment rather than buy it. The lease is for 10 years. Payments are $22,000 each December 31 beginning on December 31, Year One. Abertion has an annual incremental borrowing rate of 9 percent. The present value of an annuity due of $1 at 9 percent for 10 periods is $6.99525.

    a. Assume this lease is an operating lease. What journal entries are made in Year One and Year Two?

    b. Assume this lease is an operating lease. What is shown on the company's balance sheet at the end of Year Two?

    c. Assume this lease is a capital lease. What journal entries are made in Year One and Year Two?

    d. Assume this lease is a capital lease. What is shown on the company's balance sheet at the end of Year Two?

5. The Addams Corporation is preparing to lease several large pieces of equipment. The president has asked the company's accountant to respond to the following questions about lease accounting.

    a. How will Addams know if the lease is an operating lease or a capital lease?

    b. What is meant by off-balance sheet financing? How does off-balance sheet financing relate to the reporting of leases?

    c. Why is a discussion of substance over form often heard in connection with the financial reporting of a capital lease?

6. On January 1, Year One, Lori Inc. signed a five-year capital lease for the use of an asset. Payments are $5,000 on each January 1, beginning with Year One. Lori's incremental borrowing rate is 6 percent. The present value of an annuity due of $1 at 6 percent for 5 periods is $4.46511.

   a. Determine Lori's interest expense for Year One.

   b. Assume Lori's reported earnings for Year One before interest and taxes are $18,224. Determine Lori's times interest earned.

   c. Assume that on January 1, Year One, before signing this lease agreement, Lori reported assets of $500,000 and liabilities of $220,000. What impact did signing this contract have on the company's debt-to-equity ratio?

7. At December 30, Year One, the Eighorn Corporation has net income (and taxable income) of $400,000. The company has an effective tax rate of 30 percent. Taxes have not yet been recorded. Then, on the last day of the year, the company sells land that it bought several years ago for $70,000. The sales price is $300,000. The money will be collected in Year Three. The company opts to use the installment sales method to report this transaction for tax purposes.

   a. What does the company now report as its net income for Year One?

   b. When is the liability for the income tax on the gain on the sale of the land reported? Why is this timing appropriate?

8. The Yellow Corporation reports a deferred income tax liability of $732,000 in its December 31, Year One, balance sheet.

   a. Why are differences created between a company's reported net income and the taxable income figure shown on its income tax return?

   b. What is meant by the term "temporary tax difference"?

   c. In general, what is the meaning of a deferred income tax liability?

   d. In analyzing a company, liabilities are generally viewed as a negative. Why do company officials attempt to create deferred income tax liabilities?

9. The Greene Company has net income before income tax expense of $300,000 in Year One. However, because of differences between U.S. GAAP and the tax laws, only 60 percent of this income is taxed in Year One (to be paid on March 15, Year Two). Another 30 percent will be taxed in Year Two and the final 10 percent will be taxed in Year Nine. Assume the effective tax rate is 25 percent.

   a. What adjusting entry is recorded at the end of Year One?

   b. What amount of net income should be reported by Greene Company for Year One?

10. The Bleu Company reports a liability for "postretirement benefits" of $14 million on its December 31, Year One, balance sheet.

   a. Explain how this obligation was created.

   b. In determining this liability of $14 million, company officials worked their way through two steps. Describe those two steps.

   c. Some companies might argue that this liability should not be reported on a balance sheet. What argument would they use for this position?

11. Myrtle Inc. begins Year One with liabilities of $456,000 and stockholders' equity of $320,000. On the first day of Year One, the following occur:

   - Myrtle enters into an operating lease where it agrees to pay $50,000 per month for warehouse space. The contract is signed, and the first payment is made.
   - Myrtle borrows $103,000 in cash from Community Bank.
   - Several owners invest a total of $57,000 in cash into the company.

   a. Determine Myrtle's debt-to-equity ratio before the above transactions occur.

   b. Determine Myrtle's debt-to-equity ratio considering the effect of the above transactions.

12. In several past chapters, we met Heather Miller, who started her own business, Sew Cool. The following are the financial statements for December.

FIGURE 15.18 Sew Cool Financial Statements

Sew Cool
Income Statement
As of December 31, 20X8

Revenue	$4,000
Cost of Goods	(2,000)
Gross Profit	2,000
Other Expenses	(1,665)
Earnings before Interest and Tax	335
Interest Expense	(30)
Earnings before Tax	305
Tax Expense	(107)
Net Income	$198

FIGURE 15.19

Sew Cool
Stmt. of Retained Earnings
As of December 31, 20X8

Retained Earnings, December 1, 20X8	$500
Net Income	198
Dividends	(158)
Retained Earnings, December 31, 20X8	$540

FIGURE 15.20

Sew Cool
Balance Sheet
December 31, 20X8

Assets		Liabilities	
Current		**Current**	
Cash	$940	Accounts Payable	$900
Accounts Receivable	500	Income Tax Payable	120
Less Allowance for			
Doubtful Accounts	(20)		
Net Accounts Receivable	480		
Inventory	700		
Total Current Assets	$2,120	Total Current Liabilities	$1,020
Noncurrent		**Noncurrent**	
Equipment	$1,000	Notes Payable	$1,060
		Owners' Equity	
		Capital Stock	$500
		Retained Earnings	540
		Total Owners' Equity	$1,040
		Total Liabilities & Owners'	
Total Assets	$3,120	Equity	$3,120

Based on the financial statements determine the following:

   a. Debt-to-equity ratio.
   b. Times interest earned.

COMPREHENSIVE PROBLEM

This problem will carry through several chapters, building in difficulty. It allows students to continually practice skills and knowledge learned in previous chapters.

In Chapter 14, financial statements for February were prepared for Webworks, They are included here as a starting point for the required recording for March.

FIGURE 15.21 Webworks Financial Statements

Webworks Income Statement As of February 28	
Revenue	$19,800
Cost of Goods Sold	(10,201)
Gross Profit	9,599
Deprec. and Amort. Expense	(455)
Other Expenses and Losses	(3,760)
Investment Income (Loss)	(175)
Earnings before Interest and Tax	5,209
Interest Expense	(15)
Earnings before Tax	5,194
Tax Expense	(1,558)
Net Income	$3,636

FIGURE 15.22

Webworks Stmt. of Retained Earnings As of February 28	
Retained Earnings, February 1	$14,613
Net Income	3,636
Retained Earnings, February 28	$18,249

FIGURE 15.23

Webworks Balance Sheet February 28				
Assets			**Liabilities**	
Current			**Current**	
Cash	$4,767		Accounts Payable	$2,360
Accounts Receivable	1,800		Salaries Payable	220
Less Allowance for			Interest Payable	15
Doubtful Accounts	(180)		Unearned Revenue	600
Net Accounts Receivable	1,620			
Trading Securities, Net	1,600			
Merchandise Inventory	2,682			
Supplies Inventory	70			
Prepaid Rent	200			
Total Current Assets	$10,939		Total Current Liabilities	$3,195
Property, Plant, and Equipment			**Noncurrent**	
			Note Payable	$3,000
Equipment	$12,500			
Less Accumulated Depreciation	(1,260)			
Furniture	1,000			
Less Accumulated Depreciation	(85)			
Total P, P, and E	$12,155			
Other Noncurrent Assets			**Owners' Equity**	
Available for Sale Securities	$2,100		Capital Stock	$2,000
Licensing Agreement, Net	1,600		Retained Earnings	18,249
			Other Accumulated Comprehensive Income:	
			Unrealized Gain on Available for Sale Securities	350
			Total Owners' Equity	$20,599
			Total Liabilities & Owners' Equity	
Total Assets	$26,794		Equity	$26,794

The following events occur during March:

a. Webworks starts and completes seven more sites and bills clients for $5,000.

b. Webworks purchases supplies worth $110 on account.

c. At the beginning of March, Webworks had nineteen keyboards costing $118 each and twenty flash drives costing $22 each. Webworks uses periodic FIFO to cost its inventory.

d. On account, Webworks purchases eighty keyboards for $120 each and one hundred flash drives for $23 each.

e. Webworks sells eighty-five keyboards for $12,750 and ninety-two of the flash drives for $2,760 cash.

f. Webworks collects $5,000 in accounts receivable.

g. Webworks pays off $12,000 of its accounts payable.

h. Leon Jackson (the company's owner) determines that some of his equipment is not being used and sells it. The equipment sold originally cost $2,000 and had accumulated depreciation of $297. Webworks sold the equipment for $1,650 cash.

i. Webworks pays Nancy Po (company employee) $750 for her work during the first three weeks of March.

j. Leon Jackson and Nancy Po are having trouble completing all their work now that the business has grown. Another assistant, Juan Marcon, is hired. Webworks pays Juan $550 for his help during the first three weeks of March.

k. Webworks writes off an account receivable from December in the amount of $200 because collection appears unlikely.

l. Webworks pays off its salaries payable from March.

m. Webworks pays Leon Jackson a salary of $3,500.

n. Webworks completes the design for the bakery but not the photographer for which it was paid in February. Only $300 of the unearned revenue should be reclassified to revenue.

o. Webworks decides that more space is needed than that which is available in the home of Leon's parents (much to his parents' relief). His parents return the $200 he prepaid for March. Webworks signs a six-month lease in a nearby office building. Webworks will pay $500 at the beginning of each month, starting on March 1. The life of the building is forty years, and no bargain purchase option exists, nor do the payments come close to paying the market value of the space.

p. Webworks pays taxes of $580 in cash.

> *Required:*
>
> A. Prepare journal entries for the previous events.
>
> B. Post the journal entries to T-accounts.
>
> C. Prepare an unadjusted trial balance for Webworks for March.
>
> D. Prepare adjusting entries for the following and post them to your T-accounts.

q. Webworks owes Nancy $200 and Juan $150 for their work during the last week of March.

r. Webworks receives an electric bill for $400. Webworks will pay the bill in April.

s. Webworks determines that it has $50 worth of supplies remaining at the end of March.

t. Webworks is continuing to accrue bad debts at 10 percent of accounts receivable.

u. Webworks continues to depreciate its equipment over four years and its furniture over five years, using the straight-line method.

v. The license agreement should be amortized over its one-year life.

w. QRS Company is selling for $13 per share and RST Company is selling for $18 per share on March 31.

x. Interest should be accrued for March.

y. Record cost of goods sold.

> E. Prepare an adjusted trial balance.
>
> F. Prepare financial statements for March.

RESEARCH ASSIGNMENT

Assume that you take a job as a summer employee for an investment advisory service. One of the partners for that firm is currently looking at the possibility of investing in **SuperValu Inc.** The partner is aware that **Super-Valu** uses a lot of stores and, therefore, probably has to lease many of those sites. The partner is curious as to whether these leases are mostly capital leases or operating leases. The partner asks you to look at the 2011 financial statements for **SuperValu** by following this path:

- Go to http://www.supervalu.com.
- At the top right side of this screen, click on "About Us."
- On the right side of the next screen, click on "Investors."
- On the right side of the next screen, click on "Annual Report and Proxy Statement."
- On the next screen, click on "2011 Annual Report on 10K" to download.
- Scroll to page 36 and find the company's balance sheet as of February 26, 2011. Look at the liability section of the balance sheet and see what information is reported about "capital lease obligations."
- Scroll down to "Note 6 – Long-Term Debt" and "Note 7 – Leases." They begin on page 47. Read through the information that is provided.

a. As of the balance sheet date, what is the company reporting as its "capital lease obligations?"
b. In the future, how much cash will the company have to pay on its operating leases?
c. In the future, how much cash will the company have to pay on its capital lease obligations?

ENDNOTES

1. As explained in upper-level accounting textbooks, under certain circumstances, the lessee might use the implicit interest rate built into the lease contract by the lessor.

2. On an Excel spreadsheet, the present value of a $1 per period annuity due for seven periods at an assumed annual interest rate of 10 percent is computed by typing the following data into a cell: =PV(.10,7,1,,1).

3. Matthew Calderisi, senior editor, Accounting Trends & Techniques, 63rd edition (New York: American Institute of Certified Public Accountants, 2009), 279.

4. Many companies also report deferred income tax assets that arise because of other differences in U.S. GAAP and the Internal Revenue Code. For example, Southwest Airlines included a deferred income tax asset of $214 million on its December 31, 2010, balance sheet. Accounting for such assets is especially complex and will not be covered in this textbook. Some portion of this asset balance, although certainly not all, is likely to be the equivalent of a prepaid income tax where Southwest was required to make payments by the tax laws in advance of recognition according to U.S. GAAP.

5. The installment sales method can also be used for financial reporting purposes but only under very limited circumstances.

6. Health care and life insurance benefits paid by an employer while an employee is still working do not pose an accounting issue. The costs are known and can be expensed as incurred. These expenses are matched with the revenues being generated by the employees at the current time.

7. http://www.math.purdue.edu/academic/actuary/what.php?p=what.

In a Set of Financial Statements, What Information Is Conveyed about Shareholders' Equity?

 Video Clip

In this video, Professor Joe Hoyle introduces the essential points covered in Chapter 16.

View the video online at: http://bit.ly/hoyle16-1

1. SELECTING A LEGAL FORM FOR A BUSINESS

1.1 Creating a Corporation

Question: In the United States, businesses and other organizations must operate as one of three legal forms.[1] *A* **proprietorship** *has a single owner whereas a* **partnership** *is started and owned by two or more parties. In both of these cases, establishing the business is often an unstructured process. For example, a partnership can be created by a mere handshake or other informal agreement.*

The third legal form of organization is a **corporation**, *which is brought into existence by means of a formal request made to a state government. Incorporation creates a separate entity, one that is owned by a group of stockholders. The number of owners is usually not relevant in the operation of a corporation. Because corporations are the dominant legal form (at least monetarily) in the United States, they have been the primary emphasis throughout this text. Numerically, more proprietorships and partnerships do exist but virtually every business of any size operates as a corporation.* **How is a corporation established, and what characteristics make it attractive?**

Answer: Organizers only need to satisfy the incorporation process in one state regardless of their entity's size. To start, they submit articles of incorporation to that government along with any other necessary information.[2] Rules, regulations, and requirements vary significantly so that these procedures are more complicated in some states than others. For example, many well-known businesses are incorporated in Delaware because of the traditional ease of the laws in that state.

After necessary documents have been filed and all other requirements met, the state government issues a corporate charter that recognizes the organization as a legal entity separate from its owners. This separation of the business from its owners is what differentiates a corporation from a partnership or proprietorship. Following incorporation in one state, the entity is then allowed to operate in any other state.

As mentioned in an earlier chapter, ownership of a corporation is physically represented by shares of stock that are issued to raise funds. In general, these shares are referred to as capital stock and the owners as shareholders or stockholders. For example, by December 31, 2010, **Nucor Corporation** had issued approximately 375 million of these shares to its stockholders. Unless restricted contractually, capital stock can be exchanged freely. After being issued by a corporation, shares can be resold dozens or even hundreds of times. Operations are usually unaffected by these ownership changes. Information about the current market price of most stocks as well as considerable other information about thousands of businesses can be found at sites such as http://www.google.com/finance and http://www.yahoo.com/finance.

Thus, a corporation is able to continue in existence even after owners die or decide to switch to other investments. In partnerships and proprietorships, capital stock does not exist. Consequently, transfer of an ownership interest is much more complicated. Partnerships and proprietorships often operate only for as long as the original owners are willing and able to continue being actively involved.

---

proprietorship

A business created, owned, and operated by a single individual; business is not legally separate from its owner; it is also referred to as a sole proprietorship.

partnership

An unincorporated business created, owned, and operated by more than one individual; the business is not legally separate from its owners.

corporation

An organization that has been formally recognized by the state government as a separate legal entity so that it can sell ownership shares to raise money for capital expenditures and operations.

As a result of the legal separation of ownership and business, shareholders have no personal liability for the debts of the corporation.[3] An owner of a share of **Nucor Corporation** is not responsible for any of the liabilities of that company. Thus, the maximum loss a shareholder can suffer is the amount contributed to the corporation (or paid to a previous owner) in acquiring capital stock. The **limited liability** offered by a corporation is one of the primary reasons for its popularity.

In contrast, the owners of a partnership or proprietorship are liable personally for all business debts. No separation exists between the business and ownership. For example, a partner or proprietor could invest $1,000 but wind up losing almost any amount of money if funds are borrowed by the business that cannot be repaid. Such potential losses are especially worrisome in a partnership because of the legal concept of **mutual agency** where each partner serves as an agent for the entire organization. Thus, a partner can obligate the partnership and, if the debt is not paid when due, the creditor can seek redress from any partner. This possibility of unlimited losses typically restricts the number of potential investors because most people have a strong preference for being able to quantify the amount of risk they face.

1.2 The Double Taxation of Corporations

Question: Ownership shares of most corporations can be transferred. Thus, the life of an incorporated business can extend indefinitely as one owner leaves and another arrives. **Caswell-Massey Co.** *is a perfect example. It has been in operation now for over 250 years. According to the corporate Web site (http://www.caswellmassey.com/about/about.aspx), "Before there was the United States of America, there was* **Caswell-Massey***, the original purveyor of the finest personal care products and accessories and America's oldest operating retailer. The company was founded in Newport, Rhode Island, by Scottish-born Dr. William Hunter in 1752."*

Investors are able to move into and out of corporate investments quickly. In addition, the availability of limited liability restricts potential losses to the amounts invested. These characteristics help explain the immense popularity of the corporate form in the United States. However, a significant number of partnerships and proprietorships continue to be created each year. If no problems existed, incorporation would be the only practical option. **What disadvantages are associated with the corporation form?**

Answer: Incorporation is often a time-consuming and costly legal process. However, in most states, proprietorships and partnerships can be created informally with little effort. Owners of many small businesses may feel that the creation of a corporation is more trouble than it is worth. Furthermore, corporations are often more susceptible to a plethora of government regulations.

The most obvious problem associated with corporations is the **double taxation** of income. As noted, proprietorships and partnerships are not deemed to be separate entities. Therefore, the owners (but not the business) must pay a tax when any income is generated. However, the income is taxed only that one time when earned by the business.

For a proprietorship, Form 1040 Schedule C is an income statement attached to the owner's individual income tax return to include the business's profit or loss. A partnership does file its own tax return on Form 1065, but that is merely for information purposes; no income tax is paid. Instead, the various business revenues and expenses are assigned to the partners for inclusion on their individual tax returns. Any eventual conveyance of this income from the business to the owner does not create a second tax.

In contrast, as separate legal entities, corporations pay their own taxes by reporting all taxable income on Form 1120.[4] However, when any dividends are eventually distributed from those earnings, this transfer is also viewed as taxable income to the stockholders. Income is taxed once when earned by the corporation and again when distributed to the owners. Critics have long argued that the conveyance of the dividend is not a new earning process. To mitigate the impact of this second tax, the U. S. Congress has established a maximum tax rate of 15 percent on much of the dividend income collected by individuals. This rate is considerably lower than that applied to most other types of income (such as salaries). Whether that reduced tax rate for dividends should continue at 15 percent or be raised or lowered is the subject of intense political debate.

To illustrate, assume that income tax rates are 30 percent except for the 15 percent tax on dividends. A proprietorship (or partnership) earns a profit of $100. For this type business, the $100 is only taxable to the owner or owners when earned. Payment of the resulting $30 income tax ($100 × 30 percent) leaves $70 as the remaining disposal income. Any distribution of this money to an owner has no impact on taxes. The government has collected $30.

If a corporation reports income of $100, a tax of $30 is assessed to the business so that only $70 remains. This residual amount can then be conveyed to owners as a dividend. However, if distributed, another tax must be paid, this time by the stockholder. The second income tax is $70 times 15 percent, or $10.50. The owner is left with only $59.50 ($70.00 less $10.50) in disposal income. The government

---

limited liability

A legal characteristic associated with the ownership of a corporation whereby the maximum amount of money that can be lost is the owner's capital investment; an attribute of a corporation that does not exist with the ownership of proprietorships or partnerships.

mutual agency

A characteristic of a partnership whereby any partner can obligate other partners to an agreement without their direct consent; does not have a parallel in corporate ownership.

double taxation

A negative feature associated with the corporate form; corporate earnings are taxed when earned by the business and then taxed again when distributed to owners in the form of dividends.

has collected a total of $40.50 ($30.00 plus $10.50). The increase in the amount taken by the government is significant enough to reduce the inclination of many owners to incorporate their businesses.

TEST YOURSELF

Question:

James Erskine and Pamela White are starting a new business. They are trying to determine whether to go to the trouble of incorporating or simply shake hands to form a partnership. Which of the following is a reason to create a partnership?

a. Partnerships can raise large amounts of money more easily than corporations.

b. Partnerships offer limited liability for their owners.

c. Partnerships are not subject to double taxation of income.

d. Partnerships are more likely to have a continuous life than a corporation.

Answer:

The correct answer is choice c: Partnerships are not subject to double taxation of income.

Explanation:

Because ownership of a corporation is viewed as separate from the business, capital shares can be issued to raise money—often large sums. These shares allow frequent changes in ownership that provides an easy way for a business to exist beyond the life of the original owners. Corporations provide only limited liability for their owners, a major reason for their popularity. However, partnerships are not subject to the same double taxation effect as corporations. The owners save money.

KEY TAKEAWAY

Legally, businesses can be created to function as corporations, partnerships, or sole proprietorships. Corporations are formed by meeting the legal requirements of an individual state. In contrast, partnerships and proprietorships can be started with little formal activity. A corporation differs from these other two forms because it is an entity legally separate from its ownership. Because of that separation, the maximum possible loss for the stockholders in a corporation is limited to the amount invested. Without that separation, owners of a partnership or proprietorship face the risk of unlimited liability. Ownership shares of a corporation (capital stock) are issued to raise money for operations and growth. In many cases, these shares can be readily sold by one owner to the next, often on a stock exchange. The ability to buy and sell capital shares enables a corporation to raise funds and have a continuous life. Disadvantages associated with the corporate form include the cost and difficulty of incorporation and government regulation. The double taxation of corporate income (which is not found with partnerships and sole proprietorships) is often the biggest drawback to incorporation. This second tax effect results because dividends are taxed to the recipients, although a reduced rate is often applied.

2.   THE ISSUANCE OF COMMON STOCK

LEARNING OBJECTIVES

At the end of this section students should be able to meet the following objectives:

1. **Identify the legal rights normally held by the owners of a corporation's common stock.**
2. **Describe the responsibilities of a board of directors.**
3. **Explain the terms "authorized," "outstanding," "issued," and "par value" in relation to common stock.**
4. **Record the issuance of common stock for cash.**
5. **Record the issuance of common stock for a service or for an asset other than cash.**

2.1   Common Stock

*Question: Several accounts frequently appear in the shareholders' equity section of a balance sheet reported by a corporation. Each has its own particular meaning. For example, as of January 1, 2011, the **Kellogg Company** reported the information shown in Figure 16.1 (all numbers in millions).*

FIGURE 16.1   Shareholders' Equity—Kellogg Company as of January 1, 2011

Common stock, $0.25 par value, 1,000,000,000 shares authorized; Issued: 419,272,027 in 2010	$105
Capital in excess of par value	495
Retained earnings	6,122
Treasury stock at cost; 53,667,635 shares	(2,650)
Accumulated other comprehensive income (loss)	(1,914)
Total Kellogg Company equity	$2,158

Some of the terms shown in Figure 16.1 have been examined previously, others have not.

- *For example, "retained earnings" was described in earlier chapters as the increase in net assets generated as net income over the life of a business less any amounts distributed as dividends during that same period.*

- *In the earlier discussion of investments in available for sale securities, "accumulated other comprehensive income" was introduced because this balance sheet category reflected unrealized changes in fair value. For those investments, gains and losses caused by the rise and fall of stock prices are not included within net income. Rather, they are reported within this section of stockholders' equity.*

Common stock *has also been mentioned in connection with the capital contributed to a corporation by its owners. As can be seen in Figure 16.1, **Kellogg** communicates additional information about its common stock such as the number of authorized and issued shares as well as par value. **What is common stock?** Answering this question seems a logical first step in analyzing the information provided by a company about its capital shares.*

Answer: Common stock represents the basic ownership of a corporation. One survey found that common stock is the only type of capital stock issued by approximately 90 percent of corporations.[5] Obtaining shares of a company's common stock provides several distinct rights. However, the specific rights are set by the laws of the state of incorporation and do vary a bit from state to state, although the following are typical.[6]

common stock

A type of capital stock that is issued by every corporation; it provides rights to the owner that are specified by the laws of the state in which the organization is incorporated.

board of directors

A group that oversees the management of a corporation; the members are voted to this position by stockholders; it hires the management to run the company on a daily basis and then meets periodically to review operating, investing, and financing results and also to approve policy and strategy.

- Based on state laws and the corporation's own rules, the owners of common stock are allowed to vote on a few specified issues. By far the most prevalent is the election of the **board of directors**. As mentioned previously, these individuals represent the ownership of the corporation in overseeing the management. The board of directors meets periodically (annually, quarterly, or as necessary) to review the financial results as well as the future plans and operating strategy developed by management. The board provides guidance and changes where necessary. A list of the individuals (often ten to twenty-five) who serve in this capacity is typically included in a corporation's annual report, often just after the financial statements.

- The responsibilities of the board of directors can vary rather significantly from company to company. Some boards do little whereas others are heavily involved in policy making. For example, a note to the financial statements of **Starbucks Corporation** explained, "We may repurchase shares of **Starbucks** common stock under a program authorized by our Board of Directors." Apparently, approval of this particular program fell within the designated responsibilities of the **Starbucks** board.

- One of the most important decisions for any board of directors is the declaration of dividends. Management cannot pay dividends to shareholders without specific approval by the board. Dividends cause the company (and specifically its cash balances) to get smaller so careful consideration of the impact must be made before declaration is approved. Stockholders like to receive dividends but do not want the company's future to be imperiled as the size shrinks.

- If dividends are paid on common stock, all stockholders share in them proportionally. Although dividends are never guaranteed, the owners must be treated fairly if dividends are distributed. An owner who holds 12 percent of the outstanding common stock is entitled to 12 percent of any dividends paid on common stock. The board of directors cannot reward some common shareholders while ignoring others.

- Should the company ever be liquidated, the common stock shareholders are entitled to share proportionally in any assets that remain after all liabilities and other claims are settled. Unfortunately, most liquidations result from a severe financial crisis so that holding assets at the end of the process is rare.

2.2   Capital Stock Terminology

*Question: "Authorized," "issued," "outstanding," and "par value" are terms mentioned by the **Kellogg Company** in Figure 16.1 in describing its ownership shares.* **What terms are associated with capital stock and what do each of them mean?**

authorized shares

The maximum number of shares that a corporation can issue based on the articles of incorporation approved by the state government at the time of incorporation.

issued shares

The number of shares of a corporation that have been sold or conveyed to owners.

outstanding shares

The number of shares of a corporation that are currently in the hands of the public; it is the shares that have been issued since operations first began less any treasury shares repurchased and still held by the corporation.

Answer:

Authorized. In applying to the state government as part of the initial incorporation process, company officials indicate the maximum number of capital shares they want to be allowed to issue. This approved limit is the authorized total. Corporations often set this figure so high that they never have to worry about reaching it. However, states normally permit authorization levels to be raised if necessary.

Issued. The number of issued shares is simply the quantity that has been sold or otherwise conveyed to owners. According to Figure 16.1, **Kellogg** reports that the state of Delaware authorized one billion shares of common stock, but only about 419 million have actually been issued to stockholders as of the balance sheet date. The remaining unissued shares are still available if the company needs to raise money in the future by selling additional capital stock.

Outstanding. The total amount of stock currently in the hands of the public is referred to as the shares "outstanding." Shares are often bought back by a corporation from its stockholders and recorded as treasury stock. Thus, originally issued shares are not always still outstanding. According to the information provided, **Kellogg** has acquired nearly 54 million treasury shares. Thus, on the balance sheet date, the company has roughly 365 million shares of common stock outstanding in the hands of its stockholders (419 million issued less 54 million treasury shares). This number is quite important because it serves as the basis for dividend payments as well as any votes taken of the stockholders.

Par value. The most mysterious term on a set of financial statements might well be "par value." Decades ago, the requirement was established in many states that a par value had to be set in connection with the issuance of capital stock. This par value is printed on the face of each stock certificate and indicates (depending on state law) the minimum amount of money that owners must legally leave in the business. By requiring a par value to be specified, lawmakers hoped to prevent the declaration of a cash dividend that was so large it would bankrupt the company, leaving creditors with no chance of repayment. The owners had to leave the set par value in the company.

Traditionally, companies have gotten around this limitation by setting the par value at an extremely low number.[7] For example, **Kellogg** discloses a par value of $0.25 for its common stock, which is actually quite high. Many companies report par values that fall between a penny and a nickel. The April 30, 2011, balance sheet for **Barnes & Noble** shows a par value for its common stock of one-tenth of a penny.

> ### TEST YOURSELF
>
> **Question:**
>
> Several years ago the Catawba Corporation was incorporated. The company was authorized to issue ten million shares of $0.02 par value common stock. Currently, eight million shares remain unissued. In addition, the company is holding 25,000 treasury shares. How many shares are issued and how many shares are outstanding, respectively, for Catawba Corporation?
>
>   a. Issued—18,000,000, Outstanding—1,975,000
>
>   b. Issued—10,000,000, Outstanding—2,000,000
>
>   c. Issued—2,000,000, Outstanding—2,025,000
>
>   d. Issued—2,000,000, Outstanding—1,975,000
>
> **Answer:**
>
> The correct answer is choice d: Issued—2,000,000, Outstanding—1,975,000.
>
> **Explanation:**
>
> The Catawba Corporation was authorized to issue ten million shares but still has eight million shares unissued. Apparently, two million have been issued to date. However, 25,000 of these shares were bought back from stockholders as treasury stock. Thus, only 1,975,000 shares are outstanding (in the hands of the stockholders) at the current time.

2.3 Reporting the Issuance of Common Stock

*Question: Over the years, one residual accounting effect has remained from the legal requirement to include a par value on stock certificates. This figure continues to be used in reporting the issuance of capital stock. Thus, if **Kellogg** sells one share for cash of $46.00 (the approximate value on the New York Stock Exchange during the fall of 2011), the common stock account is increased but only by its $0.25 par value. **Kellogg** receives $46.00 but the par value is $0.25. How can this journal entry balance? **How does a company report the issuance of a share of common stock for more than par value?***

Answer: A potential stockholder contributes assets to a company to obtain an ownership interest. In accounting, this conveyance is not viewed as an exchange. It is fundamentally different than selling inventory or a piece of land to an outside party. Instead, the contribution of monetary capital is an expansion of both the company and its ownership. As a result, no gain, loss, or other income effect is ever reported by an organization as a result of transactions occurring in its own stock. An investor is merely transferring assets to a corporation to be allowed to join the ownership.

Consequently, a second shareholders' equity balance is created to report the amount received from owners above par value. As shown in Figure 16.1, **Kellogg** uses the title **capital in excess of par value** but a number of other terms are frequently encountered in practice such as "additional paid-in capital." Therefore, **Kellogg** records the issuance of a share of $0.25 par value common stock for $46 in cash as shown in Figure 16.2.[8]

par value

A number printed on a stock certificate to indicate the minimum amount of money owners must legally leave in the business; it is generally set at a low amount to avoid legal complications.

capital in excess of par value

A figure that represents the amount received by a corporation from the original issuance of capital stock that is above the par value listed on the stock certificate; it is also referred to as additional paid in capital.

FIGURE 16.2 Issuance of a Share of Common Stock for Cash

Cash	46.00	
Common stock (par value)		.25
Capital in excess of par value		45.75

On a balance sheet, within the stockholders' equity section, the amount owners put into a corporation when they originally bought stock is the summation of the common stock and capital in excess of par value accounts. This total reflects the assets conveyed to the business to gain capital stock. For **Kellogg**, this figure is $600 million as shown in Figure 16.3. That is the amount of assets received by this company from its owners since operations first began.

As mentioned in a previous chapter, the sales of capital stock that occur on the New York Stock Exchange or other stock markets are between two investors and have no direct effect on the company. Those transactions simply create a change in the ownership.

FIGURE 16.3 Kellogg Common Stock and Capital in Excess of Par Value, January 1, 2011

Common Stock	$105 million
Capital in Excess of Par Value	$495 million
Total Contributed Capital	$600 million

TEST YOURSELF

Question:

When incorporated by the state of Nebraska, Stan Company was authorized to issue ten million shares of common stock with a $0.10 par value. At first, one million shares were issued for $5 per share. Later, another four million were issued at $6 per share. What is the amount to be reported as the capital in excess of par value and also as the total of contributed capital?

a. Capital in Excess of Par Value—$500,000, Contributed Capital—$1,000,000
b. Capital in Excess of Par Value—$28,500,000, Contributed Capital—$29,000,000
c. Capital in Excess of Par Value—$28,800,000, Contributed Capital—$30,000,000
d. Capital in Excess of Par Value—$29,000,000, Contributed Capital—$30,000,000

Answer:

The correct answer is choice b: Capital in Excess of Par Value—$28,500,000, Contributed Capital—$29,000,000.

Explanation:

Stan issued one million shares for $5 each for contributed capital of $5 million. The corporation then issued four million more shares for $6 each or a total of $24 million. Total contributed capital is $29 million ($5 million plus $24 million). Common stock is recorded at the par value of these shares or $500,000 (five million shares issued with a par value of $0.10 each). The remaining $28.5 million of the contribution ($29 million less $500,000) is reported as capital in excess of par value.

2.4 Issuing Common Stock in Noncash Exchanges

*Question: Common stock is sometimes issued in exchange for property or personal services rather than for cash. Such capital contributions are especially prevalent when a small corporation is first getting started. Potential owners may hold land, buildings, machinery, or other assets needed by the business. Or, an accountant, attorney, engineer, or the like might be willing to provide expert services and take payment in stock. This arrangement can be especially helpful if the business is attempting to conserve cash. **What recording is made if common stock is issued for a service or an asset other than cash?***

Answer: The issuance of stock for a service or asset is not technically a trade[9] but merely an expansion of the ownership. However, the accounting rules are the same. The asset or the service received by the corporation is recorded at the fair value of the capital stock surrendered. That figure is the equivalent of historical cost. It reflects the sacrifice made by the business to obtain the asset or service. However, if the fair value of the shares of stock is not available (which is often the case for both new and small corporations), the fair value of the property or services received becomes the basis for reporting.

To illustrate, assume that a potential investor is willing to convey land with a fair value of $125,000 to the Maine Company in exchange for an ownership interest. During negotiations, officials for Maine offer to issue ten thousand shares of $1 par value common stock for this property. The shares are currently selling on a stock exchange for $12 each. The investor decides to accept this proposal rather than go to the trouble of trying to sell the land.

The "sacrifice" made by the Maine Company to acquire this land is $120,000 ($12 per share × 10,000 shares). Those shares could have been sold to the public to raise that much money. Instead, Maine issues them directly in exchange for the land and records the transaction as shown in Figure 16.4.

FIGURE 16.4 Issue Ten Thousand Shares of Common Stock Worth $12 per Share for Land

Land	120,000	
Common Stock ($1 par value × 10,000 shares)		10,000
Capital in Excess of Par Value ($120,000 less $10,000)		110,000

If this stock was not selling on a stock exchange, fair value might not have been apparent. In that situation, the Maine Company recognizes the land at its own fair value of $125,000 with an accompanying $5,000 increase in the capital in excess of par value account.

KEY TAKEAWAY

Common stock forms the basic ownership units of most corporations. The rights of the holders of common stock shares are set by state law but normally include voting for the board of directors, the group that oversees operations and guides future plans. Financial statements often disclose the number of authorized shares (the maximum allowed), issued shares (the number that have been sold), and outstanding shares (those currently in the hands of owners). Common stock usually has a par value although the meaning of this figure has faded in importance over the decades. Upon issuance, common stock is recorded at par value with any amount received above that balance reported in an account such as capital in excess of par value. If issued for a service or asset other than cash, the financial recording is based on the fair value of the shares surrendered. However, if a reasonable estimation of value is not available, the fair value of the asset or service is used.

3. ISSUING AND ACCOUNTING FOR PREFERRED STOCK AND TREASURY STOCK

> ## LEARNING OBJECTIVES
>
> At the end of this section students should be able to meet the following objectives:
>
> 1. Explain the difference between preferred stock and common stock.
> 2. Discuss the distribution of dividends to preferred stockholders.
> 3. Record the issuance of preferred stock.
> 4. Provide reasons for a corporation to spend its money to reacquire its own capital stock as treasury stock.
> 5. Account for the purchase and resale of treasury stock when both gains and losses occur.

3.1 Differentiating Preferred Stock from Common Stock

preferred stock

A capital stock issued by some companies that has one or more specified preferences over common shareholders, usually in the form of cash dividends.

Question: Some corporations also issue a second type of capital stock referred to as **preferred** *stock. Approximately 5–15 percent of the corporations in the United States have preferred stock outstanding but the practice is especially prevalent in certain industries.* **How is preferred stock different from common stock?**

Answer: Preferred stock is another version of capital stock where the rights of those owners are set by the contractual terms of the stock certificate rather than state law. In effect, common stockholders voluntarily surrender one or more of their legal rights in hopes of enticing additional investors to contribute money to the corporation. For common stockholders, preferred stock is often another possible method of achieving financial leverage in a manner similar to using money raised from bonds and notes. If the resulting funds can be used to generate more profit than the dividends paid on the preferred stock, the residual income for the common stock will be higher.

The term "preferred stock" comes from the preference that is conveyed to these owners. They are being allowed to step in front of common stockholders when specified rights are applied. A wide variety of such benefits can be assigned to the holders of preferred shares, including additional voting rights, assured representation on the board of directors, and the right to residual assets if the company ever liquidates.

By far the most typical preference is to cash dividends. As mentioned earlier in this chapter, all common stockholders are entitled to share proportionally in any dividend distributions. However, if a corporation issues preferred stock with a stipulated dividend, that amount must be paid before any money is conveyed to the owners of common stock. No dividend is ever guaranteed, not even one on preferred shares. A dividend is only legally required if declared by the board of directors. But, if declared, the preferred stock dividend normally must be paid before any common stock dividend. Common stock is often referred to as a residual ownership because these shareholders are entitled to all that remains after other claims have been settled including those of preferred stock.

The issuance of preferred stock is accounted for in the same way as common stock. Par value, though, often serves as the basis for stipulated dividend payments. Thus, the par value listed for a preferred share frequently approximates fair value. To illustrate, assume a corporation issues ten thousand shares of preferred stock. A $100 per share par value is printed on each stock certificate. If the annual dividend is listed as 4 percent, cash of $4 per year ($100 par value × 4 percent) must be paid on preferred stock before any distribution is made on common stock.

If ten thousand shares of this preferred stock are each issued for $101 in cash ($1,010,000 in total), the company records the journal entry shown in Figure 16.5.

FIGURE 16.5 Issue Ten Thousand Shares of $100 Par Value Preferred Stock for $101 per Share

Cash	1,010,000	
Preferred Stock (Par Value)		1,000,000
Capital in Excess of Par Value		10,000

For recording purposes, companies often establish separate "capital in excess of par value" accounts—one for common stock and one for preferred stock. Those amounts are then frequently combined in reporting the balances within stockholders' equity.

TEST YOURSELF

Question:

The Gatellan Company wants to acquire a building worth $2 million from Alice Wilkinson. The company does not have sufficient cash and does not want to take out a loan so it offers to issue 90,000 shares of its $1 par value common stock in exchange for the building. Wilkinson wants more assurance of receiving a dividend each year and asks for 18,000 shares of the company's $100 par value preferred stock paying an annual dividend rate of 5 percent. Eventually, the parties come to an agreement and the Gatellan Company records capital in excess of par value of $200,000. Which of the following happened?

a. Gatellan issued the common stock but it had no known fair value.

b. Gatellan issued the common stock and it had a $20 per share fair value.

c. Gatellan issued the preferred stock and it had no known fair value.

d. Gatellan issued the preferred stock and it had a $102 per share fair value.

Answer:

The correct answer is choice c: Gatellan issued the preferred stock and it had no known fair value.

Explanation:

In a, the asset is recorded at $2 million, the stock is its $90,000 par value, and the capital in excess is $1.91 million. In b, the asset is recorded at $1.8 million, the stock is its $90,000 par value, and the capital in excess is $1.71 million. In c, the asset is recorded at $2 million, the stock is its $1.8 million par value, and the capital in excess is $200,000. In d, the asset is recorded at $1,836,000, the stock is its $1.8 million par value, and the capital in excess is $36,000.

3.2   The Acquisition of Treasury Stock

Question: An account called **treasury stock** *is often found near the bottom of the shareholders' equity section of a balance sheet. Treasury stock represents issued shares of a corporation's own stock that have been reacquired. For example, the September 30, 2011, balance sheet for* **Viacom Inc.** *reports a negative balance of over $8.2 billion identified as treasury stock.*

An earlier story in the Wall Street Journal *indicated that* **Viacom** *had been buying and selling its own stock for a number of years: "The $8 billion buyback program would enable the company to repurchase as much as 13 percent of its shares outstanding. The buyback follows a $3 billion stock-purchase program announced in 2002, under which 40.7 million shares were purchased."*[10]

Why does a company voluntarily give billions of dollars back to stockholders in order to repurchase its own stock? That is a huge amount of money leaving the company. Why not invest these funds in inventory, buildings, investments, research and development, and the like? **Why does a corporation buy back its own shares as treasury stock?**

Answer: Numerous possible reasons exist to justify spending money to reacquire an entity's own stock. Several of these strategies are rather complicated and a more appropriate topic for an upper-level finance course. However, an overview of various ideas should be helpful in understanding the rationale for such transactions.

- As a reward for service, businesses often give shares of their stock to key employees or sell shares to them at a relatively low price. In some states, using unissued shares for such purposes is restricted legally. The same rules do not apply to shares that have been reacquired. Thus, some corporations acquire treasury shares to have available as needed for compensation purposes.

treasury stock

Issued shares of a corporation's own stock that have been reacquired; balance is shown within the stockholders' equity section of the balance sheet as a negative amount unless the shares are retired (removed from existence).

- Acquisition of treasury stock can be used as a tactic to push up the market price of a company's stock in order to please the remaining stockholders. Usually, a large scale repurchase (such as made by **Viacom**) indicates that management believes the stock is undervalued at its current market price. Buying treasury stock reduces the supply of shares in the market and, according to economic theory, forces the price to rise. In addition, because of the announcement of the repurchase, outside investors often rush in to buy the stock ahead of the expected price increase. The supply of shares is decreased while demand is increased. Stock price should go up. Not surprisingly, current stockholders often applaud a decision to buy treasury shares as they anticipate a jump in their investment values.

- Corporations can also repurchase shares of stock to reduce the risk of a hostile takeover. If another company threatens to buy sufficient shares to gain control, the board of directors of the target company must decide if acquisition is in the best interest of the stockholders.[11] If not, the target might attempt to buy up shares of its own stock in hopes of reducing the number of owners in the market who are willing to sell their shares. Here, repurchase is a defensive strategy designed to make the takeover more difficult to accomplish. Plus, as mentioned previously, buying back treasury stock should drive the price up, making purchase more costly for the predator.

3.3   Reporting the Purchase of Treasury Stock

Question: To illustrate the financial reporting of treasury stock, assume that the Chauncey Company has been in business for over twenty years. During that time, the company has issued ten million shares of its $1 par value common stock at an average price of $3.50 per share. The company now reacquires three hundred thousand of these shares for $4 each. **How is the acquisition of treasury stock reported?**

Answer: Under U.S. GAAP, several methods are allowed for reporting the purchase of treasury stock. Most companies use the cost method because of its simplicity. As shown in Figure 16.6, the acquisition of these shares is recorded by Chauncey at the $1.2 million cost (300,000 shares at $4 each) that was paid.

FIGURE 16.6   Purchase of Three Hundred Thousand Shares of Treasury Stock at a Cost of $4 Each

| Treasury Stock | 1,200,000 | |
| Cash | | 1,200,000 |

Because the money spent on treasury stock represents assets that have left the business, this balance is shown within stockholders' equity as a negative, reflecting a decrease in net assets instead of an increase.

Except for possible legal distinctions, treasury stock held by a company is the equivalent of unissued stock. The shares do not receive dividends and have no voting privileges.

3.4   Reporting the Reissuance of Treasury Stock above Cost

Question: Treasury shares can be held by a corporation forever or eventually reissued at prices that might vary greatly from original cost. If sold for more than cost, is a gain recognized? If sold for less, is a loss reported? **What is the impact on a corporation's financial statements if treasury stock shares are reissued?**

To illustrate, assume that Chauncey Company subsequently sells one hundred thousand shares of its treasury stock (shown in Figure 16.6) for $5.00 each. That is $1.00 more than these shares had cost to reacquire. Is this excess reported by Chauncey as a gain on its income statement?

Answer: As discussed previously, transactions in a corporation's own stock are considered expansions and contractions of the ownership and never impact reported net income. The buying and selling of capital stock are transactions viewed as fundamentally different from the buying and selling of assets such as inventory and land. Therefore, no gains and losses are recorded in connection with treasury stock. As shown in Figure 16.7, an alternative reporting must be constructed.

FIGURE 16.7 Sale of One Hundred Thousand Shares of Treasury Stock Costing $4 Each for $5 per Share

Cash	500,000	
Treasury Stock (Cost)		400,000
Capital in Excess of Cost—Treasury Stock		100,000

The "capital in excess of cost-treasury stock" is the same type of account as the "capital in excess of par value" that was recorded in connection with the issuance of both common and preferred stocks. Within stockholders' equity, these individual accounts can be grouped into a single balance or reported separately.

3.5 Reporting the Reissuance of Treasury Stock below Cost

Question: The first group of treasury shares was reissued for more than cost. Assume that Chauncey subsequently sells another one hundred thousand of treasury shares, but this time for only $2.60 each. The proceeds in this transaction are below the acquisition cost of $4 per share. **What recording is made if treasury stock is sold at the equivalent of a loss?**

Answer: Interestingly, the reissuance of treasury stock for an amount below cost is a transaction not well covered in U.S. GAAP. Authoritative rules fail to provide a definitive rule for reporting such reductions except that stockholders' equity is decreased with no direct impact recorded in net income. Absolute rules are not always available in U.S. GAAP.

The most common approach seems to be to first remove any capital in excess of cost recorded by the reissuance of earlier shares of treasury stock at above cost. If that balance is not large enough to absorb the entire reduction, a decrease is then made in retained earnings as shown in Figure 16.8. The $100,000 balance in capital in excess of cost-treasury stock was created in the previous reissuance illustrated in Figure 16.7.

FIGURE 16.8 Sale of One Hundred Thousand Shares of Treasury Stock Costing $4 Each for $2.60 per Share

Cash	260,000	
Capital in Excess of Cost—Treasury Stock	100,000	
Retained Earnings	40,000	
Treasury Stock (Cost)		400,000

One outcome of this handling should be noted. In earlier chapters of this textbook, "retained earnings" was defined as a balance equal to all income reported over the life of a business less all dividend distributions to the owners. Apparently, this definition is not correct in every possible case. In Figure 16.8, the retained earnings balance is also reduced as a result of a stock transaction where a loss occurred that could not otherwise be reported.

TEST YOURSELF

Question:

Several years ago, Ashkroft Inc. issued 800,000 shares of $2 par value stock for $3 per share in cash. Early in the current year, Ashkroft repurchases 100,000 of these shares at $8 per share. A month later, 40,000 of these treasury shares are sold back to the public at $10 per share. What is the total impact on reported shareholders' equity of these transactions?

a. $1,920,000 increase

b. $2,000,000 increase

c. $2,280,000 increase

d. $2,420,000 increase

Answer:

The correct answer is choice b: $2,000,000 increase.

Explanation:

The initial issuance of stock increases net assets by $2.4 million (800,000 shares × $3). The purchase of treasury stock reduces net assets by $800,000 (100,000 shares × $8). The reissuance of a portion of the treasury stock increases net assets by $400,000 (40,000 shares × $10). The individual account balances have not been computed here but the overall increase in shareholders' equity is $2 million ($2.4 million less $800,000 plus $400,000).

TEST YOURSELF

Question:

Several years ago, the Testani Corporation issued 800,000 shares of $2 par value stock for $3 per share in cash. Early in the current year, Testani repurchases 100,000 shares at $8 per share. A month later, 40,000 of these shares are sold back to the public at $10 per share. Several weeks later, after a drop in market price, 50,000 more shares of the treasury stock were reissued for $5 per share. What is the overall impact on reported retained earnings of the reissuance of the 90,000 shares of treasury stock?

a. No effect

b. $50,000 reduction

c. $70,000 reduction

d. $90,000 reduction

Answer:

The correct answer is choice c: $70,000 reduction.

Explanation:

The first batch of 40,000 shares of treasury stock was sold at $2 above cost, creating a capital in excess of cost account of $80,000. The second batch of 50,000 shares was sold at $3 below cost or $150,000 in total. In recording this second reissuance, the $80,000 capital in excess of cost is first removed entirely with the remaining $70,000 shown as a decrease in retained earnings.

KEY TAKEAWAY

A corporation can issue preferred stock as well as common stock. Preferred shares are given specific rights that come before those of common stockholders. Frequently, these rights involve the distribution of dividends. A set amount is often required to be paid before common stockholders can receive any dividends. After issuance, capital stock shares can be bought back by a company from its investors for a number of reasons. For example, repurchase might be carried out in hopes of boosting the stock price. These shares are usually reported at cost and referred to as treasury stock. In acquiring such shares, money flows out of the company so the account appears as a negative balance within stockholders' equity. When reissued above cost, the treasury stock account is reduced and capital in excess of cost is recognized. To record a loss, any previous capital in excess of cost balance is removed followed by a possible reduction in retained earnings. Net income is not impacted by a transaction in a company's own stock.

4. THE ISSUANCE OF CASH AND STOCK DIVIDENDS

LEARNING OBJECTIVES

At the end of this section students should be able to meet the following objectives:

1. Identify the various dates associated with a dividend distribution.
2. Prepare journal entries to report a cash dividend declaration and payment to stockholders.
3. Define the characteristics of a cumulative dividend.
4. Explain a company's rationale for issuing a stock dividend or stock split.
5. Record the issuance of a stock dividend

4.1 Reporting Dividend Distributions

Question: As stated in an early section of this textbook, a vast majority of investors purchase capital stock for only two reasons: price appreciation and dividend payments. Cash dividends and long-term capital gains (gains on the sale of certain investments that have been held for over one year) are especially appealing to individual investors because they are taxed at a lower rate than most other types of income.

Dividends represent the profits of a business that are being passed along to the owners. Because the corporation is effectively giving away assets, dividends require formal approval by the board of directors. This action is known as a dividend declaration. The board considers current cash balances as well as the projected needs of the business before deciding on the amount, if any, of a dividend payment. **How does a corporation report the declaration and distribution of a cash dividend?**

Answer: Dividends provide a meaningful signal to investors about the financial health of a business. Some corporations even boast about having paid a constant or rising annual dividend for many years. Unfortunately, a number of businesses have been forced recently to reduce or even eliminate their dividend distributions as a result of general economic difficulties. Such decisions typically lead to a drop in the market price of a corporation's stock because of the negative implications.

Other businesses stress rapid growth and rarely, if ever, pay a cash dividend. The board of directors prefers that all profits remain in the business to stimulate future growth. For example, **Google Inc.** reported net income of $4.2 billion (2008), $6.5 billion (2009), and $8.5 billion (2010) but paid no dividends in any of those years.

Chronologically, accounting for dividends involves several dates with approximately two to five weeks passing between each:

- The **date of declaration**
- The **date of record** (and the related ex-dividend date)
- The **date of payment** (also known as the date of distribution)

To illustrate, assume that the Hurley Corporation has one million shares of authorized common stock. Since incorporation several years ago, three hundred thousand shares have been issued to the public but twenty thousand were recently bought back as treasury stock. Thus, 280,000 shares are presently outstanding, in the hands of investors. In the current year, Hurley earned a reported net income of $780,000. After some deliberations, the board of directors votes to distribute a $1.00 cash dividend to the owner of each share of common stock.

The day on which Hurley's board of directors formally decides on the payment of this dividend is known as the date of declaration. Legally, this action creates a liability for the company that must be recognized through the journal entry shown in Figure 16.9. Dividends are only paid on shares that are outstanding so the liability balance is $280,000.

FIGURE 16.9 $1.00 per Share Dividend Declared by Board of Directors, 280,000 Shares Outstanding

Retained Earnings	280,000	
Dividends Payable		280,000

date of declaration

Date on which dividend payments are formally declared (approved) by the board of directors; it is the day on which a liability is recorded by the corporation.

date of record

Date on which stock must be held for a shareholder to be entitled to the receipt of a dividend; the date of record is specified by the board of directors when the dividend is declared.

date of payment

Date on which a cash dividend is distributed to those shareholders who held a corporation's stock on the date of record; it is also known as the date of distribution.

As discussed previously, dividend distributions reduce the amount reported as retained earnings but have no impact on net income.

When the dividend is declared by the board, the date of record is also set. Only the shareholders who own the stock on that day qualify for receipt. The ex-dividend date is the first day on which an investor is not entitled to the dividend. Because receipt of the dividend has been lost, the market price of the stock typically drops by approximately the amount of the dividend on the ex-dividend date (although myriad other market factors influence the movement of stock prices).

No journal entry is recorded by a corporation on either the date of record or the ex-dividend date because they do not represent an event or transaction. Those dates simply allow Hurley to identify the owners to whom the dividend will be paid.

On the date of payment, the corporation mails checks to the appropriate recipients. That is a simple event to record as shown in Figure 16.10.

FIGURE 16.10 Payment of $1.00 per Share Cash Dividend

| Dividends Payable | 280,000 | |
| Cash | | 280,000 |

4.2 Cumulative Preferred Stock

Question: Assume that Wington Company issues 1,000 shares of $100 par value preferred stock to an investor on January 1, Year One. The preferred stock certificate specifies an annual dividend rate of 8 percent. Thus, dividend payment to the owner is supposed to be $8 per share each year ($100 × 8 percent).

At the end of Year One, Wington faces a cash shortage and the board of directors chooses not to pay this dividend. Have the owners of the preferred shares lost the right to the Year One dividend? ***Must a corporation report a liability if a preferred stock dividend is not paid at the appointed time?***

cumulative

Feature attached to most types of preferred stock so that any dividend payments that are omitted must still be paid before the holders of common stock receive any dividends.

Answer: Preferred stock dividends are often identified on the stock certificate as **cumulative**. This term indicates that any obligation for unpaid dividends on these shares must be met before dividends can be distributed to the owners of common stock. Cumulative dividends are referred to as "in arrears" when past due.

Thus, if the dividend on the preferred shares of Wington is cumulative, the $8 per share is in arrears at the end of Year One. In the future, this (and any other) missed dividend will have to be paid before any distribution to the owners of common stock can be considered. Conversely, if a preferred stock is noncumulative, a missed dividend is simply lost to those owners. It has no impact on the future allocation of dividends between preferred and common shares.

The existence of a cumulative preferred stock dividend in arrears is information that must be disclosed through a note to the financial statements. However, the balance is not reported as a liability. Only dividends that have been formally declared by the board of directors are recorded through a journal entry.

TEST YOURSELF

Question:

The Hansbrough Company has 20,000 shares outstanding of $100 par value preferred stock with a 6 percent annual dividend rate. This company also has five million shares of $1 par value common stock outstanding. No dividends at all were paid in either Year One or Year Two. Near the end of Year Three, a cash dividend of $400,000 is scheduled to be distributed. If the preferred stock dividend is cumulative, how is this dividend allocated?

a. Preferred—$ 60,000, Common—$340,000

b. Preferred—$120,000, Common—$180,000

c. Preferred—$240,000, Common—$160,000

d. Preferred—$360,000, Common—$ 40,000

Answer:

The correct answer is choice d: Preferred—$360,000, Common—$ 40,000.

Explanation:

Owners of the preferred stock are entitled to $6 per year ($100 par value × 6 percent) or $120,000 ($6 × 20,000 shares outstanding). Because the preferred stock dividend is cumulative, dividends for Years One and Two are settled first. After those distributions, another $120,000 is paid for Year Three. A total of $360,000 is conveyed to the preferred stockholders. The remaining $40,000 dividend ($400,000 less $360,000) goes to the residual ownership, the holders of the common stock.

TEST YOURSELF

Question:

The Singler Company has 20,000 shares outstanding of $100 par value preferred stock with a 6 percent annual dividend rate. The company also has five million shares of $1 par value common stock outstanding. No dividends at all were paid in either Year One or Year Two. Near the end of Year Three, a cash dividend of $400,000 is scheduled to be distributed. If the preferred stock dividend is noncumulative, how is this dividend distributed?

a. Preferred—$60,000, Common—$340,000

b. Preferred—$120,000, Common—$280,000

c. Preferred—$240,000, Common—$160,000

d. Preferred—$360,000, Common—$ 40,000

Answer:

The correct answer is choice b: Preferred—$120,000, Common—$280,000.

Explanation:

The preferred stock dividend is noncumulative. Thus, the amounts that were missed during Years One and Two do not carry over into the future. Owners of the preferred stock are only entitled to receive a dividend distribution for the current period ($120,000 or $100 par value × 6 percent × 20,000 shares). The owners of the common stock receive the remainder of the dividend ($280,000 or $400,000 less $120,000).

4.3 Distribution of Stock Dividends

stock split

A division of each share of outstanding stock to increase the number of those shares; it is a method of reducing the market price of the stock; the process is carried out in hopes that a lower price will generate more market activity in the stock and, therefore, a faster rise in price.

stock dividend

A dividend distributed to shareholders by issuing additional shares of stock rather than cash; it increases the number of shares outstanding but each owners interest in the company stays the same; as with a stock split, it reduces the price of the stock in hopes of stimulating market interest.

*Question: A corporate press release issued by **Ross Stores Inc.** on November 17, 2011, informed the public that "its Board of Directors has approved a two-for-one* stock split *to be paid in the form of a 100%* stock dividend *on December 15, 2011 to stockholders of record as of November 29, 2011."*

*Obviously, as shown by this press release, a corporation can distribute additional shares of its stock to shareholders instead of paying only cash dividends. These shares are issued as a stock dividend or a stock split. Although slightly different in a legal sense, most companies (such as **Ross Stores**) use the terms "stock dividend" and "stock split" interchangeably.*[12] *No assets are distributed in either scenario—just more shares of the company's own stock. **Are stockholders better off when they receive additional shares of a company's stock in the form of a stock dividend?***

Answer: When a stock dividend (or stock split) is issued, the number of shares held by every investor increases but their percentage of the ownership stays the same. Their interest in the corporation remains proportionally unchanged. They have gained nothing.

To illustrate, assume that the Red Company reports net assets of $5 million. Janis Samples owns one thousand of the ten thousand shares of this company's outstanding common stock. Thus, she holds a 10 percent interest (1,000 shares/10,000 shares) in a business with net assets of $5 million.

The board of directors then declares and distributes a 4 percent stock dividend. For each one hundred shares that a stockholder possesses, Red Company issues an additional 4 shares (4 percent times one hundred). Therefore, four hundred new shares of Red's common stock are conveyed to the ownership as a whole (4 percent times ten thousand). This distribution raises the number of outstanding shares to 10,400. However, a stock dividend has no actual impact on the corporation. There are simply more shares outstanding. Nothing else has changed.

Janis Samples receives forty of these newly issued shares (4 percent times one thousand) so that her holdings have grown to 1,040 shares. After this stock dividend, she still owns 10 percent of the outstanding stock of Red Company (1,040/10,400), and the company still reports net assets of $5 million. The investor's financial position has not improved. She has gained nothing as a result of the stock dividend.

Not surprisingly, investors make no journal entry in accounting for the receipt of a stock dividend. No change has taken place except for the number of shares held.

However, the corporation does make a journal entry to record the issuance of a stock dividend although distribution creates no impact on either assets or liabilities. The retained earnings balance is decreased by the fair value of the shares issued while contributed capital (common stock and capital in excess of par value) is also increased by this same amount. Fair value is used here because the company could have issued those new shares for that amount of cash and then paid the money out as a dividend. Issuing a stock dividend creates the same overall impact.

One exception to this method of reporting is applied. According to U.S. GAAP, if a stock dividend is especially large (in excess of 20–25 percent of the outstanding shares), the change in retained earnings and contributed capital is recorded at par value rather than fair value.[13] When the number of shares issued becomes this large, fair value is no longer viewed as a reliable indicator of the financial effect of the distribution.

TEST YOURSELF

Question:

The Hazelton Corporation has 600,000 shares outstanding of $2 per share par value common stock that was issued for $5 per share but currently trades on a stock market for $9 per share. The board of directors opts to issue a 3 percent stock dividend. What will be the reported reduction in retained earnings as a result of this action?

a. Zero

b. $36,000

c. $126,000

d. $162,000

Answer:

The correct answer is choice d: $162,000.

Explanation:

As a small stock dividend (under 20–25 percent of the outstanding shares), retained earnings is decreased by the fair value of the shares issued while contributed capital goes up by the same amount. Hazelton issues 18,000 new shares (3 percent of 600,000) with a fair value of $9 each or $162,000 in total (18,000 × $9). The par value is only $36,000 (18,000 × $2) with the difference recorded as capital in excess of par value. The journal entry to record this stock dividend is as follows.

FIGURE 16.11

Retained Earnings	162,000	
Common Stock		36,000
Capital in Excess of Par Value		126,000

TEST YOURSELF

Question:

The Pitino Corporation has 600,000 shares outstanding of $2 per share par value common stock that was is-sued for $5 per share but currently trades for $9 per share. The board of directors opts to issue a 60 percent stock dividend. What will be the reported reduction in retained earnings?

a. $360,000

b. $720,000

c. $2,520,000

d. $3,240,000

Answer:

The correct answer is choice b: $720,000.

Explanation:

As a large stock dividend (over 20–25 percent of the outstanding shares), retained earnings is decreased by the par value of the shares issued while contributed capital goes up by the same amount. Pitino issues 360,000 new shares (60 percent of 600,000) with a par value of $2 each or $720,000 in total (360,000 × $2). The journal entry to record this stock dividend is as follows.

FIGURE 16.12

| Retained Earnings | 720,000 | |
| Common Stock | | 720,000 |

4.4   Why Issue a Stock Dividend?

*Question: **If no changes occur in the makeup of a corporation as the result of a stock dividend, why does a board of directors choose to issue one?***

Answer: The primary purpose served by a stock dividend (or a stock split) is a reduction in the market price of the corporation's capital stock. When the price of a share rises to a relatively high level, fewer investors are willing to make purchases. At some point, market interest wanes. This reduction in demand will likely have a negative impact on the stock price. A growing business might find that a pre-viously escalating trend in its market value has hit a plateau when the price of each share rises too high.

By issuing a large quantity of new shares (sometimes two to five times as many shares as were out-standing), the price falls, often precipitously. For example, an investor who held one hundred shares at a market price of $120 per share (total value of $12,000) might now own two hundred shares selling at $60 per share or three hundred shares selling at $40 per share (but with the same total market value of $12,000). The stockholder's investment remains unchanged but, hopefully, the stock is now more at-tractive to potential investors at the lower price so that the level of active trading increases.

Stock dividends also provide owners with the possibility of other benefits. For example, cash di-vidend payments usually drop after a stock dividend but not always in proportion to the change in the number of outstanding shares. An owner might hold one hundred shares of common stock in a cor-poration that has paid $1 per share as an annual cash dividend over the past few years (a total of $100 per year). After a 2-for-1 stock dividend, this individual now owns two hundred shares. The board of directors might then choose to reduce the annual cash dividend to only $0.60 per share so that future payments go up to $120 per year (two hundred shares × $0.60 each). Such a benefit, though, is not guaranteed. The investors can merely hope that additional cash dividends will be received.

5.   THE COMPUTATION OF EARNINGS PER SHARE

LEARNING OBJECTIVES

At the end of this section students should be able to meet the following objectives:

1. Compute and explain return on equity.
2. Discuss the reasons that earnings per share (EPS) figures are so closely watched by investors.
3. Calculate basic EPS with or without the existence of preferred stock.
4. Explain the relevance of the P/E ratio.
5. Identify the informational benefit provided by diluted EPS.

5.1   The Calculation of Return on Equity

Question: Throughout this textbook, various vital signs have been presented. They include ratios, numbers, percentages, and the like that are commonly studied by decision makers as an indication of current financial health and future prosperity. One common measure is **return on equity** (ROE). ***How does an interested party calculate the return on equity reported by a business?***

Answer: Return on equity reflects the profitability of a business based on the size of the owners' claim to net assets. It is simply the reported net income divided by average stockholders' equity for the period.

return on equity (ROE)

Ratio computed to measure the profitable use of a business's resources; it is determined by dividing net income by average stockholders' equity for the period.

$$\text{return on equity} = \text{net income/average stockholders' equity}$$

For example, **PPG Industries Inc.** began 2010 with total stockholders' equity of \$3,922 million. Partly because of a large acquisition of treasury stock and the payment of a \$360 million cash dividend, the company ended that year with stockholders' equity of only \$3,833 million. For the year ended December 31, 2010, **PPG** reported net income of \$880 million for a return on equity of 22.7 percent.

$$\text{average stockholders' equity: } (\$3,922 \text{ million} + \$3,833 \text{ million})/2 = \$3,877.5 \text{ million}$$

$$\text{return on equity: } \$880 \text{ million}/\$3,877.5 \text{ million} = 22.7\%$$

As with all such vital signs, the strength or weakness of **PPG's** 22.7 percent return on equity is difficult to evaluate in isolation. Comparison with other similar companies can be very helpful as is the trend for this particular company over time. For example, decision makers looking at **PPG** were likely to be particularly impressed with the 2010 return on equity after learning that the 2009 return on equity was 11.5 percent.

5.2   Earnings per Share and the P/E Ratio

*Question: No single "vital sign" that is computed to help investors analyze a business and its financial health is more obsessively watched than earnings per share (EPS). Corporations even call press conferences to announce their latest EPS figures. According to U.S. GAAP, public companies are required to present EPS for each period that net income is reported. As just one example, **Pfizer Inc.** disclosed basic*

EPS of $1.03 on its income statement for the year ended December 31, 2010. **Why is the EPS reported by a corporation so closely monitored by the investment community?**

Answer: The simple reason for the public fascination with EPS is that this number is generally considered to be linked to the market price of a company's capital stock. Therefore, constant and wide-scale speculation takes place about future EPS figures as a technique for forecasting future stock prices. If analysts merely predict an increase in EPS, this forecast alone can lead to a surge in the traded price of a company's shares.

A **price-earnings ratio (P/E ratio)** is even computed to help quantify this relationship. The P/E ratio is the current price of the stock divided by the latest EPS figure. It enables investors to anticipate movements in the price of a stock based on projections of earnings per share. If a company's P/E ratio is twenty and is expected to remain constant, then an increase in EPS of $1 should lead to a $20 rise in stock price.

Theories abound as to how P/E ratios should be used. Some investors only buy capital shares of companies with high P/E ratios. They believe the P/E ratio indicates businesses that the stock market has assessed as particularly strong with excellent future prospects. Other investors prefer companies with low P/E ratios because those stocks may well be undervalued by the market with more room for the price to grow.

price-earnings ratio (P/E ratio)

A ratio computed by dividing the current market price of an entity's stock by the latest earnings per share balance; it is used to help predict future stock prices based on anticipated EPS figures.

FIGURE 16.13 As of November 23, 2011, the P/E ratio for Several Prominent Companies

IBM	14.08
MetLife	5.27
Pfizer	14.52
Target	12.05

The ongoing debate as to whether EPS and the P/E ratio are over emphasized as investing tools is a controversy better left to upper-level finance courses. The fascination is certainly real regardless of whether the perceived benefits are as great as many decision makers believe.

5.3 Calculating Earnings per Share

Question: EPS is obviously a much analyzed number in a set of financial statements. **How is EPS calculated?**

Answer: EPS is a common stock computation designed to measure operating results after all other claims have been satisfied. In simplest form, EPS (often referred to as **basic EPS**) is the net income for the period divided by the weighted average number of outstanding shares of common stock. The computation allocates a company's income equally to each of its shares.

To illustrate, assume the Maris Company reports its most recent net income as $700,000. If the company has a weighted average of 200,000 shares of common stock outstanding for this period of time, EPS is $700,000/200,000 or $3.50 per share. Furthermore, if the market price of Maris Company stock is $35, then the P/E ratio is 35/3.50, or ten.

Because EPS only relates to common stock, this computation is altered slightly if any preferred stock shares are also outstanding. Preferred stock is normally entitled to a specified dividend before common stock has any claim. However, most preferred stocks get nothing other than that dividend. Therefore, in determining basic EPS, any preferred stock dividend must be removed to arrive at the portion of income that is attributed to the ownership of common stock.

basic earnings per share

A figure that must be reported by corporations that have their stock publicly traded; it is net income less preferred stock dividends divided by the weighted-average number of shares of common stock outstanding during the period.

Basic EPS

(net income – preferred stock dividend)/average number of common shares outstanding

TEST YOURSELF

Question:

Daryl Corporation's net income for the current year is reported as $450,000. Preferred stock dividends for the same period amount to $10,000. On January 1, 100,000 shares of common stock were outstanding. On July 1, 20,000 additional shares of common stock were issued. What is Daryl's EPS?

a. $3.67

b. $4.00

c. $4.40

d. $4.50

Answer:

The correct answer is choice b: $4.00.

Explanation:

The income attributed to common stock is $440,000, the reported balance of $450,000 less the $10,000 preferred stock dividend. The weighted average number of outstanding common shares for this year was 110,000. The company had 100,000 shares of common stock outstanding during the first six months and 120,000 shares for the second six months.

FIGURE 16.14

100,000 for 6 months =	600,000
120,000 for 6 months =	720,000
Total	1,320,000
Average for the year: 1,320,000/12 months =	110,000 shares
Basic Earnings per share: $440,000/110,000 shares =	$4.00

TEST YOURSELF

Question:

The latest income statement for the St. John Corporation reports net income of $828,000. Preferred dividends for the period were $30,000. On January 1, 200,000 shares of common stock were outstanding. However, on October 1, 40,000 shares of this common stock were repurchased as treasury stock. What is St. John's basic EPS?

a. $3.28
b. $3.78
c. $4.20
d. $4.73

Answer:

The correct answer is choice c: $4.20.

Explanation:

The income attributed to common stock is $798,000, the reported balance of $828,000 for the period less the $30,000 preferred stock dividend. The weighted average number of outstanding common shares for this year was 190,000. The company had 200,000 shares of common stock outstanding during the first nine months of the year but only 160,000 shares for the final three months (as a result of buying back the shares of treasury stock).

FIGURE 16.15

200,000 for 9 months =	1,800,000
160,000 for 3 months =	480,000
Total	2,280,000
Average for the year: 2,280,000/12 months =	190,000 shares
Basic Earnings per share: $798,000/190,000 shares =	$4.20

5.4   Diluted Earnings per Share

*Question: For the year ended March 31, 2011, the **McKesson Corporation** reported basic EPS of $4.65 per share. However, this company also reported a second figure, diluted EPS, which was only $4.57 per share. What is the meaning of diluted EPS?* **Why is diluted EPS also reported by some businesses along with basic EPS?**

Answer: All publicly traded companies must disclose basic EPS. Income reported for the period (after removal of any preferred stock dividends) is allocated evenly over the weighted average number of shares of outstanding common stock. Basic EPS is a mechanically derived figure based on the historically reported income and number of shares outstanding.

Many corporations also have other contractual obligations outstanding that could become common stock and, therefore, potentially affect this computation. Stock options, convertible bonds, and convertible preferred stock can each be exchanged in some manner for common stock shares. The decision to convert is usually up to the holder and out of the control of the company. If these conversions ever take place, the additional shares could cause EPS to drop—possibly by a significant amount. This potential reduction should be brought to the attention of investors.

Diluted EPS serves as a warning to decision makers of the possible impact that the existence of convertibles can have on ownership. It provides a "worst case scenario" by setting up a hypothetical computation to give weight to the possibility of such conversions. Because of the complicated steps that are involved, the actual mechanical process is better left to an intermediate accounting course. However, an understanding of the purpose of reporting diluted EPS is worthwhile at the introductory level.

Stock options, convertible bonds, convertible preferred stocks, and the like could become common stock and reduce a company's reported EPS. Thus, U.S. GAAP requires that this possible impact is calculated and shown by the reporting of a lower diluted EPS. For the **McKesson Corporation**, if all other transactions stayed the same except that its convertible items were exchanged for common stock, basic EPS would fall from $4.65 to $4.57. That is the possible dilution that could be caused by the presence of items convertible into common stock. For an investor or potential investor, that is information of interest. Including this figure alerts decision makers to the possibility of such conversions and helps them quantify the potential impact.

diluted earnings per share

Hypothetical computation that reduces basic earnings per share to reflect the possible decrease if outstanding convertible items are actually turned into common stock; it includes the potential impact of stock options, convertible bonds, convertible preferred stock, and the like to warn decision makers of the "worst case scenario" if those convertibles are ever turned into common stock.

KEY TAKEAWAY

Return on equity (ROE) is a percentage often computed by financial analysts to help evaluate the profitability of a business. It is net income divided by the average stockholders' equity for that period of time. Likewise, the reporting of earnings per share (EPS) draws an especially wide circle of interest. EPS is considered by most decision makers who are looking at a particular business. Basic EPS must be reported by every publicly traded company for each year in which net income is reported. It is the net income for the period divided by the weighted average number of common stock shares outstanding. Because EPS is only determined for common stock, any preferred stock dividends must be removed from net income as a preliminary step in this computation. The resulting EPS figure is viewed as having a major impact on the movement of the company's stock price. The price-earnings (P/E) ratio even quantifies that effect. If a corporation also has items such as stock options or convertible bonds that can be turned into common stock, their conversion could potentially have an adverse impact on EPS. Thus, if a company has any convertibles outstanding, diluted EPS must also be reported to help investors understand the possible negative impact that might result from future conversions.

Talking with a Real Investing Pro (Continued)

Following is a continuation of our interview with Kevin G. Burns.

Question: Investors in the United States seem to have an obsession about the reporting of earnings per share (EPS). Even slight movements in projected EPS figures can create significant swings in the market price of a company's stock. Do you think there is an overemphasis on EPS in the public's investing decisions? How closely do you pay attention to the EPS figures that are reported by the businesses that you are following?

Kevin Burns: This is a very good question. By now students should realize that accounting is really all about estimates. Although investors would like accounting to be objectively exact, reporting such estimates really requires an awful lot of subjectivity. For example, for many years, **General Electric** would almost always report EPS a penny or two above market expectations. This was quarter after quarter like clockwork. It got to the point where if the company didn't "beat" the estimates on the street by a penny or two, the market was disappointed. It is absurd to believe that this is meaningful. This is especially true when earnings can also be managed simply by delaying or speeding up a major transaction from one time period to another. I believe that EPS, although important, is not the ultimate piece of information that some investors seem to think. I am much more concerned about asset values, growth prospects, and what a company does with the cash it is able to generate.

Video Clip

Professor Joe Hoyle talks about the five most important points in Chapter 16.

View the video online at: http://bit.ly/hoyle16-2

6. END-OF-CHAPTER EXERCISES

QUESTIONS

1. What are the three legal forms of business found in the United States?

2. Art Heyman and Jeff Mullins create a new business that they form as a partnership. Why might they have decided not to incorporate their business?

3. Hans Iverson forms a business that earns income of $600,000 in the current year. He paid himself $400,000 purely as a reward for ownership (not a salary). How are this income and this distribution taxed if the business is formed as a sole proprietorship? How are this income and this distribution taxed if the business is formed as a corporation?

4. Jack and Jill form a business by each contributing $30,000 in cash. Jack then borrows $1 million for the business from the local bank. Unfortunately, the money is lost through a series of bad investments. If this business is formed as a corporation, what is the impact of this loss on Jill? If this business is formed as a partnership, what is the impact of this loss on Jill?

5. Arthur C. Clarke bought one share of common stock in HAL Computing on the New York Stock Exchange. What rights does Clarke gain as a result of this ownership?

6. Wilson Beckett buys a share of common stock directly from Anston Corporation for $13 in cash. Several weeks later, Beckett sells this share to Buddy O'Coron for $22 in cash. What is the impact on Anston of each of these transactions?

7. The Amskan Corporation issues common stock to several investors. On the stock certificate, a par value of $1.00 per share is listed. What is the significance of this par value figure?

8. Hogsdon Corporation was incorporated in the state of Delaware although its operations are carried out entirely in the state of Vermont. On its balance sheet, the company indicates that it has 300 million shares of common stock authorized, 188 million issued, and 174 million outstanding. What do each of these terms mean?

9. Company PR issues 1,000 shares of common stock with a $2.00 per share par value to investors for cash of $9.00 per share. What journal entry does the company record for this transaction?

10. Company PR issues 1,000 shares of common stock with a $2.00 per share par value and a $9.00 per share fair value to investors for a tract of land that has a fair value of $10,000. What journal entry does the company record?

11. Over the years, the Boyer Corporation has issued thousands of shares of its common stock. It has also bought back some of these shares as treasury stock and then reissued them later. Under what conditions do these transactions affect the company's reported net income?

12. Mike Lewis and Warren Chapman each own 50 percent of the common stock of MlWc Corporation. Ron Wyskowski wants to become an owner, so he contributes $50,000 in cash to the business for 1,000 shares of preferred stock. How might these preferred shares be different from the company's common stock? Why might the original owners have wanted to issue preferred shares rather than common shares to Wyskowski? Why might Wyskowski have wanted to acquire preferred shares rather than common shares?

13. The Vylon Corporation wants to buy enough shares of the Bitsey Corporation to gain control of its operations. Upon hearing this news, the board of directors of Bitsey immediately authorizes the purchase of 3 million shares of its common stock. Why is the company acquiring its own treasury stock?

14. The common stock of Orlent Corporation has been selling for approximately $14 per share for the past year. Stockholders are upset that the stock price has not risen for such an extended period of time. On January 19 of the current year, the board of directors authorizes the purchase of 11 million share of the company's own stock. Why was this action most likely taken?

15. A press release issued by Mason-Williams Corporation provides the following information: "On March 17, the company's Board of Directors declared a $0.60 per share cash dividend on the company's common stock to be paid to all owners on record as of March 29 with distribution on April 11." The company has 20 million shares authorized, 6 million shares issued, and 5 million shares outstanding. Make all journal entries for this cash dividend including the dates.

16. The CarlB Corporation has 30,000 shares of common stock issued and outstanding. It also has 2,000 shares of $100 par value preferred stock issued and outstanding that pays an annual 4 percent cash dividend. The dividend is neither declared nor paid in Year One. What reporting is necessary on the Year One financial statements if this preferred stock dividend is cumulative? What reporting is necessary on the Year One financial statements if this preferred stock dividend is noncumulative?

17. The MWF Corporation has 40,000 shares of common stock issued and outstanding. It also has 5,000 shares of $100 par value preferred stock issued and outstanding that pays an annual 6 percent cumulative cash dividend. No cash dividends are declared or paid in Year One but an $80,000 cash dividend is declared and paid in Year Two. How much of this cash will each share of common stock receive in Year Two?

18. A company has 100,000 shares outstanding at January 2, Year One. The company reports assets of $1.4 million and liabilities of $500,000. The company's stock is selling for $20 per share just before it issues a 20 percent dividend. Susan Marie Fonseca owns 8,000 shares of the company's stock before the dividend. What journal entry does she make when she receives the additional 1,600 shares? Why is this reporting necessary?

19. What benefit does an owner hope to receive when a corporation issues a stock dividend or a stock split?

20. The Lion Corporation has shares of $2 par value common stock outstanding that are currently selling for $29 per share. The company issues 35,000 new shares as a stock dividend. What is the reduction to be recorded in retained earnings if this issuance is a 10 percent stock dividend? What is the reduction to be recorded in retained earnings if the issuance is a 40 percent stock dividend?

21. In Year One, the Marstale Corporation reports a return on equity (ROE) of 14.7 percent. In Year Two, the ROE is 18.2 percent. How is ROE computed? What information is provided by a company's ROE?

22. A company has both common stock and preferred stock outstanding. Each of these stocks paid a cash dividend in the current year. How is basic earnings per share (EPS) computed?

23. A company reports net income of $300,000 for Year One. It started this year with 120,000 shares of common stock outstanding. However, on April 1, another 20,000 shares were issued to the public for cash. What should be reported as basic EPS?

24. A company reports a price-earnings ratio (P/E ratio) of 14.6. How is that figure determined? How might investors make use of this number?

25. The Jacston Corporation reports basic EPS of $3.80 but diluted EPS of $2.90. In general, how is diluted EPS computed? What is the significance of diluted EPS to investors?

TRUE OR FALSE

1. ____ Sole proprietorships are easier to form than corporations.

2. ____ Most businesses of any significant size are formed as corporations.

3. ____ Limited liability is a concept that applies to a corporation but not to a partnership.

4. ____ Mutual agency is a concept that applies to a corporation but not to a partnership.

5. ____ All corporations in the United States have both common stock and preferred stock.

6. ____ Par value is a term used to indicate the market value of a share of capital stock.

7. ____ The management of a corporation appoints the board of directors.

8. ____ If a company has 80,000 shares of common stock issued but only 70,000 shares outstanding, the company holds 10,000 shares of its own treasury stock.

9. ____ If a company has 80,000 shares of common stock issued but only 70,000 shares outstanding and a $1.00 per share dividend is declared, retained earnings is reduced on that date by $80,000.

10. ____ A company is going to pay a cash dividend. The liability for that dividend is first reported on the date of record.

11. ____ The Yelson Company has 20,000 shares of $50 par value preferred stock authorized but only 9,000 shares issued and outstanding. This preferred stock pays a 4 percent annual cash dividend that is cumulative. The dividend is missed in both Year One and Year Two. A liability for $36,000 should be reported on the December 31, Year Two, balance sheet.

12. ____ Jayne Wellsfield owns 10,000 shares of Hartlan Corporation that she bought for $16 per share. She sells this entire investment to Robert Cranston for $23 per share. This transaction has no financial impact on Hartlan.

13. ____ The Robertsen Corporation issues 4,000 shares of $3 par value common stock (with a fair value of $9 per share) in exchange for eight acres of land worth $5,000 per acre. Robertsen should report a gain as a result of this transaction.

14. ____ The Cordol Corporation issues 10,000 shares of its $2 par value common stock for $9 cash per share. Later, the company reacquires 2,000 shares of this stock for $10 per share. The cost method is used to record these shares. Cordol records this acquisition as an asset with a reported value of $20,000.

15. ____ The Lodroc Corporation issues 30,000 shares of its $1 par value common stock for $13 cash per share. Later, the company reacquires 4,000 shares of this stock for $15 per share. The cost method is used to record these shares. The treasury stock is reissued at $16 per share. Net income is not affected by either the reacquisition or the reissuance of these shares.

16. ____ On the ex-dividend date, the price of a company's stock on a stock exchange will have a tendency to fall.

17. ____ A company declares a cash dividend on December 18, Year One to be paid on January 22, Year Two. Working capital decreases in Year One but is not affected in Year Two.

18. ____ A cumulative dividend on preferred stock must be paid each year or a company can be forced into bankruptcy.

19. ____ An investor receives 1,000 shares of stock valued at $7 per share as a stock dividend. Dividend revenue of $7,000 should be recognized.

20. ____ The Westling Corporation is trying to decide whether to issue a 15 percent stock dividend (15,000 new shares) or a 30 percent stock dividend (30,000 new shares). The 30 percent stock dividend automatically reduces retained earnings by twice as much as the 15 percent stock dividend.

21. ____ Return on equity (ROE) is found by dividing net income for a period by the average amount of retained earnings.

22. ____ Basic earnings per share is required to be reported for all publicly-traded corporations.

23. ____ Earnings per share is found by taking the net income for the year divided by the number of common shares outstanding at the end of the year.

24. ____ The P/E ratio relates a company's reported earnings per share to the market price of its common stock.

25. ____ A company reports net income of $500,000 but pays cash dividends to preferred stock ($100,000) and common stock ($50,000). The company has 100,000 shares of common stock outstanding all year as well as 20,000 shares of preferred stock. Basic EPS is $3.50 per share.

26. ____ Diluted EPS includes the potential negative impact of convertibles on the computation of earnings per share.

MULTIPLE CHOICE

1. Bob Wills, Susan Oglethorpe, and Billie Elkins form a business and decide to have it formally recognized as a corporation. Which of the following is the most likely reason for that decision?

    a. The limited liability that is available to the owners of a corporation.

    b. The advantages of mutual agency which are only available to the owners of a corporation.

    c. The double taxation faced by partnerships and sole proprietorships.

    d. The ease of forming a corporation.

2. Which of the following rights is most typical for the owners of a corporation's common stock?

    a. The right to vote for the members of the board of directors

    b. The right to an annual dividend

    c. The right to be involved in policy making decisions

    d. The right to decide on the issuance of a cash dividend

3. Landon Corporation sold 16,000 shares of $0.50 par value common stock for $17 per share. Which of the following is the journal entry Landon should make?

    a. **FIGURE 16.16**

Cash	272,000	
Common Stock		8,000
Capital in Excess of Par Value		264,000

    b. **FIGURE 16.17**

Cash	272,000	
Common Stock		272,000

    c. **FIGURE 16.18**

Capital in Excess of Par Value	264,000	
Common Stock		264,000

    d. **FIGURE 16.19**

Cash	8,000	
Common Stock		8,000

4. Jackson Company is authorized to issue 20,000 shares of $1 par value stock. On February 1, Year One, it issues 4,000 shares for $9 per share. On July 1, Year One, the company pays a $1 per share cash dividend. On December 1, Year One, the company buys back 1,000 shares of its own stock at $11 per share. Treasury stock is reported at its cost. On a December 31, Year One, balance sheet, what is reported as Capital in Excess of Par Value?

    a. $17,000
    b. $28,000
    c. $30,000
    d. $32,000

5. Paul Mitchell purchased a licensing agreement for $40,000 from a well-known restaurant chain. Subsequently, Traylor Corporation agreed to issue 2,000 shares of its common stock to Mitchell in exchange for this licensing agreement, which now has a value of $30,000. At the time of the exchange, Traylor's $2 par value stock was selling for $14 per share. For what amount should Traylor report the licensing agreement?

    a. $4,000
    b. $28,000
    c. $30,000
    d. $40,000

6. Kramer Company is authorized by the state to issue 10,000 shares of 8 percent, $100 par value preferred stock. On January 1, Year One, Kramer issues 5,000 shares for $125 per share. On December 13, Year One, Kramer's board of directors declares the annual dividend to owners on record as of January 3, Year Two. The dividend will be distributed January 18, Year Two. What liability should Kramer Company report on its December 31, Year One, balance sheet as a result of this dividend?

    a. Zero
    b. $40,000
    c. $50,000
    d. $80,000

7. Barbara Waterman bought 10,000 shares of $2 par value common stock directly from the Towsend Corporation for $13 per share. Later she sold these shares to Benjamin Duke for $17 per share. Subsequently, he sold 2,000 of these shares back to Towsend for cash of $19 per share. The cost method is in use for the treasury stock. Just based on these transactions, what is the total amount reported by the company as its stockholders' equity.

    a. $92,000
    b. $112,000
    c. $132,000
    d. $152,000

8. The Kansas-Kentucky Corporation is started on January 1, Year One. The company issues 100,000 shares of its $1 par value common stock for $8 per share. Subsequently, the company reports net income of $40,000 each year and pays an annual cash dividend of $10,000. In Year Three, the company reacquires 10,000 of these shares for $15 each. The cost method is to be applied to the treasury stock. Several weeks later, the company reissues 1,000 shares of this stock for $17 per share. A few days later, another 2,000 shares are reissued for $12 per share. At the end of Year Three, what should the company report as its retained earnings?

    a. $84,000
    b. $86,000
    c. $88,000
    d. $90,000

9. The Gewrty Corporation issues a 50 percent stock dividend. Which of the following is true about this event?

    a. The owners are happy because they own a larger percentage of the company.
    b. The owners are happy because the stock price will be lower, which might well create an increase in the demand for the company's stock on the stock market.
    c. The owners are unhappy because the net assets have been reduced by the company's action.
    d. The owners are unhappy because some owners benefit more than others from a stock dividend.

10. The Anglewood Corporation has 200,000 shares of its $1 par value common stock outstanding. These shares currently have a market price of $15 each. The company decides to issue a 10 percent (20,000 shares) stock dividend. At the last moment, the board of directors decides to increase this stock dividend to 30 percent (60,000 shares). Which of the following is true about the impact of the change in this decision?

    a. Retained earnings will be $60,000 lower than it would have been.

    b. Retained earnings will be $90,000 lower than it would have been.

    c. Retained earnings will be $220,000 higher than it would have been.

    d. Retained earnings will be $240,000 higher than it would have been.

11. The Kearsey Corporation issues 10,000 shares of its own common stock (with a $10 per share par value) for cash of $12 per share. Several months later, the company reacquires 1,000 shares of its own stock for $15 per share. This treasury stock is to be reported using the cost method. Which of the following statements is true?

    a. If these treasury shares are later reissued for $17,000, the $2,000 gain cannot be reported on the company's income statement.

    b. The $15,000 cash outflow will be reported like a dividend as a reduction in retained earnings.

    c. The $15,000 cost of these treasury shares will be reported by the company as a noncurrent asset.

    d. When these shares are reacquired, the company's contributed capital will increase by $15,000.

12. Portor Corporation is authorized to issue 150,000 shares of its $0.25 par value common stock. It currently has 90,000 shares issued and outstanding. Portor plans to declare a stock dividend and is curious about the effect this will have on retained earnings. Portor's stock has a current market value per share of $26. Portor is trying to decide between a 5 percent stock dividend and a 40 percent stock dividend. Which of the following shows the reduction caused by each on retained earnings?

	5% Stock Dividend	40% Stock Dividend
a.	$117,000	$936,000
b.	$117,000	$9,000
c.	$1,125	$9,000
d.	$1,125	$936,000

13. Falls Church Corporation ended Year Four with revenues of $98,000 and expenses of $86,000. The company distributed a cash dividend of $8,000 during the year. No stock transactions occurred. On the year-end balance sheet, the stockholders' equity accounts total $492,000. Which of the following is Falls Church's return on equity (ROE) for the year?

    a. 2.45%

    b. 6.73%

    c. 9.18%

    d. 9.75%

14. Fleming Corporation began and ended the current year with 50,000 outstanding shares of common stock. These shares were paid a $0.20 per share cash dividend. Net income for the year totaled $480,000. The company also had 10,000 shares of preferred stock outstanding throughout the year that paid dividends of $30,000. Which of the following figures is reported as Fleming's basic earnings per share?

    a. $6.00 per share

    b. $9.00 per share

    c. $9.60 per share

    d. $10.60 per share

15. The Houston Corporation started the year with 190,000 shares of common stock but issued 40,000 more shares on April 1 of the current year. The company also has 30,000 shares of preferred stock outstanding for the entire year. During the year, net income of $710,000 was reported. Cash dividends were paid during the year; $50,000 was distributed to the owners of the preferred stock and $30,000 to the owners of the common stock. What should be reported as basic earnings per share for this year (rounded)?

    a. $2.86

    b. $2.87

    c. $3.00

    d. $3.09

16. The Zerton Corporation ends Year One with net income of $400,000 and 100,000 shares of common stock issued and outstanding. The company also has 30,000 shares of $50 par value preferred stock issued and outstanding. During the year, the company distributed a $1 per share cash dividend on its common stock and a $2 per share cash dividend on its preferred stock. Each share of preferred stock is convertible into two shares of common stock. What should the company report as its basic earnings per share (rounded)?

    a. $2.13

    b. $2.50

    c. $3.40

    d. $4.00

17. Friar Inc. reported net income for Year Five of $1,870,000. It had 600,000 shares of common stock outstanding on January 1, Year Five, and repurchased 150,000 of those shares on September 1, Year Five, as treasury stock. The company has no preferred stock. At the end of Year Five, Friar's stock was selling for $26 per share. Which of the following is Friar's price-earnings ratio on that date?

    a. 6.25

    b. 7.00

    c. 7.65

    d. 8.33

VIDEO PROBLEMS

Professor Joe Hoyle discusses the answers to these two problems at the links that are indicated. After formulating your answers, watch each video to see how Professor Hoyle answers these questions.

1. Your roommate is an English major. The roommate's parents own a chain of ice cream shops located throughout Florida. One day, while waiting for an appointment with an academic advisor, your roommate asks you the following question: "My parents started their business originally as a partnership. However, after a year or two, they switched over and had the business incorporated. Since then, they complain every year about double taxation. What does that mean? And, if double taxation is so bad, why didn't they just continue to function as a partnership? They seemed happier before they made this switch." How would you respond?

View the video online at: http://bit.ly/hoyle16-3

2. Your uncle and two friends started a small office supply store several years ago. The company has grown and now has several large locations. Your uncle knows that you are taking a financial accounting class and asks you the following question: "We are planning to build a new store in a town that is 50 miles from our headquarters. For us, this is a major expansion. We are going to need several million dollars in cash. We have looked at several options for raising this money. Our financial advisor has recommended that we issue preferred stock. I'm not totally sure what this means. And, I'm not sure why we wouldn't just be better off to issue additional shares of the corporation's common stock. Why is our financial advisor giving us this advice?" How would you respond?

View the video online at: http://bit.ly/hoyle16-4

PROBLEMS

1. Cutlass Corporation is authorized by the state government to issue 40,000 shares of $1 par value common stock. On March 15, the company issues 1,000 shares for $6 cash per share. On April 19, the company issues another 800 shares for $7 per share. Record these transactions.

2. McNair Corporation is authorized to issue 150,000 shares of 5 percent, $200 par value preferred stock. On January 22, McNair issues 32,000 shares of this preferred stock for $225 per share. The board of directors for McNair declares the annual preferred dividend on September 1, payable to owners on record as of September 17, with the money to be distributed on October 1.

    a. Record the issuance of the preferred stock.

    b. Record the declaration and payment of the dividend and provide the date for each entry.

3. Several years ago, Douglas Company issued 33,000 shares of its $1 par value common stock for $18 per share. In the current year, Douglas's board of directors approves a plan to buy back a portion of these common stock shares. Prepare journal entries for each of the following transactions and events.

    a. On Monday, Douglas buys back 2,500 shares for $35 per share.

    b. On Tuesday, Douglas reissues 1,000 shares of treasury stock for $37 per share.

    c. On Wednesday, Douglas reissues 500 shares of treasury stock for $34 per share.

    d. On Thursday, Douglas reissues 600 shares of treasury stock for $28.

    e. On Friday, the board of directors declares a cash dividend of $1.00 per share.

4. The following are a number of transactions and events for the Nielsen Corporation. For each, prepare the necessary journal entry. If no entry is required, please indicate that.

    a. The state of Delaware approves the application for incorporation made by Nielsen and authorizes 100,000 shares of common stock with a $10 per share par value.

    b. Nielsen issues the first 1,000 shares of its common stock for $12 per share in cash.

    c. On the same day as (b), Nielsen issues another 500 shares of common stock for equipment that is valued at $6,200.

    d. Nielsen's board of directors declares a $2 per share cash dividend.

    e. On the date of record for the previous dividend, Nielsen prepares a list of all owners.

    f. The date of payment arrives and Nielsen mails out all dividend distributions.

    g. A 10 percent stock dividend is declared and immediately issued after the market price of the common stock has risen to $19 per share.

    h. The company reacquires 300 shares of common stock for $16 per share in cash. Treasury stock is reported by means of the cost method.

    i. The company reissues 200 shares of its treasury stock for $17 per share in cash.

    j. The company reissues the remaining shares of treasury stock for $11 per share in cash.

    k. A 40 percent stock dividend is declared and immediately issued on a day when the fair value of the stock is $20 per share.

5. At the beginning of Year One, a company issues 40,000 shares of $2 par value common stock for $23 per share in cash. The company also issues 10,000 shares of $40 par value preferred stock that pays an annual dividend of 10 percent. No dividend is paid in Year One but a total dividend of $100,000 is distributed in Year Two.

    a. If the preferred stock dividend is not cumulative, what is reported on the financial statements about the dividend at the end of Year One?

    b. If the preferred stock dividend is not cumulative, what amount of cash dividend does each share of common stock receive in Year Two?

    c. If the preferred stock dividend is cumulative, what is reported on the financial statements about the dividend at the end of Year One?

    d. If the preferred stock dividend is cumulative, what amount of cash dividend does each share of common stock receive in Year Two?

6. The Rostinaja Company is incorporated at the beginning of Year One. For convenience, assume that the company earns a reported net income of $130,000 each year and pays an annual cash dividend of $50,000. The company is authorized to issue 200,000 shares of $3 par value common stock. At the start of Year One, the company issues 40,000 shares of this common stock for $8 per share. At the end of Year Two, the company buys back 5,000 shares of its own stock for $12 per share. The cost method is used to record these shares. At the start of Year Three, the company reissues 1,000 of these shares for $14 per share. At the start of Year Four, the company reissues the remainder of the treasury stock for $9 per share.

    a. Prepare the stockholders' equity section of this company's balance sheet as of December 31, Year One.

    b. Prepare the stockholders' equity section of this company's balance sheet as of December 31, Year Two.

    c. Prepare the stockholders' equity section of this company's balance sheet as of December 31, Year Three.

    d. Prepare the stockholders' equity section of this company's balance sheet as of December 31, Year Four.

7. Grayson Corporation is authorized by the state to sell 2 million shares of its $1 par value common stock to the public. Before Year Seven, the company had issued 60,000 shares for cash of $12 per share. During Year Seven, Grayson issued another 14,000 shares at the market value of $24 per share.

    On January 1, Year Seven, Grayson reported retained earnings of $1,950,000. During that year, Grayson earned net income of $80,000 and paid cash dividends to common stockholders of $19,000. Also, during December of Year Seven, Grayson repurchased 11,000 shares of its own stock when the market price was $22 per share.

    a. Record the issuance of the common stock in Year Seven.

    b. Determine retained earnings as of the end of Year Seven.

    c. Record the purchase of the treasury stock.

    d. Prepare the stockholders' equity section of the balance sheet as of December 31, Year Seven.

    e. Compute the company's return on equity (ROE) for Year Seven.

8. On December 28, Year One, the Pickins Corporation was formed. The articles of incorporation authorize 5 million shares of common stock carrying a $1 par value, and 1 million shares of $5 par value preferred stock. On January 1, Year Two, 2 million shares of common stock are issued for $15 per share. Also on January 1, 500,000 shares of preferred stock are issued at $30 per share.

    a. Prepare journal entries to record these transactions on January 1.

    b. On March 9, Year Two, the Pickins Corporation repurchases 100,000 common shares as treasury stock paying a price of $13 per share. During August of that year, all 100,000 treasury shares are reissued at $16 per share. Prepare journal entries to record these transactions.

    c. On November 3, Year Two, Pickins issues a 30 percent stock dividend on all outstanding shares of common stock when the market price is $50 per share. On December 1, Year Two, Pickens declares a $0.75 per share cash dividend on common stock and a $2.00 per share cash dividend on preferred stock. Payment is scheduled for December 20, Year Two, to shareholders of record on December 10, Year Two. Prepare journal entries to record the declaration and distribution of these stock and cash dividends.

9. On March 1, St. George Company declares a stock dividend on its $1 par value stock. The company had 1,000 shares outstanding on that date with a market value of $13 per share.

    a. What reduction is recorded in retained earnings if a 10 percent stock dividend is issued?

    b. What reduction is recorded in retained earnings if a 30 percent stock dividend is issued?

10. Rawlings Company has the following equity accounts at the beginning and end of Year Three:

	January 1, Year Three	December 31, Year Three
Preferred Stock, 6%, $100 par value	$2,000,000	$2,000,000
Common Stock, $1 Par Value	$160,000	$200,000
Capital in Excess of Par, Common	$12,000,000	$16,000,000
Retained Earnings	$1,100,000	$1,800,000

The common stock account increased because 40,000 shares of common stock were issued to the public on September 1, Year Three. Preferred stock was paid its dividend during the year. A cash dividend was also distributed on the common stock. Net income for the year was $1,200,000.

    a. How much cash was received when the common stock was issued during Year Three?

    b. What was the total cash dividend paid on the common stock shares during the year?

    c. What was the company's basic earnings per share for Year Three?

11. Information on Massaff Corporation's stock accounts follows:

	December 31, Year 7	December 31, Year 8
Outstanding shares of		
Common stock	300,000	330,000
Nonconvertible preferred stock	10,000	10,000

The following additional information is available about this company:

- On July 1, Year 8, Massaff issued 30,000 additional shares of common stock for cash.
- Net income for the year ended December 31, Year 8, was $750,000.
- During Year 8, Massaff paid dividends of $3.00 per share on its preferred stock. The company also paid a total cash dividend of $220,000 on its outstanding shares of common stock.

Required:

Compute Massaff's basic earnings per common share for the year ended December 31, Year 8.

12. Yesterday, the Neumann Corporation had 100,000 shares of common stock authorized, 60,000 shares issued, and 40,000 shares outstanding. The stock has a par value of $10 per share but was issued originally for $24 per share. The stock is currently selling on a stock exchange for $30 per share. Treasury stock was acquired for $25 per share. None of that stock has been reissued. It is recorded using the cost method.

Today, a stock dividend was issued. After that dividend was distributed, the Neumann Corporation reported a total for its Capital in Excess of Par Value account of $960,000. How many shares were issued in the stock dividend?

13. A company has 20,000 shares of common stock issued and outstanding. These shares have a par value of $10 per share but were issued for $17 per share. When the fair value of the shares hits $21 per share, the company declares and issues a 50 percent stock dividend. The company accidentally recorded these new shares as a small stock dividend (20 percent or less) when the issuance should have been reported as a large stock dividend. At the end of the year, the company reported total assets of $300,000, total retained earnings of $80,000, and total stockholders' equity of $220,000.

a. What was the proper amount of total assets that should have been reported?
b. What was the proper amount of total retained earnings that should have been reported?
c. What was the proper amount of total stockholders' equity that should have been reported?

14. In several past chapters, we have met Heather Miller, who started her own business, Sew Cool. The following are the financial statements for December.

FIGURE 16.20 Sew Cool Financial Statements

Sew Cool
Income Statement
As of December 31, 20X8

Revenue	$4,000
Cost of Goods	(2,000)
Gross Profit	2,000
Other Expenses	(1,665)
Earnings before Interest and Tax	335
Interest Expense	(30)
Earnings before Tax	305
Tax Expense	(107)
Net Income	$198

FIGURE 16.21

Sew Cool
Stmt. of Retained Earnings
As of December 31, 20X8

Retained Earnings, December 1, 20X8	$500
Net Income	198
Dividends	(158)
Retained Earnings, December 31, 20X8	$540

FIGURE 16.22

Sew Cool
Balance Sheet
December 31, 20X8

Assets		Liabilities	
Current		**Current**	
Cash	$940	Accounts Payable	$900
Accounts Receivable	500	Income Tax Payable	120
Less Allowance for			
Doubtful Accounts	(20)		
Net Accounts Receivable	480		
Inventory	700		
Total Current Assets	$2,120	Total Current Liabilities	$1,020
Noncurrent		**Noncurrent**	
Equipment	$1,000	Notes Payable	$1,060
		Owners' Equity	
		Capital Stock	$500
		Retained Earnings	540
		Total Owners' Equity	$1,040
		Total Liabilities & Owners'	
Total Assets	$3,120	Equity	$3,120

Based on the financial statements determine Sew Cool's return on equity (ROE).

COMPREHENSIVE PROBLEM

This problem will carry through several chapters, building in difficulty. It allows students to continually practice skills and knowledge learned in previous chapters.

In Chapter 15, financial statements for March were prepared for Webworks. They are included here as a starting point for the required recording for April.

Here are Webworks financial statements as of March 31.

FIGURE 16.23 Webworks Financial Statements

Webworks Income Statement As of March 31	
Revenue	$20,810
Cost of Goods Sold	(12,258)
Gross Profit	8,552
Deprec. and Amort. Expense	(392)
Other Expenses and Losses	(6,413)
Investment Income (Loss)	200
Earnings before Interest and Tax	1,947
Interest Expense	(15)
Earnings before Tax	1,932
Tax Expense	(580)
Net Income	$1,352

FIGURE 16.24

Webworks Stmt. of Retained Earnings As of March 31	
Retained Earnings, March 1	$18,249
Net Income	1,352
Retained Earnings, March 31	$19,601

FIGURE 16.25

Webworks
Balance Sheet
March 31

Assets		Liabilities	
Current		**Current**	
Cash	$9,027	Accounts Payable	$2,770
Accounts Receivable	1,600	Salaries Payable	350
Less Allowance for		Interest Payable	30
Doubtful Accounts	(160)	Unearned Revenue	300
Net Accounts Receivable	1,440		
Trading Securities, Net	1,800		
Merchandise Inventory	2,324		
Supplies Inventory	50		
Total Current Assets	$14,641	Total Current Liabilities	$3,450
Property, Plant, and		**Noncurrent**	
Equipment		Note Payable	$3,000
Equipment	$10,500		
Less Accumulated			
Depreciation	(1,138)		
Furniture	1,000		
Less Accumulated			
Depreciation	(102)		
Total P, P, and E	$10,260		
Other Noncurrent Assets		**Owners' Equity**	
Available-for-Sale		Capital Stock	$2,000
Securities	$2,275	Retained Earnings	19,601
Licensing Agreement, Net	1,400	Other Accumulated	
		Comprehensive	
		Income:	
		Unrealized Gain on	
		Available-for-Sale	
		Securities	525
		Total Owners' Equity	$22,126
		Total Liabilities & Owners'	
Total Assets	$28,576	Equity	$28,576

The following events occur during April:

a. Webworks starts and completes ten more sites and bills clients for $7,000.

b. Leon invites Nancy Po (an employee) to invest money in the business. She contributes $2,000 and becomes an equal owner with Leon.

c. Webworks purchases supplies worth $125 on account.

d. At the beginning of March, Webworks had fourteen keyboards costing $120 each and twenty-eight flash drives costing $23 each. Webworks uses periodic FIFO to cost its inventory.

e. Webworks purchases ninety-five keyboards for $121 each and ninety flash drives for $25 each. All purchases are on account.

f. Webworks sells eighty-seven keyboards for $13,050 and ninety of the flash drives for $2,850 cash.

g. Webworks collects $6,400 in accounts receivable.

h. Webworks pays its $500 rent.

i. Webworks pays off $14,000 of its accounts payable.

j. Webworks sells all of its shares of RST stock for $20 per share.

k. Webworks pays Juan Marcon (another employee) $700 for his work during the first three weeks of April.

l. Webworks writes off an account receivable from December in the amount of $150 because collection appears unlikely.

m. Webworks pays off its salaries payable from March.

n. Webworks pays Leon Jackson and Nancy Po a salary of $3,500 each.

o. Webworks completes the design for the photographer for which it was paid in February. The $300 of unearned revenue has now been earned.

p. Webworks pays Leon Jackson and Nancy Po a dividend of $250 each.

q. Webworks pays taxes of $372 in cash.

> *Required:*
>
> A. Prepare journal entries for the previous events.
> B. Post the journal entries to T-accounts.
> C. Prepare an unadjusted trial balance for Webworks for April.
> D. Prepare adjusting entries at the end of February for the following and post them to your T-accounts.

r. Webworks owes Juan Marcon $100 for his work during the last week of April.

s. Webworks receives an electric bill for $440. Webworks will pay the bill in May.

t. Webworks determines that it has $65 worth of supplies remaining at the end of April.

u. Webworks is continuing to accrue bad debts at 10 percent of accounts receivable.

v. Webworks continues to depreciate its equipment over four years and its furniture over five years, using the straight-line method.

w. The license agreement should be amortized over its one-year life.

x. QRS Company is selling for $14 per share on April 30.

y. Interest should be accrued for April.

z. Record cost of goods sold.

> E. Prepare an adjusted trial balance.
> F. Prepare financial statements for April.

RESEARCH ASSIGNMENT

Assume that you take a job as a summer employee for an investment advisory service. One of the partners for that firm is currently looking at the possibility of investing in **Advanced Micro Devices Inc.** The partner is aware that technology companies like **AMD** often issue a lot of stock options and other items that can be converted into shares of common stock. The partner is curious as to the potential impact such conversions might have on the company and the price of its stock. The partner asks you to look at the 2010 financial statements for **AMD** by following this path:

- Go to http://www.amd.com.
- At the top of this screen, click on "About AMD."
- In the center of the next screen, click on "Investor Relations."
- On the left side of the next screen, click on "Annual Report & Proxy."
- On the next screen, click on "2010 Annual Report" to download.
- Scroll to page 73 and find the company's statement of operations (income statement) for the year ended December 25, 2010. At the bottom of that statement, determine the basic earnings per share reported by **AMD** as well as the diluted earnings per share. In addition, note the number of common stock shares used in the computation of basic earnings per share and the number of common stock shares used in the computation of diluted earnings per share.
- Scroll down to page 81 and read the last paragraph on that page which is part of "Note 2: Summary of Significant Accounting Policies." This paragraph mentions that **AMD** has three types of instruments outstanding that can be converted into common stock.

a. For the year ended December 25, 2010, what is the amount reported for basic earnings per share and for diluted earnings per share? What is the amount of the difference in those two figures?

b. Assume that the common stock of **AMD** was selling on the New York Stock Exchange on December 25, 2010, at $8.05. What was the P/E Ratio?

c. What were the three types of convertible items that **AMD** had outstanding at this time?

d. How many shares of common stock were used in computing basic earnings per share and how many shares of common stock were used in computing diluted earnings per share? How many shares were added to arrive at diluted earnings per share as a result of the possible conversion of the items listed in the answer to (c)?

ENDNOTES

1. Over the decades, a number of variations of these legal forms have been allowed, each with its own particular characteristics. For example, limited liability companies (LLC) and limited liability partnerships (LLP) are hybrids that exhibit characteristics of both partnerships and corporations and are permitted to exist in certain states.

2. A list of the typical contents of the articles of incorporation can be found at "Articles of Incorporation," http://en.wikipedia.org/wiki/Articles_of_Incorporation.

3. When money is loaned to a corporation, especially one that is either new or small, the lender might require the owners to guarantee the debt personally. Unless such a guarantee is made, the debt is that of the corporation and not the members of the ownership.

4. Tax rules do allow smaller corporations to file their income taxes as S corporations if certain guidelines are met. S corporations follow virtually the same tax rules as partnerships so that income is only taxed one time when initially earned.

5. Matthew Calderisi, senior editor, *Accounting Trends & Techniques*, 63rd edition (New York: American Institute of Certified Public Accountants, 2009), 299.

6. Although the **Kellogg Company** has its headquarters in Battle Creek, Michigan, the company is incorporated in the state of Delaware. Thus, the laws of Delaware set the rights of the common stock shares for this company.

7. Many other laws have been passed over the years that have been much more effective at protecting both creditors and stockholders.

8. A few states allow companies to issue stock without a par value. In that situation, the entire amount received is entered in the common stock account.

9. As mentioned earlier, the issuance of capital stock is not viewed as a trade by the corporation because it merely increases the number of capital shares outstanding. It is an expansion of both the company and its ownership. That is different than, for example, giving up an asset such as a truck in exchange for a computer or some other type of property.

10. Joe Flint, "Viacom Plans Stock Buy Back, Swings to Loss on Blockbuster," *The Wall Street Journal*, October 29, 2004, B-2.

11. If the board of directors does agree to the purchase of the corporation by an outside party, the two sides then negotiate a price for the shares as well as any other terms of the acquisition.

12. As can be seen in this press release, the terms "stock dividend" and "stock split" have come to be virtually interchangeable to the public. However, minor legal differences do exist that actually impact reporting. Par value is changed to create a stock split but not for a stock dividend. Interestingly, stock splits have no reportable impact on financial statements but stock dividends do. Therefore, only stock dividends will be described in this textbook.

13. A stock dividend of between 20 and 25 percent can be recorded at either fair value or par value.

CHAPTER 17

In a Set of Financial Statements, What Information Is Conveyed by the Statement of Cash Flows?

 Video Clip

In this video, Professor Joe Hoyle introduces the essential points covered in Chapter 17.

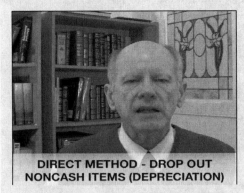

View the video online at: http://bit.ly/hoyle17-1

---

1. THE STRUCTURE OF A STATEMENT OF CASH FLOWS

LEARNING OBJECTIVES

At the end of this section, students should be able to meet the following objectives:

1. Describe the purpose of a statement of cash flows.
2. Define cash and cash equivalents.
3. Identify the three categories disclosed within a statement of cash flows.
4. Indicate the type of transactions that are reported as operating activities and provide common examples.
5. Indicate the type of transactions that are reported as investing activities and provide common examples.
6. Indicate the type of transactions that are reported as financing activities and provide common examples.

1.1 The Importance of a Statement of Cash Flows

Question: Thus far in this textbook, the balance sheet and income statement have been studied in comprehensive detail along with the computation of retained earnings. By this point, a student should be able to access a set of financial statements (on the Internet, for example) and understand much of the reported information. Terms such as "FIFO," "accumulated depreciation," "goodwill," "common stock," "bad debt expense," and the like that might have sounded like a foreign language at first should now be understandable.

Examination of one last financial statement is necessary to complete the portrait presented of a reporting entity by financial accounting and the rules of U.S. GAAP. That is the statement of cash flows. This statement was introduced briefly in an earlier chapter but will be covered here in detail. Why is it needed by decision makers? **What is the rationale for presenting a statement of cash flows?**

Answer: Coverage of the statement of cash flows has been postponed until now because its construction is unique. For this one statement, the figures do not come directly from ending T-account balances found in a general ledger. Instead, the accounts and amounts are derived from the other financial statements. Thus, an understanding of those statements is a helpful prerequisite when considering the creation of a statement of cash flows.

The delay in examining the statement of cash flows should not be taken as an indication of its lack of significance. In fact, some decision makers view it as the most important of the financial statements. They are able to see how corporate officials managed to get and then make use of the ultimate asset: cash. The acquisition of other assets, the payment of debts, and the distribution of dividends inevitably leads back to a company's ability to generate sufficient amounts of cash. Consequently, presentation of a statement of cash flows is required by U.S. GAAP for every period in which an income statement is reported.

To reiterate the importance of this information, Michael Dell, founder of **Dell Inc.**, states in his book *Direct from Dell: Strategies That Revolutionized an Industry* (written with Catherine Fredman): "We were always focused on our profit and loss statement. But cash flow was not a regularly discussed topic. It was as if we were driving along, watching only the speedometer, when in fact we were running out of gas."[1]

The income statement and the statement of cash flows connect the balance sheets from the beginning of the year to the end. During that time, total reported net assets either increase or decrease as does the entity's cash balance. The individual causes of those changes are explained by means of the income statement and the statement of cash flows.

The purpose of the statement of cash flows is virtually self-evident: It reports the cash receipts (cash inflows) and the cash disbursements (cash outflows) to explain the changes in cash that took place during the year. However, the physical structure of this statement is not self-evident. As illustrated previously, all cash flows are classified within three distinct categories. Coverage here is designed to demonstrate the logic of this classification system and the method by which the reported numbers are derived.

1.2   Cash and Cash Equivalents

cash equivalents

Short-term, highly liquid investments with original maturities of ninety days or fewer that can be readily converted into known amounts of cash.

Question: Because current assets are listed in order of liquidity, most businesses present "cash and cash equivalents" *as the first account on their balance sheets. For example, as of December 31, 2010,* **Ball Corporation** *reported holding cash and cash equivalents totaling $152.0 million. This same terminology is used on Ball's statement of cash flows which explains the drop of $58.6 million in cash and cash equivalents that took place during 2010.* **What constitutes cash and what are cash equivalents?**

Answer: Cash consists of coins, currencies, bank deposits (both checking accounts and savings accounts) and some negotiable instruments (money orders, checks, and bank drafts). Cash equivalents are short-term, highly liquid investments that are readily convertible into known amounts of cash. They are so near their maturity date that significant changes in value are unlikely. Only securities with original maturities of ninety days or fewer are classified as cash equivalents. Cash equivalents held by most companies include Treasury bills,[2] commercial paper,[3] and money market funds.

For the past few years, FASB has been considering the elimination of the cash equivalents category. If a change is made, such assets (other than cash) will likely appear on the balance sheet as temporary investments. As with all such debates, both pros and cons exist for making such an official change. For simplicity purposes, cash will be used in the examples presented throughout this chapter. However, until new authoritative rules are passed, accounting for cash equivalents is the same as that for cash.

TEST YOURSELF

Question:

Which of the following assets is least likely to be considered a cash equivalent?

a. Treasury bills

b. Commercial paper

c. Money market funds

d. Corporate bonds

Answer:

The correct answer is choice d: Corporate bonds.

Explanation:

Treasury bills, commercial paper, and money market funds are all considered to be cash equivalents as long as they can be converted into cash and had an original maturity of ninety days or fewer. Most corporate bonds have maturity dates much longer than ninety days, often many years.

1.3 Cash Flows from Operating Activities

Question: For reporting purposes all cash flows are classified within one of three categories: operating activities, investing activities, and financing activities. **What transactions are specifically identified as operating activities?**

Answer: **Operating activities** generally involve producing and delivering goods and providing services to customers. These events are those that transpire on virtually a daily basis as a result of the organization's primary function. For a business like **Barnes & Noble**, operating activities include the buying and selling of books (and other inventory items) as well as the multitude of other tasks required by that company's retail function. As shown in Figure 17.1, operating activities are those that are expected to take place regularly in the normal course of business.

> **operating activities**
>
> A statement of cash flow category used to disclose cash receipts and disbursements arising from the primary activities of the reporting organization.

FIGURE 17.1 Typical Operating Activity Cash Inflows and Outflows

Cash Inflows	Cash Outflows
Receipts from the Sale of Goods or Services	Payments for Inventory Payments to Employees Payments for Taxes Payments for Rents, Insurance, Advertising, and the Like

The net number for the period (the inflows compared to the outflows) is presented as the cash flows generated from operating activities. This figure is viewed by many decision makers as a good measure of a company's ability to prosper. Investors obviously prefer to see a positive number, one that increases from year to year. Some analysts believe that this figure is a better reflection of a company's financial health than reported net income because the ultimate goal of a business is to generate cash.

For example, **International Paper Company** reported a net loss on its income statement for the year ended December 31, 2008, of $1.282 billion (considerably worse than any of the previous five years). However, its statement of cash flows for the same period reported a net cash inflow from operating activities of $2.669 million (considerably better than any of the previous five years). That is nearly a $4 billion difference. No one could blame a decision maker for being puzzled. Did the company do poorly that year or wonderfully well?

That is the problem with relying on only a few of the numbers in a set of financial statements without a closer and more complete inspection. What caused this company to lose over $1.2 billion dollars? How did the company manage to generate nearly $2.7 billion in cash from its operating activities? In-depth analysis of financial statements is never quick and easy. It requires patience and knowledge and the willingness to dig through all the available information.

1.4   Investing Activity Cash Flows

*Question: On the statement of cash flows for the year ended August 31, 2011, **Walgreen Co.** reported that a net of over $1.5 billion in cash was spent in connection with a variety of investing activities. This company's management obviously made decisions that required the use of considerable sums of money. Details about those expenditures should be of interest to virtually any party analyzing this company. **What cash transactions are specifically identified as investing activities?***

investing activities

A statement of cash flow category used to disclose cash receipts and disbursements arising from an asset transaction other than one relating to the primary activities of the reporting organization.

Answer: **Investing activities** encompass the acquisition and disposition of assets in transactions that are separate from the central activity of the reporting organization. In simple terms, these cash exchanges do not occur as part of daily operations.

- For a delicatessen, the purchase of bread, mustard, or onions is an operating activity, but the acquisition of a refrigerator or stove is an investing activity.

- For a pharmacy, the sale of aspirin or a decongestant is an operating activity, but the disposal of a delivery vehicle or cash register is an investing activity.

All of these cash transactions involve assets but, to be classified as an investing activity, they can only be tangentially related to the day-to-day operation of the business. For example, Figure 17.2 shows the three biggest investing activity cash flows reported by **Walgreen**.

FIGURE 17.2   The Three Biggest Investing Activity Cash Flows Identified on Walgreen's Statement of Cash Flows for the Year Ended August 31, 2011

Additions to Property and Equipment	($1,213) million
Business and Intangible Asset Acquisitions, Net of Cash Received	(630) million
Proceeds from Sale of Business	442 million

Healthy, growing companies normally expect cash flows from investing activities to be negative (a net outflow) as money is invested by management especially in new noncurrent assets. As can be seen in Figure 17.2, **Walgreen Co.** spent over $1.2 billion in cash during this one year to buy property and equipment. The company apparently had sufficient cash available to fund this significant expansion.

1.5   Financing Activity Cash Flows

*Question: The third category of cash flows lists the amounts received and disbursed by a business through financing activities. For the year ended July 2, 2011, **Sara Lee Corporation** reported that its cash balance had been reduced by over $1.7 billion as a result of such financing activities. Again, that is a lot of money leaving the company. **What transactions are specifically identified in a statement of cash flows as financing activities?***

financing activities

A statement of cash flow category used to disclose cash receipts and disbursements arising from a liability or stockholders' equity transaction other than one relating to the primary activities of the organization.

Answer: **Financing activities** are transactions separate from the central, day-to-day activities of an organization that involve either liabilities or shareholders' equity accounts. Cash inflows from financing activities include issuing capital stock and incurring liabilities such as bonds or notes payable. Outflows are created by the distribution of dividends, the acquisition of treasury stock, the payment of noncurrent liabilities, and other similar cash transactions.

As can be seen in Figure 17.3, **Sara Lee's** three biggest changes in cash that resulted from financing activities were the repayments of other debt, purchases of common stock, and borrowing of other debt. Significant information about management's decisions is readily apparent from an analysis of the cash flows from both investing and financing activities.

FIGURE 17.3 The Three Biggest Financing Activity Cash Flows Identified on Sara Lee's Statement of Cash Flows for the Year Ended July 2, 2011

Repayments of Other Debt	($1,431) million
Purchases of Common Stock	(1,313) million
Borrowings of Other Debt	1,054 million

The net result reported for financing activities is frequently positive in some years and negative in others. When a company borrows money or sells capital stock, an overall positive inflow of cash is likely. In years when a large dividend is distributed or debt is settled, the net figure for financing activities is more likely to be negative.

TEST YOURSELF

Question:

The Reardon Company paid salary to its employees totaling $527,000 during the current year. Into which category on a statement of cash flows will these payments be placed?

a. Operating activities

b. Investing activities

c. Financing activities

d. Capital activities

Answer:

The correct answer is choice a: Operating activities.

Explanation:

The payment of salary is a regular operating activity. The expenditure takes place as a direct result of the day-to-day operations of the business.

TEST YOURSELF

Question:

The McGuire Company, located in Wilcox, Texas, issued 10,000 shares of its $3 par value common stock during this year for $9 in cash per share. Into which category on a statement of cash flows will this $90,000 capital contribution be placed?

a. Operating activities

b. Investing activities

c. Financing activities

d. Capital activities

Answer:

The correct answer is choice c: Financing activities.

Explanation:

This issuance of common (and preferred) stock is identified as a financing activity. It represents a change in a shareholders' equity account. However, the cash inflow is not directly related to the daily operations of the business.

TEST YOURSELF

Question:

The Staunton Corporation owns and operates several restaurants in eastern Iowa. Looking to expand operations, Staunton bought a piece of land recently for $500,000. The business paid $100,000 and a noncurrent note payable was signed for the remaining $400,000. How is this transaction reported on a statement of cash flows?

   a. Investing activity as an outflow of $100,000
   b. Investing activity as an outflow of $500,000
   c. Financing activity as an outflow of $100,000
   d. Financing activity as an outflow of $500,000

Answer:

The correct answer is choice a: Investing activity as an outflow of $100,000.

Explanation:

The purpose of the transaction is to acquire land. Land is an asset and this event did not take place as a normal part of Staunton's daily operations. Thus, the transaction is an investing activity. Because $100,000 in cash was spent for this acquisition, the transaction is reported as an outflow of that amount. The $500,000 cost of the land and the $400,000 note payable will be recorded on the corporation's balance sheet.

1.6 Disclosure of Noncash Transactions

Question: Significant investing and financing transactions can occur without any cash component. Land, for example, might be obtained by issuing common stock. Buildings are often bought through the signing of a long-term note payable with all cash payments deferred into the future. Is that information omitted entirely from the statement of cash flows? **If no cash is received or expended, should a transaction be reported on a statement of cash flows?**

Answer: All investing and financing transactions need to be reported in some manner because of the informational value. They represent choices made by the organization's management. Even if no cash is involved, such events must still be disclosed in a separate schedule (often attached to the statement of cash flows) or explained in the notes to the financial statements. This information is valuable to the interested parties who want a complete picture of the investing and financing decisions that were made during the period.

For example, on the statement for **Duke Energy Corporation** for the year ended December 31, 2010, a significant noncash transaction was identified as "accrued capital expenditures" of $361 million. Although cash was not involved, inclusion of this information was still deemed to be important.

Stock dividends and stock splits, though, are omitted entirely in creating a statement of cash flows. As discussed previously, they are viewed as techniques to reduce the price of a corporation's stock and are not decisions that impact the allocation of financial resources.

KEY TAKEAWAY

A statement of cash flows is required by U.S. GAAP whenever an income statement is presented. It explains all changes occurring in cash and cash equivalents during the reporting period. The various cash inflows and outflows are classified into one of three categories. Operating activities result from the primary or central function of the business. Investing activities are not part of normal operations and affect an asset (such as the cash acquisition of a truck or the sale of a patent). Financing activities are not part of normal operations and involve a liability or a stockholders' equity account (borrowing money on a note, for example, or the reacquisition of treasury stock). Significant investing and financing activities that do not impact cash must still be disclosed because they reflect decisions made by management.

2.   CASH FLOWS FROM OPERATING ACTIVITIES: THE DIRECT METHOD

LEARNING OBJECTIVES

At the end of this section, students should be able to meet the following objectives:

1. Identify the two methods available for reporting cash flows from operating activities.
2. Indicate the method of reporting cash flows from operating activities that is preferred by FASB as well as the one that is most commonly used in practice.
3. List the steps to be followed in determining cash flows from operating activities.
4. List the income statement accounts that are removed entirely in computing cash flows from operating activities and explain this procedure when the direct method is applied.
5. Identify common "connector accounts" that are used to convert accrual accounting figures to the change taking place in the cash balance as a result of these transactions.
6. Compute the cash inflows and outflows resulting from common revenues and expenses such as sales, cost of goods sold, rent expense, salary expense, and the like.

2.1   The Handling of Noncash and Nonoperating Transactions by the Direct Method

Question: The net cash inflow or outflow generated by operating activities is especially significant inform-ation to any person looking at an organization's financial health and future prospects. According to U.S. GAAP, that information can be presented within the statement of cash flows by either of two approaches: the **direct method** *or the* **indirect method***.*

The numerical amount of the change in cash resulting from a company's daily operations is not im-pacted by this reporting choice. The increase or decrease in cash is a fact that will not vary because of the manner of presentation. Both methods arrive at the same total. The informational value to decision makers, though, is potentially affected by the approach selected.

FASB has indicated a preference for the direct method. In contrast, reporting companies (by an ex-tremely wide margin) continue to use the more traditional indirect method. Thus, both will be demon-strated here. The direct method is more logical and will be discussed first. **How is information presented when the direct method is selected to disclose a company's cash flows from operating activities?**

Answer: The direct method starts with the entire income statement for the period. Then, each of the separately reported figures is converted into the amount of cash received or spent in carrying on this operating activity. "Sales," for example, is turned into "cash collected from customers." "Salary ex-pense" and "rent expense" are recomputed as "cash paid to employees" and "cash paid to rent facilities."

For illustration purposes, assume that Liberto Company prepared its income statement for the year ended December 31, Year One, as shown in Figure 17.4. This statement has been kept rather simple so that the conversion to cash flows from operating activities is not unnecessarily complex. For example, income tax expense has been omitted.

direct method

A mechanical method of reporting the amount of cash flows that a company generates from its operating activities; it is preferred by FASB because the information is easier to understand but it is only rarely encountered in practice.

indirect method

A mechanical method of reporting the amount of cash flows that a company generates from its operating activities; it is allowed by FASB (although the direct method is viewed as superior) but is used by a vast majority of businesses in the United States.

FIGURE 17.4 Liberto Company Income Statement Year Ended December 31, Year One

Revenues:		
Sales to Customers		$480,000
Expenses:		
Cost of Goods Sold	$250,000	
Salary Expense	60,000	
Rent Expense	30,000	
Depreciation Expense	80,000	420,000
Operating Income		60,000
Other Gains and Losses:		
Gain on Sale of		
Equipment		40,000
Net Income		$100,000

The $100,000 net income figure reported here by Liberto is based on the application of U.S. GAAP. However, the amount of cash generated by the company's operating activities might be considerably more or much less than that income figure. It is a different piece of information.

To transform a company's income statement into its cash flows from operating activities, several distinct steps must be taken. These steps are basically the same regardless of whether the direct method or the indirect method is applied.

The first step is the complete elimination of any income statement account that does not involve cash. Although such balances are important in arriving at net income, they are not relevant to the cash generated and spent in connection with daily operations. By far the most obvious example is depreciation. This expense appears on virtually all income statements but has no direct impact on a company's cash. In determining cash flows from operating activities, it is omitted because depreciation is neither a source nor use of cash. It is an allocation of a historical cost to expense over an asset's useful life. To begin the calculation of the cash flows resulting from Liberto's operating activities, the $80,000 depreciation expense must be removed.

The second step is the removal of any gains and losses that resulted from investing or financing activities. Although cash was likely involved in these transactions, this inflow or outflow is reported elsewhere in the statement of cash flows and not within the company's operating activities. For example, Liberto's $40,000 gain on the sale of equipment is germane to the reporting of investing activities, not operating activities. The cash received in this disposal is included on the statement of cash flows but as an investing activity.

Neither (a) noncash items such as depreciation nor (b) nonoperating gains and losses are included when an income statement is converted to the cash flows from operating activities.

2.2 Converting Accrual Accounts to Cash Flows—The Direct Method

Question: After all noncash and nonoperating balances are deleted, Liberto is left with four income statement accounts:

1. *Sales to customers—$480,000*

2. *Cost of goods sold—$250,000*

3. *Salary expense—$60,000*

4. *Rent expense—$30,000*

These balances all relate to operating activities. However, the numbers reflect the application of U.S. GAAP and accrual accounting rather than the amount of cash exchanged. The cash effects must be determined individually for these accounts. **How are income statement figures such as sales or rent expense converted to the amount of cash received or expended?**

Answer: *The third step in the process of determining cash flows from operating activities is the individual conversion to cash of all remaining income statement accounts. For these balances, a difference usually exists between the time of recognition as specified by accrual accounting and the exchange of* cash. A sale is made on Monday (revenue is recognized), but the money is not collected until Friday. An employee performs work on Monday (expense is recognized) but payment is not made until Friday.

These timing differences occur because accrual accounting is required by U.S. GAAP. Thus, many revenues and expenses are not recorded at the same time as the related cash transactions. In the interim, recognition of an asset or liability balance is necessary. Between the sale on Monday and the collection on Friday, the business reports an account receivable. This asset goes up when the sale is made and down when the cash is collected. Between the employee's work on Monday and the payment on Friday, the business reports a salary payable. This liability goes up when the money is earned and down when the cash payment is made. In this textbook, these interim accounts (such as accounts receivable and salary payable) will be referred to as "connector accounts" because they connect the recording mandated by accrual accounting with the cash transaction.

Each income statement account (other than the noncash and nonoperating numbers that have already been eliminated) has at least one asset or liability that is recorded between the time of accounting recognition and the exchange of cash. The changes in these connector accounts can be used to convert the individual income statement figures to their cash equivalents. Basically, the increase or decrease is removed to revert the reported number back to the amount of cash involved. As can be seen in Figure 17.5, connector accounts are mostly receivables, payables, and prepaid expenses.

FIGURE 17.5 Common Connector Accounts for Liberto's Four Income Statement Balances[4]

Income Statement Account	Balance Sheet Connector Account
Sales to Customers	Accounts Receivable
Cost of Goods Sold	Inventory and Accounts Payable
Salary Expense	Salary Payable
Rent Expense	Prepaid Rent and Rent Payable

If a connector account is an asset and the balance goes up, the business has less cash (the receivable was not collected, for example). If a connector account is an asset and goes down, the business has more cash (such as when receivables from previous years are collected in the current period). Therefore, for a connector account that is an asset, an inverse relationship exists between the change in the balance during the year and the reporting entity's cash balance.

- Increase in connector account that is an asset → Lower cash balance
- Decrease in connector account that is an asset → Higher cash balance

If a connector account is a liability and the balance goes up, the business has saved its cash and holds more (an expense has been incurred but not yet paid, for example). If a connector account is a liability and this balance falls, the business must have used its cash to reduce the debt and has less remaining. Consequently, a direct relationship exists between the change in a connector account that is a liability and the cash balance.

- Increase in connector account that is a liability → Higher cash balance
- Decrease in connector account that is a liability → Lower cash balance

2.3 Applying the Direct Method to Determine Cash Revenues and Expenses

Question: Liberto has one revenue and three expenses left on its income statement after removal of noncash and nonoperating items. To arrive at the net cash flows from operating activities, the cash inflow or outflow relating to each must be determined. Assume that the following changes took place during this year in the related balance sheet connector accounts:

- *Accounts receivable: up $19,000*
- *Inventory: down $12,000*
- *Prepaid rent: up $4,000*
- *Accounts payable: up $9,000*
- *Salary payable: down $5,000*

In applying the direct method to determine operating activity cash flows, how are the individual figures to be disclosed computed?

Answer:

- Sales to customers were reported on the income statement as $480,000. During that same period, accounts receivable increased by $19,000. Thus, less money was collected than the amount of the company's credit sales. That is the cause for a rise in receivables. To reflect the collection of less cash, a reduction is needed. Consequently, the cash received from customers was only $461,000 ($480,000 less $19,000).

- Salary expense was reported as $60,000. During that time period, salary payable went down by $5,000. More cash must have been paid to cause this drop in the liability. The amount actually paid to employees was $65,000 ($60,000 plus $5,000).

- Rent expense was reported as $30,000. Prepaid rent increased by $4,000 from the first of the year to the end. This connector account is an asset. Because this asset increased, Liberto must have paid an extra amount for rent. Cash paid for rent was $34,000 ($30,000 plus $4,000).

- Cost of goods sold has been left to last because it requires an extra step. The company first determines the quantity of inventory bought during this period. Only then can the cash payment made for those acquisitions be determined.

  - Cost of goods sold is reported as $250,000. However, the balance held in inventory fell by $12,000. Thus, the company bought $12,000 less inventory than it sold. Fewer purchases cause a drop in inventory. The amount of inventory acquired during the period was only $238,000 ($250,000 less $12,000).

  - Next, the cash paid for those purchases is calculated. As indicated, accounts payable went up $9,000. Liabilities increase because less money is paid. Although $238,000 of merchandise was acquired, only $229,000 in cash payments were made ($238,000 less $9,000).

After each of these four income statement accounts is converted to the amount of cash received or paid this period, the operating activity section of the statement of cash flows can be created by the direct method as shown in Figure 17.6.

FIGURE 17.6 Liberto Company Statement of Cash Flows for Year One, Operating Activities Reported by Direct Method

Cash Collected from Customers	$461,000
Cash Paid to Acquire Inventory	(229,000)
Cash Paid to Employees	(65,000)
Cash Paid for Rent	(34,000)
Cash Generated by Operating Activities	$133,000

Liberto's income statement reported net income of $100,000. However, the cash generated by operating activities during this same period was $133,000. The conversion from accrual accounting to operating cash inflows and outflows required three steps.

1. All noncash revenues and expenses (depreciation, in this example) were removed. These accounts do not represent cash transactions.

2. All nonoperating gains and losses (the gain on sale of equipment, in this example) were removed. These accounts reflect investing and financing activities and the resulting cash flows are reported in those sections of the statement of cash flows rather than within the operating activities.

3. All remaining income statement accounts are adjusted to the amount of cash physically exchanged this period by applying the change in each related connector account. By this process, accrual accounting figures are converted to cash balances.

TEST YOURSELF

Question:

The Giotto Company reported sales in its latest year of $800,000. Giotto held $170,000 in accounts receivable at the beginning of the period but only $144,000 at the end. Assume that all of these receivables are viewed as collectible so that no allowance is needed. What amount of cash did the company collect this period from its customers?

a. $774,000

b. $776,000

c. $824,000

d. $826,000

Answer:

The correct answer is choice d: $826,000.

Explanation:

During this year, the accounts receivable balance dropped by $26,000 ($170,000 to $144,000). Thus, more cash was collected than the amount of sales. Receivables decrease because cash is received. These additional receipts indicate that a total of $826,000 was collected from the Giotto's customers ($800,000 plus $26,000).

TEST YOURSELF

Question:

The Lessain Company reported salary expense of $345,000 on its income statement for the year ended December 31, Year One. At the beginning of that year, salary payable was shown as $31,000 but rose to $40,000 by December 31. In reporting the Lessain's cash flows generated from operating activities, what amount should be shown as the cash paid to employees?

a. $336,000

b. $345,000

c. $354,000

d. $376,000

Answer:

The correct answer is choice a: $336,000.

Explanation:

Lessain's salary payable went up by $9,000. Accrued liabilities rise because fewer payments are made than the expenses incurred. Although employees earned $345,000 during this year, only $336,000 was paid to them as salary ($345,000 less $9,000). It is this reduction in the cash payment that caused the salary payable account to increase by $9,000 during Year One.

TEST YOURSELF

Question:

The TJ Corporation reported cost of goods sold for Year One of $564,000. During that same period, this company's inventory balance rose by $22,000 while its accounts payable fell by $7,000. In creating a statement of cash flows using the direct method, what amount should be reported by the TJ Corporation as the cash spent to acquire inventory?

a. $535,000

b. $549,000

c. $579,000

d. $593,000

Answer:

The correct answer is choice d: $593,000.

Explanation:

Although cost of goods sold was reported as $564,000, the inventory on hand increased $22,000. More inventory was bought that year than sold. TJ acquired $586,000 in inventory during Year One ($564,000 sold plus the $22,000 increase). At the same time, accounts payable dropped. This decrease indicates that more in cash was paid than the amount bought. Spending an extra $7,000 caused the reduction. Thus, cash paid out this year to acquire inventory was $593,000 ($586,000 plus $7,000).

TEST YOURSELF

Question:

Sales reported by a local shoe store are $470,000. Accounts receivable decreased by $27,000 this year while unearned revenues rose by $14,000. If the direct method is used to report cash flows from operating activities, how much should be shown as the store's cash collected from its customers?

a. $429,000

b. $467,000

c. $483,000

d. $511,000

Answer:

The correct answer is choice d: $511,000.

Explanation:

A new connector account (unearned revenues) is included here. This balance represents cash received where revenue has not yet been earned. This increase indicates that $14,000 more in cash was collected from customers than the amount reported as revenue. Also, accounts receivable fell by $27,000. Receivables are reduced through collection. The shoe store must have received that much more cash than it earned. Cash received during this period is $511,000 ($470,000 plus $14,000 and $27,000).

KEY TAKEAWAY

An entity's cash flows from operating activities can be derived and reported by either the direct method or the indirect method. FASB has expressed preference for the direct method but the indirect method has been adopted by virtually all businesses in the United States. The process always begins with the income for the period (the entire income statement is used when the direct method is applied). First noncash items (such as depreciation) and then nonoperating gains and losses are eliminated entirely because they are not related to operating activity cash flows. In the direct method, the remaining revenue and expense accounts are individually converted into cash figures. For each, the change in one or more related balance sheet connector accounts is used to adjust these accrual accounting numbers to their corresponding cash balances. Thus, income statement balances are returned to their underlying cash inflows and outflows for reporting purposes.

3. CASH FLOWS FROM OPERATING ACTIVITIES: THE INDIRECT METHOD

LEARNING OBJECTIVES

At the end of this section, students should be able to meet the following objectives:

1. Explain the difference in the start of the operating activities section of the statement of cash flows when the indirect method is used rather than the direct method.
2. Demonstrate the removal of both noncash items and nonoperating gains and losses in the application of the indirect method.
3. Determine the effect caused by the change in the various connector accounts when the indirect method is used to present cash flows from operating activities.
4. Identify the reporting classification for interest revenues, dividend revenues, and interest expense in creating a statement of cash flows and explain the controversy that resulted from this handling.

3.1 The Steps Followed in Applying the Indirect Method

Question: As mentioned, most organizations do not choose to present their operating activity cash flows using the direct method despite the preference of FASB. Instead, this information is almost universally shown within a statement of cash flows by means of the indirect method. **How does the indirect method of reporting operating activity cash flows differ from the direct method?**

Answer: The indirect method actually follows the same set of procedures as the direct method except that it begins with net income rather than the business's entire income statement. After that, the same three steps demonstrated previously to determine the net cash flows from operating activities are followed although the mechanical application here is different.

1. Noncash items are removed.
2. Nonoperational gains and losses are removed.
3. Adjustments are made, based on the monetary change occurring during the period in the various balance sheet connector accounts, to switch all remaining revenues and expenses from accrual accounting to cash accounting.

3.2 Removing Noncash and Nonoperating Items—The Indirect Method

Question: In the income statement presented in Figure 17.4 for the Liberto Company, net income was reported as $100,000. This figure included depreciation expense (a noncash item) of $80,000 and a gain on the sale of equipment (an investing activity rather than an operating activity) of $40,000. **In applying the indirect method, how are noncash items and nonoperating gains and losses removed from net income?**

Answer: First, all noncash items within net income are eliminated. Depreciation is the example included here. As an expense, it is a negative component found within net income. To remove a negative, it is offset by a positive. Thus, adding back $80,000 serves to remove the impact of depreciation from the reporting company's net income.

Second, all nonoperating items within net income are eliminated. Liberto's gain on sale of equipment is reported within reported income. As a gain, it is a positive figure; it helped increase profits this period. To eliminate this gain, $40,000 must be subtracted from net income. The cash flows resulting from this transaction came from an investing activity and not an operating activity.

In applying the indirect method, as shown in Figure 17.7, a negative is removed by addition; a positive is removed by subtraction.

FIGURE 17.7 Operating Activity Cash Flows, Indirect Method—Elimination of Noncash and Nonoperating Balances

Net Income	$100,000
Eliminate:	
Depreciation Expense	+80,000
Gain on Sale of Equipment	(40,000)

- In the direct method, these two income statement amounts were simply omitted in arriving at the individual cash flows from operating activities.
- In the indirect method, they are both physically removed from income by reversing their effect.

The impact is the same in the indirect method as in the direct method; the balances are removed.

3.3 Converting Accrual Accounting Figures to Cash Balances—The Indirect Method

Question: After all noncash and nonoperating items are removed from net income, only the changes in the balance sheet connector accounts must be utilized to complete the conversion to cash. For Liberto, those balances were shown previously.

- *Accounts receivable: up $19,000*
- *Inventory: down $12,000*
- *Prepaid rent: up $4,000*
- *Accounts payable: up $9,000*
- *Salary payable: down $5,000*

Each of these increases and decreases was used in the direct method to turn accrual accounting figures into cash balances. That same process is followed in the indirect method. **In determining cash flows from operating activities, how are changes in an entity's connector accounts reflected in the application of the indirect method?**

Answer: Although the procedures appear to be different, the same logic is applied in the indirect method as in the direct method. The change in each of the previous connector accounts discloses the difference in the accrual accounting amounts recognized in the income statement and the actual changes in cash. Here, though, the effect is measured on net income as a whole rather than on the individual revenue and expense accounts.

Accounts receivable increased by $19,000. This rise in the receivable balance shows that less money was collected than the sales made by Liberto during the period. Receivables go up because customers are slow to pay. This change results in a lower cash balance. Thus, the $19,000 is subtracted in arriving at the cash flow amount generated by operating activities. The cash received was actually less than the figure reported for sales that appears within the company's net income. *Subtract $19,000.*

Inventory decreased by $12,000. A drop in the amount of inventory on hand indicates that less merchandise was purchased during the period. Buying less requires a smaller amount of cash to be paid. That leaves the cash balance higher. The $12,000 is added in arriving at the operating activity change in cash. *Add $12,000.*

Prepaid rent increased by $4,000. An increase in any prepaid expense shows that more of the asset was acquired during the year than was consumed. This additional purchase requires the use of cash; thus, the resulting cash balance is lower. The increase in prepaid rent necessitates a $4,000 subtraction in the operating activity cash flow computation. *Subtract $4,000.*

Accounts payable increased by $9,000. Any jump in a liability means that Liberto paid less cash during the period than the debts that were incurred. Postponing liability payments is a common method for saving cash to keep the reported balance high. In determining cash flows from operating activities, the $9,000 liability increase is added. *Add $9,000.*

Salary payable decreased by $5,000. Liability balances fall when additional payments are made. Such cash transactions are reflected in applying the indirect method by a $5,000 subtraction from net income. *Subtract $5,000.*

Therefore, if Liberto Company uses the indirect method to report its cash flows from operating activities, the information will be presented to decision makers as shown in Figure 17.8.

FIGURE 17.8 Liberto Company Statement of Cash Flows for Year One, Operating Activities Reported by Indirect Method

Net Income	$100,000
Eliminate:	
Depreciation Expense	+80,000
Gain on Sale of Equipment	(40,000)
Adjust Revenues and Expenses from	
Accrual Accounting to Cash:	
Increase in Accounts Receivable	(19,000)
Decrease in Inventory	+12,000
Increase in Prepaid Rent	(4,000)
Increase in Accounts Payable	+9,000
Decrease in Salary Payable	(5,000)
Cash Generated by Operating	
Activities	$133,000

As with the direct method (Figure 17.6), the total here reflects a net cash inflow of $133,000 from the operating activities of this company. In both cases, the starting spot was net income (either as the entire income statement or as the single number). Then, all noncash items were removed as well as nonoperating gains and losses. Finally, the effect of changes in the various connector accounts that bridge the time period between accrual accounting recognition and the cash exchange are included so that only the cash flows from operating activities remain.

In reporting operating activity cash flows by means of the indirect method (Figure 17.8), the following pattern can be seen.

- A change in a connector account that is an asset is reflected on the statement in the opposite fashion. As shown previously, increases in both accounts receivable and prepaid rent are subtracted while a decrease in inventory is added.

- A change in a connector account that is a liability is included on the statement in an identical change. An increase in accounts payable is added whereas a decrease in salary payable is subtracted.

A quick visual comparison of the direct method (Figure 17.6) and the indirect method (Figure 17.8) makes the two appear almost completely unrelated. However, when analyzed more closely, the same series of steps can be seen in each. They both begin with the income for the period. Noncash items and nonoperating gains and losses are removed. Changes in the connector accounts for the period are factored in so that only the cash from operating activities remains.

TEST YOURSELF

Question:

The Hemingway Company reported net income last year of $354,000. Within that figure, depreciation expense of $37,000 was included. In addition, accounts receivable increased by $11,000 during the period. What amount of cash did this company generate from its operating activities?

a. $306,000

b. $328,000

c. $380,000

d. $402,000

Answer:

The correct answer is choice c: $380,000.

Explanation:

Depreciation is a noncash expense that appears within net income as a negative. To remove it, the $37,000 figure is added. Addition counterbalances the original negative effect. The increase in accounts receivable means that customers were slow to pay this year. Credit sales were greater than the amount of cash received. The $11,000 is subtracted from net income to arrive at the lower cash figure. Thus, cash inflow from operating activities is $380,000 ($354,000 + $37,000 − $11,000).

TEST YOURSELF

Question:

The Faulkner Corporation reported net income in Year One of $437,000. Accounts receivable at the start of the period totaled $26,000 but grew to $41,000 by the end of Year One. Beginning insurance payable was $7,000 but fell to an ending balance of $4,000. What amount of cash did Faulkner collect as a result of its operating activities?

a. $419,000

b. $425,000

c. $449,000

d. $455,000

Answer:

The correct answer is choice a: $419,000.

Explanation:

Accounts receivable went from $26,000 to $41,000. The $15,000 increase indicates that credit sales were greater than cash collected. The $15,000 is subtracted from net income. Insurance payable fell by $3,000 ($7,000 to $4,000); thus, the amount paid was greater than the expense recognized. Cash was spent to reduce the liability. The $3,000 is also subtracted in arriving at the cash change. The cash inflow from operating activities is $419,000 ($437,000 net income − $15,000 and $3,000).

3.4 The Reporting of Dividends and Interest on the Statement of Cash Flows

*Question: When listing cash flows from operating activities for the year ended December 31, 2010, **EMC Corporation** (a technology company) included an inflow of nearly $103 million labeled as "dividends and interest received" as well as an outflow of over $76 million shown as "interest paid."*

Unless a company is a bank or financing institution, dividend and interest revenues do not appear to relate to its central operating function. For most businesses, these cash inflows are fundamentally different from the normal sale of goods and services. Monetary amounts collected as dividends and interest resemble investing activity cash inflows because they are often generated from noncurrent assets. Similarly, interest expense payments are normally associated with noncurrent liabilities rather than resulting from daily operations. Interest expenditures could certainly be viewed as a financing activity cash outflow.

*Dividend distributions are not in question here. They are labeled as financing activity cash outflows because they are made directly to stockholders. The issue is the classification of dividend and interest revenue collections and interest expense payments. **Why is cash received as dividends and interest and cash*** *paid as interest expense reported within operating activities on a statement of cash flows rather than as investing activities and financing activities?*

Answer: Authoritative pronouncements that create U.S. GAAP are the subject of years of intense study, discussion, and debate. In this process, controversies often arise. When FASB issued its official standard on cash flows in 1987, three of the seven board members voted against passage. Their opposition, at least in part, came from the handling of interest and dividends. On page ten of Statement 95, *Statement of Cash Flows*, these three argue "that interest and dividends received are returns on investments in debt and equity securities that should be classified as cash inflows from investing activities. They believe that interest paid is a cost of obtaining financial resources that should be classified as a cash outflow for financing activities."

The other board members were not convinced. Thus, inclusion of dividends collected, interest collected, and interest paid within an entity's operating activity cash flows became a requirement of U.S. GAAP. Such disagreements arise frequently in the creation of official accounting rules.

The majority of the board apparently felt that—because these transactions occur on a regular ongoing basis—a better portrait of the organization's cash flows is provided by inclusion within operating activities. At every juncture of financial accounting, multiple possibilities for reporting exist. Rarely is complete consensus ever achieved as to the most appropriate method of presenting financial information.

Talking With an Independent Auditor about International Financial Reporting Standards

Following is the conclusion of our interview with Robert A. Vallejo, partner with the accounting firm **PricewaterhouseCoopers**.

Question: Any company that follows U.S. GAAP and issues an income statement must also present a statement of cash flows. Cash flows are classified as resulting from operating activities, investing activities, or financing activities. Are IFRS rules the same for the statement of cash flows as those found in U.S. GAAP?

Rob Vallejo: Differences do exist between the two frameworks for the presentation of the statement of cash flows, but they are relatively minor. Probably the most obvious issue involves the reporting of interest and dividends that are received and paid. Under IFRS, interest and dividend collections may be classified as either operating or investing cash flows whereas, in U.S. GAAP, they are both required to be shown within operating activities. A similar difference exists for interest and dividend payments. These cash outflows can be classified as either operating or financing activities according to IFRS. For U.S. GAAP, interest payments are viewed as operating activities whereas dividend payments are considered financing activities.

KEY TAKEAWAY

Most reporting entities use the indirect method to report net cash flows from operating activities. This presentation begins with net income and then eliminates any noncash items (such as depreciation expense) as well as nonoperating gains and losses. Their impact on net income is reversed to create this removal. In addition, changes in each balance sheet connector account (such as accounts receivables, inventory, accounts payable, and salary payable) must also be utilized in converting from accrual accounting to cash. Changes in asset connectors are reversed in arriving at cash flows from operating activities whereas changes in liability connectors have the same impact (increases are added and decreases are subtracted). Cash transactions that result from interest revenue, dividend revenue, and interest expense are all reported within operating activities because they happen on a regular ongoing basis. However, some argue that interest and dividend collections are really derived from investing activities and interest payments relate to financing activities.

4. CASH FLOWS FROM INVESTING AND FINANCING ACTIVITIES

4.1 Determining Cash Flows from Investing Activities

*Question: As shown in Figure 17.9, **The Walt Disney Company** reported a net cash outflow of over $4.5 billion as a result of investing activities undertaken during the year ended October 2, 2010.*

FIGURE 17.9 The Walt Disney Company Investing Activity Cash Flows for Year Ended October 2, 2010

Investment in Parks, Resorts, and Other Property	($2,110) million
Proceeds from Dispositions	170 million
Acquisitions	(2,493) million
Other	(90) million
Cash used in Continuing Investing Activities	($4,523) million

*This section of **Disney's** statement of cash flows shows that a number of transactions involving assets (other than operating assets such as inventory and accounts receivable) created this $4.5 billion reduction in cash. Information about management decisions is readily available. For example, a potential investor can see that officials chose to spend over $2.1 billion in cash during this year in connection with **Disney's** parks, resorts and other property. Interestingly, this expenditure level is approximately 20 percent higher than the monetary amount invested in those assets the previous year. With a strong knowledge of financial accounting, a portrait of a business and its activities begins to become clear.*

*After the various cash amounts are determined, conveyance of this information does not appear particularly complicated. **How does a company arrive at the investing activity figures that are disclosed within the statement of cash flows?***

Answer: Here, the accountant is not interested in assets such as inventory, accounts receivable, and prepaid rent because they are included within operating activities. Instead, each of the other asset accounts (land, buildings, equipment, patents, trademarks, and the like) is investigated to determine the individual transactions that took place during the year. The amount of every cash change is identified and reported. A sale of land can create a cash inflow whereas the acquisition of a building may well require the payment of some amount of cash.

The difficulty in this process frequently comes from having to sort through multiple purchases and sales to compute the exact amount of cash involved in each transaction. At times, determining the individual cash effects can resemble the work needed to solve a puzzle with many connecting pieces. Often, the journal entries that were made originally must be replicated. Even then, the cash portion of these transactions may have to be determined by mathematical logic. To illustrate, assume that the Hastings Company reports the account balances that appear in Figure 17.10.

FIGURE 17.10 Account Balances to Illustrate Cash Flows from Investing Activities

	January 1, Year One	December 31, Year One
Balance Sheet:		
Equipment	$730,000	$967,000
Accumulated Depreciation	300,000	450,000
Income Statement:		
Depreciation Expense		230,000
Gain on Sale of Equipment		74,000

In looking through the financial records maintained by this business, assume the accountant finds two additional pieces of information about the accounts in Figure 17.10:

- Equipment costing $600,000 was sold this year for cash.
- Other equipment was acquired, also for cash.

Sale of equipment. This transaction is analyzed first because the cost of the equipment is already provided. However, the accumulated depreciation relating to the disposed asset is not known. The accountant must study the available data to determine that missing number because that balance is also removed when the asset is sold.

Accumulated depreciation at the start of the year was $300,000 but depreciation expense of $230,000 was then reported as shown in Figure 17.10. This expense was apparently recognized through the year-end adjustment recreated in Figure 17.11.

FIGURE 17.11 Assumed Adjusting Entry for Depreciation

Depreciation Expense	230,000	
Accumulated Depreciation		230,000

The depreciation entry increases the accumulated depreciation account to $530,000 ($300,000 plus $230,000). However, the end-of-year balance is not $530,000 but only $450,000. What caused the $80,000 drop in this contra asset account?

Accumulated depreciation represents the cost of a long-lived asset that has already been expensed. Virtually the only situation in which accumulated depreciation is reduced is the disposal of the related asset. Here, the accountant knows equipment was sold. Although the amount of accumulated depreciation relating to that asset is unknown, the assumption can be made that the sale caused this reduction of $80,000. No other possible decrease in accumulated depreciation is mentioned.

Thus, the accountant believes equipment costing $600,000 but with accumulated depreciation of $80,000 (and, hence, a net book value of $520,000) was sold. The amount received must have created the $74,000 gain that is shown in the reported balances in Figure 17.10.

A hypothetical journal entry can be constructed in Figure 17.12 from this information.

FIGURE 17.12 Assumed Journal Entry for Sale of Equipment

Cash	???	
Accumulated Depreciation	80,000	
Equipment		600,000
Gain on Sale of Equipment		74,000

This journal entry only balances if the cash received is $594,000. Equipment with a book value of $520,000 was sold during the year at a reported gain of $74,000. Apparently, $594,000 was the cash received. How does all of this information affect the statement of cash flows?

- A cash inflow of $594,000 is reported within investing activities. It is labeled something like "cash received from sale of equipment."

- Depreciation of $230,000 is eliminated from net income in computing the cash flows from operating activities because this expense had no impact on cash flows.

- In determining the cash flows from operating activities, the $74,000 gain is also eliminated from net income. The $594,000 cash collection comes from an investing activity rather than an operating activity.

Purchase of equipment. According to the information provided, another asset was acquired this year but its cost is not provided. Once again, the accountant must puzzle out the amount of cash involved in the transaction.

The equipment account began the year with a $730,000 balance. The sale of equipment costing $600,000 was just discussed. This transaction should have dropped the ledger account to $130,000 ($730,000 less $600,000). However, at the end of the period, the amount reported for this asset is actually $967,000. How did the cost of equipment rise from $130,000 to $967,000? If no other transaction is mentioned, the most reasonable explanation is that additional equipment was acquired at a cost of $837,000 ($967,000 less $130,000). Unless information is available indicating that part of this purchase was made on credit, the journal entry that was recorded originally must have been made as shown in Figure 17.13.

FIGURE 17.13 Assumed Journal Entry for Purchase of Equipment

Equipment	837,000	
Cash		837,000

At this point, the changes in all related accounts (equipment, accumulated depreciation, depreciation expense, and the gain on sale of equipment) have been used to determine the two transactions for the period and their related cash inflows and outflows. In the statement of cash flows for this company, the investing activities are listed as shown in Figure 17.14.

FIGURE 17.14 Statement of Cash Flows—Investing Activities

Sold Equipment	$594,000
Purchased Equipment	(837,000)
Net Cash Outflow—Investing Activities	($243,000)

TEST YOURSELF

Question:

The following accounts appear on Red Company's balance sheets at the beginning and end of Year One:

FIGURE 17.15

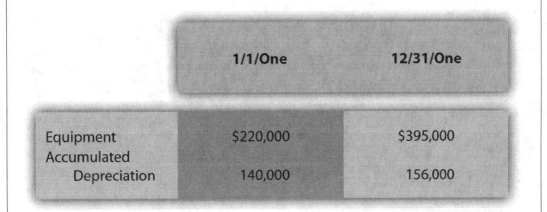

	1/1/One	12/31/One
Equipment	$220,000	$395,000
Accumulated Depreciation	140,000	156,000

During Year One, equipment with an original cost of $30,000 and accumulated depreciation of $18,000 was sold at a loss of $3,000. What is the cash received on the sale of that equipment?

a. $9,000

b. $12,000

c. $15,000

d. $16,000

Answer:

The correct answer is choice a: $9,000.

Explanation:

The book value of this equipment is $12,000 ($30,000 cost less $18,000 accumulated depreciation). Because the equipment was sold at a loss of $3,000, cash received must have been only $9,000 ($12,000 less $3,000). The transaction can also be recreated through the following entry.

FIGURE 17.16

Cash	9,000	
Loss on Sale of Equipment	3,000	
Accumulated Depreciation	18,000	
Equipment		30,000

The loss is eliminated from income in determining the cash flows from operating activities. If the direct method is used, the loss is simply omitted. If the indirect method is used, the loss (because it is a negative within net income) is added back to net income. The $9,000 cash inflow appears in the investing activity section of the statement of cash flows.

TEST YOURSELF

Question:

The following accounts appear on White Company's balance sheets at the beginning and end of Year One.

FIGURE 17.17

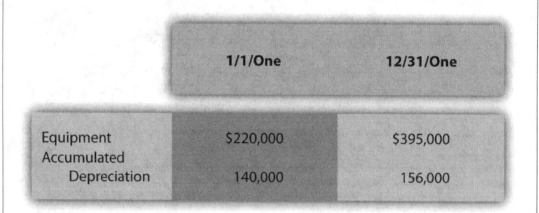

	1/1/One	12/31/One
Equipment	$220,000	$395,000
Accumulated Depreciation	140,000	156,000

One piece of equipment—with an original cost of $30,000 and accumulated depreciation of $18,000—was sold at a loss of $3,000. On a statement of cash flows, what amount should be reported as cash paid for additional equipment bought during the period?

a. $145,000
b. $175,000
c. $205,000
d. $235,000

Answer:

The correct answer is choice c: $205,000.

Explanation:

Based on the information provided, the equipment account decreased by the $30,000 cost of the asset that was sold. The reported balance would have fallen from $220,000 to $190,000. At year's end, equipment was not reported as $190,000 but rather as $395,000. With no other transactions mentioned, the $205,000 increase from $190,000 to $395,000 must have been created by purchase of additional equipment. This $205,000 acquisition appears in the investing activities section as a cash outflow.

TEST YOURSELF

Question:

The following accounts appear on Blue Company's balance sheets at the beginning and end of Year One.

FIGURE 17.18

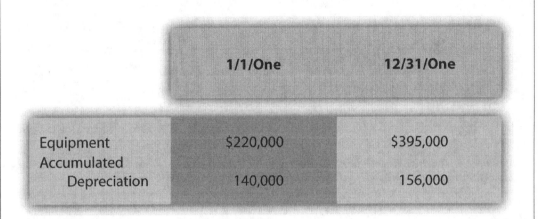

	1/1/One	12/31/One
Equipment	$220,000	$395,000
Accumulated Depreciation	140,000	156,000

Equipment with an original cost of $30,000 and accumulated depreciation of $18,000 was sold at a loss of $3,000. What is the depreciation expense recognized during the year and, if the indirect method is used, how is this reported in the statement of cash flows?

a. $19,000 is subtracted from net income

b. $28,000 is added to net income

c. $34,000 is added to net income

d. $46,000 is subtracted from net income

Answer:

The correct answer is choice c: $34,000 is added to net income.

Explanation:

Because of the sale of equipment, accumulated depreciation drops by $18,000 from $140,000 to $122,000. By the end of Year One, the account is $156,000. Accumulated depreciation only increases as a result of recording depreciation expense. The increase from $122,000 to $156,000 points to an expense of $34,000. Depreciation is a negative noncash item in net income and is removed in presenting cash flows from operating activities. With the indirect method is used, depreciation is added back.

4.2 Determining Cash Flows from Financing Activities

Question: For the year ended January 2, 2011, **Johnson & Johnson** reported a net cash outflow from financing activities of over $4.9 billion. Within the statement of cash flows, this total was broken down into seven specific categories as replicated in Figure 17.19.

FIGURE 17.19 Financing Activity Cash Flows Reported by Johnson & Johnson for Year Ended January 2, 2011

Dividends to Shareholders	($5,804) million
Repurchase of Common Stock	(2,797) million
Proceeds from Short-Term Debt	7,874 million
Retirement of Short-Term Debt	(6,565) million
Proceeds from Long-Term Debt	1,118 million
Retirement of Long-Term Debt	(32) million
Proceeds from the Exercise of Stock Options/Excess Tax Benefits	1,226 million
Net Cash Used by Financing Activities	(4,980) million

In preparing a statement of cash flows, how does a company such as **Johnson & Johnson** *determine the amounts that were paid and received as a result of its various financing activities?*

Answer: As has been indicated, financing activities reflect transactions that are not part of a company's central operations and involve either a liability or a stockholders' equity account. **Johnson & Johnson** paid over $5.8 billion in cash dividends in this year and nearly $2.8 billion to repurchase common stock (treasury shares). During the same period, approximately $7.9 billion in cash was received from borrowing money on short-term debt and another $1.1 billion from long-term debt. None of these amounts are directly associated with the company's operating activities. However, they do involve either liabilities or stockholders' equity accounts and are appropriately reported as financing activities.

The procedures used in determining the cash amounts to be reported as financing activities are the same as demonstrated above for investing activities. The change in each relevant balance sheet account is analyzed to determine cash payments and receipts. In starting this process, many liabilities such as accounts payable, rent payable, and salaries payable are ignored because they relate only to operating activities. However, the remaining liabilities and all stockholders' equity accounts must be studied. The recording of individual transactions can be replicated so that the cash effect is isolated.

To illustrate, various account balances for the Hastings Corporation are presented in the schedule included in Figure 17.20.

FIGURE 17.20 Account Balances to Illustrate Cash Flows from Financing Activities

	January 1, Year One	December 31, Year One
Balance Sheet:		
Note Payable	$680,000	$876,000
Treasury Stock	(400,000)	(300,000)
Capital in Excess of Cost	120,000	160,000
Retained Earnings	454,000	619,000
Income Statement:		
Loss on Early Extinguishment of Debt		25,000
Net Income		200,000

In examining the financial records for the Hastings Corporation for this year, the accountant finds several additional pieces of information:

1. Cash of $400,000 was borrowed by signing a note payable with a local bank.

2. Another note payable was paid off prior to its maturity date because of a drop in interest rates.

3. Treasury stock was reissued to the public for cash.

4. A cash dividend was declared and distributed.

Once again, the various changes in each account balance can be analyzed to determine the cash flows, this time to be reported as financing activities.

Borrowing on note payable. Complete information about this transaction is available. Hastings Corporation received $400,000 in cash from a bank by signing a note payable. Figure 17.21 provides the journal entry to record the incurrence of this liability.

FIGURE 17.21 Assumed Journal Entry for Signing of Note Payable

| Cash | 400,000 | |
| Note Payable | | 400,000 |

On a statement of cash flows, this transaction is listed within the financing activities as a $400,000 cash inflow.

Paying note payable. Incurring the $400,000 debt raises the note payable balance from $680,000 to $1,080,000. By the end of the year, this account only shows a total of $876,000. The company's notes payable have decreased in some way by $204,000 ($1,080,000 less $876,000). According to the information gathered by the accountant, a debt was paid off this year prior to maturity. In addition, the general ledger reports a $25,000 loss on the early extinguishment of a debt. When a bond or note is settled before its maturity, a penalty payment is often required. Once again, the journal entry for this transaction can be recreated by logical reasoning as shown in Figure 17.22.

FIGURE 17.22 Assumed Journal Entry for Extinguishment of Debt

Note Payable	204,000	
Loss on Extinguishment of Debt	25,000	
Cash		???

To balance this entry, cash of $229,000 must have been paid. Spending this amount of money to extinguish a $204,000 liability creates the $25,000 reported loss. The cash outflow of $229,000 relates to a liability and is, thus, listed on the statement of cash flows as a financing activity.

Issuance of treasury stock. This equity balance reflects the cost of all repurchased shares. During the year, the total in the T-account fell by $100,000 from $400,000 to $300,000. Apparently, $100,000 was the cost of the company's shares reissued to the public. At the same time, the capital in excess of cost balance rose from $120,000 to $160,000. That $40,000 increase in contributed capital must have been created by this issuance since no other stock transaction is mentioned. The shares were sold for more than their purchase price. The journal entry must have looked like the one presented in Figure 17.23.

FIGURE 17.23 Assumed Journal Entry for Sale of Treasury Stock

Cash	???	
Treasury Stock		100,000
Capital in Excess of Cost		40,000

If the original cost of the treasury stock was $100,000 and $40,000 was added to the capital in excess of cost, the cash inflow from this transaction had to be $140,000. Cash received from the issuance of treasury stock is reported as a financing activity of $140,000 because it relates to a stockholders' equity account.

Distribution of dividend. A dividend has been paid to the company's stockholders, but the amount is not shown in the information provided. However, other information is available. Net income for the period was reported as $200,000. Those profits increase retained earnings. As a result, the beginning balance of $454,000 increases to $654,000. Instead, retained earnings only rose to $619,000 by the end of the year. The unexplained drop of $35,000 ($654,000 less $619,000) must have resulted from the payment of the dividend. No other possible reason is given for this reduction. The appropriate journal entry is found in Figure 17.24. Hence, a cash dividend distribution of $35,000 is shown within the statement of cash flows as a financing activity.

FIGURE 17.24 Assumed Journal Entry for Payment of Dividend

| Retained Earnings (or Dividend Paid) | 35,000 | |
| Cash | | 35,000 |

In this example, four specific financing activity transactions have been identified as created changes in cash. This section of Hasting's statement of cash flows can be created in Figure 17.25. All the sources and uses of this company's cash (as related to financing activities) are apparent from this schedule. Determining the cash amounts can take some computational logic, but the information is then clear and useful.

FIGURE 17.25 Statement of Cash Flows—Financing Activities

Borrowed on Note Payable	$400,000
Extinguishment of Note Payable	(229,000)
Issuance of Treasury Stock	140,000
Distribution of Cash Dividend	(35,000)
Net Cash Outflow—Financing Activities	($243,000)

TEST YOURSELF

Question:

The Abraham Company begins the year with bonds payable having a reported balance of $600,000. The ending balance is $700,000. This company's income statement for the year reports a gain on extinguishment of bond of $9,000. During the year, new bonds were issued at their face value of $300,000. How much cash was paid for the bonds that were extinguished?

a. $191,000

b. $209,000

c. $291,000

d. $309,000

Answer:

The correct answer is choice a: $191,000.

Explanation:

The issuance of $300,000 in new debt would increase the liability balance from $600,000 to $900,000. However, the account ended the year at only $700,000. The unexplained reduction of $200,000 must have been the face value of the debt paid off ($900,000 less $700,000). Because a gain of $9,000 was recognized on this transaction, the company managed to eliminate the debt by paying only $191,000.

TEST YOURSELF

Question:

The Oregon Company's total stockholders' equity on January 1 was $870,000. By the end of the year, stockholders' equity had risen to $990,000. This company bought treasury stock this year. The shares had originally been issued for $120,000 but were reacquired for $150,000. In addition, Oregon reported net income for the year of $340,000. No other stock transactions occurred but a cash dividend was paid. How much should Oregon report on the statement of cash flows for the dividend distribution?

a. $50,000

b. $60,000

c. $70,000

d. $80,000

Answer:

The correct answer is choice c: $70,000.

Explanation:

Acquisition of the treasury stock reduces stockholders' equity by $150,000 while net income increases it by $340,000. If nothing else took place, stockholders' equity at the end of the period would be $1,060,000 ($870,000 less $150,000 but plus $340,000). Instead, the ending total is actually $990,000. Because only the dividend distribution is left to include, it must have been the amount needed to reduce stockholders' equity to its final reported total ($70,000 or $1,060,000 less $990,000).

KEY TAKEAWAY

In determining cash flows from investing activities, current assets such as inventory, accounts receivable, and prepaid rent are ignored because they relate to operating activities. The accountant then analyzes all changes that have taken place in each remaining asset such as buildings and equipment. Hypothetical journal entries can be recreated to replicate the impact of each transaction and lead to the amount of cash involved. For financing activities, a similar process is applied. Liabilities such as accounts payable, interest payable, and salaries payable are not excluded; they only impact operating activities. Monetary changes in the remaining liabilities (notes and bonds payable, for example) and all stockholders' equity accounts are analyzed. Again, the journal entries that were recorded to report individual events can be recreated so that the cash amounts are known. Once all changes in these accounts have been determined, the various sections of the statement of cash flows can be produced.

Talking with a Real Investing Pro (Continued)

Following is the conclusion of our interview with Kevin G. Burns.

Question: Many investors watch the movement of a company's reported net income and earnings per share and make investment decisions based on increases or decreases. Other investors argue that the amount of cash flows generated by operating activities is really a more useful figure. When you make investing decisions are you more inclined to look at net income or the cash flows generated by operating activities?

Kevin Burns: As I have said previously, net income and earnings per share have a lot of subjectivity to them. Unfortunately, cash flow information can be badly misused also. A lot of investors seem fascinated by the calculation of EBITDA which is the company's earnings before interest, taxes, depreciation, and amortization. I guess you could say that determining EBITDA is like blending net income and cash flows. But, to me, interest and taxes are real cash expenses so why exclude them? The biggest mistake I ever made as an investor or financial advisor was putting too much credence in EBITDA as a technique for valuing a business. Earnings are earnings and that is important information. A lot of analysts now believe that different cash flow models should be constructed for different industries. If you look around, you can find cable industry cash flow models, theater cash flow models, entertainment industry cash flow models, and the like. I think that is a lot of nonsense. You have to obtain a whole picture to know if an investment is worthwhile. While cash generation is important in creating that picture so are actual earnings and a whole lot of other financial information found in a company's annual report.

5. APPENDIX: COMPREHENSIVE ILLUSTRATION—STATEMENT OF CASH FLOWS

5.1 The Creation of a Complete Statement of Cash Flows

Question: All three sections of the statement of cash flows are presented in this chapter but in separate coverage. Now, through a comprehensive illustration, these categories will be combined into a formal and complete statement.

The following information has been uncovered within the internal records maintained by the Ashe Corporation for Year Seven. The company is a small organization that was incorporated several years ago in the western part of North Carolina.

A few of the significant financial events that occurred during the current year are as follows:

- Land that had cost Ashe $7,000 several years ago was sold to an outside buyer.
- A building was also sold but for $210,000 in cash. This property had an original cost of $230,000. Accumulated depreciation to date on this building was $30,000. This building was replaced with a new purchase made for cash during the year.
- Equipment was purchased for $44,000 in cash to replace other equipment that was sold at the beginning of the year.
- Additional cash of $110,000 was borrowed on a note payable.
- Common stock was issued to an investor for cash of $5,000.
- A cash dividend was declared and paid to the owners near the end of the year.

The accountant for the Ashe Corporation is now attempting to prepare the company's first complete set of financial statements as part of an application for a new loan. As part of this process, the accountant has created informal balance sheets (Figure 17.26) and an income statement (Figure 17.27).

FIGURE 17.26 Ashe Corporation—Beginning and Ending Balance Sheets for Year Seven

	January 1, Year Seven	December 31, Year Seven
Cash	$1,000	$27,000
Accounts Receivable	13,000	28,000
Inventory	17,000	13,000
Land	21,000	14,000
Buildings	390,000	420,000
Less Accumulated Depreciation	(120,000)	(160,000)
Equipment	36,000	50,000
Less Accumulated Depreciation	(17,000)	(20,000)
	$341,000	$372,000
Accounts Payable	18,000	22,000
Wages Payable	1,000	4,000
Interest Payable	2,000	3,000
Taxes Payable	10,000	9,000
Notes Payable	120,000	130,000
Capital Stock	50,000	55,000
Retained Earnings	140,000	149,000
	$341,000	$372,000

FIGURE 17.27 Ashe Corporation—Income Statement for Year Ended December 31, Year Seven

Sales	$274,000
– Cost of Goods Sold	(79,000)
– Wages Expense	(40,000)
– Depreciation Expense—Buildings	(70,000)
– Depreciation Expense—Equipment	(30,000)
– Interest Expense	(9,000)
– Loss on Sale of Land	(5,000)
+ Gain on Sale of Building	10,000
– Income Tax Expense	(11,000)
= Net Income	$40,000

A statement of cash flows is now needed for the Ashe Corporation. As shown in Figure 17.26, cash increased from $1,000 to $27,000 during the course of this year. That $26,000 change should be explained. How does a company construct an entire statement of cash flows? Application of the indirect method for presenting operating activities is so prevalent that company officials have decided to use it.

Operating Activities

Answer:

In both the direct and indirect methods, net cash flows from operating activities are derived by following several specific steps:

1. *Start with net income, either the balance for the period (the indirect method) or the income statement as a whole (the direct method).* Because the indirect method is being used here, the preparation of the operating activities section begins with Ashe Corporation's reported net income of $40,000 (from Figure 17.27).

2. *Remove noncash expenses.* Here, depreciation must be eliminated. This year, the reported amount is $70,000 (buildings) and $30,000 (equipment). As expenses, depreciation is a negative within net income. To remove these two negative amounts, they are added back to the net income figure. Negatives are removed by the inclusion of a positive.

3. *Remove nonoperating gains and losses because they relate to either investing activities or financing activities.* Consequently, both the loss on the sale of land ($5,000) and the gain on sale of a building ($10,000) are removed. Neither relates to an operating activity. The loss (a negative) is eliminated by an addition to net income while the gain (a positive) is offset by means of a subtraction.

4. *Convert the remaining revenue and expense balances from accrual accounting to cash accounting by adjusting for changes occurring during the year in related balance sheet connector accounts.* The identity of these connector accounts and the amount of each change is reported in Figure 17.28. The increases and decreases were computed from the beginning and ending balance sheets shown previously in Figure 17.26.

FIGURE 17.28 Ashe Corporation—Change in Connector Accounts

Income Statement Account	Connector Account	Change in Connector Account
Sales	Accounts Receivable	Increase of $15,000
Cost of Goods Sold	Inventory	Decrease of $4,000
	Accounts Payable	Increase of $4,000
Wages Expense	Wages Payable	Increase of $3,000
Interest Expense	Interest Payable	Increase of $1,000
Income Tax Expense	Taxes Payable	Decrease of $1,000

The change in each of these six connector accounts—accounts receivable, inventory, accounts payable, wages payable, interest payable, and taxes payable—is factored into the computation of cash flows from operating activities to arrive at the actual effect on cash for the period. In this way, the accrual accounting figures reported on the income statement are changed to their cash equivalents.

Accounts receivable—increase of $15,000. A receivables balance can only rise in this manner when more sales are made on credit than cash is collected. The reduction in the cash received causes the receivable to increase. *This decrease in cash collections is reflected by subtracting the $15,000 from net income.*

Inventory—decrease of $4,000. The inventory balance dropped, which indicates that less inventory was bought this year than was sold. Fewer purchases take less money, keeping the cash balance high. *The decrease in inventory and its impact on cash are reported within operating activities through an addition to net income.*

Accounts payable—increase of $4,000. Liabilities increase because more debt is acquired than the amount of cash that is paid. Slowness of payment increases accounts payable but also helps keep the company's cash balance high. *This increase in accounts payable is added to net income as another step in arriving at the cash flows from operating activities.*

Wages payable—increase of $3,000; interest payable—increase of $1,000. The balance of both of these accrued liabilities went up during this year. Once again, as with accounts payable, an increase in a liability indicates a reduction in payments. *This saving of cash is shown when using the indirect method by adding the increases in wages payable and interest payable to net income.*

Taxes payable—decrease of $1,000. A liability goes down because cash payments are made that reduce the obligation. However, those payments also shrink the amount of cash held. *This effect is mirrored by subtracted the decrease in the liability from net income.*

The steps for determining cash flows generated by operating activities have been completed (using the indirect method), and this part of the statement of cash flows can be prepared as shown in Figure 17.29.

FIGURE 17.29 Ashe Corporation—Cash Flows from Operating Activities for Year Ended December 31, Year Seven (Indirect Method)

Net Income	$40,000
Eliminate:	
Depreciation Expense—Buildings	+70,000
Depreciation Expense—Equipment	+30,000
Loss on Sale of Land	+5,000
Gain on Sale of Building	(10,000)
Adjust Revenues and Expenses from Accrual Accounting to Cash:	
Increase in Accounts Receivable	(15,000)
Decrease in Inventory	+4,000
Increase in Accounts Payable	+4,000
Increase in Wages Payable	+3,000
Increase in Interest Payable	+1,000
Decrease in Taxes Payable	(1,000)
Cash Inflow from Operating Activities	$131,000

As can be seen by comparing Figure 17.29 to the company's income statement (Figure 17.27), cash generated by operating activities ($131,000) is considerably higher than the net income reported for that same period ($40,000). Such differences are not uncommon in the business world especially since depreciation is often a large expense that does not require cash.

Investing Activities

After accounting for operating activities, only three asset accounts remain to be examined (along with accumulated depreciation balances where appropriate): land, buildings, and equipment. The accountant analyzes each individually and attempts to recreate the transactions that brought about the various changes during the year.

Land decreased by $7,000 ($21,000 to $14,000). The information provided by the accountant states that land costing $7,000 was sold but does not indicate the amount of cash received. However, the income statement discloses a $5,000 loss on the sale of land. If land costing $7,000 is sold at a loss of $5,000, only $2,000 in cash is received. The journal entry shown in Figure 17.30 was apparently recorded by Ashe Corporation for this transaction. Land is an asset, so this $2,000 inflow of cash will be reported as an investing activity.

FIGURE 17.30 Assumed Journal Entry for Sale of Land

Cash	2,000	
Loss on Sale of Land	5,000	
Land		7,000

Buildings increased by $30,000 ($390,000 to $420,000). According to the introductory information, one building with a cost of $230,000 but a net book value of $200,000 (related accumulated depreciation was identified as $30,000) was sold during this year for $210,000. The company received $10,000 more than net book value which creates the $10,000 gain that appears on the company's income statement. Because all account balances are known here, the journal entry made by the Ashe Corporation can be replicated in Figure 17.31. This transaction will be listed as a $210,000 cash inflow within investing activities on the statement of cash flows.

FIGURE 17.31 Assumed Journal Entry for Sale of Building

Cash	210,000	
Accumulated Depreciation	30,000	
Building		230,000
Gain on Sale of Building		10,000

The entry made in Figure 17.31 does not fully explain the monetary change appearing in the buildings account during this period. This sale drops that account from $390,000 to $160,000 (because of the $230,000 reduction in cost). However, the final balance for the year was not $160,000 but rather $420,000, an increase of $260,000. The introductory information does indicate that a new building was acquired as a replacement. Without mention of any other building transaction, the assumption must be made that this asset was acquired for $260,000 through the entry presented in Figure 17.32. The cash payment will be disclosed on the statement of cash flows as a $260,000 investing activity outflow.

FIGURE 17.32 Assumed Journal Entry for Purchase of Building

Buildings	260,000	
Cash		260,000

Equipment increased by $14,000 ($36,000 to $50,000). The information provided by the company's accountant states that one piece of equipment was purchased during the year for $44,000 in cash. This transaction is recorded in Figure 17.33 and identifies another cash outflow to be reported within the investing activities.

FIGURE 17.33 Assumed Journal Entry for Purchase of Equipment

Equipment	44,000	
Cash		44,000

This journal entry does not entirely explain the change that occurred in the equipment account. The beginning balance of $36,000 grew to $80,000 as a result of this $44,000 purchase. Yet, the ending balance was just $50,000. Apparently, during the year, another $30,000 reduction ($80,000 less $50,000) took place. Equipment accounts decrease as the result of a sale or some other type of disposal. Equipment was sold this period; its cost must have been the cause of this $30,000 decrease.

In recording the disposal of a long-lived asset, removal of any related accumulated depreciation is also necessary. For the equipment owned by Ashe Corporation, beginning accumulated depreciation was $17,000—a figure that increased by $30,000 due to the depreciation for that year (to a balance of $47,000). However, the ending accumulated depreciation account shows a balance of only $20,000. Another change in this contra account, a reduction of $27,000 ($47,000 less $20,000), still needs to be explained. This figure is the accumulated depreciation for the equipment that was sold. That balance was removed in recording the disposal of this asset.

Because no gain or loss on the disposal of equipment is reported in the income statement, the amount received must have been equal to the $3,000 net book value of the asset ($30,000 less $27,000). With that assumption, the journal entry shown in Figure 17.34 can be constructed. The $3,000 collection will be reported as a cash inflow from an investing activity.

FIGURE 17.34 Assumed Journal Entry for Sale of Equipment

Cash	3,000	
Accumulated Depreciation	27,000	
Equipment		30,000

All changes in the land, buildings, and equipment accounts have now been examined. Each individual transaction was recreated and the change in cash calculated. The investing activity section of the statement of cash flows can then be prepared in Figure 17.35 based on the information that has been gathered.

FIGURE 17.35 Ashe Corporation—Cash Flows from Investing Activities for Year Ended December 31, Year Seven

Sale of Land	$2,000
Sale of Building	210,000
Purchase of Building	(260,000)
Purchase of Equipment	(44,000)
Sale of Equipment	3,000
Cash Outflow from Investing Activities	($89,000)

Financing Activities

Only three accounts remain unexamined: notes payable, capital stock, and retained earnings. They are either liabilities or stockholders' equity accounts and, thus, lead to financing activities.

Notes payable increased by $10,000 ($120,000 to $130,000). The information gathered from the company disclosed the signing of a note payable for $110,000 in cash. The journal entry is made in Figure 17.36. This transaction is obviously an inflow of that amount of cash that will be reported as a financing activity.

FIGURE 17.36 Assumed Journal Entry for Signing of Note Payable

Cash	110,000	
Notes Payable		110,000

According to the beginning and ending balance sheets, notes payable did not actually increase by $110,000 but only by $10,000. Thus, another transaction must have taken place that reduced this liability by $100,000. Except in unusual situations, notes payable only decrease because of cash payments. Because no gain or loss on extinguishment of debt is reported in the income statement, Ashe Corporation must have paid exactly $100,000 to retire that same amount of debt. The journal entry is shown in Figure 17.37 and the accountant has located another financing activity cash flow (a $100,000 payment).

FIGURE 17.37 Assumed Journal Entry for Extinguishment of Note Payable

| Notes Payable | 100,000 | |
| Cash | | 100,000 |

The recording of this second transaction (Figure 17.37) leads to the appropriate change in notes payable (the $10,000 account increase was created by $110,000 in additional borrowing and a $100,000 decrease payment).

    Capital stock increased by $5,000 ($50,000 to $55,000). The information provided by the accountant states that Ashe Corporation issued stock to an investor for $5,000. This contribution created the change seen in this account, which is recorded in Figure 17.38. The business received this money and must report a financing activity cash inflow of $5,000. No other stock transactions are indicated for Ashe Corporation.

FIGURE 17.38 Assumed Journal Entry for Issuance of Capital Stock

| Cash | 5,000 | |
| Capital Stock | | 5,000 |

Retained earnings increased by $9,000 ($140,000 to $149,000). This final balance sheet account increased by $40,000 because of the net income earned by Ashe Corporation as reported on its income statement. At the end of the year, this amount is closed into retained earnings. The cash flows relating to net income have already been presented within operating activities.

    To create the overall change of $9,000, retained earnings must have also declined by $31,000. As mentioned several times in this textbook, other than net income, retained earnings are changed by virtually only one other event: the distribution of dividends. The information provided by the accountant mentions that a dividend was paid this year. That dividend must have caused the remaining $31,000 drop. Net income of $40,000 and a dividend distribution of $31,000 provide the reported increase in retained earnings of $9,000. The dividend entry is presented in Figure 17.39.

FIGURE 17.39 Assumed Journal Entry for Payment of Cash Dividend

| Retained Earnings (or Dividends Paid) | 31,000 | |
| Cash | | 31,000 |

With this final financing activity, an entire statement of cash flows can be created for the Ashe Corporation in Figure 17.40. All the transactions that affected cash during the current period are included within one of the three categories. Investors and other interested parties can gain a complete picture of the cash results of operations as well as the investing and financing decisions made by management. This portrait provides an excellent complement to the income statement, statement of retained earnings, and balance sheet.

FIGURE 17.40 Ashe Corporation—Statement of Cash Flows Year Ended December 31, Year Seven

Ashe Corporation
Statement of Cash Flows
Year Ended December 31, Year Seven

Cash flows from operating activities:		
Net income		$40,000
Eliminate:		
Depreciation expense—buildings		+70,000
Depreciation expense—equipment		+30,000
Loss on sale of land		+ 5,000
Gain on sale of building		(10,000)
Adjust revenues and expenses from		
Accrual accounting to cash:		
Increase in accounts receivable		(15,000)
Decrease in inventory		+ 4,000
Increase in accounts payable		+ 4,000
Increase in wages payable		+ 3,000
Increase in interest payable		+ 1,000
Decrease in taxes payable		(1,000)
Cash inflow from operating activities		$131,000
Cash flows from investing activities:		
	$ 2,000	
Sale of land	210,000	
Sale of building	(260,000)	
Purchase of building	(44,000)	
Purchase of equipment	3,000	
Sale of equipment		
Cash outflow from investing activities		(89,000)
Cash flows from financing activities:		
	$110,000	
Signed note payable	(100,000)	
Paid note payable	5,000	
Issued common stock	(31,000)	
Paid cash dividend		
Cash outflow from financing activities		(16,000)
Increase in cash during Year Seven		$ 26,000
Beginning cash balance, January 1, Year Seven		1,000
Ending cash balance, December 31, Year Seven		$ 27,000

Video Clip

Professor Joe Hoyle talks about the five most important points in Chapter 17.

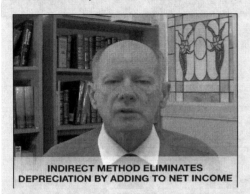

View the video online at: http://bit.ly/hoyle17-2

6.   END-OF-CHAPTER EXERCISES

QUESTIONS

1. James Hartwell is preparing financial statements for the Ashton Corporation. Hartwell wants these statements to conform to U.S. GAAP so they are more credible with decision makers. Only a balance sheet has been prepared so far. Is Hartwell required to prepare a statement of cash flows according to U.S. GAAP?

2. As of December 31, Year One, the Midlothian Corporation reports "cash" of $318,455. What might be included in this figure?

3. As of December 31, Year One, the Midlothian Corporation reports "cash equivalents" of $74,329. What might be included in this figure?

4. Sashya Douglas is analyzing a statement of cash flows reported by a company that has securities traded on the New York Stock Exchange. Is the direct method or the indirect method more likely to be seen? How can Douglas tell whether the direct method or the indirect method has been applied?

5. What are the three sections of a statement of cash flows? What types of transactions are included in each of these categories?

6. During the current year, the Durham Corporation issued 10,000 shares of $1 par value common stock with a stock market value of $18 per share in exchange for 2 acres of land. How is this transaction reported on a statement of cash flows?

7. A company reports rent expense for the current year of $74,000. Why is this figure not the same as the cash paid by the company for rent?

8. The Ames Corporation reports salary expense of $875,000. During that period of time, the salary payable balance rose by $39,000. How much cash did the company pay its employees this period?

9. The Lewiston Corporation reported cost of goods sold of $376,000 for Year One. During that period, its inventory went up by $72,000 while its accounts payable fell by $19,000. How much cash did the company pay for inventory purchases during Year One?

10. The Clarkson Corporation reported depreciation expense of $107,000 in Year One. In a statement of cash flows where the direct method is applied, how is this expense reported? If the indirect method is applied, how is this expense reported?

11. For the year ended December 31, Year One, the Maeburry Corporation reports an $85,000 gain on the sale of land. Several acres attached to a warehouse were sold during the year for cash. If cash flows from operating activities are reported by the direct method, how is this gain reported? If the indirect method is applied, how is this gain reported?

12. During the current year, the Leftowich Company reported that its accounts receivable had gone down while salary payable went up. If the indirect method is applied to determine cash flows from operating activities, how are these changes shown?

13. The Central Western Corporation reports its cash flows from operating activities by means of the indirect method. In the current year, the company's prepaid rent account increased by $11,000. At the same time, its accounts payable balance fell by $23,000. If the indirect method is used to present cash flows from operating activities, how are these two changes reported?

14. The Harbaugh Corporation paid a $39,000 cash dividend this year but also received $11,000 as a dividend from one of the company's investments. If U.S. GAAP is applied, how are these two transactions reported within a statement of cash flows? If IFRS is applied, how are these two transactions reported within a statement of cash flows?

15. The Anna Company sells a building with an original cost of $950,000 and accumulated depreciation of $400,000 to another company at a gain of $18,000. What reporting is necessary on a statement of cash flows?

16. During the current year, a company repurchases 10,000 shares of common stock that were originally issued several years ago for $32 per share. The stock is acquired this year for $37 per share. Later, in the year, 3,000 of these shares are reissued to the public for $40 each. How are these transactions reported in the statement of cash flows for this period?

TRUE OR FALSE

1. _____ A company reports cash equivalents as an asset. The term "cash equivalents" has the same meaning as "cash."

2. _____ If the cash flows from operating activities begins with "cash collected from customers," the indirect method is being applied.

3. _____ When the direct method of reporting cash flows from operating activities is applied, depreciation expense is added to net income.

4. _____ When the indirect method of reporting cash flows from operating activities is applied, a loss on the sale of equipment is added to net income.

5. _____ The Walsingham Corporation reported rent expense of $75,000 this year. At the same time, prepaid rent increased by $9,000. The company paid $84,000 in rent this period.

6. _____ The Trigger Company reported rent expense of $43,000 this year. At the same time, rent payable increases by $9,000. The company paid $52,000 in rent this period.

7. _____ A company reports net income for the current year of $200,000. During that year, depreciation expense of $30,000 was reported as well as an $8,000 gain on the cash sale of a building. In addition, accounts receivable increased by $9,000. The net cash flows from operating activities for the period was $213,000.

8. _____ A company reports cost of goods sold of $500,000. During that period, inventory fell by $34,000 while accounts payable rose by $9,000. The company paid $475,000 in cash this period for the purchase of merchandise.

9. _____ Purchasing treasury stock is an example of a financing activity.

10. _____ Significant investing and financing activities not involving cash still need to be disclosed.

11. _____ During the current year, the Baxter Corporation paid $100,000 on a long-term note payable and $13,000 in related interest expense. According to U.S. GAAP, these two payments must be shown in separate sections of a statement of cash flows.

12. _____ During the current year, the Frances Corporation paid $200,000 on a long-term note payable and $22,000 in related interest expense. According to IFRS, these two payments must be shown in separate sections of a statement of cash flows.

13. _____ Equipment costing $320,000 but with accumulated depreciation of $240,000 was sold at a loss of $22,000. The company reports a cash inflow of $58,000 as a financing activity.

MULTIPLE CHOICE

1. Where does cash that is collected from customers appear on a statement of cash flows?

    a. Operating activities section

    b. Investing activities section

    c. Financing activities section

    d. Capital activities section

2. Fritz Corporation began the year with $900,000 in accounts receivable. During the year, sales revenue totaled $7,000,000. Fritz ended the year with $750,000 in accounts receivable. How much cash did Fritz collect from its customers during the year?

    a. $6,850,000

    b. $7,150,000

    c. $7,750,000

    d. $7,900,000

3. The Willson Company pays off one of its bonds before it came due because interest rates have fallen rather significantly. Where does the cash paid to redeem a bond payable appear on a company's statement of cash flows?

    a. Operating activities section

    b. Investing activities section

    c. Financing activities section

    d. Capital activities section

4. Which of the following is true about the reporting of cash flows from operating activities?

    a. Most companies use the indirect method although FASB prefers the direct method.

    b. Most companies use the indirect method because it is preferred by FASB.

    c. Most companies use the direct method because it is preferred by FASB.

    d. Most companies use the direct method, although FASB prefers the indirect method.

5. During the current year, Rafael Corporation distributed dividends of $23,000, received cash by signing a note payable of $105,000, purchased a piece of equipment for $29,000 in cash, and received dividend income of $12,000. What is reported as Rafael's net cash inflow from financing activities for the year?

    a. $53,000

    b. $65,000

    c. $82,000

    d. $94,000

6. Happy Toy Company began Year Nine with $1,000 in inventory and $4,500 in accounts payable. During the year, Happy Toy incurred cost of goods sold of $25,000. Happy Toy ended Year Nine with $2,700 in inventory and $3,800 in accounts payable. How much cash did Happy Toy pay for its merchandise purchases during Year Nine?

    a. $22,600

    b. $24,000

    c. $26,000

    d. $27,400

7. Crystal Bell Company generated $48,900 in net income during the year. Included in this number are depreciation expense of $13,000 and a gain on the sale of equipment of $4,000. In addition, accounts receivable increased by $16,000, inventory decreased by $5,090, accounts payable decreased $4,330, and interest payable increased $1,200. Based on the above information, what is Crystal Bell's net cash inflow from operating activities?

    a. $43,860

    b. $48,900

    c. $54,120

    d. $71,940

8. Transportation Inc. incurred rent expense of $98,000 during the year on a large warehouse. During that same period, prepaid rent increased by $34,000. How much cash did Transportation pay for rent during the year?

    a. $34,000

    b. $64,000

    c. $98,000

    d. $132,000

9. The Robious Company presents cash flows from operating activities by the direct method. On its income statement for the current year, Robious reports rent expense of $60,000. This figure relates to two different buildings in use by the company. For Building One, prepaid rent went up by $9,000 during the year. For Building Two, rent payable went down by $5,000. How much cash did the company pay this year for rent?

    a. $46,000

    b. $56,000

    c. $64,000

    d. $74,000

10. A building is bought on October 1, Year One, for $500,000 in cash. It is depreciated using the straight-line method over an expected life of twenty years. A residual value of $20,000 is anticipated. The half-year convention is applied. On April 1, Year Four, the building is sold for cash at a loss of $13,000. Which of the following appears on the company's Year Four statement of cash flows?

    a. Investing activities cash inflow of $395,000

    b. Investing activities cash inflow of $415,000

    c. Investing activities cash inflow of $428,000

    d. Investing activities cash inflow of $441,000

11. The Hamster Company determines its cash flows from operating activities by the indirect method. Net income is reported for the current period as $400,000, which included depreciation expense of $70,000 and a gain on sale of land of $30,000. In addition, accounts receivable went down $2,000 during the year while accounts payable went up $7,000. What is the amount of cash generated by the Hamster Company's operating activities this year?

    a. $431,000

    b. $435,000

    c. $445,000

    d. $449,000

12. In Year One, the Karsenti Company reported net income of $30,000. Among many other accounts, the income statement included sales revenue of $500,000, cost of goods sold of $300,000, depreciation expense—equipment of $50,000, and a gain on sale of equipment of $23,000. Included on the balance sheet were a number of accounts such as bonds payable (increased $23,000), accounts payable, (decreased $6,000), retained earnings (increased $11,000), equipment (decreased $70,000), accumulated depreciation—equipment (increased $29,000), accounts receivable (decreased $17,000), and inventory (increased $3,000). No capital stock was issued or reacquired during the year. How much cash did this company spend on inventory during the year?

    a. $291,000

    b. $297,000

    c. $303,000

    d. $309,000

13. Use the same information as presented in problem 12. Using the indirect method, how much cash did Karsenti generate this year from its operating activities?

    a. $57,000

    b. $65,000

    c. $69,000

    d. $71,000

14. Use the same information as presented in problem 12. One piece of equipment was sold by Karsenti this year for cash, and none was bought. Which of the following is true about this sale of equipment?

    a. It is an investing activity cash inflow of $49,000.

    b. It is an investing activity cash inflow of $63,000.

    c. It is an investing activity cash inflow of $72,000.

    d. It is an investing activity cash inflow of $93,000.

15. Use the same information as presented in problem 12. Karsenti paid a cash dividend to shareholders this year. How should this distribution be shown on a statement of cash flows?

    a. Operating activity cash outflow of $19,000.

    b. Investing activity cash outflow of $30,000.

c. Operating activity cash outflow of $30,000.

d. Financing activity cash outflow of $19,000.

VIDEO PROBLEMS

Professor Joe Hoyle discusses the answers to these two problems at the links that are indicated. After formulating your answers, watch each video to see how Professor Hoyle answers these questions.

1. Your roommate is an English major. The roommate's parents own a chain of ice cream shops located throughout Florida. One day, while the two of you are taking a study break, your roommate asks you the following question: "I was recently looking at the financial statements my parents prepare for their business. I happened to see the statement of cash flows. I studied it more carefully because I was interested in the amount of cash that the business has been making. One of the biggest positive numbers on the entire statement was depreciation expense. It was listed right there under operating activities with a big plus sign. I don't understand. How are they able to get so much cash from depreciation? I understand how they get cash by selling ice cream, but how does a company get that cash from something called depreciation?" How would you respond?

View the video online at: http://bit.ly/hoyle17-3

2. Your uncle and two friends started a small office supply store several years ago. The company has grown and now has several large locations. Your uncle knows that you are taking a financial accounting class and asks you the following question: "We've been having cash flow problems recently. We are making roughly the same net income as in the past, but our cash reserves are shrinking. How can we possibly be selling so much merchandise and making a reasonable profit and still see our cash dwindling? This makes no sense to me. I'm mystified." How would you respond?

A warning about future increase in bad debt expense

View the video online at: http://bit.ly/hoyle17-4

PROBLEMS

1. For each of the following transactions, indicate whether the cash flows are reported in the operating activities section of the statement of cash flows, the investing activities section, or the financing activities section.

    a. Issuance of bonds payable

    b. Cash paid for interest

    c. Cash collected from customers

    d. Paid dividends

    e. Sold equipment for cash

    f. Issued preferred stock for cash

    g. Cash paid for inventory purchases

    h. Purchased a small percentage of the ownership shares of another company

    i. Cash received from dividend income

2. For each of the following transactions, indicate what is reported on the statement of cash flows and the section in which it is listed. Assume the indirect method is used to present the cash flows from operating activities.

    a. Equipment costing $33,000 but with accumulated depreciation of $14,000 is sold for cash creating a reported gain of $5,000.

    b. A note is signed at the bank on a $200,000 loan.

    c. A building with a cost of $700,000 but a net book value of only $111,000 is destroyed by fire.

    d. A new truck is acquired for $56,000 by signing a long-term note payable.

    e. A new owner invests cash of $49,000 into the business in exchange for 10,000 shares of $1 par value common stock.

    f. The first payment of $11,000 is made on the truck bought in problem 2(d). Of that total, $10,000 is paid on the note with the rest paid as interest.

    g. A building costing $530,000 with accumulated depreciation of $170,000 is sold for cash at a loss of $15,000.

3. The Starmer Corporation begins the current year with equipment costing $900,000. This figure rises to $1.2 million by the end of the period. Accumulated depreciation was $200,000 on the first of the year but $260,000 at the end. During the year, the following events took place:

    ■ Equipment costing $450,000 was bought by signing a note for $180,000 and paying cash for the remainder.

    ■ Depreciation expense recognized for the year on equipment was $110,000.

    ■ Equipment was sold during the year for cash; a gain of $13,000 was recognized.

    In connection with this company's equipment account, what will be the effects reported on the statement of cash flows?

4. Roy Company generated sales during Year Two of $120,000. Roy began the year with $56,000 in accounts receivable and ended the year with $79,000 in accounts receivable. Determine the amount of cash Roy collected from its customers during Year Two.

5. Below are figures found in the beginning and ending trial balances for the DeFaul Company for Year Three.

	1/1/3	12/31/3
Equipment	$420,000 debit	$460,000 debit
Accumulated depreciation	$350,000 credit	$370,000 credit
Note payable	$320,000 credit	$350,000 credit
Loss on sale of equipment	—	$24,000 debit

Additional information:

- A $50,000 cash payment was made on the note payable this year as well as a $20,000 payment for interest expense.
- New equipment was bought this year by signing a note payable and making a cash payment.
- Equipment costing $100,000 but with a net book value of $60,000 was sold for cash.
- The company uses the indirect method for presenting its cash flows from operating activities.

a. Based on the previous information, this company has two cash flows that need to be reported as investing activities. What are they and what monetary amount should be included?

b. Based on the previous information, this company has one cash flow that needs to be reported as a financing activity. What is it and what monetary amount should be included?

6. The Pasley Company prepares an income statement that reports cost of goods sold of $320,000, rent expense of $30,000, and salary expense of $90,000. During the year, prepaid rent went up $5,000, accounts payable went down $4,000, salary payable went up $3,000, and inventory went down $2,000.

a. What is the amount of cash the company spent this year to purchase inventory?

b. What is the amount of cash the company spent this year on rent?

c. What is the amount of cash the company paid this year to its employees as salaries?

7. Jamison Company's income statement for 20X6 is below.

FIGURE 17.41 Jamison Company Income Statement as of 12/31/X6

Jamison Company
Income Statement
As of 12/31/X6

Revenue	$76,450
Cost of Goods Sold	(40,740)
Gross Profit	35,710
Depreciation Expense	(8,240)
Other Expenses	(19,000)
Earnings Before Tax	8,470
Tax Expense	(2,076)
Net Income	$6,394

FIGURE 17.42 Selected Balance Sheet Accounts from the Beginning and End of 20X6

	1/1/X6	12/31/X6
Accounts Receivable	$32,590	$34,090
Inventory	23,100	35,020
Prepaid Expenses	13,970	11,340
Accounts Payable	39,870	44,960
Salaries Payable	22,030	17,440
Taxes Payable	12,490	11,230

Determine Jamison's net cash inflow or outflow from operating activities for this year using both the direct and indirect methods.

8. The following information is found in the year-end financial statements reported by Barney Corporation.

FIGURE 17.43 Income Statement

Sales	$300,000
Cost of Goods Sold	(100,000)
Rent Expense	(17,000)
Salary Expense	(80,000)
Depreciation Expense	(34,000)
Gain on Sale of Land	9,000
Net Income	$78,000

FIGURE 17.44 Current Asset and Liability Accounts

Accounts	January 1	December 31
Accounts Receivable	$22,000	$33,000
Prepaid Rent	8,000	2,000
Inventory	6,000	17,000
Accounts Payable	29,000	24,000
Salary Payable	40,000	44,000

Prepare the operating activities section of a statement of cash flows by means of the indirect method.

9. For each of the following transactions, indicate what is shown on a statement of cash flows as either an investing activity, a financing activity, or an operating activity. What kind of activity is it? Is it a cash inflow or outflow? How much cash is reported?

   a. One thousand shares of $1 per share par value common stock is issued for $19,000.

   b. A cash dividend of $16,000 is distributed to stockholders.

   c. A cash dividend of $9,000 is collected from another company because of the ownership of shares of stock.

   d. A $7,000 payment is made on a long-term note payable with $6,000 reducing the principal and the remaining $1,000 for interest.

   e. A building is sold with a historical cost of $400,000 and accumulated depreciation of $210,000 for cash at a loss of $17,000.

10. A company creates the following operating activities section of its statement of cash flows.

FIGURE 17.45 Company Prepared Operating Activities Cash Flows

Net Income	$90,000
Depreciation Expense	+20,000
Gain on Sale of Equipment	+11,000
Increase in Accounts Receivable	(6,000)
Decrease in Intrest Payable	+$8,000
Cash Inflow from Operations	$123,000

What was the correct amount of cash that was received during this period from the company's operating activities?

11. A company computed its cash payments for rent expense for the most recent period as $127,000, as shown next. What was the correct amount of cash the company paid for rent?

FIGURE 17.46 Company Computed Payments for Rent

Rent Expense	$120,000
Decrease in prepaid rent	(11,000)
Increase in rent payable	18,000
Cash paid for rent	$127,000

12. Killian Corporation had several transactions during the year that impacted long-term assets, long-term liabilities, and stockholders' equity. Determine if the cash amount in each of the following transactions is shown as an investing activity, as a financing activity, or as neither.

FIGURE 17.47 Determination of Cash Flow Balances

	Investing Activity	Financing Activity	Neither
Sold Common Stock			
Signed a Note Payable for Cash			
Purchased Equipment by Signing a Note Payable			
Sold Land			
Redeemed Bonds Payable			
Declared Dividends to Be Paid Next Year			
Purchased an Investment in Knox Company			

13. Ruthers Corporation began business on January 1, 20X5. The financial statements for Ruthers's first year are given here. Because 20X5 is the first year in business, the balance sheet accounts have no beginning balances.

FIGURE 17.48 Ruthers Corporation Income Statement as of 12/31/X5

Ruthers Corporation
Income Statement
As of 12/31/X5

Revenue	$14,900
Cost of Goods Sold	(6,780)
Gross Profit	8,120
Other Expenses	(3,910)
Earnings Before Tax	4,210
Tax Expense	(1,263)
Net Income	$2,947

FIGURE 17.49 Ruthers Corporation Balance Sheet 12/31/X5

Ruthers Corporation
Balance Sheet
12/31/X5

Assets		Liabilities	
Cash	$900	Accounts Payable	$1,830
Accounts Receivable	1,990	Salaries Payable	700
Inventory	2,510	Note Payable	10,000
Prepaid Expenses	577	Total Liabilities	$12,530
Land	14,000		
		Owners' Equity	
		Common Stock	4,500
		Retained Earnings	2,947
		Total Owners' Equity	7,447
		Total Liabilities & Owners'	
Total Assets	$19,977	Equity	$19,977

Additional Information:

a. Ruthers purchased land for $14,000 cash.

b. Common stock was issued for $4,500 in cash.

c. A note payable was signed for $10,000 cash.

Prepare Ruthers's statement of cash flows for 20X5 using the indirect method of calculating cash flows from operating activities.

14. Looney Company is in the process of preparing financial statements for the year ended 12/31/X9. The income statement as of 12/31/X9 and comparative balance sheets are presented here.

FIGURE 17.50 Looney Company Income Statement as of 12/31/X9

Looney Company
Income Statement
As of 12/31/X9

Sales	$6,328
Cost of Goods Sold	(4,740)
Gross Profit	1,588
Selling and Administrative Expenses	(895)
Depreciation Expense	(140)
Earnings Before Interest and Taxes	553
Interest Expense	(100)
Earnings Before Tax	453
Tax Expense	(108)
Net Income	$345

FIGURE 17.51 Looney Company Balance Sheet December 31, 20X9 and 20X8

Looney Company
Balance Sheet
December 31, 20X9 and 20X8

	20X9	20X8
Assets		
Cash	$485	$98
Accounts Receivable	960	990
Inventories	1,580	1,802
Property, Plant, and Equipment	1,710	1,620
Less: Accumulated Depreciation	(390)	(250)
Total Assets	$4,345	$4,260
Liabilities and Owners' Equity		
Accounts Payable	$200	$545
Interest Payable	50	80
Income Tax Payable	120	130
Long-Term Debt	1,500	1,430
Total Liabilities	$1,870	$2,185
Capital in Excess of Par	1,164	1,120
Common Stock, $1 Par	291	280
Retained Earnings	1,020	675
Total Owners' Equity	$2,475	$2,075
Total Liabilities and Equity	$4,345	$4,260

The following additional information has been assembled by Looney's accounting department:

a. Equipment was purchased for $90 in cash.
b. Long-term debt of $70 was issued for cash.
c. Looney issued eleven shares of common stock for cash during 20X9.

Prepare Looney's statement of cash flows as of 12/31/X9 using the direct method.

15. The following information relates to Henrich's Hat Store Inc. for the year ended December 31, 20X8.

FIGURE 17.52 Henrich's Hat Store Inc. Balance Sheet, December 31, 20X8

Henrich's Hat Store, Inc.
Balance Sheet
December 31, 20X8

	20X8	20X7
Assets		
Current Assets		
Cash	$280,000	$300,000
Accounts Receivable	750,000	690,000
Inventory	660,000	320,000
Total Current Assets	1,690,000	1,310,000
Land	300,000	0
Building and Fixtures	700,000	550,000
Less: Accumulated Depreciation	(100,000)	(80,000)
Total Assets	$2,590,000	$1,780,000
Liabilities		
Current Liabilities		
Accounts Payable	$460,000	$430,000
Taxes Payable	200,000	170,000
Total Current Liabilities	660,000	600,000
Stockholders' Equity		
Common Stock	$200,000	$150,000
Capital in Excess of Par	1,220,000	750,000
Retained Earnings	510,000	280,000
Total Stockholders' Equity	1,930,000	1,180,000
Total Liabilities and Stockholders' Equity	$2,590,000	$1,780,000

FIGURE 17.53 Henrich's Hat Store Inc. Income Statement for the Year Ended December 31, 20X8

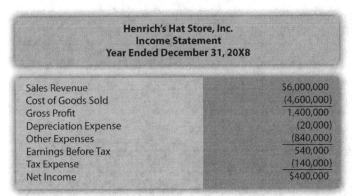

Henrich's Hat Store, Inc. Income Statement Year Ended December 31, 20X8	
Sales Revenue	$6,000,000
Cost of Goods Sold	(4,600,000)
Gross Profit	1,400,000
Depreciation Expense	(20,000)
Other Expenses	(840,000)
Earnings Before Tax	540,000
Tax Expense	(140,000)
Net Income	$400,000

Other information:

a. The company purchased a building and fixtures with cash during the year, but none were sold.

b. Dividends of $170,000 were declared and paid.

c. Cash proceeds from the sale of common stock totaled $520,000.

d. Land was purchased for $300,000 cash.

Prepare the statement of cash flows for Henrich's Hat Store Inc. for the year ended December 31, 20X8 using the indirect method of calculating cash flows from operations.

COMPREHENSIVE PROBLEM

This problem has carried through several chapters, building in difficulty. Hopefully, it has allowed students to continually practice skills and knowledge learned in previous chapters.

In Chapter 16, financial statements for April were prepared for Webworks. They are included here as a starting point for the required recording for May.

This will be your final month of preparing financial statements for Webworks. This month, the statement of cash flows will be added. To simplify the construction of that statement, fewer transactions than usual are included.

FIGURE 17.54 Webworks Financial Statements

Webworks	
Income Statement	
As of April 30	
Revenue	$23,200
Cost of Goods Sold	(12,707)
Gross Profit	10,493
Deprec. and Amort. Expense	(392)
Other Expenses and Losses	(9,045)
Investment Income (Loss)	200
Earnings Before Interest & Tax	1,256
Interest Expense	(15)
Earnings Before Tax	1,241
Tax Expense	(372)
Net Income	$869

FIGURE 17.55

Webworks	
Stmt. of Retained Earnings	
As of April 30	
Retained Earnings, April 1	$19,601
Net Income	869
Dividends	(500)
Retained Earnings, April 30	$19,970

FIGURE 17.56

Webworks Balance Sheet April 30				
Assets			**Liabilities**	
Current			**Current**	
Cash	$11,905		Accounts Payable	$3,080
Accounts Receivable	2,050		Salaries Payable	100
Less Allowance for			Interest Payable	45
Doubtful Accounts	(205)			
Net Accounts Receivable	1,845			
Merchandise Inventory	3,362			
Supplies Inventory	65			
Total Current Assets	$17,177		Total Current Liabilities	$3,225
Property, Plant, and Equipment			**Noncurrent**	
			Note Payable	$3,000
Equipment	$10,500			
Less Accumulated				
Depreciation	(1,313)			
Furniture	1,000			
Less Accumulated				
Depreciation	(119)			
Total P, P, and E	$10,068			
Other Noncurrent Assets			**Owners' Equity**	
Available for Sale Securities	$2,450		Capital Stock	$4,000
Licensing Agreement, Net	1,200		Retained Earnings	19,970
			Other Accumulated Comprehensive Income:	
			Unrealized Gain on Available for Sale Securities	700
			Total Owners' Equity	$24,670
Total Assets	$30,895		Total Liabilities & Owners' Equity	$30,895

The following events occur during May:

a. Webworks starts and completes twelve more sites and bills clients for $9,000.

b. Webworks purchases supplies worth $140 on account.

c. At the beginning of March, Webworks had twenty-two keyboards costing $121 each and twenty-eight flash drives costing $25 each. Webworks uses periodic FIFO to cost its inventory.

d. On account, Webworks purchases eighty-three keyboards for $122 each and ninety flash drives for $26 each.

e. Webworks sells 98 keyboards for $14,700 and 100 of the flash drives for $3,000 cash.

f. Webworks collects $9,000 in accounts receivable.

g. Webworks pays its $500 rent.

h. Webworks pays off $14,000 of its accounts payable.

i. Webworks sells all of its shares of QRS stock for $14 per share.

j. Webworks pays Juan $750 for his work during the first three weeks of May.

k. Webworks pays off its salaries payable from April.

l. Webworks pays the owners (Leon Jackson and Nancy Po) a salary of $4,000 each.

m. Webworks's note payable permits early payment with no penalty. Leon Jackson and Nancy Po decide to use some of their excess cash and pay off the note and interest payable. The note was paid at the beginning of May, so no interest accrued during May.

n. Webworks pays taxes of $740 in cash.

> *Required:*

>> A. Prepare journal entries for the previous events.

>> B. Post the journal entries to T-accounts.

>> C. Prepare an unadjusted trial balance for Webworks for May.

>> D. Prepare adjusting entries for the following, and post them to your T-accounts.

o. Webworks owes Juan Marcon (an employee) $200 for his work during the last week of May.

p. Webworks receives an electric bill for $450. Webworks will pay the bill in June.

q. Webworks determines that it has $70 worth of supplies remaining at the end of May.

r. Webworks is continuing to accrue bad debts at 10 percent of accounts receivable.

s. Webworks continues to depreciate its equipment over four years and its furniture over five years, using the straight-line method.

t. The license agreement should be amortized over its one-year life.

u. Record cost of goods sold.

>> E. Prepare an adjusted trial balance.

>> F. Prepare financial statements, including the statement of cash flows, for May. Prepare the operating section using the indirect method.

RESEARCH ASSIGNMENT

Assume that you take a job as a summer employee for an investment advisory service. One of the partners for that firm is currently looking at the possibility of investing in **Caribou Coffee Company Inc.** The partner is interested in knowing how much money the company has available for growth. The partner also wants to know how much growth has taken place in recent years. The partner asks you to look at the 2010 financial statements for **Caribou Coffee** by following this path:

- Go to http://www.cariboucoffee.com.
- At the bottom of this screen, click on "Our Company."
- In the upper right side of the next screen, click on "Investors."
- On the left side of the next screen, click on "Financial Reports."
- On the next screen, click on "2010 Annual Report" to download.
- Scroll to page 26 and find the company's statement of operations (income statement) for the years ended January 2, 2011, and January 3, 2010. Note the amount of net income reported for each year.
- Scroll down to page 28 and, for each of these two years, note the amount of cash inflow generated by operating activities. Then, look under Investing Activities for the cash outflows labeled as payments for property and equipment.

a. What net income is reported for each of these two years? Scan the statements of operation to determine any obvious causes for the difference in these two years.

b. What is the net cash inflow from operating activities for each of these two years? How do each of these numbers compare to the net income figures reported for the same periods of time? Scan the statement of cash flows to determine any obvious causes for the difference in these two years.

c. In each year, how much cash was spent as payments on property and equipment? What does that say about the growth of the company?

ENDNOTES

1. Michael Dell with Catherine Fredman, *Direct from Dell: Strategies That Revolutionized an Industry* (New York: HarperBusiness, 1999), 47.

2. A Treasury bill is a popular U.S. government security with a maturity date of one-year or less.

3. The term "commercial paper" refers to securities issued by corporations to meet their short-term cash needs.

4. For convenience, the allowance for doubtful accounts will not be included with accounts receivable. The possibility of bad debts makes the conversion to cash more complicated and is covered in upper-level accounting textbooks.

CHAPTER 18
Appendix: Present Value Tables

FIGURE 18.1 Present Value of $1

Periods	Rate per Period													
	1.00%	1.50%	2.00%	2.50%	3.00%	4.00%	5.00%	6.00%	7.00%	8.00%	9.00%	10.00%	11.00%	12.00%
1	0.99010	0.98522	0.98039	0.97561	0.97087	0.96154	0.95238	0.94340	0.93458	0.92593	0.91743	0.90909	0.90090	0.89286
2	0.98030	0.97066	0.96117	0.95181	0.94260	0.92456	0.90703	0.89000	0.87344	0.85734	0.84168	0.82645	0.81162	0.79719
3	0.97059	0.95632	0.94232	0.92860	0.91514	0.88900	0.86384	0.83962	0.81630	0.79383	0.77218	0.75131	0.73119	0.71178
4	0.96098	0.94218	0.92385	0.90595	0.88849	0.85480	0.82270	0.79209	0.76290	0.73503	0.70843	0.68301	0.65873	0.63552
5	0.95147	0.92826	0.90573	0.88385	0.86261	0.82193	0.78353	0.74726	0.71299	0.68058	0.64993	0.62092	0.59345	0.56743
6	0.94205	0.91454	0.88797	0.86230	0.83748	0.79031	0.74622	0.70496	0.66634	0.63017	0.59627	0.56447	0.53464	0.50663
7	0.93272	0.90103	0.87056	0.84127	0.81309	0.75992	0.71068	0.66506	0.62275	0.58349	0.54703	0.51316	0.48166	0.45235
8	0.92348	0.88771	0.85349	0.82075	0.78941	0.73069	0.67684	0.62741	0.58201	0.54027	0.50187	0.46651	0.43393	0.40388
9	0.91434	0.87459	0.83676	0.80073	0.76642	0.70259	0.64461	0.59190	0.54393	0.50025	0.46043	0.42410	0.39092	0.36061
10	0.90529	0.86167	0.82035	0.78120	0.74409	0.67556	0.61391	0.55839	0.50835	0.46319	0.42241	0.38554	0.35218	0.32197
11	0.89632	0.84893	0.80426	0.76214	0.72242	0.64958	0.58468	0.52679	0.47509	0.42888	0.38753	0.35049	0.31728	0.28748
12	0.88745	0.83639	0.78849	0.74356	0.70138	0.62460	0.55684	0.49697	0.44401	0.39711	0.35553	0.31863	0.28584	0.25668
13	0.87866	0.82403	0.77303	0.72542	0.68095	0.60057	0.53032	0.46884	0.41496	0.36770	0.32618	0.28966	0.25751	0.22917
14	0.86996	0.81185	0.75788	0.70773	0.66112	0.57748	0.50507	0.44230	0.38782	0.34046	0.29925	0.26333	0.23199	0.20462
15	0.86135	0.79985	0.74301	0.69047	0.64186	0.55526	0.48102	0.41727	0.36245	0.31524	0.27454	0.23939	0.20900	0.18270
16	0.85282	0.78803	0.72845	0.67362	0.62317	0.53391	0.45811	0.39365	0.33873	0.29189	0.25187	0.21763	0.18829	0.16312
17	0.84438	0.77639	0.71416	0.65720	0.60502	0.51337	0.43630	0.37136	0.31657	0.27027	0.23107	0.19784	0.16963	0.14564
18	0.83602	0.76491	0.70016	0.64117	0.58739	0.49363	0.41552	0.35034	0.29586	0.25025	0.21199	0.17986	0.15282	0.13004
19	0.82774	0.75361	0.68643	0.62553	0.57029	0.47464	0.39573	0.33051	0.27651	0.23171	0.19449	0.16351	0.13768	0.11611
20	0.81954	0.74247	0.67297	0.61027	0.55368	0.45639	0.37689	0.31180	0.25842	0.21455	0.17843	0.14864	0.12403	0.10367
21	0.81143	0.73150	0.65978	0.59539	0.53755	0.43883	0.35894	0.29416	0.24151	0.19866	0.16370	0.13513	0.11174	0.09256
22	0.80340	0.72069	0.64684	0.58086	0.52189	0.42196	0.34185	0.27751	0.22571	0.18394	0.15018	0.12285	0.10067	0.08264
23	0.79544	0.71004	0.63416	0.56670	0.50669	0.40573	0.32557	0.26180	0.21095	0.17032	0.13778	0.11168	0.09069	0.07379
24	0.78757	0.69954	0.62172	0.55288	0.49193	0.39012	0.31007	0.24698	0.19715	0.15770	0.12640	0.10153	0.08170	0.06588
25	0.77977	0.68921	0.60953	0.53939	0.47761	0.37512	0.29530	0.23300	0.18425	0.14602	0.11597	0.09230	0.07361	0.05882
30	0.74192	0.63976	0.55207	0.47674	0.41199	0.30832	0.23138	0.17411	0.13137	0.09938	0.07537	0.05731	0.04368	0.03338
40	0.67165	0.55126	0.45289	0.37243	0.30656	0.20829	0.14205	0.09722	0.06678	0.04603	0.03184	0.02209	0.01538	0.01075
50	0.60804	0.47500	0.37153	0.29094	0.22811	0.14071	0.08720	0.05429	0.03395	0.02132	0.01345	0.00852	0.00542	0.00346

FIGURE 18.2 Present Value of Annuity Due (annuity in advance—beginning of period payments)

Periods	Rate per Period													
	1.00%	1.50%	2.00%	2.50%	3.00%	4.00%	5.00%	6.00%	7.00%	8.00%	9.00%	10.00%	11.00%	12.00%
1	1.00000	1.00000	1.00000	1.00000	1.00000	1.00000	1.00000	1.00000	1.00000	1.00000	1.00000	1.00000	1.00000	1.00000
2	1.99010	1.98522	1.98039	1.97561	1.97087	1.96154	1.95238	1.94340	1.93458	1.92593	1.91743	1.90909	1.90090	1.89286
3	2.97040	2.95588	2.94156	2.92742	2.91347	2.88609	2.85941	2.83339	2.80802	2.78326	2.75911	2.73554	2.71252	2.69005
4	3.94099	3.91220	3.88388	3.85602	3.82861	3.77509	3.72325	3.67301	3.62432	3.57710	3.53129	3.48685	3.44371	3.40183
5	4.90197	4.85438	4.80773	4.76197	4.71710	4.62990	4.54595	4.46511	4.38721	4.31213	4.23972	4.16987	4.10245	4.03735
6	5.85343	5.78264	5.71346	5.64583	5.57971	5.45182	5.32948	5.21236	5.10020	4.99271	4.88965	4.79079	4.69590	4.60478
7	6.79548	6.69719	6.60143	6.50813	6.41719	6.24214	6.07569	5.91732	5.76654	5.62288	5.48592	5.35526	5.23054	5.11141
8	7.72819	7.59821	7.47199	7.34939	7.23028	7.00205	6.78637	6.58238	6.38929	6.20637	6.03295	5.86842	5.71220	5.56376
9	8.65168	8.48593	8.32548	8.17014	8.01969	7.73274	7.46321	7.20979	6.97130	6.74664	6.53482	6.33493	6.14612	5.96764
10	9.56602	9.36052	9.16224	8.97087	8.78611	8.43533	8.10782	7.80169	7.51523	7.24689	6.99525	6.75902	6.53705	6.32825
11	10.47130	10.22218	9.98259	9.75206	9.53020	9.11090	8.72173	8.36009	8.02358	7.71008	7.41766	7.14457	6.88923	6.65022
12	11.36763	11.07112	10.78685	10.51421	10.25262	9.76048	9.30641	8.88687	8.49867	8.13896	7.80519	7.49506	7.20652	6.93770
13	12.25508	11.90751	11.57534	11.25776	10.95400	10.38507	9.86325	9.38384	8.94269	8.53608	8.16073	7.81369	7.49236	7.19437
14	13.13374	12.73153	12.34837	11.98318	11.63496	10.98565	10.39357	9.85268	9.35765	8.90378	8.48690	8.10336	7.74987	7.42355
15	14.00370	13.54338	13.10625	12.69091	12.29607	11.56312	10.89864	10.29498	9.74547	9.24424	8.78615	8.36669	7.98187	7.62817
16	14.86505	14.34323	13.84926	13.38138	12.93794	12.11839	11.37966	10.71225	10.10791	9.55948	9.06069	8.60608	8.19087	7.81086
17	15.71787	15.13126	14.57771	14.05500	13.56110	12.65230	11.83777	11.10590	10.44665	9.85137	9.31256	8.82371	8.37916	7.97399
18	16.56225	15.90765	15.29187	14.71220	14.16612	13.16567	12.27407	11.47726	10.76322	10.12164	9.54363	9.02155	8.54879	8.11963
19	17.39827	16.67256	15.99203	15.35336	14.75351	13.65930	12.68959	11.82760	11.05909	10.37189	9.75563	9.20141	8.70162	8.24967
20	18.22601	17.42617	16.67846	15.97889	15.32380	14.13394	13.08532	12.15812	11.33560	10.60360	9.95011	9.36492	8.83929	8.36578
21	19.04555	18.16864	17.35143	16.58916	15.87747	14.59033	13.46221	12.46992	11.59401	10.81815	10.12855	9.51356	8.96333	8.46944
22	19.85698	18.90014	18.01121	17.18455	16.41502	15.02916	13.82115	12.76408	11.83553	11.01680	10.29224	9.64869	9.07507	8.56200
23	20.66038	19.62082	18.65805	17.76541	16.93692	15.45112	14.16300	13.04158	12.06124	11.20074	10.44243	9.77154	9.17574	8.64465
24	21.45582	20.33086	19.29220	18.33211	17.44361	15.85684	14.48857	13.30338	12.27219	11.37106	10.58021	9.88322	9.26643	8.71843
25	22.24339	21.03041	19.91393	18.88499	17.93554	16.24696	14.79864	13.55036	12.46933	11.52876	10.70661	9.98474	9.34814	8.78432
30	26.06579	24.37608	22.84438	21.45355	20.18845	17.98371	16.14107	14.59072	13.27767	12.15841	11.19828	10.36961	9.65011	9.02181
40	33.16303	30.36458	27.90259	25.73034	23.80822	20.58448	18.01704	15.94907	14.26493	12.87858	11.72552	10.75696	9.93567	9.23303
50	39.58808	35.52468	32.05208	29.07137	26.50166	22.34147	19.16872	16.70757	14.76680	13.21216	11.94823	10.90630	10.03624	9.30104

FIGURE 18.3 Present Value of Ordinary Annuity (annuity in arrears—end of period payments)

Periods	Rate per Period													
	1.00%	1.50%	2.00%	2.50%	3.00%	4.00%	5.00%	6.00%	7.00%	8.00%	9.00%	10.00%	11.00%	12.00%
1	0.99010	0.98522	0.98039	0.97561	0.97087	0.96154	0.95238	0.94340	0.93458	0.92593	0.91743	0.90909	0.90090	0.89286
2	1.97040	1.95588	1.94156	1.92742	1.91347	1.88609	1.85941	1.83339	1.80802	1.78326	1.75911	1.73554	1.71252	1.69005
3	2.94099	2.91220	2.88388	2.85602	2.82861	2.77509	2.72325	2.67301	2.62432	2.57710	2.53129	2.48685	2.44371	2.40183
4	3.90197	3.85438	3.80773	3.76197	3.71710	3.62990	3.54595	3.46511	3.38721	3.31213	3.23972	3.16987	3.10245	3.03735
5	4.85343	4.78264	4.71346	4.64583	4.57971	4.45182	4.32948	4.21236	4.10020	3.99271	3.88965	3.79079	3.69590	3.60478
6	5.79548	5.69719	5.60143	5.50813	5.41719	5.24214	5.07569	4.91732	4.76654	4.62288	4.48592	4.35526	4.23054	4.11141
7	6.72819	6.59821	6.47199	6.34939	6.23028	6.00205	5.78637	5.58238	5.38929	5.20637	5.03295	4.86842	4.71220	4.56376
8	7.65168	7.48593	7.32548	7.17014	7.01969	6.73274	6.46321	6.20979	5.97130	5.74664	5.53482	5.33493	5.14612	4.96764
9	8.56602	8.36052	8.16224	7.97087	7.78611	7.43533	7.10782	6.80169	6.51523	6.24689	5.99525	5.75902	5.53705	5.32825
10	9.47130	9.22218	8.98259	8.75206	8.53020	8.11090	7.72173	7.36009	7.02358	6.71008	6.41766	6.14457	5.88923	5.65022
11	10.36763	10.07112	9.78685	9.51421	9.25262	8.76048	8.30641	7.88687	7.49867	7.13896	6.80519	6.49506	6.20652	5.93770
12	11.25508	10.90751	10.57534	10.25776	9.95400	9.38507	8.86325	8.38384	7.94269	7.53608	7.16073	6.81369	6.49236	6.19437
13	12.13374	11.73153	11.34837	10.98318	10.63496	9.98565	9.39357	8.85268	8.35765	7.90378	7.48690	7.10336	6.74987	6.42355
14	13.00370	12.54338	12.10625	11.69091	11.29607	10.56312	9.89864	9.29498	8.74547	8.24424	7.78615	7.36669	6.98187	6.62817
15	13.86505	13.34323	12.84926	12.38138	11.93794	11.11839	10.37966	9.71225	9.10791	8.55948	8.06069	7.60608	7.19087	6.81086
16	14.71787	14.13126	13.57771	13.05500	12.56110	11.65230	10.83777	10.10590	9.44665	8.85137	8.31256	7.82371	7.37916	6.97399
17	15.56225	14.90765	14.29187	13.71220	13.16612	12.16567	11.27407	10.47726	9.76322	9.12164	8.54363	8.02155	7.54879	7.11963
18	16.39827	15.67256	14.99203	14.35336	13.75351	12.65930	11.68959	10.82760	10.05909	9.37189	8.75563	8.20141	7.70162	7.24967
19	17.22601	16.42617	15.67846	14.97889	14.32380	13.13394	12.08532	11.15812	10.33560	9.60360	8.95011	8.36492	7.83929	7.36578
20	18.04555	17.16864	16.35143	15.58916	14.87747	13.59033	12.46221	11.46992	10.59401	9.81815	9.12855	8.51356	7.96333	7.46944
21	18.85698	17.90014	17.01121	16.18455	15.41502	14.02916	12.82115	11.76408	10.83553	10.01680	9.29224	8.64869	8.07507	7.56200
22	19.66038	18.62082	17.65805	16.76541	15.93692	14.45112	13.16300	12.04158	11.06124	10.20074	9.44243	8.77154	8.17574	7.64465
23	20.45582	19.33086	18.29220	17.33211	16.44361	14.85684	13.48857	12.30338	11.27219	10.37106	9.58021	8.88322	8.26643	7.71843
24	21.24339	20.03041	18.91393	17.88499	16.93554	15.24696	13.79864	12.55036	11.46933	10.52876	9.70661	8.98474	8.34814	7.78432
25	22.02316	20.71961	19.52346	18.42438	17.41315	15.62208	14.09394	12.78336	11.65358	10.67478	9.82258	9.07704	8.42174	7.84314
30	25.80771	24.01584	22.39646	20.93029	19.60044	17.29203	15.37245	13.76483	12.40904	11.25778	10.27365	9.42691	8.69379	8.05518
40	32.83469	29.91585	27.35548	25.10278	23.11477	19.79277	17.15909	15.04630	13.33171	11.92461	10.75736	9.77905	8.95105	8.24378
50	39.19612	34.99969	31.42361	28.36231	25.72976	21.48218	18.25593	15.76186	13.80075	12.23348	10.96168	9.91481	9.04165	8.30450

Index